CREDITORS' RIGHTS
AND
BANKRUPTCY

CREDITORS' RIGHTS AND BANKRUPTCY

STEVE H. NICKLES
Roger F. Noreen Professor of Law
University of Minnesota Law School

DAVID G. EPSTEIN
Dean & Southeastern Bankruptcy Law Institute Professor of Law
Emory University Law School

BLACK LETTER SERIES

WEST PUBLISHING CO.
ST. PAUL, MINN.
1989

COPYRIGHT © 1989 By WEST PUBLISHING CO.
610 Opperman Drive
P.O. Box 64526
St. Paul, MN 55164–0526

Library of Congress Cataloging-in-Publication Data

Nickles, Steve H., 1949–
    Creditors' rights and bankruptcy.
        (Black letter series)
1. Debtor and creditor—United States—Outlines, syllabi, etc.
2. Bankruptcy—United States—Outlines, syllabi, etc. I. Epstein, David
G., 1943– II. Title. III. Series.
KF1501.Z9N53   1989   346.73'077   88–27939
                              347.30677

ISBN 0–314–48841–3

(N. & E.) Creditors' Rights BLS
2nd Reprint—1992

PUBLISHER'S PREFACE

This "Black Letter" is designed to help a law student recognize and understand the basic principles and issues of law covered in a law school course. It can be used both as a study aid when preparing for classes and as a review of the subject matter when studying for an examination.

Each "Black Letter" is written by experienced law school teachers who are recognized national authorities in the subject covered.

The law is succinctly stated by the author of this "Black Letter." In addition, the exceptions to the rules are stated in the text. The rules and exceptions have purposely been condensed to facilitate quick review and easy recollection. For an in-depth study of a point of law, citations to major student texts are given. In addition, a **Text Correlation Chart** provides a convenient means of relating material contained in the Black Letter to appropriate sections of the casebook the student is using in his or her law school course.

If the subject covered by this text is a code or code-related course, the code section or rule is set forth and discussed wherever applicable.

FORMAT

The format of this "Black Letter" is specially designed for review. (1) **Text.** First, it is recommended that the entire text be studied, and, if deemed necessary, supplemented by the student texts cited. (2) **Capsule Summary.** The Capsule Summary is an abbreviated review of the subject matter which can be used both before and after studying the main body of the text. The headings in the Capsule Summary follow the main text of the "Black Letter." (3) **Table of Contents.** The Table of Contents is in outline form to help you organize the details of the subject and the Summary of Contents gives you a final overview of the materials. (4) **Practice Examination.** The Practice Examination in Appendix B gives you the opportunity of testing yourself with the type of question asked on an exam.

In addition, a number of other features are included to help you understand the subject matter and prepare for examinations.

Short Questions and Answers: This feature is designed to help you spot and recognize issues in the examination. We feel that issue recognition is a major ingredient in successfully writing an examination.

Perspective: In this feature, the authors discuss their approach to the topic, the approach used in preparing the materials, and any tips on studying for and writing examinations.

Analysis: This feature, at the beginning of each section, is designed to give a quick summary of a particular section to help you recall the subject matter and to help you determine which areas need the most extensive review.

Examples: This feature is designed to illustrate, through fact situations, the law just stated. This, we believe, should help you analytically approach a question on the examination.

Glossary: This feature is designed to refamiliarize you with the meaning of a particular legal term. We believe that the recognition of words of art used in an examination helps you to better analyze the question. In addition, when writing an examination you should know the precise definition of a word of art you intend to use.

We believe that the materials in this "Black Letter" will facilitate your study of a law school course and assure success in writing examinations not only for the course but for the bar examination. We wish you success.

The Publisher

SUMMARY OF CONTENTS

APPENDICES

TABLE OF CONTENTS

APPENDICES

*

CAPSULE SUMMARY

PART ONE: OBTAINING AND ENFORCING JUDGMENTS

I. INCREASING THE ODDS OF A CREDITOR'S JUDGMENT

A creditor must generally obtain a judgment and pursue appropriate post-judgment remedies in order to seize and apply the debtor's assets in satisfaction of the creditor's claim. Not surprisingly, therefore, creditors sometimes use devices and tactics aimed at increasing their odds for success in suits against debtors.

A. OBTAINING A JUDGMENT BY COGNOVIT
1. COGNOVIT EXPLAINED
"The cognovit is the ancient legal device by which the debtor consents in advance to the holder's obtaining a judgment without notice or hearing, and possibly even with the appearance, on the debtor's behalf, of an attorney designated by the holder." *D.H. Overmyer Co. v. Frick Co.,* 405 U.S. 174, 176, 92 S.Ct. 775, 777 (1972).

2. CONSTITUTIONAL DUE PROCESS LIMITATIONS ON COGNOVITS
The use of a cognovit clause involves the debtor's waiver of her fourteenth amendment due process protections. Such a waiver, and thus a cognovit clause, is not per se invalid, but is enforceable only if the debtor "voluntarily, intelligently, and knowingly waived the rights it otherwise possessed to prejudgment notice and hearing, and * * * did so with full awareness of the legal consequences." *Overmyer,* 405 U.S. at 187, 92 S.Ct. at 783.

1

3. STATE STATUTORY LIMITATIONS

The vast majority of states restrict the use of cognovits, especially in consumer transactions, either by forbidding their use or by regulating the procedures for establishing or enforcing them.

4. F.T.C. TRADE REGULATION RULE

The Federal Trade Commission has effectively prohibited the use of cognovits in consumer credit transactions.

5. OTHER LIMITATIONS AND CONCERNS

A cognovit clause may be unconscionable, and a cognovit judgment may be denied full faith and credit in other states. Moreover, there are possible ethical problems in a lawyer seeking to get a judgment by cognovit for a creditor client, or in using a cognovit clause in a contract for services between the lawyer and a client. Finally, a creditor who obtains a cognovit judgment, knowing that her claim or the amount of it is unjustified or excessive, risks liability for malicious prosecution, although this risk is quite small.

B. SELECTING AN INCONVENIENT FORUM

If a cognovit judgment is not possible, the creditor must hope that, upon suing the debtor and giving her notice of the action, the debtor will fail to answer and default. The odds of a debtor defaulting are increased if the creditor's action is initiated and pursued in a court distant from the debtor's residence; but there are restrictions on creditors pursuing collection actions in a state other than a debtor's home.

1. JUDICIAL JURISDICTION

A creditor's judgment against a debtor will be valid in the state where rendered, and enforceable in any other state under the full faith and credit clause (U.S. Const. art. IV, § 1), only if the court rendering the judgment has *judicial jurisdiction* of the person at whom, or property at which, the proceedings are directed. Three requirements must be satisfied if a state court is to have judicial jurisdiction of a creditor's action against a debtor: (a) competence; (b) notice; and (c) contacts.

2. SELECTING AN INCONVENIENT FORUM AS AN UNFAIR TRADE PRACTICE

The Federal Trade Commission is empowered to enjoin creditors from pursuing collection actions in forums that are inconvenient for the debtor-defendants.

3. FORUM NON CONVENIENS

A creditor can be prevented from continuing an action in an inconvenient forum through the doctrine of *forum non conveniens,* which empowers a trial "court to decline to exercise a possessed jurisdiction whenever it appears that the cause before it may be more appropriately tried elsewhere." Blair, *The Doctrine of Forum Non Conveniens in Anglo–American Law,* 29 Colum.L.Rev. 1 (1929).

4. FORUM–SELECTION CLAUSES

Creditors commonly insure that venue is convenient for themselves, if not inconvenient for their debtors, by including a *forum-selection clause* in the credit contract. Such a clause specifies the state (sometimes, even a particular city or a specific court) where actions on or under the contract must be brought.

C. CHOOSING FAVORABLE LAW

A creditor can increase the chances of prevailing in the place where a judgment is sought by getting the debtor to agree at the time of contracting on the creditor's choice of law to govern the parties' transaction. As a general rule, parties to a contract are free to determine which state's substantive law will apply in resolving disputes between them; so, as a general rule, *choice-of-law clauses* are binding and enforceable, subject to certain conditions or limitations which concern (1) impropriety, mistake or the absence of bargained-for-consent in agreements choosing governing law; (2) the relationship of the parties and their transaction to the chosen state; (3) the policies of the state whose law would otherwise govern; and (4) statutory choice-of-law rules overriding the parties' agreement.

II. JUDGMENT LIENS

Virtually every state subjects the debtor's interests in certain property to a lien that arises, by force of statute, from the judgment itself.

A. HISTORY OF THE JUDGMENT LIEN

At common law a judgment could be enforced only through the judicial writ of *fieri facias* (*fi. fa.*), which directed the sheriff to satisfy a judgment from the debtor's goods and chattels. In the thirteenth century, a statute was enacted giving the creditor a choice, in enforcing a judgment, between a *fi. fa.* writ or a *writ of elegit,* which gave the creditor an interest in the debtor's lands. Eventually, the writ of *fi. fa.* was enlarged to permit the seizure and sale of not only the judgment debtor's personalty, but also her real property. The *writ of elegit* thus fell by the wayside. The notion that a debtor's lands were bound by a judgment lien survived, however; and the lien was broadened so that it spread to all of the debtor's real property that was subject to seizure and sale under a writ *fi. fa.*

B. NATURE AND ENFORCEMENT OF THE JUDGMENT LIEN
1. THE LIEN IS GENERAL RATHER THAN SPECIFIC

A *judgment lien* is not a specific lien on any of the debtor's real property. Rather, it is a general lien only. Thus, the judgment creditor receives no estate or interest in the debtor's lands, but only a power to execute and levy on the land. Yet, the rights of the creditor for this purpose relate back to the time of the judgment, so as to prime purchasers and encumbrancers who intervene between judgment and execution on the realty.

2. ENFORCEMENT IS TYPICALLY THROUGH EXECUTION

Enforcement of a judgment lien is typically through execution.

C. JUDGMENTS WHICH PRODUCE A LIEN
1. GENERALLY

As a general rule, the only type of judgment that produces a lien is a final, personal judgment of a court of record, for a definite sum of money, that can be enforced through execution against the debtor's real property.

2. DECREES FOR ALIMONY AND THE LIKE
Unless a decree for periodic payments for support or alimony specifically states that it shall constitute a lien on property, none arises in the absence of a statute declaring such decree a lien.

3. JUDGMENTS OF FEDERAL DISTRICT COURTS
"Every judgment rendered by a district court within a State shall be a lien on the property located in such State in the same manner, to the same extent and under the same conditions as a judgment of a court of general jurisdiction in such State * * *." 28 U.S.C.A. § 1962.

4. FOREIGN JUDGMENTS
A state court judgment for the recovery of money can usually be enforced in another state through a summary process that involves filing or registering the judgment with the clerk of any court of general jurisdiction within the state.

D. WHEN THE JUDGMENT LIEN ARISES
In most states, a judgment lien ordinarily arises when the judgment is docketed or otherwise indexed or recorded as prescribed by statute.

E. PROPERTY REACHED BY THE JUDGMENT LIEN
1. TYPES OF PROPERTY AFFECTED
In most states a judgment creates a general lien only on the debtor's interests in *real property,* but the states disagree on what constitutes real property for this purpose.

2. TENANCY–BY–THE–ENTIRETY PROPERTY
Property held in tenancy by the entirety is completely immune from levy and sale under execution or other collection process initiated by a creditor of one of the spouses.

3. THE GEOGRAPHICAL REACH OF A JUDGMENT LIEN
A lien of judgment does not ordinarily reach beyond the county where the judgment was rendered, but the lien will spread to another county if the judgment is there docketed or otherwise recorded.

4. AFTER–ACQUIRED PROPERTY
In most jurisdictions, the lien of judgment extends not only to interests of the debtor in property owned when the judgment was rendered, but also to interests thereafter acquired by her for as long as the judgment lien survives. The authorities disagree, however, about the relative priority of judgment liens that attach simultaneously to after-acquired property.

5. SUBSEQUENT INCREASES IN VALUE
The creditor who enjoys a judgment lien can reach any and all increases in the value of the equity in property subject to the lien.

6. PROCEEDS OF SALE OF PROPERTY ARE NOT SUBJECT TO THE LIEN
A judgment lien ordinarily does not confer on the judgment creditor any claim to proceeds of the sale of the debtor's real estate.

F. PRIORITY OF A JUDGMENT LIEN IN RELATION TO OTHER CLAIMS TO THE PROPERTY

1. JUDGMENT LIENOR VERSUS JUDGMENT LIENOR

The priority of judgment liens attaching to the same property usually corresponds to the order in which the liens were created or attached to the property; but there is disagreement on the priority of liens attaching simultaneously to after-acquired property.

2. JUDGMENT LIENOR VERSUS PURCHASER OR OTHER TRANSFEREE OF INTEREST IN THE PROPERTY

    a. Subsequent Transferees. Ordinarily, according to the familiar rule that first in time is first in right, interests in and claims to property acquired after the attachment of a judgment lien are subordinate to the lien, except that a purchase-money mortgage on after-acquired property is superior to a lien of judgment even though the judgment is prior in time.

    b. Prior Unrecorded Transfers. In most states, judgment creditors are protected by the registry laws that require the recording of conveyances affecting real estate. Consequently, if prior to judgment the debtor has sold or mortgaged real property that belonged to her, but the transfer was not recorded, the lien of judgment will attach to the property and take precedence over the secret conveyance.

3. JUDGMENT LIENOR VERSUS BANKRUPTCY TRUSTEE

As a very general rule, all liens on a debtor's property, including judgment liens, are enforceable against the debtor's estate and her trustee in bankruptcy, but the debtor's bankruptcy trustee is empowered to avoid judgment liens under some circumstances.

G. LIFE OF A JUDGMENT LIEN

1. STATUTE OF LIMITATION

A judgment lien cannot survive the running of a statute of limitation governing actions on the underlying judgment. Before this statute has run, however, the judgment creditor can renew the judgment and get a new judgment which will itself give rise to a new lien and a new limitation period.

2. DORMANCY AND REVIVOR

A judgment lien may become ineffective well before expiration of the limitations period for judgments because the lien itself becomes *dormant*. If dormancy results, the sleeping judgment lien can be *revived* through a judicial proceeding in *scire facias*. The revival of a judgment (as opposed to the renewal of a judgment) does not stop the running of a statute of limitation governing actions on judgments.

3. JUDGMENT LIEN UNAFFECTED BY DEATH OF JUDGMENT DEBTOR

The death of the judgment debtor does not terminate an attached judgment lien.

III. ENFORCING JUDGMENTS THROUGH EXECUTION

A. ISSUING THE WRIT OF EXECUTION

The process of execution to enforce a money judgment is begun by the issuance of a judicial writ of execution.

1. JUDGMENTS THAT SUPPORT ISSUANCE OF A WRIT OF EXECUTION

"[N]o valid writ of execution can be issued until a valid, final, viable, money judgment has been obtained by the creditor." W. Hawkland & P. Loiseaux, Cases and Materials on Debtor–Creditor Relations 40 (2d ed. 1979).

2. WHEN WRIT OF EXECUTION WILL ISSUE

There are three major conditions on the issuance of a writ of executions: (a) the judgment must be entered; (b) execution must not have been stayed; and (c) the time for issuing execution must not have expired.

3. HOW THE WRIT OF EXECUTION ISSUES

Typically, a writ of execution issues upon application of the judgment creditor to the clerk of the court.

4. TO WHOM THE WRIT OF EXECUTION ISSUES

The writ of execution is usually directed to the sheriff.

5. THE SHERIFF'S DUTY UNDER A WRIT OF EXECUTION

A writ of execution directs the sheriff (or other official charged with enforcing the writ) to satisfy the judgment, with interest, out of the judgment debtor's property by seizing, i.e., levying on, such property and selling it.

B. LEVYING ON THE DEBTOR'S PROPERTY
1. PROPERTY SUBJECT TO LEVY AND SALE UNDER EXECUTION

All non-exempt personal property in tangible form (including reified obligations owed the debtor) and most non-exempt real estate interests of the debtor (including contingent remainders in some circumstances) are subject to execution, whether or not the property is encumbered by a mortgage or the like. Some states also allow execution on purely intangible personal property, but in most states this kind of property is reached through the special remedy of garnishment.

2. DECIDING WHAT PROPERTY TO LEVY ON

"Some jurisdictions accord the judgment debtor the right to designate the property which should be subjected to levy and sale, while others leave that choice to the sheriff and the judgment creditor, sometimes qualified by a mandate that real property shall be levied upon only if there are no leviable chattels." S. Riesenfeld, Creditors' Remedies And Debtors' Protection 89 (4th ed. 1987).

3. HOW LEVY IS EFFECTED

The usual method of levying on real estate is filing some sort of notice of levy in the county land records. The sheriff usually effects a levy on goods that are capable of manual delivery by physically seizing and holding them until the time for sale of the property. Purely intangible rights of the debtor that are not embodied in symbolic writings are usually gathered or collected through a proceeding called garnishment, which is aimed at the debtor's obligor, rather than through execution in its usual form.

4. **ACTION FOLLOWING THE LEVY**
   a. **Sheriff Must Make a Timely Return.** The return date limits the life of a writ of execution. After its return date the writ becomes *functus officio*. So, the sheriff must act to enforce the writ before that date, and on or before that date must record her success in satisfying the judgment or describe what property she has seized toward that end.

   b. **The Meaning of a Return "*Nulla Bona*".** By making a return *nulla bona*, the sheriff indicates that she has failed to find any property of the debtor that is subject to levy and sale under execution.

   c. **Subsequent Writs.** In the event of a return *nulla bona,* or in the event that the first writ results in only partial satisfaction of the judgment, the judgment creditor may cause a second (*alias*) and further (*pluries*) writs to issue.

C. SELLING THE PROPERTY
Property on which the sheriff levies is not turned over to the judgment creditor in satisfaction of her claim. Rather, the sheriff sells the property and gives the net proceeds (after paying the costs of the sale) to the creditor. Any surplus ordinarily goes to the debtor.

1. **SUBJECT OF THE SALE**
   Property levied on by the sheriff is the subject of the sale. Yet, the sheriff is permitted to sell only so much of the debtor's property as is necessary to satisfy the execution creditor's judgment and the costs of the sale.

2. **MANNER OF SALE**
   Usually, the execution sale is by public auction.

3. **INSURING A FAIR PRICE**
   Most states provide various means of protecting judgment debtors from the sale of property at execution sales for unfairly low prices, including (a) appraisal statutes; (b) redemption; and (c) vacating an execution sale because of inadequacy of the sale price.

4. **TITLE ACQUIRED BY EXECUTION PURCHASER: "BUYERS BEWARE"**
   As a general rule, a purchaser at any execution sale acquires only such title as the debtor had.

D. LIEN OF EXECUTION
The process of execution gives rise to an execution lien that can reach any of the debtor's leviable property, including personal property.

1. **ATTACHMENT AND DURATION OF THE LIEN OF EXECUTION**
   In the majority of states, the sheriff's levy itself creates an execution lien on the property that is seized. Thus, for the purpose of determining priorities, the lien

dates from the time of the levy. In a minority of states, the lien dates from the time that the writ of execution is delivered to the sheriff.

2.   TERRITORIAL REACH OF EXECUTION LIEN
An execution lien ordinarily extends to all of the debtor's leviable property located within the bailiwick of the official to whom the writ of execution is delivered, which usually is limited to one county in the state.

3.   RELATIONSHIP BETWEEN JUDGMENT LIENS AND EXECUTION
An execution lien on real estate ordinarily relates back to a subsisting judgment lien on the property.

4.   PRIORITY OF EXECUTION LIENS
   a.   Execution Lienors *Inter Se*. In states where an execution lien arises upon delivery of the writ of execution to the sheriff, priority among execution creditors is usually determined according to the order in which their writs were delivered to the officer. In states where the lien of execution dates from the time of actual levy by the sheriff, "[t]he execution first levied * * * has the first lien on the property, though there may be others in the hands of the sheriff, which were delivered to him before the one levied." *Albrecht v. Long,* 25 Minn. 163, 172 (1878).

   b.   Prior Claims and Interests. As a general rule, an execution lien attaches to whatever title or interest the debtor has, subject to all prior equities, including existing liens, mortgages, and other claims and interests, except where a recording statute protects the execution creditor from secret interests.

   c.   Subsequent Claims and Interests. An execution lien ordinarily takes priority over subsequent claims and interests, but such priority can be lost by delay in enforcing the writ.

   d.   Execution Lienor Versus Bankruptcy Trustee. As a very general rule, all liens on a debtor's property, including execution liens, are enforceable against the debtor's bankruptcy estate and the trustee in bankruptcy; but these liens are subject to the trustee's avoiding powers and can thereby be invalidated in bankrutpcy when the conditions for avoidance are satisied.

E.   EXECUTION FROM FEDERAL COURT
Execution is the usual process for enforcing a money judgment of a federal district court.

1.   STATE PROCEDURE USUALLY GOVERNS
Generally, the procedure governing execution from federal district court "shall be in accordance with the practice and procedure of the state in which the district court is held, existing at the time the remedy is sought * * *." Fed.R.Civ.P. 69(a).

2. **STAY OF EXECUTION**
   a. **Ten–Day Waiting Period.** "[N]o execution shall issue upon a judgment nor shall proceedings be taken for its enforcement until the expiration of 10 days after its entry." Fed.R.Civ.P. 62(a).

   b. **Stay Upon Appeal.** Execution of a federal court judgment will be stayed upon the debtor's appeal of the judgment only if she provides a supersedeas bond that is approved by the court. Fed.R.Civ.P. 62(d).

3. **MARSHALS ENFORCE WRITS**
   Writs of execution issued by federal district courts are usually enforced by United States marshals. 28 U.S.C.A. § 569(b) (1968); Fed.R.Civ.P. 4(c)(1).

4. **TERRITORIAL REACH OF A FEDERAL WRIT**
   "[A] writ of execution [issued from a federal district court] may run and be served anywhere within the territorial limits of the state in which the district court is held that rendered the judgment, although a state writ of execution will not run throughout the state," 7 (pt. 2) J. Moore & J. Lucas, Moore's Federal Practice paragraph 69.04[2] at 69–17 (2d ed.1983), except that a writ obtained for the use of the United States may be executed in any state or the District of Columbia.

5. **FEDERAL EXECUTION LIENS**
   Liens of execution based on federal judgments are governed by the law of the state in which the district court is held.

IV. FINDING PROPERTY OF THE DEBTOR

The law provides remedies designed specifically to aid in discovering the debtor's hidden assets and in applying hard to reach assets in satisfaction of the creditor's judgment. A creditor's bill in equity (actually a set of creditors' bills) was the first of such remedies, but virtually every jurisdiction now has statutory substitutes of various kinds that are commonly collected under the generic heading of supplemental (sometimes supplementary) proceedings.

A. **CREDITORS' BILLS**
1. **UNSATISFIED EXECUTION AS PREREQUISITE TO A CREDITOR'S BILL**
   The general rule is that a creditor's bill cannot be brought until judgment is obtained and execution is returned wholly or partially unsatisfied.

2. **BRINGING A CREDITOR'S BILL**
   A creditor's bill is a separate action begun by filing a complaint or petition, the substance of which varies depending on the particular relief sought.

3. **FORMS OF RELIEF UNDER A CREDITOR'S BILL**
   Typical forms of relief include examination and discovery; injunction; sale of property; appointment of a receiver; assignment; and contempt.

4. **THE LIEN RESULTING FROM A CREDITOR'S BILL**
   The general rule is that, upon the commencement of a judgment creditor's bill, an equitable lien attaches to property of the debtor that is found and appropriated for the creditor's benefit. The lien is usually subordinate to then existing liens on or rights to the specific property affected by the bill, but is usually entitled to priority over claimants of the property who acquired their interests after the equitable lien attached.

5. **CREDITOR'S BILLS IN FEDERAL COURT**
   Relief in the form of a creditor's bill can be sought in federal court if the action is available to state courts under local law.

6. **DECLINE IN USE OF CREDITOR'S BILLS**
   In many states, statutes have taken over almost all of the functions of the equitable creditor's bill; but creditor's bills have not been entirely displaced and retain some utility, especially as a sturdy vehicle for setting aside fraudulent conveyances.

B. **MODERN SUPPLEMENTAL PROCEEDINGS**
1. **SUPPLEMENTAL DISCOVERY**
   A local variation of Federal Rule of Civil Procedure 69(a) is available to judgment creditors in most states. This rule provides in pertinent part that, "[i]n aid of the judgment or execution, the judgment creditor * * * may obtain discovery from any person, including the judgment debtor, in the manner provided in [the rules of civil procedure] or in the manner provided by the practice of the state in which the district court is held."

   a. **When Discovery Is Available.** The discovery procedures authorized by Rule 69(a) and its local counterparts are available to a creditor in many states as soon as she wins a judgment; the creditor need not first pursue execution.

   b. **Which Discovery Devices Are Available.** Many states permit post-judgment discovery by *any* method that the state rules of civil procedure sanction for pre-judgment discovery.

2. **SUPPLEMENTAL RELIEF**
   The local counterparts of Rule 69(a) do not in their simplest forms provide for action against property that the creditor locates through post-judgment discovery. Most states, however, have enacted a statute or series of statutes that not only permit discovery of the debtor's property, but also allow and facilitate application of the property to the creditor's judgment. This sort of law provides for various kinds of relief designed to aid the creditor in satisfying her judgment through execution or some other process. Statutes in aid of judgment or execution commonly provide for some or all of the following kinds of relief:

   - *Discovery* and *examination* of the debtor and third parties;

   - *Court orders* to facilitate satisfaction of the judgment, including orders to achieve specific objectives such as to prevent the transfer or disposition of, or interference with, property belonging to the debtor; to apply property of the debtor toward satisfaction of the judgment, whether the property is held by the debtor or some third person; to require the debtor to satisfy the judgment by installment payments; and to appoint a receiver of the debtor's property.

- *Contempt* citations against the debtor or third persons who disobey court orders in supplemental proceedings.

V. GARNISHMENT

"Garnishment (sometimes called 'trustee process') is a procedure for reaching [1] debts owed *to* the debtor * * * by a third person or [2] property *of* the debtor in the possession of a third person. The third person is described as a garnishee." W. Warren & W. Hogan, Cases and Materials on Debtor–Creditor Law 105 (2d ed. 1981). The object is to reach the assets or credits under the garnishee's control and apply them in satisfaction of the creditor's claim against the debtor.

A. GARNISHMENT PROCEDURE

Garnishment typically begins with the judgment creditor, the garnishor, filing with the court an affidavit describing the judgment, complaining that the judgment is unsatisfied, and alleging that a third person, the garnishee is indebted to, or holds property of, the judgment debtor. The judge or the court clerk then issues a garnishment summons that is served on the garnishee and the judgment debtor. Service of the summons on the garnishee creates a lien of garnishment on property of the debtor held by the garnishee and also on debts and other credits the garnishee owes the debtor. The garnishee is required to answer the garnishment summons within a stated time; and in its answer the garnishee must describe what, if any, credits or effects of the debtor it holds. If the garnishor controverts the garnishee's answer, the controverted issues are tried as other civil cases.

B. GARNISHABLE PROPERTY
1. GENERAL RULE

A judgment creditor can reach through garnishment any of the debtor's personal property, whether tangible or not, having salable worth that is held, controlled, or owed to the debtor by a third person.

2. INTANGIBLE OBLIGATIONS OWED THE DEBTOR

Wages, bank accounts, and other purely intangible obligations owed the debtor are popular targets of garnishment, but in most states contingent or unliquidated obligations cannot be garnished.

3. REIFIED PROPERTY RIGHTS (DOCUMENTS OF TITLE AND CERTIFICATED SECURITIES)

Some rights to property owned by a debtor may be reified, meaning that the law regards the debtor's rights as transferable through assignment of the paper that evidences them. A creditor usually cannot capture such property of the debtor through garnishment; instead, she must seize through execution the paper representing the debtor's rights.

4. NEGOTIABLE INSTRUMENTS

When a person's obligation to a debtor is evidenced by a negotiable instrument such as a promissory note, this obligation cannot be reached by a judgment creditor through simple garnishment of the obligor unless the instrument is produced and delivered or the obligor is indemnified.

C. DEBTOR'S PROTECTIONS
1. STATE EXEMPTIONS

Virtually every state exempts a portion of a debtor's wages from garnishment and other creditors' process.

2. FEDERAL RESTRICTIONS ON THE AMOUNT OF EARNINGS A CREDITOR CAN GARNISH

Title III of the federal Consumer Credit Protection Act limits the amount of a debtor's earnings that a creditor can garnish to 25 percent of a debtor's aggregate weekly "disposable earnings" or the amount by which her disposable earnings exceed thirty times the minimum hourly wage, whichever is less. A larger sum can be garnished to enforce orders for the support of any person, including decrees and judgments for alimony and child support; and the limitation has no application to tax debts and court orders in a Chapter 13 bankruptcy case. Moreover, the Title III limitation does not apply after the debtor has received the earnings; so it is not a true exemption statute.

3. RESTRICTIONS ON DISCHARGE FROM EMPLOYMENT DUE TO GARNISHMENT OF EARNINGS

Federal law prohibits an employer from discharging "any employee by reason of the fact that her earnings have been subjected to garnishment for any one indebtedness." 15 U.S.C.A. § 1674(a) (1982).

4. STATE LIMITATIONS ON AVAILABILITY OF GARNISHMENT

Due to the harshness of garnishment, some states severely limit the availability of the remedy and completely outlaw the garnishment of wages.

5. GARNISHING CREDITOR'S EXPOSURE TO DAMAGES FOR WRONGFUL GARNISHMENT

The debtor's remedy of wrongful garnishment protects her to some extent from a creditor's abuse of the garnishment process.

6. DUE PROCESS GUARANTEES

The debtor's property cannot be garnished, either before or after judgment, without according her due process of law.

D. MAJOR DUTIES AND RIGHTS OF GARNISHEE
1. GARNISHEE MUST ANSWER GARNISHMENT SUMMONS

Unless the neglect is excused, a garnishee who fails to timely answer a garnishment summons risks liability for (1) the full amount of the garnishor's judgment against the debtor, (2) the amount or value of the debtor's property that the judgment creditor alleged was in the garnishee's hands, or (3) the actual damages suffered by the garnishor as a result of the garnishee's neglect.

2. **GARNISHEE MUST ACCOUNT FOR DEBTOR'S PROPERTY**
   a. **Garnishment Impounds Property Owed or Held By Garnishee as of the Time Summons is Served.** After proper service of a writ of garnishment, the garnishee acts at her peril if she disposes of property of the debtor which she holds at that time, or if she pays an obligation then owing to the debtor.

   b. **Garnishment's Coverage of After–Acquired Property and Obligations.** In some states the impoundment and lien of garnishment reach only the property of the debtor that the garnishee holds or owes the debtor at the time the writ is served. Any property of the debtor thereafter received by the garnishee, or any obligation to the debtor thereafter incurred by the garnishee, is not affected by the garnishment. In other states the impoundment and lien of garnishment not only reach property held, and credits owed, by the garnishee at the time the summons is served; the garnishment also reaches property of the debtor which comes into the possession of the garnishee, and debts of the garnishee which accrue, in the interim between service on the garnishee and answer by her.

   c. **Future Wages.** Some states provide that a garnishment of wages automatically continues for a specified length of time or until the judgment is satisfied.

3. **GARNISHEE MAY QUESTION VALIDITY OF THE ORIGINAL MAIN ACTION AND GARNISHMENT PROCEEDINGS**
   A garnishee can defeat a garnishment on the basis of irregularities in the garnishment proceeding itself. Moreover, she can defend against the garnishment by challenging the validity of the creditor's judgment against the debtor.

4. **GARNISHEE MAY RAISE DEFENSES SHE COULD ASSERT AGAINST DEBTOR**
   A garnishor stands in the judgment debtor's shoes in collecting property of the debtor held or owed by the garnishee; so any defenses that the garnishee could assert against the debtor can be raised against the garnishor.

5. **OBLIGATIONS OWED GARNISHEE BY DEBTOR CAN BE SET OFF AGAINST GARNISHOR'S CLAIM**
   In accounting to a garnishing creditor, the garnishee may offset claims she has against the judgment debtor.

6. **GARNISHEE MAY ASSERT THE RIGHTS OF THIRD PARTY CLAIMANTS OF THE DEBTOR'S PROPERTY**
   There is some authority that a garnishee has "the right to offer in defense all of the rights of a third-party claimant [of the debtor's credits or property which the garnishee holds], such as an assignee." *First Wisconsin Mortgage Trust v. Wyman's, Inc.,* 139 Vt. 350, 356, 428 A.2d 1119, 1123 (1981).

7. **GARNISHEE MAY ASSERT DEBTOR'S EXEMPTIONS**
   If the debtor's credits or other property held by the garnishee are exempt from garnishment by federal or state law, the garnishee is generally permitted to assert the debtor's exemptions and thereby resist the garnishment, but the law is unclear whether the garnishee is obligated to do so.

E.   SPECIAL PROBLEMS WHEN THE GARNISHEE IS A BANK
1.   GARNISHING JOINT ACCOUNTS
The rule in most states is that a joint account can be garnished by a creditor of only one of the depositors, but only to the extent of the debtor's equitable ownership of the funds in the account.

2.   GARNISHING SPECIAL ACCOUNTS
A special bank account established by a debtor to hold another's funds, or even to hold funds of the debtor that are dedicated to a particular purpose, is generally immune from garnishment by creditors of the depositor.

3.   GARNISHING A UNIT OF THE DEBTOR'S BANK OTHER THAN THE BRANCH WHERE THE DEBTOR'S ACCOUNT IS MAINTAINED
The traditional rule is that a debtor's account can be garnished only by directing process at the branch where her account is maintained, although there is modern authority to the contrary.

4.   DECIDING THE RACE BETWEEN A CHECK IN THE COLLECTION PROCESS AND A WRIT OF GARNISHMENT AIMED AT FREEZING THE DRAWER'S ACCOUNT
   a.   Under the Uniform Commercial Code.   U.C.C. § 4–303 provides that legal process, such as a writ of garnishment, is ineffective against a bank with respect to checks which the bank pays or decides to pay before the expiration of a reasonable time after the process has been served.

   b.   Under the Bankruptcy Code.   The Bankruptcy Code expressly provides that a person who acts in good faith without actual notice or knowledge of the debtor's bankruptcy petition may transfer property of the debtor, such as by paying checks drawn by her or giving property to a garnishor, without incurring liability to the bankruptcy estate.   11 U.S.C.A. § 542(c).

F.   EFFECT OF GARNISHMENT BETWEEN GARNISHEE AND JUDGMENT DEBTOR
1.   WHERE GARNISHEE PAYS JUDGMENT CREDITOR
Ordinarily, "the finding in a garnishment proceeding is not binding on the judgment debtor except as to the amount actually paid by the garnishee." *Savepex Sales Co. v. M.S. Kaplan Co.,* 103 Ill.App.2d 481, 484, 243 N.E.2d 608, 610 (1968). The garnishee's obligation to the judgment debtor is reduced to the extent of such payment.

2.   WHERE GARNISHEE IS DISCHARGED FROM LIABILITY TO JUDGMENT CREDITOR
A garnishee's victory in a garnishment action to which the judgment debtor was not a party does not prevent a later suit by the judgment debtor against the garnishee on the obligation which the latter owes the former.

G.   PRIORITY BETWEEN GARNISHMENTS
The long-established general rule as to priority between several garnishments against the same property by different creditors is that the garnishors rank in the direct order of time of service of the garnishment summons on the garnishee; but a number of states give special preference to a garnishment to enforce a support judgment in a do-

mestic relations case and give it priority over even another creditor's earlier garnishment.

H.   PRIORITY AMONG GARNISHMENTS AND OTHER CLAIMS OR INTERESTS

In the usual case where the priority of a garnishing creditor is at issue, the other claimant is an assignee of the debtor; both parties, the garnishor and the assignee, claim a credit which the garnishee has interpleaded or has already paid to one of the claimants. If the garnishee has already paid the credit, the validity of the payment, and thus the liability of the garnishee, turns on whether the recipient was entitled to priority over the other claimant.

1.   DETERMINE FIRST IF GARNISHOR'S LIEN REACHED THE PROPERTY

Before determining priority according to the following rules, it must be decided if the garnishing creditor acquired a lien on the credit which the debtor has assigned. If not, there is no priority dispute, and the assignee prevails.

2.   ASSIGNMENT OF DEBTOR'S RIGHT AGAINST GARNISHEE MADE BEFORE CREDITOR'S GARNISHMENT

    a.   Traditional Rule—First in Time First in Right. Because a garnishment is effective only to the extent of the debtor's interest in property that is seized, the usual rule is that a garnishor's lien does not displace prior equities or rights in the property that the garnishor seeks to attach. Thus, the claim of an assignee under a valid assignment made before the garnishment is superior to any lien of the garnishing creditor.

    b.   Exception—Perfection May Be Required. In a great many states a prior assignment will prevail over a garnishment only if the assignee perfected her claim, either by notifying the obligor/garnishee of the assignment or by recording public notice of it, prior to service of the garnishment summons. Certainly, if U.C.C. Article 9 governs the debtor's assignment of her rights against the obligor/garnishee, the assignee/secured party will lose to a subsequent garnishor unless the assignee has perfected its security interest before the garnishment. See U.C.C. § 9–301(1)(b).

3.   ASSIGNMENT MADE AFTER GARNISHMENT

A garnishment prior in time to an assignment of the debtor's rights against the garnishee is also prior in right; so the debtor's rights, which the assignee takes, are burdened with the lien of garnishment.

I.   GOVERNMENT AS WAGE GARNISHEE
1.   FEDERAL GOVERNMENT

Because of the principle of sovereign immunity, the United States Government cannot be sued without its consent; for this reason, the wages of federal employees cannot be reached by garnishment against the United States, except in isolated cases where immunity has been waived. This immunity, however, does not protect deposit accounts at banks chartered by the federal government. National banks are not agencies of the United States.

2.   STATE AND LOCAL GOVERNMENTS
State and local governments also enjoy sovereign immunity, but most states explicitly permit the garnishment of wages owed by state and other local governments to their employees.

J.   WRONGFUL GARNISHMENT
A creditor risks liability for wrongful garnishment by causing seizure of her debtor's property, or property of another, through a garnishment proceeding that is not in compliance with law. The victim can recover all damages actually suffered and, in an appropriate case, can also recover punitive damages.

VI. FRAUDULENT CONVEYANCES

The source of modern fraudulent conveyance law is the Statute of 13 Elizabeth, chapter 5, enacted by Parliament in 1570. American jurisdictions either recognized the Statute of 13 Elizabeth as part of inherited common law or enacted identical or very similar versions of it. More recently, about one-half of the states adopted the Uniform Fraudulent Conveyance Act (1918), hereinafter referred to as the *UFCA*. In 1984, a successor to the UFCA was promulgated by the National Conference of Commissioners on Uniform State Laws. The proposed new statute is entitled the Uniform Fraudulent Transfer Act, *UFTA*. For the most part, the two uniform laws are very similar. Like the Statute of 13 Elizabeth, both the UFCA and the UFTA condemn transfers of property that are *actually fraudulent,* meaning that they are made with the actual, subjective intention of defrauding creditors. The two uniform statutes go further, however, and also condemn transfers that are *constructively fraudulent,* meaning that they are ineffective either because the circumstances of the conveyance conclusively imply wrongful intent, or because the law deems that creditors are wronged by the property's transfer irrespective of the intention accompanying it.

A.   CONVEYANCES THAT ARE ACTUALLY FRAUDULENT
Under both the UFCA (§ 7) and the UFTA (§ 4(a)(1)), every conveyance made and every obligation incurred with actual intent to hinder, delay, or defraud either present or future creditors is fraudulent as to both present and future creditors.

1.   THE MEANING OF "CONVEYANCE"
"Conveyance" means "every payment of money, assignment, release, transfer, lease, mortgage or pledge of tangible or intangible property, and also the creation of any lien or encumbrance." UFCA § 1. (The new UFTA substitutes "transfer" for "conveyance" but does not change the substance of the definition.)

2.   THE MEANING OF ACTUAL INTENT TO DEFRAUD
An actual intent to hinder, delay, or defraud involves calculated conduct by the debtor who acts with a conscious realization of the adverse effects of the conduct on her creditors. Circumstantial indicators of actual fraudulent intent are commonly referred to as *badges of fraud.*

3. **BADGES OF FRAUD**
    The term *badges of fraud* has long been used in referring to circumstances that are especially reliable indicators of actual intent to defraud creditors. The UFTA contains the most comprehensive and authoritative collection of badges of fraud.

4. **ROLE OF PRESUMPTIONS UNDER UFCA § 7**
    Badges of fraud are significant not only because their presence in a case is indirect evidence of intent to defraud; certain of them are so suggestive of fraud as to cause a shift in the burden of going forward with the evidence at trial of a fraudulent conveyance case. Instead of requiring the plaintiff—who is attacking the transfer—to establish the elements of a fraudulent conveyance, the defendant—who is the transferee of the property—is required to put on evidence that some necessary element is missing. This reversal of usual roles, and the badge of fraud that caused it, are often described as creating a presumption of fraud, which in some cases is conclusive and thus irrefutable.

5. **FAMILIAL RELATIONSHIP AS A BADGE OF FRAUD AND BASIS OF PRESUMPTION**
    A debtor's conveyance of property to a spouse or other family member is always suspect and is subject to more careful and closer scrutiny than a transfer between strangers. The familial relationship in itself is only a badge of fraud, however, only one indicator of actual fraudulent intent. Yet, such a relationship greatly strengthens an inference of actual fraud drawn from other suspect circumstances.

6. **GOOD CONSIDERATION NO DEFENSE IN ITSELF TO ACTUAL FRAUD**
    The giving of fair, substantial, good or otherwise sufficient consideration by a transferee of the debtor's property does not excuse an actually fraudulent transfer, but it does provide the transferee a complete defense if she herself acted in good faith.

7. **PREFERENCES**
    a. **Traditional Rule.** Neither the common law nor the UFCA condemns a debtor deliberately preferring one creditor to another. In short, a preference is not per se fraudulent. This is the rule of the common law which applies even if, as a result of the preference, the claims of other creditors will be hindered, delayed, or defeated.

    b. **UFTA Rule.** UFTA § 5(b) renders constructively fraudulent a preferential transfer to an insider who had reason to believe that the debtor was insolvent when the transfer was made. "Insider" includes a relative, a director or officer of a corporate debtor, a partner, or a person in control of a debtor.

8. **TRANSACTIONS INVOLVING EXEMPT PROPERTY**
    a. **Conveying Exempt Property.** A conveyance of property that the law exempts from creditors' process usually cannot be attacked as fraudulent no matter what the debtor's intention.

    b. **Converting Nonexempt Property to Property That Is Exempt.** A heavily indebted or insolvent debtor, a debtor who has suffered a judgment against her, or a debtor contemplating bankruptcy can freely convert nonexempt property to exempt property and so remove it from the reach of her creditors or trustee in bankruptcy. This sort of conversion is usually not fraudulent, regardless of the debtor's motive, although a few modern authorities disagree.

B. CONVEYANCES THAT ARE CONSTRUCTIVELY FRAUDULENT

In every state, certain conveyances of a debtor's property are deemed fraudulent and thus ineffective against creditors even in the absence of direct proof of an actual subjective intention to hinder, delay or defraud creditors. Such conveyances are commonly described as *constructively fraudulent.* The most common variety of constructively fraudulent conveyance is described in UFCA § 4: *a conveyance made or obligation incurred by a person who is or will be thereby rendered insolvent when the conveyance is made, or the obligation is incurred, without a fair consideration.* UFTA § 5(a) condemns the same thing, as does the law of every state either by statute or decisional rule. Although relieved of the burden of showing actual fraudulent intent, a creditor attacking a conveyance under UFCA § 4 or UFTA § 5(a) must nevertheless establish, first, that there was a "conveyance" of the debtor's property; second, that the conveyance was without "fair consideration;" and, third, that the debtor was, or then became, "insolvent."

1. CONVEYANCE

Actually and constructively fraudulent conveyances share the requirement that the challenged transfer is a "conveyance," which has the same meaning for both actual and constructive fraud. Because of this common definition, constructively fraudulent conveyances take as many different forms as conveyances made with actual fraudulent intent.

2. FAIR CONSIDERATION

   a. **Fair Consideration Means Equivalent Value.** As long as no actual fraudulent intent is involved, a debtor, whether solvent or not, can freely convey her property in exchange for *fair consideration,* which essentially means an exchange of property of equivalent value.

   b. **Comparing "Fair Consideration" in Fraudulent Conveyances Law With "Consideration" in Contracts Law.** The concept of fair consideration is both thinner and wider than the doctrine of consideration in the law of contracts.

   c. **Love and Affection.** "Love and affection" and comparable motives for making transfers of property do not constitute fair, good, valuable or otherwise sufficient consideration.

   d. **Inadequate Consideration in Foreclosure Sales of Collateral.** The usual rule of state law is that a secured creditor's foreclosure sale of collateral, if conducted according to law, is not a fraudulent conveyance solely because of the inadequacy of the price paid for the property by the buyer at the forced sale. In bankruptcy, however, a contrary tradition and rule has recently developed which holds that a perfectly legal forced sale is constructively fraudulent under bankruptcy law if the price received for the property is substantially less than the property's market value.

e.   **Whether Excessive Collateral in Secured Transactions Is Unfair Considera-tion.**   If the value of a secured creditor's collateral far exceeds the amount of the secured debt, the security arrangement can be attacked as a constructively fraudulent conveyance under the UFCA; but the new UFTA rejects this UFCA rule.

f.   **Good Faith as a Distinct Element of Fair Consideration.**   Under some existing laws, including the UFCA, the definition of fair consideration requires not only an exchange of fair equivalents; another, separate requirement is that the ex-change be made in good faith.   The new UFTA eliminates good faith as an is-sue in determining whether fair or otherwise adequate consideration has been given; but good faith on the transferee's part is an issue in determining whether the transferee has a defense to an action against her by a creditor who is wronged by a fraudulent conveyance.

g.   **Burden of Proof With Respect to Fairness of Consideration.**   Initially, the party attacking a conveyance as constructively fraudulent has the burden of proving the lack of fair consideration.   Yet, there are facts which, if proved, will cause the burden of going forward to shift to the transferee, who then must demonstrate that adequate consideration was given for the conveyance.

h.   **The Force of Recitals of Consideration.**   Recitals of consideration in contracts and deeds are virtually meaningless in deciding if fair consideration supports what is alleged to have been a constructively fraudulent transfer of property.

3.   **INSOLVENCY**
a.   **The Meaning of Insolvency.**   For purposes of fraudulent conveyances law, "[a] person is insolvent when the present fair salable value of her assets is less than the amount that will be required to pay her probable liability on her ex-isting debts as they become absolute and matured."   UFCA § 2(1).   The UFTA's definition of insolvency is identical in substance.   Under both statutes, a debtor's assets do not include exempt property.

b.   **Burden of Proof of Insolvency.**   The usual rule is that the person attacking a conveyance as constructively fraudulent has the burden of showing that the grantor did not receive fair consideration and also that the grantor was insol-vent either at the time of the conveyance or as a result of it.   Yet, there is some authority that proof of either of these elements by the attacking creditor shifts to the transferee the burden as to the other element.   Moreover, al-though the UFCA and the UFTA agree in substance on the meaning of insol-vency, the new uniform law adds that "[a] debtor who is generally not paying his or her debts as they become due is presumed to be insolvent."   UFTA § 2(b).

C.   **REMEDYING A FRAUDULENT CONVEYANCE**
The principal cure for a fraudulent conveyance is to apply the fraudulently conveyed property, or its value, to the realization of the debt which is owed the creditor.   Four remedies, or sets of remedies, are potentially involved.   All of them are directed at the property's transferee; and, as a general rule, all of the remedies can be exercised not

only against the original or first transferee, but also against a subsequent transferee, often referred to as a subgrantee.

1. **REMEDIAL OPTIONS**
   a. **Protect the Property.** Courts in appropriate cases may protect property that has been fraudulently conveyed by restraining any further disposition of it, appointing a receiver to take charge of the property, or making any other order which the circumstances of the case may require.

   b. **Ignore the Conveyance and Seize the Property.** The creditor can disregard the conveyance and attach or levy execution upon the property even though it is held by the debtor's transferee.

   c. **Sue to Set Aside the Conveyance.** Instead of ignoring the debtor's fraudulent conveyance and seizing the property from the transferee, a creditor of the debtor is more likely to sue to have the conveyance set aside so that the property can be applied in satisfaction of the creditor's claim.

   d. **Sue the Transferee for Damages.** The traditional rule is that creditors usually cannot recover damages from the transferee of a fraudulent conveyance. Their remedy is limited to recovering the property. There are numerous exceptions to this rule, however, so that a transferee or grantee must account in damages for the property's value when the creditor has a pre-existing lien on property fraudulently conveyed; the grantee has not yet paid for the property; or the grantee is unable to return the property.

2. **CREDITORS WHO CAN PURSUE REMEDIES**
   Not all of the remedies listed above are available to every creditor of a debtor who fraudulently conveys property. Whether a creditor has any remedies at all, and the nature of the remedies that are available to her, depend largely on three facts:

   • Whether or not the creditor is a "creditor" as defined by fraudulent conveyance law;

   ("Creditor" means a person having any claim, whether matured or unmatured, liquidated or unliquidated, absolute, fixed or contingent.)

   • Whether she became a creditor before or after the fraudulent conveyance; and,

   (Creditors existing at the time of the conveyance are more fully protected than subsequent creditors.)

   • Whether or not her claim has matured by the time she pursues remedies against the transferee of a fraudulent conveyance.

   (The range of a creditor's remedial options may vary depending on whether the creditor's claim has matured by the time she pursues remedies.)

3. REMEDIES OF A BANKRUPTCY TRUSTEE TO AVOID FRAUDULENT CONVEYANCES OF A BANKRUPT DEBTOR'S PROPERTY

A bankruptcy trustee has two primary tools by which she can void fraudulent conveyances of a bankrupt debtor's property and bring the property within the bankruptcy estate for distribution to creditors: The tools are Bankruptcy Code §§ 544(b) and 548, which allow the trustee to use state and federal law in avoiding fraudulent conveyances.

D. TRANSFEREE'S DEFENSES

1. COMPLETE DEFENSE OF AN INNOCENT PURCHASER FOR FAIR CONSIDERATION

When a creditor attacks a conveyance of her debtor as fraudulent, the transferee's best defense is that she is an innocent purchaser for a fair consideration. This defense is complete even if the conveyance was actually fraudulent.

2. PARTIAL DEFENSE OF AN INNOCENT TRANSFEREE WHO PAID LESS THAN FAIR CONSIDERATION

A person who has given less than fair consideration for property fraudulently conveyed to her does not qualify for protected purchaser status, but the UFCA provides that a purchaser who without actual fraudulent intent has given less than a fair consideration for the conveyance may retain the property as security for repayment. The UFTA agrees. A guilty transferee, i.e., one who participated in the fraud associated with the property's conveyance, gets no credit for the value, whether fair or not, she gave in exchange for the property.

3. PROTECTION OF SUBGRANTEES

If a transferee of fraudulently conveyed property reconveys it to a third person, this subgrantee is generally subject to the same remedies that the debtor's creditors could have pursued against the original transferee. A subgrantee is protected, however, if (1) in her own right she satisfies the requirements of a purchaser whom the law protects from creditors of the debtor, or (2) she claims the property through a protected purchaser.

VII. BULK SALES

Uniform Commercial Code Article 6 primarily regulates sales of inventory in bulk. Wholly apart from fraudulent conveyance law, and regardless of the seller's intention, a sale or other transfer that is governed by Article 6 is ineffective against any of the seller's creditors if Article 6's requirements have not been satisfied.

A. TRANSACTIONS COVERED BY ARTICLE 6

Article 6 applies when an enterprise, whose principal business is the sale of merchandise from stock, transfers a major part of its inventory in bulk and not in the ordinary course of business; and Article 6 also governs a transfer of a substantial part of the equipment of such an enterprise if it is made in connection with a bulk transfer of inventory.

B. REQUIREMENTS OF ARTICLE 6

Article 6 imposes two major conditions on the effectiveness of a bulk transfer:

1. **NOTICE MUST BE GIVEN TO THE TRANSFEROR'S CREDITORS**
    A bulk transfer governed by Article 6 is ineffective against any creditor of the transferor unless at least ten days before the transferee takes possession of the goods or pays for them, whichever happens first, she gives notice of the transfer to the transferor's existing creditors. The statute describes in detail the required contents of the notice.

2. **PROCEEDS OF THE BULK TRANSFER MUST BE APPLIED TO CREDITORS' CLAIMS**
    The official text of Article 6 conditions the effectiveness of a bulk transfer on a second major requirement which many states have elected not to adopt. This requirement, which is imposed by U.C.C. § 6–106, applies whenever a bulk transfer is for new consideration, and requires the transferee to ensure that the consideration is applied in satisfaction of the transferor's debts.

C. **CONSEQUENCES OF FAILURE TO COMPLY WITH ARTICLE 6**
1. **AS BETWEEN THE PARTIES TO THE BULK TRANSFER**
    Failure to comply with Article 6 is generally inconsequential as between the parties to the bulk transfer.

2. **AS BETWEEN THE TRANSFEROR AND HER CREDITORS**
    Article 6 does not add to or subtract from the remedies available to the transferor's creditors on their claims against the transferor.

3. **AS BETWEEN THE TRANSFEREE AND THE TRANSFEROR'S CREDITORS**
    a. **Where Proper Notice Is Not Given.**
        1) **Usual Remedy of Transferor's Creditors Is to Proceed in Rem Against the Transferred Property or Its Proceeds.** A bulk transfer is "ineffective" unless proper and timely notice is given to the transferor's creditors pursuant to Article 6. Ineffective means voidable, and an aggrieved creditor can pursue the same sorts of remedies that would be available to her had the transfer been condemned under the Uniform Fraudulent Conveyance Act of similar local law. The creditor can sue to set aside the conveyance and to have the property applied in satisfaction of her claim; she can garnish, levy or otherwise proceed directly against the property as if the transfer had never been made; or, she can pursue any other legal or equitable remedy that is available under local law to creditors in her position.

        2) **Transferee Is Generally Not Personally Liable.** When the notice requirements of Article 6 have been violated, the transferee is treated as a receiver of the goods but is not personally liable for the transferor's debts. Nevertheless, because a bulk transferee is accountable for the property to the transferor's creditors, she is personally liable to them under any state's law for the value of property that she has conveyed, confused with other goods, converted to her own use, or otherwise put beyond the reach of the transferor's creditors.

b. **Where Proceeds Are Misapplied.** In some states, the transferee is required to apply new consideration given for a bulk sale in satisfaction of the transferor's debts. In these states the transferee is personally liable for any sum that should have been distributed to a creditor pursuant to the dictates of Article 6.

c. **Where the Transferor's Creditor Is An Article 9 Secured Party.** If the transferred property is collateral for a secured claim, the security interest generaly survives, and is unaffected by, the bulk transfer. U.C.C. §§ 9–201 & 9–306(2). Thus, the secured party can hold the transferee accountable for the property.

d. **Good Faith Purchaser Status No Defense in Action Against Immediate Transferee.** When a bulk transfer is attacked by creditors of the transferor for lack of compliance with Article 6, the immediate transferee cannot successfully defend on the basis of her good faith, the absence of fraudulent intent, or the payment of a fair consideration.

4. **AS BETWEEN CREDITORS OF THE TRANSFEROR AND PERSONS CLAIMING THROUGH THE TRANSFEREE WHEN A BULK TRANSFER IS DEEMED INEFFECTIVE**

a. **General Rule of Derivative Title.** When a bulk transfer is deemed ineffective because of a failure to satisfy the notice requirements of Article 6, the transferee's rights must yield to the claims of the transferor's creditors, and so must the rights of the transferee's creditors and other persons who claim through her.

b. **Exception Protecting Bona Fide Purchasers From a Bulk Transferee.** Although the title of a bulk transferee is defective because of non-compliance with Article 6's requirements, a purchaser for value, in good faith, and without notice takes free of any such defect.

c. **Secured Party of Transferor Versus Secured Party of Transferee.** A secured party of the bulk transferee, who is a good faith purchaser, takes free of any defect in title caused by failure to comply with Article 6, but is subject to an earlier perfected security interest created by the bulk transferor.

5. **STATUTE OF LIMITATIONS**

A creditor of the transferor can neither bring an action under Article 6, nor levy on the property transferred, more than six months after the date on which the transferee took possession of the goods. If, however, the transfer was concealed, the six-month period begins to run when the transfer is discovered.

VIII. SHIELDING EXEMPT PROPERTY

A. **PERSONALTY IN GENERAL**

1. **COMMONLY EXEMPTED GOODS**

The following kinds of goods are protected from creditor process in almost every state which exempts specific types of personal property: family Bible; wearing apparel; household furnishings; tools and implements of trade or business; and a motor vehicle.

2. **COMMON LIMITATIONS ON PERSONAL PROPERTY EXEMPTIONS**
   a. **Residency Requirement.** Local personal property exemptions are normally available only to residents.

   b. **"Necessity" Requirement.** Many states limit exemptions of specific goods and other property, including some forms of income, to that which is "necessary."

   c. **Head of Family Or Household Requirement.** Many personal property exemptions are expressly restricted to a debtor who is the head of a household or family.

   d. **Value Limitation.** Statutes exempting goods usually impose value limitations, such as "one motor vehicle to the extent of a value not exceeding $2000." Applying these statutes raises three major issues: (1) the meaning of value; (2) how to measure the property's worth; and (3) the effect of excess value.

3. **PROCEDURE FOR EXEMPTING PERSONALTY**
   The typical procedure for asserting exemptions requires the debtor to claim her exemptions within a specified period, or reasonable time, after creditors' process is initiated against her.

4. **EXEMPTABILITY OF PROCEEDS**
   The proceeds of exempt property resulting from a voluntary sale thereof are usually not exempt, and property is not exempt solely for the reason that it was purchased with exempt funds.

5. **CLAIMS ENFORCEABLE AGAINST EXEMPT PERSONALTY**
   There are several classes of claims that take priority over, and are enforceable notwithstanding, the exemptions generally available to a debtor. The most common and important are (a) debts for necessaries of life; (b) claims for alimony or support; (c) tort liability; (d) purchase-money debts; and (e) tax debts.

6. **CONSENSUALLY WAIVING PERSONAL PROPERTY EXEMPTIONS**
   a. **Validity Under State Law of Waiver of Exemptions by Consent.** The well-established general rule is that, except where expressly provided otherwise by enacted law, executory waivers of exemptions are void as violative of public policy.

   b. **Waivers of Exemptions Under Federal Law.**
      1) **Unlawful as an Unfair Trade Practice.** The Federal Trade Commission has effectively prohibited waivers of and limitations on exemptions in consumer credit contracts.

      2) **Void Under Bankruptcy Code.** In bankruptcy, a waiver of exemptions in favor of a creditor holding an unsecured claim is unenforceable.

7. **CREATING CONSENUSAL SECURITY INTERESTS IN EXEMPT PERSONAL PROPERTY**

The creation of an enforceable security interest in personal property amounts to a waiver of exemption rights with respect to the property. Nevertheless, the vast majority of states, by express statutory provision or through decisional law, permit debtors to encumber exempt property not only to secure payment of the purchase price of the property, but also to secure any non-purchase money loan or other extension of credit.

8. **CHOICE OF LAW WHEN EXEMPTION LAWS CONFLICT**

Exemption laws are local in nature and have no extra-territorial force or operation; so forum law determines exemptions.

B. **INCOME EXEMPTIONS**

Every state exempts from creditors' process certain income of a debtor. The term "income" is used here in a very broad sense to mean any money or right to money received by the debtor.

1. **WAGES, SALARY, EARNINGS, AND THE LIKE**

Some part of a debtor's "wages," "salary" or "earnings" is everywhere protected as exempt, but these three terms have slightly different meanings that affect the scope of protection. For example, the compensation of an independent contractor may be salary or earnings, but is not wages. Generally, however, all three terms are limited to compensation for personal services.

2. **EMPLOYEE BENEFITS**

Exemption laws usually do not explicitly cover a variety of employee benefits that often are paid in addition to, or in lieu of, regular or ordinary compensation. Thus, such benefits are exempted only if they fit within statutes protecting more generally described compensation. In some instances where employee benefits are treated separately, as is commonly true of retirement pay, the protection may be less than that given other forms of employee compensation. Thus, for one reason or another, debtors attempt to shield employee benefits under laws exempting "wages," "salary," or "earnings."

3. **RETIREMENT BENEFITS AND OTHER TYPES OF SOCIAL SECURITY PAYMENTS**

The exemption laws of some states specifically exempt retirement pay earned in connection with certain types of employment (usually public sector employment), and most states typically exempt health and welfare assistance of various kinds. Federal law exempts retirement pay for various kinds of work performed for the United States government and a variety of health and welfare assistance paid with federal funds.

4. **PROCEEDS OF INCOME AND THE SPECIAL PROBLEM OF EXEMPT INCOME DEPOSITED IN A BANK**

The general rule is that, unless otherwise provided by statute, proceeds of property are not exempt solely because the property itself was exempt. Concomitantly, goods and real estate purchased with exempt income generally are not exempt simply because the money used to buy it was exempt. Yet, even though a bank ac-

(N. & E.) Creditors' Rights BLS—3

count amounts to proceeds of the money deposited there, exempt income remains exempt notwithstanding deposit of the funds in a checking account. Outdated authority holds, however, that income deposited in a savings account loses its exempt status.

5. **BANK'S RIGHT TO EXERCISE SETOFF AGAINST EXEMPT FUNDS IN A DEPOSIT ACCOUNT**
The majority view is that a bank cannot exercise its right of setoff against exempt funds in a debtor's account.

C. **LIFE INSURANCE**
1. **MATURED POLICIES**
   a. **Protection of Proceeds Paid to Beneficiary Other Than Insured's Estate.** Modern exemption laws, either by their express terms or as construed by the courts, typically shield life insurance proceeds from the claims of the beneficiary's own creditors and also from the claims of the insured's creditors.

   b. **Exemptability of Proceeds Paid to Insured's Estate.** Ordinarily, the insured's creditors can reach insurance proceeds paid to an insured's estate, unless an exemption law specifically shields the property from those creditors' claims.

2. **UNMATURED POLICIES**
   a. **Protection of Present Value From Creditors of the Insured.** The cash surrender value of an insurance policy is typically exempt from creditors' process.

   b. **Determining if The Substance of a Contract Matches Its Form as a Life Insurance Policy.** If the investment features of an insurance policy go beyond providing a cash surrender value, substance will control form in determining the applicability of an insurance exemption.

D. **HOMESTEAD**
A debtor's home and the underlying land, which together constitute her homestead, are exempt from creditors' process in most states if, as is usually required, the debtor has dependents who live with her and rely on her for support.

1. **NATURE OF HOMESTEAD**
In most jurisdictions, a homestead is fundamentally a privilege or right to exempt certain real property from legal process, not an estate or a vested interest in the property.

2. **PERSONS ENTITLED TO HOMESTEAD EXEMPTION**
   a. **Residency Requirement.** The homestead exemption is typically available only to local residents.

   b. **The "Head of Household" or "Family" Requirement.** In most states, the homestead exemption is available only to a debtor who heads a "household" or a "family."

3. **PROPERTY THAT QUALIFIES AS HOMESTEAD**
   a. **Occupancy and Use as Residential Home.** For property to qualify as an exempt homestead, the debtor must actually occupy the premises as her home or residence. So long as the place is and continues to be the bona fide residence of the debtor and her family, the property qualifies for the homestead exemption despite its use partly, or even chiefly, as valuable income-producing commercial property.

   b. **Property Interest.** Virtually any legal or equitable interest or claim that gives the debtor, as against someone, a right to possession of the property will support her claim of exemption under the homestead laws.

4. **SCOPE OF HOMESTEAD**
   a. **Area.** A homestead ordinarily consists of the debtor's home itself, i.e., the house in which she and her family reside, together with the underlying, and some surrounding, land and connected appurtenances. Many states, however, limit the geographical size of the homestead. Usually, the allowable size of rural homesteads is much greater than that of homesteads in a city, town or village, often referred to as urban homesteads.

   b. **Value.** Most states limit the homestead exemption in terms of dollar value, and some states combine value and area limitations.

   c. **Income From and Products of a Homestead.** The homestead exemption normally embraces rents of the property and ungathered products of the land such as minerals beneath the ground and crops growing above it.

   d. **Proceeds.** The proceeds from a sale of a homestead, whether the sale is voluntary or forced, are exempt from creditors' process for a reasonable period of time to allow the debtor to invest in another homestead, as are proceeds of an insurance policy covering casualty to the property.

5. **ESTABLISHING A HOMESTEAD**
   In most states, the right to a homestead exemption does not depend upon any formalities. A homestead is established simply by an eligible debtor's occupancy of property that qualifies as a homestead. In some states, however, an additional prerequisite to the establishment of a homestead, or to the right to assert the exemption, is a formal declaration of homestead by the debtor or, in some cases, by the debtor's spouse or both spouses.

6. **GENERAL RULE AS TO ACTIONS BLOCKED BY HOMESTEAD LAWS**
   The states largely agree that homestead exemptions protect against ordinary collection process, including judgment and execution liens and the entire execution process.

7. **EXCEPTED CLAIMS, DEBTS, AND LIENS**
   The homestead exemption is not absolute. Some types of obligations are excepted from the homestead exemption. The common major exceptions are (a) pre-existing claims, debts and liens; (b) purchase-money debts; (c) debts for improvements and

repairs; (d) mortgages; (e) taxes; (f) claims for alimony and support; (g) liabilities for fraud; (h) liabilities as a fiduciary; and (i) rights between co-owners.

8. **VOLUNTARY SALE OF PROPERTY IMPRESSED WITH HOMESTEAD**
    a. **Homestead Freely Alienable With Spouse's Consent.** A debtor's interest in homestead property is as freely alienable as any other real estate, but in most states a sale of a homestead by a married debtor is void unless the spouse consents.

    b. **Purchaser of Former Homestead Takes Free of Claims of Debtor's Creditors.** Homestead property sold by a debtor is immune from the claims of the debtor's creditors to the same extent as before the sale.

    c. **Proceeds of Homestead.** Proceeds from a voluntary sale of a homestead are themselves exempt for a short period of time to allow the debtor to acquire a new homestead.

    d. **New Homestead Acquired With Proceeds Of Old.** As a general rule, when a debtor sells her homestead and with the proceeds buys another place that she occupies as her new homestead, the new place is immune from the claims of subsequent creditors and existing creditors who could not reach the old place, and, in some states, is also shielded from intervening creditors whose claims arose between the sale of the old homestead and the acquisition of the new.

9. **LOSS OF HOMESTEAD RIGHTS**
    a. **Waiver.**
        1) **By Agreement.** An executory waiver of homestead rights for the benefit of a creditor is enforceable in a majority of states.

        2) **By Encumbering the Property.** Almost every state allows a debtor, if her spouse consents, to mortgage the homestead even for the purpose of securing nonpurchase-money debts, and permits the mortgagee to foreclosure on the homestead if debtor defaults.

        3) **By Failing to Make a Timely Assertion.** It is equally true in most states that the homestead exemption is lost forever if a person entitled to the exemption fails to assert it before the property is forcibly sold.

    b. **Break Up of Family or Household.** Even though the establishment of a homestead usually requires that the debtor be the head of a household or family, the continuation of such status is usually not a condition to the continued existence of the exemption. Once homestead rights are acquired, they are not easily lost by disintegration of the household or family which the debtor headed.

    c. **Abandonment.** A debtor loses her homestead exemption if she abandons the homestead property. Abandonment results when the debtor voluntarily leaves the homestead with the present, or later developed, definite intention never to occupy the place again as a homestead.

10. RIGHTS OF SURVIVING DEPENDENTS

The protection of a debtor's family through homestead laws does not die with the debtor. A surviving spouse and minor children are sheltered by what is commonly called the *probate homestead*. It gives the spouse a personal right to occupy and otherwise use the property throughout her lifetime even though he may have no interest of his own in it. Surviving children share this right until they reach majority age.

E. FEDERAL CONCERNS

1. STATE EXEMPTIONS APPLY IN FEDERAL COURT

Creditors' process issued from a federal district court is generally subject to exemptions provided by the law of the state where the court sits.

2. ASSERTING LOCAL EXEMPTIONS AGAINST THE UNITED STATES

Local exemptions are generally effective against the enforcement of debts owed the United States. The largest exception is that such exemptions are ineffective against federal tax debts and liens.

3. EXEMPTIONS ESTABLISHED BY FEDERAL LAW

a. Federal Exemptions That Are Generally Applicable. Federal non-bankruptcy law creates a wide array of typically narrow exemptions from creditors' process that apply without regard to the source of, or the reason for, the process. Most of the exemptions protect various forms of retirement income and social welfare benefits paid by the United States or somehow regulated by federal law.

b. Federal Bankruptcy Exemptions. A debtor in bankruptcy is allowed to exempt certain property from the bankrupt estate and thereby keep it for herself free from creditors' claims. Bankruptcy law allows the debtor to rely on local exemptions or, in the alternative, to elect a schedule of exemptions described by federal bankruptcy law itself.

4. PSEUDO EXEMPTIONS WHICH ACTUALLY ARE LIMITATIONS ON CREDITORS' RIGHTS

There are a few federal laws that appear to create exemptions but actually operate only to limit or restrict creditors' rights in certain cases. The best example is Title III of the Consumer Credit Protection Act, which restricts the amount of a debtor's wages that a creditor can garnish from the debtor's employer.

F. INALIENABLE PROPERTY EXEMPT IN FACT

As a general rule, only property that can be assigned or alienated is subject to the claims of creditors. Consequently, inalienable property generally is immune from creditors' claims even though the property is not by law explicitly designated as an exemption.

PART TWO: CREDITORS WITH SPECIAL RIGHTS

IX. SPECIAL RIGHTS UNDER STATE LAW

A. SELLERS' RIGHTS UNDER ARTICLE 2

1. RIGHT TO WITHHOLD DELIVERY OF GOODS

    a. Upon Breach. If a buyer fails to make a payment due before delivery of the goods or anticipatorily breaches the sales contract, the seller is empowered to withhold delivery of any goods directly affected and, if the breach is of the whole contract, to withhold delivery also of all of the other goods which are the subject matter of the particular contract. U.C.C. § 2–703(a).

    b. Upon Discovering Buyer's Insolvency. If a seller discovers that the buyer is insolvent, the seller may refuse to deliver the goods unless the buyer pays cash for the goods to be delivered and also for all goods already delivered. U.C.C. § 2–705(1).

2. RIGHT TO STOP DELIVERY OF GOODS IN TRANSIT

    a. Upon Breach. After goods have been delivered to a carrier or other bailee, the seller rightfully "may stop delivery of carload, truckload, planeload or larger shipments of express or freight when the buyer repudiates or fails to make a payment due before delivery * * *." U.C.C. § 2–705(1).

    b. Upon Discovery of Buyer's Insolvency. A seller can stop the delivery of any size shipment of goods that are in the possession of a carrier or other bailee upon discovering the buyer to be insolvent. U.C.C. § 2–705(1).

3. RIGHT OF UNPAID CREDIT SELLER TO RECLAIM GOODS

U.C.C. § 2–702(2) gives a credit seller a limited right to reclaim goods when she discovers that the buyer received them while insolvent.

    a. Limitations on the Right to Reclaim. The right of an unpaid credit seller to reclaim goods under U.C.C. § 2–702(2) is subject to two requirements:

        • The buyer must have been "insolvent" at the time she received the goods; and

        • The seller must make a demand for a return of the property within ten days after the buyer received it.

    b. Protection of Third Parties. A seller's right to reclaim under U.C.C. § 2–702(2) "is subject to the rights of a buyer in the ordinary course or other good faith purchaser."

    c. Effect of Buyer's Bankruptcy. A seller's § 2–702(2) right of reclamation survives the debtor's bankruptcy and is enforceable against the trustee upon two conditions: (1) the requirements of U.C.C. § 2–702(2) must be satisfied so that the seller has the right of reclamation under state law, and also (2) the separate but similar requirements of Bankruptcy Code § 546(c) must be met so as to preserve the seller's reclamation right under federal bankruptcy law.

4. RIGHT OF DISAPPOINTED CASH SELLER TO RECLAIM GOODS
There are circumstances under which a seller who delivered goods for cash may want to reclaim them from a buyer. The typical case involves a buyer who paid with a check that bounced. The seller in such a case has a right to reclaim under state law whether or not the buyer was or is insolvent. The right can be enforced in a bankruptcy case involving the buyer if certain conditions are satisfied, but the right is defeated by a good faith purchaser for value from the buyer.

B. BANKS' EQUITABLE RIGHT OF SETOFF
The non-consensual, extra-judicial, equitable *right of setoff* empowers a bank to help itself to certain deposits of its customers to satisfy debts they owe the bank.

1. BASIS AND NATURE OF THE RIGHT
A general deposit of monies with a bank, whether in a checking or savings account, creates the relationship of debtor and creditor between the bank and depositor. If a debt of the depositor to the bank becomes due, as when a loan matures or overdraft liability arises, the common law allows the bank to apply the depositor's accounts in satisfaction of the depositor's debt to the bank. This action operates as a mutual cancellation of indebtedness and is referred to as a bank's *equitable right of setoff,* which in most states exists as a matter of common law wholly apart from any statute.

2. HOW SETOFF WORKS
Setoff is a self-help remedy that is effected by a bank making appropriate bookkeeping entries. In its pure common-law form, the remedy exists even though the depositor is unaware of it and has not agreed to it. No prior approval by a court is required, and notice to the depositor is unnecessary.

3. LIMITATIONS ON THE RIGHT OF SETOFF
There are four major conditions to a bank exercising its right of setoff against a customer's deposit accounts: (a) Mutuality of obligation must exist; (b) the depositor's debt to the bank must have matured; (c) the account must be general and unrestricted; and (d) the funds in the account must belong to the debtor or the bank must be ignorant of other persons' claims.

4. PRIORITY OF SETOFF OVER OTHER CLAIMS
   a. Check Drawn Against Account. U.C.C. § 4–303(1) provides that a check has priority over a setoff if the bank has taken any of several, statutorily defined actions with respect to the check before the setoff is exercised.

   b. Lien of Garnishment on the Account. When a bank account is garnished by a creditor of the depositor, the bank is entitled to set off for itself so much of the account as is necessary to satisfy the depositor's debts to the bank that were mature at the time of the garnishment.

   c. Pledge of the Account. A depositor may pledge or otherwise assign her bank account, and the assignee takes free of the bank's right of setoff, except as to matured debts the depositor owes the bank at the time the bank is notified of the assignment.

d. Article 9 Security Interest in Proceeds Deposited in the Account. The courts disagree on whether a bank's right of setoff has priority over another creditor's U.C.C. Article 9 security interest in the debtor's account. The reason the courts disagree on the result is that they disagree on whether the source of law for resolving the priority contest is Article 9 or common law.

e. Trustee of Depositor in Bankruptcy. With some limitations, a bank's right of setoff against a depositor is valid and enforceable in the depositor's bankruptcy.

C. ARTISAN'S LIEN
1. LIEN ATTACHES TO OBJECT OF LABOR
The common law gives a person who enhances the value of goods, as by repairing the goods or fashioning a finished product from them, a lien on the object of her labor, i.e., an *artisan's lien,* which is confirmed by statute in most states.

2. LIEN ATTACHES BY LAW
An artisan's lien arises by operation of law and thus is not dependent on the debtor's consent.

3. DURATION OF THE LIEN
Under the common law, an artisan's lien ordinarily is lost if the lienor parts with possession of the property. In many states, however, statutes automatically continue an artisan's lien despite the lienor's loss of possession or permit the lienor to preserve the lien by recording an account or a notice of lien.

4. ENFORCING THE LIEN
Under the common law, the lienor's only remedy is to withhold possession of the goods from the debtor. Enacted law in a large group of states has expanded the remedies of an artisan's lienor by giving her the additional right to sell the property herself or to force a judicial sale of it.

5. PRIORITY OF THE LIEN
Under the common law, an artisan's lien is subordinate to existing liens and encumbrances unless, as is often the case, the prior lienor or encumbrancer expressly or impliedly consents to the artisan's services. When the competing claim is an Article 9 security interest, U.C.C. § 9–310 must be consulted along with any priority provision of a lien statute on which the artisan bases her claim.

D. CONSTRUCTION LIEN
Every state provides by statute that certain persons who perform work on, or supply materials for, an improvement to land under contract with the owner, or with the owner's agent, acquire liens on the land to secure payment for their work or materials.

1. BENEFICIARIES OF THE LIEN
The class of persons who are entitled to assert construction liens ordinarily includes everyone owed a debt for work and labor performed, or materials supplied,

for the improvement of real estate. This includes prime contractors, subcontractors, suppliers, artisans, and laborers.

2. **REACH OF THE LIEN**

    A construction lien attaches to the building or other improvement for which services and materials were furnished and also attaches to the lot or other tract of land on which the improvement sits.

3. **WARNING THE OWNER**

    Many modern construction lien statutes require a claimant of the lien to notify the owner before the services or materials are furnished, or shortly thereafter, that a lien can be asserted against the property if the claimant is unpaid. Sending this notice is a condition to claiming a construction lien.

4. **SIGNIFICANCE OF OWNER'S DEALINGS WITH GENERAL CONTRACTOR**

    In many states, neither the right of a supplier or laborer to assert a construction lien, nor the size of the lien she can assert, is affected by the landowner's contract with a prime or general contractor or by the landowner's payment of all or part of the contract price of the improvement to the contractor. In other states, however, the lien laws provide that neither any one lien nor the total of all liens can exceed the amount due from the owner to the prime or general contractor. The contract price between the owner and contractor establishes the owner's maximum exposure, and the owner's exposure is reduced by contract payments made in the regular course to the contractor. In a few states, the owner gets credit only for contract payments made before she receives a notice of a construction lien.

5. **PERFECTING THE LIEN**

    A construction lien claimant is usually required to make a public filing of her lien claim within three to six months after she has ceased to furnish materials or services.

6. **ENFORCING THE LIEN**

    Construction liens are ordinarily enforced by suit seeking judicial foreclosure.

7. **PRIORITY OF THE LIEN**

    a. **Among Construction Lienors Inter Se.** In most states, construction liens are on an equal footing without regard to the dates when labor or services were performed or the dates when the liens were perfected. The lienors share ratably in the proceeds of a foreclosure sale of the property to which their liens had attached.

    b. **Between Construction Liens and Other Claims.** In the larger number of states, all construction liens on the same land date from the time of visible commencement of the improvement. A construction lien is subordinate to all claims recorded prior to that time, and is superior to all claims that arise thereafter and also to all previous but unrecorded claims of which the construction lienor had no knowledge.

X. FEDERAL TAX LIEN

The United States has a lien on "all property and rights to property" of a taxpayer who "neglects or refuses to pay any tax" for which she is liable. 26 U.S.C.A. § 6321.

A. REACH OF THE LIEN
1. DEFINITION OF PROPERTY
State law controls in determining whether and to what extent a debtor has property or rights to property to which a federal tax lien can attach.

2. AFTER–ACQUIRED PROPERTY INCLUDED
The lien reaches not only property which the debtor owns when the lien arises, but also property she subsequently acquires during the life of the lien.

3. DURATION OF THE LIEN
"The Federal tax lien continues until satisfied, until expiration of the period for collecting the assessed liability, or, if the tax liability is reduced to a personal judgment against the taxpayer, until the judgment is satisfied or becomes unenforceable by reason of the running of the statute of limitations." 4 L. Casey, Federal Tax Practice § 14.26 at 367 (1982).

4. EXEMPTIONS INEFFECTIVE
The federal tax lien law contains its own schedule of property that is exempt from the lien's reach. Unless otherwise specifically provided by Congress, no other federal exemption and no state law exemptions are effective against the lien.

B. HOW THE LIEN IS CREATED
1. THREE CONDITIONS ON CREATION

The creation of a federal tax lien is subject to three conditions:

- There must be a tax assessment;

- The government must demand payment of the taxes due; and,

- The tax debtor must refuse to pay the taxes.

2. RELATION BACK TO ASSESSMENT
Although a federal tax lien does not exist until the tax debtor refuses a demand to pay taxes assessed against her, once these requirements are satisfied the lien relates back to the time the assessment was made and attaches to all property and rights to property belonging to the debtor on the date of assessment and property thereafter acquired by her during the life of the lien. For practical purposes, therefore, a federal tax lien is deemed to arise at the time of the tax assessment.

3. MAKING THE ASSESSMENT
How assessment is accomplished depends on whether liability is acknowledged, or is understated and must be discovered by the government. In the latter case the process of assessment is much longer, but can be speeded up when a jeopardy assessment is appropriate.

C. FILING NOTICE OF THE LIEN
1. PURPOSE OF FILING CONCERNS PRIORITY
The creation of a federal tax lien is *not* conditioned on the government giving public notice of the lien by filing or otherwise. Yet, the Internal Revenue Code provides for filing notice of a federal tax lien which is essential to make the lien effective against certain of the taxpayer's creditors and transferees whom Congress has decided to protect against an otherwise secret encumbrance.

2. WHERE NOTICE IS FILED
State law specifies the places to file notices of federal tax liens.

3. CONTINUOUS NOTICE
The filing of a federal tax lien will be effective continuously only if the government refiles its notice within the one-year period ending six years and 30 days after the date of the tax assessment.

D. PRIORITY OF A FEDERAL TAX LIEN
A federal tax lien, whether filed or not, is superior to any claim against, or interest in, the debtor's property that is not choate and perfected as fully as possible before the date of assessment. The largest exceptions to this general rule are created by the federal tax lien statute which protects a set of four classes of claimants from an unfiled tax lien, and protects another set of ten classes of claimants from even a filed tax lien.

1. CLAIMANTS PROTECTED BY STATUTE FROM AN UNFILED LIEN
A federal tax lien "shall not be valid as against any purchaser, holder of a security interest, mechanic's lienor, or judgment lien creditor until notice thereof * * * has been filed * * *." 26 U.S.C.A. § 6323(a).

2. CLAIMANTS PROTECTED BY STATUTE FROM EVEN A FILED LIEN
Ten classes of claimants are afforded a "super-priority" status over a federal tax lien, meaning that they have priority even though their claims arise after the lien is filed. Most of these "super-priorities," which are defined by § 6323(b), are either (1) casual and common transactions for which an individual cannot be expected to check for filed tax liens or (2) transactions which tend to increase the value of the taxpayer's property.

3. CLAIMANTS PROTECTED BY GENERAL RULE OF DECISIONAL LAW
A claimant whose lien or interest is not protected by the provisions of the federal tax lien statute is not necessarily subordinate to a tax lien. Wholly apart from the federal tax lien statute, a tax lien is subordinate to a claim that was choate and perfected as far as possible under applicable law before the tax lien arose, i.e., before the date of assessment.

E. ENFORCEMENT OF A FEDERAL TAX LIEN
1. LEVY AND DISTRAINT
The government is authorized to levy on all property subject to a federal tax lien. The right to levy includes the power of distraint and seizure by any means. The government disposes of the property as soon as practical after the seizure.

2. JUDICIAL FORECLOSURE

Alternatively, the government may enforce its lien by suing in federal court and seeking a judicial sale of property subject to the lien.

PART THREE: PREJUDGMENT OR PROVISIONAL REMEDIES

XI. ATTACHMENT

A. ATTACHMENT EXPLAINED
1. DEFINITION

Attachment is a creditor's remedy that impounds a debtor's property upon or after the commencement of suit against her in order to secure collection of the creditor's judgment *if and when* one is obtained.

2. PURPOSES HISTORICALLY AND AFTER *SHAFFER*

Historically and traditionally, a prime use of attachment was jurisdictional. If personal jurisdiction over the debtor could not be obtained, her property located in the forum was attached and in rem jurisdiction was thereby established. Because of the decision in *Shaffer v. Heitner,* 433 U.S. 186, 97 S.Ct. 2569 (1977), the presence of property in a state is no longer regarded as a sufficient basis in itself for exercising any kind of judicial jurisdiction. Thus, the role of attachment as a jurisdictional device has diminished greatly, and attachment now functions primarily as a security device.

B. AVAILABILITY OF ATTACHMENT
1. KINDS OF ACTIONS

The remedy of attachment is not generally available in every kind of action. Even under the most generous statutes, the remedy is only available in actions "for the recovery of money," which includes both tort and contract claims. Stingier statutes permit attachment only upon claims *ex contractu,* and further limitations on the kinds of actions in which the remedy is available are not uncommon.

2. GROUNDS FOR ATTACHMENT

In many states, the availability of attachment is limited not only to certain kinds of actions, but also to cases involving certain extenuating circumstances referred to as *grounds for attachment.*

3. DEBTS NOT YET DUE

In most states, the availability of attachment in an action on a contract is not conditioned on the maturity of the plaintiff's claim against the defendant. The plaintiff can sue on the contract and attachment can issue even before the debt is due if the debtor is threatening to leave the jurisdiction or to dispose of her property. Ordinarily, however, no judgment can be rendered for the plaintiff until the debt matures.

4. ATTACHMENT IN FEDERAL COURT
Generally, the remedy of attachment is available in an action in federal district court only under the circumstances and in the manner provided by the law of the state in which the district court is held.

C. MECHANICS OF ATTACHMENT
1. PLAINTIFF'S PROCEDURE
A plaintiff invokes the attachment process either at the very beginning of her lawsuit against the debtor when the complaint is filed and summons issued, or at any time during the suit before judgment. The plaintiff must file with the court an affidavit for attachment and must also post a bond.

2. ISSUANCE OF WRIT OR ORDER OF ATTACHMENT
If the plaintiff's affidavit and bond are in order, a judge or court clerk will issue a writ or order of attachment directing the sheriff to seize as much of the defendant's property as will be necessary to satisfy plaintiff's claim and the costs of the action.

3. PRE–SEIZURE NOTICE AND HEARING

Many states condition attachment on giving the defendant notice and an opportunity for a hearing prior to the seizure of property. Ordinarily, when a noticed hearing is required, the burden is on the plaintiff to establish not only that attachment is justified, but also that there is a "probability" or a "reasonable likelihood" of success in her underlying action against the defendant.

4. EX PARTE ATTACHMENT
In states which require a noticed hearing in the usual case, ex parte attachment is allowed in exceptional cases, such as when the plaintiff demonstrates that "irreparable harm" will result if the debtor is notified and attachment is delayed until after a hearing.

5. ENFORCEMENT OF WRIT OR ORDER OF ATTACHMENT
All of a debtor's property, except that exempt from execution, is subject to attachment, which requires that the sheriff actually or constructively seize sufficient property to satisfy the plaintiff's expected judgment plus costs.

6. GARNISHMENT AS MEANS OF REACHING PROPERTY HELD BY THIRD PARTIES
When property or credits of the debtor are held by a third party, they usually are attached by the creditor invoking the allied but different remedy of garnishment (or trustee's process).

7. ATTACHED PROPERTY HELD IN *CUSTODIA LEGIS*
Property that has been attached is held by the sheriff pending resolution of the plaintiff's lawsuit against the defendant.

8. DEFENDANT'S RESPONSES
   a. **Post–Seizure Hearing.** If the attachment is issued ex parte without notice to the debtor and without an opportunity for a hearing, the debtor is entitled to be heard soon after the seizure of her property so that she can challenge both

the availability of attachment in the case and the plaintiff's compliance with procedures for invoking the remedy.

b. **Posting Bond for Return of Attached Property.** Every state allows a debtor to secure the return of attached property by posting a bond of one kind or another.

c. **Challenge to Plaintiff's Bond.** The attachment laws of most states allow the defendant to attack the plaintiff's bond by challenging the sufficiency of the bond, i.e., questioning whether the amount of the bond is large enough, and also by excepting to any surety on the bond, i.e., questioning whether the person is financially sound and otherwise qualified to serve as a surety.

9. JUDGMENT FOR THE PLAINTIFF
If plaintiff prevails in the underlying action against the defendant who fails to pay the judgment, it is satisfied by the sheriff selling the attached property and applying the proceeds to the judgment, or by looking to the sureties on a bond given by the defendant for the return of the property.

10. JUDGMENT FOR THE DEFENDANT
If judgment in the main action is for the defendant, the attachment is discharged and the attached property is released and returned to her. Moreover, the plaintiff becomes liable for the defendant's costs associated with the attachment and also for the damages suffered by the defendant because of the attachment.

D. LIEN OF ATTACHMENT
1. WHEN THE LIEN ARISES
In most states, the lien of attachment arises at the time of the levy.

2. NATURE OF THE LIEN
A lien of attachment is "inchoate" or contingent prior to judgment for the plaintiff in the principal action.

3. PRIORITY OF THE LIEN
a. **Priority of Attachment Liens Inter Se.** The rule of first-in-time, first-in-right governs the priority between attachment liens on the same property. This priority is unaffected by the order in which the attaching creditors win judgments and acquire judgment liens against the debtor.

b. **Prior Interests.** Generally, an attachment lien reaches only the debtor's interest in the property and thus does not displace prior claims, rights, and interests, unless the prior interest is subject to a recording law which has not been satisfied when the attachment lien arises.

c. **Subsequent Interests.**
1) **General Rule.** An attachment lien that is perfected by judgment for plaintiff has priority over any conflicting claim, right, or interest created after the attachment lien arises, which usually is at the time of levy.

2) Exception for Federal Tax Lien. A federal tax lien has priority over an earlier inchoate attachment lien that is later perfected by judgment for the attaching creditor.

d. Bankruptcy Trustee. An attachment lien obtained against an insolvent debtor prior to the debtor's filing a bankruptcy petition is subject to avoidance as a preference under Bankruptcy Code § 547.

XII. REPLEVIN

A. DESCRIPTION OF REPLEVIN ACTION

The action in replevin is "an action for the recovery of specific personal chattels wrongfully taken and detained, or [rightfully taken but] wrongfully detained, with damages which the wrongful taking or detention has occasioned." H. Wells, A Treatise on the Law of Replevin 31–33 (1907).

1. NATURE AND ELEMENTS OF THE ACTION

a. Right to Possession in Plaintiff and Wrongful Detention by Defendant. The primary issue in a replevin action is whether, as against the defendant, the plaintiff had the exclusive right of possession of the property when the action was brought. The same issue, phrased negatively, is whether the defendant at the time was wrongfully detaining as against the plaintiff. The plaintiff cannot win by establishing that the defendant has no claim to the property; the plaintiff must establish that she herself has an immediate and unqualified right to possession, which necessarily implies that the defendant's detention is wrongful as against her.

b. Demand for Return by Plaintiff and Refusal by Defendant. In cases where the defendant's taking of the property was lawful and only the detention is complained of, *replevin in detinet*, a plaintiff ordinarily must establish that she made a demand for a return of the property and that the demand was refused by the defendant.

2. RECOVERY SOUGHT BY PLAINTIFF IN REPLEVIN ACTION

a. Property or Its Value. The principal aim of a replevin action is to recover possession of the property wrongfully taken or detained by the defendant. Traditionally, the plaintiff can recover alternatively the property's value only if the defendant is unable to return the property itself as would be true, for instance, if the defendant sold the property while the replevin action was pending.

b. Compensatory Damages for Detention. If the plaintiff prevails on the primary issue by establishing her right to possession of the property, she recovers not only the property itself but also damages for the defendant's unlawful detention, which includes loss of use and depreciation.

c. Punitive Damages. A successful plaintiff in a replevin action can recover punitive damages if the defendant's wrong in taking or detaining the property involved fraud, malice, gross negligence, or oppression.

    d. **Judgment for Debt Due Plaintiff Inappropriate.** A creditor suing to recover collateral in a replevin action cannot recover a personal judgment for the debt itself.

3. **DEFENSES OF DEFENDANT**
    a. **No Right to Possession in Plaintiff.** Because the plaintiff in a replevin action must establish that she is entitled to possession of the property sued for, the defendant can successfully defend by showing that law or contract gives her, or some third party, possessory rights superior to the plaintiff's.

    b. **Defendant Lacks Possession.** It is generally a good defense in replevin that the defendant was not in actual or constructive possession of the property at the time the action was commenced.

    c. **Counterclaims.** The general rule is that the defendant cannot counterclaim for the recovery of money damages.

B. **PROCEDURES OF THE REPLEVIN REMEDY**
1. **AVAILABILITY OF THE REMEDY**
The remedy of replevin is available in any action in which the plaintiff seeks to recover the possession of personal property.

2. **APPLICATION FOR THE REMEDY**
Plaintiff initiates the replevin remedy by filing an appropriate affidavit with the judge or clerk of the court in which the replevin action is pending.

3. **PRE–SEIZURE NOTICE AND HEARING**
In most states replevin will not be ordered except upon notice to the defendant who is given an opportunity for a hearing prior to seizure of the property in controversy.

4. **EX PARTE SEIZURE**
    a. **When Allowed.** In virtually every state where pre-seizure notice and hearing is the general rule, provision is made in general or specific terms for ordering replevin ex parte in extraordinary or unusual cases.

    b. **Post–Seizure Hearing Required.** Wherever and whenever replevin is ordered ex parte, the defendant is entitled to a hearing soon after the seizure to test the plaintiff's entitlement to the replevin remedy.

5. **RESTRAINING ORDER IN PLACE OF EX PARTE SEIZURE**
A significant number of states provide a procedural alternative to ex parte replevin in cases where the plaintiff fears that the property will be harmed or lost pending a plenary hearing on her application for the replevin remedy. At the time of notifying the defendant of the application and of a right to a preseizure hearing, the court in its discretion can issue a preliminary injunction or restraining order prohibiting the defendant from harming, concealing, or disposing of the property.

6. **PLAINTIFF'S BOND**
    Whether or not a preseizure hearing is required, the property cannot be replevied until the plaintiff posts with the sheriff a sufficient bond.

7. **ISSUANCE AND EXECUTION OF WRIT OF REPLEVIN**
    Upon satisfaction of the requirements for invoking the replevin remedy, the judge or clerk of the court in which the replevin action is filed directs the sheriff to seize the property claimed by the plaintiff. Thereafter, unless the debtor posts bond for return of the property, the sheriff is bound to deliver the property to the plaintiff after the plaintiff pays the sheriff's lawful fees for taking and keeping the property. The plaintiff thereafter keeps possession of the property pendente lite.

8. **DEFENDANT'S BOND FOR RETURN OF THE PROPERTY**
    The typical replevin statute allows a defendant from whom property has been re-plevied to regain possession of the property by posting a forthcoming bond.

9. **ULTIMATE DISPOSITION OF PROPERTY TAKEN PROVISIONALLY THROUGH RE-PLEVIN REMEDY BY PLAINTIFF IN REPLEVIN ACTION**
    a. **Judgment for Plaintiff in Replevin Action.** If the plaintiff prevails in the replevin action, the judgment awards her possession of the property which was delivered provisionally to her through the replevin remedy, and also gives her damages against the defendant for losses resulting from the defendant's wrongful taking or detention of the property.

    b. **Judgment for Defendant in Replevin Action.** If the defendant prevails in the replevin action, the judgment entitles her to recover property seized through the plaintiff's use of the replevin remedy or, in some states, to recover at her election the property's value. A judgment against the plaintiff also entitles the defendant to recover damages she suffered as a result of the provisional taking and detention of the property by plaintiff.

XIII. LIS PENDENS

A. **NATURE OF LIS PENDENS**
Technically speaking, the doctrine of lis pendens creates no lien or other interest in property. Rather, the doctrine merely puts prospective purchasers and encumbrancers on notice of pending litigation involving rights to property that is the subject of the action and binds them to the outcome of the action.

B. **STATUTES USUALLY GOVERN LIS PENDENS**
1. **STATUTES REQUIRE FILING OF NOTICE**
    Lis pendens statutes condition the effect of the doctrine on the claimant's compliance with a prescribed procedure, the main feature of which is to require the claimant file a notice of lis pendens in public records maintained for the purpose of alerting the world to property that is the subject matter of pending litigation.

2. **STATUTES IDENTIFY ACTIONS SUBJECT TO LIS PENDENS**
    Lis pendens statutes also identify the types of actions subject to the lis pendens doctrine.

C. ACTIONS SUBJECT TO LIS PENDENS

Lis pendens does not operate with respect to all lawsuits that may somehow affect rights to property. An action is constructively publicized through lis pendens only if the action is of a nature, and involves a type of property, which the law (usually a statute) describes as subject to the lis pendens doctrine.

1. TYPE OF PROPERTY

Lis pendens statutes everywhere apply the doctrine to real estate, and in some states the doctrine is also made applicable to personal property.

2. NATURE OF THE ACTION

As a very general rule, lis pendens operates only in actions in which the relief sought will *directly affect title to, or possession of, property.*

D. FILING OF LIS PENDENS NOTICE AND OTHER PROCEDURAL MATTERS
1. LIS PENDENS EFFECT REQUIRES FILING OF PROPER NOTICE

Statutes almost everywhere provide that the pendency of an action does not constitute notice to anyone other than parties to the action unless a proper lis pendens notice is filed, except that in some states purchasers and encumbrancers having actual knowledge of the action are bound by it even in the absence of such a filing.

2. WHAT IS FILED

Typically, a notice of lis pendens must be in a writing separate from the complaint or other pleadings; signed by the plaintiff, defendant, or other party who seeks to benefit from the lis pendens effect, or signed by the party's attorney; show the name of the court in which the action has been filed and the title, docket number, date of filing, and object of the action; and describe the property affected by the notice of lis pendens.

3. WHERE IS THE NOTICE FILED

A notice of lis pendens ordinarily is filed in the office of the clerk or recorder of the county where the affected property is located.

4. WHEN IS THE NOTICE FILED

A notice of lis pendens is filed when the action is commenced or at any time during the pendency of the action.

5. CANCELLATION OF LIS PENDENS

    a. Upon Judgment. If the action is decided against the person who filed the lis pendens, the judgment of the court should include an order cancelling the notice.

    b. During Pendency of Action. Any party to the action who is affected by a notice of lis pendens can by motion, at any time during the pendency of the action, request the court where the action is pending to cancel, discharge, release, or modify the lis pendens on the basis that the action or the property is not subject to lis pendens or that for some other reason the filing of the lis pendens was not in accordance with law or was otherwise wrongful.

6. LIS PENDENS IN FEDERAL DISTRICT COURT
Generally speaking, local lis pendens statutes govern actions in federal district court.

E. PERSONS BOUND BY LIS PENDENS
The typical lis pendens law provides that the notice of lis pendens binds *purchasers* and *encumbrancers* of the affected property who acquire their interests through a party to the action after the notice of lis pendens is filed or otherwise becomes effective.

F. BINDING EFFECT OF LIS PENDENS
Lis pendens gives constructive notice of the action to subsequent purchasers and encumbrancers of the subject property and so binds them to the outcome of the action. A subsequent purchaser or encumbrancer is bound in the sense that the interest she acquires will be coextensive with the interest her grantor is determined to have when the action is completed.

G. CONSTITUTIONALITY OF LIS PENDENS
Due process does not require notice and hearing prior to the filing and effectiveness of a notice of lis pendens.

PART FOUR: GUARANTEES OF DEBTOR'S PROCEDURAL DUE PROCESS RIGHTS

XIV. FOURTEENTH AMENDMENT PROTECTION

The Fourteenth Amendment to the United States Constitution commands that no "state shall deprive any person of life, liberty, or property without due process of law." Thus, any creditors' remedy that implicates the state must provide a constitutional minimum of procedural safeguards designed to guard against arbitrary and erroneous seizures of debtors' property.

A. PREREQUISITES TO FOURTEENTH AMENDMENT PROTECTION
1. STATE ACTION
Procedural due process is required by the Fourteenth Amendment only when the taking of a debtor's property is fairly attributable to the state, i.e., involves state action. State action is present in the exercise of a creditor's remedy when the taking overtly involves a state officer performing some substantial role in her official capacity. There are several alternative tests for deciding when the conduct of private parties is attributable to the state so as to establish state action. They are the (1) symbiotic relationship test; (2) close nexus test; and (3) public function test.

2. SIGNIFICANT TAKING
A debtor is not entitled to due process protection against a creditors' remedy simply because the remedy involves state action. The Fourteenth Amendment applies only when the state is involved in a *significant* taking of property, which means an interest encompassed by the Fourteenth Amendment's protection of property.

B.   MINIMUM DUE PROCESS WITH RESPECT TO PREJUDGMENT REMEDIES

After deciding that the Fourteenth Amendment protects a debtor's rights against a creditor's remedy, the next issue is whether the remedy provides the procedural safeguards required by due process.   The question, in other words, is what process is due.

1.   GENERAL RULE OF PRESEIZURE NOTICE AND HEARING

As a general rule, a seizure of a debtor's property through a creditor's exercise of a prejudgment remedy must be preceded by notice to the debtor of the impending seizure and an opportunity for the debtor to be heard in opposition to it.

2.   EXCEPTION WHEN THERE ARE OVERRIDING CREDITOR INTERESTS

In the case, *Mitchell v. W.T. Grant Co.,* 416 U.S. 600, 94 S.Ct. 1895 (1974), the Court held that when a creditor has a preexisting interest of her own in the property to be seized and the value of her interest will be threatened if the debtor is allowed to continue in possession, the property can constitutionally be seized without prior notice and hearing so long as other procedural safeguards adequately protect the interests of the debtor by adequately guarding against an erroneous or arbitrary seizure.   The *Mitchell* case thereby implies that ex parte seizure is approved on two conditions:

* An analysis of the realities of the circumstances affecting the property, and a balancing of the debtor's and creditor's interests, must support the conclusion that the creditor is entitled to "somewhat more protection" than she would receive under a procedural scheme requiring preseizure notice and hearing; and

* The procedures must effect a "constitutional accommodation" of the conflicting interests of both parties.

C.   MINIMUM DUE PROCESS WITH RESPECT TO POSTJUDGMENT REMEDIES

A debtor is not entitled to a hearing prior to seizure of her property through execution and postjudgment garnishment; but a growing number of courts have decided that, when the taking involves possibly exempt property, the debtor is minimally entitled to (1) simultaneous notice of the seizure, which notice should alert the debtor to her exemptions and to the procedure for protecting them, and also to (2) an immediate postseizure hearing at which the debtor can claim her exemptions out of property which has been seized.

D.   WAIVER OF DUE PROCESS RIGHTS

A debtor is not entitled to due process protection if she has effectively waived her Fourteenth Amendment rights.   To be effective the waiver must be "voluntarily, intelligently and knowingly made."

XV.   OTHER SOURCES OF DUE PROCESS PROTECTION

A.   FIFTH AMENDMENT DUE PROCESS

The Fifth and Fourteenth Amendments to the United States Constitution are alike in providing that no person shall be deprived of life, liberty, or property without due process of law.   The two due process clauses are different in that the Fourteenth Amendment restrains the states, while the Fifth Amendment limits the federal government and the District of Columbia.

1. **FEDERAL ACTION**
    The Fifth Amendment restricts "only the Federal Government and not private persons." *Public Utilities Com'n v. Pollak,* 343 U.S. 451, 461, 72 S.Ct. 813, 820 (1952). Therefore, in deciding if there has been a violation of the Fifth Amendment due process clause, the first issue is whether the taking involves federal action. "The standards utilized to find federal action . . . [are] identical to those employed to detect 'state action' [for purposes of the Fourteenth Amendment]." *Wenzer v. Consolidated Rail Corp.,* 464 F.Supp. 643, 647 (E.D.Pa.1979), aff'd without opin., 612 F.2d 576 (3d Cir.1979).

2. **WHAT PROCESS IS DUE**
    a. **In General—Usual Balancing Approach.** The approach to deciding what process is due under the Fifth Amendment is no different from that used when the Fourteenth Amendment due process clause applies: The procedures must effect a constitutional accommodation of the parties' conflicting interests.

    b. **Maritime Attachment.** A creditors' remedy frequently challenged under the Fifth Amendment due process clause is maritime attachment. The majority of courts facing the issue have held that maritime attachment need not provide prior notice and hearing, and some courts have gone so far as to say that the Fifth Amendment is satisfied even though the debtor or ship owner is not afforded the full panoply of other procedural safeguards that are usually necessary in the absence of prior notice and hearing.

B. STATE CONSTITUTIONAL LAW

The typical state constitution has its own clause guaranteeing that no person shall be deprived of life, liberty, or property without due process of law. Even though a creditors' remedy may pass muster under the Fourteenth Amendment as interpreted by the Supreme Court, the remedy may be invalid for failing to satisfy a local due process clause as interpreted by the state's highest court. The local high court, not the United States Supreme Court, is the final arbiter of the state constitution even when the constitutional provision at issue reads exactly like some part of the United States Constitution. A state through its own law is generally free to require greater due process protection of debtors' rights in a wider range of circumstances than does the 14th Amendment, so long as the federal constitutional rights of creditors are not thereby impaired.

C. CONTRACTUAL DUE PROCESS

A debtor can freely negotiate to include in her credit contract procedural safeguards beyond those required by law; and in such a case the creditor is contractually bound to observe the bargained-for procedures.

PART FIVE: BANKRUPTCY

XVI. OVERVIEW OF BANKRUPTCY

A. WHAT IS BANKRUPTCY LAW?
The law of bankruptcy is federal law. It is primarily, though not completely, statutory law.

1. STATUTES
There are two main federal bankruptcy statutes: the Bankruptcy Act of 1898 (the "Bankruptcy Act," which governs bankruptcy cases filed prior to October 1, 1979), and the Bankruptcy Reform Act of 1978 (the "Bankruptcy Code," which governs cases filed since October 1, 1979). The Bankruptcy Code was amended in 1984 and 1986.

2. RULES
The United States Supreme Court has promulgated Bankruptcy Rules. These rules, not the Federal Rules of Civil Procedure, govern procedure in United States bankruptcy courts.

3. STATE LAW
The Bankruptcy Code often expressly incorporates state law, and repeatedly refers to state law for application in conjunction with federal bankruptcy law.

B. FORMS OF BANKRUPTCY RELIEF
There are two basic forms of bankruptcy relief—liquidation and rehabilitation—under four chapters of the Bankruptcy Code—Chapter 7, Chapter 11, Chapter 12, and Chapter 13.

1. LIQUIDATION—CHAPTER 7
Chapter 7 is entitled "Liquidation." The title is descriptive. In a Chapter 7 case, the trustee collects the non-exempt property of the debtor, converts that property to cash, and distributes the cash to the creditors. The debtor gives up all of the non-exempt property she owns at the time of the filing of the bankruptcy petition in the hope of obtaining a discharge. A discharge releases the debtor from any further personal liability for her pre-bankruptcy debts.

2. REHABILITATION—CHAPTERS 11, 12 AND 13
Chapters 11, 12, and 13 generally deal with debtor rehabilitation, not liquidation, of the debtor's assets. In a rehabilitation case under the bankruptcy laws, creditors usually look to future earnings of the debtor, not the property of the debtor at the time of the initiation of the bankruptcy, to satisfy their claims. The debtor retains its assets and makes payments to creditors, usually from post-petition earnings, pursuant to a court approved plan.

C. BANKRUPTCY COURTS AND BANKRUPTCY JUDGES
Bankruptcy judges are appointed by the United States courts of appeals. These judges constitute a unit of the district court known as the bankruptcy court. Thus, the bankruptcy court is not really a separate court; rather, it is a part of the dis-

trict court. Accordingly, the grant of jurisdiction over bankruptcy matters is to the district court. The federal district judges then refer bankruptcy matters to the bankruptcy judges.

D. TRUSTEES

In every Chapter 7 case, every Chapter 12, every Chapter 13, and some Chapter 11 cases, there will be not only a bankruptcy judge but also a bankruptcy trustee. A bankruptcy trustee, who is usually a private citizen rather than an employee of the government, represents the bankruptcy estate which is created, as a separate legal entity, upon the filing of a bankruptcy petition. The bankruptcy trustee is the person who sues or is sued on behalf of the estate. The powers and duties of a bankruptcy trustee vary from chapter to chapter.

E. UNITED STATES TRUSTEES

The United States Trustee and her assistants, who are appointed by the United States Attorney General, perform appointing and other administrative tasks that the bankruptcy judge would otherwise have to perform, including the appointment and supervision of private trustees in chapter cases. Thus, United States Trustees are not intended as substitutes for private bankruptcy trustees. Rather, United States Trustees are more like substitutes for the bankruptcy judge with respect to supervisory and administrative details.

XVII. COMMENCEMENT AND DISMISSAL OF A BANKRUPTCY CASE

A. COMMENCEMENT
1. VOLUNTARY CASES

A voluntary bankruptcy case is commenced when an eligible debtor files a petition. No formal adjudication is necessary. The filing operates as an order for relief.

a. Eligibility Requirements.

1) Chapter 7 Cases. Chapter 7 is available to any "person," as defined in section 101(33), which includes partnerships and corporations, except that the debtor may not be a railroad, insurance company, or banking institution.

2) Chapter 11 Cases. The eligibility requirements for Chapter 11 mirror those of Chapter 7, with two exceptions: (1) railroads are eligible for Chapter 11 but (2) stockbrokers and commodity brokers are ineligible for Chapter 11.

3) Chapter 13 Cases. The debtor must be (1) an individual, who has (2) "income sufficiently stable and regular to enable such individual to make payments under a [Chapter 13 plan]," and (3) "non-contingent, liquidated" unsecured debts totalling less than $100,000 and "non-contingent, liquidated" secured debts of less than $350,000.

4) Chapter 12 Cases. Only a family farmer with sufficiently regular and stable annual income may be a debtor under Chapter 12, and only if the farmer's debts do not exceed $1.5 million. The term "family farmer" includes an individual, partnership or family-owned corporation whose principal debt and income are farm related.

b.   Insolvency Not Required. Insolvency is not a condition precedent to any form of voluntary bankruptcy.

c.   Joint Petitions. A husband and a wife may file a single joint petition for voluntary relief under any chapter that is available to each spouse.

d.   Frequent–Filer Disqualification. An individual debtor is not eligible to be a debtor under Chapter 7, 11, 12, or 13, if he or she was a debtor in a bankruptcy case within the last 180 days that was dismissed for certain reasons.

e.   Filing Fee. A debtor who files a bankruptcy petition must pay a filing fee.

2.   INVOLUNTARY CASES

Subject to certain limitations, debtors can be forced into bankruptcy by creditors filing involuntary petitions (petitions for involuntary bankruptcy) against them. Such a petition itself, however, does not entitle the creditors to relief. An order of relief against the debtor results only if she fails to answer the creditors' petition or a ground for bankruptcy is found to exist. The two alternative grounds for involuntary bankruptcy are: the debtor's insolvency or a receiver or other representative taking charge of the debtor's property.

B.   DISMISSAL

The bankruptcy court may dismiss or suspend a voluntary bankruptcy case even though it was filed by an eligible debtor; and the bankruptcy court may dismiss or suspend an involuntary bankruptcy case even though all of the requirements for initiating such a case are satisfied. Each bankruptcy relief chapter has its own dismissal provision, and the Bankruptcy Code (section 305) provides overarching additional reasons for dismissal that apply in every kind of case. In addition, the bankruptcy court may dismiss a bankruptcy case for failure to pay filing fees.

1.   CHAPTER 7 CASES

Chapter 7 cases can be dismissed upon motion "for cause" and sua sponte by the court.

2.   CHAPTER 11 CASES

In Chapter 11, like Chapter 7, the standard a bankruptcy court applies to a motion to dismiss is "for cause."

3.   CHAPTER 13 CASES

In Chapter 13, unlike Chapters 7 and 11, a debtor is given an absolute right to have his or her Chapter 13 case dismissed. Motions to dismiss filed by creditors in a Chapter 13 case are subject to the "for cause" standard.

4.   SECTION 305 DISMISSALS

In Chapter 7, 11, 12, and 13 cases, a debtor or creditors can also base a motion to dismiss on section 305. It empowers the bankruptcy court to dismiss or suspend a case if there is a foreign bankruptcy pending concerning the debtor or if "the interests of creditors and the debtor would be better served by such dismissal or suspension."

XVIII. STAY OF COLLECTION ACTIVITIES

The filing of a voluntary petition under Chapter 7, Chapter 11, Chapter 12, or Chapter 13, or the filing of an involuntary petition under Chapter 7 or Chapter 11 automatically "stays", i.e., restrains, creditors from taking further action against the debtor, the property of the debtor, or the property of the estate to collect their claims or enforce their liens. Section 362 provides for this automatic stay.

A. TIME STAY ARISES
The automatic stay is triggered by and dates from the filing of a bankruptcy petition.

B. SCOPE OF THE STAY
1. SECTION 362
a. What Is Stayed. Section 362(a) lists the conduct and actions that are stayed and, in so doing, covers virtually all creditor collection activity, including most litigation efforts of creditors directed at collecting pre-bankruptcy debts; virtually all types of secured creditor action against the property of the estate or property of the debtor; and informal collection actions such as telephone calls demanding payments and dunning letters.

b. What Is Not Stayed. Section 362(b) lists eleven kinds of actions that are not stayed.

c. Actions Against Third Persons. The automatic stay of section 362(a) only covers the debtor, property of the debtor, and property of the estate. It does not protect third parties.

2. SECTIONS 1201 AND 1301
Sections 1201 and 1301 stay collection actions against third persons who are guarantors and other codebtors if the debt is a consumer debt and the codebtor is not in the credit business.

3. SECTION 105
Section 105 grants to bankruptcy courts the power to issue orders "necessary or appropriate to carry out the provisions of this title." Courts have used this power to stay or restrain creditor action. In using section 105 the bankruptcy court is not expressly limited by the restrictions in section 362, 1201, or 1301.

C. TERMINATION OF THE STAY
1. PROPERTY NO LONGER ESTATE PROPERTY
The section 362 automatic stay ends as to particular property when the property ceases to be property of the estate or property of the debtor.

2. CASE CLOSED OR DISMISSED OR DEBTOR DISCHARGED
Otherwise, the automatic stay ends when the bankruptcy case is closed or dismissed or the debtor receives a discharge.

D. RELIEF FROM THE STAY

A bankruptcy court may grant relief from the section 362 automatic stay on request of a "party in interest," which is typically a creditor, usually a secured creditor. The grounds for relief from stay are set out in section 362(d).

1. SECTION 362(d)(1)

Section 362(d)(1) describes the most general statutory ground for relief from the stay: "for cause." There is very little case law on what constitutes "cause" for purposes of section 362(d)(1). Most of the reported section 362(d)(1) cases involve the specific example of cause set out in the statute: "lack of adequate protection of an interest in property of such party in interest." The Bankruptcy Code specifies three non-exclusive methods of providing adequate protection: i) periodic cash payments; ii) additional or substitute lien; and iii) indubitable equivalent.

2. SECTION 362(d)(2)

Under section 362(d)(2) a lien creditor can obtain relief from the stay if (1) the debtor does not have any equity in the encumbered property, AND (2) the encumbered property is not necessary to an effective reorganization.

3. RELATIONSHIP BETWEEN SECTIONS 362(d)(1) AND 362(d)(2)

Section 362(d)(1) and section 362(d)(2) are connected by the conjunction "or." A creditor is entitled to relief from the stay if she can establish reason for relief under either section 362(d)(1) or section 362(d)(2).

4. BURDEN OF PROOF IN SECTION 362(d) LITIGATION

The creditor or other party requesting the relief has the burden on the issue whether the debtor has an equity in the property. The debtor or bankruptcy trustee has the burden on all other issues.

XIX. PROPERTY OF THE ESTATE

A. WHY PROPERTY OF THE ESTATE IS AN IMPORTANT CONCEPT

Section 541 declares that the filing of a bankruptcy petition automatically creates an "estate."

B. WHAT IS PROPERTY OF THE ESTATE

The seven numbered subparagraphs of section 541 specify what property becomes property of the estate. Paragraph (1) is by far the most comprehensive and significant. Section 541(a)(1) provides, very broadly, that property of the estate includes "all legal or equitable interests of the debtor in property as of the commencement of the case," i.e., all property of the debtor as of the time of the filing of the bankruptcy petition.

1. LIMITATIONS

   a. **Interests of the Debtor.** Property of the estate is limited to "interests *of the debtor* in property."

   b. **Upon Commencement of the Case.** Estate property is limited to the debtor's interest in property that she owns "as of the commencement of the case," which means as of the filing of the petition.

2. EXCEPTIONS COVERING POST–PETITION PROPERTY

There are four significant exceptions to the rule that property acquired after the filing of a bankruptcy petition remains the debtor's property:

- Certain property acquired within 180 days after filing;

- Earnings of property;

- Proceeds; and,

- In a Chapter 12 or 13 case, wages earned and other property acquired by the debtor after the Chapter 12 or 13 filing.

XX.   EXEMPTIONS IN BANKRUPTCY

A.   WHAT PROPERTY IS EXEMPT

Under the Bankruptcy Code, all pre-bankruptcy property in which the debtor has an interest becomes property of the estate, but an individual debtor is permitted to exempt certain property from property of the estate.

1.   CHOICE OF EXEMPTION LAWS

In bankruptcy, an individual debtor may assert the exemptions to which she is entitled under state and non-bankruptcy federal law. *Alternatively,* individual debtors may claim the bankruptcy schedule of exemptions set out in section 522(d).

2.   NO CHOICE IN STATE THAT HAS "OPTED OUT"

The section 522(d) schedule of exemptions is not available to individual debtors that reside in states that have enacted "opt out" legislation, i.e., a statute precluding resident debtors from electing to utilize section 522(d). Most states have enacted such "opt out" legislation.

3.   LIMITATIONS ON CHOICE

Even in states that have not "opted out" there are statutory limitations on the debtor's choice of exemption statutes.

a.   All or Nothing. A debtor cannot select some exemptions from state law and some exemptions from section 522(d). He or she must choose either the non-bankruptcy exemptions or section 522(d).

b.   Joint Cases. Husbands and wives in joint cases filed under section 302, or in individual cases which are being jointly administered under Bankruptcy Rule 1015(b), must both elect either the non-bankruptcy exemptions or the section 522(d) exemptions. While each spouse will be entitled to separate exemptions, one cannot choose section 522(d) exemptions while the other chooses non-bankruptcy exemptions.

4.   WAIVERS OF EXEMPTIONS

Whether an individual debtor elects to claim under non-bankruptcy exemption law or under section 522(d), waivers of exemption are not enforceable.

5. CONVERTING NON–EXEMPT PROPERTY TO EXEMPT PROPERTY

The Bankruptcy Code does not expressly deal with the consequences of a debtor converting non-exempt property into exempt property on the eve of bankruptcy, but both legislative history and case law suggest that the property will be exempt.

B. SIGNIFICANCE OF EXEMPT PROPERTY IN BANKRUPTCY
1. KEEPING PROPERTY

Generally, an individual debtor is able to retain his or her exempt property. Exempt property is not distributed to creditors in the bankruptcy case and is protected from the claims of most creditors after the bankruptcy case.

2. AVOIDING ENCUMBRANCES THROUGH INVALIDATION—§ 522(f)

Some liens on exempt property that are valid outside of bankruptcy can be invalidated because of bankruptcy. The trustee's general avoiding powers can be used against liens on exempt property. More importantly, section 522(f) empowers the debtor to avoid judicial liens on any exempt property and to avoid non-possessory, non-purchase money security interests in certain household goods, tools of trade, and health aids.

3. EXTINGUISHING SECURITY INTERESTS THROUGH REDEMPTION—§ 722

Security interests in some exempt personal property not covered by section 522(f) may be extinguished through "redemption" under section 722. It authorizes an individual debtor to redeem or extinguish a lien on exempt personal property by paying the lienor the value of the property encumbered.

XXI. AVOIDING PRE–BANKRUPTCY TRANSFERS

Some transfers that are valid outside of bankruptcy can be invalidated by a bankruptcy trustee. The Bankruptcy Code empowers the bankruptcy trustee to invalidate certain pre-bankruptcy transfers. These invalidation provisions (commonly known as the trustee's avoiding powers) reach both absolute transfers such as payments of money, gifts, and sales, and security transfers such as creation of mortgages and security interests.

A. PREFERENCES (SECTION 547)

Under common law, a debtor, even an insolvent debtor, may freely make preferences among her creditors, that is, treat certain creditors more favorably than other similar creditors. Bankruptcy law, however, condemns certain preferences through section 547.

1. ELEMENTS OF A PREFERENCE—§ 547(b)

Section 547(b) sets out the elements of a preference that is voidable in bankruptcy by providing that the bankruptcy trustee may void any transfer of property of the debtor if he or she can establish:

- The transfer was "to or for the benefit of a creditor;" and

- The transfer was made for or on account of an "antecedent debt", i.e., a debt owed prior to the time of the transfer; and

- The debtor was insolvent at the time of the transfer; and

- The transfer was made within 90 days before the date of the filing of the bankruptcy petition, or was made between 90 days and 1 year before the date of the filing of the petition to an "insider"; and,

- The transfer has the effect of increasing the amount that the transferee would receive in a Chapter 7 case.

2. APPLYING § 547(b)
[See the main text for lots of examples illustrating the application of section 547(b).]

3. EXCEPTIONS—§ 547(c)
Section 547(c) excepts certain transfers from the operation of section 547(b). If a transfer comes within any of section 547(c)'s exceptions, the bankruptcy trustee will not be able to invalidate the transfer even though the trustee can establish all of the requirements of section 547(b).

The seven exceptions cover transfers that involve:

a. Contemporaneous New Value

b. Payments In The Ordinary Course Of Business

c. Enabling Loans

d. Subsequent Value

e. Floating Liens [On Inventory Or Receivables]

f. Statutory Liens

g. Small Consumer Transfers

B. SETOFFS (SECTION 553)
1. WHAT IS SETOFF
Setoff is the cancellation of cross demands between two parties that most commonly occurs between banks and their customers.

2. BANKRUPTCY AVOIDANCE OF SETOFF
Section 553 permits the avoidance of pre-petition setoffs subject to certain limitations:

a. **"Mutual Debt".** The debts must be between the same parties in the same right or capacity.

b. **"Arose Before the Commencement of the Case".** Both the debt owed to the "bankrupt" and the claim against the "bankrupt" must have preceded the filing of the bankruptcy petition.

c. **"Disallowed" (§ 553(a)(1)).** A claim that is disallowed under section 502 may not be used as the basis for a setoff.

> **d.** **"Acquired" Claims (§ 553(a)(2)).** Certain claims against the bankrupt that were acquired from a third party cannot be set off.
>
> **e.** **Build–Ups (§ 553(a)(3)).** Section 553(a)(3) precludes a setoff by a bank if:
>
> - money was deposited by the "bankrupt" within 90 days of the bankruptcy petition, and
>
> - the "bankrupt" was insolvent at the time of the setoff, and
>
> - the purpose of the deposit was to create or increase the right of setoff.
>
> **f.** **Improvement in Position (§ 553(b)).** An otherwise valid setoff that occurs within 90 days of the bankruptcy filing can be avoided to the extent that the creditor's position is improved during the period. This rule is similar to the improvement-in-position test found in the preference section 547(c)(5).

3. EFFECT OF BANKRUPTCY STAY

The filing of a bankruptcy petition automatically stays any further setoffs. Thus, exercising a right of setoff after the filing of the bankruptcy petition requires relief from the stay.

C. FRAUDULENT TRANSFERS
1. SECTION 548

The Bankruptcy Code, like non-bankruptcy law, invalidates fraudulent conveyances. The Bankruptcy Code's principal provision on fraudulent conveyances is section 548, which is very much like the non-bankruptcy fraudulent conveyance statutes considered earlier. Section 548 is based on the Uniform Fraudulent Conveyances Act, although the UFCA differs in certain significant respects.

2. SECTION 544(b)

The trustee may also use section 544(b) to invalidate fraudulent conveyances. It empowers the bankruptcy trustee to avoid any pre-bankruptcy transfer that is voidable under applicable law by a creditor holding an allowable, unsecured claim and thereby incorporates state fraudulent conveyance law into the Bankruptcy Code.

D. TRANSFERS NOT TIMELY RECORDED OR PERFECTED

A bankruptcy trustee may avoid certain pre-petition transfers that are not timely recorded or perfected. The Bankruptcy Code does not have its own public notice requirements. It does not simply invalidate all transfers not recorded within 10 days or 90 days. Rather, the Bankruptcy Code makes use of the notoriety requirements of state law in the following invalidation provisions: sections 544, 547 and 545:

1. SECTION 544(b)

Section 544(b) empowers the bankruptcy trustee to invalidate any transfer that under non-bankruptcy law is voidable as to any actual creditor of the debtor with an unsecured, allowable claim. So, if an actual unsecured creditor of the debtor can ignore or otherwise avoid a transfer under state law due to failure to satisfy local public notice requirements, the trustee can use that state law to invalidate the transfer in bankruptcy.

2. **SECTION 544(a)**

Section 544(a) focuses on the rights of hypothetical lien creditors and hypothetical bona fide purchasers of real property. Section 544(a) empowers the bankruptcy trustee to invalidate any transfer that under non-bankruptcy law is voidable as to a creditor who extended credit and obtained a lien on the date of the filing of the bankruptcy petition, or is voidable as to a bona fide purchaser of real property, whether or not such a creditor or purchaser actually exists.

3. **COMPARISON OF SECTIONS 544(a) AND 544(b)**

[See the main text for a chart comparing the two sections.]

4. **SECTION 547(e)**

Preference law, mainly through section 547(e), allows the trustee to invalidate liens that were perfected before bankruptcy but only after a consequential period of delay after the liens were created. Basically, the Bankruptcy Code's method of invalidating such liens is to "deem" that for purposes of applying the requirements of section 547(b), the date of transfers not timely recorded is the date of perfection, not the actual date of transfer. As a result of section 547(e), a delay in perfection can result in a security interest or other transfer actually given for present consideration being deemed made for an antecedent indebtedness and thus being avoided as a section 547 preference.

5. **SECTION 548(d)**

Section 548(d) is similar to section 547(e). Section 548(d) fixes the time when a transfer is deemed made for purposes of the fraudulent conveyance invalidation provisions of section 548: when the transfer is so far perfected that no subsequent bona fide purchaser of the property from the debtor can acquire rights in the property superior to those of the transferee. The purpose of section 548(d) is to prevent a fraudulent conveyance from escaping invalidation by being kept secret for over a year.

6. **SECTION 545(2)**

Section 545(2) invalidates statutory liens that are not perfected or enforceable on the date of the petition against a hypothetical bona fide purchaser, subject to any applicable state law "grace period."

E. LANDLORDS' LIENS

Sections 545(3) and 545(4) allow the trustee to avoid a statutory lien on the property of the debtor to the extent that such lien is for rent or is a lien of distress for rent.

F. DISGUISED PRIORITIES

Section 507 of the Bankruptcy Code is a priority provision; it sets out the order in which the various unsecured claims against the debtor are to be satisfied. It displaces any state priority statutes. Section 545 protects this federal priority scheme from disruption by state priority provisions that are "disguised" as statutory liens. Section 545 reaches spurious statutory liens which are in reality merely priorities.

G.   RECLAMATION UNDER U.C.C. SECTION 2–702
1.   RIGHT UNDER THE UNIFORM COMMERCIAL CODE
Uniform Commercial Code section 2–702 gives unpaid credit sellers of goods a right to recover the property from the buyer. Case law has created a similar right of reclamation for sellers paid with bad checks.

2.   BANKRUPTCY'S EFFECT ON THE RIGHT
With certain exceptions, a seller's right of reclamation under state law is valid in bankruptcy if the requirements of bankruptcy law section 546 are satisfied. The bankruptcy trustee can avoid the reclamation rights of a seller who fails to comply with section 546(c).

XXII.   POST–BANKRUPTCY TRANSFERS

A.   THE PROBLEM OF POST–PETITION TRANSFERS
During the hiatus between the filing of the bankruptcy petition and the bankruptcy trustee's taking possession of the property of the estate, the debtor will usually have possession and control of the property and might transfer all or parts of it to some third party. The significant inquiry is whether the trustee can recover this property from the debtor's transferees.

B.   GENERAL RULE REGARDING AVOIDANCE OF POST–PETITION TRANSFERS
Section 549(a) provides that, as a general rule, the trustee can avoid any unauthorized post-petition transfer of estate property. In other words, the transferees are unprotected and are accountable for the property.

C.   EXCEPTIONS PROTECTING TRANSFEREES
Section 549 protects transferees of post-petition transfers in certain circumstances.

1.   TRANSFERS AUTHORIZED
A post-bankruptcy transfer will be effective against the bankruptcy trustee if the transfer was authorized by the Bankruptcy Code or by the bankruptcy court.

2.   INVOLUNTARY CASES
Section 549(b) validates transfers by the debtor that occur after the filing of an *involuntary* bankruptcy petition and before the order for relief to the extent that the transferee gave value to the debtor after the filing of the bankruptcy petition.

3.   TRANSFERS OF REAL ESTATE
Section 549(c) provides that, in certain circumstances, a transfer of real property by the debtor after the filing of a voluntary petition or after an order for relief in an involuntary case will be effective against the bankruptcy trustee.

D.   POST–PETITION TRANSFERS OF ESTATE PROPERTY BY THIRD PARTIES
Under section 542(c), a third person who in good faith transfers property of the estate after the filing of the petition is protected from the bankruptcy trustee if the third party had "neither notice nor actual knowledge of the commencement of the case." This protection, however, only extends to the party who transfers the property of the estate; it does not protect the transferee.

XXIII. EFFECT OF BANKRUPTCY ON SECURED CLAIMS

A. WHAT IS A SECURED CLAIM
A creditor has a secured claim if it holds a lien on or has a right of setoff against "property of the estate." The claim is secured only to the extent of the value of "such creditor's interest in the estate's interest in such property."

B. INVALIDATION OF LIENS
Some liens that are valid outside of bankruptcy can be invalidated in a bankruptcy case by use of avoiding powers given to the trustee and the debtor. All that is eliminated, however, is the lien. The creditor's claim remains. Lien invalidation converts a secured claim into an unsecured claim.

C. OVERVIEW OF IMPACT OF BANKRUPTCY ON SECURED CLAIMS
In thinking about the impact of bankruptcy on secured claims, a law student or lawyer should focus on two questions:

- How can the debtor's bankruptcy filing adversely affect the holder of a secured claim?

- How can a secured claim be satisfied when the debtor is in bankruptcy?

D. WHAT CAN HAPPEN TO SECURED CLAIMS DURING BANKRUPTCY
Especially in reorganization cases, bankruptcy has major effects on a creditor that holds a valid-in-bankruptcy lien:

1. DELAY IN REALIZING ON COLLATERAL
The automatic stay of section 362 prevents a creditor from enforcing its lien against property of the estate or property of the debtor. Accordingly, a creditor will not be able to sell or even seize encumbered property from a debtor who is in bankruptcy without obtaining relief from the automatic stay.

2. DEBTOR'S USE, LEASE, OR SALE OF COLLATERAL
Section 363 provides for continued use, lease, or sale of encumbered property during bankruptcy.

3. LOSS OF PRIORITY
Subject to certain conditions, section 364(d) empowers the bankruptcy court to approve the debtor's granting a post-petition creditor a lien on encumbered property that has priority over all pre-petition liens.

4. LIMITATIONS ON FLOATING LIENS
After-acquired property clauses are expressly cut off in bankruptcy by section 552(a). On the other hand, section 552(b) generally recognizes a security interest in post-petition proceeds from pre-petition collateral.

5. RETURN OF REPOSSESSED PROPERTY
Section 542(a) compels the holder of a secured claim that has taken possession of its collateral prior to bankruptcy to return it to the debtor when she files a bankruptcy petition if the collateral is "property that the trustee may use, sell, or lease

under section 363 * * * unless such property is of inconsequential value or benefit to the estate."

E. SATISFACTION OF SECURED CLAIMS
1. OVERVIEW
    a. **Recovery of Collateral.** If the holder of a secured claim recovers its collater-
al, the secured claim is extinguished.

    b. **Payment of Amount Equal to the Value of the Collateral.** If the holder of a
secured claim does not recover its collateral, it should receive a payment equal
to the value of the collateral.

2. CHAPTER 7
There are six different ways that a Chapter 7 case can result in the holder of a
secured claim obtaining either the collateral or its cash value.

    a.   Obtaining Relief from the Automatic Stay

    b.   Abandonment by the Bankruptcy Trustee

    c.   Sale of the Collateral by the Bankruptcy Trustee and Distribution of the Pro-
ceeds from This Sale to the Holder of the Secured Claim

    d.   Redemption by Payment by the Debtor

    e.   Payments Pursuant to a Reaffirmation Agreement

    f.   Voluntary Return by Trustee

3. CHAPTERS 11, 12 AND 13
What the holder of a secured claim receives in a Chapter 11 case or a Chapter 12
case or a Chapter 13 case depends on the provisions of the plan. Within limits, a
Chapter 11 or Chapter 12 plan can modify the rights of the holder of any secured
claim. A Chapter 13 plan also can modify, subject again to certain limits, the
rights of the holder of any secured claim other than a claim secured "only by a security interest in real property that is the debtor's principal residence."

F. POSTPONEMENT OF TAX LIENS IN CHAPTER 7 CASES
In a Chapter 7 case in which the government has a tax lien that is not avoided, Section 724 applies to postpone payment of the secured tax claim until the complete payment of all claims entitled to priority under section 507(a)(1)–(6).

XXIV. CHAPTER 7 AND UNSECURED CLAIMS

A. WHAT IS A CLAIM
Generally, the Bankruptcy Code deals with "claims," not creditors. The term "claim"
is defined in section 101(4), and has alternative components of "right to payment" and
"equitable remedy for breach of performance."

1. **RIGHT TO PAYMENT**

   Any right to payment is a "claim," whether the right is contingent, unliquidated, unmatured, or disputed.

2. **EQUITABLE REMEDY**

   Some, but not all, rights to equitable remedies are claims. The test is whether the right to an equitable remedy "gives rise to a right to payment."

B. WHAT IS AN UNSECURED CLAIM

A claim is unsecured if the creditor has not obtained a consensual, judicial, or statutory lien or if the value of the property subject to such a lien is less than the amount of the creditor's claim.

C. COLLECTION OF UNSECURED CLAIMS FROM THE DEBTOR

Under section 362, the filing of a Chapter 7 petition operates as a "stay" that prevents a creditor from collecting its unsecured claim from the debtor until the bankruptcy case is closed. Under section 727, the bankruptcy court generally grants the debtor a "discharge" that prevents a creditor from collecting its claim from the debtor after the bankruptcy case is closed. The section 362 stay coupled with the section 727 discharge makes it necessary for most holders of unsecured claims to look to the "property of the estate" for the satisfaction of their claims.

D. SATISFACTION OF UNSECURED CLAIMS IN CHAPTER 7 CASES

1. **WHAT PROPERTY IS DISTRIBUTED TO HOLDERS OF UNSECURED CLAIMS IN CHAPTER 7 CASES**

   Holders of unsecured claims receive the net proceeds (reduced by usually very significant prior claims on the funds) from the bankruptcy trustee's sale of the "property of the estate."

2. **WHICH HOLDERS OF UNSECURED CLAIMS PARTICIPATE IN THE DISTRIBUTION OF PROPERTY OF THE ESTATE**

   a. **Proof of Claim.** Creditors who wish to participate in the distribution of the proceeds of the liquidation of the "property of the estate" must file a proof of claim.

   b. **Allowance.** In a Chapter 7 case, the distribution is only made to unsecured creditors whose claims are "allowed." If a proof of claim has been filed, the claim is deemed allowed "unless a party in interest objects." Section 502(b) sets out nine grounds for disallowing claims.

3. **ORDER OF DISTRIBUTION**

   Section 726 establishes the rules for distribution to the holders of unsecured claims in a Chapter 7 case. Basically, the distribution is in this order:

   - priorities under section 507

   - allowed unsecured claims which were either timely filed or tardily filed by a creditor who did not know of the bankruptcy

- allowed unsecured claims which were tardily filed by creditors with notice or actual knowledge of the bankruptcy

- fines and punitive damages

- post-petition interest on pre-petition claims

Each claim of each of the five classes must be paid in full before any claim in the next class receives any distribution. Each claimant within a particular class shares pro rata if the proceeds from the liquidation of the property of the estate is insufficient to satisfy all claims in that class.

In the very unlikely event that the sale of the "property of the estate" yields enough to satisfy each claim in each of the five "classes" listed above, the surplus is paid to the debtor.

a. Priorities. Section 507 establishes seven classes of priority claims which involve:

1) Administrative Expenses

2) Ordinary Business Expenses

3) Wage Claims

4) Employee Benefit Plans

5) Farmers And Fishermen

6) Consumer Deposits

7) Tax Claims

b. Subordination. Section 510, the subordination provision, has the effect of moving some claims further back in the line of distribution.

1) Required Subordination. Section 510 requires subordination in two instances:

- when there is a subordination agreement that would be enforceable under non-bankruptcy law; or,

- when a seller or purchaser of equity securities seeks damages or rescission.

2) Discretionary Subordination. Additionally, the court has the discretion, after notice and hearing, to subordinate any claim to another claim or claims "under principles of equitable subordination."

XXV. LEASES AND EXECUTORY CONTRACTS

The effect of bankruptcy on a debtor's leases and executory contracts is governed primarily by section 365. Under section 365, a bankruptcy trustee can:

- reject a lease or executory contract;

- assume and retain a lease or executory contract; or,

- assume and assign a lease or executory contract.

A. EFFECT OF REJECTION, ASSUMPTION, ASSIGNMENT OF LEASE OR EXECUTORY CONTRACT

1. REJECTION

If a debtor/lessee rejects a lease, the debtor has no further right to use the property, and no further personal liability on the lease. The rejection of the lease is, of course, a breach of the lease. The lessor will have an allowable unsecured claim against the bankrupt estate for back rent and future rentals.

2. ASSUMPTION

If the debtor's lease is assumed, the leasehold continues to be an asset of the estate, and the debtor can continue to use the property. Assumption covers the burdens of the lease as well as the benefits. By assuming the lease, the trustee or debtor-in-possession is obligating the estate to make all payments under the lease. This obligation is a first priority administrative expense.

3. ASSUMPTION AND ASSIGNMENT

An assumption and assignment of a lease by the trustee or debtor-in-possession "relieves the trustee and the estate from any liability for any breach of such contract or lease occurring after such assignment." After the assignment, the landlord can look only to the assignee for the payment of the post-assignment obligations under the lease.

B. PROCEDURE FOR REJECTION OR ASSUMPTION

Section 365(a) contemplates court approval of rejection or assumption. A business judgment test is usually applied.

1. CHAPTER 7 CASES

Section 365(d)(1) imposes a 60–day rule in Chapter 7 cases. Leases and executory contracts that are not assumed within 60 days after the order for relief are deemed rejected.

2. CHAPTERS 11 AND 13

Section 365(d)(4) provides the same 60–day time limit in Chapter 11 and Chapter 13 cases for leases of non-residential real property. There is no time limit in Chapter 11 and Chapter 13 cases for the assumption or rejection of residential leases, personal property leases, or other executory contracts. Such leases and contracts can be assumed or rejected in the Chapter 11 or Chapter 13 plan or can be assumed or rejected prior to the formulation of the plan.

C. LIMITATIONS ON THE REJECTION OF A LEASE OR EXECUTORY CONTRACT

There are five kinds of contracts with respect to which the power of a trustee or debtor-in-possession to reject a lease or executory contract is limited: (1) a lease of real property when the debtor is the (2) landlord; a timeshare contract; (3) an installment land sales contract; (4) collective bargaining contracts and retirement benefits in Chapter 11 cases; and (5) intellectual property licenses.

D. LIMITATIONS ON ASSUMPTION AND ASSIGNMENT
1. LEASES AND EXECUTORY CONTRACTS THAT CANNOT BE ASSUMED OR ASSUMED AND ASSIGNED

There are some leases and executory contracts that cannot be assumed and assigned: (a) A lease or contract that has terminated before bankruptcy cannot be assumed; (b) a loan commitment or other financing arrangement cannot be assumed; and (c) contracts that are not assignable under state law are not assignable in bankruptcy.

2. REQUIREMENTS FOR ASSUMPTION AND ASSIGNMENT

Paragraph (b) of section 365 sets out the requirements for assumption of a lease or executory contract *when there has been a default* other than breach of a provision relating to bankruptcy filing or insolvency. The principal requirement of section 365(b) is "adequate assurance" of future performance and a cure of all defaults or "adequate assurance" that all defaults will be promptly cured.

"Adequate assurance" is also a condition precedent to assignment of a lease or executory contract.

E. DEFINITION OF EXECUTORY CONTRACT

Section 365 applies to leases and executory contracts. The Bankruptcy Code does not define the term "lease." There is probably no need for a definition. When there is a question whether a "lease" of personal property is a disguised credit sale, bankruptcy courts look to the definition of "security interest" in UCC section 1–201(37).

Similarly, the Bankruptcy Code does not define the phrase "executory contract." Most authorities define it as a contract that is so far unperformed on both sides that the failure of either party to complete her performance would be a material breach excusing further performance from the other party.

XXVI. DISCHARGE

Bankruptcy "discharges" *certain* debtors from *certain* debts.

A. WHICH DEBTORS RECEIVE A DISCHARGE (MAINLY, OBJECTIONS TO DISCHARGE)
1. CHAPTER 7
a. **Importance of Determining Eligibility for Discharge.** In counseling a beleaguered individual debtor about Chapter 7, it is very important to ascertain her eligibility for discharge because, if the debtor is denied a discharge, she loses two ways: She will leave the bankruptcy case without her section 541 property

yet still liable for the debts she owed at the time of the filing of the bankruptcy case (less any distribution that creditors received from the trustee).

b. **Grounds for Withholding Discharge.** The grounds for withholding a discharge, i.e., objections to discharge, are set out in section 727(a).

   1) Corporation Or Partnership

     REMEMBER: Only an individual is eligible for discharge in a Chapter 7 case.

   2) Certain Fraudulent Conveyances

   3) Failing to Preserve Record

   4) Depriving Trustee of Property or Information

   5) Failing to Explain Loss of Assets

   6) Refusal to Testify

   7) Acts Affecting Bankruptcy of Insider

   8) Recent Discharge in Chapter 7 or 11 Case

   9) Recent Discharge in Chapter 13 Case

  10) Waiver of Discharge

c. **Procedure for Withholding Discharge.** Section 727(a) is not self-executing. The bankruptcy trustee or a creditor must object to discharge. Any complaint objecting to discharge must be filed within 60 days of the first date set for the meeting of creditors, unless the court "for cause" extends the time. If an objection to discharge is filed, the bankruptcy court tries the issue of the debtor's right to a discharge.

d. **Hearing After Determination Whether to Grant Discharge.** After the court has determined whether to grant a discharge, the court must hold a hearing and the debtor must appear in person. At the hearing, the court informs the debtor that a discharge has been granted, or why a discharge has not been granted.

2. **CHAPTER 11**
  a. **In General.** In Chapter 11, the confirmation of the plan operates as a discharge.

  b. **Grounds for Denying Discharge.** The grounds for denying a discharge in a Chapter 11 case are different from the grounds for denying a discharge in a Chapter 7 case. A Chapter 11 debtor will be denied a discharge only if all of the following requirements are satisfied:

    • the plan provides for liquidation of all or substantially all of the property of the estate; AND

- the debtor does not engage in business after consummation of the plan; AND

- the debtor would be denied a discharge if the case were in Chapter 7, section 1141(d)(3).

3. CHAPTER 12 AND 13

In Chapter 12 and 13 cases, unlike Chapter 11 cases, the confirmation of the plan does not effect a discharge. In Chapter 12 and Chapter 13, the debtor receives a discharge if and when she completes her payments under the plan or completes her efforts to make payments under the plan, except that the court is empowered to grant a "hardship" discharge to a debtor who has failed to make all of the payments required by her Chapter 12 or 13 plan.

B. WHICH OBLIGATIONS ARE AFFECTED BY A BANKRUPTCY DISCHARGE (MAINLY, EXCEPTIONS TO DISCHARGE)

Even when the debtor receives a discharge, she is not necessarily freed from all of her obligations. Certain obligations are not affected by a discharge.

1. CHAPTER 7

    a. Debts That Are Discharged. In a Chapter 7 case, a discharge relieves a debtor from personal liability for debts that are both

- incurred prior to the time of the order for relief and

- not within one of the ten exceptions to discharge set out in section 523.

    b. Debts That Are Excepted From Discharge. Section 523(a) sets out ten exceptions to discharge:

    1) Taxes

    2) Debts for Property Obtained Through Fraud

    3) Unscheduled Debts

    4) Liabilities as Fiduciary

    5) Domestic Obligations

    6) Liabilities for Willful And Malicious Injury

    7) Governmental Fines

    8) Education Debts

    9) DWI Debts

    10) Debts Covered by Previous Bankruptcy in Which Discharge Not Granted

    c. Procedure for Asserting Exceptions. Exceptions to discharge based on section 523(a) (2), (4), or (6) must be asserted in bankruptcy court. Unless the creditor's motion to except a debt is timely made, the debt is discharged.

When a creditor is relying on section 523(a)(1), (3), (5), (7), (8), (9) or (10), there is no requirement that the matter be heard in bankruptcy court. If no request is filed with the bankrutpcy court, the dischargeability issue may arise in connection with the creditor's collection efforts in a non-bankruptcy forum.

2. CHAPTER 11
Chapters 11 and 7 differ in two major respects with respect to determining which debts are dischargeable:

While a Chapter 7 discharge is limited to debts that arose before the date of the order for relief, a Chapter 11 discharge reaches debts that arose before the date of confirmation of the plan.

While every Chapter 7 discharge is subject to the exceptions to discharge of section 523, that provision only applies in Chapter 11 if the debtor is an individual. Section 523 does not apply if the Chapter 11 debtor is a corporation or a partnership.

3. CHAPTER 13 CASES AND CHAPTER 12 CASES
In Chapter 13 cases, determining the debts covered by the discharge depends on the nature of the Chapter 13 discharge. If the debtor has made all of the payments required by the plan and received a discharge under section 1328(a), the discharge affects all debts provided for by the plan except:

- claims for alimony and child support and

- certain long term obligations such as a house mortgage on which the payments extend beyond the term of the plan, section 1328(a).

The "hardship" discharge under section 1328(b), and *all* discharges under Chapter 12, are not as comprehensive as the section 1328(a) discharge. If the debtor receives a discharge under section 1328(b) or under section 1228(a) or (b), all of the exceptions to discharge in section 523 apply.

C. EFFECT OF A DISCHARGE
1. WHAT A DISCHARGE DOES
    a. Protection From Personal Liability. A discharge protects the debtor from any further personal liability on discharged debts.

    b. Protection From Reaffirmation Agreements. A reaffirmation agreement is an agreement to pay a debt dischargeable in bankruptcy. Section 524(c) and (d) limit the enforceability of reaffirmation agreements.

    c. Protection From Discrimination by a Governmental Unit or an Employer.
    Subject to very limited exceptions, a governmental unit may not deny a debtor a license or a franchise or otherwise discriminate against a debtor "*solely because*" the debtor

- filed for bankruptcy,

- was insolvent prior to and/or during bankruptcy, or

- refuses to pay debts *discharged* by his, her or its bankruptcy, section 525(a).

A private employer cannot fire an employee or "discriminate with respect to employment" "*solely because*" (i) the employee filed for bankruptcy, (ii) was insolvent prior to or during the bankruptcy, or (iii) refuses to pay debts *discharged* by his or her bankruptcy.

2. WHAT A DISCHARGE DOES *NOT* DO

A discharge does not cancel or extinguish debts or affect liens securing debts. It only protects the debtors from further personal liability on the debt. A bankruptcy discharge does not automatically affect the liability of other parties such as codebtors or guarantors.

3. DISCHARGE AND A DEBTOR'S LEGALLY IMPOSED PUBLIC OBLIGATIONS

a. **Obligations to Dispose of Toxic Waste.** A Chapter 7 debtor's obligation to clean-up toxic wastes is a dischargeable obligation.

b. **Court–Ordered Restitution in Criminal Cases.** Court–ordered restitution imposed in connection with a criminal defendant's sentence is excepted from discharge by section 523(a)(7), which excepts a debt that is a "fine, penalty, or forfeiture payable to and for the benefit of a governmental unit, and is not compensation for actual pecuniary loss."

XXVII.   CHAPTER 11

A. COMMENCEMENT OF THE CASE
1. FILING THE PETITION

A case under Chapter 11 is commenced by the filing of a petition by either the debtor or creditors.

a. **Voluntary Petition.** With two exceptions relating to stock-brokers/commodity brokers and railroads, any "person" that is eligible to file a voluntary bankruptcy petition under Chapter 7 is also eligible to file a petition under Chapter 11. The filing of the petition operates as an "order for relief" without an adjudication.

b. **Involuntary Petition.** The requirements for a creditor-initiated Chapter 11 case are the same as the requirements for an involuntary Chapter 7 case.

2. NOTIFYING AND ORGANIZING THE CREDITORS

a. **List of Creditors and Notice.** Section 521 obligates the debtor to file a list of creditors. Section 342 requires appropriate notice of the order for relief.

b. **Proof of Claim.** A creditor's claim in a Chapter 11 case is "deemed" filed without an actual filing of a proof of claim, unless the claim is scheduled as disputed, contingent, or unliquidated.

    c. Creditors' Meeting. The Bankruptcy Code requires a meeting of creditors at which the debtor is examined under oath.

    d. Creditors' Committee. As soon as practicable after the order for relief, the bankruptcy court appoints a committee of unsecured creditors that represents all such creditors in monitoring the administration of the case; investigating the debtor's acts and financial condition; participating in the formulation of the plan; and generally in performing such other services as are in the interest of those represented.

B. OPERATION OF THE BUSINESS

Successful rehabilitation of a business under Chapter 11 generally requires the continued operation of the business. No court order is necessary in order to operate the debtor's business after the filing of a Chapter 11 petition. Section 1108 provides that unless the court orders otherwise, the "trustee" may operate the debtor's business.

1. WHO OPERATES THE BUSINESS

    a. Debtor-in-Possession. Notwithstanding section 1108's use of the word "trustee," the debtor will remain in control of the business in most Chapter 11 cases. Pre-bankruptcy management will continue to operate the business as a "debtor-in-possession" unless a request is made for the appointment of a trustee and the court, after notice and a hearing, grants the request.

    b. Trustee. A trustee is appointed only if there is cause to doubt the ability or integrity of the debtor-in-possession or doing so is in the interest of creditors, any equity security holders, and other interests of the estate.

    c. Examiner. If a trustee is not appointed, the court may appoint an "examiner" who does not operate the business. Rather, she investigates the competence and honesty of the debtor and files a report of the investigation.

2. OBTAINING CREDIT

Section 364 deals with obtaining credit for the operation of the business in a Chapter 11 case. It provides a number of inducements to third parties to extend credit to a debtor that has filed a Chapter 11 petition:

    a. Priority in Payment Over Pre–Petition Creditors

    b. Priority in Payment Over Administrative Expenses Plus Collateral

    c. Superpriority In Collateral

3. USE OF ENCUMBERED PROPERTY

In the typical Chapter 11 case, most of the personal and real property that the debtor owns *at the time of* the filing of the Chapter 11 petition is encumbered by liens.

    a. Immunity of Post–Petition Property From Pre–Petition Liens. The personal and real property that the debtor acquires *after* the filing of the Chapter 11 petition is generally protected from pre-petition liens, although there is an exception to this rule for proceeds.

b.   Effect of Stay on Reaching Collateral. Section 362(a) stays a creditor with a lien on the property of a Chapter 11 debtor from repossessing the encumbered property.

c.   Rules as to Use of Collateral. Section 363 empowers the debtor-in-possession or trustee to use, sell, or lease encumbered property. The interest of the lien creditor is safeguarded by section 363's requirement of "adequate protection." Encumbered property that is not "cash collateral" may be used, sold, or leased in the ordinary course of business without a prior judicial determination of "adequate protection." Encumbered "cash collateral" may only be used if the court authorizes such use after notice and hearing on adequate protection. "Cash collateral" is defined in section 363(a): "cash, negotiable instruments, documents of title, securities, deposit accounts, or other cash equivalents."

C.   PREPARATION OF THE PLAN OF REHABILITATION
1.   WHO PREPARES THE PLAN

a.   When Trustee Not Appointed. In the absence of a trustee, the debtor initially has the exclusive right to file a Chapter 11 plan.

b.   When Trustee Is Appointed. If a trustee is appointed, the trustee, the debtor, a creditor, the creditors' committee, and any other party in interest may file a plan. More than one plan may be filed.

c.   When Debtor Fails to File Plan. If the debtor fails to file a plan and obtain creditor acceptances within the specified time periods, any party in interest may file a plan and more than one plan may be filed.

d.   Important Role of Creditors' Committee. No matter who files the plan, the creditors' committee will probably play a major role in negotiating and formulating the plan.

2.   TERMS OF THE PLAN
Section 1123 governs the provisions of a Chapter 11 plan. Subparagraph (a) sets out the mandatory provisions of a Chapter 11 plan ("shall"); subparagraph (b) of section 1123 indicates the permissive provisions of a Chapter 11 plan ("may").

a.   Rights Altered. A Chapter 11 plan may alter the rights of unsecured creditors, secured creditors, and/or shareholders.

b.   Classes of Claims. The plan will divide creditors' claims into classes and treat each claim in a particular class the same.

3.   FUNDING FOR THE PLAN
There are several sources of funding:

a.   Loans. Chapter 11 debtors often use money borrowed from third parties to make distributions to creditors under Chapter 11 plans.

b.   Sale of Assets. Sale of assets is another major source for Chapter 11 payments. A Chapter 11 plan may provide for the sale of all or substantially all of the debtor's assets.

    c.   **Securities.**   A Chapter 11 plan may offer creditors the debtor's debt or equity securities, rather than cash.

D. ACCEPTANCE
1. DISCLOSURE
Section 1125 requires full disclosure before postpetition solicitation of acceptances of a Chapter 11 plan. Two items are especially important in making full disclosure:

    a.   **Copy of Plan.**   Creditors and shareholders must be provided with a copy of the plan or a summary of the plan.

    b.   **Written Disclosure Statement.**   Creditors and shareholders must also be provided with "a written disclosure statement approved, after notice and a hearing, by the court as containing adequate information."

2. WHO VOTES
Creditors with claims "allowed under section 502" and shareholders with interests "allowed under section 502" vote on Chapter 11 plans.

3. IMPAIRMENT OF CLAIMS
Under section 1124 a class of claims or interests is impaired unless

- the legal, equitable, and contractual rights of the holder are left "unaltered;" or

- the only alteration of legal, equitable, or contractual rights is reversal of an acceleration on default by curing the default and reinstating the debt; or

- cash payment to (A) a creditor on the effective date of the plan is equal to the allowed amount of the claim; or (B) cash payment to a shareholder on the effective date of the plan is equal to the greater of the share's redemption price and its liquidation preference.

4. 1111(b) ELECTION

Section 1111(b) allows a creditor who is undersecured, and who thus has a secured claim and an unsecured claim, to abandon her unsecured claim and measure her secured claim by the full amount of the debt rather than by the value of the collateral. Making this election has certain advantages and disadvantages for the holder of the secured claim with respect to how her claim is treated under the Chapter 11 plan.

5. NEEDED MAJORITIES
    a.   **Class of Claims.**   A class of claims has accepted a plan when more than one half in number and at least two thirds in amount of the allowed claims actually voting on the plan approve the plan.

    b.   **Class of Interests.**   A class of interests has accepted a plan when at least two thirds in amount of the allowed interests actually voting on the plan approve the plan.

E.   CONFIRMATION

Section 1128 requires that the bankruptcy court hold a hearing on confirmation and give parties in interest notice of the hearing so that they might raise objections to confirmation.   Confirmation standards are described by section 1129.

1.   STANDARDS FOR CONFIRMATION
   a.   Plans Accepted by Every Class. A plan that has been accepted by every class of claims and every class of interests must meet all of the requirements of section 1129(a).   The additional requirements of section 1129(b) do not apply.

   b.   Plans Accepted by Less Than Every Class. Plans accepted by less than every class can be confirmed only if the additional requirements of section 1129(b) are satisfied.   Section 1129(b) requires that

   - at least one impaired class of claims has accepted the plan;

   - the plan does not discriminate unfairly;

   - the plan is fair and equitable.

2.   EFFECT OF CONFIRMATION
   a.   Plan Governs Obligations. After confirmation of a Chapter 11 plan, the debtor's performance obligations are governed by the terms of the plan.   The provisions of a confirmed Chapter 11 plan bind not only the debtor but also the debtor's creditors and shareholders "whether or not such creditor, equity security holder, or general partner has accepted the plan."   Subject to certain limitations, confirmation of a Chapter 11 plan operates as a discharge.

   b.   Limitations on Discharge. Chapter 11 withholds discharge from some debtors and some debts.   The plan may limit discharge.   The order of confirmation may limit discharge.   The exceptions to discharge in section 523 are applicable to individual debtors, but the objections to discharge in section 727 are applicable only in limited circumstances.

XXVIII.   CHAPTER 13

A.   ELIGIBILITY

A debtor may file for Chapter 13 relief if she (1) is an individual, and (2) has a "regular income," and (3) has fixed unsecured debts of less than $100,000 and fixed secured debts of less than $350,000.

B.   COMMENCEMENT OF THE CASE
1.   BY FILING VOLUNTARY PETITION
   The case begins with the filing of a bankruptcy petition.   Only the debtor may file a Chapter 13 petition.   There are no involuntary, i.e., creditor-initiated, Chapter 13 cases.

2.   STAY TRIGGERED
   The filing of a Chapter 13 petition triggers the automatic stay of section 362.

C. CODEBTOR STAY
Section 1301 restrains a creditor from attempting to collect a debt from the codebtor of a Chapter 13 debtor.

1. APPLICABILITY OF STAY
Section 1301's stay of collection activities directed at codebtors is applicable only if:

- the debt is a consumer debt, and
- the codebtor is not in the credit business.

2. TERMINATION OF STAY
This codebtor stay automatically terminates when the case is closed, dismissed, or converted to Chapter 7 or 11.

3. RELIEF FROM STAY
Section 1301(c) sets out three grounds for relief from the codebtor stay. Section 1301(c) requires notice and hearing, and requires the court to grant relief if any of the three grounds are established:

a. Codebtor Got The Consideration

b. Claim Not Paid Under Debtor's Plan

c. Irreparable Harm

D. TRUSTEES
1. APPOINTMENT
A trustee is appointed by the United States Trustee in every Chapter 13 case.

2. DUTIES AND POWERS
The trustee in a Chapter 13 case is an active trustee with many duties described by the Bankruptcy Code. Operation of the debtor's business is not among the trustee's duties, however. If a debtor engaged in business files a Chapter 13 petition, the business will be operated by the debtor, not by the trustee, "unless the court orders otherwise."

A chapter 13 trustee probably has all of the lien avoidance powers.

E. PREPARATION OF THE CHAPTER 13 PLAN
1. WHO FILES
Only a debtor may file a Chapter 13 plan.

2. CONTENTS
a. **What Plan Must Provide.** A Chapter 13 plan must provide for full payment in cash of all claims entitled to priority under section 507.

b. **What Plan May Provide.**

1) For Less Than Full Payment of Unsecured Claims

2) For Modifying Secured Claims

3. FUNDING

A Chapter 13 plan must provide for submission of "such portion of future earnings * * * of the debtor to the supervision and control of the trustee as is necessary for the execution of the plan." Payments under the plan may also be funded by sale of property of the estate.

4. PAYMENT PERIOD

Section 1322(c) limits the payment period under a Chapter 13 plan to three years except that the court may "for cause" approve a payment period of as long as five years.

F. CONFIRMATION OF THE CHAPTER 13 PLAN

In Chapter 13, creditors do not vote on the plan. Chapter 13 requires only court approval.

1. STANDARDS FOR CONFIRMATION

The standards for judicial confirmation of a Chapter 13 plan are set out in section 1325:

a. Satisfy Law

b. Payment of Filing Fee

c. Good Faith

d. Best Interests of Creditors

e. Protection of Secured Claims

f. Ability to Perform

2. BINDING EFFECT

A confirmed Chapter 13 plan is binding on the debtor and all of his creditors. Unless the plan or the order confirming the plan otherwise provides, confirmation of a plan vests all of the "property of the estate" in the debtor free and clear of "any claim or interest of any creditor provided for by the plan."

3. PERFORMANCE

After confirmation, the plan is put into effect with the debtor generally making the payments provided in the plan to a Chapter 13 trustee who acts as a disbursing agent.

4. MODIFICATION

A Chapter 13 plan can be modified after confirmation.

G. DISCHARGE

1. WHEN GRANTED

The debtor receives a discharge after completion of the payments provided for in the Chapter 13 plan.

2. EXCEPTIONS
A Section 1328(a) discharge is not subject to all of the exceptions from discharge set out in section 523. The only debts excepted from a section 1328(a) discharge are:

- allowed claims not provided for by the plan,

- certain long-term obligations specifically provided for by the plan, and

- claims for alimony and child support.

3. HARDSHIP DISCHARGE
In certain circumstances, the bankruptcy court may grant a "hardship" discharge in a Chapter 13 case even though the debtor has not completed payments called for by the plan. This section 1328(b) "hardship" discharge is not as comprehensive as a section 1328(a) discharge. A "hardship" discharge is limited by all of the section 523(a) exceptions to discharge.

4. EFFECT ON DISCHARGE IN SUBSEQUENT CASES
If a debtor receives a discharge under either section 1328(a) or section 1328(b), he may not receive a discharge in a Chapter 7 case filed within six years of the date that the Chapter 13 case was filed unless payments under the plan totalled at least 70 of the allowed unsecured claims, and the plan was the "debtor's best effort." A discharge under section 1328(a) or section 1328(b) does not affect the debtor's right to future Chapter 13 relief.

H. DISMISSAL AND CONVERSION
1. UPON DEBTOR'S REQUEST
A debtor who files a Chapter 13 petition may at any time request the bankruptcy court to dismiss the case or convert it to a case under Chapter 7.

2. UPON CREDITOR'S REQUEST
The bankruptcy court may also dismiss a Chapter 13 case or convert it to a case under Chapter 7 on request of a creditor if there is cause shown.

3. BY COURT
The bankruptcy court is empowered to convert from Chapter 13 to Chapter 11 before confirmation of the plan on request of a party in interest and after notice and hearing.

4. TREATMENT OF POST–PETITION CLAIMS AND PROPERTY UPON CONVERSION
Converting a case from Chapter 13 to Chapter 7 raises questions about the treatment of post-petition claims and post-petition property. Claims arising in the period between filing of the Chapter 13 petition and conversion to Chapter 7 are allowable claims. Cases are divided on whether property acquired in the gap between filing for Chapter 13 relief and conversion to Chapter 7 is property of the estate.

I. COMPARISON OF CHAPTERS 7 AND 13
[See the chart in the main text that compares Chapters 7 and 13.]

J.   COMPARISON OF CHAPTERS 11 AND 13
[The main text lists the comparative advantages of Chapters 11 and 13.]

XXIX.   ALLOCATION OF JUDICIAL POWER OVER BANKRUPTCY MATTERS

A.   HISTORY
1.   1898 ACT
Under the Bankruptcy Act of 1898, bankruptcy courts had limited jurisdiction which was commonly referred to as "summary jurisdiction." There was considerable uncertainty over which disputes were within the summary jurisdiction of the bankruptcy court. This uncertainty gave rise to considerable litigation.

2.   1978 CODE
Congress in 1978 decided to create a bankruptcy court with pervasive jurisdiction, but Congress also decided that this bankruptcy court should not be an Article III court.

3.   *MARATHON PIPELINE* DECISION
The Supreme Court held in 1982 that the pervasion jurisdiction of bankruptcy courts was unconstitutional because bankruptcy courts were not Article III courts.

4.   EMERGENCY RULE
In December of 1982, all of the district courts adopted an Emergency Rule on allocation of judicial power over bankruptcy matters.

5.   1984 AMENDMENTS
Congress amended the Bankruptcy Code in 1984 to deal with the problem of bankruptcy court jurisdiction. The 1984 amendments make the bankruptcy court a part of the federal district court, confer jurisdiction in bankruptcy on the district court, and allocate judicial power in bankruptcy matters between the federal district judge and the bankruptcy judge.

B.   OPERATION OF 1984 AMENDMENTS
In understanding the 1984 amendments allocating judicial powers over bankruptcy matters, it is necessary to understand three separate, new sections to United States Code title 28: sections 151, 1334, and 157.

1.   BANKRUPTCY COURT AS PART OF THE DISTRICT COURT, SECTION 151
Section 151 refers to a bankruptcy judge and a bankruptcy court as a "unit" of the district court.

2.   GRANTS OF JURISDICTION TO THE DISTRICT COURT, SECTION 1334(a) AND (b)
    a.   Jurisdiction Over "Cases". Section 1334(a) vests original and exclusive jurisdiction in the district court over all cases arising under the Bankruptcy Code. "Case" is a term of art used in both the Bankruptcy Code and the Bankruptcy Rules. "Case" refers to the entire Chapter 7, 9, 11, or 13 case—not just some controversy that arises in connection with it.

    b.   **Jurisdiction Over "Proceedings".** The term "case" is to be distinguished from the term "proceeding." A specific dispute that arises during the pendency of a case is referred to as a "proceeding." Section 1334(b) provides that the district courts have original but not exclusive jurisdiction over all civil proceedings, "arising under title 11, or arising in or related to cases under title 11."

3. **ROLE OF THE BANKRUPTCY COURT, SECTION 157**
Section 157 empowers the district judge to refer bankruptcy matters to the bankruptcy judge.

    a.   **"Core" Versus "Non–Core" Proceedings.** Section 157 differentiates between "core" and "non-core" proceedings. Generally, in core proceedings, the bankruptcy judge conducts the trial or hearing and enters a final judgment. In non-core proceedings, the bankruptcy judge still can hold the trial or hearing, but generally cannot issue a final judgment. She instead submits proposed findings of fact and law to the district court for review.

    b.   **Who Determines Whether Proceeding Is "Core" or "Non–Core".** The bankruptcy judge is empowered to determine whether a matter is a core proceeding or a non-core proceeding.

    c.   **District Court Judge's Withdrawal Of Case or Proceeding From Bankruptcy Judge.** Section 157(d) authorizes the district judge to withdraw a case or proceeding from a bankruptcy judge.

4. **ABSTENTION UNDER SECTION 1334(c)**
Withdrawal under section 157(d) moves a matter from the bankruptcy judge to the federal district judge. Abstention under section 1334 moves the litigation from the federal courts to a state court.

    a.   **Permissive.** Section 1334(c)(1) provides for permissive abstention when the district court believes that abstention would be "in the interest of justice" or "in the interest of comity with State courts or respect for State law."

    b.   **Mandatory.** Section 1334(c)(2) provides for mandatory abstention under certain circumstances.

C. **QUESTIONS ABOUT ALLOCATION OF JUDICIAL POWER UNDER THE 1984 AMENDMENTS**
Numerous questions remain unanswered about the allocation of judicial power over bankruptcy matters.

*

PERSPECTIVE

ORGANIZATION OF THIS BOOK

Most debts are timely paid. Moreover, the vast majority of delinquent debts are ultimately paid "voluntarily" as a result of some kind of bargaining between creditor and debtor. Whitford, *A Critique Of The Consumer Credit Collection System,* 1979 Wis. L. Rev. 1047, 1051–56. Thus, only in a small percentage of cases are creditors forced either to write off a debt or to pursue a remedy that will compel satisfaction of it. Why then should law schools devote an entire course to the subject of creditors' rights? First, although the percentage of coercive collection cases is small, their number is very high. Second, the haunting awareness of coercive creditors' remedies surely motivates many debtors to pay their obligations voluntarily. Third, learning about creditors' rights necessarily involves learning about debtors' rights. Fourth, the material is historically significant and intellectually challenging. Finally, some law teachers enjoy studying and researching about creditors' remedies and need an outlet for their knowledge of the subject.

For these and other reasons, there are courses in creditors' rights; and, as an aid for students taking those courses, we prepared this outline. The first half is a survey of rights and privileges, principally given by state law, that enable a creditor to impound and ultimately to apply a debtor's assets in satisfaction of the creditor's legitimate claims against the debtor. The beginning premise of this survey is a very broad general rule: A debtor's assets cannot be seized and applied in satisfaction of a creditor's claim other than by reducing the claim to judgment which is then enforced by the creditor pursuing an appropriate post-judgment remedy. Part One of this outline thus focuses on various ways and means of obtaining and enforcing judgments.

The general rule requiring a creditor to obtain and enforce a judgment as preconditions to seizing her debtor's assets has three large exceptions:

First, in many cases debtors provide collateral for their debts by agreeing to give a creditor an interest in their property to secure whatever obligation is owed. Article 9 of the Uniform Commercial Code governs the creation and enforcement of security interests in personal property or fixtures. Upon the debtor's default, the Article 9 secured party may help herself to the collateral which is the property subject to her security interest; or, in the alternative, the secured party may invoke the aid of the state in repossessing her collateral as through the remedy of replevin. The secured party then disposes of the collateral herself and applies the proceeds to the obligation which the debtor owes her. Real estate law governs when the collateral is land, and the particulars of creating and enforcing consensual liens on such property vary considerably throughout the country.

Second, some creditors by operation of law, rather than by agreement of the debtor, are given interests in, liens on, or other special rights to property of the debtor. These rights effectively create security for the creditor and allow her to reach the property without having to execute on it and, in some cases, without having to get a judgment against the debtor. Examples of these special rights are the artisan's lien, the lien of mechanics and laborers, the federal tax lien and a seller's right of reclamation.

Third, if a creditor sues to reduce her claim to judgment, she may be entitled to have property of the debtor seized and held pending the outcome of the suit for the purpose of insuring the creditor's expected judgment. This is accomplished through a pre-judgment, provisional remedy such as attachment or sequestration which, in cases where the remedy is available, can be used by any creditor whether or not she has by agreement of the debtor or by operation of law some pre-existing security for the debt owed her. These remedies are provisional in that the property seized cannot be applied in satisfaction of the creditor's claim unless and until the claim becomes a judgment.

We thoroughly discuss the last two of these three sets of exceptional remedies in Parts Two ("Creditors With Special Rights") and Three ("Pre-Judgment Provisional Remedies") of this outline.*

---

* An overall discussion of the rights and remedies of Article 9 secured parties is beyond the scope of this book. Secured transactions is a large and complex subject which can stand alone conceptually. Indeed, many law schools, law professors, and law book publishers often prefer to handle the subject as a topic unto itself. Thus, a separate book in West's Black Letter Series provides a comprehensive outline of secured transactions law, which is excluded as a general topic of this book. See R. Speidel, Sales and Sales Financing (1984) (Black Letter Series). Still, however, we frequently refer in this book to Article 9 in explaining that statute's relationship to topics that are covered generally herein.

Similarly, because most law schools devote a separate course to real estate finance, this Black Letter does not cover consensual liens on land. We recommend that you consult the works of Professors Grant Nelson and Dale Whitman, who have written both a student outline and a hornbook on the subject of real estate finance.

In Part Four we address due process limitations on the remedies discussed in the preceding parts.

Part Five surveys bankruptcy law. Bankruptcy is often a large part of a course in creditors' rights or the subject of a wholly separate course. The principal reason is that bankruptcy is very important both as a creditor's remedy and as a debtor's right.

Bankruptcy is a haven for the financially troubled debtor. There she can rid herself of most debts and get a fresh start in exchange for the liquidation of her assets and the distribution of the proceeds among her creditors; or she can get the chance to rehabilitate her financial condition through a restructuring of her obligations. An insolvent debtor who is unwilling to go into bankruptcy voluntarily may nevertheless be forced there by her creditors and required by law either to liquidate or to rehabilitate.

Whichever route the debtor takes to liquidation or rehabilitation in bankruptcy, her creditors will struggle among themselves and with the bankruptcy trustee in efforts to win the preferential treatment that bankruptcy law affords some claimants of a debtor's estate. The outcome of these struggles often depends on the interplay of federal bankruptcy law and state law governing creditors' remedies, which is another reason many creditors' rights courses and this outline cover both areas.

*

PART ONE

OBTAINING AND ENFORCING JUDGMENTS

Analysis

As a general rule, a debtor's assets cannot be seized and applied in satisfaction of a creditor's claim except by reducing the claim to judgment and enforcing the judgment through appropriate post-judgment remedies. This first part of the Black Letter thus focuses on various ways and means of obtaining and enforcing judgments.

*

INCREASING THE ODDS OF A CREDITOR'S JUDGMENT

Analysis

Remember the beginning premise for the first half of this Black Letter: As a general rule, a creditor must obtain a judgment and pursue appropriate post-judgment remedies in order to seize and apply the debtor's assets in satisfaction of the creditor's claim. Not surprisingly, therefore, creditors sometimes use devices and tactics aimed at increasing their odds for success in suits to enforce claims against debtors. One such device is the *cognovit clause* included in the credit contract signed by the debtor. Through this device the debtor consents in advance to the creditor obtaining a judgment without notifying the debtor and without giving the debtor the opportunity for a hearing. If a judgment by cognovit is not possible, the creditor might achieve much the same result by filing her action in an inconvenient forum where it is practically impossible for the debtor to defend. A debtor who is able to defend might discover that the creditor has an ace up her sleeve in the form of a choice-of-law provision buried in the credit contract. Such a provision determines which state's law will govern any dispute between the parties to the contract. As you might expect, the creditor who drafts the contract is likely to have selected the state whose law most favors her. This chapter of the outline discusses the three ways mentioned above of enhancing a creditor's chances of getting a judgment against a debtor.

A. OBTAINING A JUDGMENT BY COGNOVIT

A creditor who must sue a debtor in order to collect a claim wants to obtain a judgment against the debtor as quickly and inexpensively as possible. The fastest and cheapest method of obtaining a judgment against a debtor is by way of a *cognovit clause* in the contract between the creditor and debtor.

1. COGNOVIT EXPLAINED

a. Definition

"The cognovit is the ancient legal device by which the debtor consents in advance to the holder's obtaining a judgment without notice or hearing, and possibly even with the appearance, on the debtor's behalf, of an attorney designated by the holder." *D. H. Overmyer Co. v. Frick Co.,* 405 U. S. 174, 176, 92 S.Ct. 775, 777 (1972). This agreement by the debtor is typically part of the promissory note or other contract of indebtedness executed by her.

b. Operation

A cognovit works very simply: By means of a clause included in the credit contract, "[t]he debtor either confesses judgment in advance of default or authorizes the creditor or an attorney designated by the creditor to appear and confess judgment against the debtor. Unless the contract so provides, default is not a necessary condition precedent to the entry of judgment. * * * Judgment is rendered for the amount due shown on the face of the note [or other credit contract] plus any other charges authorized, such as attorney fees and any court costs. It can be converted into a lien on the debtor's property, which subjects the debtor's property to seizure and sale to satisfy the judgment." Statement of Basis and Purpose and Regulatory Analysis Accompanying Federal Trade Commission Rule on Credit Practices, 49 Fed. Reg. 7740, 7748–49 (1984), which rule is codified at 16 C.F.R. part 444. (Regarding conver-

85

sion of a judgment into a lien on property, see Chapters II and III, supra.) Confession of judgment in this manner is exactly what the debtor authorized by agreeing to the cognovit clause. If she wishes to dispute the creditor's claim, the debtor is in the position of having to reopen the judgment.

2. CONSTITUTIONAL DUE PROCESS LIMITATIONS ON COGNOVITS

The use of a cognovit clause involves the waiver by the debtor of her Fourteenth Amendment due process protections. That these protections can be waived in a civil action is clear. The central issue in determining the constitutionality of judgment by cognovit is the validity of the waiver.

a. Commercial Setting

The Supreme Court held in *D. H. Overmyer Co. v. Frick Co.*, 405 U.S. 174, 92 S. Ct. 775 (1972) "that a cognovit clause is not, *per se,* violative of Fourteenth Amendment due process," 405 U.S. at 187, 92 S. Ct. at 783, and affirmed entry of judgment based on such a clause in a note executed by a corporate debtor. The Court found that the debtor "voluntarily, intelligently, and knowingly waived the rights it otherwise possessed to prejudgment notice and hearing, and that it did so with full awareness of the legal consequences." 405 U.S. at 187, 92 S. Ct. at 783. From the creditor's perspective, however, *Overmyer* presented the best possible set of facts:

1) Corporate Actors

The setting was the commercial world and the actors were two corporations. The Court observed: "This is not a case of unequal bargaining power or overreaching." 405 U.S. at 186, 92 S. Ct. at 782.

2) Negotiation

Inclusion of the cognovit clause in the note executed by the debtor was negotiated by the parties. The Court noted that the agreement between the creditor and debtor, "from the start, was not a contract of adhesion." 405 U.S. at 186, 92 S. Ct. at 782.

3) Additional Consideration

The debtor received additional consideration for agreeing to the cognovit. 405 U.S. at 186–87, 92 S. Ct. at 783.

4) Possibility of Vacating Judgment

The debtor was not rendered defenseless by having executed the cognovit note. Under the applicable Ohio law, the court in which judgment is confessed "may vacate its judgment upon a showing of a valid defense, and, indeed, [the debtor in this case] had a postjudgment hearing in the Ohio court." 405 U.S. at 188, 92 S. Ct. at 783.

b. Consumer Setting
1) The *Overmyer* Caveat

The Court cautioned in *Overmyer* that "where the contract is one of adhesion, where there is great disparity in bargaining power, and where the debtor receives nothing for the cognovit provision, other legal consequences may ensue." *D.H. Overmyer Co. v. Frick Co.,* 405 U.S. 174, 188, 92 S.Ct. 775, 783 (1972) (dictum); cf. *Fuentes v. Shevin,* 407 U.S. 67, 95, 92 S. Ct. 1983, 2002 (1972) (debtor's waiver of constitutional rights with respect to replevin proceeding invalid because the waiver was buried among fine print of form contract, there was no bargaining between parties over contract's terms, the parties were far from equal in bargaining power, and there was no showing that the debtor was aware of the significance of the fine print relied on by the creditor to establish the waiver). In other words, the validity of cognovit judgments in consumer cases is highly doubtful.

2)   The *Swarb* Warning

The case *Swarb v. Lennox,* 405 U.S. 191, 92 S. Ct. 767 (1972), involved individual consumers, each of whom was a Pennsylvania resident who had signed a cognovit note. A three judge district court enjoined the enforcement of confessed judgments against a class of plaintiffs earning less than $10,000 annually. This court was unconvinced that there had been an intentional waiver of known rights by members of the class in executing cognovits. The plaintiff-debtors appealed because they had sought to have the Pennsylvania cognovit procedures declared unconstitutional on their face, not just as applied to them. The defendants did not appeal. The Supreme Court affirmed with respect to the plaintiff-appellant's appeal, holding the Pennsylvania cognovit provisions not unconstitutional on their face. The Court declined, however, to consider other aspects of the district court's decision in the absence of a cross-appeal by the defendants. Nevertheless, the Court warned that its caveat in *Overmyer* was possibly pertinent. *Swarb v. Lennox,* 405 U.S. 191, 201, 92 S. Ct. 767, 772–73 (1972). That caveat advised that cognovits might be unconstitutional when used in contracts of adhesion where there is disparity of bargaining power and the absence of anything received in return for the cognovit provision. *D.H. Overmyer Co. v. Frick Co.,* 405 U.S. 174, 188, 92 S. Ct. 775, 783 (1972).

c.   **Timing of the Determination on the Validity of the Waiver**

1)   Waiver Hearing Must Precede Judgment

The case *Isbell v. County of Sonoma,* 21 Cal. 3d 61, 145 Cal. Rptr. 368, 577 P.2d 188 (1978), cert. denied, 439 U.S. 996, 99 S. Ct. 597 (1978), is probably the most significant state court decision regarding the constitutional validity of cognovits. The plaintiff-debtors signed cognovit notes for alleged welfare overpayments. After confessed judgments were entered against them, the debtors claimed that the California laws governing cognovits were unconstitutional. The California Supreme Court agreed, reasoning that the procedure was defective in failing to provide for a prejudgment judicial determination of the validity of the debtor's waiver. This sort of provision is essential because a confession-of-judgment clause executed by the debtor does not on its face represent a voluntary, knowing and intelligent waiver of constitutional rights; and an opportunity for a postjudgment determination of the waiver's validity is not a determination at a meaningful time.

2)   The Resulting Paradox
Other courts also have held that, prior to entering a cognovit judgment, there must be a judicial determination of the validity of the debtor's waiver of her due process rights. This holding is paradoxical. "Since such a [pre-judgment determination] presumably must itself be held only after notice, requiring it as a matter of Due Process seems incompatible with *Overmyer,* and in effect nullifies the waiver agreement." Restatement (Second) of Judgments § 2, Reporter's Note on Comment i (1982).

3.   STATE STATUTORY LIMITATIONS

The vast majority of states restrict the use of cognovits, especially in consumer transactions. A few states simply forbid them in all consumer transactions. See, e.g., Ill. Ann. Stat. ch. 110, § 2–1301(c) (Smith-Hurd 1983); Ohio Rev. Code Ann. § 2323.13(E) (Page 1981); Ore. R. Civ. P. 73A(2) (1988). General, all-encompassing prohibitions are uncommon, however. Most states have adopted one or more acts designed to regulate different types of consumer transactions. These acts typically contain a section which defines the regulated transactions; a section which prohibits cognovit clauses in those sorts of transactions; and most acts contain a section which imposes a penalty for violations, including the use of a cognovit clause in a regulated transaction. See, e.g., Uniform Consumer Credit Code § 3.306 (1974 Official Text).

When the use of a cognovit is permitted, there is often some procedural regulation to satisfy. A most common regulation requires that a cognovit be a separate writing which is distinct from the bond, contract or other instrument for which judgment is confessed. See, e.g., Mich. Comp. Laws Ann. § 600.2906(1) (1986); Minn. Stat. § 548.23 (1986). Satisfying this requirement may not go very far in establishing the validity of the debtor's waiver of her fourteenth amendment due process rights. (See supra Chapter I.A.2.) Awareness of one's conduct does not necessarily imply that the person acts voluntarily and intelligently with a full understanding of the consequences.

4.   F.T.C. TRADE REGULATION RULE

The Federal Trade Commission Act empowers the Federal Trade Commission (F.T.C.) to prescribe rules defining "acts or practices which are unfair or deceptive acts or practices in or affecting commerce * * *" 15 U.S.C.A. § 57(a)(1)(B) (Supp. 1983). The F.T.C. Trade Regulation Rule on Credit Practices declares that "it is an unfair act or practice * * * for a lender or retail installment seller directly or indirectly to take or receive from a consumer [which means a natural person who seeks or acquires goods, services, or money for personal, family, or household use] an obligation that * * * [c]onstitutes or contains a cognovit or confession of judgment (for purposes other than executory process in Louisiana), warrant of attorney, or other waiver of the right to notice and the opportunity to be heard in the event of suit or process thereon." FTC Trade Regulation Rule on Credit Practices, 16 C.F.R. § 444.2 (a)(1). A lender or seller within the F.T.C's jurisdiction who violates this or any other trade regulation rule is subject to injunctions, "cease and desist" orders, and civil penalties and also is liable for damages sought by the

F.T.C on behalf of persons injured by the violation. See D. Epstein & S. Nickles, Consumer Law In A Nutshell 12–21 (1981).

5. OTHER LIMITATIONS AND CONCERNS
a. Unconscionability

A cognovit clause buried in the fine print of a contract may be unconscionable under Uniform Commercial Code § 2–302 or otherwise and thus may be unenforceable. See, e.g., *Architectual Cabinets, Inc. v. Gaster,* 291 A.2d 298, 301 (Del. Super. Ct. 1971).

b. Full Faith and Credit

Valid civil judgments entered in one state or territory are generally entitled to enforcement in any other state or territory because of the full faith and credit clause. U.S. Const. art. IV, § 1. See R. Leflar, American Conflicts Law §§ 73 & 75 (3d ed. 1977). The clause applies equally as well to cognovit judgments. See cases collected in Annot., 39 A.L.R.2d 1232 (1955); but see *Atlas Credit Corp. v. Ezrine,* 25 N.Y.2d 219, 303 N.Y.S.2d 382, 250 N.E.2d 474 (1969) (alternative basis of decision refusing enforcement of Pennsylvania cognovit judgment was that the judgment was not a "judgment" within the meaning of the full faith and credit clause).

If, however, a cognovit judgment is void under the law of the state where the judgment was entered, the judgment is not entitled to full faith and credit elsewhere. See, e.g., *Bell v. Staren & Co.,* 259 Ark. 506, 534 S.W.2d 238 (1976) (judgment confessed in Illinois could not be registered in Arkansas because the Illinois cognovit procedure had not been strictly followed); *Atlas Credit Corp. v. Ezrine,* 25 N.Y.2d 219, 230–33, 303 N.Y.S.2d 382, 392–94, 250 N.E.2d 474, 481–83 (1969) (alternative basis for refusing enforcement of Pennsylvania cognovit judgment was that an overly broad cognovit clause violates due process so that the court where the judgment was confessed was without jurisdiction of the debtor and thus the judgment is not entitled to full faith and credit). See generally R. Leflar, American Conflicts Law § 79 at 158 & 160 (3d ed. 1977).

c. Ethical Problems
1) Conflict of Interests

Cognovit judgments are typically entered by the creditor's lawyer acting to confess judgment on behalf of the debtor. The creditor and debtor, of course, have different interests. Does this conflict of interests create an ethical problem for the lawyer? See Model Code of Professional Responsibility Canon 5, EC 5–14 & 5–15, DR 5–105 (1980). An argument for dismissing any ethical concern is that Canon 5 and its ancillary rules are aimed at insuring the exercise of a lawyer's independent professional judgment on behalf of her client. This concern is not present when a lawyer for a creditor confesses judgment for the debtor because the legal representation of the debtor is so limited and ministerial in nature as to involve no exercise of judgment at all. Cf. *Blanck v. Medley,* 63 Ill. App. 211 (1896) (holding that a cognovit judgment is not invalid because the same law firm represents both the creditor and debtor inasmuch as exercising the warrant of attorney is largely a matter of form so that, practically, it is not material what attorney acts for the debtor). Moreover, there is authority explicitly holding that a cognovit judgment is not invalid because it was obtained by the creditor's lawyer. *Withers v. Starace,* 22 F. Supp. 773, 774 (E.D. N.Y. 1938); *Houpt v. Bohl,* 71 Ark. 330, 333–34, 75 S.W. 470, 470–71 (1903); cf. *Gecht v. Suson,* 3 Ill. App. 3d 183, 188, 278 N.E.2d 193, 196 (1971) (judgment confessed by law partner of creditor's attorney); but see *Sherwood v. Saratoga & Washington R. R. Co.,* 15 N.Y. 650, 652 (Barb. 1852) (the same person cannot act for plaintiff and defendant in taking judgment by confession on bond and warrant of attorney) (dictum). Finally, in executing a cognovit clause the debtor usually consents to *any* lawyer confessing judgment for her. Yet, is conduct ethical simply because it is "legal"? Is a conflict of interest cured by the clients' consent to the dual representation? Remember that, in assessing whether or not an improper conflict of interests exists, a lawyer is obligated to resolve all doubts against the propriety of the representation. Model Code of Professional Responsibility EC 5–15 (1980).

2) Using Cognovits in Collecting Attorneys' Fees
In *Hulland v. State Bar of California,* 8 Cal. 3d 440, 105 Cal. Rptr. 152, 503 P.2d 608 (1972), the court publicly reprimanded an attorney for obtaining a cognovit judgment against a client who had executed a confession of judgment in the amount of an agreed fee. Critically important was the attorney's use of the cognovit to collect more than the reasonable value of his legal services.

d. Enforcing a Cognovit As Malicious Prosecution
A creditor who obtains a cognovit judgment knowing that her claim or the amount of it is unjustified or excessive risks liability for malicious prosecution. See *March v. Cacioppo,* 37 Ill. App. 2d 235, 185 N.E.2d 397 (1962). Traditionally, however, the courts have cast a jaundiced eye on actions for malicious prosecution and the like; and the courts ordinarily treat cognovit judgments as they would treat any civil action with respect to the question whether such a proceeding establishes a basis for malicious prosecution or abuse of process. See Annot., 87 A.L.R.3d 554 (1978). Generally, therefore, the odds are against a debtor making a case for one of these torts based on a creditor having obtained a cognovit judgment against her.

B. SELECTING AN INCONVENIENT FORUM

The fastest and cheapest method of obtaining a judgment against a debtor is by way of a cognovit clause in the contract between the creditor and debtor. (See Chapter I.A., supra.) If a cognovit judgment is not possible, the creditor must hope that, upon suing the debtor and giving her notice of the action, the debtor will fail to answer and default. Most collection actions result in default judgments favoring the creditor. The odds of a debtor defaulting are increased if the creditor's action is initiated and pursued in a court distant from the debtor's residence. When a creditor sues in a state that is not the debtor's home, the debtor is likely to decide that responding is not worth the time and money. She may also mistakenly believe that a judgment rendered by a court of another state cannot affect her at home. Creditors are deterred from pursuing collection actions in a state other than a debtor's home because of various restrictions, which are discussed below, on a creditor's freedom in selecting the forum of a lawsuit.

1. JUDICIAL JURISDICTION

A creditor's judgment against a debtor will be valid in the state where rendered, and enforceable in any other state under the full faith and credit clause (U.S. Const. art. IV, § 1), only if the court rendering the judgment has *judicial jurisdiction* of the person at whom, or property at which, the proceedings are directed. Here are the requirements that must be satisfied if a state court is to have judicial jurisdiction of a creditor's action against a debtor:

a. Competence

State law must empower the court to entertain the action. There are a variety of reasons why a court as a matter of state law may lack the power or competence to decide a case. For example, "the state may not have authorized use by its courts of a given contact as a basis of judicial proceedings;" or, "the particular court may lack power over the cause of action either because of the amount of damages claimed or because of the type of action involved;" or, "the court may lack power because of venue considerations ∗ ∗ ∗ " Restatement (Second) of Conflict of Laws ch. 3, Introductory Note (1971).

b. Notice

"[A] mode of service must exist, prescribed by law and followed in the instant case, which has a reasonable tendency to give the person whose interests are to be affected actual notice of the proceeding and a fair opportunity to be heard therein." R. Leflar, American Conflicts Law § 20 at 31 (3d ed. 1977).

c. Contacts

"[A] state must have certain minimum contacts with the parties or their property in order to possess legal power to exercise authority through its courts. A judgment rendered in the absence of such contacts will not be recognized or enforced in other states ∗ ∗ ∗ [because such] action on the part of a State court violates the due process clause of the Fourteenth Amendment." Restatement (Second) of Conflict of Laws ch. 3, Introductory Note (1971).

1) Territorial Power Theory Of Jurisdiction—*Pennoyer v. Neff* and *Harris v. Balk*
For many years, constitutional law regarding jurisdiction was based on a territorial conception of judicial power. The two guiding principles of this territorial power theory are usually attributed to the case *Pennoyer v. Neff,* 95 U.S. (5 Otto) 714 (1877): "[F]irst, every state possesses exclusive jurisdiction and sovereignty over persons and property within its territory; and second, no state can exercise direct jurisdiction over persons or property outside its boundaries." Bernstine, *Shaffer v. Heitner: A Death Warrant for the Transient Rule of In Personam Jurisdiction?* 25 Vill. L. Rev. 38, 40 (1979–80).

a) *In Personam* Jurisdiction

Because of the principle that a state possesses jurisdiction over persons within the state's territory, *in personam* jurisdiction over a defendant could be acquired simply by serving the person with process while she was within the state's boundaries. The reason for her presence in the state, and the length of time she was there, were ordinarily unimportant. Her presence in the state even as a transcient was a sufficient contact to sustain *in personam* jurisdiction and to support a judgment binding her person.

b) *In Rem* Jurisdiction

If the defendant herself was not a domiciliary of the state and could not be served while in the state, *in personam* jurisdiction over her person was constitutionally impossible in the usual case unless she consented to jurisdiction. If, however, the defendant had property located in the state, that contact in and of itself was sufficient to sustain *in rem* jurisdiction and thus support a judgment affecting her interests in the property. If the lawsuit affected only the interests of particular persons in the property rather than the interests of all people, the proceeding commonly was referred to as *quasi in rem*.

In rem jurisdiction was not conditioned on the existence of real property or tangible personalty of the defendant within the state. Because of the fiction that a debt travels with the debtor, the doctrine of *in rem* jurisdiction expanded to permit "a state * * * to exercise judicial jurisdiction to apply to the satisfaction of a claim an obligation owed to the person against whom the claim is asserted if the obligor is subject to the judicial jurisdiction of the state, even though the state lacks jurisdiction over the person against whom the claim is asserted." Restatement (Second) of Conflict of Laws § 68 (1971). This Restatement provision embodies the principle of *Harris v. Balk,* 198 U.S. 215, 25 S. Ct. 625 (1905). The *Harris* case is the basis of the following example:

> *Example:* A has a simple contract claim against B who has a simple contract claim against C. A resides in Maryland. Both B and C reside in North Carolina, and neither of them has any connection with Maryland. C travels to Maryland for a visit, and thereby subjects herself to *in personam* jurisdiction of the Maryland courts. While in Maryland C is served with process in an action begun by A to "attach" or "garnish" property of B. (A state, through the process of attachment or garnishment, seizes and holds property for the purpose of applying it in satisfaction of a claim against the property's owner. See Part Three of this outline where we discuss attachment and garnishment as prejudgment, provisional creditors' remedies.) In the case of an intangible debt such as C's obligation to B, service on

the obligor is equivalent to seizing the property and bringing it within the court's control. Thus, because of the service on C while in Maryland, that state would acquire *in
rem* jurisdiction over C's debt to B; and, if the Maryland
court determined that B was obligated to A, then C would
be bound to pay to A the sum that C owed B (up to the
amount of A's judgment against B).

2) Expanding *In Personam* Jurisdiction—*International Shoe Co. v. Washington*
Under the doctrine of *Pennoyer v. Neff,* 95 U.S. (5 Otto) 714 (1877), a
court could not render a judgment personally binding on a defendant who
was domiciled elsewhere and who had not consented to jurisdiction unless
the defendant had some presence within the physical boundaries of the
court's jurisdiction. This territorial limitation on *in personam* jurisdiction
was removed by the decision in *International Shoe Co. v. Washington,* 326
U.S. 310, 66 S.Ct. 154 (1945). In this case the Supreme Court decided
that the State of Washington could exercise personal jurisdiction over a
foreign corporation even though its activities in Washington were so minimal that, under earlier cases, the corporation had no presence in the
state. The Court did not justify its decision on the basis of the territorial
power theory of jurisdiction. In effect, that theory was abandoned to the
extent it limited a state's exercise of *in personam* jurisdiction. The Court
concluded that the defendant's presence within the territory of the forum
was not constitutionally required as a prerequisite to a personal judgment
against her. All that due process required, if the defendant is not present
in the forum, is that she have other "minimum contacts with it such that
the maintenance of the suit does not offend 'traditional notions of fair
play and substantial justice.'" 326 U.S. at 316, 66 S. Ct. at 158, *quoting
Milliken v. Meyer,* 311 U.S. 457, 463, 61 S. Ct. 339, 343 (1940). Because of
International Shoe, "the relationship among the defendant, the forum, and
the litigation, rather than the mutually exclusive sovereignty of the States
on which the rules of *Pennoyer* rest, became the central concern of the inquiry into personal jurisdiction." *Shaffer v. Heitner,* 433 U.S. 186, 204, 97
S.Ct. 2569, 2580 (1977). State sovereignty continues to limit personal jurisdiction, *World-Wide Volkswagen Corp. v. Woodson,* 444 U.S. 286, 292–94,
100 S. Ct. 559, 564–66 (1980), but not to the extent of altogether precluding extra-territorial exercises of judicial power as under the rule of *Pennoyer.*

3) Restricting *Quasi In Rem* Jurisdiction—*Shaffer v. Heitner*
Until recently, *International Shoe's* "minimum contacts/fundamental fairness" theory of jurisdiction was thought by many to supplement rather
than to displace the traditional theory of territorial power. If the defendant could not be served in the forum, had no property there and was
domiciled elsewhere, jurisdiction could nevertheless be asserted over her if
she had sufficient other contacts with the forum so that subjecting her to
jurisdiction was fair and just. Fairness and justice were not considered,
however, when personal jurisdiction was based on service within the forum

state or when *in rem* jurisdiction was based on the presence of the defendant's property there. The common belief was that, despite *International Shoe,* the traditional theory of territorial power was alive and well and sufficient in itself to sustain jurisdiction.

The decision in *Shaffer v. Heitner,* 433 U.S. 186, 97 S. Ct. 2569 (1977), caused everyone to rethink the relationship between the "minimum contacts/fundamental fairness" and "territorial power" theories of judicial jurisdiction. In this case, plaintiff filed a shareholder's derivative suit in Delaware. *Quasi in rem* jurisdiction was established over nonresident defendants by attaching their stock in the Delaware corporation. According to forum law, the situs of stock in Delaware corporations was Delaware. These defendants moved to quash service, arguing that their contacts with Delaware were too few and insubstantial to support that state's exercise of jurisdiction over them under the standard of *International Shoe.* The state courts rejected this argument. They concluded that the territorial power doctrine of *Pennoyer v. Neff* and *Harris v. Balk* survived the decision in *International Shoe* and supported Delaware's assertion of *quasi in rem* jurisdiction.

The Supreme Court reversed, concluding that "all assertions of state-court jurisdiction must be evaluated according to the standards set forth in *International Shoe* and its progeny." 433 U.S. at 212, 97 S. Ct. at 2584. Thus, just as a state's assertion of personal jurisdiction beyond its boundaries is limited by the "minimum contacts/fundamental fairness" standard of *International Shoe,* so is a state's other assertions of jurisdiction, including *quasi in rem* jurisdiction over property within its boundaries as in *Shaffer.* The Court also concluded that, generally and on the facts before it, exercising *quasi in rem* jurisdiction solely on the basis of the defendant having property in the forum is unfair and thus unconstitutional. 433 U.S. at 212–16, 97 S. Ct. at 2584–86.

4) Principal Ramifications Of *Shaffer*
   a) *Shaffer* Rules Any Assertion of *Quasi in Rem* Jurisdiction
      Shaffer involved the attachment of corporate stock which forum law deemed located in the forum state. Apparently, however, the principle of the case applies in any *quasi in rem* action without regard to the type or nature of the property. Even in a case where the defendant owns realty in the forum, the property's presence there is not a sufficient contact in and of itself to sustain jurisdiction if *International Shoe*'s standards of fairness and justice are not satisfied. Consequently, cases to the contrary such as *Ownbey v. Morgan,* 256 U.S. 94, 41 S. Ct. 433 (1921), may have been overruled. (In concurring opinions, however, Justices Powell and Stevens suggested that *Shaffer* should not be interpreted to invalidate *in rem* jurisdiction where real estate is involved.)

b) **Physical Presence in a State Is No Longer a Basis For *in Personam* Jurisdiction**

The Court in *Shaffer* stated broadly that "*all* assertions of state-court jurisdiction must be evaluated according to the standards set forth in *International Shoe* and its progeny." 433 U.S. at 212, 97 S. Ct. at 2584. The intention may have been "to declare the territorial power theory [of *Pennoyer*] completely obsolete [even as it applies to *in personam* jurisdiction]. Physical presence is no longer either necessary or sufficient for *in personam* actions or for *in rem* actions. Presence in the state and personal service, then, apparently are no longer sufficient bases for the exercise of personal jurisdiction over a nonconsenting, transient resident." Casad, *Shaffer v. Heitner: An End to Ambivalence in Jurisdiction Theory?* 26 Kan. L. Rev. 61, 77 (1977); but see *Oxmans' Erwin Meat Co. v. Blacketer,* 86 Wis. 2d 683, 687–88, 273 N.W.2d 285, 287 (1979) ("In our view the United States Supreme Court has not imposed a 'minimum contacts' requirement on a state's assertion of jurisdiction over a natural person upon whom personal service within the state has been achieved.") (dictum).

c) ***Seider* Doctrine Dead**

An early casualty of the *Shaffer* decision was the *Seider* doctrine, *Seider v. Roth,* 17 N.Y.2d 111, 269 N.Y.S.2d 99, 216 N.E.2d 312 (1966), "under which a liability insurance policy was regarded as a debt owed to the insured and subject to garnishment by anyone asserting a claim against him covered by the policy. In theory, such quasi-in-rem jurisdiction could have been asserted wherever the insurance company did business. In practice, however, it was allowed only in the state in which the plaintiff resided ∗ ∗ ∗ [and] effectively permitted a plaintiff to litigate in his home state and under its substantive law with respect to a foreign accident." Louis, *The Grasp of Long Arm Jurisdiction Finally Exceeds Its Reach,* 58 N.C. L. Rev. 407, 418–19 (1980). The *Seider* doctrine fell victim to *Shaffer* in the case *Rush v. Savchuk,* 444 U.S. 320, 100 S. Ct. 571 (1980), which is the basis of this example:

> ***Example:*** Two Indiana residents, R and S, were involved in a single-car accident in Indiana. S was the passenger in the car driven by R. The car is insured by a company that does business in Minnesota. S moves to Minnesota and there files suit against R, who has no contacts with Minnesota. *Quasi in rem* jurisdiction is asserted by attaching in Minnesota the contractual obligation of the insurance company to defend and indemnify R in connection with the suit. Jurisdiction is lacking, however, because there are not sufficient contacts, ties or relations between R and Minnesota to satisfy the fairness standard of *International Shoe.*

5) Principal Exceptions to *Shaffer*
   a)   Presence of Property Remains a Factor to Consider
   Applying the standards of *International Shoe* to all assertions of jurisdiction probably means that, in the typical case, a state cannot exercise jurisdiction over a defendant simply because she has an interest
   in property located there. Nevertheless, the presence of defendant's
   property is one contact or tie with the forum that can be considered
   along with others in deciding the fairness of exercising jurisdiction
   over her. This contact is especially important and strongly favors jurisdiction when:

      i) Controversy Concerns The Property Itself
      The presense of property in a state strongly favors jurisdiction if
      "claims to the property itself are the source of the underlying
      controversy between the plaintiff and the defendant * * *"
      Shaffer v. Heitner, 433 U.S. 186, 207, 97 S. Ct. 2569, 2581 (1977).
      This category of cases includes pure *in rem* actions to determine
      and affect the interests of all persons in the designated property,
      and also *quasi in rem* actions where the plaintiff is seeking to se-
      cure a pre-existing claim in the property and to extinguish, or es-
      tablish the nonexistence of, similar interests of particular persons.
      Id. at 207 n.24, 97 S. Ct. at 2581 n.24.

      ii) Controversy Is Related To Defendant's Ownership Of The Proper-
      ty
      The presence of property in a jurisdiction is also an especially
      important factor when "the defendant's ownership of the property
      is conceded but the cause of action is otherwise related to rights
      and duties growing out of that ownership [as in suits for injury
      suffered on the land of an absentee owner] * * *" Id. at 208,
      97 S. Ct. at 2582.

      iii) The Property Is Real Estate
      The principle of *Shaffer* arguably applies in any *quasi in rem* ac-
      tion without regard to the type or nature of the property, which
      would mean that even the presence of real estate in the forum is
      not a sufficient contact in and of itself to sustain jurisdiction.
      Cases to the contrary such as *Ownbey v. Morgan*, 256 U.S. 94, 41
      S. Ct. 433 (1921), thus would be overruled. In concurring opin-
      ions, however, Justices Powell and Stevens suggested that *Shaffer*
      should not restrict *in rem* jurisdiction over real estate by courts
      in the state where the land is located.

   b)   Security for Foreign Proceeding
   The Court in *Shaffer* suggested that a state where property is located
   might have jurisdiction to attach that property, by use of proper procedures (see Part Four, infra, on the constitutional validity of procedures for attachment), as security for a judgment being sought in a
   forum where the litigation could be maintained consistently with *In-*

ternational Shoe. Id. at 210, 97 S. Ct. at 2583. See, e.g., *Carolina Power & Light Co. v. Uranex,* 451 F. Supp. 1044 (N.D. Cal. 1977). (Moreover, if a state where property is located itself has jurisdiction under *International Shoe,* then that state can provide for attaching the property so as to secure the plaintiff's expected judgment. *Shaffer* effectively limits the use of attachment and like remedies in obtaining jurisdiction; the case does not restrict the use of such remedies in securing judgments in cases where jurisdiction is constitutionally valid.)

c)   Enforcing Foreign Judgments
"Once it has been determined by a court of competent jurisdiction that the defendant is a debtor of the plaintiff, there would seem to be no unfairness in allowing an action to realize on that debt in a State where the defendant has property, whether or not that State would have jurisdiction to determine the existence of the debt as an original matter." *Shaffer v. Heitner,* 433 U.S. 186, 210–11 n.36, 97 S. Ct. 2569, 2583 n.36 (1977).

d)   No Other Forum Available
The Court left open in *Shaffer* "the question whether the presence of a defendant's property in a State is a sufficient basis for jurisdiction when no other forum is available to the plaintiff." *Id.* at 211 n.37, 97 S. Ct. at 2583 n.37. Does this mean no other forum in the United States or none anywhere in the world? See *Louring v. Kuwait Boulder Shipping Co.,* 455 F. Supp. 630 (D. Conn. 1977) (no other forum in the United States).

e)   Maritime Attachment
When a maritime or admiralty action is filed in federal court, federal procedure provides for *quasi in rem* jurisdiction through attachment of a defendant's property within the district if the defendant herself cannot be found there. F.R.C.P. Supplemental Rule B(1). Jurisdiction asserted under this rule, solely on the basis of the presence of defendant's property within the court's jurisdiction, appears at first glance to violate *Shaffer.* It can be argued, however, that *Shaffer* would not bar *quasi in rem* jurisdiction under Rule B if *in personam* jurisdiction could not be acquired in any forum in the United States. See supra Ch. I.B.1.c.(5)(D); *Amoco Overseas Oil v. Compagnie Nationale Algerienne,* 605 F.2d 648, 655 (2d Cir. 1979). It also can be argued that *Shaffer* is totally inapposite to any assertion of jurisdiction based on Rule B attachment because admiralty jurisdiction rests traditionally on principles and concerns altogether different from "land-based" jurisdiction. *Trans-Asiatic Oil Ltd. v. Apex Oil Co.,* 743 F.2d 956 (1st Cir. 1984); *Grand Bahama Petroleum Co., Ltd. v. Canadian Transportation Agencies, Ltd.,* 450 F. Supp. 447 (W.D. Wash. 1978).

Federal procedure also gives a federal district court *in rem* jurisdiction in any action to enforce a maritime lien against a vessel present within the district. F.R.C.P. Supplemental Rule C(1)(a). Jurisdiction is based solely on the presence of the property within the district. Even if *Shaffer* applies, its "minimum contacts" requirement arguably is satisfied in such an *in rem* action even though there are no connections between the owners of interests in the vessel and the jurisdiction where the action is maintained. First, in an admiralty *in rem* action under Rule C, the defendant is the vessel itself, and "the theory of the ship's own liability is sufficient to confer *in rem* jurisdiction without regard to the contacts its owner may have with the district." *Merchants Nat. Bank v. Dredge General G.L. Gillespie,* 663 F.2d 1338, 1350 n.18 (5th Cir. 1981), cert. dismissed, 456 U.S. 966, 102 S. Ct. 2263 (1982). Second, the claim which the plaintiff pursues in a Rule C *in rem* action, i.e., the maritime lien, is related to the property. The Court in *Shaffer* suggested that the presence of property within the jurisdiction may well support any kind of judicial jurisdiction when the plaintiff's claim is related to the property. For a basic introduction to jurisdiction in admiralty cases, and also to maritime liens and attachment, see F. Maraist, Admiralty In A Nutshell 83–105, 327–58 (1983).

2. SELECTING AN INCONVENIENT FORUM AS AN UNFAIR TRADE PRACTICE

A creditor's judgment against a debtor will be enforceable only if the court rendering the judgment has judicial jurisdiction of the case and the parties. (See Chapter I.B.1., supra.) The requirement of judicial jurisdiction thus limits a creditor's freedom in selecting the forum for its collection actions against debtors. Another limitation is the Federal Trade Commission Act, 15 U.S.C.A. §§ 41–77 (1973 & Supp. 1988) which empowers the FTC to prevent unfair or deceptive acts or practices in commerce. In *Spiegel, Inc. v. F. T. C.,* 540 F.2d 287 (7th Cir. 1976), the court held that the FTC has the power to prevent large retail businesses from suing customers for delinquent credit accounts in a court distant from the consumer's residence.

The *Spiegel* case focused on that company's practice of using Illinois courts to sue defaulting retail mail order purchasers who were residents of other states. These purchasers had no contacts with Illinois other than their dealings with Spiegel, whose principal place of business was Chicago. The court conceded that the questioned practice was perfectly proper under Illinois law and assumed that courts in Illinois had jurisdiction. The court nevertheless concluded that the FTC had acted properly in enjoining Spiegel from continuing the practice of bringing suits in Illinois against distant mail order purchasers. Because the debts involved were relatively small, the defendants simply could not justify the great expenses of hiring counsel in Illinois and traveling there to defend themselves. Thus, Spiegel's practice was unfair inasmuch as nonresident debtors were effectively deprived of a meaningful opportunity to defend themselves in court.

3. *FORUM NON CONVENIENS*

The Federal Trade Commission is empowered to enjoin creditors from pursuing collection actions in forums that are inconvenient for the debtor-defendants. (See Chapter I.B.2., supra.) The FTC's resources are limited, however, and its staff can police the activities of only a small number of creditors. Nevertheless, apart from considerations of judicial jurisdiction and action by the FTC, a creditor can be prevented from continuing an action in an inconvenient forum through the doctrine of *forum non conveniens.* This doctrine of civil procedure empowers a trial "court to decline to exercise a possessed jurisdiction whenever it appears that the cause before it may be more appropriately tried elsewhere." Blair, *The Doctrine of Forum Non Conveniens in Anglo-American Law,* 29 Colum. L. Rev. 1 (1929). Application of the doctrine of *forum non conveniens* rests largely within the trial court's discretion. In exercising its discretion the court will consider the residence of the parties, their interests and the effects of the choice of forum on each of them, and the interests of the local public in having local disputes decided locally while avoiding the costs of lawsuits having little connection with the forum. F. James, Civil Procedure § 12.29 at 657–60 (2d ed. 1977). Although judicial jurisdiction and the doctrine of *forum non conveniens* are distinct constructs providing different limitations on a creditor's choice of forums, the distinction between them has blurred considerably since the decisions in *International Shoe* and *Shaffer* which established fairness (including convenience) as the test for all assertions of jurisdiction. (See Chapter I.B.1., supra.) Moreover, at least for purposes of deciding judicial jurisdiction, "modern transportation and communication" undercut a defendant's claim of inconvenience in any case. *World-Wide Volkswagen Corp. v. Woodson,* 444 U.S. 286, 293, 100 S. Ct. 559, 565 (1980), *quoting* the case *McGee v. International Life Ins. Co.,* 355 U.S. 220, 222–23, 78 S. Ct. 199, 201 (1957).

4. FORUM–SELECTION CLAUSES

A device that is commonly used by creditors to insure venue that is convenient for themselves, if not inconvenient for their debtors, is to include a *forum-selection clause* in the contract. Such a clause specifies the state (sometimes even a particular city or a specific court) where actions on or under the contract can be brought. The effect, if the clause is enforced, is to deny jurisdiction to courts in other states where there are sufficient contacts so that, constitutionally and consistent with long-arm statutes and jurisdictional rules, the action could be heard. The general rule, which applies both in state and federal courts, is as follows:

> [A] forum selection clause is presumptively valid and will be enforced unless the party objecting to its enforcement establishes (1) that it is the result of fraud or overreaching, (2) that enforcement would violate a strong public policy of the forum, or (3) that enforcement would in the particular circumstances of the case result in litigation in a jurisdiction so seriously inconvenient as to be unreasonable.

In re Diaz Contracting, Inc., 817 F.2d 1047, 1051 (3d Cir. 1987), quoting *Coastal Steel Corp. v. Tilghman Wheelabrator Ltd.,* 709 F.2d 190, 202 (3d Cir.), cert. denied, 464 U.S. 938, 104 S. Ct. 349 (1983), citing *M/S Bremen v. Zapata Off-Shore Co.,* 407 U.S. 1, 92 S. Ct. 1907 (1972).

Example: A New York maufacturer sells equipment to a corporate buyer in Florida. The contract provides that any dispute between the parties will be adjudicated only in New York. Buyer is unhappy with the equipment and sues the manufacturer in Florida. The manufacturer moves to dismiss the action on the basis of the forum-selection clause. The action will probably be dismissed if the parties were of equal bargaining strength in executing the contract. See, e.g., *Manrique v. Fabbri*, 493 So.2d 437 (Fla. 1986), in which the court observed that "[f]orum selection clauses * * * do not 'oust' courts of their jurisdiction [but rather] * * * present the court with a legitimate reason to refrain from exercising that jurisdiction." Id. at 439–40.

An issue that has divided the authorities is whether a federal court sitting in diversity can enforce a forum-selection clause, and thereby refuse to hear the action because of the parties selection of forum, when the state in which the court sits has a strong public policy against such clauses. In the case *Stewart Organization, Inc. v. Ricoh Corp.*, 810 F.2d 1066 (11th Cir. 1987), affirmed, ___ U.S. ___, 108 S. Ct. 2239 (1988) (issue of venue of federal court action is a matter of federal procedure), the court held that a federal court need not defer to the state public policy against forum-selection clauses in circumstances where (1) the purpose of the policy is to protect state court jurisdiction and (2) the action is brought in federal rather than state court.

WARNING: That the parties' contract establishes venue for actions between them does not mean that the designated forum has jurisdiction over the parties. There must be sufficient contacts with the forum so that the court is empowered, constitutionally and consistent with state long-arm statutes and the like, to hear the matter, or the parties must have consented to jurisdiction. See Chapter I.B.1., supra. A forum-selection clause does not necessarily amount to consent to jurisdiction. Moreover, where there are no contacts with the forum state, a forum-selection clause may be deemed an insufficient basis on which to predicate jurisdiction. *McRae v. J.D./M.D. Inc.*, 511 So.2d 540 (Fla. 1987).

C. CHOOSING FAVORABLE LAW

If a creditor in pursuing collection actions must give debtors a meaningful opportunity to defend themselves in court, the odds against a default judgment lessen. A creditor can increase the chances of prevailing in any event, and on its terms, by getting the debtor to agree, at the time of contracting, to the creditor's choice of substantive law that will govern the parties' transaction. As a general rule, parties to a contract are free to determine which state's substantive law will apply in resolving disputes between them. A creditor, of course, will "bargain" for applying the law of a state with which she is most familiar, or the law of a state which she believes is most likely to declare the contract fully enforceable against the debtor. Choice-of-law clauses in contracts are especially important with regard to interest rates. Maximum interest rates vary widely among the states. Given a choice among governing laws, a creditor is quite likely to choose the law of the state having the highest ceiling on interest rates. Choice of law is a matter that must be agreed to by the debtor; but, especially in consumer credit transactions, the debtor's bargaining power is usually such that she cannot resist a creditor's choice of law. The enforcement of contractual choice-of-law clauses is subject, however, to a number of very real conditions or limitations including the following:

1. **IMPROPRIETY, MISTAKE OR THE ABSENCE OF BARGAINED FOR CONSENT IN AGREEMENTS CHOOSING GOVERNING LAW**

    A choice-of-law clause in a contract will not be enforced if consent to inclusion of the clause was obtained improperly as by misrepresentation, duress, or undue influence, or by mistake. Such a clause in an adhesion contract will be closely scrutinized by the forum court which may not enforce the provision if doing so would cause substantial injustice. See Restatement (Second) of the Law of Conflicts of Law § 187, Comment b.

2. **RELATIONSHIP TO THE CHOSEN STATE**

    Ordinarily, at least with regard to matters the parties themselves are not free to determine, there must be a "substantial" or "reasonable" relationship between the chosen state and the parties or their transaction in order for a choice of law clause to be enforced with respect to matters of contract validity. *Id.*, § 187(2)(a); U.C.C. § 1–105(1). The parties cannot choose the law of "a place which has no normal relation to the transaction and to whose law they would not otherwise be subject." *Seeman v. Philadelphia Warehouse Co.*, 274 U.S. 403, 408, 47 S. Ct. 626, 628 (1927); U.C.C. § 1–105 comment 1.

3. **RESPECTING POLICIES OF THE STATE WHOSE LAW WOULD OTHERWISE GOVERN**

    The law of the chosen state cannot be applied if another state, whose law would govern in the absence of an effective choice of law by the parties, has a materially greater interest than the chosen state in having its law applied. Restatement (Second) of the Conflict of Laws § 187(2)(b) (1971).

4. **STATUTORY CHOICE OF LAW RULE OVERRIDING PARTIES' AGREEMENT**

    A statute of the forum state may require the court to apply local law in resolving a contract dispute notwithstanding the parties' agreement that a different state's law should govern their transaction. For example, see Uniform Consumer Credit Code (U.C.C.C.) § 1–201 (1974 Official Text).

    Example: C, an individual consumer who resides in Iowa, establishes a charge account with R, a mail order retailer located in Illinois. The credit agreement between C and R states that it is an Illinois contract governed by Illinois law. C charges the price of consumer goods to her account and fails to pay for them. R sues C in Iowa to collect the price of the goods and accrued finance charges. The finance charges imposed by R are excessive under Iowa law but well within the limits of Illinois law. Iowa law provides, however, that Iowa's ceiling on finance charges will apply to all charge accounts entered into by Iowa residents. The Iowa court must apply the Iowa law on finance charges and doing so neither violates R's due process rights nor imposes an undue burden on interstate commerce. See, e.g., *Aldens, Inc. v. Miller*, 466 F. Supp. 379 (S.D. Iowa 1979), aff'd, 610 F.2d 538 (8th Cir. 1979); *Whitaker v. Spiegel, Inc.*, 95 Wash. 2d 408, 623 P.2d 1147 (1981).

REVIEW QUESTIONS

1. Apart from state law, what is the key issue in determining the validity of a cognovit judgment?

2. Two Indiana residents, R and S, were involved in a single-car accident in Indiana. S was the passenger in the car driven by R. The car is insured by a company that does business in Minnesota. S moves to Minnesota and there files suit against R, who has no contacts with Minnesota. *Quasi in rem* jurisdiction is asserted by attaching in Minnesota the contractual obligation of the insurance company to defend and indemnify R in connection with the suit. Does the Minnesota court have judicial jurisdiction of the case?

3. T or F   A creditor can pursue a lawsuit against a debtor in any court that has judicial jurisdiction over the parties.

4. T or F   Parties to a contract can select any state's law to govern disputes between them.

*

II

JUDGMENT LIENS

Analysis

The principal value of a judgment as a creditor's remedy lies not in the intrinsic effects of a judgment as a final resolution of the parties' dispute. Rather, a judgment's importance as a creditor's remedy lies in the judgment's extrinsic attributes or effects "which are bestowed thereon by the common law [and by statute] for the purpose of enabling the judgment creditor to proceed to a forced but orderly collection." Riesenfeld, *Collection of Money Judgments in American Law—A Historical Inventory and a Prospectus*, 42 Iowa L.Rev. 155, 156 (1957). Professor Riesenfeld has categorized these extrinsic effects as actionability, executability and creation of a lien. Id. "Actionability" refers to the status of a judgment as a new and independent cause of action in itself which supersedes the creditor's original claim against the debtor. "Executability" is the attribute of a judgment enabling the creditor to invoke the coercive powers of the state and cause the seizure and sale of the debtor's property in satisfaction of the judgment. To help insure that property of the debtor is available for execution should the creditor's judgment not be satisfied voluntarily, virtually every state subjects the debtor's interests in certain property to a lien that arises, by force of statute, from the judgment itself. This judgment lien is the focal point of the following discussion.

A. HISTORY OF THE JUDGMENT LIEN

At common law a judgment could be enforced only through the judicial writ of *fieri facias (fi. fa.)*, which directed the sheriff to satisfy a judgment from the debtor's goods and chattels. "[E]xcept for debts due the king, the lands of the debtor were not liable to the satisfaction of a judgment against him, and consequently no lien thereon was acquired by a judgment. This was in accordance with the policy of the feudal law introduced into England after the Conquest, which did not permit the feudatory to charge, or to be deprived of, his lands for his debts, lest thereby he should be disabled from performing his stipulated military service, and which, moreover, forbid the alienation of a feud without the lord's consent." *Hutcheson v. Grubbs*, 80 Va. 251, 254 (1885).

"As the social and commercial life of the English people changed and became more complex it became necessary to enact a statute giving to the creditor the security by way of a lien as known to the modern law. This first finds expression in the statute of Westminster 2, 13 Edw. I. [1285], commonly known as the statute *de mercatoribus*." *Beatty v. Cook*, 192 Iowa 542, 544–45, 185 N.W. 360, 361 (1921). This statute required a creditor to choose the method of enforcing the judgment. The choice was between a *fi. fa.* writ, described above, or a *writ of elegit* " 'on which the sheriff shall deliver to him all the chattels of the debtor, saving only his oxen, and beasts of the plow, and half of his land, till the debt be levied upon a reasonable price or extent.'" 2 A. Freeman, A Treatise on the Law of Judgments § 916 at 1929 (1925). The writ of elegit enabled the judgment creditor "to obtain a term of years in one half of the debtor's lands [a moiety] for a period appraised to be long enough to satisfy the judgment debt from the rents and profits of the land thus 'extended.'" Riesenfeld, *Enforcement of Money Judgments in Early American History,* 71 Mich. L. Rev. 691, 694 (1973). Moreover, in consequence of this writ and in aid of it, a moiety of the debtor's land was deemed bound by a lien that arose upon the rendition of judgment.

Eventually, the writ of *fi. fa.* was enlarged to permit the seizure and sale of not only the judgment debtor's personalty, but also her real property. The writ of elegit thus fell by the wayside. The notion that a debtor's lands were bound by a judgment lien survived, however; and the lien was broadened so that it spread to all of the debtor's real property that was subject to seizure and sale under a writ *fi. fa.*

B. NATURE AND ENFORCEMENT OF THE JUDGMENT LIEN

1. THE LIEN IS GENERAL RATHER THAN SPECIFIC

A *judgment lien* is not a specific lien on any of the debtor's real property. Rather, the lien is a general lien only. Thus, the judgment creditor receives no estate or interest in the debtor's lands. All the judgment creditor acquires as a result of the lien is "'a mere power to make his general lien effectual by following up the steps of the law and consummating his judgment by an execution and levy on the land.'" 2 A. Freeman, A Treatise on the Law of Judgments § 915 at 1925 (1925). Because a judgment lienor "has a mere general lien, he cannot, like a mortgagee or other holder of a specific lien, sue for waste as injures his security, nor is he entitled to possession of the property * * * [or to] recover crops produced upon it, or timber cut from it * * *" Id. at 1926. Nevertheless, when a judgment lien is enforced through execution by levying on and selling the property, "the title of the creditor for this purpose relates back to the time of the judgment, so as to cut out intermediate encumbrances." Id.

2. ENFORCEMENT IS TYPICALLY THROUGH EXECUTION

As suggested above, enforcement of a judgment lien is typically through execution. The whole subject of execution is fully outlined below (see Chapter III). Basically, *execution* is the process whereby a state official (usually the sheriff) is directed by way of an appropriate writ to seize and sell so much of the debtor's nonexempt property as is necessary to satisfy a judgment. If the sheriff levies on property that is subject to a judgment lien, the judgment creditor's claim to this property relates back to the time when her judgment lien attached. *Hames v. Archer Paper Co.,* 45 Tenn. App. 1, 8, 319 S.W.2d 252, 255 (1958). This "relation back" feature of the relationship between judgment liens and the process of execution largely explains a judgment lien's efficacy as a creditor's remedy. See Chapter II. F., infra, for a discussion of the judgment lien's priority over other claims to the propery.

In some states, the judgment creditor may elect to enforce her lien through foreclosure proceedings rather than through execution; and, in a few states, foreclosure is the exclusive method of enforcement.

C. JUDGMENTS WHICH PRODUCE A LIEN

1. GENERALLY

As a general rule, the only type of judgment that produces a lien is a final, personal judgment of a court of record, for a definite sum of money, that can be enforced through execution against the debtor's real property.

2. DECREES FOR ALIMONY AND THE LIKE

"We believe the general rule to be that * * * 'unless a decree for periodical payments for support or alimony specifically states that it shall constituite a lien on property, none arises, in the absence of a statute declaring such decree a lien.'" *Brieger v. Brieger,* 197 Kan. 756, 759, 421 P.2d 1, 3 (1966) (quoting Annot., 59 A.L.R.2d 656, 660 (1958)). Most states have statutes that expressly or impliedly deal with the matter. A typical statute explicitly provides, or is interpreted to provide, that a decree for alimony or support will constitute a lien in the same manner and under the same circumstances as any other money judgment. In construing this sort of statute, however, the courts disagree on whether a lien attaches for future installments of alimony or support, or only for matured installments. See cases collected in Annot., 59 A.L.R.2d 656 (1958). The court held in the *Brieger* case, cited above, that a judgment providing for periodic support payments does not create a lien for installments not yet due; a lien arises only when the installments become final judgments, which occurs when they are due and unpaid.

3. JUDGMENTS OF FEDERAL DISTRICT COURTS

a. Federal Money Judgments Are Treated Like State Court Judgments

Federal law provides:

> Every judgment rendered by a district court within a State shall be a lien on the property located in such State in the same manner, to the same extent and under the same conditions as a judgment of a court of general jurisdiction in such State, and shall cease to be a lien in the same manner and time. Whenever the law of any State requires a judgment of a State court to be registered, recorded, docketed or indexed, or any other act to be done, in a particular manner, or in a certain office or county or parish before such lien attaches, such requirements shall apply [to federal judgments] only if the law of such State authorizes the judgment of a court of the United States to be registered, recorded, docketed, indexed or otherwise conformed to rules and requirements relating to judgments of the courts of the State.

28 U.S.C.A. § 1962 (1982). For a collection of cases construing § 1962, see Annot., 18 A.L.R. Fed. 568 (1974).

As § 1962 clearly provides, docketing and similar steps that are necessary under state law to create a judgment lien apply to federal judgments only if the state makes it possible for a creditor with a federal judgment to satisfy the local requirements. States cannot impose conditions on the attachment of federal court judgment liens that are more stringent than those applicable to state court judgment liens. If they do, a federal judgment will of itself create a lien on the defendant's property. In such a case, no state law requirements, such as docketing, need be satisfied. Also, the lien in such a case will not be limited to the county where the district court sits; rather, the lien will spread throughout the district court's entire jurisdiction. *Rhea v. Smith,* 274 U.S. 434, 47 S. Ct. 698 (1927).

b. Federal Judgments for Condemnation Are Treated Differently

Unless federal law provides otherwise, state requirements as to the recording, indexing and performance of others acts necessary to create a judgment lien are inapplicable to federal judgments of condemnation; and 28 U.S.C.A. § 1962 (1982), quoted above, does not govern condemnation judgments. Thus, as against subsequent transferees, the United States acquires good title to condemned land upon the entry of the judgment of condemnation and payment into court of the compensation awarded for the taking. *Norman Lumber Co. v. United States,* 223 F.2d 868 (4th Cir.), cert. denied, 350 U.S. 902, 76 S. Ct. 181 (1955).

4. FOREIGN JUDGMENTS

A state court judgment for the recovery of money can usually be enforced in another state through a summary process that involves filing or registering the judgment with the clerk of any court of general jurisdiction within the state. Uniform Enforcement of Foreign Judgments Act § 2 (1964). A judgment so filed has the same effect as a judgment of a local court, id., which means that the filing creates a judgment lien to the same extent that local law provides for such a lien. Similarly, a judgment of a federal district court can be registered in any other such court and has "the same effect as a judgment of the district court of the district where registered and may be enforced in like manner." 28 U.S.C.A. § 1963 (1982). A judgment of a federal district court creates a lien to the same extent and under the same conditions as a state court judgment. 28 U.S.C.A. § 1962 (1982).

D. WHEN THE JUDGMENT LIEN ARISES

1. GENERALLY

In some states, a lien of judgment arises and attaches to the debtor's property as soon as the judgment is rendered. In most states, however, the lien does not arise until the judgment is docketed or otherwise indexed or recorded as prescribed by statute. A *docket* is a book or set of records in which the judge or clerk of court notes briefly all the proceedings in a case. There may be a separate judgment docket which lists alphabetically the names of judgment debtors, the amount of each judgment, and the precise time the judgment was entered.

2. REGISTERED LAND

In some states, a judgment lien does not attach to the debtor's interests in registered land until the judgment is noted on the certificate of title to the land. See Minn. Stat. § 508.63 (1986).

E. PROPERTY REACHED BY THE JUDGMENT LIEN

1. TYPES OF PROPERTY AFFECTED

a. Lien Generally Reaches Only Real Property

In all but seven states (Kentucky, Maine, Massachusetts, Michigan, New Hampshire, Rhode Island and Vermont), a judgment creates a general lien on the debtor's interests in real property. In three states (Alabama, Georgia and Mississippi), the judgment lien reaches both real and personal property. In California, certain types of business personalty are subjected to the lien of judgment if the judgment creditor files a notice of judgment lien with the Secretary of State. Elsewhere, a different sort of lien attaches to personal property through the process of execution, which is discussed below. See Chapter III, infra.

b. Disagreement as to What is Real Property

What constitutes real property for judgment lien purposes varies somewhat from state to state. The following are examples of interests that are considered real property for judgment lien purposes in some states, but not in others:

- Equitable interests such as the vendee's or vendor's interest under a contract to sell real property;

- Leasehold interests;

- Reversionary interests and contingent remainders;

- Beneficial interests in land trusts;

- Shares in a cooperative apartment;

- Crops growing on, or harvested from, land that is subject to the judgment lien;

- Timber cut from land that is subject to the judgment lien;

- Oil and gas leaseholds and other mineral rights.

2. TENANCY BY THE ENTIRETY PROPERTY

In most of the twenty-some states that still recognize tenancies by the entirety, property so held is completely immune from levy and sale under execution or other collection process initiated by a creditor of one of the spouses. Thus, a creditor's judgment against one spouse does not create a lien on that person's interest in real property held by her as a tenant by the entirety. See *United States v. Gurley*, 415 F.2d 144 (5th Cir. 1969).

3. THE GEOGRAPHICAL REACH OF A JUDGMENT LIEN

A lien of judgment ordinarily does not reach beyond the county where the judgment was rendered. Usually, however, whether the lien originally arose upon rendition or docketing of the judgment, the lien will spread to another county if the judgment is there docketed or otherwise recorded.

4. AFTER–ACQUIRED PROPERTY

a. Judgment Liens Reach After-Acquired Property

In most jurisdictions, the lien of judgment extends not only to interests of the debtor in property owned when the judgment was rendered, but also to interests thereafter acquired by her for as long as the judgment lien survives. (Regarding the duration of judgment liens, see Chapter II. G. infra.)

b. Priority Between Judgment Liens Attaching to After-Acquired Property

The authorities disagree about the relative priority of judgment liens on after-acquired property.

> *Example:*   In January, A obtains a judgment against D and dockets her judgment in Orange County. In May, B obtains a judgment against D and this judgment, too, is docketed in Orange County. D owns no property in Orange County until November when she buys realty there. As soon as D acquires her interest in the real estate, the liens of A and B attach simultaneously to the property. Whose lien has priority, A's or B's?

A few courts would answer that A has priority because she was the first to acquire and docket her judgment. The majority of courts would hold, however, that the liens are of equal rank because they actually attached to the property at the same time. Yet, in many states, the creditor who is the first to enforce her lien through execution (which involves levying on and selling the property) will thereby achieve priority. In other states, such diligence is not rewarded; no matter which judgment lienor forces a sale of the after-acquired property, each of them shares pro rata in the sale proceeds. See *Hulbert v. Hulbert,* 216 N.Y. 430, 440–42, 111 N.E. 70, 73–74 (1916); *Zink v. James River Nat. Bank,* 58 N.D. 1, 11–13, 224 N.W. 901, 905–06 (1929).

5. SUBSEQUENT INCREASES IN VALUE

"If the creditor can thus reach wholly distinct parcels of property which the debtor did not even own when the abstract of judgment was recorded [i.e., after-acquired property discussed above], a fortiori he can reach any and all increases in the value of the equity in property owned by the debtor at the time of such recordation and already subject to the lien." *Kinney v. Vallentyne,* 15 Cal. 3d 475, 479, 124 Cal. Rptr. 897, 899, 541 P.2d 537, 539 (1975).

> *Examples:*   N prevailed in a tort action against D. N then recorded her judgment in Contra Costa County where D and his wife owned realty which was community property. Thereafter, D and his wife were divorced and D's wife was awarded the real estate.
>
> Several years later, N sought to enforce her judgment against the realty now owned exclusively by D's former wife. Held: N's judgment lien attached to the property when she recorded her judgment; this lien survived the award of the property to D's former wife; and N is entitled to reach any increase in the equity in the property that occurs before she enforces her lien. "[D]uring the life of the lien the

transferee contributes to the equity in the property at his peril." *Kinney v. Vallentyne,* supra.

6. PROCEEDS OF SALE OF PROPERTY ARE NOT SUBJECT TO THE LIEN

Because a judgment lien is not a specific charge on particular property, it ordinarily does not confer on the judgment creditor any claim to proceeds of the sale of the debtor's real estate. The judgment lien entitles the creditor only to proceed against the real property itself. (The judgment creditor may, however, be entitled to enforce the lien on the land against the purchaser. See the discussion of the priority of a judgment lien in Chapter II.F., infra. Moreover, she may be able to reach the purchase price through the process of execution or garnishment. Both of these remedies are discussed below. See Chapters III and V, infra.)

F. PRIORITY OF A JUDGMENT LIEN IN RELATION TO OTHER CLAIMS TO THE PROPERTY

1. JUDGMENT LIENOR VERSUS JUDGMENT LIENOR
a. Usual Rule
The priority of judgment liens attaching to the same property usually corresponds to the order in which the liens were created or became attached to the property. In most states, therefore, judgment liens are ranked according to the order in which the judgments were docketed or otherwise recorded. (See Chapter II.D., supra, for a discussion of when a judgment lien arises.)

b. Exception: Liens Attaching Simultaneously to After-Acquired Property
As noted above (II.E.4.b.), when judgment liens attach at the same time to after-acquired property, the dates the liens were created are unimportant in determining priority. The courts either declare that the liens are of equal rank or award priority to the diligent judgment creditor who first levies on the property.

2. JUDGMENT LIENOR VERSUS PURCHASER OR OTHER TRANSFEREE OF INTEREST IN THE PROPERTY
a. Subsequent Transferees
1) General Rule
Ordinarily, according to the familiar rule that first in time is first in right, interests in and claims to property acquired after the attachment of a judgment lien are subordinate to the lien. "If the debtor since [the judgment lien first attached] has made any conveyance or encumbrance, or suffered a judgment, attachment or other lien, or has been subjected to any action or proceeding seeking to affect his title to the land * * *, such conveyance, lien or proceeding is unavailing against the judgment lien * * *". 2 A. Freeman, A Treatise on the Law of Judgments § 973 at 2046–47 (1925).

2)   Exception: Purchase-Money Mortgages
A purchase-money mortgage on after-acquired property is superior to a lien of judgment even though the judgment is prior in time. *Emery v. Ward,* 68 Colo. 373, 191 P. 99 (1920).

b.   Prior Unrecorded Transfers

1)   Where Registry Laws Protect Judgment Lienors
In most states, judgment creditors are protected by the registry laws that require the recording of conveyances affecting real estate. Consequently, if prior to judgment the debtor has sold or mortgaged real property that belonged to her, but the transfer was not recorded, the lien of judgment will attach to the property and take precedence over the secret conveyance. In some states, the judgment creditor must have no actual knowledge of the unrecorded interest to be given priority.

2)   Where Registry Laws Do Not Protect Judgment Lienors
Where the registry laws do not protect judgment creditors, their judgment liens are subordinate to earlier unrecorded conveyances of the debtor's real property interests. This result is based on the generally true proposition that the lien of judgment attaches only to the debtor's real interest in the property. In other words, the judgment creditor slips into the debtor's shoes with respect to the state of the property's title; consequently, as against third parties, a judgment lien is no stronger than the debtor's rights against them, except where registry and similar laws provide otherwise. Nevertheless, a person who buys the property when the judgment lien is enforced through execution will likely be the sort of purchaser protected by the registry laws; so, the buyer through a judgment lienor may take free of an earlier, unrecorded interest even though the lienor herself was subject to the interest. The lienor's position is not improved, however, if she buys the property herself at the execution sale. A creditor who is the successful bidder at a judicial sale and who credits the debtor's obligation with the amount of the bid is not generally considered to be a *bona fide* purchaser within the protection of the registry laws. 2 A. Freeman, A Treatise on the Law of Judgments § 972 (1925). There are cases that follow a contrary rule, however, and hold that a judgment creditor who purchases at a proper sale on his own valid judgment takes free of prior secret equities of which the creditor had no notice. See *Pugh v. Highley,* 152 Ind. 252, 53 N.E. 171 (1899). The court reasoned in *Pugh* that the judgment creditor's position is no different from that of a purchaser who is a stranger to the judgment debtor: "The judgment creditor purchaser has parted with value and has changed his position for the worse. He has paid to the sheriff the amount of his bid in cash, actually or constructively; for, if he merely receipts for payment of his judgment in whole or in part, the transaction in contemplation of law is the same as if he had paid the sheriff in cash and the sheriff had paid him in cash." Id. at 254, 53 N.E. at 172.

3.   JUDGMENT LIENOR VERSUS BANKRUPTCY TRUSTEE
As a very general rule, all liens on a debtor's property, including judgment liens, are enforceable against the debtor's estate and her trustee in bankruptcy. There are many exceptions to this rule. The bankruptcy trustee and the bankrupt debtor herself are empowered by federal bankruptcy law to avoid certain liens and other transfers of interests in the debtor's property. The greatest threats to the enforceability of a judgment lien in bankruptcy are these provisions of the federal Bankruptcy Code: § 522(f) [11 U.S.C.A. § 522(f) (1979)], which allows the debtor to avoid judicial liens on exempt property, and § 547(b) [11 U.S.C.A. § 547(b) (1979)], which allows the trustee to avoid preferential transfers, including liens occurring usually within 90 days before the bankruptcy petition is filed. Parts of Chapters XX and XXI, infra, of this outline are given over to a thorough explanation of §§ 522(f), 547(b) and the other avoiding powers in bankruptcy.

G.   LIFE OF A JUDGMENT LIEN

1.   STATUTE OF LIMITATION
a.   Lien Terminates Upon Expiration of Period for Enforcing Judgments
Just as states limit actions on contracts, negotiable instruments, and other types of debts, they similarly limit action on a judgment, which is a form of debt. Ten years is the typical period during which an action on a judgment must be commenced. A judgment lien cannot survive the running of such a statute of limitation.

b.   Renewal of Judgment Creates New Lien
Before this statute has run, however, the judgment creditor can institute a new action based on the debtor's failure to pay the existing judgment. Prosecuting this new action, which essentially is an action for debt, is referred to as *renewing* the judgment. If the creditor prevails—as she surely will unless the debtor has satisfied the original judgment—a new judgment will be rendered that will itself give rise to a new lien and a new limitations period. The authorities disagree on whether the lien of a renewal judgment should relate back to the original judgment. This disagreement extends to the case in which there is no gap between the expiration of the original judgment lien and the creation of the new one.

2.   DORMANCY AND REVIVOR
a.   Suspension of Judgment Lien Due to Dormancy
A judgment lien may become ineffective well before the running of the statute of limitation governing actions on judgments. Under the common law, a judgment lien became *dormant* a year and a day after the rendition of the judgment because, after that time, execution process, which is the usual vehicle for enforcing judgments and judgment liens, would not issue in the absence of an earlier effort to enforce the judgment. In effect, the law presumed that a judgment was satisfied during the 366–day period. A large number of states now have statutes that, in one way or another, effectively delay dormancy for a period of time that is longer than a year and a day, but shorter than the

usual statute of limitation governing actions on judgments. A statute may straightforwardly declare that a judgment lien is effective for three, five, or more years. The same effect is achieved by a statute that permits the enforcement of judgments through execution for a comparable period of time following the rendition or docketing of a judgment.

b.   Waking a Dormant Judgment Lien Through Revivor

If dormancy nevertheless results, the sleeping judgment lien can be *revived* through a judicial proceeding in *scire facias*. In some states, but not all of them, a revivor proceeding can be instituted prior to dormancy so that the lien never sleeps. In any event, whether the lien is reconfirmed through such a proceeding before or after the onset of dormancy, there is the important question of whether or not the revived lien relates back to the time of its birth and, in so doing, subordinates the claims of intervening purchasers or creditors. The authorities disagree. For a case deciding against relation back when dormancy had occurred before revival was undertaken, see *Brieger v. Brieger,* 197 Kan. 756, 421 P.2d 1 (1966).

In some states where statutory law explicitly declares that a judgment lien is effective for a certain period of time, the law is unclear on whether or not its purpose is simply to postpone dormancy. The murkiness creates doubt about the revivability of the judgment lien after the specified period expires.

In other states, the declared life span of a judgment lien is the same as both the period of limitation applicable to actions on judgments and the time during which a judgment is enforceable through execution. In such a state a judgment lien cannot be extended through revival. Whether or not the judgment can be renewed, thus giving rise to a new lien, is a separate issue. Renewal is generally possible, however, which suggests that a revival proceeding and a renewal action are significantly different. They are, as is explained in the next paragraph.

c.   Effect of Revival Upon Statute of Limitation

There is general agreement that the revival of a judgment does not stop the running of a statute of limitation governing actions on judgments; and, if the period of limitation expires without the creditor having renewed her judgment, the judgment lien expires forever along with the judgment itself. The reasoning is that, unlike an action to renew a judgment, a revival action does not produce a new judgment; rather, a revival action continues the original suit and revitalizes the original judgment and lien solely for the purpose of removing dormancy as a bar to execution. *Aetna Casualty and Surety Co. v. Brunsmann,* 77 Ill. App. 2d 219, 222 N.E.2d 527 (1966); see also *Union Nat. Bank v. Lamb,* 337 U.S. 38, 69 S. Ct. 911 (1949). Revival and renewal actions also are different procedurally. Revival involves a rather summary exercise of a court's continuing jurisdiction over a matter properly before it at some earlier time. A renewal action is an altogether separate lawsuit requiring a fresh basis of jurisdiction and proper venue. *Owens v. McCloskey,* 161 U.S. 642, 16 S. Ct. 693 (1896).

Example: C obtained a judgment against D in 1980. State law provides that a judgment becomes dormant three years after it is rendered but that a dormant judgment can be revived for additional periods of three years. State law also provides that any action to enforce a judgment must be brought within ten years after rendition of the judgment. In 1989, C revived her judgment lien which had become dormant. In 1991, D acquired real property in the county where C's judgment was docketed. No lien attaches to this property because the statute of limitation on the enforcement of judgments had run. The revival did not create a new judgment and lien or extend the statute of limitation governing the original judgment.

3. JUDGMENT LIEN UNAFFECTED BY DEATH OF JUDGMENT DEBTOR

The death of the judgment debtor does not terminate a judgment lien which has attached to property. Although the means of enforcing the lien might change after the debtor's death, the lien itself survives and is effective against heirs or others who succeed to ownership of the encumbered real estate. *Corporation of America v. Marks,* 10 Cal. 2d 218, 73 P.2d 1215 (1937) (judgment creditor need not file a claim against judgment debtor's estate in order to enforce judgment lien against persons who inherited the encumbered property).

REVIEW QUESTIONS

1. When does a judgment lien arise?

2. C gets a judgment against D in County Y and dockets the judgment there. Does the lien of C's judgment reach D's lake property in County X?

3. C dockets a judgment against D in County X where the real estate records reflect that D owns lake property. These records do not reveal that, in an unrecorded transaction, D sold the property to Z one year before C won her judgment. Does C's judgment lien reach the lake property?

4. C records a judgment against D in County X where D owns lake property. D sells the property to A who sells it to B. Can C enforce her lien of judgment against B? Does C's judgment lien attach to the proceeds of either sale?

5. O and P both acquired and docketed judgments against D in County X where D owns lake property. O's judgment was first in time. How would you rank the judgment creditors' liens on the lake property? How would you rank their liens attaching to real property later acquired by D in County X?

6. C obtains a judgment against D in State A where the statute of limitations governing the enforcement of judgments is 20 years. Seven years later, C revives her judgment which had become dormant. Four years later, C files her judgment in State B where D has moved. State B's statute of limitations on the enforcement of judgments is ten years. If State B's statute of limitations is the controlling law, does the statute bar the enforcement of C's judgment there?

ENFORCING JUDGMENTS THROUGH EXECUTION

Analysis

115

Judgments are not self-executing. Creditors must take action to enforce them. The standard method of enforcing money judgments is execution, the process whereby a state actor (usually a sheriff) seizes and sells property of a debtor in satisfaction of a judgment against the debtor.

A. ISSUING THE WRIT OF EXECUTION

The process of execution to enforce a money judgment is begun by the issuance of a judicial writ of execution.

1. JUDGMENTS THAT SUPPORT ISSUANCE OF WRIT OF EXECUTION
a. Final Money Judgments
"[N]o valid writ of execution can be issued until a valid, final, viable, money judgment has been obtained by the creditor." W. Hawkland & P. Loiseaux, Cases and Materials on Debtor-Creditor Relations 40 (2d ed. 1979).

b. Of Courts Competent to Issue Execution
Execution cannot issue from a court that lacks the authority to enforce its judgments by the aid of a writ of execution. Yet, "[i]t may be assumed, as a general proposition, that every judicial tribunal having jurisdiction to pronounce judgment has authority to award execution. Exceptions to this rule must rest upon some clear and positive statutory limitation." 1 A. Freeman, A Treatise on the Law of Executions § 10 at 30 (3d ed. 1900).

2. WHEN WRIT OF EXECUTION WILL ISSUE
a. The Judgment Must Be Entered
Under early common law, the debtor's land was not affected by a judgment until the judgment had been docketed. Execution could issue against the debtor's personalty, however, as soon as the judgment was signed. The modern trend is to condition execution against any of the debtor's property on formalization of the judgment such as by docketing.

Example: In P's suit against D, the court wrote an opinion letter on May 18 declaring judgment for P. The court clerk received this letter the next day, but the judgment was not noted in the civil docket until May 31. Five days earlier, on May 26, P had caused execution to issue against land belonging to D; the property was subsequently sold by the sheriff to satisfy P's judgment. D argued that the proceedings against the land were void because the execution preceded the formal entry of the judgment. D prevailed on these facts in the case *Jackson v. Sears, Roebuck and Co.,* 83 Ariz. 20, 315 P.2d 871 (1957). By statute and rule of procedure in Arizona, a judgment is not effective for purposes of execution until the court clerk notes the judgment in the civil docket book.

b. Execution Must Not Be Stayed

1) Automatic Stay

Some states provide for an automatic stay of execution, such as ten or thirty days following the entry of judgment, see Ark. R. Civ. P. 62(a) (1988) (10 days); Tex. R. Civ. P. 627 (1988) (30 days), which often coincides with the time for making a motion for a new trial.

2) Effect Of Appeal

In most states, execution will be stayed while a judgment is appealed only if the trial or appellate court issues a *supersedeas writ,* which is usually conditioned on the appellant furnishing a bond as security for the appellee's judgment.

c. The Time for Issuing Execution Must Not Have Expired

1) Common-Law Rule

"By the common law, a plaintiff who had obtained a judgment in a personal action was compelled to attempt to execute it within a year and a day. If he failed to do so, the right to execution upon that judgment was forever gone." 1 A. Freeman, A Treatise On The Law Of Executions § 27 at 88 (3d ed. 1900).

2) Modern Statutory Rule

The common law rule has been changed by statute. A not unusual period within which execution must issue is now ten years, which in several states coincides with the length of the statute of limitations governing judgments. In other states, however, the execution period is shorter than the time for enforcing judgments. If the execution period lapses before the creditor has taken any steps toward collecting her judgment, the judgment becomes dormant; as a consequence, the creditor cannot execute against the debtor's property without first reviving the judgment. Revival is usually accomplished by a summary procedure that may involve nothing more than making a simple motion to revive the judgment. Of course, any attempt at revival must be made before expiration of the limitation period for the enforcement of the judgment.

3. HOW THE WRIT OF EXECUTION ISSUES

Typically, a writ of execution issues upon application of the judgment creditor to the clerk of the court that rendered the judgment or, in some states, the clerk of any other court in which the judgment has been docketed. The issuance of a writ of execution is essentially a ministerial act by the clerk. The clerk exercises no discretion in passing on the judgment creditor's application, and the writ cannot be denied for reasons other than failing to satisfy requirements of procedure and form.

4. **TO WHOM THE WRIT OF EXECUTION ISSUES**

In most states, the writ of execution is directed to the sheriff or, if the sheriff is absent from her jurisdiction or is interested in the case, some other county official, such as the coroner. Ordinarily, the writ can be addressed to any such official in the state.

5. **THE SHERIFF'S DUTY UNDER A WRIT OF EXECUTION**

A writ of execution names the parties in the case, refers to the judgment, identifies the court that rendered the judgment, states the amount of the judgment not yet paid, and directs the sheriff (or other official charged with enforcing the writ) to satisfy the balance of the judgment, with interest and costs, out of the judgment debtor's property by seizing, i.e., levying, on the property and selling it.

B. LEVYING ON THE DEBTOR'S PROPERTY

1. **PROPERTY SUBJECT TO LEVY AND SALE UNDER EXECUTION**
   a. **General Rule**

   "In general it may be said that all non-exempt personal property in tangible form may be taken at execution. In some states intangible personal property also is subject to execution, but most states hold otherwise and permit such property to be taken from the third-party obligor (i.e., the person obligated to the debtor on the account receivable, contract right or chose in action) only through garnishment or some similar third-party process." W. Hawkland & P. Loiseaux, Cases and Materials on Debtor-Creditor Relations 41 (2d ed. 1979). "Most non-exempt real estate interests are subject to execution, including non-possessory interests like vested remainders." Id. at 43.

   b. **Obligations Owed the Debtor**

   Execution reaches money, negotiable instruments and other obligations owed the debtor that have been reified, which means that an intangible right has been embodied in a writing and that transfer of the writing effects a transfer of the right itself. In most states, however, execution is not the process used to reach purely intangible obligations owed the debtor such as accounts and contract rights. This type of property is reached through garnishment or some similar third-party process. In garnishment, the creditor in effect sues a third party who holds property of, or who owes an obligation to, the debtor. The purpose of the suit is to force the third person, i.e., the garnishee, to release the debtor's property for the creditor's benefit or to pay to the creditor whatever sum the garnishee owes the debtor. Chapter V, infra, outlines fully the garnishment process, which in most states is both a pre- and post-judgment creditor's remedy.

   Whatever process is used to reach obligations owed the debtor, a common question is whether the process can reach unliquidated and contingent claims of the debtor:

1) Unliquidated Claims

Whether the debtor's intangible property is reached through execution or third party process, even unliquidated obligations owed the debtor are leviable. *Meacham v. Meacham*, 262 Cal. App. 2d 248, 68 Cal. Rptr. 746 (1968) (unliquidated contract right); *Woody's Olympia Lumber, Inc. v. Roney*, 9 Wash. App. 626, 513 P.2d 849 (1973) (undetermined and unliquidated tort claim).

2) Contingent Debts

"When a debt has a present existence, although payable at some future day, it * * * may be reached by * * * [execution]; but the rule is otherwise where the debt rests upon a contingency that may or may not happen, and over which the court has no control." *Boisseau v. Bass' Adm'r*, 100 Va. 207, 210, 40 S.E. 647, 649 (1902).

The issue in the *Boisseau* case was whether or not the debtor had a leviable interest in an insurance policy. The policy apparently had no cash value, and the insurer had no obligations to the insured debtor until premiums for 20 full years had been paid. Debtor died, however, before the expiration of the 20 years but not until after the creditor had caused execution to issue. The court held that the creditor's execution did not reach the insurance policy because the policy did not constitute a present, fixed liability upon the insurer to pay the debtor anything; nor did it create any present indebtedness that the debtor could demand within the 20 years. Until the 20 years had expired the interest of the debtor in the policy was wholly contingent.

c. Contingent Remainder Interests in Land

"[T]he general rule is that all possible interests in land, contingent or otherwise, which are real and substantial, are subject to seizure and sale on execution, and that generally if the interest is assignable it is subject to execution. Where the contingencies are such, however, as to render the interest in the specific property a mere remote possibility, the difficulty in determining the value of the interest for sale upon execution gives strong practical and legal reasons for denial of the right to so levy." *Adams v. Dugan*, 196 Okl. 156, 159, 163 P.2d 227, 230–31 (1945). In the *Adams* case, Father died and his real estate passed to a Trustee who was authorized to dispose of the property. Initial beneficiary of trust was Mother, to whom trust income was payable. Upon Mother's death, income was to be paid to Children, one of whom was George. Before Mother's death a creditor of George caused the sheriff to execute on George's undivided one-third interest as remainderman in the real property that formed the corpus of the trust. Trustee sued to enjoin the sheriff's sale of the land. Trustee prevailed. The court reasoned that, inasmuch as George may never acquire any interest beyond that of a remainderman, the value to be placed presently on his contingent interest can be nothing more than mere speculation.

d. Exempt Property

Every state constitutionally or statutorily exempts some of a debtor's property from creditors' process, including execution. Exempt property ordinarily includes, for example, a homestead in real property, a certain amount of wages, some insurance, and a selection of goods that often includes a Bible and personal clothing. Federal law also provides for exemptions. Moreover, some forms of property which may not be exempted by statute may nevertheless be immune from process because of decisional law holding that the debtor's interest in the property is not alienable and thus is not leviable. Examples include property held by the entirety, spendthrift trusts, and causes of action or damages for personal injury. Exemptions and the like are outlined in detail in Chapter VIII infra.

e. Collateral

The debtor's property that is encumbered by a security interest of some kind is not for that reason immune from process. Ordinarily, the property may be levied on and the debtor's interest may be sold. U.C.C. § 9–311 makes this clear in the case of personal property that is collateral. Yet, if the debtor has defaulted under her agreement with the secured party so that this creditor is entitled to possession of the collateral under U.C.C. § 9–503, the property may not be leviable under execution issued by another creditor, at least not when the secured party's interest has priority over the other creditor's claim. *Murdock v. Blake,* 26 Utah 2d 22, 484 P.2d 164 (1971); cf. *Knapp v. McFarland,* 462 F.2d 935 (2d Cir. 1972) (sheriff can constructively levy on collateral held by a pledgee but cannot actually seize the property inasmuch as that would interfere with the pledgee's lawful possession).

Ordinarily, when the debtor's interest in collateral is sold under execution issued by a creditor other than the secured party, the sale is subject to the security interest if the interest is perfected and is entitled to priority over the execution creditor. This is not true in every state, however. For instance, Delaware law provides that the sale of collateral under execution is free and clear of all liens theretofore existing. *Maryland Nat. Bank v. Porter-Way Harvester Mfg. Co.,* 300 A.2d 8 (Del. 1972).

2. DECIDING WHAT PROPERTY TO LEVY ON

"Some jurisdictions accord the judgment debtor the right to designate the property which should be subjected to levy and sale, while others leave that choice to the sheriff and the judgment creditor, sometimes qualified by a mandate that real property shall be levied upon only if there are no leviable chattels." S. Riesenfeld, Creditors' Remedies And Debtors' Protection 89 (4th ed. 1987).

3. HOW LEVY IS EFFECTED
a. Real Estate

The usual method of levying on real estate is filing some sort of notice of levy in the county land records.

b. Goods

1) Physical Seizure Required Where Possible

To effect a levy, the sheriff physically seizes goods that are capable of manual delivery and holds them until the time for sale of the property. If the goods cannot easily be carted away by the sheriff, she may constructively levy on them as by posting notices that the property is in *custodia legis*, i.e., in custody of the law. Another form of constructive levy is filing a copy of the execution or other notice in the public records that give constructive notice of security interests created under Article 9 of the U.C.C. Minnesota provides for this form of levy on bulky articles. Minn. Stat. § 550.13 (1986).

2) Goods Covered by Documents of Title

When goods of the debtor are covered by a negotiable document of title, such as a warehouse receipt or a bill of lading, a creditor's process cannot compel the debtor's bailee, who actually holds the goods, to release them until the document of title is surrendered to her or impounded by a court. U.C.C. § 7–602.

c. Intangibles

1) Reaching Intangibles Through Garnishment

Purely intangible rights of the debtor that are not embodied in symbolic writings cannot, of course, be physically seized. They are usually gathered or collected through a proceeding called garnishment, which is aimed at the debtor's obligor, rather than through execution in its usual form. See Chapter V infra.

2) Negotiable Instruments

Negotiable instruments, such as notes and checks, made payable to the debtor evidence obligations owed to her. Yet, under modern practice, these debts are not collected for the creditor's benefit by garnishing the instruments' makers, drawers, or other obligors. Instead, because the rights against the obligors are embodied in the instruments, the sheriff seizes the instruments, and sells or enforces them, and pays the proceeds to the creditor.

3) Securities

Levies on stock and other securities owned by the debtor are governed by a host of special rules in Article 8 of the U.C.C. The basic rules are that a levy on a certificated security requires actual seizure and that, whenever uncertificated securities are involved, an effective levy is made by serving process upon the person controlling transfer. U.C.C. § 8–317(1) & (2).

An important exception applies when levying on a certificated security in the possession of a secured party who is holding the property as collateral for an obligatation owed it by the debtor. In this event, actual seizure is not required. Levy is effected through legal process on the secured party, U.C.C. § 8–317(3), such as by serving a copy of the writ of execution on the secured party and causing the issuance against it of a restraining no-tice. *Knapp v. McFarland,* 462 F.2d 935 (2d Cir. 1972).

4. ACTION FOLLOWING THE LEVY
a. Sheriff Must Make a Timely Return
1) The Meaning of a "Return"
The writ will specify the period of time prescribed by statute (usually 60 or 90 days) within which the sheriff must make a *return* of the writ. In making a return, the sheriff reports her success in satisfying the judgment or the property she has seized toward that end.

In describing the property seized under a writ of execution, the sheriff must do so with "particularity and distinctness" in a manner as will rea-sonably identify it or afford a means of identification. *W.E. Stephens Manufacturing Co. v. Miller,* 429 S.W.2d 384 (Ky. 1968). If the description is inadequate, the execution is ineffective.

2) The Effect of a Sale After the Return Date
The return date limits the life of the writ. After its return date, a writ becomes functus officio, i.e., a task performed, whether or not the sheriff actually returns the writ. Thus, if a sheriff levies on property after the return date of the execution and sells the property, the sale is void. *Hicks v. Bailey,* 272 S.W.2d 32 (Ky. 1954) The rule in a majority of juris-dictions, however, is that "a sale of property, whether real or personal, af-ter the return date of the writ of execution is valid and not subject to at-tack so long as the property sold was levied on before the return date." S. Riesenfeld, Cases and Materials on Creditors' Remedies and Debtors' Protection 87 (3d ed. 1979).

b. The Meaning Of A Return "Nulla Bona"
By making a return *nulla bona,* the sheriff indicates that she has failed to find any property of the debtor that is subject to levy and sale under execu-tion.

c. Subsequent Writs
In the event of a return nulla bona, or in the event that the first writ results in only partial satisfaction of the judgment, the judgment creditor may cause a second (*alias*) and further (*pluries*) writs to issue. "It is not necessary that the plaintiff should be able to point to any specific statutory provision giving him a right to an additional writ. It is sufficient that the judgment in his favor remains wholly or partly unsatisfied and that the time within which exe-cution may issue thereon has not terminated. The right to such further writs * * * may be regarded as a common-law right." 1 A. Freeman, A Treatise on the Law of Executions § 48 at 222 (3d ed. 1900).

C. SELLING THE PROPERTY

Property on which the sheriff levies is not turned over to the judgment creditor in satisfaction of her claim. Rather, the sheriff sells the property and gives the net proceeds, after paying the costs of the sale, to the creditor. Any surplus ordinarily goes to the debtor.

1. SUBJECT OF THE SALE

Property levied on by the sheriff is the subject of the sale. Yet, the sheriff is permitted to sell only so much of the debtor's property as is necessary to satisfy the execution creditor's judgment and the costs of the sale. In *Griggs v. Miller,* 374 S.W.2d 119 (Mo. 1963), the sheriff levied on and sold the debtor's 322 acre farm, valued at $50,000 to $90,000, to satisfy a $2000 judgment. The court cancelled the execution sale because, " '[i]f the property can be divided without prejudice, and a part will sell for the debt and costs, a part only shall be sold.' " Id. at 124 (quoting *Gordon v. Hickman,* 96 Mo. 350, 356, 9 S.W. 920, 92122 (1888)).

2. MANNER OF THE SALE

Usually, the execution sale is by public auction. The sheriff's conduct of the sale is thoroughly regulated in most states by detailed statutes prescribing when the sale shall take place, how the sale will be advertised, and how and where it will be conducted.

3. INSURING A FAIR PRICE

Most states have statutes designed to protect judgment debtors from the sale of property at execution sales for unfairly low prices.

    a. Appraisal Statutes

    These statutes generally provide (1) that an appraisal of the subject property must be made before the sale and (2) either that an execution sale must produce not less than a stated percentage of the appraised value or that a stated percentage of the appraised value must be credited on the debt.

    b. Redemption

      1) The Right of Redemption

      Redemption is another statutory device providing some protection against inadequate bidding. Generally, the right of redemption extends only to the execution debtor or her grantee and is limited to the repurchase, within a stated time and at a stated price, of real property. Some states, however, permit redemption of personal property; and some states have extended the right of redemption to junior lienors of the debtor.

      2) Redemption of Real Property Reinstates Judgment Lien

      Where real property is sold under execution to enforce a judgment lien, the lien will be reinstated upon redemption of the property by the execution debtor or her grantee. *Ford v. Nokomis State Bank,* 135 Wash. 37, 237 P. 314 (1925).

c. Vacating An Execution Sale Because Of Inadequacy Of Sale Price
While most states do not require judicial confirmation of an execution sale, the court from which the execution issued may, for sufficient cause shown, vacate a sale. As a general rule, however, "mere inadequacy of price, where the parties stand on an equal footing and there are no confidential relations between them, is not, in and of itself, sufficient to authorize vacation of the sale unless the inadequacy is so gross as to be proof of fraud or shocks the conscience of the court." *Wiesel v. Ashcraft,* 26 Ariz. App. 490, 494, 549 P.2d 585, 589 (1976). In the *Wiesel* case, a mortgagor asked the court to set aside the sheriff's sale of his home. The property was purchased by two employees of the original mortgagee who bid one dollar more than the mortgage debt. This amount was less than half of the property's fair market value. Nevertheless, the court upheld the sale.

Although the mere inadequacy of price is not sufficient in itself to vacate an execution sale, it may be considered together with other circumstances; and slight irregularities, when coupled with the low price, may well justify setting aside the sale.

4. TITLE ACQUIRED BY EXECUTION PURCHASER: "BUYER BEWARE"
As a general rule, a purchaser at any execution sale acquires only such title as the debtor had.

a. Where the Debtor Had No Title
There are no warranties of title implied in a forced sale of property such as an execution sale. The rule of *caveat emptor* applies. Thus, if the debtor had no title whatsoever and the execution buyer must account to the property's true owner, there is no right of reimbursement from the judgment creditor.

b. Where the Debtor's Title Was Encumbered
1) General Rule
The purchaser at an execution sale stands in the debtor's shoes with respect to infirmities of title. Generally, therefore, the purchaser takes the title subject to such liens and encumbrances and the like as the property was affected (subject to) in the hands of the execution debtor. See the vast collection of cases at Annot., 68 A.L.R. 659 (1930). There are exceptions, however.

2) Exception: Where Law Provides for Execution Sales Free and Clear of Encumbrances
In Delaware, the purchaser of goods at an execution sale takes title free and clear of all liens theretofore existing. *Maryland Nat. Bank v. Porter-Way Harvester Mfg. Co.,* 300 A.2d 8 (Del. 1972).

Example: Seller of equipment obtained judgment against the Buyer for the price of the goods and caused the equipment to be seized and sold under execution. The equipment was subject to a prior, perfected Article 9 security interest in favor of Bank, whose claim to the property was superior to the Seller's claim.

See U.C.C. § 9–301(1)(b). The execution sale nevertheless discharged the Bank's interest. "Chattels sold at an execution sale should be sold free and clear of all encumbrances in order to ensure the highest price and to stimulate bidding. The creditor with the highest priority is not prejudiced in his reliance on the value of the chattel to secure the debt since he is satisfied first from the proceeds." Id. at 12.

3) Exception: Where Recording Laws Provide Protection of the Purchaser
A) Real Estate
Recording statutes in many jurisdictions protect buyers of real estate at execution sales from secret liens and interests. If the statute does not explicitly include such buyers as a class protected from unrecorded interests, decisional law may categorize execution buyers as bona fide purchasers, which is a class of claimants always protected by recording statutes.

B) Goods
An execution buyer of goods, as a buyer not in the ordinary course of business, should take free of an unperfected security interest in the property to the extent that she gives value and receives delivery of the goods without knowledge of the security interest. U.C.C. § 9–301(1)(c).

4) Exception: Where Buyer Is Sheltered by Judgment Creditor's Priority
Even if a purchaser at an execution sale is herself unprotected by real estate recording statutes or U.C.C. Article 9, she should take free of any encumbrances that were subordinate to the execution creditor's lien on the property.

> *Example:* Bank acquired an Article 9 security interest in Debtor's boat. Creditor got a judgment against Debtor and caused the sheriff to levy execution on the boat. This levy gave Creditor an execution lien on the property. (See Chapter III. D. infra.) At the execution sale of the boat, a Bank representative appeared and announced the existence of the Bank's security interest. Buyer purchases the boat and takes free of the Bank's interest even though she knew of it. Buyer is not shielded by U.C.C. § 9–301(1)(c), which protects innocent, non-ordinary course buyers from unperfected security interests, but Buyer is sheltered by the priority of Creditor's execution lien over the Bank's security interest under U.C.C. § 9–301(1)(b).

c. **Where Debtor's Title Was Subject to Latent Equities or Other Defects in Title**
Even in jurisdictions where judgment creditors qua lienors and buyers at execution sales are protected against secret encumbrances and conveyances, they may not be protected against other latent equities or other assorted defects in

the debtor's title. S. Riesenfeld, Cases and Materials on Creditors' Remedies and Debtors' Protection 137 (3d ed. 1979).

D. LIEN OF EXECUTION

A creditor's judgment, when docketed, typically creates a lien on the debtor's real property. See Chapter II supra. Only in a few states does the judgment lien reach personal property. Virtually everywhere, however, the process of execution gives rise to an execution lien that can reach any of the debtor's leviable property, including personal property.

1. ATTACHMENT AND DURATION OF THE LIEN OF EXECUTION
a. Majority Rule
1) Lien Attaches at Time of Levy

In the majority of states, the sheriff's levy itself creates an execution lien on the property that is seized. Thus, for the purpose of determining priorities, the lien dates from the time of the levy.

2) Life of the Lien

If there is no levy before the writ's return date, so that the writ becomes *functus officio,* no lien is created. If, however, the sheriff seizes property before the writ expires, a lien arises upon levy; but this lien does not continue indefinitely. "At common law this lien survived a return on which the levy was endorsed and continued until the sale of the chattels, unless the creditor released the chattels or engaged in dilatory tactics constituting a waiver or abandonment of his rights. A few jurisdictions have adopted specific limitations on the duration of levy liens." S. Riesenfeld, Creditors' Remedies and Debtors' Protection 173 (3d ed. 1979); see, e.g., Cal. Civ. Proc. Code § 688 (1980) (one year) (repealed by Stats. 1982, c. 1364, § 1), which was applied in the case *Puissegur v. Yarbrough,* 29 Cal. 2d 409, 175 P.2d 830 (1946); see also *Domby v. Heath,* 327 Mich. 29, 41 N.W.2d 325 (1950) (lien of execution expires five years after levy); *Woods v. Wilson,* 341 Mo. 479, 108 S.W.2d 12 (1937) (execution lien expires at the end of second term of court after issuance).

b. Minority Rule
1) Lien Attaches at Time Writ Is Delivered

In a minority of states, the lien dates from the time that the writ of execution is delivered to the sheriff. In some of these jurisdictions the execution lien is described as a general, inchoate lien attaching to all the debtor's leviable property within the county, which is made specific or perfected by levy; in other jurisdictions the levy is seen as creating a specific lien that relates back to the delivery of the writ to the sheriff. In any event, for the purpose of determining priorities, the execution lien dates from the time of delivery of the writ to the sheriff.

2) Lien Reaches After-Acquired Property

As long as the writ of execution is in force, the lien attaches to after-acquired property of the debtor. Thus, leviable property acquired by the debtor after the writ is delivered to the sheriff may be seized by the sheriff and sold under execution.

3) Life of the Lien

Where the execution lien arises upon delivery of the writ to the sheriff, the lien terminates after the writ's return day if there has been no levy or sooner if the writ is returned nulla bona. *In re Continental Midway Corp.*, 185 F. Supp. 867 (D. Md. 1960); *Illi, Inc. v. Margolis*, 267 Md. 30, 296 A.2d 412 (1972). An *alias* writ creates a lien from that writ's delivery to the sheriff and does not in every jurisdiction extend the life of the original lien.

If the sheriff successfully levies, any general lien that arose upon delivery of the writ is extinguished; a specific lien continues only on the property the sheriff has seized. 2 J. Poe, Pleading and Practice § 668 (4th ed. 1969); A. Freeman, A Treatise on the Law of Judgments §§ 268 & 269 (1876). This specific lien ordinarily continues until the property is sold unless its life is cut short by a statute limiting the period of the lien's existence.

2. TERRITORIAL REACH OF EXECUTION LIEN

An execution lien ordinarily extends to all of the debtor's leviable property located within the bailiwick of the official to whom the writ of execution is delivered, which usually is limited to one county in the state. Florida law has been interpreted, however, to subject all of a debtor's leviable property, wherever located in the state, to a lien of execution upon delivery of the writ to any sheriff. *In re Vero Cooling & Heating, Inc.*, 11 B.R. 359 (Bkrtcy.S.D. Fla. 1981) (interpreting Fla. Stat. Ann. § 56.031 (West 1969)); but see *In re Belize Airways Ltd.*, 19 B.R. 840 (Bkrtcy.S.D. Fla. 1982) ("Florida adheres to the common law rule that an execution lien is obtained on the personal property of the debtor, located in a particular county, when the writ of execution is delivered to the sheriff of that county.").

3. RELATIONSHIP BETWEEN JUDGMENT LIENS AND EXECUTION

Remember that judgment liens on real estate are usually enforced through execution. See Chapter II supra. The question thus arises whether the judgment creditor's priority as to such collateral dates from the time the judgment lien first attached or from the time of execution. Professor Riesenfeld reports that "[a] sheriff's sale held under an execution issued and levied for the enforcement of the judgment creating the lien will pass the debtor's title as of the date when the judgment lien attached, *if such lien still subsists at the time of the sale.*" S. Riesenfeld, Cases and Materials on Creditors' Remedies and Debtors' Protection 129 (3d ed. 1979).

Example: Cobbs recovered a judgment against Bower on April 25, 1876. Board recovered a judgment against the same debtor on December 12, 1877. Both Cobbs and Board acquired judgment liens on Bower's real estate. State law provided that any lien of judgment terminates after ten years from the date of the judgment. The Cobbs judgment was enforced through execution issued on April 13, 1886, whereby the sheriff sold land of the debtor on May 15, 1886. The Board judgment was similarly enforced on August 6, 1877, by the sheriff selling the same parcel of land. The question is which execution buyer has the better title to the land. The winner is the buyer who purchased the property at the Board sale. By the time of the sale to enforce the Cobbs judgment, there was no lien on the property. Ten years had passed from the time the Cobbs judgment was obtained. Causing execution to issue within the ten-year period did not have the effect of continuing the judgment lien. *Wells v. Bower,* 126 Ind. 115, 25 N.E. 603 (1890).

The result in *Wells* is easily understood if the execution itself did not create a lien on the land or if it gave rise to a lien that lapsed upon expiration of the ten-year period. In some states, an execution lien attaches to real estate just as it does to personal property. In these states it is possible, if the execution lien attaches before the judgment lien expires, that the former lien will relate back to the inception of the latter. *Bank of Missouri v. Wells & Bates,* 12 Mo. 361 (1849). There is substantial authority to the contrary, however.

4. PRIORITY OF EXECUTION LIENS
a. Execution Lienors *Inter Se*
1) Where Lien Dates From Delivery
In states where an execution lien arises upon delivery of the writ of execution to the sheriff, priority among execution creditors is usually determined according to the order in which their writs were delivered to the officer. But, if writs are delivered to different officers, as in the case where sheriffs of different counties pursue the same property, priority between the execution creditors is determined in some states according to the order in which levies are made.

2) Where Lien Dates From Levy
In states where the lien of execution dates from the time of actual levy by the sheriff, "[t]he execution first levied * * * has the first lien on the property, though there may be others in the hands of the sheriff, which were delivered to him before the one levied." *Albrecht v. Long,* 25 Minn. 163, 172 (1878). This rule applies even though the universal rule is that executions should be levied in the order in which the writs are received.

b. Prior Claims and Interests
1) General Rule
As a general rule, an execution lien attaches to whatever title or interest the debtor has, subject to all prior equities, including existing liens, mortgages, and other claims and interests.

2) **Exception: Where Recording Statute Protects Execution Creditor From Secret Interests**

a) **Real Property**

Real estate recording statutes in some states include execution creditors among the classes protected from unrecorded conveyances. In these jurisdictions, an execution lien would thus have priority over any unrecorded interest required to be recorded.

b) **Personal Property**

i) **General Rule**

An Article 9 security interest is subordinate to the rights of one who became a lien creditor (as through execution) before the security interest was perfected. U.C.C. § 9–301(1)(b). This Code provision determined the outcome in the case *Heinicke Instruments Co. v. Republic Corp.*, 543 F.2d 700 (9th Cir. 1976). In the *Heinicke* case, Bergman made a loan to Block and received an Article 9 security interest in stock of Heinicke Instruments Co. Block was then president and a director of Heinicke. The stock was never actually delivered to Bergman, who had to take possession of the stock in order to perfect his security interest. A lien creditor attached the stock and was awarded priority under U.C.C. § 9–301(1)(b). The court rejected Bergman's argument that the issuing company was his agent for possession of the stock.

ii) **Exception: Delay In Perfecting Purchase-Money Security Interest Is Excused**

A lien creditor does not prevail over a purchase-money security interest that is unperfected when the lien attaches if the security interest is thereafter perfected by filing either before or within ten days after the debtor receives possession of the collateral. U.C.C. § 9–301(2). This provision has been amended in some states to allow the secured party twenty days of grace rather than only ten. A purchase-money security interest is a security interest taken or retained by the seller of the collateral to secure all or part of its price, or taken by a person who, by making advances or incurring an obligation, gives value to enable the debtor to acquire rights in or, use of the collateral if such value is in fact so used. U.C.C. § 9–107.

So, if ABC Equipment Co. sells a bulldozer on credit and retains a security interest in the goods, it has ten (or twenty) days after the debtor takes possession of the collateral within which to file a financing statement and thereby perfect its interest. If it perfects within that period, ABC will have priority over a subsequent execution creditor, even one who becomes a lien creditor before ABC files its financing statement.

The same result would follow if the buyer had borrowed the purchase price of the bulldozer from a bank that was given a security interest in the property. The bank's interest in such a case would be a purchase money security interest under U.C.C. § 9–107(b), and thus would be entitled to the extraordinary protection of § 9–301(2).

c.   Subsequent Claims and Interests

1)   General Rule

An execution lien ordinarily takes priority over subsequent claims and interests. This rule generally applies not only in states where the lien dates from the time of levy, but also in most jurisdictions that adhere to the rule that an execution lien dates from the time the writ is delivered to the sheriff. In the latter jurisdictions, the result in some cases is to subject even bona fide purchasers to a lien that exists only secretly between the time of the writ's delivery and the time of the sheriff's levy.

2)   Limitation on the General Rule: Loss of Priority Through Delay in Enforcing the Writ

A creditor may lose a priority gained by first delivery (or first levy) if the execution becomes "dormant." The classic explanation of dormancy, as the term is used in this context, is that given by the court in *Excelsior Needle Co. v. Globe Cycle Works,* 48 A.D. 304, 309–310, 62 N.Y.S. 538, 540–41 (1900): "The law is quite clear that the object of the execution is to enforce the judgment debt, and not to convert it into a security upon the property, and still allow the judgment debtor to prosecute his business regardless of the lien of execution." In the words of a leading commentary, " 'it is not the mere issuing or delivery of the writ which creates a lien, but an issuing and delivery for the purpose of execution. The execution of a writ for the purpose of making or keeping it effective as a lien cannot stop with a mere levy upon the property. If the officer is instructed by the plaintiff not to sell till further orders, the lien of the execution and levy becomes subordinate to that of any subsequent writ placed in the officers' hands for service.' * * * The law, therefore, seems to be settled that *any direction by the execution creditor to the sheriff which suspends the lien or delays the enforcement of the levy renders the execution dormant against subsequent creditors or bona fide purchasers.* However veiled may be the direction, however much it may be founded on a humane desire to protect the debtor, if it is tantamount to a mandate or instruction to the sheriff to withhold the execution of his process, during the interim that he accedes to this demand the levy ceases to be effective. That doctrine rests on public policy, and is necessary to prevent fraud, and it should receive a fairly rigorous enforcement." 2 A. Freeman, A Treatise on the Law of Executions § 206 (3d ed. 1900).

Not every delay in enforcing a writ of execution results in subordination of the execution lien, however. In *Illi, Inc. v. Margolis,* 267 Md. 30, 296 A.2d 412 (1972), two creditors caused the sheriff to levy execution on goods of the debtor; but the creditors directed the sheriff to leave the property with the debtor as long as the debtor made weekly payments on the judgments against him. The goods remained with the debtor for a period of six months, at the end of which the debtor conveyed her property to a trustee pursuant to an assignment for the benefit of creditors. The trustee argued that she was entitled to priority over the execution creditors whom, the trustee argued, had permitted their execution liens to become dormant. The court rejected the argument: "A speedy levy was made and nothing these [execution creditors] subsequently did was inconsistent with or indicated a relinquishment of that purpose. Their acceptance of the payments was consonant with the maintenance of the levy and was neither a constructive abandonment of it nor an abuse of the writ. This distinguishes the case here [from another case] where, under affirmative instructions of the creditor, no activity was ever undertaken to consummate the lien. We are not now confronted by a case where there was total inaction after the lien was consummated as the installment payments were accepted to reduce the debt. We recognize that through lack of good faith in obtaining the writ or improper action or inaction in executing it priorities can be lost. Likewise, a case may arise where the lien is left dormant for such an inordinate time as to evidence abandonment of it, but we do not think the six month delay here, coupled with the active pursuit of payment, creates such a case." Id. at 42, 296 A.2d at 419.

3) **Displaced Exception to the General Rule: Subsequent Purchase Money Security Interest**
In *Robinson v. Wright,* 90 Colo. 417, 9 P.2d 618 (1932), in which there was a conflict between a purchase-money chattel mortgage retained by the seller of goods and an execution lien on the property that arose before the mortgage was recorded upon delivery of the writ to the sheriff, the court held that the chattel mortgage had priority. The court reasoned that the debtor never had an interest in the property that was subject to the execution lien. This holding is clearly displaced by Article 9 of the Uniform Commercial Code. U.C.C. § 9–311 establishes that the debtor's rights in collateral, including collateral secured by a purchase money security interest, can be transferred voluntarily or involuntarily to other creditors. If the *Robinson* case should arise under Article 9, the execution creditor would prevail, § 9–301(1)(b) (negative implication), unless the security interest was automatically perfected or protected under § 9–301(2) (superpriority where perfection is within ten days after debtor took possession of the collateral).

d. **Execution Lienor Versus Bankruptcy Trustee**
As a very general rule, all liens on a debtor's property, including execution liens, are enforceable against the debtor's estate and her trustee in bankruptcy. There are many exceptions to this rule. The bankruptcy trustee and sometimes the bankrupt debtor herself are empowered by federal bankruptcy law to avoid certain liens and other transfers of interests in the debtor's property. The greatest threats to the enforceability of an execution lien in bankruptcy are these provisions of the federal Bankruptcy Code: § 522(f) (11 U.S.C.A. § 522(f)), which allows the debtor to avoid judicial liens on exempt property,

and § 547(b) (11 U.S.C.A. § 547(b)), which avoids preferential transfers, including liens, occurring usually within 90 days before the bankruptcy petition is filed. Chapters XX and XXI, infra, of this outline provide thorough explanations of §§ 522(f), 547(b) and the other powers of avoidance in bankruptcy.

E. EXECUTION FROM FEDERAL COURT

Federal Rule of Civil Procedure 69(a) provides that "[p]rocess to enforce a judgment for the payment of money shall be a writ of execution, unless the court directs otherwise."

1. STATE PROCEDURE USUALLY GOVERNS

Generally, the procedure governing execution from federal district court "shall be in accordance with the practice and procedure of the state in which the district court is held, existing at the time the remedy is sought * * *." Fed. R. Civ. P. 69(a).

a. Consult Law of State Where Enforcement Sought

Rule 69(a) directs that enforcement of a federal writ of execution is governed by the procedure of the state *in which the district court is held.* This directive is easily applied when enforcement of a judgment is sought in the state where the judgment was rendered. But which state's law governs enforcement of a federal judgment in a state other than the one in which the judgment was rendered? Ordinarily, the governing law in such a case is that of the state in which enforcement of the judgment is sought, not that of the state where the judgment was rendered. 12 C. Wright & A. Miller, Federal Practice and Procedure § 3012 at 65 (1973). Enforcement in the other state, however, will usually require registration of the judgment there.

b. Federal Law May Override State Procedure

There is a caveat to the general rule that state procedure governs execution issued from federal court. State procedure will not apply to the extent that "any statute of the United States governs." Fed. R. Civ. P. 69(a). "Thus if there is an applicable federal statute, it is controlling, as is also any relevant Civil Rule, since those rules have the force of a statute." 12 C. Wright & A. Miller, Federal Practice and Procedure § 3012 at 63 (1973). "In the main, though, federal statutes do not deal with most problems; and relative to some problems merely provide, indirectly or directly, that state law shall govern." 7 (pt. 2) J. Moore & J. Lucas, Moore's Federal Practice paragraph 69.04[2] at 69–18 (1983). Mentioned next are a few of the federal statutes that deal with some aspects of execution and override state law.

2. STAY OF EXECUTION
a. Ten-Day Waiting Period

"[N]o execution shall issue upon a judgment nor shall proceedings be taken for its enforcement until the expiration of 10 days after its entry." Fed. R. Civ. P. 62(a).

b. Stay Upon Appeal

Execution of a federal court judgment will be stayed upon the debtor's appeal of the judgment only if she provides a supersedeas bond that is approved by the court. Fed. R. Civ. P. 62(d).

3. MARSHALS ENFORCE WRITS

Writs of execution issued by federal district courts are usually enforced by United States marshals. 28 U.S.C.A. § 569(b) (1968); Fed. R. Civ. P. 4(c)(1).

4. TERRITORIAL REACH OF A FEDERAL WRIT
a. General Rule: State-Wide Reach

"[A] writ of execution [issued from a federal district court] may run and be served anywhere within the territorial limits of the state in which the district court is held that rendered the judgment, although a state writ of execution will not run throughout the state." 7 (pt. 2) J. Moore & J. Lucas, Moore's Federal Practice paragraph 69.04[2] at 69–17 (2d ed. 1983); see Fed. R. Civ. P. 4(f).

b. Exception Permitting Nation-Wide Reach

"While a writ of execution cannot generally be executed beyond the territorial limits of the state in which the issuing court sits, a writ obtained for the use of the United States may be executed in any state or the District of Columbia." 11 Fed. Proc., L. Ed. 31:62 at 247 (1982); see 28 U.S.C.A. § 2413. In such a case, "[s]ince Rule 69 [of the Federal Rules of Civil Procedure] makes applicable 'the practice and procedure of the state in which the district court is held,' the law of Pennsylvania, authorizing attachment execution upon bank deposits, permitted execution of that kind in New York on a judgment in favor of the United States from a district court in Pennsylvania, even though New York law did not allow that relief." 12 C. Wright & A. Miller, Federal Practice and Procedure § 3012 at 65 (1973) (summarizing *United States ex rel. Marcus v. Lord Electric Co.,* 43 F. Supp. 12 (W.D. Pa. 1942)).

5. FEDERAL EXECUTION LIENS

Liens of execution based on federal judgments are governed by the law of the state in which the district court is held. 10 Cyclopedia Of Federal Procedure § 36.23 at 260 (F. Poore & E. Koeber 3d ed. 1968). Federal Rule of Civil Procedure 69(a) is consistent with this view in that it refers broadly to the "*procedure* on execution" in deferring to state law for the rules on execution that will be observed in federal court.

a. Attachment of Federal Execution Liens

The most recent cases suggest that the time at which a federal execution lien attaches depends on the law of the state where the judgment is being executed. Thus, the court in *In re Cone,* 11 B.R. 925, 928–29 (Bkrtcy. M.D. Fla. 1981), applied Florida law and concluded that, just as the execution of state court judgments results in an execution lien upon delivery of the writ to the sheriff, the execution of a federal judgment in Florida will create an execution lien upon delivery of the writ to the United States marshal. On the other hand, the court in *S. Birch & Sons Constr. Co. v. Capehart,* 192 F. Supp. 330, 332 (D. Alaska 1961) applied Alaska law and concluded that a federal execution lien did not arise until the United States marshal actually levied the execution. Though the court in the latter case did not cite any federal authority for its application of Alaska law, the court in *In re Cone* mentioned both Federal Rule of Civil Procedure 69(a) and 28 U.S.C.A. § 1962.

b. Territorial Reach of Federal Execution Liens
In those states that follow the rule that an execution lien attaches upon delivery of the writ to the appropriate officer, questions will arise as to the territorial reach of the federal execution lien upon delivery of the writ to the United States marshal. Neither statutory nor decisional law provides certain answers. The logical possibilities are that (1) the territorial reach would be coextensive with the district which the United States marshal serves, see 28 U.S.C.A. § 569(a) (general powers and duties of marshals), or (2) the territorial reach could be state-wide by analogy to 28 U.S.C.A. § 1962 (providing state-wide reach of judgment liens in some cases) or Fed. R. Civ. P. 4(f) (providing for state-wide service of process including writs of execution).

REVIEW QUESTIONS

1. T or F   The sheriff acts automatically to collect a money judgment entered against a debtor.

2. Who issues a writ of execution?

3. What property of a debtor can be seized and sold through execution process?

4. T or F   Property seized under a writ of execution is turned over to the judgment creditor.

5. What is the significance of the return date of a writ of execution?

6. What kind of a return does a sheriff make when she has been unable to locate property of the debtor to seize and sell under a writ of execution?

7. How does a sheriff levy on IBM stock owned by the debtor?

8. T or F   The debtor can redeem any of her property that is seized under process of execution.

9. T or F   An execution sale can be set aside if the price paid for the property is very low in relation to its market value.

10. D owns lake property that is mortgaged to X. Can this property be seized and sold through execution process to satisfy a judgment of Z aganist D?

11. If the property referred to in Question 10 is sold at an execution sale, will the buyer take free of, or subject to, X's mortgage?

12. When does the lien of execution arise?

13. How does the lien of execution discussed in this chapter differ from the lien of judgment discussed in Chapter II?

14. D financed the purchase of a piece of heavy equipment with a loan from Local Bank. The loan was secured by an Article 9 security interest in the equipment. C won a judgment against D and initiated execution to enforce her judgment. The sheriff levied on the automobile and was preparing to sell it. Local Bank perfected its security interest and intervened in the execution proceeding, claiming that it had a better right to the equipment. Whose claim is entitled to priority, Local Bank's security interest or C's execution lien?

15. T or F   Execution to enforce judgments rendered by federal district courts is governed by state enforcement procedures.

*

IV

FINDING PROPERTY OF THE DEBTOR

Analysis

Consider this not unlikely case: A creditor wins a judgment, which the debtor ignores. The creditor thus causes execution to issue against the debtor's property. The sheriff dutifully acts to enforce the writ of execution but, alas, returns it *nulla bona* or unsatisfied. The judgment creditor is surprised and puzzled because she knows of the debtor's high standard of living. The creditor comes to you, her lawyer, for an explanation. The answer to the riddle is simple: A *nulla bona* return means only that the sheriff was unsuccessful in locating leviable assets of the debtor, not that the debtor has no such property. The debtor may well have nonexempt assets that are out of the sheriff's sight or easy reach. To find this property and apply it in satisfaction

137

of the judgment, the creditor need not surreptitiously shadow the debtor's every move or hire a private detective to stake out the debtor's home and office. The law provides remedies designed specifically to aid in discovering the debtor's hidden assets and in applying hard-to-reach assets to satisfy the creditor's judgment. A creditor's bill in equity (actually a set of creditors' bills) was the first of such remedies, but virtually every jurisdiction now has statutory substitutes of various kinds that are commonly collected under the generic heading of supplemental (sometimes supplementary) proceedings.

A. CREDITORS' BILLS

At early common law, execution from a law court would not reach the judgment debtor's intangible property, such as choses in action, or the debtor's equitable assets, such as a beneficial interest in property held in trust. Execution also would not reach property of the debtor held by third persons. The English Chancery thus developed a remedy for reaching these forms of a judgment debtor's property. This remedy is the judgment creditor's bill (sometimes referred to as a creditor's suit), which is the equitable counterpart to execution and garnishment at law. To help ferret out the debtor's equitable and hidden assets, equity also permitted the creditor, through a bill of discovery, to bring the debtor into court to answer questions under oath about the extent of the debtor's property and its whereabouts. There was a third bill available to creditors in equity through which they could set aside fraudulent conveyances of a debtor's property and remove all manner of legal obstructions blocking the normal execution process at law. These three equitable bills are frequently combined in practice and often referred to collectively by courts and commentators as a single creditor's bill or a creditor's suit. The following discussion adopts this common usage of the term "creditor's bill".

1. UNSATISFIED EXECUTION AS PREREQUISITE TO A CREDITOR'S BILL

The general rule is that a creditor's bill cannot be brought until judgment is obtained and execution is returned wholly or partially unsatisfied. The principal reason is the ancient requirement that legal remedies must be exhausted before equitable remedies are invoked. A "court of equity does not interfere to enforce the payment of debts until the creditor has exhausted all the remedies known to the law to obtain satisfaction on the judgment. It is essential, in order to give the court jurisdiction * * *." *Adsit v. Butler,* 87 N.Y. 585, 587 (1882). This requirement is still recited in recent cases involving creditors' bills despite the merger of law and equity in federal courts and in most states. *United States ex rel. Goldman v. Meredith,* 596 F.2d 1353, 1357 (8th Cir.), cert. denied sub nom., *Goldman v. Merrill Lynch, Pierce, Fenner & Smith,* 444 U.S. 838, 100 S.Ct. 76 (1979); *Schaeffer v. Zaltsman,* 29 Ill. App. 3d 1011, 1013–14, 331 N.E.2d 212, 214 (1975); *Young v. Wilkinson,* 22 Ill. App. 2d 304, 315, 160 N.E.2d 709, 714 (1959); but see *Huntress v. Estate of Huntress,* 235 F.2d 205, 208, 61 A.L.R.2d 682, 686 (7th Cir. 1956) (applying Fed. R. Civ. P. 18(b)). Nevertheless, there have always been exceptions to the general rule that the bringing of a creditor's bill in equity is conditioned on an unsatisfied execution at law. Among the most important exceptions are these two:

a. Exception Where Debtor Is a Nonresident

1) The Exception

There is substantial authority for the view that nonresidence or absence of the debtor from the jurisdiction obviates the necessity of a prior judgment at law, at least where such nonresidence or absence renders it impossible or impracticable to obtain a judgment. See cases collected in Annot., 38 A.L.R. 269 (1925); cf. *Shuck v. Quackenbush,* 75 Colo. 592, 603, 227 P. 1041, 1044 (1924) (holding that, without the prior recovery of a judgment at law and the return of execution unsatisfied, a general unsecured creditor could maintain a creditor's bill to reach his debtor's equitable interest in real estate where the debtor was a nonresident and a fugitive from justice and the equitable realty interest was his only property); but see *Hamburger Apparel Co. v. Werner,* 17 Wash. 2d 310, 135 P.2d 311 (1943). In the *Hamburger* case a creditor sought to reach the debtor's interest in an insurance policy, which really was an annuity contract. Because the debtor was a nonresident, the creditor filed a creditor's bill aimed at the insurer. The court recognized that, in essence, the action was in the nature of a garnishment (See infra Chapter V.), the statutory requirements of which had not been satisfied by the creditor. The court affirmed the dismissal of the creditor's bill because the garnishment "statute cannot be avoided by the subterfuge of bringing an equitable action against one alleged to be indebted to the principal defendant, or to have property in his possession belonging to the debtor." Id. at 320, 135 P.2d at 316.

2) Caveat: Remember *Shaffer v. Heitner*

In maintaining an equitable creditor's bill, a court is bound as in any other case to satisfy due process requirements. Accordingly, the court's exercise of jurisdiction with respect to the debtor or her property—whether *in rem* or *in personam*—must meet the "minimum contacts/fundamental fairness" test of *International Shoe Co. v. Washington,* 326 U.S. 310, 66 S. Ct. 154 (1945). See *Shaffer v. Heitner,* 433 U.S. 186, 97 S. Ct. 2569 (1977). Both of these cases and the whole subject of judicial jurisdiction are discussed earlier in Chapter I.B.1. *Shaffer* teaches that exercising even *quasi in rem* jurisdiction solely on the basis of the defendant having property in the forum is violative of due process requirements. Id. at 209, 87 S. Ct at 2582. Consequently, an action in the nature of a creditor's bill to reach and apply a debtor's property in satisfaction of a general creditor's claim cannot be maintained if the sole basis of the court's jurisdiction is the presence of the debtor's property in the state. There is no problem with *Shaffer,* however, if the creditor's bill is viewed (though it usually is not) as merely an extension of the creditor's main action for which a solid jurisdictional basis existed, or if the creditor's bill fits within the exception to *Shaffer* that relaxes due process requirements when the purpose of acquiring jurisdiction is to enforce a judgment.

b. Exception Where Creditor Seeks to Set Aside Fraudulent Conveyance

A debtor's fraudulent conveyance of property is void as against her creditors. (See infra Chapter VI.) Thus, if the property is real estate, the lien of the creditor's judgment (see supra Chapter II) will reach the property notwithstanding the conveyance; if the property is goods or chattels, it can be reached through execution. Yet, in either case, there is a cloud on the property's title, i.e., the bogus claim of the transferee. Most courts have long held that a creditor can sue in equity to remove such a cloud, and can have the property applied in satisfaction of her claim, without first having execution issued and returned unsatisfied. One line of authority demands, however, that the creditor cause execution to issue before seeking equitable relief; another line of authority, at least when the property involved is real estate, requires only that the creditor have a judgment. *Schofield v. Ute Coal & Coke Co.,* 92 Fed. 269 (8th Cir. 1899); *Wadsworth v. Schisselbaur,* 32 Minn. 84, 19 N.W. 390 (1884). A few cases permit a creditor to pursue a bill to set aside a fraudulent conveyance even before a judgment is recovered if the creditor has attached the subject property creating a lien in her favor. 4 J. Pomeroy, A Treatise On Equity Jurisprudence § 1415 at 1069 (S. Symons 5th ed. 1941). (Regarding attachment and attachment liens, see Chapter XI.) One commentator argued that there should be no such prerequisites whatsoever when a creditor seeks equity's aid in setting aside a fraudulent conveyance. "The requirement that the creditor first obtain a judgment at law before he can come into equity and have the conveyance set aside, seems to place a useless burden upon the creditor. Since he must of necessity come into equity eventually, why not allow him to come in the first instance * * *." Note, *Creditors' Rights in Equity,* 29 Mich. L. Rev. 1057, 1059 (1931). Modern rules and statutes agree, putting virtually no obstacles of any kind in the path of defrauded creditors suing to set aside fraudulent conveyances. See, e.g., Fed. R. Civ. P. 18(b); *American Sur. Co. of New York v. Conner,* 251 N.Y. 1, 7, 166 N.E. 783, 785 (1929) (concluding that the Uniform Fraudulent Conveyance Act abrogates the ancient rule whereby a judgment and lien were essential preliminaries to equitable relief against fraudulent conveyances); see also infra Chapter VI.

2. BRINGING A CREDITOR'S BILL

A creditor's bill is a separate action begun by filing a complaint or petition, the substance of which varies depending on the particular relief sought. A creditor seeking the widest possible relief will typically allege the inadequacy of legal relief, set forth every imaginable kind of equitable property and interests as belonging to the debtor, and describe if possible any particular assets sought to be reached and the positions of all persons made parties. The action will join as parties the judgment debtor and all persons holding any interests in or claims to the assets, or who will be affected by the relief asked. The prayer will ask that the defendant be compelled to make discovery of his property and that all dispositions of property made by him for his own benefit or in fraud of creditors be set aside. The prayer will also ask for any type of equitable decree, whether *in rem* or *in personam* in operation, that will procure the application of the assets to the satisfaction of plaintiff's judgment. Through summons or other appropriate process, all parties to the action will be served. D. Riddle, The Law and Practice in Proceedings Supplemental to Execution 2 (2d ed. 1882); Fornoff, *The Creditor's Bill,* 16 Ohio St. L. J. 32, 33 (1955).

3. **FORMS OF RELIEF UNDER A CREDITOR'S BILL**
Commenting on the utility of the creditor's bill, one author wrote: "It is not one clear-cut remedy, such as a judgment for debt or a decree of specific performance. It opens the arsenal door, and the creditor can pick a poinard or a field piece." Fornoff, *The Creditor's Bill,* 16 Ohio St. L. J. 32, 32 (1955). "The relief to be granted, whether intermediate or final, seems to include a large segment of the forms which an equity court may make available. * * * The arsenal door is indeed ajar, once the suit is begun." Id. at 33. Typical forms of relief include the following:

a. **Examination And Discovery**
The debtor can be brought before the court and questioned about her property and financial affairs.

b. **Injunction**
The court can enjoin the debtor and third parties from disposing of property that might be applied to the creditor's judgment.

c. **Sale of Property**
The court can effect a sale of non-exempt property uncovered through the proceeding or recovered from a fraudulent transferee so that the proceeds of the property can be applied in satisfaction of the creditor's claim.

d. **Receiver**
A receiver can be appointed to hold property of the debtor pending the outcome of the proceedings or to find and apply property of the debtor in satisfaction of the creditor's judgment.

e. **Assignment**
The debtor can be required to assign all her property to the receiver (even property that has not been disclosed) so as to facilitate the receiver's work.

f. **Contempt**
Anyone disobeying court orders issued in connection with the creditor's bill risks being held in contempt of court.

4. **THE LIEN RESULTING FROM A CREDITOR'S BILL**
a. **When the Lien Attaches**
The law judges had their lien of execution; the chancellors, not to be outdone, deemed that an equitable lien or equitable levy resulted from a creditor's bill, which is equity's counterpart to execution. The general rule is that, upon the commencement of a judgment creditor's bill, an equitable lien attaches to property of the debtor that is found and appropriated for the creditor's benefit. *Sterling Sav. and Loan Ass'n v. Schultz,* 71 Ill. App. 2d 94, 109, 218 N.E.2d 53, 61 (1966) (filing of creditor's bill resulted in a lien on the judgment debtor's beneficial interest under a land trust); *Nowka v. Nowka,* 157 Neb. 57, 66, 58 N.W.2d 600, 605 (1953) (service of process beginning a creditor's action to subject an equitable estate to the payment of a judgment gives a specific lien on the property that the creditor seeks to reach); *Cannon Mills, Inc. v. Spivey,*

208 Tenn. 419, 425, 346 S.W.2d 266, 269 (1961) (lien attaches by the filing of a creditor's bill without more). As the cited cases suggest, for the purpose of determining when an equitable lien arises from a creditor's bill and for other purposes, the definition of "commencement" varies among the states. In some places an action is commenced upon filing the action; in other places commencement awaits service of the necessary process.

1) Description of Property May Be Required
Some cases suggest that the lien arises whether or not property is specifically described in the creditor's bill. Sometimes, however, the lien's priority over other claims (especially other subsequent claims) depends on the bill describing the property involved in the priority dispute. Consequently, as property is discovered through use of a creditor's bill, the cautious creditor will amend her bill by including a description of the newfound property. The creditor may be required, alternatively or additionally, to file in some public place a separate written notice of her lawsuit and claim to the property. See, e.g., *Shuck v. Quackenbush,* 75 Colo. 592, 601–02, 227 P. 1041, 1045 (1924) (equitable lien arises upon commencement of creditor's bill and filing of notice of lis pendens).

2) Relationship Between Equitable Lien and Legal Lien on Same Property
When a creditor's bill is used against leviable property, the creditor may already have a lien, as will be the case when the property is real estate subject to the lien of judgment. Nevertheless, the creditor may also acquire an equitable lien on the property. But see *Chautauque County Bank v. Risley,* 19 N.Y. 369, 374 (1859) (creditor pursuing equitable remedy abandons the lien of her judgment). This equitable lien may be of more lasting value than the lien of judgment. In *Thomas v. Richards,* 13 Ill. 2d 311, 148 N.E.2d 740 (1958), the creditor won a judgment and shortly thereafter filed a creditor's bill seeking to reach certain real estate that the debtors had earlier deeded to a son. The litigation remained dormant for more than seven years, and the creditor's original judgment lien expired. The court held, however, that the equitable lien resulting from the creditor's bill survived. "[I]t was wholly unimportant that the final decree establishing the [equitable] lien and ordering a sale was not rendered until long after the judgment at law had ceased to be a lien * * * upon the real estate of the judgment [debtor]." Id. at 318, 148 N.E.2d at 744. The *Thomas* case is the subject of Recent Decisions, *Creditor's Suit,* 47 Ill. B. J. 503 (1959). Compare *Miller & Co. v. Melone,* 11 Okl. 241, 255–58, 67 P. 479, 483–84 (1901) (the filing of a creditor's bill does not suspend or toll the running of a statute of limitations governing the vitality of the judgment itself). For a collection of cases similar to *Miller & Co.,* see Annot., *Suspension or Removal of Bar of Statute of Limitations as Against Judgment,* 21 A.L.R. 1038, 1049–53 (1922).

b. **Priority of the Lien**
The law regarding the priority of an equitable lien relative to other claims to and interests in the debtor's property is unclear. In fact, the law on this sub-

ject is a mess, principally because of the overlap among common law, equitable, and statutory remedies; the overlay of legal and equitable rights and interests; and the lack of uniformity among the states with respect to relevant governing principles. The almost endless number of possible combinations of claims, claimants and jurisdictions means that there are very few common denominators in cases deciding the priority of equitable liens. Bear this in mind when considering the following *very* general rules which, as far as general rules go, are uncommonly unreliable.

1) Inferiority to Existing Liens and Rights
   An equitable lien arising from a creditor's bill is usually subordinate to then existing liens on or rights to the specific property affected by the bill. Note, *Priorities of Creditors Under Judgment Creditor's Bills,* 42 Yale L. J. 919, 928 (1933). The equitable lien may, however, have priority over an existing interest that has not been recorded as required by law if the equitable lienor is within the class of persons intended to be protected by the recording statute.

   > *Example:* David purchased 40 acres of land in Colorado and, while indebted, fraudulently conveyed the property to his wife, Cora. On August 16, 1916, David and Cora deeded the land to the Quackenbushes. Before this transaction was recorded, Shuck filed a creditor's bill seeking to subject the 40 acres to the satisfaction of a claim (based on a foreign judgment) against David. Shuck prevailed in the action, and the property was sold to him in a court ordered sale. The Quackenbushes eventually recorded their deed and sued to quiet title to the property. The court held that Shuck's rights were superior because he acquired an equitable lien on the property before the Quackenbush deed was recorded. "[O]ur recording act, as between the holder of an unrecorded deed and the holder of an incumbrance such as an equitable lien, prefers the latter * * *." *Shuck v. Quackenbush,* 75 Colo. 592, 606, 227 P. 1041, 1047 (1924).

2) Superiority Over Subsequent Claimants
   Except where recording statutes dictate otherwise, the beneficiary of an equitable lien resulting from a creditor's bill is usually entitled to priority over claimants of the property who acquired their interests after the equitable lien attached. See, e.g., *Sterling Sav. and Loan Ass'n v. Schultz,* 71 Ill. App. 2d 94, 109, 218 N.E.2d 53, 61 (1966) (property transferred from one spouse to another under court order); *Cannon Mills, Inc. v. Spivey,* 208 Tenn. 419, 429–30, 346 S.W.2d 266, 271 (1961) (property levied on under writ of execution). This result may be conditioned, however, on the creditor's bill containing a specific description of the property. Ward, *Ordering the Judicial Process Lien and the Security Interest Under Article Nine: Meshing Two Different Worlds: Part I—Secured Parties and Post-Judgment Judicial Process Creditors,* 31 Me. L. Rev. 223, 256–57 (1980).

Subordinating the rights of subsequent claimants is supported by the common law doctrine of *lis pendens*. This doctrine provides that those who acquire interests in property involved in litigation take subject to the outcome, at least when the property is real estate. J. Moore & W. Phillips, Debtors' and Creditors' Rights 2187 (4th ed. 1975). "Its purpose is to prevent a judgment or decree from being rendered futile by an alienation of the property in litigation." J. Hanna & J. MacLachlan, Creditors' Rights and Corporate Reorganization 78 (Consolid. 5th ed. 1957). Modern statutes in many states now condition the lis pendens effect on the recording of a written notice of lis pendens. These statutes typically apply only when the property in dispute is real estate. Moreover, the statutory lis pendens, like the common law doctrine, typically protects only bona fide purchasers and encumbrancers for value, not other claimants such as judgment creditors and buyers at forced sales.

Example: C filed a judgment creditor's bill on October 18, 1957, in an effort to reach and apply to its claim certain real estate in which the debtor had an interest. The bill specifically described the land. On October 23, AOC won a judgment against the debtor and levied on the land. On November 1, C recorded notice of its creditor's bill in the county register's office. On January 10, the property was sold to satisfy AOC's judgment. AOC itself bid in the property and was given a deed to the land. Thereafter, two other creditors of the debtor redeemed the property from AOC. These two creditors claimed that AOC had priority over C because C's notice was recorded after AOC acquired it lien; the creditors then argued that, inasmuch as they claimed through AOC, they too should have priority over C. The court disagreed. C acquired a lien upon filing its creditor's bill, and the recording statute protected only bona fide purchasers and encumbrancers for value. AOC did not fit into either of these categories of protected persons. *Cannon Mills, Inc. v. Spivey*, 208 Tenn. 419, 429, 346 S.W.2d 266, 271 (1961).

3)   Priority Among Equitable Lienors *Inter Se* Each Acting For Herself
As concerns the debtor's nonexempt property that is immune from levy under execution, the judgment creditor who, acting for herself, is the first in time to initiate a creditor's bill is entitled to priority over others who later pursue the same remedy for themselves. See, e.g., *Travelers Indem. Co. v. First Nat. Bank*, 368 So.2d 836, 839 (Miss. 1979); see also Note, *Receivers at the Instance Of Judgment Creditors and Priorities Incident Thereto*, 17 Va. L. Rev. 45, 49 (1930); Note, *Priorities Among Judgment Creditors Pursuing Statutory and Equitable Remedies in New York*, 29 Colum. L. Rev. 504, 504–05 (1929); Note, *Priorities of Creditors Under Judgment Creditor's Bills*, 42 Yale L. J. 919, 927 (1933).

4) **Pro Rata Sharing When Creditors Either Actually or Constructively Join Together In Pursuing a Creditor's Bill**
Rather than pursuing a bill alone, a creditor may file the action on behalf of herself and other creditors of the debtor. This sort of proceeding is sometimes referred to as a general creditors' bill or suit. The initiating creditor may make her suit representative or may simply invite other creditors to intervene. In any event, whenever creditors proceed collectively in this fashion they ordinarily share the spoils ratably. See *Cannon Mills, Inc. v. Spivey*, 208 Tenn. 419, 425, 346 S.W.2d 266, 269 (1961); see also 1 G. Glenn, Fraudulent Conveyances And Preferences § 93 (Rev. ed. 1940); J. Moore & W. Phillips, Debtors' And Creditors' Rights 2–95 (1966). Pro rata distribution may sometimes be ordered by the court, as when a bill is maintained as an application for a general or administrative receivership, or when applicable law permits a nonjudgment creditor to pursue a creditor's bill only on condition that property appropriated thereby is held for all claimants. Note, *Priorities of Creditors Under Judgment Creditor's Bills*, 42 Yale L. J. 919, 921–23 (1933).

5) **Priority Between Equitable Liens of Creditor's Bills and Legal Liens of Judgment or Execution**
One might think that a priority conflict between an equitable lien of a creditor's bill and a legal (or "at law") lien of judgment or execution is impossible, inasmuch as creditor's bills are designed for reaching property beyond the scope of legal liens. Such a conflict is possible, however. For example, consider this case: Judgment Creditor A causes execution to issue, but for whatever reason the execution is returned unsatisfied and she files a creditor's bill. Judgment Creditor B is luckier and successfully levies execution on goods belonging to the debtor. The goods are subject to A's equitable lien which attached before B's execution lien. Nevertheless, B wins the priority contest because she "is said to have shown superior vigilance by securing an actual levy where [A, though senior in time,] failed." Note, *Priorities Among Judgment Creditors Pursuing Statutory and Equitable Remedies in New York*, 29 Colum. L. Rev. 504, 507 (1929).

The result might be different should A act unselfishly. If A files a general creditors' bill for the benefit of herself and all other creditors, B could not achieve priority for itself by winning the race to establish a legal lien on the property. Once the equitable lien attached under A's general creditors' bill, "thereafter no creditor could acquire any priority but all must share pro rata in the proceeds." *Cannon Mills, Inc. v. Spivey*, 208 Tenn. 419, 425, 346 S.W.2d 266, 269 (1961). If the property is real estate, A might achieve priority even if she filed the creditor's bill only for herself. If the judgments of both A and B created judgment liens on the land (See supra Chapter II.) in the order suggested by their names, A could rely on her judgment lien instead of the equitable lien of her creditor's bill. In so doing A could claim priority under the usual rule that judgment liens rank chronologically. But see *Chautauque County Bank v. Risley*, 19 N.Y. 369, 374 (1859) (observing in dictum that a creditor who pursues the equitable remedy abandons the lien of her judgment). B could not achieve priority by filing a creditor's bill before A acts to enforce her judgment lien. *Eldridge, Dunham & Co. v. Post,* 20 Fla. 579, 583 (1884).

5. CREDITORS' BILLS IN FEDERAL COURT

Federal Rule of Civil Procedure 69(a) provides essentially that the enforcement of judgments in federal district court shall be in accordance with the practice and procedure of the state in which the district court is held. Thus, relief in the form of a creditor's bill can be sought in federal court if the action is available in state courts under local law. *United States ex rel. Goldman v. Meredith,* 596 F.2d 1353, 1357 (8th Cir.), cert. denied sub nom., *Goldman v. Merrill Lynch, Pierce, Fenner & Smith,* 444 U.S. 838, 100 S. Ct. 76 (1979).

6. DECLINE IN USE OF CREDITORS' BILLS

Several statutory developments have limited the need for and use of true creditors' bills in equity. In most states, the writ of execution has been extended to equitable interests in property and intangible property. (See supra Chapter III.) Garnishment is also available in most states for the collection of judgments from property of the debtor held by third parties. (See infra Chapter V.) Moreover, virtually every state now provides by procedural rules or statutes that creditors can not only examine debtors in court about their property and its whereabouts, but can also conduct wide-ranging, out-of-court discovery of almost anyone who might know of or hold nonexempt property of the debtor. (See infra Chapter IV.B.1.) In addition, a number of states have statutorily provided for applying any property so discovered toward satisfaction of the creditor's judgment. (See infra Chapter IV.B.2.) Very often, legislative provisions for discovery of a debtor's property and application of it are part of the same statutory scheme, which is generally referred to as supplemental proceedings. Statutes, therefore, have taken over almost all of the functions of the equitable creditor's bill.

Creditor's bills have not been entirely displaced, however. They remain available in many states despite the enactment of statutory supplemental proceedings, at least where such proceedings do not furnish an adequate remedy. Indeed, a number of states' laws providing for supplemental proceedings expressly declare that such proceedings are cumulative remedies available in addition to other existing remedies. Ark. Code Ann. § 16–66–419 (1987); Ill. Ann. Stat. ch. 110, § 2–1402 (Smith-Hurd 1983). Not only are creditors' bills still available, they also retain some utility, especially as a sturdy vehicle for setting aside fraudulent conveyances. Nevertheless, creditors prefer the modern statutory substitutes, which achieve in a simpler and more summary process virtually all the purposes of the old creditor's bill.

B. MODERN SUPPLEMENTAL PROCEEDINGS

The equitable creditors' bills discussed above (Chapter IV.A.) have largely been displaced by modern supplementary or supplemental proceedings, which cover much of the same ground as the old creditors' bills through a wide range of statutes and procedural rules. The details of these proceedings vary significantly among the states, but their general contours are everywhere very much alike in that most states provide for two broad types of supplemental proceedings. One type, referred to here as supplemental discovery, provides for questioning persons, including the debtor, who might have information that could be useful in locating nonexempt property of the debtor. The other type of supplemental proceedings, referred to here as supplemental relief, goes one step further and provides for applying to the creditor's judgment whatever property is discovered. Unlike a creditor's bill, which is a separate action in itself, supplemental proceedings are a continuation of the creditor's original action against the debtor. *Mitchell v. Godsey,* 222 Ind. 527, 539, 53 N.E.2d 150, 154 (1944).

1. SUPPLEMENTAL DISCOVERY

A local variation of Federal Rule of Civil Procedure 69 is available to judgment creditors in most states. This rule provides in pertinent part that, "[i]n aid of the judgment or execution, the judgment creditor * * * may obtain discovery from any person, including the judgment debtor, in the manner provided in [the rules of civil procedure] or in the manner provided by the practice of the state in which the district court is held." Fed. R. Civ. P. 69(a). In some states the legislature has enacted a statute similar to this rule, and in other states the rule or some form of it has been adopted by the highest court as a rule of local procedure.

a. When Discovery Is Available

The discovery procedures authorized by Federal Rule of Civil Procedure 69(a) and its local counterparts are available to a creditor in many states as soon as she wins a judgment; the creditor need not first pursue execution.

b. Which Discovery Devices Are Available

The states disagree about the types of discovery devices that are available to judgment creditors under local variations of Federal Rule of Civil Procedure 69(a). Many states have simply copied the current version of the Rule and thus permit post-judgment discovery by *any* method that the state rules of civil procedure sanction for pre-judgment discovery. Idaho R.Civ. P. 69; Minn. R. Civ. P. 69; Nev. R. Civ. P. 69. Other states only permit the taking of depositions. Colo. R. Civ. P. 69(i); Tenn. R. Civ. P. 69.

2. SUPPLEMENTAL RELIEF

The local counterparts of Federal Rule of Civil Procedure 69(a) do not in their simplest forms provide for action against property that the creditor locates through post-judgment discovery. Most states, however, have enacted a statute or series of statutes that not only permit discovery of the debtor's property, but also allow and facilitate application of the property to the creditor's judgment. This sort of law provides for various kinds of relief designed to aid the creditor in satisfying her judgment through execution or some other process. Statutes in aid of judgment or execution commonly provide for some or all of the following kinds of relief:

a. Discovery of the Debtor and Third Parties

Statutes governing supplemental proceedings sometime empower the court to order the debtor or third persons to submit to discovery by the creditor. This sort of provision does not always duplicate supplemental discovery, which is discussed earlier in this chapter.

A few states have no separate supplemental discovery law. Discovery is available, if at all, through and according to the terms of a statute providing comprehensively for supplemental proceedings. Moreover, in many states that do provide separately for supplemental discovery, the only discovery device available thereunder is the deposition. A judge empowered to order discovery upon a creditor's petition in a proceeding to enforce a judgment may not be so limited with respect to discovery devices that the creditor can use.

b.   Examination of the Debtor
Upon the judgment creditor's request, the court can order examination of the debtor.

1)   Method
In most states the court's order requires the debtor to appear and account for her property before the court or a judicially appointed referee. Fla. Stat. Ann. § 56.29(2) (West Supp. 1984); Or. Rev. Stat. §§ 23.710 & 23.720(1)(a) (1983); Wis. Stat. Ann. § 816.03(1)(a) (West 1977).

2)   When Available
Some states allow a court to order examination of the debtor anytime after a judgment is rendered for the creditor. Ariz. Rev. Stat. § 12–1631 (1982); Hawaii Rev. Stat. § 636–4 (1985). In other states, however, such an order can issue only after execution has issued and has been returned unsatisfied. Idaho Code § 11501 (1979); N.C. Gen. Stat. §§ 1–352 to –352.2 (1983). The requirement of a *nulla bona* return may be excused in some jurisdictions upon proof by the creditor that the debtor has property which she unjustly refuses to apply to the judgment. Ohio Rev. Code Ann. § 2333.10 (Page 1981); S.C. Code Ann. § 15–39–310 (Law. Co-op. 1977). The requirement may also be excused when the debtor threatens conduct intended to hinder, delay or defraud creditors. Ala. Code §§ 6–6–181(a), –182 (1977).

3)   Arresting a Debtor Who May Abscond
If the creditor can show a danger of the debtor absconding, the court can order the debtor's arrest and force her to appear before the court where she will be examined with regard to her property. Minn. Stat. § 575.03 (West Supp. 1988); Okla. Stat. Ann. tit. 12, § 844 (West Supp. 1988); Wash. Rev. Code Ann. § 6.32.010 (West Supp. 1988). In some states the debtor's arrest is also conditioned on the creditor showing reason to believe that the debtor has property which she unjustly refuses to apply to the judgment. Wis. Stat. Ann. § 816.05 (West 1977). The debtor's release is usually conditioned on the posting of bond to insure against her absconding with, or disposing of, her property. Id. § 816.07.

c.   Examination of Third Parties
The statutes governing supplemental proceedings typically provide for examining not only the debtor, but also third parties who are not obligated to the judgment creditor.

1) **Obligors of the Debtor and Persons Believed to Hold Property of the Debtor**
   When a third person is obligated to the debtor or possibly holds property of the debtor, the judgment creditor can petition the court for an order requiring the person to submit to discovery or to appear before the court or a referee for examination. Ark. Code Ann. § 16–66–418(2) (1987); Ky. Rev. Stat. § 426.381(1) (1972); Mich. Comp. Laws Ann. § 600.6110(1) (West 1987); Wyo. Stat. § 1–17–405 (1987).

   The issuance of this sort of court order is conditioned (1) on proof by affidavit or otherwise that the third person is obligated to the debtor or holds property of the debtor and also, in some states, (2) on the issuance or return of execution. A few states add an extra condition, which is that the value of the obligation owed, or the property held, by the third person exceed a statutory minimum amount (usually $10 to $50).

2) **Other Third Parties**
   Some states allow the examination of any person for the purpose of uncovering or locating nonexempt property of the debtor. Ala. Code §§ 6–6–180, –183 (1975); Ill. Ann. Stat. ch. 110, § 2–1402(a) (Smith-Hurd 1983).

d. **Court Orders to Facilitate Satisfaction of Judgment**
Statutes providing for supplemental proceedings typically empower courts to issue orders facilitating satisfaction of the creditor's judgment. Orders can be issued to achieve the following specific objectives:

- To prevent the transfer or disposition of, or interference with, property belonging to the debtor, N.Y. Civ. Prac. Law § 5222 (Consol. 1978 & Supp. 1988) (debtor and third parties may be enjoined); N.D. Cent. Code § 28–25–12 (1974) (same); Or. Rev. Stat. § 23.730 (1983) (debtor may be enjoined).

- To apply property of the debtor toward satisfaction of the judgment whether the property is held by the debtor or some third person, West's Fla. Stat. Ann. § 56.29(5) (1969); Mass. Gen. Laws Ann. ch. 224, §§ 16 & 17 (West 1979 & Supp. 1983); Neb. Rev. Stat. § 25–1572 (1979).

   If the third person claims an adverse interest in the property, the court in some states cannot determine title to the property as part of the proceeding for supplemental relief. Some other action must be pursued in order to determine who has the better right to the property. Ariz. Rev. Stat. Ann. § 12–1635 (1982) (judgment creditor must initiate action against the adverse claimant); Minn. Stat. Ann. § 575.06 (1982) (receiver must proceed against the claimant); Wis. Stat. Ann. § 716.08 (West 1977) (same); but see Cal. Civ. Pro. Code §§ 708.180, .190) (West 1987) (subject to some exceptions, court may determine interests in property when there is an adverse claimant if the judgment creditor so requests); N.Y. Civ. Prac. Law § 5225(b) (Consol. 1978) (court can permit adverse claimants to intervene whereupon the proceeding for supplemental relief is converted into a plenary test of whom has the highest right to the disputed property).

- To require the debtor to satisfy the judgment by installment payments, Me. Rev. Stat. Ann. tit. 14, §§ 3127–3129 (1964 & Supp. 1983); R.I. Gen. Laws 1969, § 9–28–5.

Thus, in *Mitchell v. Godsey,* 222 Ind. 527, 53 N.E.2d 150 (1944), the court affirmed the trial judge's order that the debtor pay ten per cent of her salary each month to the judgment creditor. Id. at 544–45, 53 N.E.2d at 156.

- To appoint a receiver of the debtor's property, Cal. Civ. Pro. Code § 708.620 (West 1987); N.J. Stat. Ann. §§ 2A:17–66 to 2A:17–68 (West 1987).

Judgment creditors sometimes ask for a receiver to collect the debtor's receivables or to find and sell property that is not easily reached through ordinary execution. Where the appointment of a receiver is specifically authorized by the statute governing supplemental proceedings, the creditor is excused from the usual requirement of showing that other remedies are inadequate. *D.W.L., Inc. v. Goodner-Van Eng'g Co.,* 373 P.2d 38, 43 (Okla. 1962).

e. Contempt as a Means of Deterring Disobedience by the Debtor

A debtor risks a contempt citation by disobeying a court order and, therefore, is effectively compelled to follow any orders issued in supplemental proceedings. The consequences of disobedience can be severe. In *First Nat. Bank v. Reoux,* 9 A.D.2d 1005, 194 N.Y.S.2d 546 (1959), the debtor was examined during supplemental proceedings hearings but refused to answer questions regarding his actions while out of the country. The debtor was thus found in contempt. The punishment was a fine equalling the amount of the creditor's judgment and also imprisonment, which was to continue until such time as the debtor determined to answer the questions put to him. Id. at 1066, 194 N.Y.S.2d at 548. The report of the *First Nat. Bank v. Reoux* case does not suggest that the debtor asserted a constitutional privilege against self-incrimination. This privilege applies in supplemental proceedings against a judgment debtor, *Busby v. Citizens Bank,* 131 Ga. App. 738, 740–41, 206 S.E.2d 640, 641 (1974); *First Nat. City Bank v. Pal,* 72 A.D.2d 716, 421 N.Y.S.2d 889 (1979); but the privilege can be waived expressly or impliedly. An implicit waiver can result from a course of conduct whereby the debtor agrees to give the creditor access to the debtor's accounting books and other financial records. *Morgan v. United States Fidelity & Guar. Co.,* 222 So. 2d 820, 829–30 (Miss. 1969). For more on contempt as a creditors' remedy, see Rendleman, *Compensatory Contempt to Collect Money,* 41 Ohio St. L. J. 625 (1980).

f. Supplemental Relief in Aid of Judgment or Execution Not a Vehicle for Attacking Fraudulent Conveyances

The traditional rule is that supplemental relief in aid of judgment or execution is not the appropriate remedy for setting aside a fraudulent conveyance of the debtor's property. The principal reason is that such a proceeding is summary and is not a full-dress plenary action to which the defendants are entitled. *Greater Valley Terminal Corp. v. Goodman,* 415 Pa. 1, 6, 202 A.2d 89, 93 (1964). There is a creditor's bill designed for voiding fraudulent conveyances, see supra Chapter IV.A.1.b.; and, the Uniform Fraudulent Conveyances Act (1918), which many states have adopted, expressly recognizes that a defrauded creditor has a cause of action to set aside a fraudulent conveyance. Uniform Fraudulent Conveyance Act §§ 9 & 10 (1918).

REVIEW QUESTIONS

1. What is the purpose of a creditor's bill?

2. What is the difference between a creditor's bill and a general creditors' bill?

3. Why might a creditor benefit from having an equitable lien on real estate resulting from the filing of a creditor's bill when the real estate already is subject to a lien of the creditor's judgment?

4. What is the difference between a creditor's bill and supplemental proceedings?

5. What are the two major types of supplemental proceedings?

6. What relief is available through a creditor's bill that generally is unavailable through supplemental proceedings?

*

V

GARNISHMENT

Analysis

Intangible property of a debtor, such as a debt owed her by someone else, cannot usually be reached through ordinary execution. Actually seizing such property is quite literally impossible. Moreover, execution is not really designed for reaching property in the hands of someone other than the judgment debtor. "It does not give one subject to it the opportunity to object, except on very basic matters, such as the judgment being executed is void. Where property claimed to be owned by the judgment debtor is in the hands of a third party, there is a good chance that the latter has some special interest in it or may even own it outright. The third party ought to have an opportunity to establish his or her rights to this property before it is summarily taken, and this is essentially the reason that execution cannot be used to reach it. Rather, a special proceeding, both in the nature of process and an adversary suit, was devised to allow judgment creditors to reach property of the defendant in the hands of third persons. This process is called 'garnishment' in most states * * *" W. Hawkland & P. Loiseaux, Cases and Materials in Debtor-Creditor Relations 61 (1979). "Garnishment (sometimes called 'trustee process') is a procedure for reaching [1] debts owed *to* the debtor * * * by a third person or [2] property *of* the debtor in the possession of a third person. The third person is described as a garnishee." W. Warren & W. Hogan, Cases and Materials on Debtor-Creditor Law 105 (2d ed. 1981). Garnishment is available in most states both before and after judgment. Although this part of the outline focuses on postjudgment garnishment, much of the discussion also applies to prejudgment garnishment. See infra Chapter XI.C.6. Some courts conceptualize postjudgment garnishment not as an original suit, but as an ancillary proceeding in the nature of execution to satisfy a prior judgment. *Rush v. Simpson,* 373 So.2d 1105, 1107 (Ala.Civ.App.), cert. denied, 373 So.2d 1108 (Ala.1979); *Sharum v. Dodson,* 264 Ark. 57, 61, 568 S.W.2d 503, 505 (1978). Other courts have an opposite view. They see postjudgment garnishment not as a process of execution, but as an independent suit by the judgment debtor in the name of the judgment creditor against the garnishee. *Butler v. Butler,* 219 Va. 164, 165–66, 247 S.E.2d 353, 354 (1978). Yet, no matter how postjudgment garnishment is regarded by the courts, the object is always the same: to reach the assets or credits under the garnishee's control and apply them in satisfaction of the creditor's claim against the debtor.

A. GARNISHMENT PROCEDURE

Garnishment typically begins with the judgment creditor, the garnishor, filing with the court an affidavit describing the judgment, complaining that the judgment is unsatisfied, and alleging that a third person, the garnishee is indebted to, or holds property of, the judgment debtor. The judge or the court clerk then issues a garnishment summons that is served on the garnishee and the judgment debtor. Some states have special rules that govern the garnishment of earnings. A not uncommon example is the requirement that the debtor receive notice of a garnishment of wages ten days in advance of service on the garnishee. See, e.g., Minn. Stat. § 571.41(5) (1986 & Supp. 1987); N.D. Cent. Code § 32–09.1–04 (Supp. 1983). During this time the debtor may pay the judgment, contest the garnishment or assert any federal or state exemptions of earnings.

Service of the summons on the garnishee creates a lien of garnishment on property of the debtor held by the garnishee and also on debts and other credits the garnishee owes the debtor.

The garnishee is required to answer the garnishment summons within a stated time, usually 20 or 30 days. Failure to answer may result in contempt proceedings or a default judgment, which may require the garnishee to pay the full amount of the garnishor's judgment against the debtor. In its answer the garnishee must describe what, if any, credits or effects of the debtor it holds. The garnishee may then tender to the court the debtor's property and credits and pray for discharge from any further liability to the garnishor.

If the garnishor controverts the garnishee's answer, the controverted issues are tried as other civil cases. At trial the garnishee may assert any defenses available to it. If the answer is not controverted, the answer is taken as true. If the garnishee is obligated to the debtor, the court will render judgment against the garnishee for the amount of the obligation. Similarly, any property of the principal debtor that the garnishee holds will be ordered turned over to the court or the sheriff for sale in satisfaction of the garnishor's judgment.

B. GARNISHABLE PROPERTY

1. GENERAL RULE
Each state's garnishment law specifies the types of property that can be garnished. A fairly safe general rule is that a judgment creditor can reach through garnishment any of the debtor's personal property, whether tangible or not, having salable worth that is held, controlled, or owed to the debtor by a third person.

2. INTANGIBLE OBLIGATIONS OWED THE DEBTOR
Wages, bank accounts, and other purely intangible obligations owed the debtor are popular targets of garnishment. In most states, however, contingent or unliquidated obligations cannot be garnished. See, e.g., *Walker v. Paramount Engineering Co.,* 353 F.2d 445, 450 (6th Cir. 1965) (under both federal and Michigan law, when future performance of a contract is necessary before money payable thereon becomes due, the right to payment is conditioned upon performance and thus is not subject to garnishment until the condition has been fulfilled); *Cummings General Tire Co. v. Volpe Constr. Co.,* 230 A.2d 712, 713 (D.C.App. 1967) (cannot garnish right to payment under contract until performance is completed); *National Sur. Corp. v. Gillette,* 194 Kan. 604, 606–07, 400 P.2d 681, 683–84 (1965) (cannot garnish cash surrender value of life insurance policy where the debtor has not done what is required to force payment of that value by insurer).

The usual rule that a verdict won by a debtor is not subject to garnishment is sometimes explained by comparing a verdict to an unliquidated claim. See *Bassett v. McCarty,* 3 Wash. 2d 488, 496–97, 101 P.2d 575, 579 (1940). The states disagree on whether a judgment in favor of a debtor against a third person is subject to garnishment by the debtor's judgment creditor. Compare *McIlroy Bank v. First Nat. Bank,* 252 Ark. 558, 560, 480 S.W.2d 127, 128 (1972) (judgment debtor is not subject to process of garnishment of the judgment) with *Florida Steel Corp. v. A. G. Spanos Enterprises, Inc.,* 332 So. 2d 663, 664 (Fla. Dist. Ct. App. 1976) (judgment obtained on unliquidated claim can be garnished when final and no longer subject to appeal).

Although obligations owed a debtor are subject to garnishment only when they are certain and liquidated, maturity of the obligation is not everywhere required, at least not when the maturity depends solely on the passage of time. Of course, in no event can the garnishee be required to actually pay to the garnishor an obligation owed the debtor until the obligation has matured.

3. REIFIED PROPERTY RIGHTS (DOCUMENTS OF TITLE AND CERTIFICATED SECURITIES)
Some rights to property owned by a debtor may be reified, meaning that the law regards the debtor's rights as transferable through assignment of the paper that evidences them. A creditor usually cannot capture such property of the debtor without seizing the paper representing the debtor's rights. Thus, when goods belonging

to a debtor are held by a bailee who issued a negotiable document covering the goods, the creditor acquires no rights to the property without surrendering the document to the bailee. U.C.C. § 7–602. Similarly, a valid levy on certificated securities belonging to a debtor depends on seizure of the certificates. Garnishing the issuer will usually not suffice. Id. § 8–317(1).

4. NEGOTIABLE INSTRUMENTS

When a person's obligation to a debtor is evidenced by a negotiable instrument such as a promissory note, can this obligation be reached by a judgment creditor through simple garnishment of the maker of the note, or must the creditor seize the note itself? [Instruments belonging to the debtor such as notes and checks which are held by a third person are subject to garnishment. See, e.g., *Equitable Life Assurance Soc. of the United States v. Cassel*, 188 So. 2d 351, 352 (Fla. Dist. Ct. App. 1966); Skalecki v. Frederick, 31 Wis. 2d 496, 502–03, 143 N.W.2d 520, 522–23 (1966); see also Annot., *Note or Check Itself as Subject of Levy and Seizure Under Attachment or Garnishment*, 41 A.L.R. 1003 (1926).] The maker of the note is exposed to double liability should she pay the instrument without a surrender of it. Her payment to the garnishor would be no defense against a holder in due course of the instrument seeking to enforce it. U.C.C. § 3–305. "Ordinarily," therefore, "the garnishee is entitled to have the paper produced and delivered up before payment; and * * * before judgment against him, he is entitled to this, or an indemnity as in case of a lost note, unless all danger of his being compelled to pay it a second time has passed." J. Rood, A Treatise On the Law of Garnishment § 135 (1896); see also *West v. Baker*, 109 Ariz. 415, 417, 510 P.2d 731, 733 (1973) (the maker of a negotiable instrument can not be charged as a garnishee except upon a showing which will clearly protect him against the holder for the reason that the maker should not be exposed to the risk of double liability); see generally Annot., *Construction, Application, and Effect of Statute Exempting from Garnishment Debt Evidenced by Negotiable Instrument*, 71 A.L.R. 581 (1931).

C. DEBTOR'S PROTECTIONS

Garnishment is an effective remedy, especially when the debtor has a source of income that the creditor can tap. There is a down side of the remedy, however. Siphoning all of a debtor's income will leave her destitute, and there will be little incentive for her to continue working. Also, garnishment is a headache for employers. In many cases, they decide that firing an employee is more economical than spending the time and money required to answer and comply with a garnishment summons. For all of these reasons, garnishment can have the effect of shifting to the government, and thus to the public, the responsibility of financially supporting debtors. Guarding against this effect are two devices that partially shield the salary and job of a debtor when her employer is garnished: (1) federal and state restrictions on property of a debtor that is subject to creditor process and (2) laws that restrict an employer's freedom to discharge an employee because the employee's wages have been garnished. These devices and other laws designed to protect debtors from unfair or abusive garnishment process, or the harsh consequences of it, are discussed here.

1. **STATE EXEMPTIONS**

   All states, either by constitution or statute, exempt certain property of debtors from creditors' process. Property designated in these exemption laws cannot be reached by creditors through judicial collection efforts, including garnishment. Virtually every state specifically provides for the exemption of a portion of a debtor's wages. Wage and other exemptions of debtors' property under state and federal law are the subjects of a separate chapter of this outline. See infra Chapter VIII.

2. **FEDERAL RESTRICTIONS ON THE AMOUNT OF EARNINGS A CREDITOR CAN GARNISH**

   Title III of the federal Consumer Credit Protection Act, 15 U.S.C.A. § 1671 et seq. (1982), limits the amount of a debtor's earnings that a creditor can garnish. Under Title III, creditors can garnish only 25 percent of a debtor's aggregate weekly "disposable earnings" or the amount by which her disposable earnings exceed thirty times the minimum hourly wage, whichever is less. Id. § 1673(a). A larger sum can be garnished to enforce orders for the support of any person, including decrees and judgments for alimony and child support: 50% of the disposable earnings of a debtor who is supporting a spouse or dependent other than a person with respect to whose support such garnishment is issued; and 60% of the disposable earnings of a debtor who is not supporting such a person. The 50% becomes 55% and the 60% increases to 65% if payment of the support order is more than three months delinquent. Id. § 1673(b).

   a. **The Meaning of "Earnings"**

      Title III only restricts the garnishment of "earnings." In the abstract, this term could have a very broad meaning. In the Title III context, however, earnings means compensation for personal services, 15 U.S.C.A. § 1672(a), that is remitted in periodic payments. *Kokoszka v. Belford*, 417 U.S. 642, 650, 94 S. Ct. 2431, 2436 (1974). Thus, amounts owed to a debtor under an equipment rental agreement or lease are not earnings because the compensation is not for personal services. *Gerry Elson Agency, Inc. v. Muck*, 509 S.W.2d 750 (Mo. App. 1974). A worker's tax refund may be traceable to compensation for personal services, but the refund itself is not "earnings" within Title III, which protects only "periodic payments of compensation needed to support the wage earner and his family on a week-to-week, month-to-month basis." *Kokoszka v. Belford*, 417 U.S. 642, 650, 94 S. Ct. 2431, 2436 (1974); but cf. *Riley v. Kessler*, 2 Ohio Misc. 2d 4, 441 N.E.2d 638 (Ohio Ct. Com. Pl. 1982) (vacation pay constitutes earnings under Title III). Title III expressly provides, however, that the term "earnings" includes pension and retirement benefits paid periodically to a debtor. 15 U.S.C.A. § 1672(a); see also *Ward v. Ward*, 164 N.J. Super. 354, 396 A.2d 365 (1978) (private pension); *Villano v. Villano*, 98 Misc. 2d 774, 414 N.Y.S.2d 625 (Sup. Ct. 1979) (federal pension).

   b. **The Meaning of "Disposable Earnings"**

      The maximum amount of earnings that a creditor can garnish is determined under Title III not on the basis of total earnings, but on the basis of a smaller sum labeled "disposable earnings," which means earnings less deductions "required by law to be withheld." 15 U.S.C.A. § 1672(b) (1982).

Examples: D's salary is $10,800 a year. Yet, D does not receive $900 a month. Rather, D's "take-home pay" is only $700 a month because of the following deductions: $130 for taxes, $50 for social security, and $20 for Blue Cross. Only the $130 for taxes and the $50 for social security are deductions "required by law." D's "disposal earnings," therefore, amount to $720 a month or $180 a week. Title III limits the amount that D's creditors can garnish to 25 percent of $180 or $45 a week.

Suppose that D is obligated under a divorce decree to make monthly payments of alimony and child support. Should these payments be deducted from D's gross earnings in determining the amount of D's disposal earnings for Title III purposes? No. *First Nat. Bank v. Hasty,* 415 F. Supp. 170 (E.D. Mich. 1976), aff'd without opin., 573 F.2d 1310 (6th Cir. 1977).

c. The Meaning of "Garnishment"

Title III protects a person's earnings only from "garnishment," which the law itself defines as "any legal or equitable procedure through which the earnings of any individual are required to be withheld for payment of any debt." 15 U.S.C.A. § 1672(c) (1982).

d. Exceptions to the Usual Restriction

The general or usual rule of Title III is that creditors cannot garnish more than 25 percent of a debtor's disposable earnings or the amount by which those earnings exceed thirty times the minimum hourly wage, whichever is less. This rule has three exceptions. It does not apply in the case of:

1) TAXES: any debt due for any state or federal tax, 15 U.S.C.A. § 1573(b) (1)(C);

2) BANKRUPTCY: any order arising out of a Chapter 13 bankruptcy case, such as an order directing the debtor's employer to pay all or part of the debtor's earnings to a bankruptcy trustee for distribution to creditors, id. § 1573(b) (1) (C); and,

3) SUPPORT ORDER: a court or administrative order under state law for the support of any person. Id. § 1573(b)(1) (A). This exception is unlike the other two. In cases of tax debts and bankruptcy orders, there is no limitation on the amount of wages that can be garnished. In the case of a support order, Title III establishes a limitation that is different from the limitation established by the general rule. The general rule limits the amount to 25 percent of the debtor's disposable earnings; in the case of support orders, the limitation is raised to as much as 65% of those earnings, depending on whether the debtor is already supporting a spouse or dependent child, and depending also on how long the debtor has been delinquent in making support payments. 15 U.S.C.A. § 1673(b)(2).

e.   Giving Effect to Local Priorities Under Title III

The general rule of state law is that a garnishment is effective from the time of service on the garnishee and that later claims on the debtor's property held by the garnishee are subordinate to the rights of the garnishor. The rule has exceptions which are discussed later in this chapter of the outline. For example, in many states a garnishment to collect alimony or child support has priority over a garnishment to collect a contract debt regardless of the order in which the garnishments were served. See infra Chapter V.G.2. Also, the garnishee may offset her claims against the debtor before turning over the debtor's property to the garnishor. See infra Chapter V.D.5. Title III does not displace these local priorities. *Long Island Trust Co. v. United States Postal Service,* 647 F.2d 336 (2d Cir. 1981) (involving support garnishment); *Marshall v. District Court,* 444 F. Supp. 1110 (E.D. Mich 1978) (same); *Sears, Roebuck & Co. v. A.T. & G. Co., Inc.,* 66 Mich. App. 359, 239 N.W.2d 614 (1976) (involving garnishee's right of set-off). These same cases also teach, however, that the subordinate garnishor is still bound by the limitations of Title III. Thus, if the debtor owes a debt to a garnishee who is the debtor's employer, the maximum amount of the debtor's earnings that a garnishor can take is the difference between 25% of the debtor's disposable earnings and the employer's set-off. Consequently, if the garnishee's set-off is more than 25% of disposable earnings, the garnishor will receive nothing. *Sears, Roebuck & Co. v. A.T. & G. Co., Inc.,* 66 Mich.App. 359, 239 N.W.2d 614 (1976). (Does this case effectively treat the amount of a garnishee's setoff as a deduction required by law in determining a debtor's disposal income? Or, does the case effectively equate a garnishee's set-off with a garnishment? If two garnishments are outstanding against an employer of the debtor, can the garnishors together take 50% of the debtor's disposable earnings, or are they limited collectively to 25% of those earnings?) Similarly, if a creditor garnishes to enforce a contract debt and the debtor's former spouse garnishes to enforce a support order (under which the former spouse can reach as much as 65% of the debtor's disposable earnings), the creditor is limited to the difference between 25% of the debtor's disposable earnings and the amount of the support garnishment. *Long Island Trust Co. v. United States Postal Service,* 647 F.2d 336 (2d Cir. 1981); *Marshall v. District Court,* 444 F. Supp. 1110 (E.D. Mich. 1978).

f.   Title III is Not a True Exemption Statute Inasmuch as Protection Ends When Earnings Are Paid to Debtor

Title III is often referred to as a federal exemption statute. In a very important sense, however, this characterization is wrong. As a general rule, income that is exempt from creditors' process retains that status after the income is paid to the debtor. Thus, if the debtor deposits in a bank account wages that are exempt under state law, the account is not subject to garnishment to the extent that the balance consists of the protected income. See infra Chapter VIII.B.4. Courts interpreting Title III have held, however, that the federal statute does not protect earnings once the debtor has received them. See, e.g., *Edwards v. Henry,* 97 Mich. App. 173, 293 N.W.2d 756 (1980). See also discussion and authorities cited infra Chapter VIII.B.4. This conclusion might make sense if, as is not the case, the funds were federal monies not yet put to their intended use. See generally *Palmiter v. Action, Inc.*, 733 F.2d 1244 (7th Cir. 1984) (federal grant monies held by a nonprofit community service organization are not subject to garnishment until they have been paid out for purposes for which they were appropriated). The conclusion could be understood, too, if, as the courts have concluded, the real purpose of Title III is to protect employers from the hassel of dealing with garnishments. Yet, the Congress enacted Title III's restrictions on wage garnishments because of the cause-and-effect relationship between such process and consumer bankruptcies. If garnishment leads to bankruptcy, the true reason is not because the debtor's employer was garnished, but because the debtor is left with no income to support herself and her family. This calamity can result from the garnishment of the debtor's bank account just as easily as from the garnishment of her employer.

3. RESTRICTIONS ON DISCHARGE FROM EMPLOYMENT DUE TO GARNISHMENT OF EARNINGS

Federal law prohibits an employer from discharging "any employee by reason of the fact that her earnings have been subjected to garnishment for any one indebtedness." 15 U.S.C.A. § 1674(a) (1982). This prohibition gives only limited protection, however. It does not protect a debtor from discharge if her employer is garnished by more than one creditor or by the same creditor for more than one debt. Also, although the statute imposes criminal liability on an employer who violates the rule against discharge, id., § 1674(b), civil enforcement is left exclusively to the United States Secretary of Labor. The statute neither explicitly nor implicitly gives an employee a private cause of action against an employer who has fired her in violation of § 1674(a). See *Le Vick v. Skaggs Companies, Inc.*, 701 F.2d 777, 779 (9th Cir. 1983), overruling, *Stewart v. Travelers Corp.*, 503 F.2d 108, 113–14 (9th Cir. 1974); *McCabe v. City of Eureka*, 664 F.2d 680, 683 (8th Cir. 1981); *Smith v. Cotton Bros. Baking Co., Inc.*, 609 F.2d 738, 742 (5th Cir.1980), cert. denied, 449 U.S. 821, 101 S.Ct. 79 (1980); but see *Ellis v. Glover & Gardner Constr. Co.*, 562 F. Supp. 1054, 1056–65 (M.D. Tenn. 1983) (implying private cause of action under § 1674(a)). In some states, local law provides greater protection of employees whose wages are garnished. In Minnesota, for example, "[n]o employer may discharge any employee by reason of the fact that her earnings have been subjected to garnishment or execution." Minn. Stat. § 571.61(1) (1986). This law prevents firing an employee regardless of the number of debts for which her employer is garnished. Also, the law gives an employee a private cause of action should she be fired because of a garnishment of her wages. The damages are twice the amount of wages lost as a result of the wrongful termination, and the employee is entitled to an order requiring her reinstatement. Id. § 571.61(2). Local statutes such as Minnesota's are not preempted by the less protective federal law. See 15 U.S.C.A. § 1677 (1982).

4. STATE LIMITATIONS ON AVAILABILITY OF GARNISHMENT

Garnishment is among the most drastic creditors' remedies in terms of the adverse consequences the debtor may suffer. The flow of a debtor's income can be interrupted, and good relations with her employer, if not her job itself, can be jeopardized because of the annoyance caused the employer. Due to the harshness of the remedy, South Carolina and Texas have almost completely outlawed the garnishment of wages.   S.C. Code Ann. §§ 37–5–104 & 37–5–106 (Law. Co-op. 1976) (prohibits garnishment of unpaid wages to enforce collection of debt arising from a consumer transaction); id. § 15–39–410 (Law. Co-op. 1976) (all of the earnings of a debtor for her personal services are exempt); Tex. Const. art. 16, § 28 & Tex. Stat. Ann. art. 4099 (Vernon 1966) (current wages for personal services are not subject to garnishment).   Other states severely limit the availability of garnishment, especially prejudgment garnishment.   Texas also is an example of a state which requires that, in some cases, a creditor must exhaust security given for a debt before pursuing garnishment against the debtor.   See Tex. Civ. Prac. & Rem. Code § 63.001 (Vernon 1986), formerly Tex. Stat. Ann. art. 4076 (Vernon 1966), formerly Tex. Rev. Stat. art. 3783 (1925), as construed in *Teague v. Fairchild,* 15 S.W.2d 585, 587–88 (Tex. Comm. App.), opinion adopted by Supreme Court of Texas, 15 S.W.2d 589 (1929).   This construction of the Texas law has been followed in a number of more rcent cases, including *Weihausen v. First Nat. Bank,* 501 S.W.2d 477 (Tex. Civ. App. 1973).   Compare Arizona where garnishment and any other attachment to enforce a contract for the payment of money is allowed as long as the contract is not *fully* secured by collateral.   Ariz. Rev. Stat. Ann. §§ 12–1521 & 12–1571 (1982), as construed in *Kaminski v. Walpole,* 10 Ariz. App. 260, 458 P.2d 127, 128–29 (1969) (citing similar, though not identical, statutes in other states).   Texas also prohibits post-judgment garnishment when the creditor knows that the debtor has property in her own hands sufficient to satisfy the judgment.   See *G–W–L, Inc. v. Juneau,* 486 S.W.2d 812, 814 (Tex. Civ. App. 1972).

5.   GARNISHING CREDITOR'S EXPOSURE TO DAMAGES FOR WRONGFUL GARNISHMENT

The debtor's remedy of wrongful garnishment protects her to some extent from a creditor's abuse of the garnishment process.   The topic of wrongful garnishment is outlined separately at the end of this chapter, infra, Chapter V.J.

6.   DUE PROCESS GUARANTEES

Garnishment overtly involves public officials exercising the coercive power of the state to effect a significant taking of a debtor's property.   For this reason, the debtor's property cannot be garnished, either before or after judgment, without according her due process of law.   This protection is guaranteed by the Fourteenth Amendment to the United States Constitution.   Similar guarantees can be found in many state constitutions.   Two entire chapters of this Black Letter are devoted to constitutional limitations on creditors' remedies, including pre- and postjudgment garnishment.   See infra Chapters XIV and XV.

D.   MAJOR DUTIES AND RIGHTS OF GARNISHEE

1.   GARNISHEE MUST ANSWER GARNISHMENT SUMMONS

Unless the neglect is excused, a garnishee who fails to timely answer a garnishment summons risks liability for (1) the full amount of the garnishor's judgment against the debtor, *Buzbee v. Overby,* 191 Kan. 112, 116–17, 379 P.2d 250, 253–54 (1963);   or (2) the amount or value of the debtor's property that the judgment creditor alleged was in the garnishee's hands, *Carter v. Helena Marine Service, Inc.,* 251

Ark. 876, 877, 475 S.W.2d 528, 529 (1972); or (3) the actual damages suffered by the garnishor as a result of the garnishee's neglect. *Ware v. Phillips,* 77 Wash. 2d 879, 883, 468 P.2d 444, 447 (1970); see also Ark. Code Ann. §§ 16–110–406 & 16–110–407 (1987) (failure or refusal to answer renders garnishee liable to garnishor for the full amount of the garnishor's claim against the debtor, except where garnishee is a financial institution in which case it is liable only to the extent of the garnishee's obligation to the debtor or the value of the property held); Minn. Stat. § 571.53 (1986) (garnishee who fails to answer is liable for an amount not exceeding creditor's judgment against debtor or 110 percent of the amount claimed in the garnishee summons, whichever is the smaller).

2. **GARNISHEE MUST ACCOUNT FOR DEBTOR'S PROPERTY**
    a. **Garnishment Impounds Property Owed or Held by Garnishee as of the Time Summons is Served**
        The unquestioned general rule is that, after proper service of a writ of garnishment, the garnishee acts at her peril if she disposes of property of the debtor which she holds at that time, or if she pays an obligation then owing to the debtor. Such property and credits are impressed with a lien of garnishment upon service of the writ, and thus are impounded by the garnishment for the purpose of applying them to the creditor's judgment.

    Examples: JC caused a writ of garnishment to issue against G, whom the court determined had in its possession a stock of merchandise belonging to the debtor, JD. After service of the garnishment, G sold the merchandise to a stranger to the proceedings. G will be liable to JC for the value of the goods. The same result follows if, after service of the writ, G mingles JD's merchandise with G's own goods so that JD's property cannot be distinguished and delivered for JC's benefit. "Since the plaintiff [creditor] acquires by his proceeding a lien upon the effects, the garnishee * * * could be proceeded against, either in an original suit or an ancillary proceeding, for the conversion of the property upon which he has acquired such lien." *Holloway Seed Co. v. City Nat. Bank,* 92 Tex. 187, 192, 47 S.W. 95, 97 (1898).

    G owes JD $500. JC wins a judgment against JD and garnishes the debt which G owes JD. Despite having received the garnishment summons, G satisfies the $500 debt by paying that amount to JD. G is liable to JD for $500 and may be held in contempt of court.

    Same facts as in the immediately preceding problem except that G pays JD by mailing JD a check on the day before the summons is served. The check is not paid by G's bank, however, until several days after service of the garnishment summons on G. G is not liable to JC. "The general rules * * * are that payment by check suspends the judgment debtor's remedy against the garnishee and, as long as the check is not dishonored, defeats a subsequent garnishment; and the garnishee-drawer of the check released from his control has no duty or obligation to stop payment thereon for the benefit of the garnishor." *Pearson Grain Co. v. Plains Trucking Co., Inc.,* 494 S.W.2d 639, 641 (Tex. Civ. App. 1973).

b.   Garnishment's Coverage of After-Acquired Property and Obligations

In some states the impoundment and lien of garnishment reach only the assets that the garnishee owes the debtor at the time the writ is served.   Any property of the debtor thereafter received by the garnishee, or any obligation to the debtor thereafter incurred by the garnishee, are not affected by the garnishment.   See, e.g., *Smith v. Crocker First Nat. Bank,* 152 Cal. App. 2d 832, 834, 314 P.2d 237, 239 (1957); *Cummings General Tire Co. v. Volpe Const. Co.,* 230 A.2d 712, 713–14 (D.C. App. 1967); *National Surety Corp. v. Gillette,* 194 Kan. 604, 606, 400 P.2d 681, 683 (1965); *Johnson v. Dutch Mill Dairy,* 237 Minn. 117, 121, 54 N.W.2d 1, 3 (1952).

Example: Bank was served on March 4 as garnishee in a proceeding begun by JC–1. At that time, Bank owed nothing to the debtor, JD. On March 7, property of JD was sold and the proceeds were paid to Bank as clerk of the sale.   Thereafter, but before the proceeds were turned over to JD, another creditor of the debtor, JC–2, garnished the bank.   JC–2 is entitled to the sale proceeds which Bank owed JD; JC–1's garnishment did not reach the proceeds because, at the time JC–1's garnishment was served on the Bank, the Bank had not yet received the property. *Marengo State Bank v. West,* 132 Ill. App. 2d 106, 108, 267 N.E.2d 527, 528 (1971).   The court in this case applied the rule that the garnishment "lien only attaches to property of the debtor in the garnishee's hands *as of the exact moment* the service of the summons is made."   W. Hawkland & P. Loiseaux, Cases and Materials on Debtor-Creditor Relations 74 (2d ed. 1979).

In other states the impoundment and lien of garnishment not only reach property held, and credits owed, by the garnishee at the time the summons is served; the garnishment also reaches property of the debtor which comes into the possession of the garnishee, and debts of the garnishee which accrue, in the interim between service on the garnishee and answer by her.   See, e.g., *Weiner v. Shredded Steel Products, Inc.,* 334 S.W.2d 390, 393 (Mo. App. 1960); *Keeran v. Salley,* 244 S.W.2d 663, 666 (Tex. Civ. App. 1951).   In a few states, the period of the garnishee's accountability is even longer, extending to the time of judgment in the garnishment action. *Fico, Inc. v. Ghingher,* 287 Md. 150, 161, 411 A.2d 430, 437 (1980); *Fleming v. Quaid,* 204 Pa. Super. 19, 22, 201 A.2d 252, 255 (1964).   The court in *Bassett v. McCarty,* 3 Wash. 2d 488, 493, 101 P.2d 575, 577 (1940), took a middle position, holding that a writ of garnishment impounds (1) any and all money or goods of the debtor in the hands of the garnishee at the date of service of the writ and at any time thereafter until service of the garnishee's answer and (2) "moneys or goods *coming into the garnishee's hands at any time before trial,* pursuant to any contract or agreement creating an obligation to pay such money or hold such goods, *provided that* such contract or agreement subsisted as an obligation at the time of service of the writ or of the answer, or at any time between those dates." Id. at 493, 101 P.2d at 577 (emphasis added).

c. Future Wages

Under any of the several rules governing the coverage of after-acquired property by a garnishment, satisfying a judgment by garnishing the debtor's wages may involve a series of garnishments. In the interest of economy, some states thus provide that a garnishment of wages automatically continues for a specified length of time or until the judgment is satisfied. For example, under North Dakota's recently overhauled garnishment statute, a wage garnishment can be perpetuated for a period of 60 days without further action by the creditor. N.D. Cent. Code § 32–09.1–21 (Supp. 1987). For a discussion of this provision and its narrow scope, see Laurence, *North Dakota's New Rules Respecting Garnishment and The Property Exempt Therefrom,* 58 N. D. L. Rev. 183, 194–97 (1982). In Louisiana, a garnishment of wages automatically covers both accrued and future earnings for such time as is necessary to satisfy the garnishor's judgment. La. Rev. Stat. Ann. §§ 13:3921 & 13:3923 (West 1968 & Supp. 1988), construed in *Grand v. Kado,* 279 So. 2d 811, 813–14 (La. App. 1973). In Arkansas, a lien of garnishment on wages extends to subsequent earnings for as long as three months after service of process on the garnishee *if* the debtor consents. Ark. Code Ann. § 16–110–415(b)(1) (1987).

3. GARNISHEE MAY QUESTION VALIDITY OF THE ORIGINAL MAIN ACTION AND GARNISHMENT PROCEEDINGS

A garnishee can defeat a garnishment on the basis of irregularities in the garnishment proceeding itself. Moreover, she can defend against the garnishment by challenging the validity of the creditor's judgment against the debtor. The garnishee has an interest in seeing that the judgment is valid so that she will be protected in her payment to the garnishor. *Ebey v. Southern Health Benefit Foundation for Employees & Dependents,* 377 So. 2d 421, 423 (La. App. 1979). Thus, a creditor's attempt to garnish will be blocked if the garnishee shows that the creditor's judgment against the debtor was rendered by a court which did not have jurisdiction over the debtor. *Clemmons v. Travelers Ins. Co.,* 88 Ill. App. 3d 201, 208, 410 N.E.2d 445, 450 (1980), aff'd, 88 Ill. 2d 469, 430 N.E.2d 1104 (1981). If a void judgment goes unchallenged by a garnishee who satisfies the garnishment, the garnishee is liable to the debtor for having surrendered the debtor's property to a person who legally had no right to it. *O'Toole v. Helio Products, Inc.,* 17 Ill. App. 2d 82, 84, 149 N.E.2d 795, 796 (1958).

4. GARNISHEE MAY RAISE DEFENSES SHE COULD ASSERT AGAINST DEBTOR

Service of garnishment has the effect of an equitable assignment to the garnishor of the debtor's rights against the garnishee. *Almi, Inc. v. Dick Corp.,* 31 Pa. Cmwlth. 26, 34, 375 A.2d 1343, 1348 (1977). Consequently, a garnishor stands in the judgment debtor's shoes in collecting property of the debtor held or owed by the garnishee. Thus, any defenses that the garnishee could assert against the debtor can be raised against the garnishor, including defenses such as those going to the existence of the debtor's rights vis-a-vis the garnishee and the enforceability of any such rights.

5. OBLIGATIONS OWED GARNISHEE BY DEBTOR CAN BE SET OFF AGAINST GARNISHOR'S CLAIM

"The authorities generally * * * recognize the right of offset; that is, if the [debtor] is indebted to the garnishee for some amount and the garnishee has in his hands any goods, credits, or money belonging to the [debtor], then the garnishee can keep enough of the same to satisfy his claim against the [debtor]." *Bray v. Ed Willey & Son,* 239 Ark. 855, 856–57, 395 S.W.2d 342, 343–44 (1965); see also *Sears Roebuck & Co. v. A.T. & G. Co., Inc.,* 66 Mich. App. 359, 368, 239 N.W.2d 614, 618 (1976); cf. *Fireman's Fund Ins. v. Plaza Oldsmobile Ltd.,* 596 F. Supp. 657 (E.D. N.Y. 1984) (when execution is aimed at debtor's obligor, the obligor can offset debts owed her by debtor). Only matured debts can be offset by the garnishee, however. *Mattek v. Hoffmann,* 272 Wis. 503, 506, 76 N.W.2d 300, 302 (1956). The courts disagree as to whether the debts must have matured by the time the writ of garnishment is served. Compare, e.g., *Prince v. West End Installation Service, Inc.,* 575 S.W.2d 831, 832–33 (Mo. App. 1978) (debts must have been mature when summons served) with *Valley Nat. Bank v. Hasper,* 6 Ariz. App. 376, 379–80, 432 P.2d 924, 927–28 (1967) (bank could offset amount due it under contract which bank accelerated after service of garnishment writ) and *Messall v. Suburban Trust Co.,* 244 Md. 502, 507–09, 224 A.2d 419, 421–22 (1966) (garnishee can offset any debt that becomes due prior to trial in garnishment proceeding). As to claims against the debtor that do not even arise until after service of the garnishment, the courts disagree. Some courts have concluded that a garnishee's right of setoff becomes fixed as of the time the writ is served. *Rockey v. McCauley,* 148 Colo. 331, 333, 366 P.2d 138, 140 (1961). Others hold that the critical time is the date when the garnishee's answer is filed. *Estridge v. Janko,* 96 Ga. App. 246, 99 S.E.2d 682 (1957). Other courts have adopted middle positions. In *Harpster v. Reynolds,* 215 Kan. 327, 331, 524 P.2d 212, 215 (1974), the court recited the rule that postservice claims cannot be offset except when the claim arises out of the very contract upon which the garnishee's liability to the garnishor is based. The court in *Eger Block & Redi-Mix Co. v. Wheeler,* 207 So. 2d 698, 699 (Fla. Dist. Ct. App. 1968), announced an even wider exception, allowing the garnishee to offset subsequent claims that arose out of *any* contracts that were in existence prior to the garnishment. Inasmuch as the garnishor is acting essentially as an assignee of the debtor's claim against the garnishee, why not look to the U.C.C. for guidance? Article 9 provides that an assignee's rights against the obligor, referred to as an account debtor under Article 9, "are subject to (a) all the terms of the contract between the account debtor and assignor and *any defense or claim arising therefrom;* and (b) *any other defense or claim* of the account debtor against the assignor *which accrues before the account debtor receives notification of the assignment.*" U.C.C. § 9–318(1) (emphasis added).

6. GARNISHEE MAY ASSERT THE RIGHTS OF THIRD PARTY CLAIMANTS OF THE DEBTOR'S PROPERTY

There is some authority that a garnishee has "the right to offer in defense all of the rights of a third-party claimant [of the debtor's credits or property which the garnishee holds], such as an assignee. Such rights must have accrued before the service of the [garnishment] process, [however,] because such service freezes the funds and forbids any change in ownership pending determination of the responsibility of [the garnishee]." *First Wisconsin Mortgage Trust v. Wyman's, Inc.,* 139 Vt. 350, 356, 428 A.2d 1119, 1123 (1981).

7. GARNISHEE MAY ASSERT DEBTOR'S EXEMPTIONS

If the debtor's credits or other property held by the garnishee are exempt from garnishment by federal or state law, the garnishee is generally permitted to assert the debtor's exemptions and thereby resist the garnishment. See, e.g., *Elbert Sales Co. v. Granite City Bank,* 55 Ga. App. 835, 836, 192 S.E. 66, 68 (1937); *Wilmer v. Mann,* 121 Md. 239, 248, 88 A. 222, 225 (1913); *Sears, Roebuck & Co. v. A.T. & G. Co., Inc.,* 66 Mich. App. 359, 367, 239 N.W.2d 614, 618 (1976) (garnishee asserted on debtor's behalf federal law limiting garnishment of wages to 25% of debtor's disposal earnings); *Texas Co. v. Asphalt Distrib. Co.,* 224 Mo. App. 1192, 1196, 33 S.W.2d 1003, 1004 (1931); *Seventy-First Street & Broadway Corp. v. Thorne,* 10 N.J. Misc. 99, 101, 157 A. 851, 852 (1932); *Oklahoma Nat. Bank v. Lingo,* 131 Okl. 209, 210, 268 P. 257, 258 (1928); *Eastern Lithographing Corp. v. Neville,* 203 Pa. Super. 21, 24, 198 A.2d 391, 393 (1964) (rules of civil procedure authorize garnishee to resist attachment by asserting defense of immunity from execution); cf. *Milne v. Shell Oil Co.,* 129 Vt. 375, 278 A.2d 741 (1971) (garnishee justified in paying to debtor that part of debtor's wages exempt from process). In Mississippi, if the garnishee raises the debtor's right to an exemption, the judgment debtor is summoned to court and the garnishment proceedings are stayed until the debtor's right to the exemption is finally determined. *Brondum v. Rosenblum,* 151 Miss. 91, 97–98, 117 So. 363, 364 (1928); *Howell v. Moss Point Furniture Co.,* 136 Miss. 399, 408, 101 So. 559, 560 (1924); *Illinois Cent. R.R. Co. v. Badley,* 94 Miss. 437, 439–40, 49 So. 114, 114 (1909).

A different question is whether a garnishee is ever required to assert the debtor's exemptions. Is a garnishee liable to the debtor to the extent that the garnishee hands over or pays exempt property to the garnishor? It would seem that, when property is immune from seizure by the garnishor, the garnishor has no legal right to it, and that a garnishee who nevertheless surrenders the property to the garnishor has thus converted the property. There is, however, no general rule based on this reasoning. But see *School Dist. No. 4 v. Gage,* 39 Mich. 484, 486 (1878) ("The garnishee cannot without the debtor's consent subject his rights to any unlawful burden.") Whether a garnishee is required to assert the debtor's exemptions more often turns on the language of the pertinent garnishment and exemption statutes. Compare *Dunlop v. First Nat. Bank,* 399 F. Supp. 855, 858 (D. Ariz. 1975) (even if debtor's wages deposited in a bank account were exempt under federal law, there is nothing in the law that places on the bank a duty to assert the exemption) with *Libby Furniture & Appliance Co. v. Nabors,* 86 Ill. App. 2d 381, 386, 230 N.E.2d 28, 31 (1967) (garnishment statute imposes upon employer the duty to ascertain and claim for the employee the benefit of the wage exemption to which employee is entitled). See generally *Hodgson v. Christopher,* 365 F. Supp. 583 (D. N.D. 1973) (federal wage exemption law preempts state statute allowing employer to surrender debtor's wages in excess of the maximum amount prescribed by law).

Apart from any statutorily imposed duty of a garnishee to assert a debtor's exemptions, a few courts through decisional law have imposed such a duty. See, e.g., *Ogle v. Barron,* 247 Pa. 19, 24–25, 92 A. 1071, 1073 (1915) and cases quoted therein; *Ingram v. Summers,* 29 S.W.2d 447, 450 (Tex. Civ. App. 1930) ("The law appears to us to be that where the funds sought to be garnished are exempt, it is the duty of the garnishee to set up such a defense in his answer."). See also *Southern Ry. Co. v. Fulford,* 125 Ga. 103, 104–05, 54 S.E. 68, 68–69 (1906) (garnishee's duty to assert debtor's exemptions limited to those exemptions the garnishee has knowledge or notice of); *Armour Packing Co. v. Wynn,* 119 Ga. 683, 685, 46 S.E. 865, 866 (1904) (same).

A large problem with requiring a garnishee to assert a debtor's exemptions is that a debtor often has some discretion in selecting exempt property. For example, a debtor in some states is allowed to exempt a certain dollar amount of personal property and must chose the specific property that will be beyond her creditor's reach. This sort of decision cannot and should not be made by a garnishee. For this reason, the court in *John H. Schroeder Wine & Liquor Co. v. Willis Coal & Mining Co.,* 179 Mo. App. 93, 161 S.W. 352 (1913), distinguished between laws that allow the debtor to choose to exempt specific types of property from laws that grant a flat percentage exemption (e.g., wages exemptions) and held that the garnishee only has a duty to assert the latter type of exemption in which case no "personal privilege of the debtor" is involved. Id. at 101–103, 161 S.W. at 354–55. Other courts rely on the more general doctrine that the judgment debtor may waive the right to claim exemptions and that exemptions are, therefore, a personal privilege of the judgment debtor that may not be asserted by a garnishee. See, e.g., *Seitz v. Starks,* 136 Mich. 90, 95, 98 N.W. 852, 854 (1904); *Osborne v. Schutt,* 67 Mo. 712, 714 (1878); *Dinkins v. Cruden-Martin Woodenware Co.,* 99 Mo. App. 310, 320, 73 S.W. 246, 249 (1903); *Conley v. Chilcote,* 25 Ohio St. 320, 324 (1874); *Pennsylvania R. Co. v. Bell,* 22 Ohio App. 67, 69–70, 153 N.E. 293, 293 (1925). Still another court has simply concluded, without elaboration, that garnishees cannot assert their creditors' rights to exemptions. *Holbrook v. Fyffe,* 164 Ky. 435, 440, 175 S.W. 977, 979 (1915).

Where there is no absolute duty upon the garnishee to assert the debtor's exemptions, or where the garnishee is precluded from asserting them, the garnishee may at least be required to notify the debtor if the debtor is unaware of the garnishment proceedings so that she has the opportunity to assert her exemptions. See *Agnew v. Cronin,* 148 Cal. App. 2d 117, 126–29, 306 P.2d 527, 533–35 (1957) (duty upon garnishee to notify judgment debtor of garnishment process reported to be the prevailing law, yet in this case garnishee was a conspirator in a scheme calculated to rob debtor of the funds held by the garnishee and to deprive debtor of the opportunity to assert exemption; *Russell v. Hamilton,* 174 S.W. 705, 705–06 (Tex. Civ. App. 1915) (garnishee has duty to either make the defense of exemption or have the judgment debtor notified so that she can make her own defense). When the debtor is aware of the garnishment, however, some authorities hold flatly that "it

is the duty of the debtor, not the garnishee, to promptly claim an exemption."
Wilmington Trust Co. v. Barry, 338 A.2d 575, 579 (Del. Super. Ct. 1975).

E. SPECIAL PROBLEMS WHEN THE GARNISHEE IS A BANK

A deposit of money in a bank account makes the bank a debtor of the depositor. This sort of debt owed by banks is a favorite target for garnishment by creditors of bank customers. A host of special problems arise when a bank is a garnishee. Among the most significant such problems are these:

1. GARNISHING JOINT ACCOUNTS

H and W maintain a joint checking account at Bank. Both H and W desposit their salaries in this account and the funds are commingled. Can a creditor of H or W garnish this account for a debt on which the other joint depositor is not liable? The rule in most states is that a joint account can be garnished by a creditor of only one of the depositors, but only to the extent of the debtor's equitable ownership of the funds in the account. For a vast collection of cases, see Annot., 11 A.L.R.3d 1465, 1473–74 (1967).

2. GARNISHING SPECIAL ACCOUNTS

A special bank account established by a person to hold another's funds is generally immune from garnishment by creditors of the depositor. Thus, a lawyer's trust account cannot be reached by the lawyer's creditors. More surprising is that, in some states, a depositor can immunize an account of her own funds by dedicating the account to some special purpose. Suppose, for example, that D maintains two checking accounts at her bank. One account is used for paying routine living expenses. The other account was established by the debtor solely for the purpose of collecting funds that the bank would draw on twice annually in paying the debtor's real estate taxes and home insurance premiums. Can D's creditor garnish the special account? The general rule in some jurisdictions is that a deposit made expressly for a particular purpose is not subject to, and cannot be diverted from such purpose by garnishment to satisfy the depositor's general obligations. (A special account is subject, however, to garnishment by a creditor for whose benefit the special deposit was made. Annot., 8 A.L.R. 4th 998, 1002 (1981).) Similarly, there is substantial authority holding that, when a client's funds are held by her lawyer in some special capacity, the funds are immune from garnishment by the client's creditors. See Annot., 35 A.L.R.3d 1094, 1104–13 (1971).

3. GARNISHING A UNIT OF THE DEBTOR'S BANK OTHER THAN THE BRANCH WHERE THE DEBTOR'S ACCOUNT IS MAINTAINED

Branch banks in some states are for many purposes treated as separate institutions. See, e.g., U.C.C. § 4–106 (branches are separate banks for many purposes under Articles 3 & 4). Until recently, this treatment made sense when a creditor sought to garnish a debtor's bank account. Branches have often maintained their own deposit ledgers and in other ways have operated independently of one another. Thus, the courts have been legitimately concerned that any other treatment could cause great confusion, especially at banks with many branches. Traditionally, therefore, the rule has been that a debtor's account can be garnished only by directing process at the branch where her account is maintained. For a collection of cases, see Annot., 12 A.L.R.3d 1088, 1089 (1967). Today, however, computerization allows a bank to consolidate all of its deposit ledgers and other records of customer transactions. Many financial institutions now keep account of all their customers' banking activities through a central processing division. In some cases branches do not even see checks that are drawn against them by bank customers. All checks presented for payment are routed to central data processing or some comparable unit of the bank where all of the bank's check clearing activities have been centralized. For descriptions of modern methods of keeping track of customers' accounts in the banking business, see, e.g., *Idah-Best, Inc. v. First Security Bank of Idaho,* 99 Idaho 517, 520–22, 584 P.2d 1242, 1245–47 (1978); *South Sound Nat. Bank v. First Interstate Bank,* 65 Or. App. 553, 554–55, 672 P.2d 1194, 1195 (1983). After considering these sorts of changes in the handling by banks of customers' accounts, the court in *Digitrex, Inc. v. Johnson,* 491 F. Supp. 66 (S.D. N.Y. 1980), held that a depositor's funds can be levied on at a branch other than the one at which she maintains her account. Id. at 69. For a discussion of this case and the issue it raises, see Korn, *Attachment of Bank Deposits in the Electronic Age: The Doctrine of Digitrex,* 100 Banking L. J. 607 (1983).

4. DECIDING THE RACE BETWEEN A CHECK IN THE COLLECTION PROCESS AND A WRIT OF GARNISHMENT AIMED AT FREEZING THE DRAWER'S ACCOUNT

a. Under the Uniform Commercial Code

Suppose that D draws a check payable to P's order. P cashes the check at her bank, which then sends the check to D's bank for payment. Just before the check arrives at D's bank, a writ of garnishment is served on the bank by one of D's creditors. D's bank is obligated to its customer to honor checks that are properly payable. On the other hand, the service of a garnishment summons impounds all of the debtor's property held by the garnishee. By paying the check, therefore, the bank will become liable to the garnishor. By refusing to pay the check, the bank risks liability to its customer for wrongful dishonor. The bank's problem is compounded because one hand cannot immediately communicate with the other. Service of the writ on a bank officer only in theory gives notice to the bank as a whole. In reality, some time is necessary in order to make the writ known to the persons who can actually freeze the customer's account. In recognition of this reality, U.C.C. § 4–303 provides that legal process, such as a writ of garnishment, is ineffective against a bank with respect to checks which the bank pays or decides to pay before the expiration of a reasonable time after the process has been served. U.C.C. § 4–303(1). Thus, a bank is not always liable to a garnishor for paying a check after service of the garnishment summons. Liability turns not on the precise moment when the writ was served, but rather on the bank's action within a reasonable time after the service. If, however, the bank has not paid or made the decision to pay a check drawn against the debtor's account before the expiration of a reasonable time after service of a garnishment summons, the bank becomes liable to the garnishor by paying the check. In this case, the check should be dishonored. The bank then need not worry about incurring liability to its customer inasmuch as the dishonor is legally justified, not wrongful. See, e.g., *Chandler v. El Paso Nat. Bank,* 589 S.W.2d 832, 836 (Tex. Civ. App. 1979).

b. Under the Bankruptcy Code
Before the adoption of the Bankruptcy Reform Act of 1978, bankruptcy law could have been construed as providing that a bank that paid a debtor's checks after the filing of the bankruptcy petition was liable to the debtor's bankrupt estate regardless of whether the bank had been given notice of the filing of the bankruptcy petition. See *Bank of Marin v. England,* 385 U.S. 99, 101–02, 87 S. Ct. 274, 276–77 (1966). The Supreme Court, however, in the *Bank of Marin* case, refused to so construe the law. Id. at 103, 87 S. Ct. at 277. Relying on the principle that parties should have notice before they are deprived of property, and reasoning that the payee of the check can be held liable as receiving a voidable preference, the Court held that the bank's authority to pay checks drawn by its customers is not revoked until the bank has received notice of the bankruptcy action. The new Bankruptcy Code codifies the holding of *Bank of Marin* by expressly providing that a person who acts in good faith without actual notice or knowledge of the debtor's bankruptcy petition may transfer property of the debtor, such as by paying checks drawn by her or giving property to a garnishor, without incurring liability to the debtor's bankrupt estate. 11 U.S.C.A. § 542(c) (1982).

F. EFFECT OF GARNISHMENT BETWEEN GARNISHEE AND JUDGMENT DEBTOR

1. WHERE GARNISHEE PAYS JUDGMENT CREDITOR
a. Garnishee Gets Credit for Amount it is Ordered to Pay
At least when the judgment debtor has notice of the garnishment, the garnishee's obligation to the judgment debtor is reduced by the amount the garnishee pays the garnishor as a result of a judgment in the garnishment proceeding. *Oppenheimer v. Dresdner Bank A.G.,* 50 A.D.2d 434, 440–41, 377 N.Y.S.2d 625, 631–32 (1975). Compare *Richard v. Industrial Trust Co.,* 85 R.I. 292, 301–04, 130 A.2d 549, 554–55 (1957), suggesting that a garnishee gets credit for amounts paid to garnishor only if judgment debtor is a party to the garnishment proceeding. However, "the garnishee is not protected when he makes payment under a garnishment judgment if the original judgment against the principal debtor [i.e., the judgment debtor] is void." *O'Toole v. Helio Products, Inc.,* 17 Ill. App. 2d 82, 84, 149 N.E.2d 795, 796 (1958).

b. Judgment Debtor Not Bound By Finding in Garnishment Proceeding as to Amount of Garnishee's Obligation to Judgment Debtor
Ordinarily, "the finding in a garnishment proceeding is not binding on the judgment debtor except as to the amount actually paid by the garnishee." *Savepex Sales Co. v. M.S. Kaplan Co.,* 103 Ill. App. 2d 481, 484, 243 N.E.2d 608, 610 (1968); accord, *Low v. Arnstein,* 73 Ill. App. 215, 216 (1897).

Example: G won judgment against S for $27,000 and garnished a debt K owed S. The court in the garnishment proceeding determined that

K owed S $2420 and K was ordered to pay that sum to G. Thereafter, S sued K, alleging that K actually owed S almost $14,000. K argued in defense that the prior garnishment proceeding was res judicata and that its payment of $2420 to G acquitted it of all demands by S. This argument fails. "[A] judgment against a garnishee is not conclusive as to the amount of his indebtedness to the judgment debtor in the garnishment proceedings and does not constitute a bar to an action by that judgment debtor against the garnishee to recover the residue over and above the amount paid by the garnishee pursuant to the judgment in garnishment." *Savepex Sales Co. v. M.S. Kaplan Co.,* 103 Ill. App. 2d 481, 483, 243 N.E.2d 608, 610 (1968).

2. WHERE GARNISHEE IS DISCHARGED FROM LIABILITY TO JUDGMENT CREDITOR

A garnishee's victory in a garnishment action to which the judgment debtor was not a party does not prevent a later suit by the judgment debtor against the garnishee on the obligation which the latter owes the former. This sort of suit is not barred even when the garnishee won the garnishment action by convincing the court that she was not obligated to the judgment debtor.

G. PRIORITY BETWEEN GARNISHMENTS

1. GENERAL RULE GOVERNING CREDITOR GARNISHMENTS

The long-established general rule as to priority between several garnishments against the same property by different creditors is that the garnishors rank in the direct order of time of service of the garnishment summons on the garnishee. *Grant v. Reed,* 167 Kan. 289, 295, 205 P.2d 955, 959 (1949) (dictum); *Grand v. Kado,* 279 So. 2d 811, 814 (La. App. 1973); *Fico, Inc. v. Ghingher,* 287 Md. 150, 162, 411 A.2d 430, 437–38 (1980); *Northwestern Nat. Ins. Co. v. William G. Wetherall, Inc.,* 267 Md. 378, 387, 298 A.2d 1, 7 (1972); J. Rood, A Treatise on the Law of Garnishment § 188 (1896); but see *Citizens & Southern Nat. Bank v. Wray,* 144 Ga. App. 769, 242 S.E.2d 365 (1978) (prior judgment creditor takes ahead of a subsequent judgment creditor even though the latter creditor first causes a summons of garnishment to issue because, under Georgia law, judgment creates lien on all of debtor's personal, as well as her real, property).

2. SUPER–PRIORITY FOR SUPPORT GARNISHMENTS

A number of states give special preference to a garnishment to enforce a support judgment in a domestic relations case and give it priority over even a prior garnishment. See, e.g., *Long Island Trust Co. v. United States Postal Serv.,* 647 F.2d 336, 339 (2d Cir. 1981) (applying New York law); *Shannon v. Shannon,* 386 So. 2d 184, 185 (La. App. 1980) (special priority for garnishment to enforce judgment for child support).

H. PRIORITY AMONG GARNISHMENTS AND OTHER CLAIMS OR INTERESTS

In the usual case where the priority of a garnishing creditor is at issue, the other claimant is an assignee of the debtor; both parties, the garnishor and the assignee, claim a credit which the garnishee has interpleaded or has already paid to one of the claimants. If the garnishee has already paid the credit, the validity of the payment, and thus the liability of the garnishee, turns on whether the recipient was entitled to priority over the other claimant.

1. DETERMINE FIRST IF GARNISHOR'S LIEN REACHED THE PROPERTY

Before determining priority according to the following rules, it must be decided if the garnishing creditor acquired a lien on the credit which the debtor has assigned. If not, there is no priority dispute, and the assignee prevails. In deciding if the garnishor acquired a lien on the property that the debtor assigned, it will often be important to check the local rule regarding garnishment's coverage of after-acquired property and obligations. See supra Chapter V.D.2.b. Suppose, for example, that after the service of a garnishment summons but before the garnishee answers, the garnishee becomes indebted to the judgment debtor. The debtor then assigns her right against the garnishee. Is there a priority dispute? The answer is no in those jurisdictions where a garnishment reaches only the property and credits of the debtor in the garnishee's hands at the moment the garnishment summons is served. Assignee prevails. If, however, local law extends the reach of garnishment to property and credits of the debtor coming into the hands of the garnishee before she answers the summons, the garnishor acquires an interest in the assigned property. In this case the winner of the priority conflict is determined according to the following rules.

2. ASSIGNMENT OF DEBTOR'S RIGHT AGAINST GARNISHEE MADE BEFORE CREDITOR'S GARNISHMENT

a. Traditional Rule—First in Time First in Right

Because a garnishment is effective only to the extent of the debtor's interest in property that is seized, the usual rule is that a garnishor's lien does not displace prior equities or rights in the property that the garnishor seeks to attach. Thus, the claim of an assignee under a valid assignment made before the garnishment is superior to any lien of the garnishing creditor. See, e.g., *Hare v. Hartley*, 349 So. 2d 1151, 1152 (Ala. 1977); *Iser Elec. Co. v. Ingran Constr. Co.*, 48 Ill. App. 3d 110, 120, 362 N.E.2d 771, 779 (1977); *Briley v. Madrid Improvement Co.*, 255 Iowa 388, 390–92, 122 N.W.2d 824, 825–26 (1963); *Southwestern Bell Tel. Co. v. Crown Ins. Co.*, 416 S.W.2d 705, 709 (Mo. App. 1967); *Russell v. Fred G. Pohl Co.*, 7 N.J. 32, 39, 80 A.2d 191, 194 (1951); *Higgs v. Amarillo Postal Employees Credit Union*, 358 S.W.2d 761, 763 (Tex. Civ. App. 1962); see also Restatement (Second) of Contracts §§ 341(1) & 342 (1981).

b. Exception—Perfection May Be Required

In a great many states a prior assignment will prevail over a garnishment only if the assignee perfected her claim, either by notifying the obligor/garnishee of the assignment or by recording public notice of it, prior to service of the garnishment summons. See, e.g., *Colt Industries Operating Corp. v. Cobb,* 646 F.2d 200, 202 (5th Cir. 1981); *Oper v. Air Control Prods., Inc. of Miami,* 174 So. 2d 561, 563 (Fla. App. 1965); *Union Livestock Yards, Inc. v. Merrill Lynch, Pierce, Fenner & Smith, Inc.,* 552 S.W.2d 392, 397 (Tenn. App. 1976); see also Restatement (Second) of Contracts § 341(2) (1981) (protects obligor/garnishee from double liability where she pays garnishor before receiving notice of the assignment). Certainly, if U.C.C. Article 9 governs the debtor's assignment of her rights against the obligor/garnishee, the assignee/secured party will lose to a subsequent garnishor unless the assignee has perfected its security interest before the garnishment. See U.C.C. § 9–301(1)(b). Conversely, if the assignee's security interest is perfected before garnishment, the assignee prevails. See, e.g., *Rural Gas, Inc. v. Shepek,* 205 Kan. 397, 400, 469 P.2d 341, 343 (1970); *Earl Dubey & Sons, Inc. v. Macomb Contracting Corp.,* 97 Mich. App. 553, 554–56, 296 N.W.2d 582, 587–88 (1980).

3. ASSIGNMENT MADE AFTER GARNISHMENT

a. Traditional Rule—First in Time First in Right

First, no one doubts that, despite garnishment of debtor's rights against the garnishee, the debtor can thereafter assign what rights she has in the property. See, e.g., *Spriggs v. Goodrich,* 74 Wyo. 183, 185, 285 P.2d 1103, 1105 (1955), reh'g denied, 74 Wyo. 185, 289 P.2d 648 (1955). On the other hand, everyone agrees that a garnishment prior in time to an assignment of the debtor's rights against the garnishee is also prior in right if the garnishment created a valid lien. Thus the debtor's rights which the assignee takes are burdened with the lien of garnishment. *Green v. Robertson,* 80 Ark. 1, 7–8, 96 S.W. 138, 140 (1906); *Crow v. Yosemite Creek Co.,* 149 Cal. App. 2d 188, 190, 308 P.2d 421, 422 (1957); *Keeran v. Salley,* 244 S.W.2d 663, 666 (Tex. Civ. App. 1951). This rule is founded on the basic principle of derivative title, i.e., no one can convey a title better than her own.

b. Similar Rule Where Tangible Property Is Involved

1) Cases Involving Goods

The usual principle, that no one can convey a better title than she herself holds, also applies when the garnishee holds tangible property of the debtor. For example, suppose that the garnishee is in possession of a boat belonging to the debtor. After service of the garnishment summons on the garnishee, the boat is sold or subjected to a security interest. The purchaser takes the property subject to the lien of garnishment. See U.C.C. § 9–301(1)(b); *McConnell v. Babcock,* 49 S.D. 616, 618–19, 208 N.W. 160, 161 (1926) (involving garnishment of crops which purportedly were mortgaged along with the land on which they grew); but see *Maxwell v. Bank of New Richmond,* 101 Wis. 286, 288, 77 N.W. 149, 150 (1898) (service of garnishment summons creates equitable levy or lien on property of debtor held by garnishee but bona fide purchaser for value without notice takes free of the lien).

2) Exception Where Negotiable Instruments Involved

There are exceptions to the rule of derivative title so that, in some cases, a transferee of property acquires greater rights than those of the transferor. The best example is the holder in due course of a negotiable instrument under U.C.C. Article 3. Such a person takes the instrument free from all adverse claims to the property. U.C.C. §§ 3–302(1) & 3–305(1). Suppose, for example, that a judgment debtor pledged to a bank a negotiable instrument payable to the debtor's order. The bank is garnished by a judgment creditor of debtor. Thereafter, the note is negotiated to a second pledgee or other transferee. This second transferee will take the instrument free of the garnishor's lien if the transferee is a holder in due course. Of course, the garnishee-bank may nevertheless be liable to the garnishor for not holding the note for the garnishor's benefit. See supra Chapter V.D.2.

I. GOVERNMENT AS WAGE GARNISHEE

1. FEDERAL GOVERNMENT

a. General Rule of Immunity

Because of the principle of sovereign immunity, the United States Government cannot be sued without its consent; for this reason, the wages of federal employees cannot be garnished so long as the wages remain in the hands of the United States, *Buchanan v. Alexander,* 45 U.S. (4 How.) 20 (1846), except in isolated cases where immunity has been waived. (The principle of *Buchanan* is really much larger. The case has been used to support the broad notion that federal monies cannot be garnished no matter who holds them until they have been paid out for their intended purposes. *Palmiter v. Action, Inc.,* 733 F.2d 1244 (7th Cir. 1984).)

b. Waivers of Immunity

1) Based on Legislation Creating Federal Agencies

"The most frequent basis for finding a waiver of [sovereign] immunity * * * has been congressional enactment of statutes authorizing federal agencies to sue and be sued in courts of competent jurisdiction. [T]he words 'sue and be sued' normally embrace all civil process incident to legal proceedings, including garnishment procedures." *May Department Stores Co. v. Smith,* 572 F.2d 1275, 1277 (8th Cir. 1978). For instance, the Supreme Court decided in *Federal Housing Administration v. Burr,* 309 U.S. 242, 60 S. Ct. 488 (1940), that consent to sue or be sued in the Federal Housing Act [12 U.S.C.A. § 1702 (1982)] includes consent to garnish the wages of Federal Housing Administration employees. Id. at 247–49, 60 S.Ct. at 491–92. Based on similar language in Postal Reorganization Act of 1970, i.e., 39 U.S.C.A. § 401 (1982), courts have held that the wages of United States Postal Service workers can be garnished. See, e.g., *Goodman's Furniture Co. v. United States Postal Service,* 561 F.2d 462, 465 (3d Cir. 1977) (per curiam); *May Department Stores Co. v. Williamson,* 549 F.2d 1147, 1147–48 (8th Cir. 1977). For other cases pro and con on the issue of garnishing postal employees' wages, see cases collected in Annot., 38 A.L.R. Fed. 546 (1978). Yet, when "sue and be sued" language is narrowly drawn and not phrased in general terms, the courts are likely to conclude that the waiver of immunity does not extend to garnishment proceedings. See, e.g., *May Department Stores Co. v. Smith*, 572 F.2d 1275, 1278 (8th Cir. 1978) (Veterans Administration is immune from garnishment to enforce state court judgments against the agency's employees). In addition to the breadth of "sue and be sued" language in the law establishing the federal agency, another critical factor in determining whether the wages of a federal agency's employees can be garnished is the extent to which the agency resembles a private enterprise in the commercial world. *May Department Stores Co. v. Williamson*, 549 F.2d 1147, 1148 (8th Cir. 1977).

2) **Based on the Purpose of the Garnishment—Garnishing Federal Employees' Wages for Alimony and Child Support**
The fear that garnishment of federal employees' wages will somehow adversely affect the public good is outweighed in a few cases where the purpose of the garnishment is especially compelling. The best example is § 659(a) of the Social Security Act, 42 U.S.C.A. § 659(a) (1983), which subjects to garnishment any money paid by the United States, or any of its parts, to any individual (including members of the armed services) when the garnishment is for the enforcement of awards of child support or alimony. For a collection of cases interpreting this law, see Annot., 44 A.L.R. Fed. 494 (1979).

The waiver of governmental immunity effected by § 659(a) is quite narrow, however. For instance, when the United States is garnished under the provision, the federal government cannot be dragged into an action against the garnishor challenging the validity of the divorce decree and thus, indirectly, the garnishor's right to support. *Overman v. United States*, 563 F.2d 1287 (8th Cir. 1977). According to the court in the *Overman* case, the government's liability under § 659(a) is not so wide. Id. at 1291. Indeed, liability is so slim under § 659 that the United States is not answerable because of the provision when it honors a garnishment order issued by a court having no jurisdiction over the garnishment debtor so long as the order is "regular on its face." *United States v. Morton*, 467 U.S. 822, 104 S. Ct. 2769 (1984).

c. **National Banks as Garnishees**
Deposit accounts at banks chartered by the federal government are not immune from garnishment. The banks themselves, however, enjoy a degree of immunity. For instance, a provision of the National Bank Act provides in part that "no attachment, injunction, or execution, shall be issued against [any national banking association] or its property before final judgment in any suit, action, or proceeding, in any State, county, or municipal court." 12 U.S.C.A. § 91 (1945). Even this shield, however, does not protect customers' accounts at national banks, and such accounts are subject to garnishment when and how-

ever local law allows. See *Earle v. Conway,* 178 U.S. 456, 20 S. Ct. 918 (1900). "Congress intended only to prevent state judicial action, prior to final judgment, which would have the effect of seizing the *bank's* property. *Third Nat. Bank v. Impac Ltd., Inc.,* 432 U.S. 312, 323, 97 S. Ct. 2307, 2314 (1977) (emphasis added). Compare *A.E. Nelson & Co. v. Haggett's Sport Shop, Inc.,* 120 N.H. 515, 519–20, 418 A.2d 1273, 1276 (1980) (creditor could garnish property of debtor held by bank but not property of the bank which included proceeds of foreclosure sale of collateral).

2. STATE AND LOCAL GOVERNMENTS

State and local governments can also raise the defense of sovereign immunity, but the immunity of both levels of government can be waived by state statute. Most states explicitly permit the garnishment of wages owed by state and local municipal governments to their employees. See, e.g., Ariz. Rev. Stat. Ann. § 12–1601 (1982); Minn. Stat. §§ 571.45 & 571.46 (1986); N.H. Rev. Stat. Ann. §§ 512.9 & 512.9–a (1983).

J. WRONGFUL GARNISHMENT

1. DEFINING THE WRONG

A creditor is potentially liable for wrongful garnishment in any case where she causes a seizure of her debtor's property, or property of another, through a garnishment proceeding that is not in compliance with law. (Wrongful garnishment is a species of wrongful attachment or wrongful execution, depending on whether the garnishment is effected before or after judgment. See supra Chapter III regarding execution, which is a post-judgment remedy, and infra Chapter XI regarding attachment, which is a pre-judgment remedy that looks like execution but is not so generally available.) As a matter of commom law, malice and want of probable cause are sometimes listed as necessary elements of the wrong because the common law views wrongful garnishment as essentially a form of abuse of process or malicious prosecution. Where the cause of action is given or implied by a statute that does not mention these elements, maliciousness and the like need not always be shown. Thus, wrongful attachment or garnishment is somewhat akin to, though sometimes broader than, the torts of abuse of process and malicious prosecution. See *White Lighting Co. v. Wolfson,* 68 Cal. 2d 336, 348–49, 66 Cal. Rptr. 697, 704–05, 438 P.2d 345, 352–53 (1968) (distinguishes four different types of wrongful attachment or garnishment).

Creditors have been found liable for wrongful garnishment when:

- the debt due the garnishor was not justly due;

- the statutory grounds for garnishment, said to exist by garnishor, did not in fact exist;

- the salary of a debtor's wife was garnished for a debt owed solely by her husband;

- garnishment issued without creditor making any attempt to personally serve the debtor;

- debtor was not in default on obligation for which her funds were garnished;

- the garnishment was obtained pursuant to a statute which previously had been declared unconstitutional;

- the creditor employed garnishment to enforce a judgment which had been vacated by the debtor's appeal or which was void for lack of jurisdiction over the debtor;

- more of the debtor's property was garnished than was necessary to secure the debt she owed the garnishor.

This list merely illustrates some of the ways in which wrongful garnishment is committed; it is by no means exclusive.

2. MEASURING THE DAMAGES

A victim of wrongful garnishment can recover whatever actual damages she suffered. Actual damages may include damages for mental anguish, embarrassment, humiliation, anxiety, general inconvenience and the like; injury to credit or business relations; loss of profits; loss of the use of funds which were wrongfully garnished; and attorneys' fees incurred in fighting the garnishment. If the creditor acted maliciously, or if other aggravating circumstances attended the wrongful garnishment, exemplary damages can be awarded, too.

REVIEW QUESTIONS

1. How is garnishment begun?

2. What is the consequence of a garnishee failing to answer a garnishment summons?

3. What is the consequence of a garnishee paying accrued wages to a judgment debtor after service of garnishment summons aimed at the debtor's wages?

4. D earns gross pay of $900 a month. She nets only $700 a month, however, because the following amounts are deducted from each monthly pay check: $130 for taxes, $50 for social security, and $20 for health insurance. Under federal law, what is the maximum amount of D's wages that can be garnished to satisfy a judgment on a contract debt?

5. What is the maximum amount that can be garnished under federal law to enforce an order for the support of D's former spouse?

6. T or F   Federal restrictions on the garnishment of wages do not protect a debtor's salary once it has been paid to her.

7. What is the liability of an employer who violates federal law by firing an employee because of a single garnishment of her wages?

8. At 10:00 a.m., Bank is served with a garnishment summons aimed at D's checking account. At 11:00 a.m., Bank pays a check drawn on the account. Is Bank liable to the garnishing creditor for the amount of the check?

9. Creditor A garnished D's bank account on February 3 to enforce a judgment on a contract debt. Creditor B garnished the same account the next day to enforce a similar judgment against D. Which garnishment is entitled to priority?

10. Does the answer to Question 9 change if Creditor B is D's former spouse whose garnishment is for the purpose of enforcing a support order?

11. T or F   The wages of a person who works for the United States Postal Service can be garnished even though she is a federal employee.

12. Does the answer to Question 11 change if the person is an employee of the United States Department of Defense?

*

VI

FRAUDULENT CONVEYANCES

Analysis

2. *Partial Defense of an Innocent Transferee Who Paid Less Than*
   Fair Consideration
3. *Protection of Subgrantees*

———————

Rather than see their property seized by creditors, debtors sometimes convey their property to friends or relatives for little or no consideration or with the understanding that the debtor shall continue to have the use and benefit of the property. Since Roman law, such attempts to defraud creditors have been ineffective. The source of modern fraudulent conveyance law is the Statute of 13 Elizabeth, chapter 5, enacted by Parliament in 1570. This law condemned any conveyance of property made with the intent "to delay, hinder or defraud" creditors. As interpreted and applied, the Statute of 13 Elizabeth, and its more modern counterparts, render fraudulent conveyances voidable by creditors of the debtor, not absolutely void. Such a conveyance thus remains enforceable between the parties to it.

American jurisdictions either recognized the Statute of 13 Elizabeth as part of inherited common law or enacted identical or very similar versions of it. More recently, about one-half of the states have adopted the Uniform Fraudulent Conveyance Act (1918), hereinafter referred to as the *UFCA*. In 1984, a successor to the UFCA was promulgated by the National Conference of Commissioners on Uniform State Laws. The new model statute is entitled the Uniform Fraudulent Transfer Act, hereinafter referred to as the *UFTA*. For the most part, the two uniform laws are very similar.

Like the Statute of 13 Elizabeth, both the UFCA and the UFTA condemn transfers of property that are *actually fraudulent,* meaning that they are made with the actual, subjective intention of defrauding creditors. The two uniform statutes go further, however, and make ineffective against creditors certain conveyances of property without regard to the grantor's actual subjective intention. This latter class of conveyances, which are *constructively fraudulent,* are ineffective either because the circumstances of the conveyance conclusively imply wrongful intent, or because the law deems that creditors are wronged by the property's transfer irrespective of the intention accompanying it. This chapter reviews the elements of both actually and constructively fraudulent conveyances; the remedies available to creditors who are protected against such conveyances; and the defenses of transferees against whom the remedies are directed. The basis of most of the discussion is the UFCA, the principles of which are very similar to the statutory or common law of states that have not enacted the uniform statute. Major differences between the UFCA and its successor, the UFTA, are mentioned.

A version of the UFCA has long been part of the federal bankruptcy laws and presently appears as § 548 of the Bankruptcy Code. See 11 U.S.C.A. § 548 (1979) & Supp. 1988). Section 548 is one of many tools used by trustees to avoid prebankruptcy transfers of a debtor's property. Another such tool is § 544(b), which in effect allows a trustee to invoke state fraudulent conveyance law to invalidate a transfer. Section 544(b) is useful when the letter of the state law, or judicial interpretations of it, condemn a wider range of transfers than § 548. These bankruptcy provisions are discussed fully in Chapter XXI infra.

A. CONVEYANCES THAT ARE ACTUALLY FRAUDULENT

"Every conveyance made and every obligation incurred with actual intent, as distinguished from intent presumed in law, to hinder, delay, or defraud either present or future creditors, is fraudulent as to both present and future creditors." UFCA § 7. The new Uniform Fraudulent Transfer Act repeats this rule. See UFTA § 4(a)(1).

1. THE MEANING OF "CONVEYANCE"

The first requirement in attacking a transfer of property as a fraudulent conveyance is to establish that the transfer was a "conveyance" as defined for purposes of fraudulent conveyance law. The term is very broad, including "every payment of money, assignment, release, transfer, lease, mortgage or pledge of tangible or intangible property, and also the creation of any lien or encumbrance." UFCA § 1. (The new UFTA substitutes "transfer" for "conveyance" but does not change the substance of the definition.) Thus, fraudulent conveyances take many different forms such as:

- a husband's gift to his wife of all his real estate after a creditor of the husband wins a judgment against him, *Reade v. Livingston,* 3 Johns. Ch. 481 (N.Y. Ct. Chan. 1818);

- a debtor's fire sale of an intangible account shortly before her creditor garnished the obligor of the account, *Osawa v. Onishi,* 33 Wash. 2d 546, 206 P.2d 498 (1949);

- a legatee's renunciation of her interest in a decedent's estate so that her share would pass to relatives rather than to her creditors, *In re Kalt's Estate,* 16 Cal. 2d 807, 108 P.2d 401 (1940);

- a change in the beneficiary of a life insurance policy from the debtor's estate to a family trust, *Fidelity Trust Co. v. Union Nat. Bank,* 313 Pa. 467, 169 A. 209 (1933);

- the giving of collateral to secure a debt, *In re Allied Development Corp.,* 435 F.2d 372 (7th Cir. 1970) (secured creditor and debtor agreed not to record security interest so that other creditors would not learn of the security arrangement); *Sullivan v. Ginsberg,* 180 Ga. 840, 181 S.E. 163 (1935) (same); *M. & N. Freight Lines, Inc. v. Kimbel Lines, Inc.,* 180 Tenn. 1, 170 S.W.2d 186 (1943) (parties created a security interest in debtor's property for the purpose of discouraging execution and levy by general creditors); and,

- a private foreclosure sale of real property collateral. *Mission Bay Campland, Inc. v. Sumner Fin. Corp.,* 731 F.2d 768 (11th Cir. 1984) (where underlying debt was invalid).

2. THE MEANING OF ACTUAL INTENT TO DEFRAUD

An actual intent to hinder, delay, or defraud involves calculated conduct by the debtor who acts with a conscious realization of the adverse effects of the conduct on her creditors. *In re Allied Development Corp.*, 435 F.2d 372, 376 (7th Cir. 1970). The debtor's ultimate intention need not be to defraud; "[i]t is sufficient * * * that the purpose, motive or intent was to hinder and delay." *M. & N. Freight Lines, Inc. v. Kimbel Lines, Inc.*, 180 Tenn. 1, 4, 170 S.W.2d 186, 187 (1943). "Direct evidence is not essential, however, for said intent may be established by circumstances which indicate its existence." *Alan Drey Co., Inc. v. Generation, Inc.*, 22 Ill. App. 3d 611, 618, 317 N.E.2d 673, 679 (1974). Indicators of actual fraudulent intent are often referred to as *badges of fraud*.

3. BADGES OF FRAUD

Litigators have always had a difficult job proving that a transfer was made with actual intent to defraud creditors. Direct evidence of subjective intentions is hard to adduce. Thus, intent to defraud usually must be established through circumstantial evidence. The term *badges of fraud* has long been used in referring to circumstances that are especially reliable indicators of an intent to defraud creditors.

a. Badges Identified in *Twyne's Case*

The courts began to identify badges of fraud as early as 1601 in the famous decision known as *Twyne's Case* [1601], 3 Coke 80b, 76 Eng. Rep. 809. In this case P was indebted to T for 400 pounds and to C for 200 pounds. C sued P and, while the action was pending, P secretly conveyed to T by deed of gift all of his chattels (worth 300 pounds) in satisfaction of T's claim. P, however, remained in possession of some of the property, i.e., some sheep, and treated this property as his own. C obtained a judgment against P, but when the sheriff sought to levy on the sheep, friends of P stopped the execution by asserting that the sheep belonged to T. C then sued T to set aside the gift of the sheep from P to T as a fraudulent conveyance. The court held that the gift was fraudulent, basing its findings of an intent to defraud on these circumstances or badges of fraud:

- the conveyance was general in that all of P's, the debtor's, assets were involved;

- the debtor continued in possession of the sheep and dealt with them as his own;

- the conveyance was made while a suit against the debtor was pending;

- the transaction was secret; and,

- T, the transferee, took the property in trust for the debtor.

None of these aspects of the case was itself condemned as fraudulent by the Statute of 13 Elizabeth, which was applied in the case; yet, they all added up to an actual intent to defraud creditors which the statute did condemn.

b. **Badges Identified by UFTA**

Unlike the UFCA, the newer UFTA provides a nonexclusive catalogue of factors appropriate for consideration by a court in determining whether the debtor had an actual intent to hinder, delay or defraud one or more creditors. This catalogue of factors, which appears as UFTA § 4(b), includes most of the badges of fraud that were recognized in Twyne's case and in other cases decided under the Statute of 13 Elizabeth and also additional badges recognized in cases decided under UFCA § 7. Courts should consider whether:

- The transfer or obligation was to an insider;

- The debtor had retained possession or control of the property transferred after the transfer;

- The transfer or obligation was disclosed or concealed;

- Before the transfer was made or obligation was incurred, the debtor was sued or threatened with suit;

- The transfer was of substantially all the debtor's assets;

- The debtor had absconded;

- The debtor had removed or concealed assets;

- The value of the consideration received by the debtor was reasonably equivalent to the value of the asset transferred or the amount of the obligation incurred;

- The debtor was insolvent or became insolvent shortly after the transfer was made or the obligation was incurred;

- The transfer had occurred shortly before or shortly after a substantial debt was incurred; and

- The debtor had transferred the essential assets of the business to a lienor who had transferred the assets to an insider of the debtor.

UFTA § 4(b).

4. ROLE OF PRESUMPTIONS UNDER UFCA § 7

Badges of fraud are significant not only because their presence in a case is indirect evidence of intent to defraud; certain of them are so suggestive of fraud as to cause a shift in the burden of going forward with the evidence at trial of a fraudulent conveyance case. Instead of requiring the plaintiff—who is attacking the transfer—to establish the elements of a fraudulent conveyance, the defendant—who is the transferee of the property—is required to put on evidence that some necessary element is missing. This reversal of usual roles, and the badge of fraud that caused it, are often described as creating a presumption of fraud, which in some cases is conclusive and thus irrefutable.

(N. & E.) Creditors' Rights BLS—8

By describing the intent necessary to violate UFCA § 7 as "actual intent, as distinguished from intent presumed as a matter of law," the drafters of the Uniform Fraudulent Conveyance Act sought to avoid "all possibility of a presumption of law * * *" 7A Uniform Laws Annotated 162 (1978) (Commissioners' Prefatory Note To The UFCA). Similarly, the drafters of the new UFTA take the position that the presence of one or more badges of fraud does not create a presumption of actual fraudulent intention. UFTA § 4 comment 5. Nevertheless, courts applying the UFCA continue to recognize presumptions, and to shift evidentiary burdens accordingly, both in cases of alleged actual fraud, see V. Countryman, Cases and Materials on Debtor and Creditor 151–52 (2d ed. 1974), and also in cases involving charges of constructive fraud. See infra Chapter VI.B. The result is that, very often, the presence of facts establishing constructive fraud of some kind, where the debtor's actual subjective intent is immaterial, will also establish a presumption of actual fraud which the debtor cannot refute. An example may be *Fidelity Trust Co. v. Union Nat. Bank,* 313 Pa. 467, 169 A. 209 (1933), cert. denied, 291 U.S. 680, 54 S. Ct. 530 (1934), in which the court concluded that a financially embarrassed debtor was guilty of both actual and constructive fraud in substituting a family trust for his estate as the beneficiary of a life insurance policy. The court began its explanation of this conclusion by observing that "[p]rima facie, a voluntary conveyance by one in debt is fraudulent as to creditors." Id. at 472, 169 A. at 212.

Finding that a debtor's conveyance was both actually, as well as constructively, fraudulent is significant because there are fewer defenses to actual fraud. Regarding defenses to constructive fraud, see infra Chapter VI.B. Also, the limitation period might vary depending on whether actual or constructive fraud is the basis of the action. See *Hearn 45 St. Corp. v. Jano,* 283 N.Y. 139, 27 N.E.2d 814 (1940) (ten-year period of limitations for constructive fraud applies rather than six-year period when both types of fraud are alleged). The standard of proof may vary, too: "substantial evidence" for constructive fraud and "clear and satisfactory" proof for actual fraud. *Sparkman & McLean Co. v. Derber,* 4 Wash. App. 341, 481 P.2d 585 (1971) (applying the UFCA).

5. FAMILIAL RELATIONSHIP AS A BADGE OF FRAUD AND BASIS OF PRESUMPTION
A debtor's conveyance of property to a spouse or other family member is always suspect and is subject to more careful and closer scrutiny than a transfer between strangers. The familial relationship in itself is only a badge of fraud, however, only one indicator of actual fraudulent intent. Yet, such a relationship greatly strengthens an inference of actual fraud drawn from other circumstances. Some courts go so far as to conclude that a familial relationship coupled with another badge of fraud, such as substantial indebtedness at the time of the transfer or the lack of fair consideration for the transfer, creates a presumption of actual fraud. See, e.g., *Reade v. Livingston,* 3 Johns. Ch. 481, 500 (N.Y. Ct. Chan. 1818) (transfer by spouse for inadequate consideration); *Patterson v. Patterson,* 167 W. Va. 1, 15, 277 S.E.2d 709, 717–18 (1981) (transfer of property by father to daughter for grossly inadequate consideration is fraudulent), overruled on different point, sub nom. *LaRue v. LaRue,* 304 S.E.2d 312, 321–22 (W. Va. 1983).

Example: Late in 1807, Reade obtained a judgment against H.G.L. The next year H.G.L. conveyed his lands to Aspinwall in trust for H.G.L.'s wife. H.G.L. had no other property to satisfy Reade's judgment. H.G.L. argued that the transfer was pursuant to an oral agreement with his wife's father. Under this agreement, which was made prior to the marriage, H.G.L. was to "settle" on the wife and her children a large amount of property. Any unwritten agreement in consideration of marriage was unenforceable. Thus, there was no valuable consideration for the settlement. In effect, the settlement was voluntary, meaning that it was a gift. The applicable rule in such a case "is, that if the party be indebted at the time of the voluntary settlement, it is presumed to be fraudulent in respect to such debts, and no circumstance will permit those debts to be affected by the settlement, to repel the legal presumption of fraud." *Reade v. Livingston,* 3 Johns. Ch. 481, 500 (N.Y. Ct. Chan. 1818).

Although a transfer of property by a debtor to a family member is viewed with great suspicion, the law of fraudulent conveyances does not absolutely prohibit a debtor from transferring her property even to close relatives so long as the transactions are free of fraud and upon fair consideration. *Sullivan v. Dixon,* 280 Md. 444, 449, 373 A.2d 1245, 1248 (1977).

Example: Ms. Barker promised to marry Mr. Conner if he would make provision for her future. He agreed, promising to convey to her certain real estate and a quantity of jewelry. The night of the marriage, Conner handed to Barker the jewelry and the deed, and told his wife they were hers. Several months later, Conner, who worked as a bank manager, was arrested for embezzlement. Barker had the marriage annulled. The surety on Conner's fidelity bond made good the bank's losses; and then, as the assignee of the bank's rights, the surety sued Conner. As part of this action the surety sought to reach the jewelry and real estate which Conner had given Barker. None of this property was purchased with embezzled funds. The surety contended that the transfer involved a fraud upon creditors. The New York Court of Appeals disagreed. *American Surety Co. v. Conner,* 251 N.Y. 1, 166 N.E. 783 (1929). The transfer of the property was made in exchange for a promise of marriage, which as a matter of common law is valuable consideration. The annulment destroyed the marriage contract but did not erase the two years of marriage which immeasurably benefitted Conner.

6. GOOD CONSIDERATION NO DEFENSE IN ITSELF TO ACTUAL FRAUD

The giving of fair, substantial, good or otherwise sufficient consideration by a transferee of the debtor's property is not in itself a defense to actual fraud. *Sullivan v. Ginsberg,* 180 Ga. 840, 845, 181 S.E. 163, 165 (1935); *Bolten v. Colburn,* 389 S.W.2d 384, 390 (Mo. App. 1965). It only suggests the lack of actual fraudulent intent on the debtor's part in making the conveyance. If the trier of fact nevertheless determines on the basis of all the evidence that the debtor acted with such intent, a transferee who was aware of the intent cannot preserve the conveyance by evidence that she gave good consideration in exchange for the debtor's property.

Examples: Sullivan, a director of Brandimist, Inc., agreed to make the company a loan. To secure the loan, the corporate debtor gave Sullivan a security interest in a substantial amount of the corporation's personal property. The parties agreed that Sullivan would not record his security interest so as not to disturb other creditors of the debtor. A few months later Sullivan foreclosed and sold all of the collateral to himself for a nominal sum. On these facts the court held in *Sullivan v. Ginsberg*, 180 Ga. 840, 181 S.E. 163 (1935), that the security arrangement was made with the intention on the debtor's part to delay and defraud its creditors and that this intention was known to Sullivan. Because of this actual fraud, the conveyance was void as to creditors of the debtor even though Sullivan had taken the security, and foreclosed on it, to protect large loans he had made to the debtor.

JC won a $98,000 judgment against D. Shortly thereafter, D sold to B its only valuable asset, which was a magazine subscription list. The purchase price was $150,000, none of which sum was paid to JC. On these facts the court concluded in *Alan Drey Co., Inc. v. Generation, Inc.*, 22 Ill. App. 3d 611, 317 N.E.2d 673 (1974), that D acted with actual fraudulent intent in selling the property to B. Because B was aware of this intention, JC was entitled to recover damages from B which in this case equalled the amount of JC's judgment against D.

Nevertheless, fair or otherwise adequate consideration, coupled with good faith on the transferee's part, gives her a complete defense against the debtor's creditors even if the debtor's intention in making the transfer was actually to defraud them. See Chapter VI.D. infra.

7. PREFERENCES
a. Traditional Rule
Outside of bankruptcy and in the absence of express statutory prohibition, even an insolvent debtor may convey part or all of her property to a bona fide creditor to the extent of satisfying an honest debt. Deliberately preferring one creditor to another is not per se fraudulent. This is the rule of the common law which applies even if, as a result of the preference, the claims of other creditors will be hindered, delayed, or defeated. See, e.g., *Blumenstein v. Phillips Ins. Center, Inc.*, 490 P.2d 1213, 1221–22 (Alaska 1971); *Mohar v. McLelland Lumber Co.*, 95 Idaho 38, 42, 501 P.2d 722, 727 (1972); *Bank of Commerce v. Rosemary & Thyme, Inc.*, 218 Va. 781, 785, 239 S.E.2d 909, 912 (1978); but see Note, *Good Faith and Fraudulent Conveyances*, 97 Harv. L. Rev. 495 (1983) (author discusses recent trend of invalidating preferences as fraudulent conveyances on basis of grantor's lack of good faith in preferring one creditor to another). Moreover, it makes no difference that the debtor's intent in making the preference was to deter or hinder another creditor (even one with a judgment), or that the preferred creditor was aware she was receiving a preference.

> ***Example:*** D owes $1243 to First National Bank, $576 to Sears, $938 to VISA, and $1000 to F, a friend and electrician who rewired her house. Disregarding encumbered assets, D's only valuable property is a savings account with a $1000 balance. She withdraws the $1000 and uses the money to pay F. D decided to pay F rather than another of her other unsecured creditors because F is a friend and also because D figured that F needed the money more than any of the other creditors. On these facts there is no evidence that D acted with actual fraudulent intent in paying F. A mere preference standing alone is not fraudulent or indicative of actual fraud.

b. UFTA Rule

The Uniform Fraudulent Transfer Act (1984) creates a limited exception to the traditional rule that preferences are not fraudulent. UFTA § 5(b) renders constructively fraudulent a preferential transfer to an insider who had reason to believe that the debtor was insolvent when the transfer was made. Regarding constructively fraudulent conveyances in general, see infra Chapter VI.B. "Preferential transfer" means a transfer by an insolvent debtor for or on account of an antecedent debt. "Insider" includes a relative, a director or officer of a corporate debtor, a partner, or a person in control of a debtor. The premise of UFTA § 5(b) is that "an insolvent debtor is obligated to pay debts to creditors not related to him before paying those who are insiders." UFTA Prefatory Note.

8. TRANSACTIONS INVOLVING EXEMPT PROPERTY

a. Conveying Exempt Property

A conveyance of property that the law exempts from creditors' process (see infra Chapter VIII) usually cannot be attacked as fraudulent no matter what the debtor's intention. The reasoning behind this rule is that creditors are unharmed by the conveyance inasmuch as they could not have reached the exempted property had the conveyance not been made. See, e.g., *Oppenheim v. Goodley,* 148 Cal. App.2d 325, 327, 306 P.2d 944, 945 (1957) (homestead); *Demartini v. Demartini,* 385 Ill. 128, 135, 52 N.E.2d 138, 141 (1943) (homestead); *Hall Roberts' Son, Inc. v. Plaht,* 253 Iowa 862, 865, 114 N.W.2d 548, 549 (1962) (same); *Century Indem. Co. v. Mead,* 121 Vt. 434, 439, 159 A.2d 325, 328 (1960) (social security payments). The same rule applies to property that is immune from creditors' process under the common law. See, e.g., *Flirt v. Kirpatrick,* 278 Ala. 61, 64, 175 So. 2d 755, 758 (1965) (statutory right of redemption); *Oliver v. Givens,* 204 Va. 123, 127, 129 S.E.2d 661, 663–64 (1963) (proceeds of the sale of realty held by spouses as tenants by the entireties).

b. Converting Nonexempt Property to Property That Is Exempt

The more surprising general rule is that a heavily indebted or insolvent debtor, a debtor who has suffered a judgment against her, or a debtor contemplating bankruptcy can freely convert nonexempt property to exempt property and so remove it from the reach of her creditors or trustee in bankruptcy. This sort of conversion usually is not fraudulent, regardless of the debtor's motive. See, e.g., *In re Dudley,* 72 F. Supp. 943 (S.D. Cal. 1947), aff'd, 166 F.2d 1023

(9th Cir. 1948) (Warren & Hogan at 121); *Putnam Sand & Gravel Co. v. Albers*, 14 Cal. App. 3d 722, 92 Cal. Rptr. 636, 639 (1971); *Quigley v. Kennedy & Ely Insurance, Inc.*, 207 So. 2d 431, 433 (Fla. 1968); *O'Brien v. Johnson*, 275 Minn. 305, 308, 148 N.W.2d 357, 360 (1967); see also Resnick, *Prudent Planning or Fraudulent Transfer? The Use of Nonexempt Assets to Purchase or Improve Exempt Property on the Eve of Bankruptcy*, 31 Rutgers L. Rev. 615 (1978).

A few modern cases have bucked the general rule, however, by suggesting that conversion on the eve of bankruptcy is suspect and will not always be tolerated. *In re Reed*, 11 B.R. 683, 687–88 (Bkrtcy.N.D. Tex. 1981), aff'd, 700 F.2d 986 (5th Cir. 1983); *In re Zouhar*, 10 B.R. 154, 156 (Bkrtcy.D. N.M. 1981); *In re Mehrer*, 2 B.R. 309, 312 (Bkrtcy.E.D. Wash. 1980); see also Note, 14 Tex. Tech. L. Rev. 648 (1983). Also, a few legislatures have rejected the general rule. See, e.g., Ill. Rev. Stat. ch. 110, § 12–1001 (Smith-Hurd 1984) (normally exempt property is not exempt if the debtor purchased the property with the intent of converting nonexempt property into exempt property).

B. CONVEYANCES THAT ARE CONSTRUCTIVELY FRAUDULENT

In every state, certain conveyances of a debtor's property are deemed fraudulent and thus ineffective against creditors even in the absence of proof of an actual subjective intention to hinder, delay or defraud creditors. Such conveyances commonly are described as *constructively fraudulent*. They are ineffective either because the circumstances of the conveyance conclusively imply wrongful intent, or because protected creditors are wronged in light of the circumstances of the conveyance irrespective of the intention accompanying it. In some states, such as those where the only enacted law on fraudulent conveyances is a simple statute like the Statute of 13 Elizabeth, constructively fraudulent conveyances have been identified by the courts recognizing badges of fraud that give rise to conclusive presumptions of fraud which cannot be rebutted even by evidence of the most innocent intentions. In other states, such as those adopting the UFCA, the enacted law explicitly identifies classes of constructively fraudulent conveyances.

Both the UFCA and its successor, the new UFTA, identify three classes of constructively fraudulent conveyances. According to these uniform laws, a transfer made or obligation incurred without adequate consideration is ineffective against protected creditors under the following circumstances:

- The debtor was left by the transfer or obligation with unreasonably small assets for a transaction or the business on which the debtor was engaged;

- The debtor intended to incur, or believed that she would incur, more debts than she would be able to pay; or,

- The debtor was insolvent at the time or as a result of the transfer or obligation.

The UFCA adds to this list certain obligations incurred, and certain transfers of property made, by an insolvent partnership. UFCA § 8. The UFTA has no comparable provision specifically aimed at transfers by, or obligations of, partnerships. The new uniform law adds, however, a class of constructively fraudulent transfer not found in the UFCA: a preferential transfer by an insolvent insider to a creditor who had reasonable cause to believe the debtor to be insolvent. UFTA § 5(b). See discussion of preferences as fraudulent conveyances, Chapter VI.A.7. supra.

Singled out for discussion below is the most common variety of constructively fraudulent conveyance, which is identified in UFCA § 4: *a conveyance made or obligation incurred by a person who is or will be thereby rendered insolvent when the conveyance is made, or the obligation is incurred, without a fair consideration.* UFTA § 5(a) condemns the same thing, as does the law of every state either by statute or decisional rule. Remember that, because this sort of conveyance is constructively fraudulent, actual intent to hinder, delay, or defraud creditors is not an element of the wrong. *Bullard v. Aluminum Co. of America,* 468 F.2d 11, 14 (7th Cir. 1972); *United States v. West,* 299 F. Supp. 661, 664 (D. Del. 1969). Behind UFCA § 4 is the notion that a debtor must be just before she is generous. S. Riesenfeld, Cases and Materials on Creditors' Remedies and Debtors' Protection 385 (3d ed. 1979); Clark, *The Duties of the Corporate Debtor to its Creditors,* 90 Harv. L. Rev. 505, 510 (1977).

Although relieved of the burden of showing actual fraudulent intent, a creditor attacking a conveyance under UFCA § 4 or UFTA § 5(a) must nevertheless establish, first, that there was a "conveyance" of the debtor's property; second, that the conveyance was without "fair consideration;" and, third, that the debtor was, or then became, "insolvent." These elements, which are discussed below, are also components of other types of constructively fraudulent conveyances condemned by the UFCA and the UFTA, and of conveyances that are fraudulent under decisional or nonuniform, statutory law. What follows, therefore, is relevant beyond UFCA § 4.

1. **CONVEYANCE**

Actually and constructively fraudulent conveyances share a requirement: a finding that the challenged transfer is a "conveyance" as defined by the law of fraudulent conveyances. The definition of the term is shared, too. " 'Conveyance' [for purposes of any kind of fraud covered by the UFCA] includes every payment of money, assignment, release, transfer, lease, mortgage or pledge of tangible or intangible property, and also the creation of any lien or encumbrance." UFCA § 1. Because of this common definition, constructively fraudulent conveyances take as many different forms as conveyances made with actual fraudulent intent. See supra Chapter VI.A.1. The most typical forms, however, are sales of goods and real estate, and security arrangements involving either type of property as collateral for loans or other advances of credit. The more complex and interesting issues are associated with the latter form.

2. **FAIR CONSIDERATION**

a. **Fair Consideration Means Equivalent Value**

As long as no actual fraudulent intent is involved, a debtor, whether solvent or not, can freely convey her property in exchange for *fair consideration.* The giving of such consideration immunizes a transfer from attack as a constructively fraudulent conveyance. The UFCA provides that "[f]air consideration is given for property, or obligation, (a) [w]hen in exchange for such property, or obligation, as a fair equivalent therefor, and in good faith, property is conveyed or an antecedent debt is satisfied, or (b) [w]hen such property, or obligation is received in good faith to secure a present advance of antecedent debt in amount not disproportionately small as compared with the value of the property, or obligation obtained." UFCA § 3. In short, fair consideration requires an exchange of property having equivalent value. Whatever the debtor gets in exchange must fairly represent the value of the property transferred. *Montana Ass'n of Credit Management v. Hergert,* 181 Mont. 442, 451–52, 593 P.2d 1059, 1064 (1979). Of course, the usual measure of "the value of the property transferred" is its market value.

Example: A financially desperate debtor, Mc, accepted an offer of $25,000 for business property which had been listed with realtors for prices ranging from $45,000 to $75,000. The buyer was a person whom Mc had asked for a loan. This person had refused to make the loan, as had a number of other people. In addition to paying the purchase price of the property, the buyer paid back taxes of $1234 and allowed Mc to retain possession of the property rent free for three months. The sale did not solve Mc's financial troubles, however. Upon Mc's bankruptcy, the trustee sought to void the sale as a fraudulent conveyance, claiming that it was a sale by an insolvent for less than fair consideration. Both sides produced expert testimony by realtors as to the value of the property Mc had sold. The estimates ranged from $42,000 to $29,000. The trial court valued the total consideration received by Mc at $27,234, and ruled that this amount was fair consideration. The holding on appeal was that the difference between the estimates of market value and the actual purchase price was insufficient to upset the trial court's ruling. *Kielb v. Johnson,* 23 N.J. 60, 127 A.2d 561 (1956).

b. **Comparing "Fair Consideration" in Fraudulent Conveyances Law With "Consideration" in Contracts Law**
   1) Where "Fair Consideration" Is Narrower Concept
      In some respects, the concept of fair consideration is not as broad as the doctrine of consideration in the law of contracts which binds parties to an agreement whenever they have bargained for an exchange.

      a) Comparing Values
         Traditional contracts doctrine holds that the value of things exchanged is irrelevant. Not so in the law of fraudulent conveyances, which requires that the exchange must involve property of equivalent values. Thus, that which is good or valuable consideration to support a contract will not necessarily protect an insolvent debtor's conveyance of property from attack as constructively fraudulent. See, e.g., *North Carolina Nat. Bank v. Evans,* 296 N.C. 374, 378, 250 S.E.2d 231, 234 (1979) (mere inadequacy of price is not sufficient to set aside contract but price must be sufficient in itself to sustain transfer by an insolvent debtor); cf. *Zellerbach Paper Co. v. Valley Nat. Bank,* 13

Ariz. App. 431, 435, 477 P.2d 550, 554 (1970) (granting additional collateral of six parcels of corporate realty upon receiving a two-month extension on an $11,000 note is not fair consideration).

Even in the law of fraudulent conveyances, however, there is room for some disparity between the value of the property transferred and the value of whatever is received in exchange. The courts frequently recite that the value given in exchange for property is not unfair unless it "startles a correct mind" or "shocks the conscience" or "moral sense". *Zellerbach Paper Co. v. Valley Nat. Bank,* 13 Ariz. App. 431, 436, 477 P.2d 550, 555 (1970), appeal after remand, 18 Ariz. App. 301, 501 P.2d 570 (1972); *White v. Nollmeyer,* 151 Mont. 387, 406, 443 P.2d 873, 883 (1968). In any event, the comparative values are determined from the standpoint of the transferor's creditors, which essentially means that, in case of doubt, err in the creditors' favor.

b)   Value Moving to Third Person
In the law of contracts, a bargained for promise or performance is consideration even though the promise or performance is given to a third person. Restatement (Second) of Contracts § 71(4) (1981). The same rule does not always apply in deciding if fair consideration was given for a transfer attacked as a fraudulent conveyance.

Example: B controlled all of the stock of L, Inc. The company was sold to C, who gave B a promissory note for most of the purchase price. C satisfied the note by giving B property from L's inventory of merchandise. In effect, therefore, L paid for itself. Eventually, L, Inc. filed bankruptcy. The trustee sued B to have declared null and void the conveyances of merchandise. The court held that the conveyances were fraudulent because they were made by an insolvent without fair consideration. Indeed, L received no consideration whatsoever. C did, of course, but consideration received by a third party is not counted in determining the fairness of the consideration received by the transferor. *Steph v. Branch,* 255 F. Supp. 526, 531 (E.D.Okl. 1966), aff'd, 389 F.2d 233 (10th Cir. 1968); see also *Bullard v. Aluminum Co. of America,* 468 F.2d 11, 14 (7th Cir. 1972) (transfers made to benefit third parties are not considered as made for fair consideration).

On the other hand, the courts have been unwilling to declare that a leveraged buyout (LBO) of a company is fraudulent in the absence of actual fraud. In an LBO the buyers of a company use the company's own assets as collateral to secure a loan to them for the purchase price of the company. In effect, the company finances its own acquisition by giving the buyers' lender a consensual lien on all of the company's property. Very often the company is insolvent before, or as a result of, this security transfer. Because the loan flows to and directly benefits only the buyers, it could be argued that the company itself gets no fair consideration for the lien. Therefore, if the company was or became insolvent, the security transfers is constructively fraudulent. The courts do not generally agree, however. Regarding the application of fraudulent conveyance law to LBOs, the Ninth Circuit recently reported:

> The few courts that have looked at the reach of fraudulent conveyance law in the context of LBOs have based their decision, implicitly at least, on whether there was evidence of actual fraud. Thus, those transactions in which all was "above board" to begin with have been "ratified" by the courts even though the creditors may have suffered in the end. In *Credit Managers Ass'n v. Federal Co.*, 629 F.Supp. 175 (C.D.Cal.1985), the court dealt with an attack on an LBO transaction * * *. The court, after noting the possibility that fraudulent conveyance law could vitiate all LBOs, refused to employ this approach and declined to overturn the LBO.
>
> In contrast, when the LBO was intentionally designed to defraud the creditors, the courts have had little difficulty in finding the transaction fraudulent. In *United States v. Gleneagles Inv. Co.*, 565 F.Supp. 556 (M.D.Pa.1983), for example, the court found violations of both the intentional and constructive fraud sections of the UFCA. This decision was upheld by the Third Circuit in *United States v. Tabor Court Realty Corp.*, 803 F.2d 1288 (3d Cir. 1986), *cert. denied*, ___ U.S. ___, 107 S.Ct. 3229, 97 L.Ed.2d 735 (1987), which relied substantially on the suspicious circumstances surrounding the transaction that evidenced actual intent to defraud.
>
>   * * *
>
> [W]e hesitate to utilize constructive intent to frustrate the purposes intended to be served by * * * a legitimate LBO. Nor do we think it appropriate to utilize constructive intent to brand most, if not all, LBOs as illegitimate. We cannot believe that virtually all LBOs are designed to "hinder, delay, or defraud creditors."

Kupetz v. Wolf, 845 F.2d 842, 847–48 (9th Cir.1988). Of course, contrary to the court's implication in *Kupetz*, a transfer that is constructively fraudulent is nonetheless so despite a real intent to defraud. Moreover, the decision in *Tabor Court* was largely based on nothing more "suspicious" than the lender's knowledge that its consensual lien on the target company's assets would leave little or no free assets for the company's other creditors. *United States v. Tabor Court Realty Corp.*, 803 F.2d 1288, 1295–97 (3d Cir.1986), *cert. denied*, ___ U.S. ___, 107 S.Ct. 3229 (1987). If this kind of knowledge on the lender's part is sufficient to defeat an LBO, virtually every LBO is in trouble, and the decision in *Tabor Court* is essentially a decision that fraudulent conveyance law applies to LBOs and that, on the whole and as a policy matter, the economic benefits of LBOs do not outweigh the potential harm to general creditors of the target companies. On this policy matter and other issues concerning the application of fraudulent conveyance law to LBO's, see Baird & Jackson, *Fraudulent Conveyance Law and Its Proper Domain*, 38 Vand.L.Rev. 829 (1985); Carlson, *Leveraged Buyouts in Bankruptcy*, 20 Ga.L.Rev. 73 (1985).

c) Executory Promise

An executory or unperformed promise is consideration in the law of contracts if the promise is bargained for. There is some debate, however, as to whether such a promise amounts to fair consideration in the law of fraudulent conveyances. The new UFTA addresses this issue by providing that value includes an unperformed promise other than one "made otherwise than in the ordinary course of the promisor's business to furnish support to the debtor or another person." UFTA § 3(a). Even under the UFTA, however, there remains the question as to when this sort of value is *equivalent* value sufficient to immunize a conveyance from attack as constructively fraudulent.

2) Where Fair Consideration Is Broader Concept

In one respect the concept of fair consideration in fraudulent conveyance law is broader than the doctrine of consideration in contracts law. Past consideration is usually no consideration at all in the field of contracts. Yet, a conveyance of property to satisfy or secure an antecedent debt usually amounts to fair consideration in the law of fraudulent conveyances if the exchange involves fair equivalents.

c. **Love and Affection**

The law of fraudulent conveyances and contracts doctrine agree that "love and affection" and comparable motives for making transfers of property do not constitute fair, good, valuable or otherwise sufficient consideration. Concerning the law of fraudulent conveyances, see *United States v. West*, 299 F. Supp. 661, 666 (D. Del. 1969) (no fair equivalent is exchanged when the conveyance is simply for natural love and affection); *Jahner v. Jacob*, 252 N.W.2d 1, 5–6 (N.D. 1977) (same).

d. **Inadequate Consideration in Foreclosure Sales of Collateral**

1) Traditional Rule

A secured creditor's privately conducted foreclosure sale of collateral can, of course, be attacked as a fraudulent conveyance if the sale is conducted in a manner designed to actually defraud the debtor's other creditors. 2 L. Jones, The Law of Chattel Mortgages and Conditional Sales § 802 (6th ed. R. Bowers 1933) (with respect to fraud of secured creditor and buyer); *Sheffield Progressive, Inc. v. Kingston Tool Co., Inc.*, 10 Mass. App. 47, 405 N.E.2d 985 (1980) (with respect to fraud of secured creditor and the debtor).

On the other hand, a secured creditor's foreclosure sale of collateral, if conducted according to law, has traditionally been immune from attack as a constructively fraudulent conveyance solely on the basis of the inadequacy of the price paid for the property by the buyer at the forced sale. The tradition was broken in the case *Durrett v. Washington Nat. Ins. Co.,* 621 F.2d 201 (5th Cir. 1980). The court held in this bankruptcy case that a privately conducted, perfectly legal forced sale of real property was constructively fraudulent under bankruptcy law simply because the price received for the property was less than 70% of the property's market value.

2) *Durrett* Breaks Tradition
In *Durrett,* supra, Durrett borrowed $180,000 from Southern Trust & Mortgage Co. Durrett's note was secured by a deed of trust on realty. The deed of trust contained a provision for a privately conducted public sale of the collateral in the event of Durrett's default. The secured obligation was assigned to Washington National Insurance Co. Durrett eventually defaulted and the mortgagee sold the property for $115,400, an amount equal to the balance of the mortgagor's obligation. The market value of the property at the time of forced sale was $200,000. A few days later Durrett filed for relief in bankruptcy.

As debtor-in-possession, Durrett attacked the foreclosure sale and sought to set it aside under § 67d of the Bankruptcy Act. See 11 U.S.C.A. § 67d (repealed in 1978). (The old Bankruptcy Act rather than the new Bankruptcy Code applied because the facts giving rise to the case arose before the Code's effective date.) Section 67d was the Bankruptcy Act's adaptation of the UFCA. Subsection 67d(2) of the Bankruptcy Act was comparable to UFCA § 4, condemning as fraudulent every transfer made within one year prior to bankruptcy if made without fair consideration by a debtor who is or will be thereby rendered insolvent. The federal district court dismissed Durrett's complaint, but this judgment was vacated and the case remanded by the appellate court.

Although there was not even a hint of irregularity with respect to the disposition of the collateral, the Fifth Circuit concluded that the foreclosure sale price was not a fair consideration for the property, that the foreclosure sale was itself a distinct transfer by the debtor who was insolvent at the time, and thus that the sale was voidable as a fraudulent conveyance. With respect to the transfer issue, the Fifth Circuit conceded that there was a transfer when the mortgage was created; but the court believed there was a second transfer upon the mortgagor's surrender of possession in connection with, and as a result of, the foreclosure sale. This belief was founded on the bankruptcy law's broad definition of "transfer," which is not materially different from the UFCA's definition of conveyance.

3) Implications of *Durrett* for Bankruptcy Law of Fraudulent Conveyance
The Fifth Circuit's reasoning in *Durrett* is not restricted to § 67d(2) of the old Bankruptcy Act. The provision is copied in § 548 of the new Bankruptcy Code. 11 U.S.C.A. § 548(a)(2) (1979). Moreover, the *Durrett* reason-

ing is not restricted to private foreclosure sales. It applies equally as well to judicial mortgage foreclosures. *In re Hulm,* 738 F.2d 323 (8th Cir. 1984). The reasoning can also extend to forced sales of personal property. But see *In re Ewing,* 33 B.R. 288 (Bkrtcy. W.D. Pa. 1983), rev'd, 36 B.R. 476 (W.D. Pa. 1984), aff'd w/o opin., 746 F.2d 1466 (3d Cir. 1984), cert. denied, 469 U.S. 1214, 105 S. Ct. 1189 (1985) (transfer of pledged stock occurred when security interest created, not when foreclosed, for § 548 purposes). *Durrett* thus implies that any foreclosure sale to enforce a secured debt of an insolvent debtor is subject to attack in bankruptcy as a fraudulent conveyance whenever the price paid for the property is less than 70% of the property's market value. It makes no difference that fair consideration was given when the mortgage was created, or that the foreclosure sale complied in every respect with the parties' agreement and any applicable law.

Not everyone agrees, however, that the decision in *Durrett* is sound. See, e.g., *In re Madrid,* 21 B.R. 424, 425–27 (9th Cir. Bkrtcy.App. 1982), aff'd sub nom. *Madrid v. Lawyers Title Ins. Corp.,* 725 F.2d 1197 (9th Cir. 1984) (Bankruptcy Code's § 548(a)(2) should not be construed so as to upset a foreclosure sale solely because of inadequacy of price); Alden, Gross & Borowitz, *Real Property Foreclosure as a Fraudulent Conveyance: Proposals for Solving the Durrett Problem,* 38 Bus. Law. 1605 (1983); Coppel & Kann, *Defanging Durrett: The Established Law of "Transfer",* 100 Banking L. J. 676 (1982); Note, *Mortgage Foreclosure As Fraudulent Conveyance: Is Judicial Foreclosure an Answer To The Durrett Problem?* 1984 Wis. L. Rev. 195.

4) **Implications of *Durrett* for State Law of Fraudulent Conveyances**
Bankruptcy Act § 67d(2), which was the basis of the *Durrett* decision, is identical to UFCA § 4 and also to counterparts under other forms of state fraudulent conveyance laws. Nevertheless, because *Durrett* was decided under federal bankruptcy law, the decision is not controlling precedent in any jurisdiction on the meaning of "fair consideration" under state fraudulent conveyance law. Moreover, the reasoning in *Durrett* probably will not be persuasive to courts interpreting such local law. Their habit, which will prove difficult to break, is to apply the traditional rule that a validly conducted foreclosure sale cannot be set aside as a fraudulent conveyance solely for inadequacy of price. See Chapter VI.B.2.d.(1).

This traditional rule of state law is confirmed by the Uniform Fraudulent Transfer Act (1984). The drafters of this new uniform law were clear in their rejection of *Durrett.* They made sure that the reasoning of the case would not invade state law by specifically providing that "a person gives a reasonably equivalent value [i.e., fair consideration] if the person acquires an interest of the debtor in an asset pursuant to a regularly conducted, noncollusive foreclosure sale or exercise of a power of sale for the acquisition or disposition of the interest of the debtor upon default under a mortgage, deed of trust, or security agreement." UFTA § 3(b). In effect, therefore, whether the asset sold is personal or real property, the price bid at a public foreclosure sale determines the fair value of the property sold. Id. comment 5. Thus, the high bidder who buys the property always will have given a fair consideration, and for this reason the sale to her cannot be set aside as constructively fraudulent. This conclusion and UFTA § 3(b) apply to foreclosure sales of personal property as well as real estate. Nevertheless, the new uniform law also provides explicitly that the enforcement of a security interest in compliance with U.C.C. Article 9, which governs secured transactions in personal property, cannot be avoided as a constructively fraudulent transfer. UFTA § 8(f)(2).

e. Whether Excessive Collateral in Secured Transactions Is Unfair Consideration

1) Rule of the UFCA and Comparable Laws

A secured creditor can have too much collateral because, if the value of the collateral far exceeds the amount of the secured debt, the security arrangement can be attacked as a constructively fraudulent conveyance. The giving of a security interest in real or personal property is a conveyance, UFCA § 1; and this sort of conveyance, like any other, is fraudulent if the conveyance is made by an insolvent debtor without a fair consideration. UFCA § 4. Fair consideration in a secured transaction means that the amount of the secured debt is not disproportionately small as compared with the value of the collateral. UFCA § 3(b). See *Zellerbach Paper Co. v. Valley Nat. Bank,* 13 Ariz. App. 431, 436, 477 P.2d 550, 555 (1970) (debt is disproportionately small when it is 56% less than the value of the security); see also *American Fidelity Co. v. Harney,* 351 Mass. 163, 217 N.E.2d 905 (1966).

In determining if a secured debt is disproportionately small as compared to the value of the collateral, the nature of the collateral should be considered; and "the less stable the collateral, the more collateral a creditor is entitled to demand." *Clarkson Co. Ltd. v. Shaheen,* 533 F. Supp. 905, 928 (S.D. N.Y. 1982) (involving pledge of common stock of corporation).

2) Rule of the UFTA

The new UFTA rejects the UFCA rule described above which enables a creditor to attack a security transfer as a constructively fraudulent conveyance on the ground that the value of the property transferred is disproportionate to the debt secured. The drafters of the UFTA reasoned "that when a transfer is for security only, the equity or value of the asset that exceeds the amount of the debt secured remains available to unsecured creditors and thus cannot be regarded as the subject of a fraudulent transfer merely because of the encumbrance resulting from an otherwise valid security transfer." UFTA § 4 comment 3.

f. Good Faith as a Distinct Element of Fair Consideration

Under some existing laws, the definition of fair consideration requires not only an exchange of fair equivalents; another, separate requirement is that the exchange be made in good faith. UFCA § 3. "[A] transfer lacking in good faith is fraudulent * * * even though fair equivalent value may have been present. And the question of good faith depends * * * on whether the 'transaction carries the earmarks of an arms-length bargain.' " *Bullard v. Aluminum Co. of America,* 468 F.2d 11, 13 (7th Cir. 1972), quoting *Holahan v. Henderson,* 277 F. Supp. 890, 899 (W.D. La. 1967), aff'd, 394 F.2d 177 (5th Cir. 1968). The UFCA does not clearly explain whether good faith is required of the transferor, the transferee, or both of them, although the statute implies that the requirement in the definition of fair consideration applies to the transferee. The authorities generally agree that, on the question of fair consideration, the issue is the the transferee's good faith. See 1 G. Glenn, Fraudulent Conveyances and Preferences § 294 et seq. (rev. ed. 1940).

The new UFTA eliminates good faith as an issue in determining whether fair or otherwise adequate consideration has been given. Good faith on the transferee's part remains an issue, however, in determining whether there is a defense to an action against her by a creditor who is wronged by a fraudulent conveyance. See UFTA § 8, and Chapter VI.D. infra.

g. **Burden of Proof With Respect to Fairness of Consideration**
Initially, the party attacking a conveyance as constructively fraudulent has the burden of proving the lack of fair consideration. *Matusik v. Large,* 85 Nev. 202, 205, 452 P.2d 457, 458 (1969); *Warwick Municipal Emp. Credit Union v. Higham,* 106 R.I. 363, 368, 259 A.2d 852, 855 (1969); *Hove v. Frazier,* 79 S.D. 551, 554, 115 N.W.2d 217, 219 (1962). Yet, there are facts which, if proved, will cause the burden of going forward to shift to the transferee, who then must demonstrate that adequate consideration was given for the conveyance. The burden shifts, for example, if the conveyance recites merely a nominal consideration, *Kindom Uranium Corp. v. Vance,* 269 F.2d 104, 108 (10th Cir. 1959); if the grantor was insolvent, failing, or financially embarrassed at the time of the conveyance; *Alabama Credit Corp. v. Deas,* 417 F.2d 135, 139 (5th Cir. 1969); or, even if the transferor was simply in debt when the conveyance was made. *Massey-Ferguson, Inc. v. Finocchiaro Equipment Co., Inc.,* 496 F. Supp. 655 (E.D. Pa. 1980), aff'd, 649 F.2d 859 (3d Cir. 1981). Shifting to the transferee the burden of proof (at least the task of producing evidence if not that of persuading the trier of fact) should for policy reasons be easily accomplished. After all, the transferee has readier access to the facts underlying the issue of the adequacy of consideration received by the transferor.

h. **The Force of Recitals of Consideration**
The consideration recited in a property deed is presumed to be true and accurate, but parol evidence is admissible in court to show that the real consideration is some amount other than that recited. Moreover, recitals such as "and other good and valuable consideration" mean nothing, and such recitals alone are given no weight in deciding if fair consideration supports what is alleged to have been a constructively fraudulent transfer of property. See, e.g., *Everett v. Gainer,* 269 N.C. 528, 530, 153 S.E.2d 90, 93 (1967).

3.   INSOLVENCY
A creditor cannot so loudly complain about a debtor's conveyance of property for less than fair consideration if the debtor is not then or thereafter insolvent. Sol-

vency of the debtor despite the conveyance implies the ownership of sufficient other assets to satisfy creditors' claims.

a.   The Meaning of Insolvency

For purposes of fraudulent conveyances law, "[a] person is insolvent when the present fair salable value of her assets is less than the amount that will be required to pay her probable liability on her existing debts as they become absolute and matured." UFCA § 2(1). The UFTA's definition of insolvency is identical in substance. UFTA § 2(a). A debtor's assets do not include property that is exempt from liability for her debts. UFCA § 1. The same is true under the UFTA. See UFTA § 2(a). For discussion of exempt property, see infra Chapter VIII.

Debts are not always measured by their face amounts. For example, the liability of a debtor as a surety for another person may be discounted due to the contingent nature of the suretyship debt. *Matter of Xonics Photochemical, Inc.,* 841 F.2d 198, 199–201 (7th Cir.1988). Such discounting makes easier the protection of up-stream and cross-stream guaranties between affiliated entities. For more on this problem, see Blumberg, *Intragroup Guaranties Under the Uniform Fraudulent Transfer Act,* 9 Cardozo L.Rev. 685 (1987). Also, the surety-debtor's assets might include its rights of subrogation to the creditor's claims against the principal and collateral for the debt, and the right to contribution from other co-obligors.

Proving the financial condition of a debtor as of the exact time a conveyance was made is usually quite difficult. Thus, "we have a rule that evidence of insolvency on a given day is also competent to prove that the same condition existed at a previous date which is reasonably near ∗ ∗ ∗." 1 G. Glenn, Fraudulent Conveyances and Preferences § 229(b) (rev. ed. 1940). Applying this rule, the court concluded in *Zellerbach Paper Co. v. Valley Nat. Bank,* 13 Ariz. App. 431, 477 P.2d 550 (1970), that a $40,000 deficit in the debtor's net worth at the end of 1965 is prima facie evidence of insolvency as of September 7, 1965.

b.   Burden of Proof of Insolvency

The usual rule is that the person attacking a conveyance as constructively fraudulent has the burden of showing that the grantor did not receive fair consideration and also that the grantor was insolvent either at the time of the conveyance or as a result of it. *Neubauer v. Cloutier,* 265 Minn. 539, 543–44, 122 N.W.2d 623, 628 (1963). Yet, there is some authority that proof of either of these elements by the attacking creditor shifts to the transferee the burden as to the other element. *Alabama Credit Corp. v. Deas,* 417 F.2d 135, 139 (5th Cir. 1969) (proof of debt or insolvency shifts burden to transferee to show fairness of consideration); *In re Security Products Co.,* 310 F. Supp. 110, 117 (E.D. Mo. 1969) (a conveyance by a debtor for no or nominal consideration is presumptively fraudulent and transferee has burden of showing the debtor's solvency); *Odom v. Luehr,* 226 Miss. 661, 664, 85 So.2d 218, 219 (1956) (same); *Fernandez v. Zullo,* 263 Or. 13, 17–18, 500 P.2d 705, 707 (1972) (same). This helps to explain the assertion by some courts that, when a conveyance is attacked on the theory of constructive fraud, the plaintiff makes a prima facie case by showing *either* that the grantor was insolvent at the time of the transfer (or was made so by the transfer), or that no fair consideration was exchanged. See, e.g., *Carraco Oil Co. v. Roberts*, 397 P.2d 126, 129 (Okl. 1964). In *United States v. West*, 299 F. Supp. 661 (D. Del. 1969), the court was not willing to embrace fully the idea of shifting the burden of proof on the insolvency question simply by proof that the debtor received less than fair consideration for the conveyance. The court determined, however, that such a shift occurred when the claimant-creditor showed, in addition to inadequate consideration, that the transferee of the property was a close relative of the debtor. The court took this position in recognition of " 'the notorious tendency of spouses [and other close relatives] to aid each other in enjoying secretly reserved property interests and to be generous to each other before they are just to creditors.' " Id. at 665.

Although the UFCA and the UFTA agree in substance on the meaning of insolvency, i.e., liabilities exceed assets, the new uniform law adds that "[a] debtor who is generally not paying his or her debts as they become due is presumed to be insolvent." UFTA § 2(b). "The presumption imposes on the party against whom the presumption is directed the burden of proving that the nonexistence of insolvency as defined in § 2(a) [liabilities exceed assets] is more probable than its existence." Id. comment 2.

C. REMEDYING A FRAUDULENT CONVEYANCE

After concluding that a debtor has made a fraudulent conveyance of property, the next step for the lawyer of a protected creditor is to find a cure for the wrong her client has suffered. The principal cure is to apply the fraudulently conveyed property, or its value, to the realization of the debt which is owed the creditor. 1 G. Glenn, Fraudulent Conveyances and Preferences §§ 74 & 239 (rev. ed. 1940). Four remedies, or sets of remedies, are potentially involved. In effect, they all are directed at the property's transferee; and, as a general rule, all of the remedies can be exercised not only against the original or first transferee, but also against a subsequent transferee, often referred to as a subgrantee.

1. **REMEDIAL OPTIONS**
   a. **Protect the Property**
      Courts in appropriate cases may protect the property which has been fraudulently conveyed by restraining any further disposition of it, appointing a receiver to take charge of the property, or making any other order which the circumstances of the case may require. UFCA § 10; UFTA § 7(a)(3).

   b. **Ignore the Conveyance and Seize the Property**
      The creditor can disregard the conveyance and attach or levy execution upon the property even though it is held by the debtor's transferee. The theory is that, because the law deems that the conveyance was void, the creditor is free to simply ignore it and proceed as if the conveyance had not been made. UFCA § 9. If the creditor has yet to get a judgment against the debtor, she has

the sheriff seize the property through a writ of attachment, assuming that provisional remedy is available to her. Regarding attachment, see infra Chapter XI. If she has already won a judgment against the debtor, the seizure is through the process of execution, which culminates in a forced sale of the property to satisfy the creditor's claim. Regarding the process of execution, see supra Chapter III. Ignoring the transfer is always a risky, and sometimes an expensive, approach, however. The creditor might be proved wrong in her belief that the conveyance to the transferee was fraudulent. If the creditor is wrong, she will face liability for conversion of the transferee's property. The sheriff may face liability, too. Thus, the sheriff probably will require the creditor to post an indemnity bond as a condition of seizing the property from the transferee. Moreover, the buyers at a forced sale will substantially discount the property's value if there is an outstanding dispute regarding the property's ownership. For all these reasons, the risky approach of ignoring the conveyance and proceeding against the property through attachment or execution is used less often than the much safer approach of bringing an action to set aside the conveyance as fraudulent.

c. **Sue to Set Aside the Conveyance**
Instead of ignoring the debtor's fraudulent conveyance and seizing the property from the transferee, a creditor of the debtor is more likely to sue to have the conveyance set aside so that the property can be applied in satisfaction of the creditor's claim. This action will most likely be in the nature of a creditor's bill, which is a remedy discussed earlier in this Black Letter. See supra Chapter IV.A. If the creditor does not yet have a judgment against the debtor, the action to set aside the fraudulent conveyance can be joined with the primary suit on the debt.

If the debtor's transferee has herself conveyed the property to a third person, this second conveyance does not put the property beyond the creditor's reach. The subsequent transferee's right and title to the property is, of course, derivative. Thus, if the title of the debtor's transferee is void as against the creditor because of violation of fraudulent conveyance law, then so too is the title of the subsequent transferee, unless she has the protection of a bona fide purchaser. *United States v. Ressler,* 433 F. Supp. 459, 465 (S.D. Fla. 1977); *United States v. West,* 299 F. Supp. 661 (D. Del. 1969).

Example: The Wests were indebted to the federal government as guarantors for a loan made to a company they controlled. Before default on the loan, the Wests transferred to their son, David, certain realty. There was no fair consideration for this transfer. David thereafter conveyed the property to his brother, Douglas. The United States got a judgment against the Wests and executed on the real estate now owned nominally by Douglas. Before the property was sold to satisfy the government's judgment, Douglas petitioned for a stay of the sale. The question was whether or not the transfers of the property should be set aside in favor of the United States. On these facts, the court held for the government in *United States v.*

West, 299 F. Supp. 661 (D. Del. 1969). The conveyance between the Wests and David was constructively fraudulent because the grantors were insolvent and received less than fair consideration for the property. There was no discussion as to whether Douglas was a bona fide purchaser. Presumably, he was not because there was no mention of evidence that he paid David a fair consideration for property.

d. Sue the Transferee for Damages

The traditional rule is that creditors generally cannot recover damages from the transferee of a fraudulent conveyance. Their remedy is limited to recovering the property. *Kuzmicki v. Nelson,* 101 Cal. App.2d 278, 279, 225 P.2d 233, 234 (1950) (transferee of fraudulent conveyance is not liable to the transferor's creditors on any account unless transferee disposes of things conveyed to her), followed in *Stearns v. Los Angeles City School District,* 244 Cal. App. 2d 696, 710, 53 Cal. Rptr. 482, 497 (1966) (creditor of debtor who fraudulently conveyed property is relegated to rights against the property and cannot recover damages from transferee who still holds property); *Bomanzi of Lexington, Inc. v. Tafel,* 415 S.W.2d 627, 631 (Ky. 1967) (specifically, transferee is not liable on transferor's debt to creditor who seeks to void a fraudulent conveyance); *David v. Zilah,* 325 Mass. 252, 254, 90 N.E.2d 343, 345 (1950) (same).

The UFTA may break tradition. The literal language of this new uniform law appears to provide that, to the extent a transfer is voidable, the creditor in any case may recover judgment for the value of the asset transferred or the amount of the creditor's claim, whichever is less, instead of recovering the property itself. UFTA § 8(b). In states that enact the UFTA, the courts might interpret this provision as permitting the recovery of damages against a transferee only in those exceptional cases in which even the traditional rule permits such a recovery.

There are numerous exceptions to the general rule that a transferee of a fraudulent conveyance is accountable only for the property itself and is not liable for damages. The three most important exceptions are these:

1) **When Creditor Has Preexisting Lien on Property Fraudulently Conveyed**
   Most states allow a creditor who has a lien on property fraudulently conveyed to recover the property's value against persons who prevent execution of the lien.

2) **When Grantee Has Not Yet Paid for the Property**
   If the debtor has not yet been paid for the fraudulently conveyed property, the transferee can be charged as a garnishee.

3) **Where Grantee Is Unable to Return the Property**
   A transferee of fraudulently conveyed property is accountable for the value of the property if she is unwilling or unable to return the property intact, as when she has reconveyed it. *Hallack v. Hawkins,* 409 F.2d 627, 630 (6th Cir. 1969); *Sullivan v. Ginsberg,* 180 Ga. 840, 843, 181 S.E. 163,

166 (1935); *Third Nat. Bank v. Keathley,* 35 Tenn.App. 82, 242 S.W.2d 760, 769 (1951). In cases where a reconveyance has occurred, the value of the property is often measured by the price paid by the second transferee. *Aggregates Associated, Inc. v. Packwood,* 58 Cal.2d 599, 605, 25 Cal. Rptr. 545, 551, 375 P.2d 425, 431 (1962); *Leachman v. Cobb Development Co.,* 226 Ga. 103, 105, 172 S.E.2d 688, 690 (1970), appeal after remand, 229 Ga. 207, 190 S.E.2d 537 (1972). The recovery of the price is sometimes based on the theory that the transferee is a trustee of the fraudulently conveyed property and its proceeds. Yet, where the property is reconveyed for less than its value, the creditor is not limited to the price received, but may recover the value of the property at the time the fraudulent transferee received it. *Post v. Browne,* 279 App.Div. 922, 926, 110 N.Y.S.2d 595, 597 (1952), aff'd, 304 N.Y. 610, 107 N.E.2d 92 (1952).

In *Alan Drey Co., Inc. v. Generation, Inc.,* 22 Ill. App. 3d 611, 317 N.E.2d 673, 680 (1974), the debtor, acting with an actual intention to defraud creditors, sold a magazine subscription list. The court held the buyer liable for damages based on the property's value. There is language in the opinion suggesting that liability was imposed on the buyer because of the buyer's awareness of the seller's fraudulent intention. The buyer itself was guilty of actual fraud. Yet, the real basis for imposing liability on the buyer may well have been that the list could not be returned in any meaningful sense because it had been used.

2. CREDITORS WHO CAN PURSUE REMEDIES

Not all of the remedies listed above are available to every creditor of a debtor who fraudulently conveys property. Whether a creditor has any remedies at all, and the nature of those which are available to her, depend largely on three facts: first, whether or not the creditor is a "creditor" as defined by fraudulent conveyance law; second, whether she became a creditor before or after the fraudulent conveyance; and third, whether or not her claim has matured by the time she pursues remedies against the transferee of a fraudulent conveyance.

a. Defining "Creditor"

Under the Uniform Fraudulent Conveyances Act, fraudulent conveyances of property, whether actual or constructive, give rise to remedies only in favor of "creditors." UFCA §§ 9 & 10. The same is true under the new UFTA § 7. " 'Creditor' is a person having any claim, whether matured or unmatured, liquidated or unliquidated, absolute, fixed or contingent." UFCA § 1; accord, UFTA § 1(3) & (4). This definition is very broad and includes not only persons having contract claims against the debtor, but also those having any other sort of claim, including tort claims not yet reduced to judgment. *Jahner v. Jacob,* 252 N.W.2d 1, 5 (N.D. 1977).

This definition of creditor, which does not require that the person have a judgment against the debtor, resolves a debate that long divided the courts, i.e., whether or not a creditor without a judgment against her debtor has the right to sue to set aside a fraudulent conveyance by the debtor or pursue other remedies against the transferee. Many courts believed that the pursuit of such remedies were conditioned on the creditor having a judgment against the debtor. Some courts further conditioned the remedies, requiring preliminarily that execution be issued and returned nulla bona. See, e.g., *Wagner v. Law*, 3 Wash. 500, 28 P. 1109 (1892). The explanation for these conditions is that, traditionally, the usual vehicle for setting aside a fraudulent conveyance has been a creditor's bill in equity. For a full review of creditors' bills, see supra Chapter IV.A. Ordinarily, of course, equity would not act unless remedies at law had been exhausted. Thus, a creditor's bill to set aside a fraudulent conveyance could not be maintained until the creditor got a judgment and sought unsuccessfully to enforce the judgment through execution at law. Some courts very early refused to follow this maxim in cases where it inhibited an action to set aside a fraudulent conveyance. Most courts, however, adhered to it until modern procedure brought about the merger of law and equity, or until the enactment locally of the Uniform Fraudulent Conveyances Act or some similar statute which makes remedies available to a creditor without regard to whether or not her claim against the debtor has been reduced to judgment. Thus, it is now clear that, while pursuing an action to establish a judgment against the debtor, a creditor can simultaneously sue to set aside a fraudulent conveyance by the debtor. The creditor need not postpone attacking the conveyance until such time as she wins a judgment against the debtor.

b. Existing Creditors More Fully Protected Than Future Creditors

The class of creditors protected against a conveyance made with actual fraudulent intent is broad. The conveyance is fraudulent not only as to the debtor's creditors whose claims exist at the time of the conveyance, but also as to those persons who become creditors of the debtor after the conveyance has been made. UFCA § 7; see also *Sullivan v. Ginsberg*, 180 Ga. 840, 843, 181 S.E. 163, 166 (1935). Some classes of constructively fraudulent conveyances also are voidable by both existing and future creditors. Yet, when the constructive fraud consists of an insolvent debtor making a transfer without fair consideration, the conveyance is fraudulent only as to existing or present creditors. UFCA §§ 1 & 7. The new UFTA similarly gives greater protection to creditors whose claims arose before the fraudulent transfer. Compare §§ 4 & 5.

c. Range of Remedial Options May Vary Depending on Whether Creditor's Claim Has Matured

Whenever a conveyance is fraudulent as to a creditor, the range of her remedial options often varies under existing law depending on whether her claim has matured by the time she seeks a remedy. Compare UFCA §§ 9 & 10. The most important difference is that a creditor whose claim has not matured is not entitled to ignore the conveyance and seize the property through attachment or garnishment. She may, however, sue to set aside the conveyance, which remedy is also available as well to a creditor with a matured claim. The UFCA also restricts the availability of protective remedies, such as injunctions against transfer and the appointments of receivers, to creditors with matured claims.

The new UFTA eliminates as "unnecessary and confusing" the UFCA's "differentiation between the remedies available to holders of matured claims and those holding unmatured claims." UFTA Prefatory Note. See UFTA § 7.

3. REMEDIES OF A BANKRUPTCY TRUSTEE TO AVOID FRAUDULENT CONVEYANCES OF A BANKRUPT DEBTOR'S PROPERTY

A bankruptcy trustee has two primary tools by which she can void fraudulent conveyances of a bankrupt debtor's property and bring the property within the estate for distribution to general creditors. One of these tools is § 548 of the Bankruptcy Code, 11 U.S.C.A. § 548 (1979 & 1988 Supp.), which is based on the Uniform Fraudulent Conveyances Act. Bankruptcy Code § 548 and the UFCA invalidate basically the same types of transfers. Another tool of a trustee for voiding fraudulent conveyances is § 544(b), 11 U.S.C.A. § 544(b) (1979). This provision of the Bankruptcy Code does not specifically provide for the invalidation of fraudulent conveyances. Rather it empowers the bankruptcy trustee to avoid any prebankruptcy transfer that is voidable under applicable law by a creditor holding a legitimate, unsecured claim against the debtor. In effect, therefore, § 544(b) incorporates state fraudulent conveyance law into the Bankruptcy Code. This is useful to a trustee even if the applicable state law is the Uniform Fraudulent Conveyance Act. For instance, under § 548, the trustee may only avoid fraudulent conveyances made within one year of the filing of the bankruptcy petition. Under state fraudulent conveyance law, which a trustee can wield because of § 544(b), the limitations period is much longer, usually three to six years. Much more is said about Bankruptcy Code §§ 544(b) and 548 later in this Black Letter. See infra Chapter XXI. One last point that should be mentioned here is that, upon voiding a fraudulent conveyance under either § 548 or 544(b), the bankruptcy trustee need not settle for a return of the property. She can recover the property's value "if the court so orders". Bankruptcy Code § 550(a), 11 U.S.C.A. § 550(a) (1984). Nothing in the section explains when such an order is appropriate.

D. TRANSFEREE'S DEFENSES

1. COMPLETE DEFENSE OF AN INNOCENT PURCHASER FOR FAIR CONSIDERATION

When a creditor attacks a conveyance of her debtor as fraudulent, the transferee's best defense is that she is an innocent purchaser for a fair consideration. This defense is complete. A fraudulent conveyance of property to such a purchaser cannot be set aside or reached by the debtor's creditors, and the transferee is not accountable in any other respect to them. Whether the conveyance was actually or constructively fraudulent makes no difference. If the transferee gave fair consideration, this fact alone usually will protect her completely against allegations of constructive fraud because the lack of fair consideration is a necessary element of most constructively fraudulent conveyances. Yet, even if the conveyance was actually fraudulent, an innocent purchaser for fair consideration is fully protected. The UFCA expressly provides that, no matter what type of fraud is involved, the debtor's creditors have no rights against a "purchaser for fair consideration without knowledge of the fraud at the time of the purchase." UFCA § 9. The UTFA has a similar provision. See UFTA § 8(a).

a. Defining "Purchaser"

The Uniform Fraudulent Conveyance Act does not define the critical term "purchaser." The term is not limited to buyers of property, however. For example, a person acquiring a security interest in property through a transaction that is fraudulent as to the debtor's creditors is a purchaser who can assert the defense of bona fide purchaser. *Perfect Photo Equities, Inc. v. American Corp.,* 42 Del. Ch. 372, 375, 212 A.2d 808, 810 (1965) (pledgee of personal property); *First State Bank v. Bear,* 172 Neb. 504, 509, 110 N.W.2d 83, 85 (1961) (real estate mortgagee); but see *American Sec. & Trust Co. v. New Amsterdam Cas. Co.,* 246 Md. 36, 41, 227 A.2d 214, 216 (1967) (chattel mortgagee is not a purchaser). There is even authority that the definition of the term "purchaser" for purposes of fraudulent conveyances law includes a person in the position of a "lien creditor", *City of New York v. Johnson,* 137 F.2d 163 (2d Cir. 1943), which stretches the term's meaning beyond the limits of Uniform Commercial Code's definition of purchaser. See U.C.C. §§ 1–201(32) & (33) (limited to persons acquiring an interest in property through a *voluntary* transaction).

b. The Need for Innocence

1) Requirement That Purchaser Lack Notice or Knowledge of Fraud in the Transfer

Courts traditionally have agreed that, for purposes of fraudulent conveyances law, protected purchaser status is conditioned on the purchaser's ignorance of the fraud involved in the transfer. Courts have disagreed, however, as to whether the requirement is a lack of *notice* of the fraud or a lack of *knowledge* of it. There is a difference. See F. Wait, A Treatise on Fraudulent Conveyances §§ 369–382 (2d ed. 1889).

The Uniform Fraudulent Conveyance Act protects only those purchasers who take without *knowledge* of the fraud. UFCA § 9. The statute does not define knowledge; but in modern statutes the term usually means more than notice of a fact, see Uniform Commercial Code § 1–201(25) (knowledge means actual knowledge but notice also includes what a person has reason to know from all the facts and circumstances known to him at the critical time), and considerably more than constructive notice, such as that which emanates from a publicly recorded document. There is substantial authority suggesting, however, that under the UFCA a purchaser knows too much, and so is unprotected, if she had mere notice of the fraud associated with the transfer of the property she holds. *Rozan v. Rozan,* 129 N.W.2d 694, 709 (N.D. 1964) (knowledge of facts and circumstances that would put a prudent person on inquiry is equivalent of all facts which would be developed by reasonable inquiry); *Columbia International Corp. v. Perry,* 54 Wash.2d 876, 879, 344 P.2d 509, 511 (1959) (same); see also *Meyer v. General American Corp.,* 569 P.2d 1094, 1097 (Utah 1977) (construing UFCA with nonuniform language explicitly conditioning a purchaser's protection on lack of "notice" rather than "knowledge"). Of course, even if knowledge is interpreted to require actual awareness rather than simply reason to know, the latter standard might be applied anyway as part of a good faith requirement which the purchaser must satisfy if she is to win protection under the UFCA. See *Sparkman and McLean Co. v. Derber,* 4 Wash. App. 341, 481 P.2d 585 (1971). *O'Neill v. Little,* 107 N.J. Super. 426, 434, 258 A.2d 731, 735 (1969).

2)   **The Related Requirement of Good Faith**
Protection of a purchaser of fraudulently conveyed property has always depended in part on the purchaser's good faith in acquiring the property. Under the Uniform Fraudulent Conveyance Act, the good faith requirement is a component of "fair consideration," UFCA § 3, which a purchaser must give in exchange for a conveyance in order to qualify for protected purchaser status.   UFCA § 9.

Good faith (as an element of fair consideration) and lack of knowledge of fraud are theoretically distinct prerequisites to that status under the UFCA, which lists both requirements in § 9. Not surprisingly, however, the two requirements are often inextricably linked in the cases.   Stop and think for a minute.   Can you imagine a case where a person could be said to have taken in good faith if she had knowledge of the fraud associated with the property conveyed to her?   A more likely case involves a purchaser who lacks good faith despite complete ignorance of her grantor's fraud in making a particular conveyance.

Example: Eisenberg made a loan to Allied. The loan was secured by a real estate mortgage on real estate owned by the debtor. Acting with actual fraudulent intent, these parties deliberately withheld the mortgage from the public record. Nine months later, Eisenberg assigned the mortgage to Bank. Allied eventually went bankrupt, and its trustee sought to void the mortgage as a fraudulent conveyance. The Bank argued the defense of bona fide purchaser because, as a matter of fact, it was totally unaware of the delay in recording the mortgage. There was nevertheless a finding that the Bank lacked good faith in accepting an assignment of the Allied mortgage from Eisenberg because, at the time of the assignment, the Bank: (1) knew that Allied was seeking Chapter 11 relief in bankruptcy; (2) had filed claims therein; (3) was aware that Allied had recently been involved in a check kiting scheme; (4) was familiar with previous irregular conduct of Allied with respect to financial transactions; (5) had previously rejected collateral in the form of any security originating with Allied.   "In the face of this background the [Bank] accepted the assignment o[f] the mortgage without a title search, did not get an opinion on the title, and made no investigation of the facts or circumstances surrounding the issuance of the mortgage. An examination of title would have disclosed the delay in recording." *In re Allied Development Corp.,* 435 F.2d 372, 376 (7th Cir. 1970). The court concluded that these "circumstances surrounding the [Bank's] acceptance of the assignment demonstrates *lack of good faith* on the part of the [Bank]." Id. at 376. Could you just as easily argue that the circumstances demonstrate the Bank's *notice* of the delay? Would notice of the delay have been notice of the fraudulent motive of Eisenberg and Allied? If not, why should notice of the delay destroy the Bank's good faith? Was the finding of lack of good faith really based at all on what the Bank would have discovered had it examined title? Do you see how easy it is to confuse the notice and good faith requirements?

c. The "Fair Consideration" Requirement

Regardless of a purchaser's innocence, she is not a protected purchaser of fraudulently conveyed property unless she gave what the common law refers to as "valuable consideration," F. Wait, A Treatise on Fraudulent Conveyances § 209 (2d ed. 1889), or, under the Uniform Fraudulent Conveyance Act, "fair consideration." See UFCA §§ 3, 9 & 10. The concept is discussed earlier in this chapter. See supra Chapter VI.B.2. Review that discussion so as not to forget that fair consideration for purposes of fraudulent conveyance law is something different from the doctrine of consideration under contracts law.

2. PARTIAL DEFENSE OF AN INNOCENT TRANSFEREE WHO PAID LESS THAN FAIR CONSIDERATION

A person who has given less than fair consideration for property fraudulently conveyed to her does not qualify for protected purchaser status. She is vulnerable to the claims of the debtor's creditors whether the conveyance was actually or constructively fraudulent. The usual consequence of not being a protected purchaser is that the conveyance is set aside in favor of the debtor's creditors, which leaves the transferee with, at most, a cause of action against her transferor to recover the less than fair, though possibly substantial, consideration the transferee paid. This result, which amounts to an unrecoverable forfeiture in many cases, is terribly harsh if the transferee was an innocent participant in a debtor's fraudulent scheme. Thus, the Uniform Fraudulent Conveyance Act provides that "[a] purchaser who without actual fraudulent intent has given less than a fair consideration for the conveyance * * * may retain the property * * * as security for repayment." UFCA § 9(2). The effect of this provision is to give the transferee a lien on the property for the amount she paid for it. Accord, UFTA § 8(d)(1).

Example: G owed $18,500 to D under a real estate contract. Shortly before J sued D to collect a promissory note, D assigned the real estate contract to M. This assignment was made by D with actual fraudulent intent to hinder her creditors, but M was unaware of the fraud. M was not a fully protected purchaser, however, because she paid only $11,000 for the real estate contract, which was less than fair consideration. J sued to set aside the assignment, whereupon G interpleaded the sum she owed to the winner of the contest between J and M. The court held that, although the conveyance was fraudulent and should be set aside, M was entitled under UFCA § 9(2) to receive from the money deposited with the court the amount actually paid for the real estate contract. *Osawa v. Onishi,* 33 Wash. 2d 546, 206 P.2d 498 (1949).

A guilty transferee, i.e., one who participated in the fraud associated with the property's conveyance, gets no credit for the value, whether fair or not, she gave in exchange for the property. See, e.g., *Citizens Bank & Trust Co. v. Rockingham Trailer Sales, Inc.,* 351 Mass. 457, 460–61, 221 N.E.2d 868, 870–71 (1966); *Blount v. Blount,* 231 Miss. 398, 428–32, 95 So. 2d 545, 559–61 (1957). On the other hand, even a guilty transferee may be allowed to recoup certain expenses incurred in preserving the property See generally 1 G. Glenn, Fraudulent Conveyances and Preferences §§ 249–258 (rev. ed. 1940). In one of the most recent cases to address this issue, however, the Wisconsin Supreme Court declared: "While even a guilty grantee may have a lien for maintenance and preservation of property from tax and other liens as a condition for relief to a creditor seeking to set aside the conveyance, it would seem that the rule as applied to a guilty grantee does not extend to payments which were derived from income from the property. A guilty grantee may recover only the payments for essential maintenance and preservation of the property made out of the grantee's pocket and before the commencement of an action by creditors to set aside the conveyance." *Running v. Widdes,* 52 Wis. 2d 254, 261, 190 N.W.2d 169, 173 (1971).

3. PROTECTION OF SUBGRANTEES

If a transferee of fraudulently conveyed property reconveys it to a third person, this subgrantee is generally subject to the same remedies that the debtor's creditors could have pursued against the original transferee.

a. Where Subgrantee Is Herself a Protected Purchaser

If a subgrantee in her own right satisfies the requirements of a purchaser whom the law protects from creditors of the debtor, the subgrantee of course enjoys whatever protection the law affords to such a purchaser. The rule is sometimes stated in these terms: Although a transferee of fraudulently conveyed property has only voidable title that is subject to defeat by creditors of the transferor, the transferee neverthess has the power to convey good title to a purchaser who, unlike the transferee, fits within a protected class. *United States v. Fidelity & Deposit Co.,* 214 F.2d 565, 570 (5th Cir. 1954) (mortgagee); *In re Paolini,* 11 B.R. 317, 319 (Bkrtcy.W.D. N.Y. 1981); *McCoy v. Love,* 382 So.2d 647, 648 (Fla. 1979); *Mathis v. Blanks,* 212 Ga. 226, 227, 91 S.E.2d 509, 512–13 (1956); *Hart v. Parrish,* 244 S.W.2d 105, 109 (Mo. 1951) (mortgagee); *Kennedy v. Dillon,* 97 N.H. 76, 77, 80 A.2d 394, 395–96 (1951) (mortgagee).

Example: United fraudulently conveyed its assets to Sheraton, which ultimately went bankrupt. A creditor of United, the City of New York, filed a claim against Sheraton's estate to reach the property United conveyed to the bankrupt. The bankruptcy trustee, who had the status of a lien creditor, objected to the City's claim. The court held that the trustee as lien creditor was a bona fide purchaser who took the property free of New York City's claim. *City of New York v. Johnson,* 137 F.2d 163 (2d Cir. 1943).

The result in the above example might be different in jurisdictions where a lien creditor is not thought of as a "purchaser" within the protection of fraudulent conveyance laws. Moreover, even where a lien creditor is a purchaser, the result might be different if the grantor's creditor acquires a lien of its own on the property before attachment of the lien of the grantee's creditor. See *Booth v. Bunce,* 33 N.Y. 139, 157 (1865) (dictum); *In re Vanity Fair Shoe Corp.,* 84 F. Supp. 533, 534 (S.D.N.Y. 1949), aff'd, 179 F.2d 766 (2d Cir. 1950) (dictum in case where prior lien of grantor's creditor was voided because of grantee's bankruptcy).

b.　Where Subgrantee Is Sheltered by an Earlier Transferee's Protection
If the subgrantee of fraudulently conveyed property does not herself fit within a class of persons whom the law protects against claims of the debtor's creditors, she nevertheless is shielded from these claims to the extent that someone through whom she holds the property, usually her immediate transferor, was a protected purchaser. *Smith v. Popham,* 266 Or. 625, 641, 513 P.2d 1172, 1179 (1973); F. Wait, A Treatise on Fraudulent Conveyances and Creditors' Bills § 384 (2d ed. 1889); see also UFTA § 8(a) (not even an actually fraudulent conveyance is "voidable ＊ ＊ ＊ against a person who took in good faith and for a reasonably equivalent value *or against any subsequent transferee* ").

REVIEW QUESTIONS

1. For the purpose of making it more difficult for creditors to reach her assets, D traded 10,000 shares of IBM stock to R in exchange for real estate of equal value. At all times D was solvent. Is the exchange a fraudulent conveyance as against A to whom D owed a debt at the time of the exchange? As against B to whom D became indebted after the exchange?

2. Are the answers to Question 1 different if D made the exchange solely for legitimate business reasons while insolvent?

3. Solely for legitimate business reasons, D exchanged stock for real estate worth about half the value of the stock. Is the conveyance of the stock fraudulent as against any of D's creditors?

4. D traded 10,000 shares of IBM stock to her brother in exchange for real estate worth only about half the value of the stock. At all times D was solvent. Is the conveyance of the stock fraudulent?

5. While insolvent, D borrowed $100,000 from B and secured the loan with a mortgage on previously unencumbered real estate worth $200,000. Does this secured transaction amount to a fraudulent conveyance as against any of D's creditors?

6. D defaulted on the loan referred to in Question 5, and B thus foreclosed the mortgage at a regularly conducted forced sale as permitted by the terms of the mortgage and by law. The real estate, which had appreciated in value, sold for $90,000, which equalled the balance due on the loan. D, of course, was insolvent.

Is the mortgage foreclosure a fraudulent conveyance as against any of D's creditors?

7. D's assets totalled $250,000. Her principal creditors were A and B, each of whom she owed $150,000. D liquidated, paid A in full, and distributed most of the balance of the proceeds to creditors owed small amounts of money. Can B attack the payment to A as a fraudulent conveyance?

8. Is the answer to Question 7 different if A is D's brother?

9. For the purpose of preventing her creditors from reaching her assets, D sold 10,000 shares of IBM stock and purchased with the proceeds a large home where she resided with her family. The stock could have been reached by creditors through execution process; the home cannot be reached through execution or other process because it is exempt from the claims of creditors. Is the sale of the stock a fraudulent conveyance?

10. What remedies are generally available to protected creditors for curing a fraudulent conveyance?

11. Even if the conveyance of the stock in Question 1 was actually fraudulent, can R sustain the conveyance and prevent A or B from setting it aside by showing that she, R, was a totally innocent purchaser? Is the answer the same if the real estate which R traded was worth only half the value of the stock?

12. Suppose that R was not an innocent purchaser for fair consideration in Question 11. Can creditor A or B recover damages from R rather than set aside aside the conveyance of the stock?

VII

BULK SALES

Analysis

Uniform Commercial Code Article 6 regulates certain sales of inventory and equipment in bulk. The purpose of the statute is to protect creditors of a seller who disposes of a major part of her stock in trade. The principal fear is that the seller will pocket the proceeds and disappear without paying her creditors. Nothing or very little will be left of the seller's property which now belongs to the seller's transferee. The sale may be voidable as an actually or constructively fraudulent conveyance. Yet, wholly apart from fraudulent conveyance law, and regardless of the seller's intention, the transfer will be ineffective against any of the seller's creditors if Article 6 applies and its requirements have not been satisfied.

A. TRANSACTIONS COVERED BY ARTICLE 6

1. SALES OF INVENTORY
Article 6 applies when an enterprise, whose principal business is the sale of merchandise from stock, transfers a major part of its inventory in bulk and not in the ordinary course of business. U.C.C. §§ 6–102(1) & (3).

Example: OR is a brick dealer having several places of business. It sold virtually all of its inventory at one location to EE. The sale represented, however, only about one-third of OR's total inventory at all business locations. The parties did not comply with Article 6; and thus, if the statute applies to the sale of inventory to EE, the transfer is ineffective as against OR's creditors. In the case *In re Albany Brick Co., Inc.,* 12 U.C.C. Rep. Serv. 165 (Bkrtcy.M.D. Ga. 1972), the court concluded that, for purposes of determining the scope of Article 6, the term "enterprise" embraces OR's total operation and not only the one location where the transferred property had been located. The court also held that a "major part" of an enterprise's inventory means more than 50% of the goods. Consequently, the court held that Article 6 did not apply to OR's transfer of bricks to EE.

2. SALES OF EQUIPMENT
"A transfer of a substantial part of the equipment of such an enterprise is a bulk transfer if it is made in connection with a bulk transfer of inventory, but not otherwise." U.C.C. § 6–102(2).

B. REQUIREMENTS OF ARTICLE 6

Article 6 imposes two major conditions on the effectiveness of a bulk transfer:

1. NOTICE MUST BE GIVEN TO THE TRANSFEROR'S CREDITORS
A bulk transfer governed by Article 6 is ineffective against any creditor of the transferor unless at least ten days before the transferee takes possession of the goods or pays for them, whichever happens first, she gives notice of the transfer to the transferor's existing creditors. U.C.C. § 6–105. These creditors include all of those holding claims based on transactions or events occurring before the notice of the bulk transfer is given. Id. § 6–109(1).

a. Purpose of the Notice
The notice requirement is the heart of Article 6. U.C.C. § 6–105 comment 1. Behind it is the notion that, upon being alerted to an impending bulk transfer,

the transferor's creditors can take steps to impound the proceeds if they think that is necessary. U.C.C. § 6–101 comment 4.

b. Contents of the Notice

Article 6 spells out the details of the notice in U.C.C. § 6–107. Generally, the notice must advise the transferor's creditors that a bulk sale is planned between parties whose names and addresses are stated. The notice must also advise whether or not all debts of the transferor are to be timely paid in full as a result of the transaction. If these debts will not be so paid, or if there is doubt on that point, additional information must be supplied, including (a) the location and general description of the property to be transferred and the estimated total of the transferor's debts; (b) an address where a schedule of property transferred and a list of the transferor's creditor may be inspected; (c) whether the transfer is to pay existing debts and, if so, the amount of such debts and to whom owing; (d) whether the transfer is for new consideration and, if so, the amount of such consideration and the time and place of payment; and (e) if the transfer is for new consideration, the notice must also explain the time and place for the transferor's creditors to file their claims for payment in states where the transferee is responsible for paying proceeds of a bulk transfer to such creditors.

c. Source of Information Contained in the Notice—Required List of Creditors and Schedule of Property

Article 6 requires the transferor to prepare a list of her existing creditors and furnish it to the transferee. U.C.C. § 6–104(1)(a). The list must include the creditors' addresses and the amounts of their claims. Id. § 6–104(2). The list must be signed and sworn to by the transferor, id., which is an incentive to include all of her creditors. If, however, the list is incomplete or inaccurate, the transfer is not rendered ineffective unless the transferee is shown to have had knowledge. Id. § 6–104(3). *Adrian Tabin Corp. v. Climax Boutique, Inc.,* 40 A.D.2d 146, 338 N.Y.S.2d 59 (1972), aff'd, 34 N.Y.2d 210, 356 N.Y.S.2d 606, 313 N.E.2d 66 (1974) (transfer not ineffective under Article 6 despite transferee's reliance on transferor's lie that there were no creditors). The parties to the bulk transfer must also prepare a schedule of the property to be transferred. Id. § 6–104(1)(b). The transferee must preserve the list of creditors and the schedule of property for six months following the transfer, and she must permit inspection of the documents by any of the transferor's creditors. Id. § 6–104(1)(c).

2. PROCEEDS OF THE BULK TRANSFER MUST BE APPLIED TO CREDITORS' CLAIMS

The official text of Article 6 conditions the effectiveness of a bulk transfer on a second major requirement which many states have elected not to adopt. This requirement, which applies whenever a bulk transfer is for new consideration, makes it the transferee's duty to ensure that the consideration is applied in satisfaction of the transferor's debts. The beneficiaries of this duty include persons who are identified on the list of creditors furnished by the transferor and also other creditors who file timely claims with the transferee. U.C.C. § 6–106(1). A pro rata distribution is required if the new consideration is insufficient to pay fully the claims of all these creditors. Id. § 6–106(3). The transferee may avoid the many possible headaches associated with satisfying the claims herself by paying the new consideration into the registry of an appropriate court and interpleading the transferor's creditors. Id. § 6–106(4).

C. CONSEQUENCES OF FAILURE TO COMPLY WITH ARTICLE 6

1. AS BETWEEN THE PARTIES TO THE BULK TRANSFER
Article 6 is designed to protect third parties, principally creditors of the transferor. It has nothing to do with the rights and remedies of the immediate parties to a bulk transfer. See, e.g., *Herrick v. Robinson,* 267 Ark. 576, 595 S.W.2d 637, 645 (1980) (buyer of property could not rescind contract of sale on basis of seller's failure to comply with Article 6); *State ex rel. Nilsen v. Ben Jacques Chevrolet Buick, Inc.,* 16 Or. App. 522, 520 P.2d 366, 367 (1974) (Article 6 generally has no effect on contractual liability); *Walkon Carpet Corp. v. Klapprodt,* 89 S.D. 172, 231 N.W.2d 370, 373 (1975) (Article 6 does not go to the validity of the transferor-transferee transaction). Thus, as between these parties, there is generally no consequence of failure to comply with Article 6. Possible exceptions include cases in which compliance with the statute was an express condition of the parties' agreement, and also cases in which one of the parties is rendered liable to a third person because of the other party's failure to comply with Article 6's requirements.

2. AS BETWEEN THE TRANSFEROR AND HER CREDITORS
Article 6 does not add to or subtract from the remedies available to the transferor's creditors on their claims against the transferor. *Johnson v. Mid States Screw & Bolt Co.,* 733 F.2d 1535, 1536 (11th Cir. 1984) (creditor who was not notified of bulk sale as Article 6 requires could not maintain action against his debtor, the bulk transferor, solely on the basis that Article 6 was violated because Article 6 creates only an in rem action against transferee); *West Denver Feed Co. v. Ireland,* 38 Colo. App. 64, 551 P.2d 1091, 1093 (1976).

3. AS BETWEEN THE TRANSFEREE AND THE TRANSFEROR'S CREDITORS
a. Where Proper Notice Is Not Given
1) Usual Remedy of Transferor's Creditors Is to Proceed in Rem Against the Transferred Property or its Proceeds
A bulk transfer is "ineffective" unless proper and timely notice is given to the transferor's creditors pursuant to Article 6. U.C.C. § 6–105. Ineffective means voidable, and an aggrieved creditor can pursue the same sorts of remedies that would be available to her had the transfer been condemned under the Uniform Fraudulent Conveyance Act or similar local law. The creditor can:

- sue to set aside the conveyance and to have the property applied in satisfaction of her claim, *H.L.C. Imports Corp. v. M & L Siegel, Inc.,* 98 Misc.2d 179, 413 N.Y.S.2d 605, 606 (1979) (dictum);

- garnish, levy or otherwise proceed directly against the property as if the transfer had never been made, U.C.C. § 6–104 comment 2 (creditors can disregard the transfer and levy on the goods as still belonging to the transferor), § 6–111 comment 2 (judgment creditor of transferor may levy execution on the property); *Johnson v. Vincent Brass & Aluminum,* 244 Ga. 412, 260 S.E.2d 325, 326–27 (1979) (creditor of bulk transferor who did not receive notice of the bulk sale can pursue in rem garnishment action against transferee who knew of creditor's claim against transferor);

- request on behalf of her and all other creditors the appointment of a receiver to take control of the transferred goods, id.; or,

- pursue any other legal or equitable remedy that is available under local law to creditors in her position. See, e.g., *Pastimes Pub. Co. v. Advertising Displays,* 6 Ill. App. 3d 414, 286 N.E.2d 19 (1972) (proceeds of bulk sale subjected to equitable lien in favor of transferor's creditors).

2)   Transferee Is Generally Not Personally Liable

When the notice requirements of Article 6 have been violated, the transferee is treated as a receiver of the goods. As such she holds the property for the transferor's creditors and must surrender the property to them for the purpose of satisfying their claims. The transferee is not, however, personally liable for the transferor's debts. See, e.g., *Johnson v. Mid States Screw & Bolt Co.,* 733 F.2d 1535, 1536 (11th Cir. 1984) (Article 6 creates only an *in rem* garnishment action against the transferee) (dictum); *American Express Co. v. Bomar Shoe Co.,* 127 Ga. App. 837, 838, 195 S.E.2d 479, 480 (1973); *Continental Cas. Co. v. Burlington Truck Lines, Inc.,* 70 Ill. App. 2d 405, 408, 217 N.E.2d 293, 295–96 (1966) (dictum); *H.L.C. Imports Corp. v. M & L Siegel, Inc.,* 98 Misc. 2d 179, 181–82, 413 N.Y.S.2d 605, 606 (N.Y. Civ. Ct. 1979); but see *National Bank of Royal Oak v. Frydlewicz,* 67 Mich. App. 417, 241 N.W.2d 471 (1976) (transferor's creditor was an Article 9 secured party and thus had a conversion claim against the transferee for interfering with secured party's rights, including right to possession, under Article 9).

Nevertheless, because a bulk transferee is accountable for the property to the transferor's creditors, she is personally liable to them for the value of property that she has conveyed, confused with other goods, converted to her own use, or otherwise put beyond the reach of the transferor's creditors. See *Associated Creditors' Agency v. Dunning Floor Covering, Inc.,* 265 Cal. App. 2d 558, 562, 71 Cal. Rptr. 494, 497 (1968); *Cornelius v. J & R Motor Supply Corp.,* 468 S.W.2d 781, 783–84 (1971); *Anderson & Clayton Co. v. Earnest,* 610 S.W.2d 846, 848 (Tex. Civ. App. 1980); but see *Bill Voorhees Co., Inc. v. R & S Camper Sales of Birmingham, Inc.,* 605 F.2d 888, 891–92 (5th Cir. 1979) (transferee is not personally liable for disposed bulk property to a creditor who does not receive notice of the bulk sale).

In any event, upon accounting to a creditor of the transferor, a transferee of a failed bulk sale is entitled to indemnification from the transferor. *Johnson v. Mid States Screw & Bolt Co.*, 733 F.2d 1535, 1537 (11th Cir. 1984).

b.   Where Proceeds Are Misapplied
In some states, the transferee is required to apply new consideration given for a bulk sale in satisfaction of the transferor's debts.   In these states the transferee is personally liable for any sum that should have been distributed to a creditor pursuant to the dictates of Article 6. U.C.C. § 6–106(1).   This obligation runs not to all possible creditors of the transferor who may appear at any time in the future, but only to creditors existing before the sale who are identified either in the list of creditors furnished by the transferor or through the timely filing of claims with the transferee. Id. § 6–106 comment 3. Nevertheless, any creditor who is a beneficiary of this obligation may enforce it for the benefit of all other such creditors.   Id. § 6–106(1) (last sentence).

c.   Where the Transferor's Creditor Is an Article 9 Secured Party
If the transferred property is collateral for a secured claim, the security interest generally survives, and is unaffected by, the bulk transfer.   Uniform Commercial Code §§ 9–201 & 9–306(2).   Thus, the secured party can hold the transferee accountable for the property even if the secured party's interest is unperfected.   U.C.C. § 9–301(1)(c) would seem to subordinate the security interest to the rights of the bulk transferee; but U.C.C. § 6–104(1) controls, making the bulk transfer ineffective against any "creditor" which includes a secured creditor.   U.C.C. § 1–201(12).   See *National Bank of Royal Oak v. Frydlewicz*, 67 Mich. App. 417, 241 N.W.2d 471 (1976).   Because a non-complying bulk transfer is ineffective against a general, unsecured creditor, there is no justification for an anomalous holding that the Code should provide otherwise whenever the transferor's creditor is secured.   Yet, the secured party may find that she need not enforce her interest against the transferee if the proceeds of bulk sale received by the transferor-debtor are sufficient to satisfy the secured debt. The security interest will attach to the proceeds of the bulk sale received by the transferor-debtor, U.C.C. §§ 9–306(1) & (2), and this proceeds interest will prevail over the claims of the transferor's general creditors.   U.C.C. § 9–201; *William Iselin & Co., Inc. v. Delta Auction & Real Estate Co.*, 433 So. 2d 911 (Miss. 1983).   If, however, these proceeds are insufficient to satisfy the secured debt, or if the transferor absconds with them, the secured party can in either event go after the original collateral in the hands of the bulk transferee.

d.   Good Faith Purchaser Status No Defense in Action Against Immediate Transferee
When a bulk transfer is attacked by creditors of the transferor for lack of compliance with Article 6, the immediate transferee cannot successfully defend on the basis of her good faith, the absence of fraudulent intent, and the payment of a fair consideration. *Danning v. Daylin, Inc.*, 488 F.2d 185, 190 (9th Cir. 1973); *Darby v. Ewing's Home Furnishings,* 278 F. Supp. 917, 919 (W.D.

Okl. 1967). This sort of defense may be effective, however, for a subsequent transferee. See infra Chapter VI.C.3.d.(2).

4. AS BETWEEN CREDITORS OF THE TRANSFEROR AND PERSONS CLAIMING THROUGH THE TRANSFEREE WHEN A BULK TRANSFER IS DEEMED INEFFECTIVE

a. General Rule of Derivative Title

When a bulk transfer is deemed ineffective because of a failure to satisfy the notice requirements of Article 6, the transferee's rights must yield to the claims of the transferor's creditors. They can recover the property from her. A different issue is whether or not the transfer is also ineffective against the transferee's creditors and other persons who claim the property through the transferee. The general answer is "yes" because title is derivative. A person cannot ordinarily acquire rights in property that are greater or better than the rights of her transferor. There are many exceptions to the rule of derivative title, however, and one such exception is § 6–110(2), which protects bona fide purchasers from bulk transferees.

b. Exception Protecting Bona Fide Purchasers From a Bulk Transferee

Although the title of a bulk transferee is defective because of non-compliance with Article 6's requirements, a purchaser for value, in good faith, and without notice takes free of any such defect. U.C.C. § 6–110(2). This is the bona fide purchaser defense of Article 6, which allows such a person to hold bulk property free of the claims of the original transferor's creditors. Those creditors cannot recover the property from the bona fide purchaser even though the bulk transfer between her transferor and the original transferor was ineffective under Article 6. This exception is broad because the Uniform Commercial Code's definitions of the operative terms are wide. "Value" includes, but is not limited to, common-law consideration. U.C.C. § 1–201(44). "Good faith" is loosely defined to mean "honesty in fact," U.C.C. § 1–201(19), which is a subjective, rather than an objective, test. "Purchaser" includes any person taking any sort of interest in property through any voluntary transaction. U.C.C. §§ 1–201(32) & (33). The term thus includes not only a buyer of property, but also a person who acquires an Article 9 security interest in property. The term purchaser does not include, however, a creditor who acquires a lien on property through attachment, execution or the like because she does not acquire her interest through a voluntary transaction. Her interest is created without the consent of the property's owner.

Examples: OR owns a shoe store. She sells all of her inventory to EE in a transaction that is subject to Article 6. No notice is given to OR's creditors. EE purchases the inventory with money borrowed from Bank. The loan is secured by EE giving the Bank an Article 9 security interest in the goods. The Bank is totally unaware of any irregularity in the transaction between OR and EE. OR's creditors learn of the bulk transfer and seek to recover the inventory from Bank, which has taken possession of the property upon EE's default. The bulk transfer is generally ineffective against OR's creditors, U.C.C. § 6–105; but the Bank, as a bona fide purchaser, nevertheless wins under § 6–110(2) and so can dispose of the inventory to satisfy the secured debt. *Mayfield Dairy Farms, Inc. v. McKenney,* 612 S.W.2d 154 (Tenn. 1981).

Same facts as above except that the person who claims through EE is not a secured party. The claimant is a judgment creditor of EE who levied execution on the inventory shortly after EE took possession of the goods. This creditor thus asserts a lien of execution on the inventory. In this case, § 6–110(2) will not protect EE's creditor because a lien creditor is not a "purchaser" as the Uniform Commercial Code defines the term. But cf. *City of New York v. Johnson,* 137 F.2d 163 (2d Cir. 1943) (lien creditor is a purchaser under pre-U.C.C., New York statute protecting bona fide purchasers of property, including subsequent transferees of property sold in bulk); *In re Gruber,* 345 F. Supp. 1076 (E.D. N.Y. 1972) (bulk transferee's trustee in bankruptcy, as lien creditor, prevails over creditor of transferor despite non-compliance with Article 6).

c. **Secured Party of Transferor Versus Secured Party of Transferee**
Suppose that the inventory disposed of by the bulk transferor is subject to a security interest in favor of one of her creditors. Upon acquiring the goods, the transferee grants a security interest in the property to one of her creditors. The bulk sale is ineffective as to the transferee, however, because the notice requirements of Article 6 were not satisfied. The transferee's secured party, as a bona fide purchaser, takes free of that defect, however. U.C.C. § 9–110(2). The defect in the transfer is all that she takes free of, however; she does not take the property free of the security interest in favor of the transferor's secured party. A security interest ordinarily survives a bulk transfer of the collateral. U.C.C. §§ 9–201 & 9–306(2). Thus, despite the defective bulk sale and the good faith and innocence of the ultimate purchaser (the transferor's secured party), the goods are subject to two security interests. The question of which one has priority over the other will be decided under Article 9. More than likely, the priority contest will be decided under U.C.C. § 9–312, the general rule of which is that security interests rank according to priority in time of filing or perfection. U.C.C. § 9–312(5)(a). See *In re McBee,* 714 F.2d 1316 (5th Cir. 1983) (right result but court wrong in suggesting through dictum that secured party is not a "purchaser").

5. **STATUTE OF LIMITATIONS**
Because Article 6 imposes unusual obligations on transferees of property, a short statute of limitations is provided. A creditor of the transferor can neither bring an action under Article 6, nor levy on the property transferred, more than six months after the date on which the transferee took possession of the goods. If, however, the transfer was concealed, the six-month period begins to run when the transfer is discovered. U.C.C. § 6–111.

REVIEW QUESTIONS

1. D sold her restaurant to B, pocketed the proceeds, and disappeared. D and B did not comply with Uniform Commercial Code Article 6. Is the sale of the business ineffective against D's creditors?

2. Identify the two major conditions on the effectiveness of a bulk transfer governed by the official version of Article 6.

3. D agreed to sell her snowmobile business to B. The principal asset was D's large stock of snowmobiles, all of which were included in the sale. B sent notice of the proposed sale to D's creditors who were included on a list prepared by D. The list did not include State Bank, a major creditor of D. After the sale was completed, State Bank learned of it when trying to collect the debt which D owed it. Is the sale ineffective as against State Bank?

4. Reconsider Question 3. Is the answer different if State Bank was included on the list of creditors but B neglected to give the bank notice of the sale?

5. Continue with Question 4. If the sale is ineffective as against State Bank, what are its rights as against B?

6. Continue with Question 5. What are State Bank's rights as against purchasers from B who bought snowmobiles included in the sale between D and B?

*

VIII

SHIELDING EXEMPT PROPERTY

Analysis

As a matter of common law, all of a debtor's property of whatever nature is subject to payment of her debts. By constitution or statute, however, all states give debtors a right to retain some of their property free from the claims of creditors. Such a statutory or constitutional provision is known as an exemption. Exemption laws normally protect only debtors who are natural persons and, in some states, only property which is used for personal rather than business purposes. Exempt property cannot be reached by creditors through judicial collection efforts. A three-pronged purpose is commonly attributed to exemption statutes: protection of the debtor, protection of the debtor's family, and protection of society. By allowing the debtor to retain certain property free from appropriation by creditors, exemption statutes give a debtor a chance to support herself so that she will not become a burden on the public.

All states exempt certain personal property from creditor process. Two of the most important personal property exemptions are those protecting a debtor's income and insurance. The single most important exemption, however, is the homestead exemption, which protects a debtor's home. The following discussion deals separately with these three classes of exempt property. It begins, however, with a brief explanation of some very important issues concerning personal property exemptions in general. This chapter ends with a note about exemptions provided by federal law and a mention of non-exempt property that is nevertheless immune from creditor process.

A. PERSONALTY IN GENERAL

All states exempt certain personal property from creditor process, but they go about it in several different ways. The various methods of identifying exempt property include:

by *type,* e.g., the family Bible, tools of the debtor's trade, wearing apparel;

by *value,* e.g., any personal property of a value not to exceed $5000: see, e.g., Ark. Const. art. 9, §§ 1 & 2 ($200 or $500, depending on whether the debtor is unattached or married or head of a family); Ga.Code Ann. § 44–13–1 (1988 Supp.) (any real or personal property or both in the amount of $5000); Fla. Const. art. 10, § 4 (personal property to the value of $1000);

by both *type and value,* e.g., an automobile with a value of not more than $2000: see, e.g., Iowa Code Ann. § 627.6(10) (West 1988 Supp.) (any combination of the following property, not to exceed $10,000 of the debtor's rights therein, such as musical instruments, implements and tools of trade, implements of husbandry, and a motor vehicle); Minn.Stat. § 550.37(12a) (1986) (one motor vehicle not exceeding the value of $2000);

by *type or value,* as in Mississippi where the debtor can exempt a long list of specifically identified property or any tangible property not exceeding $6500 in total value, Miss.Code Ann. § 85–3–1 (1988 Supp.).

Moreover, there is very little uniformity among the states with respect to the types and amounts of exempted personal property. In most states, however, specific provision is made for the exemption of wages and other income and, also, life insurance. Because of this special treatment and the importance of the property involved, income and insurance, as exempted personal property, are dealt with separately in this part of the outline.

1. COMMONLY EXEMPTED GOODS

There is much variety in the states' exemption laws. Nevertheless, the following kinds of goods are protected from creditor process in almost every state which exempts specific types of personal property:

- Family Bible;

- Wearing apparel;

- Household furnishings;

- Tools and implements of trade or business; and,

- A motor vehicle.

The major problem in applying these exemptions is determining their scope, which is basically a definitional problem. Most courts are usually very generous to debtors by broadly defining the key terms of such exemptions.

2. COMMON LIMITATIONS ON PERSONAL PROPERTY EXEMPTIONS

a. Residency Requirement

Personal property exemption statutes in many states expressly provide that their protection extends only to residents of the jurisdiction. Moreover, there is decisional law holding that "where an exemption statute is not expressly or impliedly made applicable to non-residents it will not be given effect in their favor." *Smith v. Georgia Granite Corp.,* 186 Ga. 634, 198 S.E. 772, 775 (1938);

but see *Laurencic v. Jones,* 180 So.2d 803, 805 (1965) (exemption statute applies to nonresidents unless the statute is expressly confined to residents).

b.   "Necessity" Requirement

Many states limit exemptions of specific goods and other property, including some forms of income, to that which is "necessary." Necessary does not always mean indispensible, however. Courts have recently held, for example, that necessary wearing apparel can include a $3000 diamond ring, *In re Westhem,* 642 F.2d 1139 (9th Cir.1981), and a $2500 mink coat. *In re Perry,* 6 B.R. 263 (Bkrtcy.W.D.Va.1980). The authorities disagree about the proper perspective from which to judge the necessity of property to a debtor. There is authority for a "reasonable person" or some similar standardized test, Uniform Exemption Act § 6(b) & Comment 7 ("reasonably necessary" as limitation on exemptions for certain monies and other property); there is also authority for judging necessity from the vantage point of the particular debtor taking into account her peculiar needs and station in life. See *Independence Bank v. Heller,* 275 Cal.App.2d 84, 79 Cal.Rptr. 868 (1969) (court will consider the station in life of the owner and the manner of comfortable living to which he has become accustomed).

c.   Head of Family or Household Requirement

Many personal property exemptions are expressly restricted to a debtor who is the head of a household or family. The same restriction is commonly connected with the homestead exemption, which shields a family's abode from creditors' process. The homestead exemption is outlined below. See infra Ch. VIII.D. The details respecting the "head of a family" or "household" requirement are saved for discussion there because most of the law dealing with this requirement originates in cases involving the homestead exemption. This standard, pat explanation will suffice for now: Family or household " 'means a collection of persons [at least two] living together under one head, under such circumstances or conditions that the head is under a legal or moral obligation to support the other members, and the other members are dependent upon him for support. * * * It is not necessary that the relation of husband and wife, or of parent and child, should exist in order to constitute a family [or household] having a head, within the meaning of the exemption laws. The exemption extends to one who has residing with him those so connected with him by blood, or ties of residence and association, as to become part of his household, and who have no residence but that which they enjoy under his favor, and whom he is under a legal or moral duty to support.' " *Hurt v. Perryman,* 173 Tenn. 646, 122 S.W.2d 426, 427 (1938).

d.   Value Limitation

Statutes exempting goods usually impose value limitations. An example is the Minnesota exemption covering "one motor vehicle to the extent of a value not exceeding $2000." Minn.Stat. § 550.37(12a) (1986). The plain and simple exterior of this very common sort of statute hides three major issues, all of which are usually presented whenever the statute is applied:

1) The Meaning of Value

When a statute exempts "a widget not exceeding $2000 in value," does "value" mean the worth of the property itself, or the value of the debtor's interest, i.e., equity, in the property?

> *Example:* D owns an automobile worth about $5500. Bank has a perfected security interest in the vehicle to secure a $3500 loan. JC wins a $2000 judgment against D. State law permits D to exempt a motor vehicle to the extent of $2000 in value. Can JC levy execution on the car, or is the property exempt?

In most states, the answer to the question is that JC cannot levy on the automobile. The property is totally immune from creditor's process because the value protected is the value of the debtor's equity. The debtor's equity is determined by subtracting from the worth of the property the amount of liens and security interests that encumber it and, according to some authorities, that are superior in rank to the lien of the creditor attempting to execute on the property. In the present case, D's equity is $2000 ($5500 worth minus $3500 security interest = $2000), which is exactly the size of the allowed exemption. Thus, because JC's execution lien would be subordinate to the Bank's security interest, U.C.C. § 9–301(1)(b), there is no increment of value that JC can reach and apply to her judgment.

2) Measuring the Property's Worth

In determining the worth of property for the purpose of applying an exemption having a value limitation, the usual measure is the property's market value. Market value "is not what the owner could realize at a forced sale, but the price he could obtain after reasonable and ample time, such as would ordinarily be taken by an owner to make a sale of like property." *Wade v. Rathbun,* 23 Cal.App.2d Supp. 758, 760, 67 P.2d 765, 766 (1937).

3) The Effect of Excess Value

When an item's value, or the debtor's equity in it, exceeds the limitation contained in an exemption law covering like property, the consequence is not to deprive the debtor of the exemption altogether. Rather, the property can be seized and sold under creditors' process, but the creditor is entitled to claim only such excess value as was actually received from the sale. See, e.g., *Gutterman v. First Nat. Bank,* 597 P.2d 969, 972–74 (Alaska 1979); *Maschke v. O'Brien,* 142 Pa.Super. 559, 563, 17 A.2d 923, 924 (1941); but see *Miller v. Dixon,* 176 Neb. 659, 665, 127 N.W.2d 203, 206 (1964).

3. PROCEDURE FOR EXEMPTING PERSONALTY

The procedure for asserting exemptions varies from state to state. Typically, the burden is on the debtor to claim her exemptions within a specified period, or reasonable time, after creditors' process is initiated against her. In some states the claim is made before any of the debtor's property is seized under execution, and the sheriff cannot levy on that which the debtor has set aside as exempt. In other states, however, the sheriff levies first and the debtor is in the position of having to retrieve property she claims as exempt. Of course, disagreements among the debtor, the sheriff and creditors will often arise as to the exemptability of particular assets, and thus there are procedures for raising the issue and having it determined by the court. In any event, the right to exempt property from creditors' process may be waived by failing to follow the prescribed procedure for claiming exemptions. See, e.g., *Nationwide Finance Corp. v. Wolford,* 80 Nev. 502, 396 P.2d 398 (1964); *Dakota Nat. Bank of Fargo v. Salzwedel,* 71 N.D. 643, 3 N.W.2d 468 (1942); *Hild Floor Mach. Co. v. Rudolph,* 156 Pa.Super. 102, 39 A.2d 457 (1944); *Rames v. Norbraten,* 65 S.D. 269, 272 N.W. 826 (1937). The procedures, however, must satisfy Fourteenth Amendment due process requirements for protecting the debtor's interest in exempt property. See *Finberg v. Sullivan,* 634 F.2d 50 (3d Cir. 1980). For discussion of constitutional issues associated with debtors' rights and creditors' remedies, see infra Chapters XIV and XV.

4. EXEMPTABILITY OF PROCEEDS
a. Proceeds of Sale of Exempt Personalty
"The rule generally adopted by the courts of this country is that the proceeds of exempt property resulting from a voluntary sale thereof are not exempt in the absence of a statute providing for such exemption." *Gillett State Bank v. Knaack,* 229 Wis. 179, 182, 281 N.W. 913, 914 (1938).

b. Property Purchased With Exempt Funds
Except where provided otherwise by statute, property is not exempt solely for the reason that it was purchased with exempt funds.

5. CLAIMS ENFORCEABLE AGAINST EXEMPT PERSONALTY
The reasons for satisfying a creditor's claim are sometimes more compelling than the policies behind shielding part of the debtor's wealth through exemption laws. This sort of balancing act is not performed on an ad hoc basis in every collection case. Nevertheless, there are several classes of claims that take priority over, and are enforceable notwithstanding, the exemptions generally available to a debtor. The usually impenetrable shield of exemptions which protects a minimum amount of the debtor's estate from creditors' process must yield fully or partly to the enforcement of these claims, the most important of which are mentioned here.

a. Debts for Necessaries of Life
Some exemption statutes provide in express terms that no exemption, or a reduced exemption, applies when the claim is for necessaries of life furnished for the debtor or her family. The classic examples are food and clothing. Although the word "necessary" is variously defined, no court has held that an article is necessary only when it is indispensible to sustain life.

The exact language of the necessaries exception to exemption laws is not always the same; and the courts are prone to rely on variant wording as an excuse to limit the scope of the exception. This judicial tendency should not surprise anyone. Exemptions laws are liberally construed in favor of debtors; a logical corollary of this rule of construction is that escapes from exemptions laws will be narrowed whenever and however possible.

IMPORTANT CAVEAT: Title III of the Consumer Credit Protection Act, 15 U.S.C.A. § 1671 et seq. (1982), which restricts the garnishing of wages, see supra Chapter V.C.2., establishes a maximum amount of a debtor's earnings that a creditor can garnish even when the debt is for necessaries of life. *J.J. MacIntyre Co. v. Duren,* 118 Cal.App.3d Supp. 16, 173 Cal.Rptr. 715 (1981).

b. Claims for Alimony or Support

As a general rule, "statutes and constitutional provisions exempting * * * property from legal process are usually construed, absent a specific * * * provision to the contrary, to be inapplicable as against a claim for alimony or support." *Pope v. Pope,* 283 Md. 531, 535, 390 A.2d 1128, 1131 (1978) (statute invalidating encumbrances on any right to unemployment compensation does not prohibit lien for alimony). This general rule applies to virtually every kind of exemption law, whether federal or state, even though the language of the law provides no explicit or implied authority for excepting alimony and support claims.

c. Tort Liability

Some exemption laws, by their express terms or as interpreted, limit their protection to debtors in actions based on contract. Such laws, therefore, do not shield the debtor's property in actions based on tort. *Miller v. Minturn,* 73 Ark. 183, 83 S.W. 918 (1904) (malpractice action against a doctor was a tort claim despite doctor's promise of careful and skillful treatment, which would have supported an action *ex contractu*); *Huckabee v. Stephens,* 29 Ala.App. 259, 195 So. 295 (1940) (action for damages for negligent or wanton or willful personal injury).

d. Purchase Money Debts

Exemption laws in some states provide that, in an action brought for the purchase price of property, the property shall not be exempt from creditors' process. See, e.g., Ark. Const. art. 9, § 1; N.D.Cent.Code § 28–22–14 (1974).

e. Taxes

As a general rule, exemption laws do not apply to tax debts. Exemptions are ordinarily effective against other kinds of debts owed governments, except as otherwise expressly provided by statute.

6. CONSENSUALLY WAIVING PERSONAL PROPERTY EXEMPTIONS
a. Validity Under State Law of Waiver of Exemptions by Consent

Creditors often ask debtors to waive the benefit of exemption laws so that none of the debtor's property will be shielded from execution and other process should the creditor be forced to sue on the debt. To this end, consumer credit contracts of various kinds commonly include waiver of exemptions clauses. The exemption laws of a few states authorize the waiver of some or all exemptions, See, e.g., Ala. Const. art. 9, § 210 & Ala.Code § 6–10–120 (1977); Minn. Stat. § 550.37(19) (1986) (but validity of waiver conditioned upon debtor's signature of prescribed form). The statutes of other states condemn such a waiver. See, e.g., Mont.Code Ann. § 25–13–601 (1983) (outlawing waiver of statutory exemption from execution in an unsecured promissory note); Ohio Rev.Code Ann. § 2329.66.1 (Page 1981) (every promise, agreement, or contract to waive the exemption laws of this state is void). The enacted laws of most states, however, are silent on the waiver issue; but the well-established general rule is that, except where expressly provided otherwise by enacted law, executory waivers of exemptions are void as violative of public policy. See, e.g., *Celco, Inc. of America v. Davis Van Lines, Inc.,* 226 Kan. 366, 598 P.2d 188 (1979); *Mayhugh v. Coon,* 460 Pa. 128, 331 A.2d 452 (1975).

b. Waivers of Exemptions Under Federal Law
1) Unlawful as an Unfair Trade Practice
The Federal Trade Commission has ruled that "[i]n connection with the extension of credit to consumers in or affecting commerce, * * * it is an unfair act or practice within the meaning of [the Federal Trade Commission Act] for a lender or retail installment seller directly or indirectly to take or receive from a consumer an obligation that * * * constitutes or contains an executory waiver or a limitation of exemption from attachment, execution or other process on real or personal property held, owned by, or due to the consumer, unless the waiver applies solely to property subject to a security interest executed in connection with the obligation." FTC Trade Regulation Rule On Credit Practices, 16 C.F.R. § 444.2(a)(2) (1987).

2) Void Under Bankruptcy Code
The largest number of American bankruptcies, by far, are liquidation proceedings involving individuals. In this sort of proceeding, all of the debtor's assets that are not subject to valid liens are collected, disposed of, and the proceeds are distributed to creditors. The debtor gets to keep exempt property, however. Moreover, any waiver of exemptions favoring a creditor holding an unsecured claim is voided by federal law, 11 U.S.C.A. § 522(e) (1988 Supp.), which means that the waiver will be unenforceable despite state law to the contrary.

7. CREATING CONSENSUAL SECURITY INTERESTS IN EXEMPT PERSONAL PROPERTY
The creation of an enforceable security interest in personal property amounts to a waiver of exemption rights with respect to the collateral. Indeed, the Louisiana courts have referred to the granting of a security interest in exempt property as "an implied waiver through conduct." *Aetna Finance Co. v. Antoine,* 343 So.2d 1195, 1197 (La.App.1977). Nevertheless, the vast majority of states, by express statutory provision or through decisional law, permit debtors to encumber exempt property not only to secure payment of the purchase price of the property, but also to secure any non-purchase money loan or other extension of credit.

8. CHOICE OF LAWS PROBLEMS

a. General Rule Applies Forum's Exemption Laws

"[T]he weight of authority in this country clearly holds that the exemption laws are local in nature and have no extraterritorial force or operation. They are not part of the contract, are related to the remedy, and [are] subject to the law of the forum." *Foley v. Equitable Life Assur. Soc.*, 173 Misc. 1031, 1033, 19 N.Y.S.2d 502, 504 (1940); see also Restatement (Second) of Conflict of Laws § 132 (1971).

> ***Example:*** While employed in State A, D was injured at work. She recovered $75,000 in a worker's compensation settlement, took her pension, and moved to State B. A judgment was entered against her in State B and execution was issued there. The judgment creditor garnished D's savings account maintained at a State B thrift institution. This account contained the proceeds of the worker's compensation settlement. The settlement and its proceeds are completely exempt from execution under the laws of State A. The laws of State B do not protect the settlement at all. Under the general rule, the exemption laws of State B govern in this case, which means that the savings account is unprotected from creditors' process.

B. INCOME EXEMPTIONS

Every state exempts from creditors' process certain income of a debtor. Federal law also protects part of a debtor's income in some cases. The term "income" is used here in a very broad sense to mean any money or right to money received by the debtor. Thus, income includes everything from wages and stock dividends to termination pay and retirement and disability benefits. Another example is life insurance, the cash value and proceeds of which are very popular exemptions. Insurance exemptions of this nature are discussed infra Chapter VIII.C. No state exempts every type of income, however, and the states widely disagree on the forms of income to protect. Most states agree, however, at a very general level, that the law should protect some of the direct fruits of a debtor's labor. Disagreement reappears in the statutory language used to define these fruits. Some states exempt "wages," while others protect "salary" or "earnings." Some statutes shield both "wages and salary," thereby suggesting a difference in the meaning of the two words. As scores of reported decisions make clear, there is indeed a difference; and a state's choice among words of this sort in describing exempt property can well determine not only whether the state shields a broad or narrow range of income, but also whether the category of people protected from creditors' process is large or small. An equally important issue with regard to the exemption of income is whether the protection continues as exempted income changes form.

1. WAGES, SALARY, EARNINGS, AND THE LIKE

Many states' exemption laws protect income in the form of "wages." "[G]iven its widest scope, the word 'wages' includes 'that which is pledged or paid for work or other services', * * * [and] when given its narrower scope, as is more customarily the case, the word means 'pay given for labor, usually manual or mechanical, at short stated intervals, as distinguished from salaries or fees.'" *In re Green,* 34 F.Supp. 791, 793 (W.D.Va.1940). Narrowly defined, the term "wages" does not cover the compensation received by people engaged in a large number of employment activities. For example, the court concluded in *Norman v. Goldman,* 173 A.2d 607 (Del.Super.1961), that the word "wages," as used in a statute exempting such income from execution, is not synonymous with "salary" and that the salary received by a salesperson was thus not exempt from garnishment proceedings. But see *A. Joseph Baltin & Co. v. Griffith,* 52 Lanc.Rev. 35, 36 (Pa.Com.Pl.1950) (travelling salesperson's commissions constitute wages which are exempt from attachment); cf. *Bair v. Newgeon,* 40 Pa.D. & C. 245, 29 Del. County R. 548 (Pa.1940) (the term "wages" or "salary" covers pay for mental or manual labor, including architect's compensation and counsel fees). For another example, the term "wages" may not cover the pay of an independent contractor. *Pitts v. Dallas Nurseries Garden Center, Inc.,* 545 S.W.2d 34 (Tex.Civ.App.1976); *Brasher v. Carnation Co. of Texas,* 92 S.W.2d 573 (Tex.Civ.App.1936).

Some states' exemption laws expressly protect salaries, as well as wages; these laws are more easily interpreted to exempt income such as a legislator's salary, *Georges v. Wegrocki,* 122 N.J.L. 109, 4 A.2d 274 (1939); a musician's royalties, *Sheryl Records, Inc. v. Pickens,* 431 Pa. 299, 245 A.2d 454 (1968); a physician's fee, *Eastern Lithographing Corp. v. Neville,* 203 Pa.Super. 21, 198 A.2d 391 (1964); or a lawyer's fee. *Bell v. Roberts,* 150 Pa.Super. 469, 28 A.2d 715 (1942).

Even broader protection of income is provided by statutes exempting "earnings." These laws exempt not only wages and salary, but also income that arguably does not fit within those two narrower categories. *Williams v. Sorenson,* 106 Mont. 122, 75 P.2d 784 (1938) (mileage and travelling expenses of a public official are earnings within meaning of exemption law); *Russell M. Miller Co. v. Givan,* 7 Utah 2d 380, 325 P.2d 908 (1958) (compensation received by self-employed car dealer is earnings entitled to exemption). See also *Le Font v. Rankin,* 167 Cal.App.2d 433, 334 P.2d 608 (1959) (compensation of self-employed professional or non-professional debtor, who in this case was a tax consultant, is earnings with meaning of exemption statute).

Nevertheless, statutes exempting "earnings" are not all inclusive. The typical statute of this sort protects only those earnings that the debtor reaps from her "personal services." The term personal services is somewhat slippery, too. Money received solely from a return of invested capital, such as stock dividends or income from rental property, is certainly not "wages" as the term is ordinarily defined, *United States v. Hackett,* 123 F.Supp. 106, 107 (W.D.Mo.1954) (rent is not wages), but may fall within a very broad definition of "earnings." But cf. *Johnson v. Williams,* 235 Iowa 688, 691, 17 N.W.2d 405, 406 (1945) (defines earnings narrowly to mean fruits of labor unaided by capital). Clearly, however, stock dividends and rent, even if classified as earnings, are not derived from personal services and thus would not be exempt property under statutes shielding earnings or compensation for "personal services." See, e.g., *Gerry Elson Agency, Inc. v. Muck,* 509 S.W.2d 750

(Mo.App.1974) (rent owed for lease of equipment is not compensation for personal services and so is not earnings for purposes of federal restrictions on garnishment).

2. EMPLOYEE BENEFITS

Exemption laws usually do not explicitly cover a variety of employee benefits that are paid in addition to, or in lieu of, regular or ordinary compensation. Thus, such benefits are exempted only if they fit within statute protecting more generally described compensation. In some instances where they are treated separately, as is commonly true of retirement pay, the protection may be less than that given other forms of employee compensation. Therefore, for one reason or another, debtors often attempt to shield this sort of income under laws exempting "wages," "salary," or "earnings." Success may well depend in part, but not always, on which of these terms is used in the exemption law. For example, compare *Employees Credit Union, Inc. v. Glanton,* 176 N.E.2d 926 (Ohio Mun.1961) (separation allowance provided for in union contract constitutes personal earnings of employee) with *In re Howe,* 381 F.Supp. 1025 (D.Fla.1974) (readjustment pay is not wages). Yet, the use of the term "earnings" in an exemption statute which protects a debtor's compensation for employment activities does not necessarily guarantee that the law covers employee benefits. Even if the benefits are earnings, other language in the statute can defeat the law's applicability to any income other than regular or ordinary employee compensation. For example, in *Electrical Workers v. IBEW–NECA Holiday Trust Fund,* 583 S.W.2d 154 (Mo.1979), the court concluded that an employee's interest in a trust used to collect and allocate holiday or vacation funds amounts to additional earnings of the employee. Cf. *Riley v. Kessler,* 2 Ohio Misc.2d 4, 441 N.E.2d 638 (1982) (vacation pay is "earnings" for purposes of federal restrictions on garnishment). Yet, in *Legier v. Legier,* 357 So.2d 1203 (La.App.1978), the court decided that such an interest was not protected by a statutory exemption of a percentage of a debtor's weekly disposable earnings. This decision was not based on the conclusion that holiday or vacation pay was outside the meaning of "earnings." Rather, the basis was that, because the statute refers to earnings for any *week* and to an employee's *pay period,* it must apply only to regularly paid earnings that are often and regularly paid (weekly, bi-weekly or monthly) and not those benefits that accumulate over a more extended period of time. Id. at 1206 cf. *Kokoszka v. Belford,* 417 U.S. 642, 94 S.Ct. 2431 (1974), reh'g denied, 419 U.S. 886, 95 S.Ct. 160 (1974) (income tax refund is not earnings for purposes of federal restrictions on garnishment because the refund is not compensation paid regularly and periodically and needed for the daily support of family); *Arrow S Credit Union v. Harrell,* 109 Ill.App.2d 59, 248 N.E.2d 312 (1969) (separation allowances are not wages received for services rendered in a particular pay period).

3. RETIREMENT BENEFITS AND OTHER TYPES OF SOCIAL SECURITY PAYMENTS

The exemption laws of some states specifically exempt retirement pay earned in connection with certain types of public sector employment such as teaching, law enforcement or other government service. Benefits of every kind paid by police and fire associations and other fraternal benefit associations are commonly exempted, too. Also, state law typically exempts health and welfare assistance of various kinds including (1) disability benefits from government or a private insurer, (2) worker's compensation awards, (3) supplemental security income such as old-age pensions and unemployment compensation, and (4) other forms of relief or general assistance. Federal law exempts retirement pay for various kinds of work performed for the United States government and a variety of health and welfare assistance paid with federal funds. Exemptions under federal law are discussed infra Chapter VIII.E.2. For a collection of cases on the exemptability of employee retirement pension benefits, see Annot., 93 A.L.R.3d 711 (1979).

4. **PROCEEDS OF INCOME AND THE SPECIAL PROBLEM OF EXEMPT INCOME DEPOSITED IN A BANK**
   a. **Proceeds of Exempt Income Generally**
      The general rule is that, unless otherwise provided by statute, proceeds of property are not exempt solely because the property itself was exempt. Concomitantly, property purchased with exempt income is generally not exempt simply because the money used to buy it was exempt.

   b. **Exempt Income Generally Retains Protection Upon Deposit in Checking Account**
      A bank account really represents a credit which the bank owes its customer. Technically speaking, therefore, when exempt income is deposited in a bank account, the debtor exchanges it for another form of intangible property, i.e., the obligation of the bank to pay the balance or any part of it upon the customer's demand. This obligation thus amounts to proceeds of the income. Under the usual rule governing proceeds of exempt property, the bank account would not be protected, in the absence of a statute to the contrary, simply because the account is funded by deposits of exempt income. Yet, considering the financial practices of modern society, the whole purpose of the usual income exemption would be defeated by a rule that lifts the exemption when the income is deposited in a bank account. This conclusion is shared by the vast majority of courts, which hold that exempt income remains exempt notwithstanding deposit of the funds in a checking account. The amount of exempt funds in the account, which is determined by equitable principles of tracing, will be protected.

   c. **(Antique) Exception When Exempt Income Is Deposited in a "Savings Account"**
      Although the majority of courts agree that exempt income remains exempt when deposited in a *checking account,* there is substantial authority that exempt income will lose its protection if deposited in a *savings account* or something similar. See, e.g., *Hale v. Gravallese,* 340 Mass. 722, 166 N.E.2d 557 (1960); *Auditor General v. Olezniczak,* 302 Mich. 336, 4 N.W.2d 679 (1942); *In re Bowen,* 141 Ohio St. 602, 49 N.E.2d 753 (1943). The cases have long supported a broad principle that exempt income remains exempt as long as it continues in the form of money, but that the exemption is lost whenever the income takes the form of an investment. Traditionally, the courts have thought of a savings account as an investment which is not exempt even though the funds comprising the account were themselves exempt. The reasoning has been that, by placing income in a savings account, a debtor intends for the funds to set there and collect interest and not be used to meet the essential

needs of the debtor and her family, which needs the exempt income is supposed to serve.

Courts can no longer use traditional labels in deciding whether exempt status follows funds into the debtor's account at a financial institution. The last few years have brought about a substantial relaxation of government regulation of banking enterprises and activities. As a direct consequence, clear lines no longer divide commercial banks and thrift institutions. Banks pay interest on checking accounts. Savings and loan associations permit customers to draw drafts against savings accounts. In these modern times, the test for determining the exemptability of an account filled with exempt income should be whether the account is under the debtor's control and totally accessible by her so that she can use the funds to meet her own and her dependents' essential daily needs.

The customer's ability to access an account unconditionally may in itself support exempting the account to the extent that it contains exempt funds. Even under the traditional rule that refuses to protect exempt income in a savings account, the courts have always recognized an exception if the debtor can make withdrawals on demand whenever she wishes. *Porter v. Aetna Casualty & Surety Co.,* 370 U.S. 159, 82 S.Ct. 1231 (1962); *Security Nat. Bank v. McColl,* 79 Nev. 423, 385 P.2d 825 (1963).

5. BANK'S RIGHT TO EXERCISE SETOFF AGAINST EXEMPT FUNDS IN A DEPOSIT ACCOUNT

Because a general deposit of funds in a bank account creates a debt from the bank to the depositor, the account may be offset against debts the depositor owes the bank. The details about this right of setoff, which is a potent remedy for banks, are explained elsewhere in the outline. See infra Chapter IX.B. The remedy is largely unregulated in most states and is subject to few limitations. Yet, the majority of courts hold that a bank cannot exercise its right of setoff against exempt funds in a debtor's account notwithstanding the absence of an explicit provision to this effect in the exemption laws. See *Kruger v. Wells Fargo Bank,* 11 Cal.3d 352, 367–69, 113 Cal.Rptr. 449, 458–61, 521 P.2d 441, 450–53 (1974). This holding follows from a more general proposition that applies to all creditors, not just banks: a setoff of mutual debts will not be allowed where it would defeat a debtor's exemption rights.

C. LIFE INSURANCE

Interests in, or rights under, life insurance policies are everywhere protected to some degree from creditors' process, but the states widely disagree on the extent and effect of life insurance exemptions. Differences exist with regard to (1) the classes of persons who can claim the exemption, (2) the classes of creditors against whom the exemption is effective, and (3) the nature and amount of the interests and rights that are shielded from process. The basic issues that arise in connection with life insurance exemptions are more easily understood by dealing separately with matured and unmatured policies.

1. MATURED POLICIES

a. Protection of Proceeds Paid to Beneficiary Other Than Insured's Estate

A life insurance policy matures when the insured dies. Upon her death, the insured loses interest in the exemptability of the avails of the policy. The beneficiary's interest increases dramatically. Before the policy matured, the beneficiary's rights under the policy amounted to little more than an expectancy, nothing she could count on and thus nothing of much value to anyone. Now she has a certain and definite right to the proceeds of the policy. More than one set of creditors will try and take the proceeds from her.

1) From the Claims of the Beneficiary's Creditors

Modern exemption laws, either by their express terms or as construed by the courts, typically shield life insurance proceeds from the claims of the beneficiary's own creditors. "Provisions of this type vary a great deal in structure and scope. They are frequently limited as to amount, as to the class of protected beneficiaries, as to the category of creditors affected thereby, as to the type of payments, or as to several of these factors." Riesenfeld, *Life Insurance and Creditors' Remedies in the United States,* 4 U.C.L.A.L.Rev. 583, 602 (1957).

Example: P obtained a judgment against L & S, husband and wife. They moved to exempt certain life insurance policies that covered L's life and were payable to S. Applicable law exempts from the claims of the insured's creditors amounts payable under any insurance policy made for the benefit of a dependent relative. P argued that the exemption law is inapplicable when the beneficiary, too, is a debtor. P lost the argument. The court held that the exemption law applied and protected the insurance policies. "We think it would be destructive of the benevolent policy of this statute to permit the creditor of the insured or of the beneficiary, or of both, to reach the policies or their cash value." *Consumers Time Credit, Inc. v. Remark Corp.,* 248 F.Supp. 158, 161 (E.D.Pa.1965).

2) From the Claims of the Insured's Creditors

The beneficiary of a life insurance policy must defend the proceeds not only against the claims of her own creditors, but also from the claims of the insured's creditors. The insured's creditors will argue that their debtor's money was used to pay the premiums on the insurance policy and that, therefore, they can in effect trace the contributions and the fruit of the policy into the hands of the beneficiary. This argument usually fails because most states explicitly exempt proceeds of life insurance paid to a beneficiary from the claims of the insured's creditors.

b. Exemptability of Proceeds Paid to Insured's Estate

Whether or not insurance proceeds paid to an insured's estate are exempt from process of her creditors' depends upon the wording of the applicable exemption laws. Ordinarily, the insured's creditors can reach such proceeds unless an exemption law specifically shields the property from them. Compare

Lee v. Potter, 193 Ark. 401, 404, 100 S.W.2d 252, 253 (1937) (creditors of insured not barred from participating in insurance proceeds paid to estate by exemption statute preventing them from reaching insurance proceeds paid to third person) with *In re Hazeldine's Estate,* 225 Iowa 369, 280 N.W. 568 (1938) (life policies payable to insured's estate or insured's administrator were subject to exemption statute providing that the avails of any life insurance are not subject to the deaths of the deceased and thus the proceeds inured to benefit of insured's heir). Because few states have exemption laws shielding insurance proceeds paid to an insured's estate, the creditors of an insured can reach such proceeds in most states.

2. UNMATURED POLICIES

a. Protection of Present Value From Creditors of the Insured

An unmatured insurance policy covering the life of a debtor can have present value that her creditors may want to seize and apply to their claims. For example, the policy may have a *cash surrender value.* This means that the insured can demand of the insurer a sum of money, that is equal to the policy's cash surrender value, in lieu of continued coverage of the insured's life. Very often, when an insurer pays the cash surrender value of a policy, the transaction is described as a loan to the insured. The insurance policy is dormant and unenforceable while the loan is outstanding. Upon repayment of the loan, the insurance is restored. If, however, the insured dies before repayment, the beneficiary takes nothing.

Creditors of a debtor whose life is insured by a policy having a present cash surrender or loan value may view that feature of the policy as a leviable asset. In many states, however, on one theory or another, the cash surrender value of an insurance policy is exempt from creditors' process. The exemption results not only under statutes explicitly protecting an insured's interest in a life insurance policy, but also under laws protecting a beneficiary's claim, however contingent, to the proceeds and avails of such a policy.

> *Example:* T's life was covered by a $5000 insurance policy. After twenty years T was to receive $5000; if T died before that time, his wife was to receive the money. The policy also provided for a cash surrender value beginning in the second year of coverage, increasing in amount each year. In an effort to enforce a judgment against T, J had the sheriff sell T's interest in the policy. The buyer then sued the insurer to recover the policy's cash surrender value. The insurer prevailed because the policy was exempt. The court relied on two exemption statutes. One of them protected proceeds of a policy received by a beneficiary. The other statute provided that a policy payable to a married woman inures to her separate use and benefit. *Slurszberg v. Prudential Insurance Co.,* 15 N.J.Misc. 423, 192 A. 451 (1936); see also *Dellefield v. Block,* 40 F.Supp. 616 (S.D. N.Y.1941).

A principal reason for exempting the cash surrender value of a life policy is that, if the insured's creditors could force the debtor to cash in the policy, the beneficiary—who is usually a close relative and often a dependent—would be left unprotected if the insured died before reinstating the policy's coverage. Creditors have been unable to overcome the exemption even in cases where the insured debtor retained the right willy nilly to change the beneficiary or surrender the policy for its present cash value. An interesting question, on which there is surprising little law, is whether the exemption that prevents creditors from forcing an insured to cash in a life policy also prevents them from seizing the money that an insured debtor receives upon voluntarily cashing in the policy for some purpose other than paying her creditors. Probably not. See *Bank of Brule v. Harper,* 141 Neb. 616, 627, 4 N.W.2d 609, 616 (1942); see also *Kuhn v. Wolf,* 59 Ohio App. 15, 19, 16 N.E.2d 1017, 1019 (1938) (but exemption law apparently applied only to matured policies). The reason for preventing a forced surrender does not apply in the case of a surrender freely affected. Moreover, the usual rule applicable to exemptions generally is that proceeds of exempt property are not themselves exempt. See supra Chapter VIII.A.4.

b. Determining if the Substance of a Contract Matches Its Form as a Life Insurance Policy

A debtor's savings account, a certificate of deposit belonging to her, or her portfolio of stocks, per se, is usually not exempt from the claims of creditors. In most states, however, a policy of insurance covering her life is exempt in and of itself. Does this insurance exemption apply if the policy also serves as an investment for the insured? The answer is usually "yes" if the investment feature is merely a cash surrender value. If the investment features are more extensive, however, substance will control over form in determining the applicability of insurance exemptions.

Examples: Insured purchased an insurance policy covering her life. If she died within 20 years, her spouse would receive $5000. If the insured survived, she would receive the money. The policy also provided a cash surrender value beginning in the second year, increasing in amount each year. This policy is within the protection of the exemption laws. Although it contains "investment features so far as the endowment provision is concerned, nevertheless, the policy contains a definite life insurance feature * * *" *Slurszberg v. Prudential Insurance Co.,* 15 N.J.Misc. 423, 425, 192 A. 451, 454 (1936).

Debtor purchases insurance policy providing that, upon the insured's death, named beneficiaries will receive the proceeds. The policy also provides that $104.50 of the second, third, fourth and fifth annual premiums will be deposited in a special fund for investment in certain named corporate stocks. The dividends from the investment in the stock are payable to the insured, but no part of the dividends are payable to the beneficiaries named in the policy. The funds that accumulate in the special fund are not protected by an exemption law covering " '[a]ll moneys paid or payable to a resident of this state as the insured or beneficiary designated under any insurance policy.'" *Cluck v. Mack,* 253 Ark. 769, 771, 489 S.W.2d 8, 9 (1973). As to the funds in the special account, "the policy * * * was to pay dividends to the policyholder as an investor and not 'as the insured or beneficiary designated under any insurance policy * * *'" Id. The court gratuitously added a confusing caveat: "[W]e hasten to add that the dividends here involved were not a mere incident of the life policy for such dividends would be exempt." Id. In support of this caveat, the court cited *Allen v. Central Wisconsin Trust Co.,* 143 Wis. 381, 127 N.W. 1003 (1910) (the payment of annual dividends to beneficiary of paid up life policy does not destroy policy's essential character as a purely life insurance contract).

D. HOMESTEAD

A debtor's home and the underlying land, which together constitute her homestead, are exempt from creditors' process in most states if, as is usually required, the debtor has dependents who live with her and rely on her for support. The original purpose of this homestead exemption was "to protect helpless women and children from the improvident acts of an improvident husband" and is "founded in a wise public policy * * * [that it is] better that wives and children should have shelter and a place to live than that a creditor should have his debt * * *" *Leonard v. Whitman,* 249 Ala. 205, 209, 30 So.2d 241, 244 (1947). A more credible justification, which better fits modern times, is that the exemption protects "the general economic welfare of all citizens, creditors and debtors alike, by promoting the stability and security of our society." *Wilkinson v. Carpenter,* 277 Or. 557, 565, 561 P.2d 607, 611 (1977).

1. NATURE OF HOMESTEAD

In most jurisdictions, a homestead is fundamentally a privilege or right to exempt certain real property from legal process, not an estate or a vested interest in the property. There are, however, additional consequences of establishing a homestead that give the appearance of an estate in land. First, if the debtor entitled to the exemption is married, she cannot convey the property without her spouse's consent. Second, if the debtor predeceases her spouse, the homestead survives in his favor and gives him what is essentially, though not technically, a life estate in the land free of the same claims from which it was exempt while the debtor was alive. This claim of the survivor is often referred to as a *probate homestead.* In many states, surviving children are entitled during their minority to share possession of the probate homestead with the surviving spouse.

2. PERSONS ENTITLED TO HOMESTEAD EXEMPTION
a. Residency Requirement

In many states, the homestead exemption is available only to local residents either because the law expressly so provides, or because of the decisional rule that nonresidents of the state cannot claim the exemption unless the homestead law explicitly extends itself to them. In any event, a residency requirement is typically imposed indirectly through the general rule that a house is not a homestead unless it is the residence of the debtor who lives there with her family.

b. The "Head of Household" or "Family" Requirement

In most states, due to the original purpose of homestead laws to protect debtors' dependents, the homestead exemption is available only to a debtor who heads a "household" or a "family." "To constitute a 'family' within the meaning of the homestead laws there must be two or more persons residing together under one head or manager, with the legal or moral obligation on the part of the person who occupies the position as head of the house or family to support one or more of the other members, and there must be a state of dependency, at least partial, on the part of the one receiving such support. The family relationship must be of a permanent and domestic character, and the living together must not be merely a temporary expedient rendered necessary or desirable by reason of temporary conditions. And one who claims a homestead right in premises * * * has the burden of establishing it." *State v. Haney,* 277 S.W.2d 632, 636–38 (Mo.1955).

A few states provide an exemption of residential real estate for anyone who owns a home. See, e.g., Ariz.Rev.Stat.Ann. § 33–1101 (1987) (homestead exemption available to any "resident" who is 18 or older); Mich. Const. art. 10, § 3 (a homestead in the amount of not less than $3500 of "every resident of this state" is exempt); N.H.Rev.Stat.Ann. § 480:1 (Supp.1987) ("every person" is entitled to $5000 worth of her homestead); Or.Rev.Stat. § 23.240 (1983) (homestead is exempt from liability for the debts of "owner"); Tenn.Code Ann. § 26–2–301(a) (1980) ("any individual"). The California Constitution directs the legislature to protect a certain portion of the homestead of every head of a family in the state, Cal. Const. art. 20, § 1.5, but the state has gone further and exempts some portion of every person's dwelling. Cal.Civ.P.Code § 704.710 et seq. (1987). A larger exemption applies in some cases involving married couples.

3. PROPERTY THAT QUALIFIES AS HOMESTEAD

Ordinarily, a debtor can exempt as her homestead only the real property that she occupies as a home and in which she has an interest. "It requires *both* ownership and occupancy to constitute a homestead." *Lutz v. Kehr,* 333 S.W.2d 61, 63 (Mo. 1960) (emphasis added).

a. Occupancy and Use as Residential Home

For property to qualify as an exempt homestead, the debtor must actually occupy the premises as her home or residence. This requirement explains the often cited maxim that a debtor cannot at the same time have two homesteads. See, e.g., *Corcoran v. Andrews,* 195 So.2d 767, 770 (La.App.1967). A corollary is that she cannot have " 'two places, either of which at [her] election [she] may claim as [her] homestead.' " *Horn v. Gates,* 155 Neb. 667, 53 N.W.2d 84, 87 (1952).

1) ## Unconventional Homes

Originally, homestead laws everywhere protected only real estate and contemplated the exemption of nothing other than traditional houses and service buildings constructed on land and affixed permanently thereto. At the time, of course, there were no widely used housing alternatives. Courts in some states have stretched these traditional laws to cover unconventional forms of housing such as mobile homes and condominiums. In other states, legislatures have amended homestead laws to explicitly cover a wider range of housing forms. Here is California's laundry list of types of dwellings in which a debtor can have a protected interest: housing that can qualify for the homestead exemption.

> "(1) A house together with the outbuildings and the land upon which they are situated.

> "(2) A mobilehome together with the outbuildings and the land upon which they are situated.

> "(3) A boat or other waterborne vessel.

> "(4) A condominium, as defined [elsewhere] * * *

> "(5) A planned development, as defined [elsewhere] * * *

> "(6) A stock cooperative, as defined [elsewhere] * * *

> "(7) A community apartment project, as defined [elsewhere] * * *"

Cal.Civ.P.Code § 704.710(a) (West Supp.1983) (definition of "dwelling" which is part of the definition of "homestead"). For a similar, though much shorter, list, see Ariz.Rev.Stat.Ann. § 33–1101(A) (West Supp.1983) (including dwelling on real estate, apartment of a horizontal property regime, and mobile home plus land where the home is located).

2) ## Property Used as Home and Also as Place of Business

A homestead, by definition, refers to a dwelling place that is the debtor's residence, together with the land on which the place is situated. *King v. Sweatt*, 115 F.Supp. 215, 217 (W.D.Ark.1953); *Gann v. Montgomery*, 210 S.W.2d 255 (Tex.Civ.App.1948). With rare exceptions, a debtor's place of business per se is not exempt under homestead laws. How then does the law handle the case in which the debtor's home and her business, or some part of it, are located at the same place? The general rule is that, so long as the place is and continues to be the bona fide residence of the debtor and her family, the property qualifies for the homestead exemption despite its use partly, or even chiefly, as valuable income-producing commercial property. See, e.g., *Jordan v. Jordan*, 217 Ark. 30, 228 S.W.2d 636 (1950) (sheetiron business building on same lot as debtor's house); *Buckels v. Tomer*, 78 So.2d 861 (Fla.1955) (much of land on which debtor resided was held by her solely for the purposes of speculation and eventual sale); *Heil Co. v. Lavieri*, 205 So.2d 21 (Fla.App.1967) (homestead consisted of commercial building in which debtor lived on second floor and used first floor as showroom, offices, and garage); *Jones v. Johnson,* 80 Ga.App. 340, 55 S.E.2d 904 (1949) (a farm devoted to agricultural uses is not such a commercial enterprise that would deny debtor homestead right); *O'Brien v. Johnson,* 275 Minn. 305, 148 N.W.2d 357 (1967) (homestead included commercial property consisting of stores and apartments).

b. **Property Interest**

The courts are fond of saying by way of dicta that a debtor must own the property that she claims as her exempt homestead. Do not interpret this loose talk as meaning that the debtor must hold fee title. See, e.g., *Sterling Savings & Loan Ass'n v. Schultz,* 71 Ill.App.2d 94, 218 N.E.2d 53, (1966) (unnecessary that debtor have fee title upon which to predicate her homestead right); *Barnes v. City of Detroit,* 379 Mich. 169, 150 N.W.2d 740 (1967) (same). It is true that the debtor must have some interest in or claim to the property for, if she has none, there is nothing belonging to the debtor that potentially could be seized and applied in satisfaction of her creditor's claim. Yet, virtually any legal or equitable interest or claim that gives her, as against someone, a right to possession of the property will support her claim of exemption under the homestead laws. Practically speaking, "[o]ccupancy and not title is the essential consideration in determining whether [a debtor] has a homestead," *Wambeke v. Hopkin,* 372 P.2d 470, 472 (Wyo.1962); and, " 'if the debtor's possessory right is of sufficient value to be coveted by her creditors, it is of sufficient value to the debtor herself to have it protected under the homestead law.' " *First Nat. Bank v. Boyd,* 378 F.Supp. 961, 963 (D.Ariz.1974).

Thus, for example, a homestead can be claimed with respect to property in which the debtor's possession is based on:

- A lease for a term of years, *In re Hellman,* 474 F.Supp. 348 (D.Colo.1979);

- Month-to-month tenancy, *Capitol Aggregates, Inc. v. Walker,* 448 S.W.2d 830 (Tex.Civ.App.1969);

- An equitable estate such as that retained by a grantor under a deed intended as a mortgage, *Galpatrick v. Hatter,* 258 P.2d 1200, 1203 (Okl.1953);

- The rights of a purchaser under an executory contract for the sale of land, *Childs v. Lambert,* 230 Ark. 366, 323 S.W.2d 564, 566 (1959); *Adams v. Evans,* 343 Mich. 94, 72 N.W.2d 131, 133 (1955); *Lueptow v. Guptill,* 56 Wis.2d 396, 202 N.W.2d 255, 258 (1972); or,

- A claim to or interest in property held jointly with another, *Bradley v. Scully,* 255 Cal.App.2d 101, 62 Cal.Rptr. 834 (1967) (property held in joint tenancy); *Trimble v. Trimble,* 224 Tenn. 571, 458 S.W.2d 794 (1970) (land held by entireties).

For scores of additional cases, see Annots., 74 A.L.R.2d 1355 (1960); 89 A.L.R. 511 (1934).

4. SCOPE OF HOMESTEAD

a. Area

A homestead ordinarily consists of the debtor's home itself, i.e., the house in which she and her family reside, together with the underlying, and some surrounding, land and connected appurtenances. Many states, however, limit the geographical size of the homestead. The limitations differ greatly among the states, varying from one-half acre to more than 100 acres. Usually, the allowable size of rural homesteads is much greater than that of homesteads in a city, town or village, often referred to as urban homesteads.

b. Value

In a small minority of states, there is no ceiling on the dollar value of a homestead. As a consequence, exemption laws " 'may be greatly abused, and permit great moral frauds.' " *O'Brien v. Johnson,* 275 Minn. 305, 309, 148 N.W.2d 357, 360 (1967) (debtor successfully exempted real estate worth $100,000 yielding a gross income of $1600 even though the exemption was asserted for the express purpose of evading her creditors). Most states limit the homestead exemption in terms of dollar value. Some states combine value and area limitations.

1) Determining and Measuring Value

Usually, the value of a homestead is determined as of the time when the exemption is asserted. Value for purposes of homestead exemption laws is measured by the amount of the debtor's equity in the property, which is the market value less encumbrances.

Example: D lives in a state where a debtor's homestead is exempt to the value of $20,000. A general creditor, C, wins a judgment against D for $10,000 and wants to levy on and sell D's house, which D owns alone and claims as her homestead. The market value of D's home is $100,000, and there is a $85,000 purchase money mortgage against the property. D's homestead is fully protected against C's process because the value of the property for exemption purposes is $15,000, which amount is less than the $20,000 maximum allowable value of a homestead.

The formula generally used by the courts in determining if the value of a debtor's homestead is within the allowable maximum is to add together the maximum allowable homestead exemption and the encumbrances on the property and subtract the sum from the market value of the debtor's interest in the property, i.e., $MV - (HS + E)$. If the difference is zero or a negative amount, all of the debtor's equity is fully protected by the homestead exemption. To the extent that the difference is a positive amount, the value of the debtor's interest in her homestead exceeds the value limitation, and this excessive value can be reached by creditors.

2)   Creditors Reaching Excess Value
If the debtor's interest in her homestead exceeds the maximum allowable exemption, a judgment creditor's claim is enforceable against the excess value. The rule in most states is that the creditor's lien of judgment attaches to, and is enforceable against, the homestead to the extent of the excess value. Applying the excess value of a homestead to the claims of lien creditors is normally accomplished in one of two ways: In some states, when division of the land is possible, only so much as is necessary to satisfy the claims of creditors is sold. The part reversed to the debtor must include the dwelling house. If the value of the homestead, after being reduced to its lowest practical area, is still excessive and the remainder is insufficient to pay lien creditors, the whole place is sold. From the proceeds the debtor is paid the amount of her homestead exemption, and the balance is distributed among the creditors. Any surplus goes to the debtor. In other states, however, the property is sold and the proceeds are distributed as just described without first attempting to carve out a homestead that is within the maximum allowable value. Whenever a normal size urban homestead is involved, the latter procedure will of necessity be followed everywhere because the tract of land is too small for division. Of course, whatever procedure is followed, the rights of any encumbrancers who have superior interests in the homestead are respected accordingly.

c. **Income From and Products of a Homestead**
1)   Rents Received From Lease of Homestead Property
A debtor is not precluded from exempting as her homestead the place where she lives simply because she leases part of the property. See supra Ch. VIII.D.3.a.(2). Moreover, the general rule is that the rental income is itself exempt.

2)   Minerals and Crops
A homestead embraces not only the dwelling house and the surface land on which it sits, but also extends to ungathered products of the land such as minerals beneath the ground and crops growing above it. A reason for extending the homestead protection to unsevered crops and minerals is that, "to permit a levy, it would of necessity require the use and occupation of the homestead by the executioning creditor, and this would, to such extent, subject the homestead to levy." *West v. United States Fidelity & Guaranty Co.,* 298 S.W. 652, 653 (Tex.Civ.App.1927). Once the products of the land are severed, however, neither they nor their proceeds are sheltered by the debtor's homestead exemption. The courts have long reasoned that minerals and crops are real estate for as long as they remain bound to the earth; upon being taken from the earth, however, the property becomes personalty.

d. Proceeds

1) Sale Proceeds

The prevailing rule, which is established by statute in many states, is that the proceeds from a sale of a homestead, whether the sale is voluntary or forced, are exempt from creditors' process for a reasonable period of time to allow the debtor to invest in another homestead.

2) Insurance Proceeds

By force of decisional or statutory law, the homestead exemption ordinarily extends to proceeds paid under an insurance policy covering casualty to the property. This protection of insurance proceeds may be conditioned, however, on an intent to apply the proceeds within a reasonable time toward a new or repaired homestead.

5. ESTABLISHING A HOMESTEAD

In most states, the right to a homestead exemption does not depend upon any formalities. A homestead is established simply by an eligible debtor's occupancy of property that qualifies as a homestead. See, e.g., *Mercer v. Mercer*, 365 P.2d 554, 557 (Okl.1961) (selection of homestead determined by spoken declaration, ownership, possession and occupancy will impress land with the character of a homestead); *Lueptow v. Guptill*, 56 Wis.2d 396, 405, 202 N.W.2d 255, 260 (1972) (right to homestead does not depend on its formal exercise but only on occupancy and use).

In some states, however, an additional prerequisite to the establishment of a homestead, or to the right to assert the exemption, is a formal declaration of homestead by the debtor or, in some cases, by the debtor's spouse or the debtor and her spouse jointly. See, e.g., Ariz.Rev.Stat.Ann. § 33–1102 (1987 Supp.); Va.Code § 34–6 (1984). The formality typically involves giving public notice that a homestead is claimed, as by filing a prescribed document in the real estate records of the county where the property is located. The procedures vary, however. In Utah, for example, the debtor has a choice of filing a declaration in the county land records or serving a declaration of homestead upon the officer conducting an execution prior to the time stated in the notice of execution. Utah Code Ann. § 78–23–4 (1987 Supp.).

In a few states, making a formal declaration of homestead is a substitute for actual occupancy rather than an additional prerequisite to the establishment or assertion of a homestead. In Washington, for example, property is established as a homestead "[f]rom and after the time the property is occupied as a permanent residence by the owner or the declaration is filed for record if unimproved real property * * *" Wash.Rev.Code Ann. § 6.12.080 (1988 Supp.). This declaration must be accompanied, however, by an intention to occupy the property someday as a residence. Id. § 6.12.045(2).

In California, a debtor's dwelling is exempt to some extent whether or not she formally declares a homestead. Yet, a procedure for declaring a homestead is prescribed by statute, and the incidents of the debtor's exemption depend on whether or not she has made a formal declaration. Compare Cal.Civ.Proc.Code §§ 704.710–

704.850 (West 1987) (article covering homestead exemptions) with id. Cal.Civ.Proc. Code §§ 704.910–704.990 (article covering declared homesteads).

6. **GENERAL RULE AS TO ACTIONS BLOCKED BY HOMESTEAD LAWS**
    There is much variation among the states in describing the types of evils that are held at bay by homestead laws. The descriptions range from the simple "attachment or execution" [Hawaii Rev.Stat. § 651–92(a)] or "judicial sales" [Iowa Code Ann. § 561.16 (West 1950 & 1988 Supp.)] to the wordy "attachment, judgment, levy or judgment sale" [Ill.Stat.Ann. ch. 110, § 12–901 (1984)] or the forceful "levy and sale by virtue of *any process whatever* under the laws" [Ga.Code Ann. § 44–13–1 (Michie 1987 Supp.) (emphasis added)]. Despite these differences in language, the states largely agree on the primary purpose of homestead laws: to prevent, without regard to the nature of the debt, the seizure and sale of a debtor's home (or some part of it) by a creditor trying to reach the property through ordinary collection process, including judgment and execution liens and the entire execution process.

7. **EXCEPTED CLAIMS, DEBTS AND LIENS**
    "The exemption from execution is the heart of every homestead statute, but the exemption is not an absolute one, and there are many situations in which the property may be subjected to judicial process. 'Social or economic policies which outweigh the desire to protect the home dictate that many liabilities of the owner be enforceable against [her] homestead because of the nature of the transaction out of which they arise.'" Haskins, *Homestead Exemptions,* 63 Harv.L.Rev. 1289, 1299 (1950). In the typical state, most of the liabilities that take priority over a debtor's homestead rights are explicitly spelled out in the homestead statute. The courts have added a few through decisional law. The states must largely agree on the nature and importance of social and economic polices to be weighed against the homestead right because the major exceptions to the exemption are pretty much the same everywhere.

    a. **Pre-existing Claims, Debts and Liens**
        Generally speaking, notwithstanding broad language in many homestead laws providing that the property is free from creditors' process for any and all claims of creditors, any debt that becomes a lien before a homestead is established is enforceable against the property. *Chariton Feed and Grain, Inc. v. Kinser,* 794 F.2d 1329 (8th Cir.1986). When the debt was created is unimportant. If, on the other hand, the homestead is established before the creditor gets a judgment lien on the property, the homestead exemption is enforceable against the creditor. When the debt accrued is again immaterial. See, e.g., *Holahan v. Nugent,* 198 F.2d 653, 655–56 (5th Cir.1952) (applying Louisiana law); *In re Haas,* 165 F.Supp. 488, 490 (D.Colo.1958); *Volpitta v. Fields,* 369 So.2d 367, 369 (Fla.App.1979); *Mahalko v. Arctic Trading Co., Inc.,* 29 Wash. App. 411, 413–14, 628 P.2d 859, 861 (1981) (dicta). Many courts reason that, after a homestead is established, no lien can attach to the property, except when the property exceeds the value or size limitations imposed by homestead laws. (Regarding these limitations, see supra Ch. VIII.D.4.a. & b.) Even then a creditor's lien attaches only to the excess, not the whole.

Thus, to decide whether a debt is enforceable against a homestead, determine when the debt became, or would have become, a lien on the property and when the homestead was established. Thereafter apply the old first-in-time, first-in-right rule which applies throughout the law. A wholly separate issue concerns the time by which a debtor, whose homestead rights outrank a creditor's claims to the property, must assert her homestead or forfeit the exemption. This issue is considered later. See infra Chapter VIII.D.9.a.(3).

b. Purchase-Money Debts

Homesteads are typically unprotected from judicial process to enforce some or all forms of purchase-money debts. "Purchase-money is the equivalent for the thing bought. It is a term employed in homestead laws to express the debt owing by the purchaser for [her] homestead. It is the unpaid price of the land [or other property that is her home]." R. Waples, A Treatise on Homestead and Exemption 331 (1893). Purchase-moneys debt include (1) the obligation owed a seller for the price of property she has sold on credit, see, e.g., *Corn Belt Products Co. v. Mullins,* 172 Neb. 561, 571, 110 N.W.2d 845, 851 (1961) (employer could foreclose real estate contract where it had purchased property and sold it to employee who resided there as a homesteader), and also (2) the obligation owed a bank or any other lender when it has made a loan to enable the borrower to buy certain property and the money is actually used for that purpose. See, e.g., *Martin v. First Nat. Bank,* 279 Ala. 303, 184 So.2d 815, 818–19 (1966) (that a mortgage is made to a person other than a vendor does not alone prevent its being a purchase money mortgage). See also, e.g., *Langley v. Reames,* 210 Ark. 624, 628, 197 S.W.2d 291, 293 (1946) (grandfather allowed to enforce purchase money debt against his granddaughter and her husband where grandfather had advanced money for purchase of homestead); *Hill v. Hill,* 185 Kan. 389, 399, 345 P.2d 1015, 1024 (1959) (money borrowed from son and paid to vendor of homestead is purchase money); *Dillard v. Dillard,* 341 S.W.2d 668, 671–73 (Tex.Civ.App.1960) (father who loaned money toward purchase of homestead by son and daughter-in-law could enforce his purchase money debt against the couple's home).

A purchase-money debt is not created, however, when property is purchased with the proceeds of a loan that was made for no particular purpose, see, e.g., *Starr v. City Nat. Bank,* 159 Ark. 409, 413, 252 S.W. 356, 357 (1923) (no purchase-money debt arises when a debtor bought homestead with the proceeds of a general loan which was not made for the specific purpose of buying the property); or that was made for the purpose of buying particular property is used either to buy something else or for some other purpose.

c. Debts for Improvements and Repair

To the same extent as other real estate, homesteads usually are liable to seizure and sale for debts incurred for work done and materials furnished in improving or repairing the property.

d. Mortgages

Most states permit a debtor to mortgage her homestead; and, if she defaults, the property is not protected by homestead exemption laws against a foreclosure sale to enforce the mortgage. This is true even when the mortgage secures a non-purchase money debt.

e. Taxes

Homestead exemption laws typically do not protect the property from claims and liens for taxes, but the meaning of the term "taxes" as used in this context varies among the states. There is general agreement, however, that the term includes taxes assessed against, or relating directly to, the homestead property. Notwithstanding state law on this issue, however, a homestead exemption is not effective against a federal tax lien which can be enforced against a taxpayer's interest in homestead property even though she owns it jointly with another who has no tax liability. *United States v. Rodgers,* 459 U.S. 1013, 103 S.Ct. 369 (1982).

f. Claims for Alimony and Support

Reasoning that the purpose of homestead exemption laws is to protect the family of the debtor as well as the debtor herself, some courts hold that, unless such a law clearly provides otherwise, it will not shield a debtor's homestead from claims for alimony or support unless the debtor has become the head of another household.

g. Fraud

The courts are fond of saying that a homestead cannot be a shield for fraud or theft. They usually mean that if funds obtained by fraud or theft are somehow invested in a homestead, the property is not immune from the claims of those persons whom the debtor defrauded.

h. Liabilities as a Fiduciary

Homestead laws in some states do not apply against liabilities that a debtor incurs due to her breach of fiduciary duties.

i. Rights Between Co–Owners

A homestead law merely creates an exemption as a protection against the creditors of an owner of property; the law has no relevancy as between joint owners of the property. Thus, for example, a tenant in common's homestead right does not defeat a cotenant's right to partition or accounting for rents and profits; and a homestead law does not preclude a court in a divorce case from ordering a sale or division of real estate jointly owned by the parties.

8. VOLUNTARY SALE OF PROPERTY IMPRESSED WITH HOMESTEAD
a. Homestead Freely Alienable With Spouse's Consent

A debtor's interest in homestead property is freely alienable by her just as any other real estate, but most states require the debtor's spouse, whom the homestead exemption also protects, to join in the conveyance even though the spouse is not a joint owner. A sale of a homestead by a married debtor is void in the absence of the spouse's consent.

b.   Purchaser of Former Homestead Takes Free of Claims of Debtor's Creditors
Homestead property sold by a debtor is immune from the claims of the debtor's creditors to the same extent as before the sale.

c.   Proceeds of Homestead
There is authority that the proceeds of a voluntary sale of homestead property are not exempt unless made so by enacted law. Yet, many states by statute shield such proceeds for a short period of time to allow the debtor to acquire a new homestead.

d.   New Homestead Acquired With Proceeds of Old
As a general rule, when a debtor sells her homestead and with the proceeds buys another place that she occupies as her new homestead, the new place is immune from the claims of subsequent creditors, existing creditors who could not reach the old place, and, in some states, intervening creditors whose claims arose between the sale of the old homestead and the acquisition of the new.

9.   LOSS OF HOMESTEAD RIGHTS
a.   Waiver
   1)   By Agreement
   An executory waiver of homestead rights for the benefit of a creditor is enforceable in a majority of states. But see *Iowa Mutual Insurance Co. v. Parr,* 189 Kan. 475, 370 P.2d 400 (1962) (waiver of homestead in executory agreement violates public policy). States that permit such a waiver typically require concurrence of the debtor's spouse. A few states that prohibit executory waivers of homestead rights nevertheless permit waiving homestead protection in favor of a creditor with a judgment. In any event, a debtor's waiver of exemptions in favor of an unsecured creditor is ineffective in bankruptcy. 11 U.S.C.A. § 522(e); *In re Musser,* 24 B.R. 913 (W.D.Va.1982).

   2)   By Encumbering the Property
   Almost every state allows a debtor, if her spouse consents, to mortgage the homestead even for the purpose of securing non-purchase money debts and permits the mortgagee to foreclose on the homestead if the debtor defaults.

   3)   By Failing to Make a Timely Assertion
   The law in most states is that the homestead exemption is an absolute right that may be asserted at any time before the property is sold under execution or other process. It is equally true in most states that the homestead exemption is lost forever if a person entitled to claim it fails to do so before the property is sold. Typically, a dependent of the debtor is as qualified as the debtor herself to claim the exemption.

b.   Break Up of Family or Household
In most states, a debtor acquires homestead rights only if she is the head of a household or family. See supra Chapter VIII.D.2.b. It thus seems logical that the loss of this status would result in loss of the homestead rights. Some

cases support this deduction but the courts in a much larger number of cases do not adhere strictly to it or follow a contrary rule. The truth is that once homestead rights are acquired, they are not easily lost by some disintegration of the household or family which the debtor headed. Desertion of the debtor by her spouse, a divorce, death of family members, or other causes may leave the debtor alone in the home. Her homestead rights nevertheless will be preserved if, despite the debtor's physical isolation and loss of an actual household to manage, she continues to provide support to persons who still depend on her. Some states are even more protective of the debtor and follow the rule that, "when the homestead character has once attached, it may continue for the benefit of a single individual who is the sole surviving member of the family." *Filtsch v. Curtis*, 205 Okl. 67, 70, 234 P.2d 377, 379 (1950). Where this rule is followed, the homestead rights of a debtor who has lost her household will continue even without a showing that someone continues to depend on her.

c. Abandonment

A debtor loses her homestead exemption if she abandons the homestead property. *Abandonment* results when the debtor voluntarily leaves the homestead with the present, or later developed, definite intention never to occupy the place again as a homestead. The debtor's intention is critically important. Leasing the homestead, moving away from it, or even acquiring another house at the new location, does not amount to abandonment if the debtor in good faith maintains the intention of eventually returning to the homestead. In the absence of this intention, there is an abandonment.

> *Example:* P docketed a judgment against the Bs on July 10, 1958. No lien attached to the Bs' house situated in the county where the judgment was docketed because they occupied the place as their homestead. In the first part of August, 1959, Mr. B moved to another state and found work there. A few weeks later, Mrs. B shut down the house, moved out the couple's furniture, listed the house for sale with a broker, and left town to join her husband in the other state. The house sold in October. These are the facts in *Fleischhauer v. Bilstad*, 233 Or. 578, 379 P.2d 880 (1963). The issue was whether the Bs abandoned their homestead in August, 1959. If so, P's lien thereupon attached to the property in August and was enforceable against the buyer who purchased the property in October. The court held that Bs' removal to the other state constituted an abandonment because there was no evidence "that when the Bilstad's, with their children, moved to California they intended ever to return to make the premises in question their 'actual abode' or 'to reoccupy the same as a homestead.'" Id. at 592, 379 P.2d at 886. The result in *Fleischhauer* is not inconsistent with the earlier reported rule that homestead property sold by a debtor is immune from the claims of the debtor's creditors to the same extent as before the sale. See supra Chapter VIII.D.8.b. This rule assumes that the debtor has not abandoned her homestead prior to the sale.

10. RIGHTS OF SURVIVING DEPENDENTS

The protection of a debtor and her family through homestead laws does not die with the debtor. A surviving spouse and minor children are sheltered by what commonly is called the *probate homestead*. A surviving spouse is given a personal and individual right to occupy and otherwise use the property throughout her lifetime even though he may have no interest of his own in it. Surviving children share this right until they reach majority age. The property remains immune from the claims of the debtor's creditors, and also from the claims of possession of the debtor's devisees or heirs, until the children become adults and thereafter for the life of the surviving spouse unless he voluntarily abandons the property. Abandonment of a probate homestead by a surviving spouse is not easily found: he need not occupy the property; he may lease it; he may remarry and move into another home with his new spouse. None of these facts in itself establishes an abandonment. A surviving spouse abandons his probate homestead, however, if he attempts to convey his homestead rights, which are personal to him and thus are not transferable. Upon abandonment, if there are no surviving minor children, the debtor's interest in the property passes to her devisees or heirs subject to the decedent's debts.

E. FEDERAL CONCERNS

1. STATE EXEMPTIONS APPLY IN FEDERAL COURT

Creditors' process issued from a federal court generally is subject to exemptions provided by the law of the state where the court sits. See Fed.R.Civ.P. 64 & 69(a). This is true even when the United States seeks to enforce a judgment in its favor, *Fink v. O'Neil,* 106 U.S. (16 Otto) 272, 1 S.Ct. 325 (1882), so long as the exemption would apply against the state as a judgment creditor. *United States v. Miller,* 229 F.2d 839 (3d Cir.1956).

2. ASSERTING LOCAL EXEMPTIONS AGAINST THE UNITED STATES

Apart from cases involving federal tax liens, there is very little law on the issue whether or not the enforcement of debts owed the United States is subject to local exemption laws. Apparently, however, even though the federal government ordinarily sues in federal court, local exemption laws are generally effective against the United States, see Fed.R.Civ.P. 69(a), *Fink v. O'Neil,* 106 U.S. (6 Otto) 272, 1 S.Ct. 325 (1882). There are exceptions, of course, including cases where (1) federal law preempts local exemptions, as is true with respect to the enforcement of federal tax liens, *Fried v. New York Life Ins. Co.,* 241 F.2d 504 (2d Cir.1957), cert. denied, 354 U.S. 922, 77 S.Ct. 1382 (1957) (state may not interfere with power of Congress to levy and then to collect federal income taxes), and (2) the local exemptions are not effective against claims owed the state. *United States v. Miller,* 229 F.2d 839, 841 (3d Cir.1956) (if the state exemption statute is not applicable to the state in its transactions with persons in the state's field of activity, it is equally inapplicable to the United States dealing with local persons within the federal government's field of activity).

3. EXEMPTIONS ESTABLISHED BY FEDERAL LAW

a. Federal Exemptions That Are Generally Applicable

Federal non-bankruptcy law creates a wide array of typically narrow exemptions from creditors' process that apply without regard to the source of, or the reason for, the process. Most of the exemptions protect various forms of retirement income and social welfare benefits paid by the United States or somehow regulated by federal law. Examples are: veterans' benefits, 38 U.S.C.A. § 3101(a); social security old age and disability benefits, 42 U.S.C.A. § 407(a); disability and death benefits paid to government employees injured while in the performance of their duties, 5 U.S.C.A. § 8130; federal civil service retirement, 5 U.S.C.A. § 8346(a); compensation and benefits paid under the Longshoremen's and Harbor Workers' Compensation Act, 33 U.S.C.A. § 916; annuities paid pursuant to the Railroad Retirement Act, 45 U.S.C.A. § 231m(a); and annuities paid to members of the armed forces or their survivors, 10 U.S.C.A. §§ 1440 & 1450(i). Federal law also establishes that, as a general rule, a foreign nation's property within the United States is exempt from creditors' process except as otherwise provided by statute or international agreement. 28 U.S.C.A. § 1609.

b. Federal Bankruptcy Exemptions

A debtor in bankruptcy is allowed to exempt property from the bankrupt estate and thereby keep it for herself free from creditors' claims. The Bankruptcy Code provides as a matter of federal law a generous list of exempt property, including a $7500 interest in a residence and an assortment of personalty, that a debtor can remove from the bankrupt estate unless the state of the debtor's domicile has limited its citizens to local exemptions. See 11 U.S.C.A. § 522. Most states have done so, which means that the federal schedule of exemptions is not available to most debtors in bankruptcy. Exemptions in bankruptcy are discussed more thoroughly infra Chapter XX.

4. PSEUDO EXEMPTIONS WHICH ACTUALLY ARE LIMITATIONS ON CREDITORS' RIGHTS

There are a few federal laws that appear to create exemptions but actually operate only to limit or restrict creditors' rights in certain cases. The best example is Title III of the Consumer Credit Protection Act, 15 U.S.C.A. § 1671 et seq., which limits the amount of a debtor's wages that a creditor can garnish. See supra Chapter V.C.2. This law tends to increase the burdens on an employer as garnishee because she must be careful to comply with the law's restrictions when answering a garnishment summons. Nevertheless, the courts have concluded that Title III is designed solely to protect employers from the hassles associated with the garnishment of their employees' wages. *Miller v. Monrean,* 507 P.2d 771, 773–74 (Alaska 1973). Consequently, once an employee receives her wages, Title III no longer protects them to any extent. See, e.g., *Usery v. First Nat. Bank of Arizona,* 586 F.2d 107 (9th Cir.1978); *Dunlop v. First Nat. Bank of Arizona,* 399 F.Supp. 855 (D.Ariz.1975); *Edwards v. Henry,* 97 Mich.App. 173, 293 N.W.2d 756 (1980); *John O. Melby & Co. Bank v. Anderson,* 88 Wis.2d 252, 276 N.W.2d 274 (1979). The law thus is not a true exemption statute. It is rather a temporary shelter over part of a debtor's wages that collapses when the wages leave the employer's control.

F. INALIENABLE PROPERTY EXEMPT IN FACT

As a general rule, only property which can be assigned or alienated is subject to the claims of creditors. Consequently, inalienable property generally is exempt in fact from creditors' claims even though the property is not by law explicitly designated as an exemption. Examples of property of this sort are a debtor's unliquidated claim for damages for personal injury, Plumb, *The Recommendations of the Commission on the Bankruptcy Laws—Exempt and Immune Property,* 61 Va.L.Rev. 1, 43–47 (1975); a beneficiary's rights in a spendthrift trust, *Helmsley–Spear, Inc. v. Winter,* 74 A.D.2d 195, 426 N.Y.S.2d 778 (1980), aff'd, 52 N.Y.2d 984, 438 N.Y.S.2d 79, 419 N.E.2d 1078 (1981); and a cotenant's interest in property held by the entirety. See cases collected in Annot., 75 A.L.R.2d 1172 (1961). This property is not inalienable in every state, yet it may be immune from creditors' claims for other reasons such as public policy, the nature of the property interest, or because it is covered by an exemption statute.

REVIEW QUESTIONS

1. What are the common limitations on exemptions of personal property?

2. What kinds of claims and debts generally are not subject to laws exempting personal property?

3. T or F   Executory waivers of personal property exemptions and homestead rights generally are enforceable.

4. T or F   A debtor voluntarily can encumber exempt personal property and her homestead, and the mortgage or other security interest she creates can be enforced against the property by the secured creditor upon the debtor's default in paying the secured debt.

5. Why might a debtor attempt to protect her wages under a state law exempting income rather than under Title III of the federal Consumer Credit Protection Act which restricts the amount of wages a creditor can garnish?

6. To what extent is life insurance ordinarily exempt from creditors' process?

7. D owns a house in the city, where she regularly resides with her children, and also a one-acre plot of land in the country where she plans to build a vacation home for her and the kids. Can D exempt the country property from the claims of her creditors by designating it as her homestead?

8. Can D in Question 7 claim the country place as her homestead once the vacation home is built on the land?

9. Can D in Question 7 claim the city house as her homestead if the first floor part is used by her or a lessee as a place of business?

10. Could D in Question 7 claim the city house as her homestead if she had no dependents?

11. Suppose that D in Question 7 sold the city house which had qualified as her homestead? Does the buyer of the property take subject to the pre-existing claims of D's creditors?

12. Are the proceeds of the sale in Question 11 exempt by the homestead law to the same extent as the house itself?

PART TWO

CREDITORS WITH SPECIAL RIGHTS

Analysis

*

IX

SPECIAL RIGHTS UNDER STATE LAW

Analysis

257

6. *Enforcing the Lien*
7. *Priority of the Lien*

A. SELLERS' RIGHTS UNDER ARTICLE 2

The remedies that U.C.C. Article 2 gives a seller of goods are not limited to actions for the recovery of money damages. Article 2 also gives a seller a few rights with respect to the goods themselves that allow a seller to prevent the delivery of goods to a buyer who is in breach of the sales contract or who is insolvent and, under very limited circumstances, to retrieve goods already delivered to a buyer.

1. RIGHT TO WITHHOLD DELIVERY OF GOODS
a. Upon Breach
If a buyer fails to make a payment due before delivery of the goods or anticipatorily breaches the sales contract, the seller is empowered to withhold delivery of any goods directly affected and, if the breach is of the whole contract, to withhold delivery also of all of the other goods which are the subject matter of the particular contract. U.C.C. § 2–703(a).

b. Upon Discovering Buyer's Insolvency
If a seller discovers that the buyer is insolvent, the seller may refuse to deliver the goods unless the buyer pays cash for the goods to be delivered and also for all goods already delivered. U.C.C. § 2–702(1).

2. RIGHT TO STOP DELIVERY OF GOODS IN TRANSIT
a. Upon Breach
After goods have been delivered to a carrier or other bailee, the seller rightfully "may stop delivery of carload, truckload, planeload or larger shipments of express or freight when the buyer repudiates or fails to make a payment due before delivery * * *" U.C.C. § 2–705(1).

b. Upon Discovery of Buyer's Insolvency
A seller can stop the delivery of any size shipment of goods that are in the possession of a carrier or other bailee upon discovering the buyer to be insolvent. U.C.C. § 2–705(1).

3. RIGHT OF UNPAID CREDIT SELLER TO RECLAIM GOODS
A seller of goods loses her interest in the property upon its delivery to the buyer. Title to the goods passes from the seller to the buyer upon delivery, U.C.C. § 2–401(2); and, as a general rule, the seller has no claim to the goods after delivery unless she has retained an Article 9 security interest, which requires the buyer's consent. U.C.C. § 9–203(1). A narrow exception to this rule is U.C.C. § 2–702(2), which provides a credit seller with a limited right to reclaim goods when she discovers that the buyer received them while insolvent.

a. Limitations on the Right to Reclaim

The right of an unpaid credit seller to reclaim goods under U.C.C. § 2–702(2) is subject to two requirements:

1) **Buyer Must Be Insolvent**

   The buyer must have been "insolvent" at the time she received the goods. Insolvent means that the buyer "either has ceased to pay her debts in the ordinary course of business or cannot pay her debts as they become due or is insolvent within the meaning of the federal bankruptcy law." U.C.C. § 1–201(23). Under bankruptcy law, insolvent generally means that a person's liabilities exceed her assets. 11 U.S.C.A. § 101(31)(A) (1986).

2) **Seller Must Make Timely Demand**

   A seller's right to reclaim goods from an insolvent buyer is triggered only by the seller making a demand for a return of the property within ten days after the buyer received it. This rigid time limitation does not apply, however, if the buyer makes a written misrepresentation of solvency to the seller within three months prior to the delivery of the goods. "To fall within the exception the statement of solvency must be in writing, addressed to the particular seller and dated within three months of the delivery." U.C.C. § 2–702 comment 2.

b. Protection of Third Parties

A seller's right to reclaim under U.C.C. § 2–702(2) "is subject to the rights of a buyer in the ordinary course or other good faith purchaser."

Examples: S is an electronics wholesaler who made a credit sale of personal computers to B, an electronics retailer. B was insolvent when she received the goods, which S discovered within a week after delivery. S immediately demanded return of the property. B had already sold five of the computers to customers of her business. S can reclaim the computers that B has not yet sold, but S cannot reach the five computers purchased by customers of B because they are buyers in the ordinary course and as such are immune from S's right of reclamation.

Same facts as the preceding example except that B had given Bank an Article 9 security interest in all of her inventory of computers and other stock. When S seeks to retrieve the computers that B has not yet sold, Bank objects on the basis that the computers are inventory and thus part of its collateral. Bank wins. The Bank qua secured party is a good faith purchaser, and S's right of reclamation is subject to the claims of such a person.

Suppose that the computers sold by S to B are claimed not by a secured party, but by a judgment creditor of B who has levied execution on all of B's inventory. Is S's right of reclamation subject to the claim of the lien creditor? U.C.C. § 2–702(3) does not protect the lien creditor because a lien creditor is not a buyer in the ordinary course or a good faith purchaser. The lien creditor's protection, if any, must come from extra-Code law, and the law of most states does not protect a lien creditor from the right of a debtor's creditor to reclaim under U.C.C. § 2–702(2).

c. Effect of Buyer's Bankruptcy

Whether or not the bankruptcy of a buyer cuts off a seller's U.C.C. § 2–702(2) right of reclamation is a very complicated question. The simple answer is "no" in most cases if two sets of requirements are satisfied: (1) the requirements of U.C.C. § 2–702(2) must be satisfied so that the seller has the right of reclamation under state law, and also (2) the requirements of Bankruptcy Code § 546(c), 11 U.S.C.A. § 546(c), must be met so as to preserve the seller's reclamation right under federal bankruptcy law. Preservation of the right is accomplished through § 546(c) because the provision immunizes the right from attack under the trustee's major avoiding powers. The requirements of Bankruptcy Code § 546(c), which are a little different from those of U.C.C. § 2–702(2), are these:

- The seller must have sold the goods to the buyer-debtor within the *ordinary course* of the seller's business;

- The buyer-debtor must have received the goods while *insolvent* within the meaning of the Bankruptcy Code, which requires that the debtor's liabilities exceed her assets, 11 U.S.C.A. § 101(29)(A);

- The seller must have demanded reclamation *in writing;*

- The written demand for reclamation must have been made *before* ten days after the buyer-debtor received the goods.

4. RIGHT OF DISAPPOINTED CASH SELLER TO RECLAIM GOODS

There are circumstances under which a seller who delivered goods for cash may want to reclaim them from a buyer. The typical case involves a buyer who paid with a check that bounced. The seller in such a case has a right to reclaim under state law whether or not the buyer was or is insolvent.

a. Basis of the Right

Under the common law, a buyer who pays for goods with a worthless check acquires only voidable title which is ineffective against the seller. The seller thus has the right to reclaim the goods from the buyer. The right of a seller to reclaim under these circumstances is recognized impliedly by U.C.C. §§ 2–507(2) (buyers rights against a seller where payment is due on delivery are conditional on payment) and 2–511(3) (payment by check is conditional and is defeated as between the parties by dishonor of check).

b.   Limitations on the Right

Unlike § 2–702(2) which requires a credit seller to demand the goods within ten days after the buyer has received them, the sections implying a cash seller's right of reclamation impose no conditions. Nevertheless, the drafters' commentary provides that the ten-day limit of U.C.C. § 2–702(2) also applies whenever a cash seller seeks to reclaim goods because the buyer's check failed. U.C.C. § 2–507 comment 3. Not all courts consider this commentary binding. In *Burk v. Emmick,* 637 F.2d 1172 (8th Cir. 1980), the court held that the ten-day limitation did not apply to a reclaiming cash seller when the rights of third parties are not involved and there is no prejudice to the buyer.

c.   Protection of Third Parties

A cash seller's right to reclaim is defeated as to goods acquired from the buyer by a good faith purchaser for value because, even though the buyer only has voidable title to the goods, she has the power to convey good, full, and complete title to a BFP. U.C.C. § 2–403(1). Good faith purchaser for value includes a buyer in the ordinary course of business, and also a creditor having or acquiring an Article 9 security interest in the goods through an agreement with the buyer. See, e.g., *In re Samuels & Co., Inc.,* 526 F.2d 1238 (5th Cir. 1976).

d.   Effect of the Buyer's Bankruptcy

Like a reclaiming credit seller, an unpaid cash seller usually may reclaim goods despite the buyer's bankruptcy if the seller qualifies for the right to reclaim under state law and also satisfies the federal bankruptcy law requirements of Bankruptcy Code § 546(c), 11 U.S.C.A. § 546(c), which are described above as part of the discussion of reclamation by a credit seller from an insolvent buyer.

B.   BANKS' EQUITABLE RIGHT OF SETOFF

A bank is uniquely positioned to use a very powerful remedy to enforce payment of notes or other obligations owed it by depositors. It is the non-consensual, extra-judicial, equitable *right of setoff,* by which a bank can help itself to certain deposits of its customers to satisfy debts they owe the bank.

1.   BASIS AND NATURE OF THE RIGHT

A general deposit of monies with a bank, whether in a checking or savings account, creates the relationship of debtor and creditor between the bank and depositor. The bank acquires legal title to the money but becomes obligated to pay an equivalent sum to the depositor. If a debt of the depositor to the bank becomes due, as when a loan matures or overdraft liability arises, the common law allows the bank to apply the depositor's account in satisfaction of the depositor's debt to it. This action operates as a mutual cancellation of indebtedness and is referred to as a bank's *equitable right of setoff,* which in most states exists as a matter of common law wholly apart from any statute.

2. HOW SETOFF WORKS

Setoff is a self-help remedy that is effected by a bank making appropriate book-keeping entries. In its pure common-law form, the remedy exists even though the depositor is unaware of it and has not agreed to it. No prior approval by a court is required, and notice to the depositor is unnecessary.

3. LIMITATIONS ON THE RIGHT OF SETOFF

a. Mutuality of Obligation Must Exist

"The law is clear that a bank's right to set-off or apply funds exists only where, with respect to both debt and deposit, the bank and depositor are in a debtor-creditor relationship and there is a mutuality of demands." *Get It Kwik of America, Inc. v. First Alabama Bank,* 361 So.2d 568, 571 (Ala. Civ. App. 1978). In other words, "for set-off to be permissible, there must be mutu-ality of obligation between the debtor and his creditor, as well as between the debt and the fund on deposit. Debts to be used as setoffs must be due to and from the same persons in the same capacity." *Spratt v. Security Bank,* 654 P.2d 130, 136 (Wyo. 1982).

For this reason, a bank's setoff rights against a trustee as an individual do not extend to funds held by her in trust; a corporation's account cannot be set off for the debts of its stockholders or for the debts of its parent corporation; and a partnership's debts cannot be satisfied by offsetting the individual account of one of the partners.

Modern cases tend to hold, however, that the mutuality of obligation require-ment does not prevent a bank from setting off a debtor's interest in a joint ac-count to satisfy the debtor's individual obligation; and the requirement does not preclude an offset of a person's individual account to satisfy a note on which she is jointly and severally liable with another party.

b. Depositor's Debt Must Have Matured

A bank's right of setoff does not arise until the depositor's indebtedness to the bank has matured, i.e., is due and owing. Moreover, the indebtedness "must be certain, already reduced to precise figures or capable of being liquidated by calculation without the aid of a court or jury to estimate them." *Faber, Coe & Gregg, Inc. v. First Nat. Bank,* 107 Ill. App. 2d 204, 246 N.E.2d 96 (1969). In a minority of jurisdictions, including Iowa and Texas, a bank can apply a depositor's account to unmatured obligations if and when the depositor becomes insolvent.

The right of setoff does not depend on the nature of the debt. Any kind of obligation a depositor owes can be satisfied by setoff as soon as the obligation matures. The only significant exception is created by federal law: an account cannot be offset to satisfy a depositor's bank credit card indebtedness arising in connection with a consumer credit transaction unless the depositor has pre-viously agreed in writing to such action as a means of paying her credit card account. 15 U.S.C.A. § 1666h (1982).

c.   Account Must Be General and Unrestricted

The right of setoff applies only to a *general, unrestricted* account or deposit, which exists "[w]hen money or its equivalent is deposited in a bank without any special agreement * * * On the other hand a deposit made for some special application or disposition is a *special* deposit and when a bank knowingly accepts a deposit for a specific purpose, it cannot thereafter divert it for its own benefit or otherwise act to defeat the purpose for which the deposit was made. A special deposit, or one made for a specific purpose, differs from a general deposit in that title to the special deposit does not pass to the bank, and the relationship created by the deposit is that of bailor and bailee, rather than that of creditor and debtor. It is generally recognized that whether a deposit in bank is a special or general one is dependent upon the mutual intentions and understandings of the parties, as revealed by their agreements and all of the circumstances of the case involved." *Martin v. First State Bank,* 490 S.W.2d 208, 211 (Tex. Civ. App. 1973) (emphasis in original).

Examples: D opened an account and deposited money for the purpose of paying taxes and insurance on land purchased under a contract for deed from S. The purpose of the account was designated in the deposit agreement. The account is special and cannot be offset by the bank to satisfy D's debts to it.

An IRA (individual retirement account) is a special account. *First Nat. Bank v. Philp's Estate,* 106 Ill. App. 3d 360, 436 N.E.2d 15 (1982).

"The law is equally well-settled that a deposit in a bank made in the ordinary course of business is presumed to be a general account. The burden of proof is upon the depositor to overcome this presumption and to establish by proof that the deposit was made upon such terms or under such conditions as to constitute a special account or an account for a specific purpose." *Coyle v. Pan American Bank,* 377 So.2d 213, 216 (Fla. App. 1979).

d.   Funds in the Account Must Belong to the Debtor

When a bank has knowledge or notice that funds in a depositor's account do not belong to her, or that a third party has an interest in the funds, the account may not be offset against the depositor's obligations to the bank. The courts disagree on whether or not the bank can offset the account if the bank is ignorant of the third party's interest. The older cases uphold an offset of an account containing a third party's funds if the bank acted in good faith and without notice of the third party's interest. The trend among the recent cases, however, is to disallow the offset even if the bank had no notice of the third party's interest unless the bank can show that it relied to its detriment on the appearance that the funds belonged to its depositor, as by loaning money against the account or extending the maturity of a debt or releasing collateral in reliance on the account.

4. PRIORITY OF SETOFF OVER OTHER CLAIMS
a. Check Drawn Against Account

A bank is liable to its customer for wrongful dishonor if the bank unjustifiably bounces a customer's check. U.C.C. § 4–402. A legitimate reason for bouncing a check is that the account has insufficient funds to cover the item. When an insufficiency, and the resulting dishonor of a check, are caused by the bank's exercise of a right of setoff, the customer may argue that payment of the check had priority over the setoff and thus that the bank's dishonor of the check was wrongful. This sort of priority conflict is governed by U.C.C. § 4–303(1) which provides that a check has priority over a setoff if the bank has taken any of the following steps with respect to the check before the setoff is exercised:

- accepted or certified the check;

- paid the check in cash;

- settled for the check without reserving a right to revoke the settlement and without having such right under statute, clearing house rule, or agreement;

- completed the process of posting the check to the indicated account of the customer or otherwise has evidenced by examination of such indicated account and by action its decision to pay the check;

- become accountable for the amount of the check under U.C.C. §§ 4–213(1) (d) & 4–302 dealing with the bank's responsibility for late return of checks.

Example: D draws a check to P. P presents the check to D's bank for payment. The bank examines D's account and determines that there are sufficient funds to pay the check. The bank marks the check "PAID", debits D's account for the amount of the check, and files it in the records of D's account. The bank very shortly thereafter decides to offset D's account for an obligation owed the bank. The check is retrieved, the "PAID" mark is cancelled, the check is stamped "DISHONORED" and returned to P, the credit taken from D's account to pay the check is returned to the account, and the whole account is offset to satisfy D's debt to the bank. The bank is liable to D for wrongful dishonor, and some courts and commentators suggest that the bank is also liable to P.

b. Lien of Garnishment on the Account

When a bank account is garnished by a creditor of the depositor, the bank is entitled to set off for itself so much of the account as is necessary to satisfy the depositor's debts to the bank that had matured at the time of the garnishment. In a few states, statutory law extends the right of setoff against a garnishing creditor to unmatured debts owed by the depositor to the bank.

Example: JC obtains a $5000 judgment against D and garnishes D's account at Bank. At the time of the garnishment, the account balance is $4000, but D has defaulted on a $2000 loan from the Bank to her. JC is entitled to $2000 of the account. The Bank can withhold for itself $2000 of the account to satisfy the $2000 loan which was due and owing at the time of garnishment.

c. Pledge of the Account

A depositor may pledge or otherwise assign her bank account, and the assignee takes free of the bank's right of setoff except as to matured debts the depositor owes the bank at the time the bank is notified of the assignment.

d. Article 9 Security Interest in Proceeds Deposited in the Account

An Article 9 secured party's security interest in collateral continues in proceeds of the property. U.C.C. §§ 9–306(1) & (2). Thus, if a creditor has a security interest in a car which the debtor sells, the interest attaches by law to the sale proceeds received by the debtor. This security interest in the proceeds follows the money if it is deposited in a bank account. To what extent can the bank offset these proceeds to satisfy a debt owed it by the depositor? The issue phrased differently is whether the bank's right of setoff has priority over another creditor's Article 9 security interest in the account. There is vast disagreement among the courts on this issue. Some courts decide the priority dispute under the common law by applying the local rule that governs the right of a bank to offset funds that belong to someone other than the depositor. See supra Ch. IX.B.3.d. Thus, the outcome will turn on whether the bank knew, or had notice, of the security interest and, in some states, on whether the bank detrimentally changed its position in reliance on a belief that the funds belonged solely to the depositor. Other courts decide the dispute by applying Article 9's general rule of priority, U.C.C. § 9–201. Literally applied, this rule holds that a security interest prevails over all other claims except where the U.C.C. provides otherwise. Because the U.C.C. does not provide protection for a bank's right of setoff, the security interest in the account is entitled to priority.

e. Trustee of Depositor in Bankruptcy

With some limitations, a bank's right of setoff against a depositor is recognized in bankruptcy. 11 U.S.C.A. § 553. If, however, the right has not been exercised prior to the filing of a bankruptcy petition by or against the depositor, the bank cannot effect the setoff without first getting permission from the bankruptcy court. Permission is necessary because setoff is an action automatically stayed by the filing of a bankruptcy petition. 11 U.S.C.A. § 362(a)(7). The limitations on setoff in bankruptcy are discussed infra Chapter XXI, and the automatic stay in bankruptcy is discussed infra Chapter XVIII.

C. ARTISAN'S LIEN

1. LIEN ATTACHES TO OBJECT OF LABOR

The common law gives a person who enhances the value of goods, as by repairing the goods or fashioning a finished product from them, a lien on the object of her labor. The purpose is to secure the value of the services and materials that went into repairing or otherwise caring for the goods. This lien is referred to as an *artisan's lien*. A great many states have codified the lien and in so doing have confirmed the lien's availability to persons who perform services with respect to motor vehicles of all kinds. The Arkansas statute is a good example:

> All blacksmiths, horseshoers, wheel-wrights, automobile repairmen, machine shops, farm implement repairmen, automotive storagemen, firms and corporations, who perform or have performed work or labor for any person, firm, or corporation, or who have furnished any materials or parts for the repair of any vehicle or farm implement, including tires, and all other motor accessories and bodies for automobiles, trucks, tractors, airplanes and all other motor propelling conveyances, or who stores on his or its premises any automobile, truck, tractor, airplane, or other automotive vehicle, if unpaid for same, shall have an absolute lien upon the product or object of their labor, repair, or storage and upon all such wagons, carriages, automobiles, trucks, tractors, airplanes, farm implements, and other articles repaired or stored and all horses or other animals shod by them, for the sums of money due for such work, labor, storage, and for such materials furnished by them and used in such product, the shoeing and repairing, including the furnishing of tires and all other accessories and bodies for automobiles, trucks, tractors, airplanes and all other motor propelled vehicles.

Ark. Code Ann. § 18–45–201 (1987).

2. LIEN ATTACHES BY LAW

An artisan's lien arises by operation of law and thus is not dependent on the debtor's consent. There is some question, however, about whether the lien attaches to goods in which the debtor has a limited interest. This issue can arise, for example, when an artisan repairs goods for a debtor who only leases the property or has subjected it to an Article 9 security interest. In *Associates Financial Services Co. v. O'Dell*, 491 Pa. 1, 417 A.2d 604 (1980), the court held that an artisan was not entitled to a lien on a tractor for towing and storage services because the financing company which had a security interest in the vehicle had not consented to the services. The court reasoned that the attachment of an artisan's lien was conditioned on the "owner" of the property consenting to the artisan's services, and that the owner for this purpose was the secured party.

The holding in *O'Dell* is questionable for three reasons. First, the debtor was at least part owner of the tractor because she held title to the property. Second, there is a great deal of contrary, common-law authority to the effect that, where one has ownership or comparable rights in a vehicle possessed and operated with her permission by another, the owner, for this reason alone, consents by implication to the latter acting so as to subject the vehicle to a lien for repairs. Third,

Article 9, which governs the creation and priority of security interests in personal property, explicitly provides that the existence of a security interest in collateral does not stop the debtor from further encumbering the property either voluntarily or involuntarily. U.C.C. § 9–311.

3. DURATION OF THE LIEN

Under the common law, an artisan's lien ordinarily is lost if the lienor parts with possession of the property. In many states, however, statutes automatically continue an artisan's lien despite the lienor's loss of possession or permit the lienor to preserve the lien by recording an account or a notice of lien.

4. ENFORCING THE LIEN

Under the common law, the lienor's only remedy is to withhold possession of the goods from the debtor. Enacted law in a large group of states has expanded the remedies of an artisan's lienor by giving her the additional right to sell the property herself or to force a judicial sale of it.

5. PRIORITY OF THE LIEN

Under the common law, an artisan's lien is subordinate to existing liens and encumbrances unless, as is often the case, the prior lienor or encumbrancer expressly or impliedly consents to the artisan's services. The reports are filled with cases in which a conditional vendor of a vehicle or a chattel mortgagee was found to have consented to an artisan's repair work simply by allowing the debtor to keep and operate the collateral. Where the artisan's lien has been codified, the typical statute gives the lienor priority over all claims or, at least, priority over all claims except previously recorded interests.

When the competing claim is an Article 9 security interest, U.C.C. Article 9 must be consulted along with any priority provision of an applicable artisans' lien statute. U.C.C. § 9–310 gives priority to "a person [who] in the ordinary course of his business furnishes services or materials with respect to goods subject to a security interest [and who has] a lien upon goods in [his] possession * * * given by statute or rule of law for such materials or services * * * unless the lien is statutory and the statute expressly provides otherwise." Thus, so long as an artisan retains possession of the property, her lien unquestionably is superior even to an earlier perfected security interest unless the artisan's lien is governed by a statute that expressly gives priority to a conflicting encumbrance like a security interest.

When an artisan loses possession of the property, her lien may continue on the basis of statutory authority; but U.C.C. § 9–310, by its literal terms, does not directly decide the priority dispute between a nonpossessory artisans' lien and a security interest. Nevertheless, a few courts have relied on the negative implication of § 9–310 in concluding that a nonpossessory artisan's lien is subordinate to a prior, perfected security interest. See, e.g., *Balzer Mach. Co. v. Klineline Sand & Gravel Co.,* 271 Or. 596, 533 P.2d 321 (1975).

D. CONSTRUCTION LIEN

Every state provides by statute that certain persons who perform work on, or supply materials for, an improvement to land under contract with the owner, or with the owner's agent, acquire liens on the land to secure payment for their work or materials. The first such statute was enacted by Maryland almost 200 years ago. The law applied only to the part of the state which was being ceded to the United States to constitute the District of Columbia. The purpose was to facilitate the speedy construction of the new capital city. This first law, and all others since enacted, are "designed to encourage construction by ensuring that those who contribute to a project are compensated for their efforts." *Barry Properties, Inc. v. Fick Bros. Roofing Co.*, 277 Md. 15, 18, 353 A.2d 222, 225 (1976).

1. BENEFICIARIES OF THE LIEN

Construction liens are often referred to as *mechanics' liens*. Nevertheless, their protection is not limited to laborers. The class of persons who are entitled to assert construction liens ordinarily includes everyone owed a debt for work and labor performed, or materials supplied, for the improvememt of real estate. This includes prime contractors, subcontractors, suppliers, artisans, and laborers. In some states, the protected class also includes sub-subcontractors even though they never dealt with the owner or the owner's agent with respect to the improvement. For a collection of cases dealing with the right of a sub-subcontractor to assert a construction lien, see Annot., 24 A.L.R.4th 963 (1983).

2. REACH OF THE LIEN

A construction lien attaches to the building or other improvement for which services and materials were furnished and also attaches to the lot or other tract of land on which the improvement sits.

3. WARNING THE OWNER

Many modern construction lien statutes require a claimant to notify the owner before the services or materials are furnished, or shortly thereafter, that a lien can be asserted against the property if the claimant is unpaid. Sending this notice is a condition to claiming a construction lien.

4. SIGNIFICANCE OF OWNER'S DEALINGS WITH GENERAL CONTRACTOR

In many states, neither the right of a supplier or laborer to assert a construction lien nor the size of the lien she can assert is affected by the landowner's contract with a prime or general contractor or by the landowner's payment of all or part of the contract price of the improvement to the contractor. Therefore, a landowner may have to pay twice for the same improvement or suffer the loss of her property through sale to enforce unpaid construction liens. In any event, however, lien liability is limited to the real estate; construction lien laws do not impose personal liability on the landowner.

In other states, however, the lien laws provide that neither any one lien nor the total of all liens can exceed the amount due from the owner to the prime or general contractor. The contract price between the owner and contractor establishes the owner's maximum exposure, and the owner's exposure is reduced by contract payments made in the regular course to the contractor. In a few states, the owner gets credit only for contract payments made before she receives a notice or claim of a construction lien.

5. PERFECTING THE LIEN

A construction lien claimant usually is required to file a claim, notice or statement of lien within three to six months after she has ceased to furnish materials or services. The statement is filed in the town or county where the land is located, and the lien claimant also may be required to send a copy to the owner. This filing typically preserves the lien for a period of six months to two years during which time suit must be brought to enforce it.

6. ENFORCING THE LIEN

Construction liens are ordinarily enforced by suit seeking judicial foreclosure.

7. PRIORITY OF THE LIEN

a. Among Construction Lienors Inter Se

In most states, construction liens are on an equal footing without regard to the dates when labor or services were performed or the dates when the liens were perfected. The lienors share ratably in the proceeds of a foreclosure sale of the property to which their liens have attached.

b. Between Construction Liens and Other Claims

In the larger number of states, contruction liens date from the time that actual work on the improvement by someone was first visible on the land. A construction lien is subordinate to all claims recorded prior to that time, and is superior to all claims that arise thereafter and also to all previous but unrecorded claims of which the construction lienor had no knowledge. IMPORTANT: A construction lien's priority dates from the time of first visible work by someone on the improvement no matter when the lienor herself actually supplied services or materials.

Example: O and C made a contract on March 1 under which C was to oversee the construction of a building on land owned by O. C hired a team of laborers to prepare the site for construction, and the team began digging on April 1. On April 10, O borrowed money from Bank and secured the loan by giving Bank a mortgage on the real property where the improvement was being built. Bank immediately recorded its mortgage. On April 15, Z supplied concrete used in the foundation for the building. Z satisfied all the requirements of local law for claiming and perfecting a construction lien. Z's lien dates from April 1 and has priority over Bank's mortgage.

REVIEW QUESTIONS

1. T or F   Uniform Commercial Code Article 2 allows a credit seller to reclaim goods which have been delivered to the buyer whenever the buyer fails to make a payment due on the price.

2. Seller took a postdated check in payment for goods sold to Buyer. After holding the check for a week as requested by Buyer, Seller deposited the check in her bank which soon reported that the check had bounced. Buyer's bank dishonored the check because Buyer's account had insufficient funds to cover the item. Can seller reclaim the goods?

3. As between a seller of goods asserting a right of reclamation and a secured party of the buyer asserting a security interest in the property, which claimant usually has the better right to the goods?

4. D borrowed money from Bank where D maintains a checking account. D agreed to repay the loan in twelve monthly installments. If D defaults in making the third installment payment, can the Bank offset D's checking account?

5. Is the answer to Question 4 different if the account is maintained jointly by D and another person?

6. A agreed to sell widgets belonging to B in exchange for a 10% commission. A sold the property and deposited the proceeds, save the commission, in her bank account. The bank offset this account to satisfy a matured loan which the bank had made to A. B sued the bank to recover the proceeds of the widgets. Who prevails?

7. R repaired D's car, but D refused to pay the repair bill. What are R's remedies as an artisan lienor?

8. Suppose that D in Question 7 stubbornly resists paying the repair bill, and R enforces her artisan's lien by keeping possession of the car. D also defaults in repaying the bank that financed her purchase of the car. The bank has a security interest in the car and wants its collateral. Which claim to the car is entitled to priority, R's lien or the bank's security interest?

9. Explain how a landowner in some states might be forced to pay twice for an improvement to real estate because of construction lien laws protecting laborers and suppliers.

10. D asks Bank for a loan and offers real estate as collateral. Where should Bank look to determine if there might be construction liens entitled to priority over its mortgage?

X

FEDERAL TAX LIEN

Analysis

The United States has a lien on "all property and rights to property" of a taxpayer who "neglects or refuses to pay any tax" for which she is liable. 26 U.S.C.A. § 6321 (1967).

A. REACH OF THE LIEN

The federal tax lien reaches all "property and rights to property, whether real or personal, belonging to [the tax debtor]," 26 U.S.C.A. § 6321 (1967).

1. DEFINITION OF PROPERTY

State law controls in determining whether and to what extent a debtor has property or rights to property to which a federal tax lien can attach.

2. AFTER–ACQUIRED PROPERTY INCLUDED

The lien reaches not only property which the debtor owns when the lien arises, but also property she subsequently acquires during the life of the lien.

3. DURATION OF THE LIEN

"The Federal tax lien continues until satisfied, until expiration of the period for collecting the assessed liability, or, if the tax liability is reduced to a personal judgment against the taxpayer, until the judgment is satisfied or becomes unenforceable by reason of the running of the statute of limitations." 4 L. Casey, Federal Tax Practice § 14.26 at 367 (1982). See also 26 U.S.C.A. § 6322 (1967). Assessed tax liabilities ordinarily must be collected within six years following assessment, 26 U.S.C.A. § 6502(a) (1967), unless some event tolls this period of collection or the taxpayer agrees to extend it.

4. EXEMPTIONS INEFFECTIVE

The federal tax lien law contains its own schedule of property that is exempt from the lien's reach. 26 U.S.C.A. § 6334(a) & (d) (1967 & Supp. 1984). Unless otherwise specifically provided by Congress, no other federal exemption and no state law exemptions are effective against the lien.

B. HOW THE LIEN IS CREATED

1. THREE CONDITIONS ON CREATION

The creation of a federal tax lien is subject to three conditions:

- there must be a tax assessment;
- the government must demand payment of the taxes due; and,
- the tax debtor must refuse to pay the taxes.

2. RELATION BACK TO ASSESSMENT

Although a federal tax lien does not exist until the tax debtor refuses a demand to pay taxes assessed against her, once these requirements are satisfied the lien relates back to the time the assessment was made and attaches to all property and rights to property belonging to the debtor on the date of assessment and property thereafter acquired by her during the life of the lien. For practical purposes, therefore, a federal tax lien is deemed to arise at the time of the tax assessment.

3. MAKING THE ASSESSMENT
a. Acknowledged Liability
When a person files a return acknowledging liability in excess of remittances, assessment involves nothing more than the notation of the acknowledged tax liability on a list in the office of the district director of Internal Revenue. 26 U.S.C.A. § 6203 (Supp. 1984). Assessment in the instance of acknowledged liability will occur almost immediately after the return is received. Demand follows "as soon as practicable, and within 60 days." 26 U.S.C.A. § 6303(a) (1967).

b. Understated Liability
1) Usual Assessment Case

Where tax liability is understated on the return, considerably more time will elapse between the filing of the return and the assessment, i.e., the notation of the tax liability on a list in the office of the district director of the Internal Revenue Service. First, the tax liability must be discovered through an audit of the return. After the tax liability is discovered by an audit, the actual assessment of the liability for purposes of creating a federal tax lien is postponed for at least ninety days. The IRS will send a notice of the deficiency to the tax debtor by certified or registered mail. 26 U.S.C.A. § 6212(a) (1988 Supp.). The Internal Revenue Code bars formal assessment of the deficiency until at least ninety days after the "statutory notice" or "ninety day letter" is sent. Id. § 6213(a). This delay protects the debtor's right to contest the deficiency in the Tax Court before being forced, through the government's exercise of the federal tax lien, to pay the amount that the IRS claims is due. If the tax debtor files a petition in the Tax Court, assessment and thus the creation and enforcement of a federal tax lien are further barred until the Tax Court's decision becomes final.

2) Jeopardy Assessment

The usual right to stay assessment of a deficiency by petitioning the Tax Court for a redetermination of tax due is lost in a case where the IRS believes that the assessment or collection of a deficiency will be "jeopardized by delay." 26 U.S.C.A. § 6861(a) (1967). When a jeopardy assessment is made, immediate payment of the deficiency can be demanded and, if payment is not made, property subject to the federal tax lien can be seized by the government without any notice of an intention to make the levy. 26 U.S.C.A. § 6331(a) & (d) (1967 & Supp. 1984).

C. FILING NOTICE OF THE LIEN

1. PURPOSE OF FILING CONCERNS PRIORITY
The creation of a federal tax lien is not conditioned on the government giving public notice of the lien by filing or otherwise. Yet, the Internal Revenue Code pro-

vides for filing notice of a federal tax lien. See 26 U.S.C.A. § 6323(f) (1967 & Supp. 1984). The purpose of the filing is not to make the lien effective against the taxpayer. An unfiled tax lien, though "secret" to the world generally, nevertheless exists and is fully effective against the taxpayer and also against some claimants of the taxpayer's property. Filing is required to make the lien effective against certain of the taxpayer's creditors and transferees whom Congress has decided to protect against an otherwise secret encumbrance. Filing concerns priority and nothing else. Priority of the federal tax lien is discussed below.

2. WHERE NOTICE IS FILED

Congress has invited the states to designate the places for filing notices of federal tax liens: "In the case of real property, in one office within the State (or the county, or other governmental subdivision), as designated by the laws of such State, in which the property subject to the lien is located; and [i]n the case of personal property, whether tangible or intangible, in one office within the State (or the county, or other governmental subdivision), as designated by the laws of such State, in which the property subject to the lien is situated." 26 U.S.C.A. § 6323(f)(1)(A) (1967 & Supp. 1984). "The federal law is neutral on whether the states shall designate an office at the state, county, or town (and city) level, so long as only one office is designated with respect to particular real estate and one office with respect to all the personal property of a particular taxpayer." W. Plumb, Federal Tax Liens 60–61 (3d ed. 1972). In a state which has declined this invitation or made an invalid designation, all notices of federal tax liens must be filed "[i]n the office of the clerk of the United States district court for the judicial district in which the property subject to the lien is situated * * *." 26 U.S.C.A. § 6323(f)(1)(B) (1967 & Supp. 1984).

Every state has designated places for filing federal tax lien notices. Some of them, such as Minnesota, have done so by enacting either the 1966 or 1978 version of the Uniform Federal Lien Registration Act or some variation of the model law. Minnesota's statute provides:

- "notices of liens upon real property * * * shall be filed in the office of the county recorder of the county in which the real property subject to the liens is situated.

- "notices of federal liens upon personal property, whether tangible or intangible, * * * shall be filed as follows: (1) if the person against whose interest the lien applies is a corporation or a partnership whose principal executive office is in this state, * * * in the office of the secretary of state; (2) in all other cases, in the office of the county recorder of the county where the person against whose interest the lien applies resides at the time of filing of the notice of lien."

Minn. Stat. § 272.481 (1986).

3. CONTINUOUS NOTICE

The filing of a federal tax lien will be effective continuously only if the government refiles its notice within the one-year period ending six years and 30 days after the date of the tax assessment. Further extensions are achieved by refiling within the one-year period ending with the expiration of six years after the close of the preceding required refiling period. 26 U.S.C.A. § 6323(g)(3) (1967 & Supp. 1984).

D. PRIORITY OF A FEDERAL TAX LIEN

Case law establishes a very general rule governing the priority of a federal tax lien in relation to the claims of the debtor's creditors and transferees: A federal tax lien, whether filed or not, is superior to any claim against, or interest in, the debtor's property that is not choate and perfected as fully as possible before the date of assessment. The largest exceptions to this general rule are created by the federal tax lien statute which protects a set of four classes of claimants from an unfiled tax lien, 26 U.S.C.A. § 6323(a) (1967), and another set of ten classes of claimants from even a filed tax lien. Id. § 6323(b).

1. CLAIMANTS PROTECTED BY STATUTE FROM AN UNFILED LIEN

A federal tax lien "shall not be valid as against any purchaser, holder of a security interest, mechanic's lienor, or judgment lien creditor until notice thereof * * * has been filed * * *." 26 U.S.C.A. § 6323(a) (1967).

a. Purchaser

For purposes of the federal tax lien law, the term " 'purchaser' means a person who, for adequate and full consideration in money or money's worth, acquires an interest (other than a lien or security interest) in property which is valid under local law against subsequent purchasers without actual notice." Id. § 6323(h)(6). The term includes a lessee of property and also a buyer or lessee under an executory contract or an option contract.

Examples: On January 10, the IRS obtains a tax lien against T because of an assessment made then which T has refused after demand to pay. On February 2, X buys Greenacre from T. On March 3, the IRS files its tax lien. The IRS cannot seize Greenacre to satisfy T's tax debt.

On January 10, the IRS obtains a tax lien against T. On February 2, the lien is filed. On March 3, X buys Greenacre from T. The IRS can seize Greenacre to satisfy T's tax debt.

On January 10, the IRS obtains a tax lien against T. On February 2, X leases Greenacre from T for ten years. On March 3, the IRS files the tax lien. X as lessee is a "purchaser" and thus her leasehold interest is protected against the IRS.

b. Security Interest

For purposes of the federal tax lien law, "[t]he term 'security interest' means any interest in property acquired by contract for the purpose of securing payment or performance of an obligation or indemnifying against loss or liability." 26 U.S.C.A. § 6323(h)(1) (1967). A security interest is deemed to exist, however, only from the point at which it is properly perfected under local law so as to have priority over a subsequent lien creditor and only to the extent that the holder has actually parted with money or money's worth. Id.

Examples: Federal tax lien arises on January 10. S makes a secured loan to the taxpayer on February 2 and perfects a non-purchase money Article 9 security interest in certain personal property of the taxpayer or records a non-purchase money mortgage on real estate belonging to the taxpayer. On March 3, the IRS files the tax lien. S's security interest or mortgage prevails.

Same facts as above except that S perfects or records on March 5. The IRS would have priority. S did not obtain a security interest as defined in the federal tax lien act until she perfected or recorded, which was after the IRS had filed the tax lien.

1)   Future Advances Under Pre-Existing Security Arrangement
Suppose that an Article 9 secured party (SP) has a perfected security interest in D's equipment to which a tax lien attaches. Before the tax lien is filed, the secured debt is $50,000. After the filing, the debt increases to $75,000 because of an additional loan made by SP pursuant to a future-advance clause in the security agreement between SP and D. SP's security interest is clearly entitled to priority over the tax lien to the extent of $50,000. The question is whether or not the remainder of the security interest, i.e., that part reflecting the additional advance of $25,000, is likewise safe from the lien. The answer under § 6323(a) is that SP's future advance interest is subordinate to the tax lien. Under the tax law's definition of security interest, SP was not holding a $75,000 perfected interest at the time the tax lien was filed. 26 U.S.C.A. § 6323(h)(1) (1967). At that time SP's interest was only $50,000, and SP takes priority only to that extent. Nevertheless, an exception to § 6323(a) protects the $25,000 advance if it was made within 45 days of the tax lien filing and without actual knowledge of the filing. Id. § 6323(d). This protection extends only to advances secured by collateral existing at the time of the lien filing. If, however, the collateral is commercial financing security such as inventory or accounts, advances made after the tax lien filing may also be protected under another provision of the tax lien law, § 6323(c), which is discussed next.

2)   After-Acquired Collateral
Suppose that D's debt to SP is secured by D's inventory to which a federal tax lien attaches. After the tax lien is filed, D acquires additional inventory to which the tax lien attaches by operation of law. SP's interest also attaches to the new inventory under an after-acquired property clause in the security agreement between her and the debtor. Under § 6323(a), the tax lien is entitled to priority. See 26 C.F.R. § 301.6323(a)–1 (1987) (priority for tax lien implied where third-party claim does not fit within any of the § 6323 exceptions). A security interest cannot attach until the debtor has rights in the collateral. The debtor had no rights in the new

collateral until after the tax lien filing. Thus, SP did not become a holder of a perfected security interest in the fresh collateral until after the filing. The tax law, however, protects security interests in "commercial financing security" acquired within 45 days after the tax lien filing. 26 U.S.C.A. § 6323(c). Commercial financing security means (1) paper of a kind ordinarily arising in commercial transactions, (2) accounts receivable, (3) mortgages on real property, and (4) inventory. The secured party's actual knowledge or lack of knowledge makes no difference in the operation of this exceptional provision. With respect to collateral acquired within the 45–day period, the secured party is entitled to priority even if she knew of the tax lien; but the secured party's innocence is no defense to the superiority of the tax lien in collateral acquired after the 45–day period. If the secured party cannot prove that the collateral was acquired before the 46th day after the tax filing, the IRS wins notwithstanding the secured party's lack of knowledge of the tax lien. See, e.g., *Rice Investment Co. v. United States,* 625 F.2d 565 (5th Cir. 1980); *Texas Oil & Gas Corp. v. United States,* 466 F.2d 1040 (5th Cir. 1972).

For purposes of § 6323(c), if not for all other purposes, an account that is collateral is not acquired by the debtor before the time she makes the contract to supply the goods or services for which the debtor earns the right to payment and probably no sooner than the time the goods or services are actually sold or supplied. See *Texas Oil & Gas Corp. v. United States,* 466 F.2d 1040 (5th Cir. 1972). The lien law regulations declare that inventory is acquired for purposes of § 6323(c) when title to the property passes to the debtor. 26 C.F.R. § 301.6323(c)-1(d) (1987).

Proceeds of collateral that is acquired within the 45–day period are protected even if the proceeds are produced beyond the 45–day period if the secured party has a continuously perfected security interest in the proceeds under local law. Id. Thus, if the debtor acquired accounts that were collateral on the 30th day after the tax lien filing, payments on the accounts would be protected even if the payments were collected on the 50th day following the filing. Similarly, where inventory acquired within the 45–day period "subsequently undergoes transfomation in character and form, such as the evolution of raw materials into final products and eventually cash proceeds, * * * the creditor does not lose his security interest in the value of that property which was owned on the 45th day. Implicit in this conclusion, however, is the fact that the creditor would have no rights to the 'value-added' to the product after the 45th day by the addition of either labor or *parts subsequently acquired.*" *Donald v. Madison Industries, Inc.,* 483 F.2d 837, 845 (10th Cir. 1973) (emphasis in original).

When the collateral is commercial financing security, this same provision, § 6323(c), also protects future advances made by the secured party within 45 days after the filing of a tax lien and before she had actual knowledge of the tax filing. There is no time limitation under § 6323(c) as to advances made pursuant to an "obligatory disbursement agreement" entered into before the tax lien filing. In any event, however, the advances are protected only to the extent they are secured by collateral of any kind acquired before the tax lien filing or by commercial financing security acquired within 45 days after the filing. *Texas Oil & Gas Corp. v. United States,* 466 F.2d 1040 (5th Cir. 1972).

3) **Purchase-Money Security Interests in Property Acquired After Tax Lien Filing**
The federal tax lien law makes no explicit exception for purchase-money security interests in property acquired by the debtor after the filing of a tax lien. The legislative history of the law suggests, however, that such interests should be preferred: "Although so-called purchase money mortgages are not specifically referred to under present law, it has generally been held that these interests are protected whenever they arise. This is based upon the concept that the taxpayer has acquired property or a right to property only to the extent that the value of the whole property or right exceeds the amount of the purchase money mortgage. This concept is not affected by the bill." Committee on Finance, Federal Tax Lien Act of 1966, S. Rep. No. 1708, 89th Cong., 2d Sess. p. 4 (1966); see also B. Clark, The Law Of Secured Transactions Under The Uniform Commercial Code paragraph 5.4 (1980).

c. **Mechanic's Lienor**
"The term 'mechanic's lienor' means any person who under local law has a lien on real property (or on the proceeds of a contract relating to real property) for services, labor, or materials furnished in connection with the construction or improvement of such property. * * * [A] person has a lien on the earliest date such lien becomes valid under local law against subsequent purchasers without actual notice, but not before he begins to furnish the services, labor, or materials." 26 U.S.C.A. § 2623(h)(2).

Examples: On January 1, D began the work of improving her home by adding a room. On February 1, M provided materials used in making the improvement. On March 1, a federal tax lien was filed against D. On June 1, M filed notice of a construction lien granted by state law to anyone providing labor or materials for the improvement of real property. The lien dates from the time work is first commenced on the improvement by anyone and is effective against all persons if notice of the construction lien is filed within six months of the time when the supplier provides materials for the improvement. M's supplier's lien has priority over the federal tax lien.

Same facts as above except that the federal tax lien was filed on January 15. Even though M's lien dates from January 1 under state law, the tax lien has priority. "As against the federal tax lien * * * the mechanic's lien priority cannot date back before the particular lienor began his services or the supplying of materials, even if as against other parties his lien is good under local law from the commencement of the building project or from the date of the contract." W. Plumb, Federal Tax Liens 152 (3d ed. 1972).

d. Judgment Lien Creditor

The federal tax lien act does not define "judgment lien creditor," which is the last of the four classes of claimants who take priority over an unfiled tax lien. The Regulations provide, however, that a judgment lien creditor is "a person who has obtained a valid judgment, in a court of record and of competent jurisdiction, for the recovery of specifically designated property or for a certain sum of money. In the case of a judgment for the recovery of a certain sum of money, a judgment lien creditor is a person who has perfected a lien under the judgment on the property involved. A judgment lien is not perfected until the identity of the lienor, the property subject to the lien, and the amount of the lien are established. * * * If recording or docketing is necessary under local law before a judgment becomes effective against third parties acquiring liens on real property, a judgment lien under such local law is not perfected with respect to real property until the time of such recordation or docketing. If under local law levy or seizure is necessary before a judgment lien becomes effective against third parties acquiring liens on personal property, then a judgment lien under such local law is not perfected until levy or seizure of the personal property involved." 26 C.F.R. § 301.6323(h)-1(g) (1987). In effect, therefore, a judgment lien creditor includes not only a creditor in whose favor there is a lien of judgment, but the term also includes an execution lienor.

Examples: A tax deficiency is assessed against D on January 1 and D thereafter refuses the IRS's demand for payment. JC wins a judgment against D on June 1. Federal tax lien is filed on June 2. JC dockets her judgment on June 3. State law gives JC a lien on all real estate of D in the county in which the judgment was rendered, which lien is effective against third parties from the time the judgment is docketed. The federal tax lien has priority.

In an effort to enforce a judgment against D, JC causes execution to issue against D's property, and the sheriff dutifully seizes D's car on January 15. A federal tax lien was filed on January 30 following the debtor's refusal to satisfy an assessment made the previous year. JC's lien of execution prevails over the federal tax lien.

On June 1, IRS assessed a tax deficiency against D which was not paid on demand. On July 1, P filed suit against D and obtained an attachment lien on D's farm to secure the judgment which P expected to win. (Attachment liens are discussed infra Chapter XI.) On August 3, the IRS filed a tax lien. On September 9, P obtained and docketed a judgment against D. Consequently, P acquired a lien of judgment on D's farm which related back to the time the attachment lien was obtained. The tax lien has priority. The attachment lien was not a judgment lien because it was not supported by a judgment. Moreover, the attachment lien was not perfected before the tax lien filing inasmuch as the amount of the lien was not established until judgment was rendered against D.

A tax deficiency was assessed against D on January 1. D later refused a demand to pay the taxes due. On June 1, JC caused execution to issue in enforcement of a judgment against D. On June 15, the IRS filed a tax lien. On June 30, the sheriff levied on D's car pursuant to the execution initiated by JC. State law provides that an execution lien dates from the time the writ is delivered to the sheriff. Despite this state law, the federal tax lien will be entitled to priority if the decision is that, as a matter of federal law, the execution lien was not perfected until the time of levy.

The federal Bankruptcy Code gives a bankruptcy trustee the rights and powers of a creditor who obtained a judicial lien as of the date that the bankruptcy petition is filed. 11 U.S.C.A. § 544(a) (1988 Supp.). Consequently, the trustee in the bankruptcy of a taxpayer is a judgment lien creditor for purposes of the tax lien law, § 6323(a). Thus, a tax lien which has not been filed before the taxpayer's bankruptcy will be invalidated by the trustee. See *United States v. Speers,* 382 U.S. 266, 86 S. Ct. 411 (1965) (decided under the § 70(c) of the Bankruptcy Act which is no different from Bankruptcy Code § 544(a)). Tax liens also are vulnerable under other provisions of the bankruptcy laws. See infra Chapters XXI & XXIII.

2. CLAIMANTS PROTECTED BY STATUTE FROM EVEN A FILED LIEN

Ten classes of claimants are afforded a "super-priority" status over a federal tax lien, meaning that they are given priority even though their claims arise after the lien is filed. Most of these "super-priorities," which are defined by § 6323(b), are either casual and common transactions for which an individual cannot be expected to check for filed tax liens, or they are transactions which tend to increase the value of the taxpayer's property. The protected classes are described generally in the following list. See the federal tax lien law and accompanying regulations for details about additional qualifications applicable to each class.

- Innocent purchasers of, or holders of security interests in, securities;
- Innocent purchasers of motor vehicles;
- Purchasers of goods at retail in the ordinary course of the seller's trade or business;
- Innocent purchasers of consumer goods for less than $250 in casual sales;
- Holders of liens securing the price of the repair or improvement of goods which continuously have been in the lienor's possession;
- Certain liens securing real property taxes, special assessments for public improvements, or charges for utilities or public services furnished by government or a governmental instrumentality;

- Mechanics' liens for repair or improvement of a personal residence if the contract price is $1000 or less;

- Attorneys' liens against a judgment or settlement, whether the lien arises by contract or by law;

- Insurers' claims for advances innocently made to keep life insurance in force;

- Innocently created security interests in passbook accounts.

3. CLAIMANTS PROTECTED BY GENERAL RULE OF DECISIONAL LAW

A claimant whose lien or interest is not protected by the provisions of the federal tax lien statute is not necessarily subordinate to a tax lien. Wholly apart from the federal tax lien statute, a tax lien is subordinate to a claim that was choate and perfected as far as possible under applicable law before the tax lien arose, i.e., before the date of assessment. Consider, for example, the claim of a landlord asserting a statutory lien for rent on a debtor's personal property in a case where, under state law, the lien dates from a point that is prior to the tax assessment against the debtor. Such a lien is not within any of the classes of claims which are protected by the federal tax lien act. See, e.g., *United States v. Globe Corp.*, 113 Ariz. 44, 546 P.2d 11 (1976). Yet, if the landlord can establish that her lien was choate and perfected as fully as possible under state law before the date of tax assessment against the debtor, then the landlord's lien will have priority over the tax lien. A lien or other claim becomes choate, which is defined and determined as a matter of federal law, when the identity of the lienor, the property subject to the lien, and the amount of the lien are established with exactness, certainty, and finality.

Establishing choateness is often a problem for the kinds of lienors not explicitly protected by the tax lien act and especially for landlords asserting statutory liens for rent. As explained by the leading authority on federal tax liens: "State laws vary greatly in the terms of the protection afforded landlords' liens arising by operation of law. But under the federal doctrine of 'choateness,' even the strongest of them will probably be subordinated to tax liens arising either before or after the accrual of the rent obligation for one, if not all, of the following reasons: There is at least a theoretical possibility, * * * until final judgment, of a dispute regarding the amount owing. Moreover, local law may confine the operation of its lien to rent covering a limited period of time, such as six months. And at the time the intervening tax lien arises, the actual period—in terms of precise dates—for which a landlord's lien may be enforced will not have been determined, again creating a lack of specificity. At the time the intervening tax lien arises, the landlord's lien may also be inchoate because the *property subject to it* has not been sufficiently identified. This may be because the landlord is permitted to distrain only upon sufficient property to satisfy his claim. If the amount of the claim has not been rendered certain, then the portion of the property that can be reached is not specific. Or the difficulty may be due to the fact that prior to enforcement, the lessee can defeat the landlord's lien as to certain property by removing it from the premises. Indeed, the presence of this circumstance and each of those related above seemed to provide the Supreme Court with independent reasons justifying subordination of a landlord's lien, even though the Government's rights arose after the landlord had initiated enforcement proceedings." W. Plumb, Federal Tax Liens 167–68 (3d ed. 1972). See, e.g., *United States v. Globe Corp.,* 113 Ariz. 44, 546 P.2d 11 (1976).

E. ENFORCEMENT OF A FEDERAL TAX LIEN

1. LEVY AND DISTRAINT

The government is authorized to levy on all property subject to a federal tax lien if an assessed tax debt is not paid within ten days following demand for payment. 26 U.S.C.A. § 6331(a) (1980). There is no ten-day grace period in the case of a jeopardy assessment. The right to levy includes the power of distraint and seizure by any means. Id. § 6331(b) (Supp. 1984). The taxpayer is not entitled to a pre-seizure hearing, and the government ordinarily is not required to give prior notice of the levy. Notice follows the levy. Id. § 6335(a) (1980). The taxpayer's property can be seized from anyone in possession of it, id. § 6332 (1980 & Supp. 1988), including a claimant whose lien or interest in the property is entitled to priority over the federal tax lien which the levy is intended to enforce. The government must begin the process of disposing of the property "as soon as practical after the seizure ✳ ✳ ✳." Id. § 6335(b) (1967). The taxpayer can redeem real or personal property prior to sale by paying the taxes she owes together with expenses of the levy; a right of redemption after sale applies only to real estate. Id. § 6337(a) & (b) (1980). If property seized by the government does not belong to the taxpayer or a third person has rights in the property superior to the tax lien, the true owner or claimant with priority can prevent a sale and recover the property by suing in federal court. Id. § 7426 (Supp. 1988).

2. JUDICIAL FORECLOSURE

Instead of enforcing a tax lien through levy and distraint as described above, the government may enforce its lien by suing in federal court and seeking a judicial sale of property subject to the lien. 26 U.S.C.A. § 7403 (1967 & Supp. 1988). A court can order foreclosure to enforce a tax lien on a debtor's interest in the property even though (1) the debtor's interest is exempt under state law, (2) another person owing none of the tax liability owns the property jointly with the debtor, and (3) this other person's interest is also exempt under state law. *United States v. Rodgers,* 461 U.S. 677, 103 S. Ct. 2132 (1983).

REVIEW QUESTIONS

1. Which of the following events are conditions to the creation and enforcement of a federal tax lien against a taxpayer?

    (a) Assessment of deficiency

    (b) Demand for payment

(c) Refusal to pay

(d) Filing of tax lien notice

2. T or F A federal tax lien exists and dates from the time a tax assessment is made.

3. T or F Federal tax lien notices are filed with the clerk of the federal district court of the judicial district in which the taxpayer resides.

4. On January 10, the IRS obtains a tax lien against T Television City. On February 2, the IRS properly files a tax lien notice. On March 3, X buys a television set from T's inventory. Does X take the set free, or subject to, the federal tax lien?

5. On May 3, the IRS assessed a tax deficiency against F, a farmer. F refuses the goverment's demand that she pay the taxes. On June 1, S extends credit to T and obtains a non-purchase money security interest in F's combine. S perfects its interest on June 5. On August 1, the IRS files notice of its tax lien. Does the tax lien or S's security interest have priority?

6. Is the answer to Question 5 different if S waits until August 15 to perfect her security interest?

7. In January, S obtained a security interest in all of T's accounts, now owned and thereafter acquired. S perfected her interest on February 2. On March 3, IRS obtained a tax lien against T and properly filed notice of the lien on April 4. T continued to generate additional accounts. Does S's security interest of the tax lien have priority as to accounts that arise on May 5? On June 6?

8. Would the answers to Question 7 be different if S's collateral was equipment rather than accounts?

9. On January 1, S loans D $10,000 and takes a security interest in T's accounts. The security agreement has a future-advances clause. S properly perfects her security interest on February 2. A federal tax lien arises against T on March 3 and notice of the lien is filed on April 4. On May 5, S makes an additional loan of $5000 to T so that the total of the secured debt is $15,000. What is the extent of S's priority over the federal tax lien?

10. Would the answer to Question 9 be different if S's collateral was equipment rather than accounts?

*

PART THREE

PREJUDGMENT OR PROVISIONAL REMEDIES

Analysis

This part of the Black Letter covers the most important prejudgment, provisional remedies, which are available even to unsecured creditors in some cases. Provisional remedies of this kind create the third exception to the general rule that a creditor can seize a debtor's property only through the process of executing a judgment. These remedies are ancillary to a suit to collect a debt or enforce a lien or other special right and have the effect of impounding the debtor's property before judgment to insure the availability after judgment of sufficient assets from which to satisfy the creditor's claim.

*

XI

ATTACHMENT

Analysis

A general, unsecured creditor usually cannot satisfy her claim by seizing assets of the debtor until the creditor gets a judgment and then pursues an appropriate post-judgment remedy. The time between the accrual of a claim and entry of a judgment on the claim is often very long. During this period the debtor may dispose of her property, or other persons may take it in satisfaction of their claims. Thus, when the creditor finally wins a judgment, the debtor may be judgment proof. In the exceptional cases, however, through the process known as *attachment,* the creditor can cause a pre-judgment seizure of the debtor's property. At the time a creditor files suit, or at some point during the action, the sheriff will take and hold, i.e., attach, so much of the debtor's property as will be necessary to satisfy the creditor's expected judgment. Property or credits of the debtor held by a third person can be impounded, too, usually by the creditor invoking a pre-judgment version of garnishment (Garnishment is discussed fully in Chapter V supra.) If the creditor prevails in the action, she then can satisfy her judgment from the property which the sheriff attached or which the garnishee holds. Attachment thus serves as a creditor's remedy by creating security for the creditor and by simultaneously putting pressure on the debtor to settle. Historically, attachment also has served as a device for acquiring judicial jurisdiction over property. The importance of attachment as a jurisdictional device has diminished greatly, however, since the decision in *Shaffer v. Heitner,* 433 U.S. 186, 97 S.Ct. 2569 (1977), which is discussed fully in Chapter I.B.1. supra.

The discussion in this chapter focuses on attachment as a security device and assumes that there are no problems with judicial jurisdiction.

A. ATTACHMENT EXPLAINED

1. DEFINITION

Attachment is an extraordinary, statutory remedy which "is purely ancillary to the main suit, has nothing to do with the merits, and is a summary, anticipatory method of impounding defendant's assets to facilitate collection of the judgment against him, *if and when* one be obtained." *Lubrication Engineers, Inc. v. Parkinson,* 341 S.W.2d 876, 878 (Mo.App.1961).

2. PURPOSES HISTORICALLY AND AFTER *SHAFFER*

At early common law, attachment was a form of process to compel the defendant to appear and answer actions against her. The defendant's personal appearance was essential because the law did not generally permit default judgments. The writ of attachment commanded the sheriff to attach the property of the defendant to compel her to appear. If she appeared the property was returned to her; if she failed to appear, the property was forfeited.

In the 17th century, the nature of attachment changed somewhat in that attached property was no longer released upon the appearance of the defendant. The property remained attached until after judgment for the plaintiff was satisfied. But cf. *Nakasone v. Randall,* 129 Cal. App.3d 757, 760–61, 181 Cal. Rptr. 324, 326–27 (1982) (attachment against defendant based on nonresidency must be released if she appears personally in the action). The purpose of attachment thus expanded to include providing security for a plaintiff's expected judgment.

Until very recently, however, securing judicial jurisdiction remained an equally important purpose of attachment. If personal jurisdiction could not be obtained over a defendant, the presence of the defendant's property in the state was sufficient in itself to give the state's courts *quasi in rem* jurisdiction over the defendant's interest in the property. Even if the defendant did not appear personally, the action against her would proceed and a judgment for plaintiff, which frequently was acquired by default, would be enforced against the attached property. This procedure was especially useful in actions against nonresidents. Acquiring *quasi in rem* jurisdiction over nonresidents based on their having property in the state was so common that the process had a special name: *foreign attachment.*

Nonresidency of a defendant remains a basis for attachment. Yet, because of the decision in *Shaffer v. Heitner,* 433 U.S. 186, 97 S. Ct. 2569 (1977), discussed supra in Chapter I.B.1., the presence of property in a state is no longer regarded as a sufficient basis in itself for exercising any kind of judicial jurisdiction. Jurisdiction *quasi in rem* is now tested by the same standard that long has governed the exercise of jurisdiction *in personam,* i.e., fair play and substantial justice. *Quasi in rem* jurisdiction through attachment is still possible. *Unitech USA, Inc. v. Ponsoldt,* 91 A.D.2d 903, 905, 457 N.Y.S.2d 526, 529 (1983). Yet, if the defendant's contacts with the state are sufficient to support *quasi in rem* jurisdiction, they also will be sufficient in most cases to support *in personam* jurisdiction. Jurisdiction *in personam* is preferred because it will support a personal judgment against the defendant.

So you see that the role of attachment as a jurisdictional device has diminished greatly because of *Shaffer.* As a result of that decision, attachment now functions primarily as a security device "to allow unsecured creditors a procedure ancillary to their action by which to ensure that the alleged debtor's assets are not dissipated prior to the time the creditor can obtain and enforce the anticipated judgment on his claim." *North Hollywood Marble Co. v. Superior Court,* 157 Cal. App.3d 683, 690, 204 Cal. Rptr. 55, 59 (1984).

B. AVAILABILITY OF ATTACHMENT

In most states, attachment is available only in certain kinds of actions and even then only upon a showing of special statutory grounds.

1. KINDS OF ACTIONS

The remedy of attachment is not generally available in every kind of action. Local variations are great on this and every other point of attachment law. The most generous statutes make attachment available in any "action for the recovery of money," which includes both tort and contract claims. Stingier statutes permit attachment only upon claims *ex contractu,* thereby embracing all claims arising from a contract, express or implied, and excluding those arising from a tort (claims *ex delicto*). Some statutes allow attachment upon either a claim *ex contractu* or *ex delicto* but establish different requirements or grounds of attachment for the two types of claims. In a few states, attachment is available in a contract action only if the debt is fully or partially unsecured. A few other states, however, specifically provide for attachment by secured creditors. In any event, attaching a defendant's property is proper and effective only if the action is of a kind in which local law makes the remedy available.

Examples: Local law permits attachment "upon all complaints containing a money demand against the estate of the defendant" and also in divorce actions to secure claims for alimony. Wife sues for divorce seeking alimony and a conveyance of her husband's interest in certain real estate. Wife can attach the realty for the purpose of securing her claim for alimony but not for the purpose of securing her demand for a conveyance of the property. "Where the statute so provides, a remedy by attachment is limited to actions to recover a sum of money only, and in such a case it cannot be employed as a means of recovering specific property." *Atlas Garage & Custom Builders, Inc. v. Hurley,* 167 Conn. 248, 258, 355 A.2d 286, 291 (1974).

D defrauded P by obtaining property from P through an unlawful trick or scheme. P sued and caused the attachment of D's real and personal property. This attachment was improper even under a statute authorizing the remedy "whenever the plaintiff * * * has a just claim against the defendant, that is due." The statute allows attachment only when the plaintiff's claim arises *ex contractu.* This interpretation follows from a well-established principle that an attachment statute covers claims *ex delicto* (tort claims) only when such coverage is clearly expressed. In this case, plaintiff's claim for fraud is *ex delicto,* and thus attachment is not allowed. *United States v. J. Tirocchi & Sons, Inc.,* 180 F. Supp. 645 (D. R.I. 1960).

In selling a business to P, D concealed the fact that the place where the business had been operating could no longer be occupied. P could not find a suitable location elsewhere, and thus the business was of no value to her. Alleging fraud and deceit, P sued D to recover the sum paid for the business and caused a writ of garnishment to issue against D. (For now, think of garnishment as a form of attachment used to reach property of the defendant which is possessed or controlled by a third party.) The remedy of attachment or garnishment was properly available to P only if her action was one for "debt." A suit for damages for tort is not an action for debt. Nevertheless, P's attachment was allowed in this case. A claim arising out of contract express or implied is within the rubric of "action for debt." "The instant suit is not, except incidentally or in the alternative, an action for tort * * * The action arises out of the contract between the plaintiff and the defendant * * * In substance and effect the plaintiff waives the tort and brings an action upon a promise [i.e., contract] implied in law * * *" *Cleveland v. San Antonio Bldg. & Loan Ass'n,* 148 Tex. 211, 216, 223 S.W.2d 226, 229 (1949).

2. GROUNDS FOR ATTACHMENT

In many states, attachment is limited not only to certain kinds of actions, as described above. The remedy is also limited to cases involving certain extenuating circumstances referred to as *grounds for attachment*. Very typical is the District of Columbia law, under which the grounds for attachment are that the defendant:

- Is a foreign corporation or a nonresident;

- Has been absent from the District for at least six months;

- Evades services of process;

- Has removed, or is about to remove, some or all of her property from the District so as to defeat just claims against her;

- Has assigned or secreted her property, or is about to do so, in fraud of creditors; or

- Fraudulently contracted the debt or incurred the obligation.

D.C. Code Ann. § 16–501 (1981).

3. DEBTS NOT YET DUE

In most states, the availability of attachment in an action on a contract is not conditioned on the maturity of the plaintiff's claim against the defendant. The plaintiff can sue on the contract and attachment can issue even before the debt is due if the debtor is threatening to leave the jurisdiction or to dispose of her property. Ordinarily, however, no judgment can be rendered for the plaintiff until the debt matures.

4. ATTACHMENT IN FEDERAL COURT

Generally, the remedy of attachment is available in an action in federal district court only under the circumstances and in the manner provided by the law of the state in which the district court is held. Fed. R. Civ. P. 4(e) & 64; *United States v. J. Tirocchi & Sons, Inc.,* 180 F. Supp. 645 (D. R.I. 1960).

C. MECHANICS OF ATTACHMENT

1. PLAINTIFF'S PROCEDURE

a. When Attachment Can Be Sought

A plaintiff can invoke the attachment process either at the very beginning of her lawsuit against the debtor when the complaint is filed and summons issued, or at any time during the suit before judgment. The typical statute authorizes attachment "at or after the commencement of the action" or "at the time of issuing the summons or at any time afterwards."

b. Affidavit Required

Attachment is initiated by the plaintiff filing an affidavit with the judge or clerk of court which shows, among other things, the name and residence of the defendant, the nature of the plaintiff's action, the amount of the claim against the defendant, and the grounds on which the attachment is based. In many states, the test of the sufficiency of the affidavit is whether the plaintiff's claim and the grounds for the attachment "clearly appear" from allegations of "specific facts."

A typical affidavit will look like this:

> STATE OF ILLINOIS ⎫
> _____ County   ⎬ ss.
>   ⎭

AB, being duly sworn, says: That (here state if affiant is agent or attorney of the creditor; if the action is by an individual or corporation, the name of the individual or corporation, and if the action is by a firm, the name of the partners) has a just claim against (name of debtor), on account of (here state facts giving rise to the cause of action and amount of the claim), and the affiant believes (the name of the creditors) is entitled to recover of (name of debtor), after allowing all just credits and set-offs _____ dollars and _____ cents, which is now due, and that he, she or it has good reason to believe and does believe that (name of debtor) (here state facts which give rise to some one or more of the causes [or grounds] which authorize an attachment). (Name of debtor) resides at (here state the residence of the debtor if known, or if not, that the affiant has made diligent inquiry and cannot ascertain his or her or its place of residence).

Affiant has personal knowledge that the foregoing statements are true.

/s/ _____

Subscribed and sworn to before me this _____ day of _____, _____,

/s/ _____

My commission expires _____, _____.

c. Bond Required

Virtually every state conditions the issuance of attachment on the plaintiff furnishing a corporate bond, or a bond with two individual sureties, in the amount of twice the plaintiff's claim or double the value of the property to be attached. The bond is to the effect that, if the defendant recovers judgment, or if the attachment is wrongfully issued, the plaintiff will pay all costs that may be awarded to the defendant and all damages which she may sustain by reason of the attachment not exceeding the amount of the bond.

d.   Strict Compliance With Procedures Necessary

Attachment is both a harsh and extraordinary remedy, and the courts thus require strict compliance with the procedural prerequisites. Every court would agree with the opinion expressed in the case *Lubrication Engineers, Inc. v. Parkinson,* 341 S.W.2d 876 (Mo.App.1961): "[S]ince attachment proceedings were unknown at common law and are creatures of the statutes, * * * strict compliance with applicable statutory requirements is essential * * *. Thus, with our statutes and now our rules of civil procedure expressly requiring * * * an affidavit be filed before a writ of attachment issues, there is no room for doubt but that, where no affidavit has been theretofore filed in the case, issuance of a writ or attachment is unauthorized and any writ issued under such circumstances is void." Id. at 878–879.

2.   ISSUANCE OF WRIT OR ORDER OF ATTACHMENT

If the plaintiff's affidavit and bond are in order, a judge or court clerk will issue a writ or order of attachment directing the sheriff to seize as much of the defendant's property as will be necessary to satisfy plaintiff's claim and the costs of the action. The typical writ looks very much like the following form which is prescribed by law for use in Alabama:

The State of Alabama
_____ County }

To Any Sheriff of the State of Alabama:

Whereas A.B. (or C.D., as the agent or attorney of A.B., as the case may be) hath complained on oath to me, E.F., judge of the circuit court of said state (or district court judge, or judge of the probate court or clerk of the circuit court of said county or as the case may be), that G.H. is (or will be, as the case may be) justly indebted to the plaintiff in the sum of _____ dollars, and the plaintiff having made affidavit and given bond as required by law in such cases, you are hereby commanded to attach so much of the estate of G.H. as will be of value to satisfy said debt and costs, according to the complaint, and such estate, unless replevied, so to secure that the same may be liable to further proceedings thereon, to be had in the circuit court for the county of _____, to be held at the courthouse thereof; when and where you must make known how you have executed this writ.

Witness my hand, this, etc.

E.F., clerk.

Ala. Code § 6–6–40 (1975).

3.   PRE–SEIZURE NOTICE AND HEARING

Until rather recently, attachment statutes did not require giving the debtor notice and an opportunity for a hearing prior to the seizure. The Supreme Court's reappraisal in the 1960's and 1970's of debtors' due process rights, see infra Chapter XIV, prompted a break with tradition. About half the states have amended their attachment laws so as to condition attachment on giving the defendant notice and an opportunity for a hearing prior to the seizure of property. Ordinarily, when a noticed hearing is required, the defendant is informed that attachment will issue unless she quickly requests a hearing. At the hearing, the burden is on the plaintiff to establish not only that attachment is justified, but also that there is a "probability" or a "reasonable likelihood" of success in her underlying action against the defendant. These two standards have essentially the same meaning which implies a favorable chance for success. Either standard is satisfied if the claim is not of such insubstantial character as clearly to foreclose a reasonable possibility of recovery. *Northeast Investment Co., Inc. v. Leisure Living Communities, Inc.,* 351 A.2d 845, 852 (Me.1976).

4. EX PARTE ATTACHMENT

In about half the states, there is no requirement of a noticed hearing prior to an attachment of a debtor's property. In the other half of the states, where attachment laws require a noticed hearing in the usual case, ex parte attachment is allowed in exceptional cases. The description of exceptional cases varies considerably among these states. In some states, ex parte attachment will issue whenever the plaintiff demonstrates that "irreparable harm" will result if the debtor is notified and attachment is delayed until after a hearing, or that giving the defendant an opportunity for a noticed hearing would "seriously impair" the attachment remedy. In other states where newly amended attachment laws require a noticed hearing in the usual case, the presence of the traditional grounds for attachment is not a condition on the availability of attachment generally; rather, a debtor threatening to remove herself or her property from the state, or to destroy or conceal her property, is a reason justifying ex parte attachment. In a few states, the traditional grounds for attachment remain a general requirement for allowing the remedy in any case, and an additional showing of irreparable harm or its equivalent is necessary to justify ex parte attachment.

5. ENFORCEMENT OF WRIT OR ORDER OF ATTACHMENT

All of a debtor's property, except that exempt from execution, is subject to attachment. The sheriff takes physical custody of personal property when possible. Personalty that cannot actually be seized is attached in some states by the sheriff leaving a copy of the attachment writ or order with the person in possession of the property or, under more modern statutes in other states, by filing a notice of some kind in the place where a financing statement would be filed to perfect an Article 9 security interest in the property. A sheriff ordinarily attaches real property by filing a copy of the writ of attachment or some other notice of attachment in the appropriate real estate records.

The sheriff normally is required to make an inventory of property she attaches, to have the property appraised, and to return the inventory and appraisal to the official who issued the writ or order of attachment. The debtor may also receive a copy of the inventory.

6. GARNISHMENT AS MEANS OF REACHING PROPERTY HELD BY THIRD PARTIES

When property or credits of the debtor are held by a third party, they usually are reached by the creditor invoking an allied but different remedy of garnishment (or trustee's process). Garnishment as a post-judgment remedy is discussed earlier, see supra Chapter V. Garnishment procedure, and the rights and duties of a garnishee, are much the same whether the remedy is pursued before or after judgment. In some states, pre-judgment garnishment is simply a proceeding ancillary to attachment and is available only in the kinds of actions and upon the special grounds that will support attachment. In these states, the common characterization of pre-judgment garnishment as a "species of attachment," *Van Maanen v. Van Maanen*, 360 N.W.2d 758, 761 (Iowa 1985), is quite accurate.

In other states, garnishment is an entirely independent remedy with its own terms of availability. In any event, pre-judgment garnishment serves to warn the garnishee, who is the target of the remedy, that the plaintiff/creditor claims the right to have the property of the debtor that the garnishee holds, or the credit that the garnishee owes the debtor, applied in satisfaction of the plaintiff's claim. The garnishee is thus bound to hold the property or credit pending the outcome of plaintiff's action, and, if the plaintiff prevails, the property will be used to satisfy the judgment. In most states, however, the garnishee has the option of surrendering to the court whatever property of the debtor she holds or paying into the registry of the court whatever obligation she owes the debtor. By exercising this option the garnishee is released from any further accountability to the garnishing creditor.

7. ATTACHED PROPERTY HELD IN *CUSTODIA LEGIS*

Property that has been attached or taken from a garnishee is held by the sheriff pending resolution of the plaintiff's lawsuit against the defendant. Only rarely will any of it be sold prior to a judgment for the plaintiff and then only if the property is perishable, threatens to decline significantly in value, or is unduly expensive to keep.

8. DEFENDANT'S RESPONSES

a. Post-Seizure Hearing

If the attachment is issued ex parte without notice to the debtor and without an opportunity for a hearing, the debtor is entitled to be heard soon after the seizure of her property so that she can challenge both the availability of attachment in the case and the plaintiff's compliance with procedures for invoking the remedy. Such a challenge is mounted in most states through a motion to quash, vacate, or dissolve the attachment, or by the debtor filing her own controverting affidavit which is, in effect, an answer to, and denial of, the affidavit filed by the plaintiff to initiate the attachment. In some jurisdictions, any attacks on the attachment must be made before an answer is filed in the main action because answering to the merits waives defects or irregularities in the attachment proceeding.

The common practice in an earlier day was to require a defendant to post a bond as a prerequisite to attacking an attachment of her property. The bond, which required sureties, was intended to take the place of the attached property as security for the plaintiff's expected judgment. Attitudes have changed on the fairness of such a bonding requirement, and it is not a part of modern attachment practice. Compare *Ownbey v. Morgan,* 256 U.S. 94, 41 S. Ct. 433 (1921) with *Cleveland v. San Antonio Bldg. & Loan Ass'n,* 148 Tex. 211, 223 S.W.2d 226 (1949).

At the hearing on the defendant's post-seizure challenge to the attachment, the plaintiff ordinarily has the burden of showing cause for the attachment and of establishing that she probably will, or is likely to, succeed in the underlying action against the defendant. If the plaintiff fails in either respect, the attachment will be discharged; property levied on will be returned to the defendant; and she will have a right to recover from the plaintiff, or against the plaintiff's bond, her costs and the damages she suffered because of the attachment. The plaintiff's underlying action against the defendant will proceed, however. A discharge of the attachment has no effect on the merits of the principal lawsuit. See *Peter Fischer Import Motors v. Buckley,* 121 Ill. App. 3d 906, 909–10, 460 N.E.2d 346, 349 (1984).

Example: P chartered an oil drilling rig to D, an Iranian company. P filed suit against D in New York alleging that D had failed to abide by the charter and had wrongfully exercised exclusive dominion and control over the rig. Upon commencement of the action, P caused the ex parte attachment of D's New York bank accounts. As required by New York law, P moved within five days to confirm the attachment, which involved a noticed hearing at which P had the burden of establishing the grounds for the attachment, the need for continuing the levy, and the probability of success on the merits. The grounds were present inasmuch as P had demanded a money judgment and D was a foreign corporation. The attachment was discharged, however, because P failed to satisfy the court of the continuing need for the levy by failing to establish sufficient insecurity of enforcement of a potential judgment. D "is presently doing substantial business and is party to many long-term contracts with United States customers. The proceedings in this case indicate that it has at least upwards of $700 million on deposit with New York banking institutions. The possibility that [D] will remove all of its funds from New York and revise all of its contracts to provide for payments outside of the United States is simply too remote to justify continuing the pre-judgment attachment in this case." *Reading & Bates Corp. v. National Iranian Oil Co.,* 478 F. Supp. 724, 727 (S.D. N.Y. 1979).

b. Posting Bond for Return of Attached Property
Every state allows a debtor to secure the return of attached property by posting a bond of one kind or another. For this purpose there are two forms of bonds. First, there are "forthcoming" or "delivery" bonds, which are to the effect that, if judgment is for the plaintiff, the property will be surrendered to satisfy the judgment; otherwise, the surety on the bond will be liable to the plaintiff for the value of the property. Giving this type of bond will secure re-

lease of the property from the custody of the sheriff, but there is no release from the lien of attachment that resulted from the sheriff's levy on the property. The other form of bond is the "discharging" or "dissolution" bonds. They provide that the defendant in the attachment suit will satisfy whatever judgment may be entered against her in the action and that, if she does not, the surety will pay the judgment. A bond of this type not only releases the property from the sheriff's custody but also releases the property from the lien of attachment.

c. Challenge to Plaintiff's Bond

The attachment laws of most states allow the defendant to attack the plaintiff's bond by challenging the sufficiency of the bond, i.e., questioning whether the amount of it is large enough, and also by excepting to any surety on the bond, i.e., questioning whether the person is financially sound and otherwise qualified to serve as a surety. These questions are raised by the defendant filing a motion to modify the attachment, and the matter is decided by the court in a hearing upon notice to the plaintiff.

9. JUDGMENT FOR THE PLAINTIFF

If plaintiff prevails in the underlying action against the defendant who fails to pay the judgment, it is satisfied by the sheriff selling the property she attached and applying the proceeds to the judgment. If a discharging bond was given to release the attached property, the plaintiff can look to the sureties on the bond for payment of the judgment. If a deficiency remains and the judgment is *in personam* against the defendant, the balance of the judgment is satisfied through the usual process of execution.

10. JUDGMENT FOR THE DEFENDANT

If judgment in the main action is for the defendant, the attachment is discharged and all of the attached property is released and returned to her. Moreover, the plaintiff becomes liable for the defendant's costs associated with the attachment and also for the damages suffered by the defendant because of the attachment. If the plaintiff defaults in paying these costs and damages, the defendant can look for payment to the sureties on plaintiff's bond.

D. LIEN OF ATTACHMENT

Attachment provides security for the plaintiff's expected judgment not only by the sheriff impounding property of the defendant; security also results from a lien which attaches to any real or personal property that is levied on regardless of how the levy is accomplished.

1. WHEN THE LIEN ARISES

In most states, the lien of attachment arises at the time of the levy. Where levy on real estate is accomplished by some kind of recording, an attachment lien on such property is not created until the recording is made. When the sheriff levies through prejudgment garnishment or otherwise on property or credits held by a third party, the lien arises when the third party is served with appropriate process.

2. NATURE OF THE LIEN

A lien of attachment is "inchoate" or contingent prior to judgment in the principal action. If the defendant prevails, the lien evaporates, and the law deems that it never existed. If the plaintiff prevails, the lien is thus "perfected," and its effectiveness against the debtor and third parties dates from the time it first arose as an inchoate claim.

3. PRIORITY OF THE LIEN

a. Priority of Attachment Liens Inter Se

The rule that first in time is first in right governs the priority between attachment liens on the same property. This priority is unaffected by the order in which the attaching creditors win judgments and acquire judgment liens against the debtor.

Example: A files suit against D and attaches Blackacre. B files suit against D and attaches the same property. B gets judgment which creates a lien of judgment on Blackacre. A thereafter gets judgment which also creates such a lien on the property. A has priority because she was the first to attach Blackacre. *City Nat. Bank v. Traffic Engineering Associates, Inc.,* 166 Conn. 195, 348 A.2d 637 (1974). The same rule applies when the dispute involves personal property. *Petri v. Sheriff of Washoe County,* 87 Nev. 549, 491 P.2d 43 (1971).

Usually, the winner of the first-in-time race is determined either by the order in which attachments were levied or by the order in which the writs were issued. The authorities disagree. Yet, the attachment laws of many states explicitly direct that attachments shall be levied in the order in which the sheriff receives the writs.

b. Prior Interests

Generally, an attachment lien reaches only the debtor's interest in the property and thus does not displace prior claims, rights, and interests. If, however, the prior interest is subject to a recording law which has not been satisfied when the attachment lien arises, the attachment will have priority if an attaching creditor is within the class of claimants that the recording law is designed to protect.

Example: D borrowed money from SP and secured the loan by giving SP a security interest in widgets. SP failed, however, to perfect the security interest by filing a financing statement or by taking possession of the property. Thereafter, JC sued D on a contract debt and attached the widgets. JC ultimately got a judgment in the action. JC is entitled to priority over SP. See U.C.C. § 9301(1)(b); cf. *Heinicke Instruments Co. v. Republic Corp.,* 543 F.2d 700 (9th Cir. 1976) (security interest in securities, which interest had not been perfected by the secured party taking possession of the collateral, was subordinate to attachment lien). The result would be the same if SP had perfected its interest before JC won judgment, unless SP's interest was a purchased money security interest perfected within 10 days after D took possession of the widgets. U.C.C. § 9–301(2). The result would be different if SP had perfected its interest before JC attached the widgets.

c. Subsequent Interests
1) General Rule
An attachment lien that is perfected by judgment for plaintiff has priority over any conflicting claim, right, or interest created after the attachment lien arises, which usually is at the time of levy. See, e.g., *In re Gibbons*, 459 A.2d 938 (R.I. 1983). The judgment makes the attachment lien final and relates the effectiveness of the lien back to the date of its inchoate origin.

> ***Examples:*** On February 2, C sues D for $2000, obtains a writ of attachment and causes the sheriff to levy on D's horse. On March 3, B, who is ignorant of C's attachment, buys the horse from D for $3000. On April 4, C obtains judgment against D. C's rights to the horse prevail over B's.
>
> A sued D and properly attached Blackacre which belonged to D. Before the A v. D action was concluded, B sued D and won a judgment against D. B's judgment created a final and specific lien on Blackacre. A thereafter won a judgment against D, and A's judgment, too, created a lien on Blackacre. A's claim, however, relates back to the time of her attachment of the property, and A thus is entitled to priority over B. The result is the same even if B's lawsuit against D had been filed before A's action. *Atlas Garage & Custom Builders, Inc. v. Hurley,* 167 Conn. 248, 355 A.2d 286 (1974).

2) Exception for Federal Tax Lien
A federal tax lien has priority over an earlier inchoate attachment lien that is later perfected by judgment for the attaching creditor. Inchoate interests are ineffective against federal tax liens, and the lien of the attaching creditor is inchoate prior to judgment for her. Moreover, as against a federal tax lien, there can be no relation back of the perfected attachment lien to the time of its inchoate origin.

> ***Example:*** In October, 1946, M sued S on an unsecured note and attached land of the defendant. In December, 1946, the United States filed notices of federal tax liens. In April, 1947, M won judgment, which was recorded in the next month. The tax liens have priority. *United States v. Security Trust & Sav. Bank,* 340 U.S. 47, 71 S. Ct. 111 (1950).

d. Bankruptcy Trustee
Attachment benefits a single creditor at the expense of the debtor and other creditors. A debtor deprived by attachment of the use of important property

may decide to file bankruptcy. Moreover, attachment may motivate the debtor's other creditors to initiate involuntary bankruptcy proceedings. Under the Bankruptcy Code, an attachment lien obtained against an insolvent debtor within 90 days of the filing of the bankruptcy petition is an invalid preference voidable by the trustee. 11 U.S.C.A. § 547 (1979). For more on the avoidance of preferences in bankruptcy, see infra Chapter XXI.

REVIEW QUESTIONS

1. T or F   The plaintiff can attach property of the defendant in any case in which a judgment for money damages is sought.

2. Identify the usual procedural prerequisities to the issuance of a writ of attachment.

3. Does the sheriff sell attached property immediately after it is seized, or does the sale usually take place only after the attaching creditor obtains a judgment in the main action against the defendant?

4. How might a defendant respond procedurally to an ex parte attachment of her property?

5. What is similar about forthcoming or delivery bonds and discharging or dissolution bonds? How are the two types of bonds different?

6. An attachment lien is not perfected until judgment for the plaintiff. Yet, for purposes of determining priority against third parties' claims, an attachment lien perfected by judgment dates from the time

    (a) the writ of attachment was issued.

    (b) the writ was received by the sheriff.

    (c) the sheriff levied on the property pursuant to the writ of attachment.

7. A sued D and attached Blackacre. D mortgaged Blackacre to B who properly recorded the mortgage. A obtained a judgment in the action against D and the judgment was properly docketed. A now seeks to apply Blackacre in satisfaction of the judgment. Is A's claim to Blackacre, or B's, entitled to priority?

8. D gave A a non-purchase money security interest in widgets. B sued A and attached the widgets. A perfected her security interest by filing pursuant to U.C.C. Article 9. Does A or B have priority of interest in the widgets?

REPLEVIN

Analysis

Replevin refers to both an action and a provisional, prejudgment remedy. When a person sues to recover possession of specific goods or chattels in which she claims an interest and an immediate right to possession, the suit is often referred to as a *replevin action*. The replevin action is largely statutory today, but it began as a common-law remedy to recover chattels taken through distress, which refers to the seizure of property of a debtor to force or secure satisfaction of the obligation. For example, early common law allowed a landlord to take property of a tenant who had defaulted in rent. The property taken, and the process of taking it, was known as distress. Replevin was a tenant's remedy for abuses of distress. Today, a replevin action is available as a means of recovering goods or chattels unlawfully detained by any person for any reason, whether or not the defendant acquired possession rightfully.

As soon as a replevin action is begun, the plaintiff can ask that the property in dispute be taken from the defendant and delivered to her pending the outcome of the action. This provisional taking of the property which is the subject matter of the suit is often referred to as the *replevin remedy.* If the plaintiff in a replevin action is entitled to the replevin remedy, the sheriff will be directed through a *writ of replevin, order of delivery,* or *writ of possession* to take from the defendant the property for which the plaintiff sues and to deliver the property to the plaintiff who will hold it until the main action is decided. If judgment in the action is for plaintiff, she keeps the property. If judgment is for defendant, the property is returned to her, and she recovers damages resulting from the dispossession. Other names for the replevin remedy, if not also the replevin action, include "claim and delivery," "detinue," "revendication," and "seizure of subject property."

A. DESCRIPTION OF REPLEVIN ACTION

The action in replevin is defined in a classic treatise thusly: "Replevin is an action for the recovery of specific personal chattels wrongfully taken and detained, or [rightfully taken but] wrongfully detained, with damages which the wrongful taking or detention has occasioned. It lies for all goods and chattels wrongfully taken or detained, and may be brought whenever one person claims chattel property in the possession of another, whether his property in the goods be absolute or qualified, provided he has the right of possession at the time the suit is begun. The primary object of the action is to recover the specific chattels which have been wrongfully taken or detained. Though judgment for damages usually follows a judgment for the property as a matter of course, the contest is about the specific things; the recovery of the thing, and not the damages, is the primary object. The secondary object is to recover a sum of money which shall be equivalent to the value sued for, in case the property itself is not delivered to the plaintiff upon the writ; compensation for the injury which the plaintiff has sustained by the wrongful detention of his goods is also recoverable, as in cases when the goods themselves are recovered. It may be said to be the proper form of action, in all cases where the plaintiff, having a general or special property, with the right to the immediate possession of chattels personal which are wrongfully detained by another, desires to recover the specific goods, and this without reference to whether they were wrongfully taken or not." H. Wells, A Treatise on the Law of Replevin 31–33 (1907).

1. **NATURE AND ELEMENTS OF THE ACTION**
   a. **Right to Possession in Plaintiff and Wrongful Detention by Defendant**
      Replevin is a possessory action. The primary issue is whether, as against the defendant, the plaintiff had the exclusive right of possession of the property

when the action was brought. The same issue, phrased negatively, is whether the defendant at the time was wrongfully detaining as against the plaintiff. The plaintiff cannot win by establishing that the defendant has no claim to the property; the plaintiff must establish she has an immediate and unqualified right to possession, which necessarily implies that the defendant's detention is wrongful. Thus, the courts often recite the maxim that, in a replevin action, the plaintiff's recovery depends on the strength of her own claim to possession of the goods, not the weakness of the defendant's claim. Usually, however, a right to possession is accompanied by an interest in the property, which explains why it is frequently said that a plaintiff in a replevin action must establish ownership or some other interest in the property in addition to an immediate right of possession. This also explains why a general, unsecured creditor cannot avail herself of replevin: She has no interest in property of the debtor and thus no right to possess any of it. Nonetheless, a replevin action is not decided by comparing the nature or quality of interests held by the parties. Even a plaintiff who establishes herself as "owner" of the disputed property cannot recover for that reason alone. Neither title nor any lesser interest necessarily carries with it an exclusive right of possession, which right the plaintiff in a replevin action must establish.

Examples: A has title to an aircraft. She leases the property to B for a term of two years. Before expiration of the lease term, A sues to replevy the property from B who has not breached the lease agreement. Judgment for B. B's proprietary interest is less substantial than A's. Yet, as long as B complies with the lease, her right to possession of the leased property is superior to the lessor's.

S sells and delivers goods to B. Title thus passes to B. S, however, reserves a security interest in the goods to secure payment of the purchase price by B. B fails to pay the price when due, and S sues to replevy the goods. Judgment for S. Although S does not have title, S qua secured party has the right to possession of her collateral upon the debtor's default. U.C.C. § 9–503.

b. Demand for Return by Plaintiff and Refusal by Defendant

In cases where the defendant's taking of the property was lawful and only the detention is complained of (*replevin in detinet*), a plaintiff ordinarily must establish that she made a demand for a return of the property and that the demand was refused by the defendant. There are many exceptions to this requirement, however, as in a case where a demand for the property's return would be a useless or futile act. Also, the requirement may have been abolished altogether by a statute which codifies the replevin action and fails to mention the need for a demand and refusal. *Brunswick Corp. v. Sposato,* 120 R.I. 673, 389 A.2d 1251, 1253 (1978).

Proof of demand and refusal by the plaintiff is never required in cases of *replevin in cepit,* which involve both a wrongful taking and an unlawful detention by the defendant.

2. RECOVERY SOUGHT BY PLAINTIFF IN REPLEVIN ACTION

a. Property or Its Value

The principal aim of a replevin action is to recover possession of the property wrongfully detained by the defendant. Traditionally, the plaintiff can recover alternatively the property's value only if the defendant is unable to return the property itself as would be true, for instance, if the defendant sold the property while the replevin action was pending.

Some states provide by statute, however, that judgment in a replevin action must be in the alternative for the property or its value, without regard to the defendant's ability to effect a return in specie, if the plaintiff invoked the replevin remedy (See infra Chapter XII.B.), but the defendant kept possession of the property pendente lite by posting bond.

In any event, if the plaintiff has a limited interest in the property, such as a security interest, any recovery of value in lieu of the property itself is limited to the value of her interest. *Martin v. Coker,* 204 Miss. 576, 589, 37 So.2d 772, 774–75 (1948). Thus, if the plaintiff is a secured party who is owed $6500 and the collateral she is seeking to replevy is worth $10,000, any alternative judgment for value cannot exceed $6500.

b. Compensatory Damages for Detention

If the plaintiff in a replevin action prevails on the primary issue by establishing her right to possession of the property, she recovers not only the property itself but also damages for the defendant's unlawful detention.

1) Loss of Use

The primary measure of damages for unlawful detention is the value of the loss of use of the property during the period it was unlawfully detained by the defendant. Typically, the basis for calculating this loss is the property's fair rental value. Damages for loss of use are not limited by the value of the property. *Harris v. Dixon Cadillac Co.,* 132 Cal.App. 3d 485, 490–92, 183 Cal.Rptr. 299, 301–02 (1982); *Universal C.I.T. Credit Corp. v. Jones,* 227 N.W.2d 473, 479 (Iowa 1975); *Morfeld v. Bernstrauch,* 216 Neb. 234, 241–43, 343 N.W.2d 880, 885 (1984). Recovery for loss of use cannot exceed, however, rentals actually paid by the plaintiff for substitute property during the period of unlawful detention. *Rose v. U.S. Nat. Bank,* 218 Neb. 97, 100, 352 N.W.2d 594, 597 (1984). Moreover, the plaintiff is obligated to mitigate her damages, and her recovery will be reduced accordingly if she fails in this regard. *Culligan Rock River Water Cond. Co. v. Gearhart,* 111 Ill.App.3d 254, 443 N.E.2d 1065 (1982).

Although rental value is the usual basis for determining damages for loss of use, "lost profits may be used as a measure where such profits are ascertainable with a reasonable degree of certainty." *Wolff v. Slusher,* 161 Ind.App. 182, 189–90, 314 N.E.2d 758, 763 (1974); but cf. *Widgren v. Massie,* 352 N.W.2d 420, 426 (Minn.App.1984) (damages for loss of use did not include lost wages). Lost profits and damages for loss of property cannot both be recovered, however. *Rocky Mountain Turbines v. 660 Syndicate,* 623 P.2d 758, 762 (Wyo.1981).

2) Depreciation

Depreciation of the property during its unlawful detention is also recoverable by a successful plaintiff in a replevin action. This recovery is not an alternative measure of loss of use; it is rather a separate and additional element of damages.

c. Punitive Damages

A successful plaintiff in a replevin action can recover punitive damages if the defendant's wrong in taking or detaining the property involved fraud, malice, gross negligence, or oppression. See, e.g., *Haskins v. Shelden,* 558 P.2d 487 (Alaska 1976); *Hallmark v. Stillings,* 648 S.W.2d 230 (Mo.App.1983).

d. Judgment for Debt Due Plaintiff Inappropriate

When a secured party sues to replevy collateral, or any other creditor sues to recover from a debtor property in which the creditor has an interest, the creditor cannot recover in the replevin action a personal judgment for the debt itself. *Road Material and Equipment Co. v. McGowan,* 229 Miss. 611, 91 So.2d 554 (1956). Any personal judgment for damages in a replevin action is restricted to losses occasioned by the wrongful detention of the property by the defendant and, in an appropriate case, to recovery of the property's value, as when the defendant is unable to return the property.

3. DEFENSES OF DEFENDANT

a. No Right to Possession in Plaintiff

Because the plaintiff in a replevin action must establish that she is entitled to possession of the property sued for, the defendant can successfully defend by showing that law or contract gives her possessory rights superior to the plaintiff's. Moreover, traditional doctrine holds that right to possession in a third person is a good defense in a replevin action even though the third person is not a party to the action and, as between the plaintiff and defendant, the former's claim to the property is better than the latter's. J. Cobbey, A Practical Treatise on the Law of Replevin 784–787 (2d ed. 1900); *Erwin v. Potts,* 216 Miss. 593, 63 So.2d 50 (1953). This doctrine has been rejected or greatly diluted by exceptions in some states where, therefore, the real issue in a replevin action is the relative possessory rights of the parties to the litigation, not whether the plaintiff has an exclusive right to possession as against the world. See, e.g., *Lieber v. Mohawk Arms, Inc.,* 64 Misc.2d 206, 314 N.Y.S.2d 510 (Sup. Ct.1970). A universally recognized exception is that right to possession in a third person cannot be set up as a defense in a replevin action by one who is a mere trespasser or who obtained possession of the goods by her own wrongful act. In such a case, the plaintiff need only show prior rightful possession in order to prevail against the wrongdoer.

b. Defendant Lacks Possession

It is generally a good defense in replevin that the defendant was not in actual or constructive possession of the property at the time the action was commenced. A defendant in possession cannot, however, defeat the replevin action by subsequently disposing of the property after being sued for its return. The action continues and the defendant, though she cannot return the property, will be liable for the property's value and damages for the wrongful taking or detention.

c. Counterclaims

Because the primary issue in a replevin action is the right to possession of the property sued for, the general rule is that the defendant cannot counterclaim for the recovery of money damages, even though her claim may be directly related to the transaction whereby she obtained possession of the goods. *Sandy Isles of Miami, Inc. v. Futernick,* 154 So.2d 355 (Fla.App.1963); *Martin v. Phelps,* 115 Ga.App. 552, 155 S.E.2d 447 (1967); *Standard Finance Corp. v. Breland,* 249 Miss. 413, 163 So.2d 232 (1964); *Paetow v. Van Erp,* 54 A.D.2d 976, 388 N.Y.S.2d 669 (1976); but see *National City Bank v. Fleming,* 2 Ohio App. 3d 50, 440 N.E.2d 590 (1981). Similarly, set-offs cannot be asserted. *Standard–Toch Chemicals, Inc. v. Victor Paint Co. Eastgate Corp.,* 367 Mich. 640, 116 N.W.2d 745 (1962). A counterclaim can be asserted, however, if it forms the basis of a specific charge against the property so as to give the defendant a right to possession, *Stoner v. Verhey,* 335 N.W.2d 636 (Iowa App.1983), or if it otherwise goes to the right of the plaintiff to recover the specific property. *Southside Atlantic Bank v. Lewis,* 174 So.2d 470, 472 (Fla.App.1965) (dicta); *Novak Food Service Equipment, Inc. v. Moe's Corned Beef Cellar, Inc.,* 121 Ill. App.3d 902, 460 N.E.2d 443 (1984) (defendant's claim of material breach of sales agreement went to essence of plaintiff's right to replevy the goods); *Mack Trucks, Inc. v. Taylor,* 227 Or. 376, 362 P.2d 364 (1961).

Examples: A repairs B's car. B refuses to pay the repair bill. A refuses to release possession of the car. B sues A to replevy the car. A counterclaims based on B's breach of the contract of repair and seeks damages. A's counterclaim should be dismissed.

Same facts except that A asserts artisan's lien for value of services rendered in repairing the car. See supra Chapter IX.C. This lien can properly be raised in defense of B's claim of replevin.

S sells goods to B on credit and reserves a security interest in the property to secure payment of the purchase price. B fails to pay the price when due. S sues to replevy the goods. B counterclaims for damages as to accepted goods because of breach of warranty by S. See U.C.C. § 2–714. This counterclaim cannot be asserted in the replevin action unless B's damages equal or exceed the debt owed S, in which case the counterclaim is permissible because "if proved the defendant owes no debt to the plaintiff and thus plaintiff would have no claim to possession of the property." *Mack Trucks, Inc. v. Taylor,* 227 Or. 376, 362 P.2d 364, 371 (1961).

Same facts except that B has not accepted the goods, or has revoked her acceptance of them, so that she has the rights provided by U.C.C. § 2–711. In this case, B can defend against S's replevin action without regard to the amount of her damages if she has paid anything toward the price of the goods. A buyer's remedies upon rightful rejection of the goods, or upon justified revocation of acceptance, include the right to keep the goods and sell them as a way of recovering payments made on their price. U.C.C. § 2–711(3). This right of possession can be asserted as a defense to S's replevin action.

B. PROCEDURES OF THE REPLEVIN REMEDY

The remedy of replevin is a privilege peculiar to the plaintiff in a replevin action. "Upon affidavit being filed [alleging among other things] that he is * * * entitled to immediate possession [of the property in controversy], he can demand that it be delivered to him under the first process issued in the case, leaving the title or right of possession to be investigated afterwards." H. Wells, A Treatise on the Law of Replevin 37 (1907).

1. AVAILABILITY OF THE REMEDY

The remedy of replevin is available in any action in which the plaintiff seeks to recover the possession of personal property. The remedy can be sought when summons is issued in the main action or thereafter until judgment (until trial in some states and until the defendant answers in others) for the purpose of having the subject property delivered to the plaintiff pendente lite.

Ordinarily, however, *replevin will not lie:*

- For any property taken in the collection of taxes, assessments, etc.;

- For any property seized under execution, attachment, or other process unless the property is exempt from process or otherwise is not subject to the process under which it was seized; or,

- By the original defendant in replevin for property taken in the action and delivered to the plaintiff who still holds it.

2. APPLICATION FOR THE REMEDY

Plaintiff initiates the replevin remedy by filing an affidavit with the judge or clerk of the court in which the replevin action is pending, which affidavit minimally alleges, states, or shows:

- A description of the property in controversy, its value and location;

- The plaintiff's interest in the property;

- The property has not been taken for tax, assessment, or fine; and has not been taken under attachment or execution or, if it has, the exempt status of the property;

- The defendant's wrongful detention of the property, and the plaintiff's right to immediate possession of it.

3. PRESEIZURE NOTICE AND HEARING

In most states replevin will not be ordered except upon notice to the defendant who is given an opportunity for a hearing prior to seizure of the property in controversy. In some states, after a plaintiff has filed an affidavit for replevin, the matter is routinely set for hearing and the defendant is informed of the date and place. In other states, the defendant is notified of the plaintiff's request for immediate possession of the property and informed that replevin will issue accordingly unless the defendant quickly responds and demands a hearing. In any event, the usual purpose of the hearing is to determine if there is a reasonable probability that plaintiff is entitled to possession of the property and will thus prevail in the main action. The burdens of proof and persuasion are on the plaintiff. If she succeeds in meeting these burdens, the court will order delivery of the property to her pendente lite.

4. EX PARTE SEIZURE
a. When Allowed

The usual practice in most states is to give a defendant notice and an opportunity for a hearing prior to ordering the provisional seizure through the replevin remedy of property in her possession. Yet, in virtually every state where preseizure notice and hearing is the general rule, provision is made in general or specific terms for ordering replevin ex parte in extraordinary or unusual cases. Typically, the replevin statute describes the kinds of situations in which ex parte replevin is allowed. The most common examples are in cases in which:

- the plaintiff can demonstrate that the property in controversy is threatened by immediate removal, transfer or injury;

- the property is perishable and will likely perish before a hearing can be held;

- the defendant acquired the property by theft or as a result of some other criminal conduct;

- the defendant has validly waived her right to a preseizure hearing, and the plaintiff can show that statutory and constitutional requirements for a valid waiver of this right have been satisfied. (A few states such as Illinois will not enforce under any circumstances a waiver of the right by a consumer. See Ill.Code Civ.Proc. ch. 110 § 19–105 (1984)).

In a minority of states, ex parte seizure is the norm. Preseizure notice and hearing are never demanded under the terms of the replevin statute. In a few of these states, however, the replevin remedy is available only in extraordinary cases such as where there is an immediate danger of harm to or loss of the property which the plaintiff seeks to recover in the replevin action.

b.   Post–Seizure Hearing Required
Wherever and whenever replevin is ordered ex parte, the defendant is entitled to a hearing soon after the seizure to test the plaintiff's entitlement to the replevin remedy.

5.   RESTRAINING ORDER IN PLACE OF EX PARTE SEIZURE
A significant number of states provide a procedural alternative to ex parte replevin in cases where the plaintiff fears that the property will be harmed or lost pending a plenary hearing on her application for the replevin remedy. At the time of notifying the defendant of the application and a right to a preseizure hearing, the court in its discretion can issue a preliminary injunction or restraining order prohibiting the defendant from harming, concealing, or disposing of the property. The penalties for violating such an order may include criminal sanctions.

6.   PLAINTIFF'S BOND
Whether or not a preseizure hearing is required, the property cannot be replevied until the plaintiff posts with the sheriff a bond to the effect that plaintiff will prosecute the action with diligence and, if the defendant prevails in the replevin action, plaintiff will account for the property and pay any damages that the defendant may have suffered because of the dispossession. The typical statute requires that the bond equal twice the value of the property to be seized and that it be backed by two or more sufficient sureties. The typical statute also provides a procedure whereby the defendant can challenge the sufficiency of the bond and, when appropriate, force the plaintiff to increase the amount of the bond or provide more or better security.

7.   ISSUANCE AND EXECUTION OF WRIT OF REPLEVIN
Upon satisfaction of the requirements for invoking the replevin remedy, the judge or clerk of the court in which the replevin action is filed directs the sheriff to seize the property claimed by the plaintiff. This direction commonly is called an *order* or *writ of possession* or *replevin*. The writ is directed to the sheriff of the county where the property is located. She is ordered to find and take custody of the property even if doing so requires her, consistent with the Constitution, to break open and enter a building or other enclosure. The sheriff then holds the property for a short period during which the defendant may regain possession of the property by posting a redelivery bond. If by the end of the period the defendant has failed to secure return of the property, the sheriff is bound to deliver it to the plaintiff after the plaintiff pays the sheriff's lawful fees for taking and keeping the property. The plaintiff thereafter keeps possession of the property pendente lite.

8.   DEFENDANT'S BOND FOR RETURN OF THE PROPERTY
The typical replevin statute allows a defendant from whom property has been replevied to regain possession of the property before the sheriff delivers it to the plaintiff by posting a forthcoming bond. The bond, which usually is backed by two or more sureties, is insurance for plaintiff which guarantees performance of a judgment against defendant in the replevin action. The bond commonly is in an amount equalling twice the value of the property which has been seized; and the bond is to the effect that the property will be delivered to plaintiff if she takes

judgment, or its value if delivery is not possible, and that the plaintiff will be paid
whatever damages she may recover against the defendant.

9. **ULTIMATE DISPOSITION OF PROPERTY TAKEN PROVISIONALLY THROUGH RE-
    PLEVIN REMEDY BY PLAINTIFF IN REPLEVIN ACTION**
    a. **Judgment for Plaintiff in Replevin Action**
        1) Generally
            If the plaintiff prevails in the replevin action, the judgment awards her
            permanent possession of the property which was delivered provisionally to
            her through the replevin remedy. The plaintiff also is awarded damages
            against the defendant for losses resulting from the defendant's wrongful
            taking or detention of the property. See supra Chapter XII.A.2. If the
            defendant resisted the provisional replevy of the property by posting a
            forthcoming bond, the sureties on the bond are accountable to the plaintiff
            if the defendant defaults in satisfying the judgment against her. Remem-
            ber, too, that if the defendant kept the property pendente lite by posting
            bond, the plaintiff in some states is allowed at her option to recover the
            value of the property rather than the property itself.

        2) Where Plaintiff is a Secured Party
            If the plaintiff in a replevin case is an Article 9 secured party pursuing
            collateral, she wants possession of the property for the purpose of dispos-
            ing of it in satisfaction of the secured debt. See U.C.C. § 9–503. The ac-
            tion and remedy of replevin are a means of gaining possession of the col-
            lateral through "action" under U.C.C. § 9–503 in cases where self-help
            repossession is unattractive or impossible. The secured party does not
            want to keep the property permanently and usually has no right to per-
            manent possession. She is obligated to dispose of the collateral unless
            there is an agreement between the debtor and her that the secured party
            will retain the collateral in total satisfaction of the secured debt. Such
            agreements are very rare. Thus, a replevin judgment for a secured party
            is a means to an end and not the end itself.

    b. **Judgment for Defendant in Replevin Action**
        If the defendant prevails in the replevin action, the judgment entitles her to
        recover property seized through the plaintiff's use of the replevin remedy or,
        in some states, to recover at her election the property's value. A judgment
        against the plaintiff also entitles the defendant to recover damages she suf-
        fered as a result of the provisional taking and detention of the property by
        plaintiff. The defendant's damages are calculated according to substantially
        the same measures used in determining the damages of a successful plaintiff
        in a replevin action. See supra Chapter XII.A.2. Remember that satisfaction
        of a judgment for defendant is guaranteed by the bond which plaintiff was re-
        quired to post as a condition of invoking the replevin remedy.

REVIEW QUESTIONS

1. What is the relationship between the replevin action and the replevin remedy?

2. T or F Success in a replevin action does not depend on the plaintiff establishing that she is the owner of the disputed property.

3. T or F The replevin remedy is ordinarily available to a plaintiff in an action for the recovery of goods and chattels only in extraordinary cases, such as when the defendant is threatening to dispose of or remove the property.

4. What is done with property pending the outcome of the replevin action after the sheriff seizes it pursuant to a writ of replevin?

5. Are damages recoverable in a replevin action?

*

XIII

LIS PENDENS

Analysis

The rule of *res judicata* is that the judgment of a court binds only persons who are parties to the action. The doctrine of *lis pendens* (which means "pending suit") creates an exception to this rule when the action directly affects title to property. In such a case the "litigation, either by its own force under the common law or through a statutory notification procedure, puts potential purchasers or encumbrancers of property on notice, and that notice binds them to the judgment rendered." Laurence, *Lis Pendens,* 56 N.D.L. Rev. 327 (1980). Thus, when a person sues to establish a claim or right as to property that is protected by lis pendens, a conveyance of the property by the other party while the action is pending cannot adversely affect the claimant's rights as ultimately determined through the litigation. In this sense, lis pendens facilitates the desired relief and so can be fairly characterized as a remedy.

A. NATURE OF LIS PENDENS

Technically speaking, the doctrine of lis pendens creates no lien or other interest in property. Rather, the doctrine merely puts prospective purchasers and encumbrancers on notice of pending litigation involving rights to property that is the subject of the action. Typically, however, the party to the action who benefits from lis pendens has no legally recognizable claim except as a result of the litigation. The litigation will not conclude until after consummation of the transfers against which the beneficiary is protected. In a sense, therefore, as against purchasers and encumbrancers pendente lite, the beneficiary's claim is given retroactive effect. The end result is basically the same as giving the beneficiary a lien from the time she is first protected by the lis pendens doctrine.

B. STATUTES USUALLY GOVERN LIS PENDENS

The common law created the lis pendens doctrine; but as a common-law creature the doctrine worked unfairly against third persons. Any one who purchased or encumbered property that was subject to litigation was bound by the outcome of the action even though she had no actual knowledge of the litigation and no reliable means of discovering that the property was involved in litigation. For this reason, most states long ago enacted statutes designed mainly to protect third parties by limiting the effects of lis pendens. Lis pendens statutes have two chief purposes:

1. STATUTES REQUIRE FILING OF NOTICE
Lis pendens statutes condition the effect of the doctrine on the claimant's compliance with a prescribed procedure, the main feature of which is the requirement that the claimant file a notice of lis pendens in public records maintained for the purpose of alerting the world to property that is the subject matter of pending litigation.

2. STATUTES IDENTIFY ACTIONS SUBJECT TO LIS PENDENS
Lis pendens statutes also identify more clearly than the common law, and sometimes more broadly, the types of actions subject to lis pendens.

C. ACTIONS SUBJECT TO LIS PENDENS

Lis pendens does not operate with respect to all lawsuits that may somehow affect rights to property. An action is constructively publicized through lis pendens only if the action is of a nature, and involves a type of property, which the law (usually a statute) describes as subject to the lis pendens doctrine.

1. TYPE OF PROPERTY

At common law, the doctrine of lis pendens operated only against real estate. Most states now have lis pendens statutes. These statutes everywhere continue to apply the doctrine of lis pendens to real estate, and in some states the doctrine is also made applicable to personal property.

2. NATURE OF THE ACTION

a. In General: Actions Affecting Title to or Possession of Property

There is no common description of the nature of the actions that are subject to lis pendens. The states disagreed somewhat on the applicability of the doctrine in its common-law form, and statutory codifications of the doctrine also differ in this regard. As a very general rule, however, lis pendens operates only in actions in which the relief sought will *directly affect title to, or possession of, property*. This description makes lis pendens proper not only in actions involving questions of title to property, but also in actions " 'which are brought to establish an equitable estate, interest, or right in specific * * * property or to enforce any lien, charge, or encumbrance against it, * * * although at the commencement of the suit there is no present vested interest, claim or lien in or on the property which it [the action] seeks to charge.' " *General Electric Credit Corp. v. Winnebago of New Jersey, Inc.,* 149 N.J. Super. 81, 86, 373 A.2d 402, 404 (1977).

Examples of actions subject to the lis pendens doctrine include these:

- complainant seeks to enforce adherence to building criteria contained in protective covenants covering specific real estate, *Hammersley v. District Court,* 199 Colo. 442, 610 P.2d 94 (1980);

- a vendee sues for specific enforcement of a contract for the conveyance of property, *Goldstein v. Ray,* 118 Cal. App. 3d 571, 173 Cal. Rptr. 550 (1981);

- an owner of realty sues to establish an easement appurtenant to adjoining land, *Taylor v. Lanahan,* 73 Ill. App. 3d 829, 392 N.E.2d 425 (1979); see also *416 Properties, Inc. v. Stampler,* 19 A.D.2d 801, 243 N.Y.S.2d 321 (1963) (suit to annul easement agreement appropriate for lis pendens);

- the object of the action is to impress a constructive trust on property, *Polk v. Schwartz,* 166 N.J. Super. 292, 399 A.2d 1001 (1979); *Pegram v. Tomrich,* 4 N.C.App. 413, 166 S.E.2d 849 (1969); *Hughes v. Houston Northwest Medical Center,* 647 S.W.2d 5 (Tex. Civ. App. 1982);

- the court is asked to set aside a conveyance as fraudulent or otherwise wrongful and ineffective against petitioner, *Boca Raton Land Development, Inc. v. Sparling,* 397 So. 2d 1053 (Fla. App. 1981); *Bennett v. Bennett,* 62 A.D.2d 1154, 404 N.Y.S.2d 171 (1978); *North Carolina Nat. Bank v. Evans,* 296 N.C. 374, 250 S.E.2d 231 (1979);

- plaintiff seeks relief under statute providing equitable and legal remedies (including imposition of equitable lien) for any person who makes improvements to land in good faith and under erroneous belief that she is owner of the land, *Okuda v. Superior Court,* 144 Cal. App. 3d 135, 192 Cal. Rptr. 388 (1983).

b. Actions for Money Damages Only

Lis pendens is not available in an action in which the plaintiff seeks a personal judgment for money damages *only* even though such a judgment, if obtained and properly docketed, will create a lien upon the defendant's land. See Chapter II, supra. Thus, courts have determined that lis pendens is not available:

- In a suit alleging wrongful termination and various breaches of contract when the complaint sought solely monetary damages with the exception of a generalized claim for "such additional relief as this Court deems just and proper", *Lowell Staats Mining Co., Inc. v. Pioneer Uravan, Inc.,* 596 F. Supp. 1428 (D. Colo. 1984);

- When the purchasers under a contract for the sale of land sued the sellers for breach of the contract and sought nothing more than damages for the breach, *Keith v. Bratton,* 738 F.2d 314, 316 n.2 (8th Cir. 1984);

- When a general contractor sued a land developer alleging breach of joint venture, breach of fiduciary duty, and for an accounting after their deal fell apart and the developer hired a different contractor to proceed with the project, *Construction General, Inc. v. Richard Schwarz/Neil Weber, Inc.,* 354 N.W.2d 877 (Minn. App. 1984);

- In an action to enforce a promissory note even though court had power to enter judgment creating lien on real estate, *Mauer v. Rohde,* 257 N.W.2d 489 (Iowa 1977); see also *Mammoth Cave Production Credit Ass'n v. Gross,* 141 Ariz. 389, 687 P.2d 397 (App. 1984) (action by a credit association against debtor on a note executed in connection with a mortgage which the plaintiff did not seek to foreclose); *Otten v. Birdseye,* 527 P.2d 925 (Colo. App. 1974) (suit to recover under terms of loan not challenging defendant's title to property); *Lord v. Jeffreys,* 22 N.C.App. 13, 205 S.E.2d 563 (1974) (action to recover commission due on sale of real estate and damages for breach of contract);

- When the complaint is to register a judgment for money damages rendered by a court of another state, *Tortu v. Tortu,* 430 So. 2d 531 (Fla. App. 1983);

- In an action seeking reimbursement of value of improvements placed upon defendant's property, *Settoon v. Settoon,* 413 So. 2d 634 (La. App. 1982);

- When the plaintiff sues in tort for damages arising when her vehicle struck defendant's cow, *Gatewood v. Bosch,* 2 Kan. App. 2d 474, 581 P.2d 1198 (1978);

- In a suit against an estate to preserve a tort claim pending against the decedent at the time of her death, *Estate of Patten v. Batchelor,* 664 S.W.2d 698 (Tenn. App. 1983).

If money damages are sought additionally or alternatively to relief that would directly affect title to property and by itself would support lis pendens, the claim for money damages usually does not make lis pendens inapplicable. See, e.g., *Okuda v. Superior Court,* 144 Cal. App. 3d 135, 192 Cal. Rptr. 388 (1983); *Balsam v. Axelrod,* 102 Misc. 2d 1000, 424 N.Y.S.2d 814 (Sup. Ct. 1979).

c. Divorce Actions

The cases disagree on the extent to which a general lis pendens law applies in a divorce action. Compare *Atlas Garage and Custom Builders, Inc. v. Hurley,* 167 Conn. 248, 355 A.2d 286 (1974) (lis pendens inapplicable in divorce action in which plaintiff sought alimony and a conveyance of specific property); *Schofield v. Fearon,* 169 Ga. App. 924, 315 S.E.2d 452 (1984) (lis pendens filed by wife in divorce action in which she sought certain real estate of husband could not tie up the property and affect sales by him prior to final decree of divorce) with *Clopine v. Kemper,* 140 Colo. 360, 344 P.2d 451 (1959) (divorce action in which an equitable share of real and personal property of parties was sought is proper subject of lis pendens); *Joneson v. Joneson,* 251 Iowa 825, 102 N.W.2d 911 (1960) (divorce action is subject to lis pendens where specific property is described and sought to be charged with payment of alimony); *Jones v. Jones,* 249 Miss. 322, 161 So. 2d 640 (1964) (spouse's right to alimony constitutes such interest in husband's realty as will permit her to invoke lis pendens statute to protect such interest).

d. Actions Concerning Leases of Real Estate

Whether lis pendens applies in an action concerning rights in a leasehold of real estate depends primarily on whether the lis pendens law is limited to actions concerning realty (including possession thereof) and, if so, whether a lease of land is considered for purposes of lis pendens an interest in real property or, at least, something that affects real property within the meaning of the lis pendens law. On this latter issue, the cases are divided. Compare, e.g., *Gyurek v. 103 East 10th Owners Corp.,* 128 Misc.2d 384, 490 N.Y.S.2d 415 (1985) (right to possession of apartment pursuant to lease is not an interest in real property but is deemed to be personalty) with *Parker v. Superior Court,* 9 Cal. App. 3d 397, 88 Cal. Rptr. 352 (1970) (a leasehold being an estate in real property nevertheless comes within scope of lis pendens statute which covers "action concerning * * * the right of possession of real property" even though leasehold is, in contemplation of law, personal property).

D. FILING OF LIS PENDENS NOTICE AND OTHER PROCEDURAL MATTERS

1. LIS PENDENS EFFECT REQUIRES FILING OF PROPER NOTICE

a. General Rule

Under the common law, the filing of an action to which the doctrine of lis pendens applied was itself notice of the lawsuit that bound purchasers and encumbrancers of the property. Statutes almost everywhere now provide that the pendency of an action does not constitute notice to anyone, other than parties to the action, unless a proper lis pendens notice is filed.

b. Exception

In some states, a purchaser or encumbrancer of property involved in litigation is bound by the outcome of the action even in the absence of a filed notice of lis pendens if the purchaser or encumbrancer has actual knowledge of the pendency of the action when she acquires her interest. See, e.g., *Carpenters District Council v. Morse,* 455 F. Supp. 535, 536 (E.D. Mich. 1978); *Packard Bell Electronics Corp. v. Theseus,* 244 Cal.App.2d 355, 53 Cal. Rptr. 300, 305 (1966); *Glynn v. Dubin,* 13 Utah 2d 163, 165, 369 P.2d 930, 931 (1962).

2. WHAT IS FILED

Lis pendens statutes commonly require a notice of lis pendens:

- To be in a writing separate from the complaint or other pleadings;

  Caveat: In some states the complaint or another pleading can serve the added function of a notice of lis pendens if the pleading contains the necessary information and is filed in the place designated by law for recording notices of actions affecting property.

- Signed by the plaintiff, defendant, or other party who seeks to benefit from the lis pendens effect, or signed by the party's attorney;

- Show the name of the court in which the action has been filed and the title, docket number, date of filing, and object of the action; and

- Describe the property affected by the notice of lis pendens.

3. WHERE IS THE NOTICE FILED

A notice of lis pendens ordinarily is filed in the office of the clerk or recorder of the county where the affected property is located. This official may maintain a separate book or other system exclusively for the recording of lis pendens notices, or the official may merge such notices with other systems kept for the purpose of recording interests in, or claims to, property.

4. WHEN IS THE NOTICE FILED

Typically, a notice of lis pendens is filed when the action is commenced or at any time during the pendency of the action. "[A] prematurely filed notice of lis pendens is a nullity." *Keith v. Bratton,* 738 F.2d 314, 316 (8th Cir. 1984). In some states, however, a lis pendens notice can be filed even before an action is begun so long as an action is seasonably brought to enforce the claim that prompted the lis pendens filing.

5. CANCELLATION OF LIS PENDENS

a. Upon Judgment

If the action is decided against the person who filed the lis pendens, the judgment of the court should include an order cancelling the notice.

b. During Pendency of Action

Any party to the action who is affected by a notice of lis pendens can by motion at any time during the pendency of the action request the court where the action is pending to cancel, discharge, release, or modify the lis pendens on the basis that the action or the property is not subject to lis pendens or that for some other reason the filing of the lis pendens was not in accordance with law or was otherwise wrongful. Lis pendens statutes in some states make the same sort of provision for persons claiming an interest in the property who are not parties to the action. Where there is no specific provision for non-parties, they can challenge a lis pendens by intervening in the action and thereafter moving to cancel the lis pendens or by suing to quiet title to the property.

6. LIS PENDENS IN FEDERAL DISTRICT COURT

"When the law of a State requires a notice of an action concerning real property pending in a court of the State to be registered, recorded, docketed, or indexed in a particular manner, or in a certain office or county or parish in order to give constructive notice of the action as it relates to the real property, and such law authorizes a notice of an action concerning real property pending in a United States district court to be registered, recorded, docketed, or indexed in the same manner, or in the same place, those requirements of the State law must be complied with in order to give constructive notice of such an action pending in a United States district court as it relates to real property in such State." 28 U.S.C.A. § 1964.

E. PERSONS BOUND BY LIS PENDENS

The typical lis pendens law provides that the notice of lis pendens binds *purchasers* and *encumbrancers* of the affected property who acquire their interests through a party to the action after the notice of lis pendens is filed or otherwise becomes effective.

1. TERMS "PURCHASERS" AND "ENCUMBRANCERS" BROADLY CONSTRUED

The word "purchasers" may be, and often is, construed broadly to include anyone acquiring any interest in property through a sale or similar transaction. Thus, a notice of lis pendens filed in an action seeking specific performance of a contract to sell land is effective against a subsequent lessee of the property from the defendant seller. *Goldstein v. Ray,* 118 Cal. App. 3d 571, 173 Cal. Rptr. 550 (1981).

The term "encumbrancer" is not limited to mortgagees; it also may include a person who claims an interest in the property through a construction lien or other statutory lien.

2. PERSON MUST CLAIM THROUGH A PARTY TO THE ACTION
Lis pendens binds only purchasers and encumbrancers pendente lite who are immediate or remote transferees of a party to the action. 1 A. Freeman, A Treatise of the Law of Judgments §§ 526–527 & 529 (1925).

3. ONLY PENDENTE LITE INTERMEDDLERS AFFECTED
a. General Rule
Lis pendens does not affect a person who traces her interest to a conveyance that becomes effective prior to the commencement of the suit or, where the law requires it, prior to the filing of a notice of lis pendens. 1 A. Freeman, A Treatise of the Law of Judgments § 528 (1925); *Tinnon v. Tanksley,* 408 S.W.2d 98 (Mo. 1966); *Four-G Corp. v. Ruta,* 56 N.J. Super. 52, 151 A.2d 546 (1959).

b. Exception Caused by Recording Laws
Yet, if the law requires recordation of the conveyance through which the person claims her interest, she may be bound by a lis pendens notice that becomes effective before the conveyance is recorded. See, e.g., *D–K Inv. Corp. v. Sutter,* 19 Cal. App. 3d 537, 96 Cal. Rptr. 830 (1971); *Jones v. Jones,* 249 Miss. 322, 161 So. 2d 640 (1964); *J. & S. Corp. v. Mortgage Associates, Inc.,* 41 Wis. 2d 418, 164 N.W.2d 221 (1969). There is contrary authority, however. See, e.g., *Freligh v. Maurer,* 111 So. 2d 712 (Fla. App. 1959); cf. *Lamarche v. Rosenblum,* 50 A.D.2d 636, 374 N.Y.S.2d 443 (1975) (where lis pendens claimant had actual knowledge of prior unrecorded claim).

F. BINDING EFFECT OF LIS PENDENS

The doctrine of lis pendens creates no lien, nor does it prevent anyone—not even a party to the action—from disposing of her interest in the property that is the subject of the action. Lis pendens merely gives constructive notice of the action to subsequent purchasers and encumbrancers of the subject property and so binds them to the outcome of the action. A subsequent purchaser or encumbrancer is bound in the sense that the interest she acquires will be coextensive with the interest her grantor is determined to have when the action is completed. This binding effect occurs even though the purchaser or encumbrancer is not made a party to the action. In other words, when lis pendens applies, a purchaser or encumbrancer pendente lite stands in no better position or attitude than her grantor occupies at the conclusion of the litigation.

Example: A agreed to sell Blackacre to B. A breached the contract. B sued for specific performance and, upon commencing the action, properly filed a notice of lis pendens. A conveyed the property to C who recorded the deed. B won her action against A. The conveyance by A to C is ineffective. C takes nothing. The result is the same if (1) A mortgaged Blackacre to C, see generally *Bodner v. Brickner,* 29 A.D.2d 441, 288 N.Y.S.2d 342 (1968); (2) A leased Blackacre to C, see generally *Goldstein v. Ray,* 118 Cal. App. 3d 571,

173 Cal. Rptr. 550 (1981); *Wagner v. Wagner,* 249 Iowa 1310, 90 N.W.2d 758 (1958); (3) C was a creditor of A who acquired a judgment lien against Blackacre after B filed the lis pendens, see generally *Stearns v. Los Angeles City School District,* 244 Cal. App.2d 696, 53 Cal. Rptr. 482 (1966).

G. CONSTITUTIONALITY OF LIS PENDENS

In theory, the doctrine of lis pendens does not prevent anybody from disposing of her interest in the property that is the subject of the action; in practice, however, as the California Supreme Court has recognized, "the filing of a lis pendens usually clouds the title to the property and prevents its transfer until the litigation is resolved or the lis pendens is expunged." *Malcolm v. Superior Court,* 29 Cal. 518, 520 n.2, 629 P.2d 495, 497 n.2, 174 Cal. Rptr. 694, 696 n.2 (1981); accord, *Beefy King Intern., Inc. v. Veigle,* 464 F.2d 1102, 1104 (5th Cir. 1972) (lis pendens is only a notice but the effect on the owner of the property is "constraining"). Because the filing of a lis pendens notice effectively restricts the free alienability of the subject property, lis pendens statutes have been attacked as unconstitutional under the due process clause of the Fourteenth Amendment of the United States Constitution. Most of these attacks have been unsuccessful for several reasons. First, the Fourteenth Amendment restains only state action, which arguably is lacking in the operation of a lis pendens scheme. *Jerry's Sport Center, Inc. v. Novick,* 122 N.H. 636, 448 A.2d 404 (1982). Second, there is serious doubt that restricting the free alienability of real property amounts to a taking that is protected by the Fourteenth Amendment. *Empfield v. Superior Court,* 33 Cal. App. 3d 105, 108 Cal. Rptr. 375 (1973); cf. *Spielman-Fond, Inc. v. Hanson's Inc.,* 379 F. Supp. 997 (D. Ariz. 1973), aff'd mem., 417 U.S. 901, 94 S. Ct. 2596 (1974) (a construction lien effects no protected taking when the owner is not deprived of possession and use). Finally, several courts have determined that, even if the Fourteenth Amendment applies so that due process is required, the procedures for invoking lis pendens are constitutionally sufficient. *Chrysler Corp. v. Fedders Corp.,* 670 F.2d 1316 (3d Cir. 1982); *Williams v. Bartlett,* 189 Conn. 471, 457 A.2d 290 (1983). Yet, a lis pendens scheme that passes muster under the federal Constitution may fail the test of due process imposed by a state constitution. *Hercules Chemical Co., Inc. v. VCI, Inc.,* 118 Misc.2d 814, 462 N.Y.S. 2d 129 (1983).

The next two chapters, infra Chapters XIV & XV, discuss more fully the issues of when due process is required of creditors' remedies generally and what procedures satisfy the requirements.

REVIEW QUESTIONS

1. A made a loan to B. B promised to secure the loan by giving A a mortgage on real property which B owned. B reneged on this promise. When B defaulted in repaying the loan, A sued and claimed an equitable lien on the real estate. Upon commencing the action, A filed a notice of lis pendens covering the real estate. Thereafter, B sold the land to C. The litigation between A and B resulted in the court recognizing an equitable lien in A's favor. Is this lien valid against C who was not a party to the action?

2. Would the answer be the same if A had not filed a notice of lis pendens?

3. Same facts as Question 1 except that B conveyed the land to C before the transaction between A & B. What result?

PART FOUR

GUARANTEES OF DEBTORS' PROCEDURAL DUE PROCESS RIGHTS

Analysis

For present purposes, due process refers to the procedural aspects of a creditors' remedy that guard against unlawful or unjustified uses of the remedy. Creditors will argue that the effectiveness and efficiency of a creditors' remedy are inversely related to the number and complexity of due process requirements. Debtors will counter that there is also an inverse relationship between the sophistication of such requirements and the risk that the remedy will be used arbitrarily or erroneously. The next two chapters mainly explore when and how constitutional law applies to mediate these conflicting concerns.

*

FOURTEENTH AMENDMENT PROTECTION

Analysis

The Fourteenth Amendment to the United States Constitution commands that no "state shall deprive any person of life, liberty, or property without due process of law." Thus, any creditors' remedy that implicates the state must provide minimum procedural safeguards designed to guard against arbitrary and erroneous seizures of debtors' property. These safeguards are not static but rather change over time. As the Supreme Court observed in *Sniadach v. Family Finance Corp.,* 395 U.S. 337, 89 S. Ct. 1820 (1969), "[t]he fact that a procedure would pass muster under a feudal regime does not mean that it gives necessary protection to all property in its modern forms." Id. at 340, 89 S. Ct. at 1822.

In *Sniadach,* the debtor challenged the Wisconsin prejudgment garnishment statute, which at the time was essentially identical to the garnishment laws of virtually all the other states. The standard procedure, which had been around for decades, allowed a creditor to garnish and thus freeze a debtor's bank account at the inception of a suit to collect the debt. The debtor received no prior notice, and she had no opportunity for a hearing before the account was frozen. If the creditor prevailed in the main action, the account was applied in satisfaction of the judgment. In the interim the debtor lost the use of her money unless she posted a bond guaranteeing payment of a judgment against her. Although this procedure was ancient and had withstood constitutional attacks many times before, the Supreme Court held in *Sniadach* that that procedure violated "the fundamental principles of due process" because the debtor did not receive notice and a hearing prior to the seizure of her property.

The *Sniadach* case brought about a reappraisal of the constitutionality of all creditors' remedies. Pre- and postjudgment remedies of every sort and special creditors' rights of every kind have been tested, and are still being tested, under the doctrine of *Sniadach* and its progeny, which includes *Fuentes v. Shevin,* 407 U.S. 67, 92 S. Ct. 1983 (1972); *Mitchell v. W.T. Grant Co.,* 416 U.S. 600, 94 S. Ct. 1895 (1974); and *North Georgia Finishing, Inc. v. Di-Chem, Inc.,* 419 U.S. 601, 95 S. Ct. 719 (1975). Taken together, these cases apply to the creditors' rights area the traditional balancing approach of procedural due process law, which determines what process is due in each case by weighing the interests of the parties and also the interests of the government. See generally *Cleveland Board of Education v. Loudermill,* 470 U.S. 532, 105 S.Ct. 1487 (1985); *Mathews v. Eldridge,* 424 U.S. 319, 335, 96 S. Ct. 893, 903 (1976); *Boddie v. Connecticut,* 401 U.S. 371, 91 S. Ct. 780 (1971). As interpreted and applied, however, by legislatures and lower courts, *Sniadach* and its progeny establish the general rule that, when the Fourteenth Amendment applies, a debtor's property cannot be taken from her until she is notified and has had an opportunity to be heard. A procedural scheme less protective of the debtor's interest that allows ex parte seizure is sufficient only in exceptional cases.

Yet, in many cases involving some very important creditors' remedies, debtors' rights are not protected by the doctrine of *Sniadach* and its progeny due to the inapplicability of the Fourteenth Amendment. The Fourteenth Amendment limits only *state action,* and it limits state action only when the taking involves a *significant property interest.* When a creditor pursues a remedy that does not implicate the state, i.e., involves purely private action, or when the property interest affected by the pursuit of the remedy is de minimis, the debtor is not entitled to Fourteenth Amendment procedural due process. The same is true whenever the debtor effectively has waived her due process rights. The following discussion considers instances when the Fourteenth Amendment fails to apply, as well as the necessary process that must be afforded a debtor whenever her rights are protected by the Fourteenth Amendment.

A. PREREQUISITES TO FOURTEENTH AMENDMENT PROTECTION

1. STATE ACTION

Procedural due process is required by the Fourteenth Amendment only when the taking of a debtor's property is fairly attributable to the state, i.e., involves state action. The due process clause provides no protection against purely private action. There are two parts to the proper approach for deciding if conduct amounts to state action:

> First, the deprivation must be caused by the exercise of some right or privilege created by the state or by a rule of conduct imposed by the state or by a person for whom the state is responsible. * * * Second, the party charged with the deprivation must be a person who may fairly be said to be a state actor. This may be because he is a state official, because he has acted together with or has obtained significant aid from state officials, or because his conduct is otherwise chargeable to the state.
>
> Although related, these two principles are not the same. They collapse into each other when the claim of a constitutional deprivation is directed against a party whose official character is such as to lend the weight of the state to his decisions. The two principles diverge when the constitutional claim is directed against a party without such apparent authority, i.e., against a private party.

Lugar v. Edmondson Oil Co., Inc., 457 U.S. 922, 937, 102 S. Ct. 2744, 2754 (1982).

a. Involvement of State Officials

State action is present in the exercise of a creditor's remedy when the taking overtly involves a state officer performing some substantial role in her official capacity. Therefore, a debtor is entitled to due process protection against any creditors' remedy such as garnishment, attachment, or replevin which involves a sheriff or other state official seizing property of the debtor upon the command of a court.

There is authority that state action exists when a public official is involved not only when the law requires it, but also when the official's aid is requested by a creditor pursuing an otherwise purely private remedy. See, e.g., *Walker v. Walthall,* 121 Ariz. 121, 588 P.2d 863 (App. 1978) (sheriff present when Article 9 secured party repossessed collateral); *Callen v. Sherman's, Inc.,* 182 N.J. Super. 438, 442 A.2d 626 (1982) (constable assisted in landlord's distress of tenant's goods); but compare *Wright v. National Bank,* 600 F. Supp. 1289 (N.D. N.Y. 1985) (passive participation of police in secured party's repossession not sufficient official involvement to constitute state action).

State action cannot be predicated on just any official involvement. The officer must play a substantial role in enforcing the creditor's remedy, which means that her performance must entail more than mere ministerial acts. *Flagg Brothers v. Brooks,* 436 U.S. 149, 160–61 n.10, 98 S. Ct. 1729, 1735–36 n.10 (1978). The courts disagree on whether the involvement of the state through public recordation and the like is sufficient official involvement with a creditor's remedy to constitute state action. Compare, e.g., *Gibson v. Dixon,* 579 F.2d 1071 (7th Cir. 1978) (the participation of public officials in the transfer of paper title to a vehicle repossessed and sold by a secured party under U.C.C. §§ 9–503 & 9–504 does not amount to state action) with *Chrysler Corp. v. Fedders Corp.,* 670 F.2d 1316 (3d Cir. 1982) (state's role in recording lis pendens smacks of state action sufficient to invoke the Fourteenth Amendment); *Williams v. Bartlett,* 189 Conn. 471, 478 n.5, 457 A.2d 290, 293–94 n.5 (1983) (same); but see *Jerry's Sport Center, Inc. v. Novick,* 122 N.H. 636, 448 A.2d 404 (1982) (cannot find state action in filing of lis pendens even though creditor used standard forms supplied by court and recorded by Registrar of Deeds).

b.   Attributing Conduct of Private Parties to the State

Any creditor almost always acts pursuant to a state-created right or privilege when she takes property of a debtor in the exercise of a creditors' remedy. Reliance on, or action pursuant to, state law does not of itself establish state action, however, if the creditor is a private party. Conduct by a private party amounts to state action only when there is "something more"; otherwise, "private parties could face constitutional litigation whenever they seek to rely on some state rule governing their interactions with the community surrounding them." *Lugar v. Edmondson Oil Co., Inc.,* 457 U.S. 922, 937, 102 S. Ct. 2744, 2754 (1982). What more is required to convert private action into state action for due process purposes varies with the circumstances. There is no uniform or unitary test. Instead, there is a collection of tests or approaches or, more precisely, "methods of analyzing and appraising the facts and circumstances of a particular case." *Gerena v. Puerto Rico Legal Services, Inc.,* 697 F.2d 447, 449 n.2 (1st Cir. 1983). These different methods cannot always be reconciled and sometimes produce inconsistent results.

1)   Symbiotic Relationship Test

"Under the symbiotic relationship test, * * * actions of a private party are attributable to the * * * government if the government 'has so far insinuated itself into a position of interdependence with [the private entity] that it must be recognized as a joint participant in the challenged activity * * *.'" *Gerena v. Puerto Rico Legal Services, Inc.,* 697 F.2d 447, 451 (1st Cir. 1983). See *Burton v. Wilmington Parking Authority,* 365 U.S. 715, 81 S. Ct. 856 (1961). "The dispositive factor * * * [is] the 'extent and nature of the overall relationship between the (government) and the private enterprise * * * [establishing] an inextricably-linked relationship * * *.'" *Miller v. Indiana Hospital,* 562 F. Supp. 1259, 1276 (W.D. Pa. 1983). Under such circumstances there is no need to show state involvement in the specific action being challenged because "the state is charged with all actions of the private party." *Gerena v. Puerto Rico Legal Services, Inc.,* 697 F.2d 447, 451 (1st Cir. 1983). It now seems clear, however, that a symbiotic relationship cannot be founded solely on state funding and regulation of the private actor even when the regulation is extensive and the actor receives virtually all of its income from government sources. *Rendell-Baker v. Kohn,* 457 U.S. 830, 102 S. Ct. 2764 (1982); *Community Med. Center v. Emergency Med. Services,* 712 F.2d 878 (3d Cir. 1983). The necessary connections may be established, however, where there is a "complete intermingling of state and private actors" and the state financially benefits from the interaction, although a financial reward is not absolutely required. *Krynicky v. University of Pittsburgh,* 742 F.2d 94 (3d Cir. 1984).

2) Nexus Test

"Unlike the symbiotic relationship test, which looks at the overall relationship among the parties, the close nexus approach attempts to determine whether the state can be deemed responsible for the *specific* conduct [which allegedly involves a taking without due process]." *Community Med. Center v. Emergency Med. Services,* 712 F.2d 878, 881 (3d Cir. 1983). State action exists under this test when "there is a sufficiently close nexus between the [government] and the challenged action of the [private party] so that the action of the latter may be fairly treated as that of the [government] itself." *Jackson v. Metropolitan Edison Co.,* 419 U.S. 345, 351, 95 S. Ct. 449, 453 (1974). "Thus, the government can be held responsible for the private act only when it has compelled the act by law or when it has 'provided such significant encouragement, either overt or covert, that the choice must in law be deemed to be that of the [government].'" *Miller v. Indiana Hospital,* 562 F. Supp. 1259, 1277 (W.D. Pa. 1983), quoting *Blum v. Yaretsky,* 457 U.S. 991, 1004, 102 S. Ct. 2777, 2786 (1982). On the other hand, "[m]ere approval of or acquiescence in the initiatives of a private party is not sufficient to justify holding the State responsible for those initiatives under the terms of the Fourteenth Amendment." *Blum v. Yaretsky,* 457 U.S. 991, 1004, 102 S. Ct. 2777, 2786 (1982). Also, the fact that the private party receives government funding is not determinative of state action. *Rendell-Baker v. Kohn,* 457 U.S. 830, 102 S. Ct. 2764 (1982). Finally, the mere fact the state regulates the private party—even if the regulation is extensive and detailed—does not by itself convert the private party's conduct into state action. *Jackson v. Metropolitan Edison Co.,* 419 U.S. 345, 95 S. Ct. 449 (1974). In sum, indirect governmental involvement does not convert what otherwise would be private conduct into state action. *Johnson v. Educational Testing Service,* 754 F.2d 20, 23–25 (1st Cir. 1985). Rather, there must be such a close link between the regulation and the specific challenged action "that it can in actuality be viewed more as the action of the * * * government than that of [the private party]." *Warren v. Government Nat. Mortgage Ass'n,* 611 F.2d 1229, 1233 (8th Cir. 1980). The state must be involved with the activity to such an extent that the activity at issue may be fairly treated as that of the state. *Id.* at 1234.

3) Public Function Test

There is state action when a private party exercises "powers traditionally exclusively reserved to the State" or powers that are "traditionally the exclusive prerogative of the State." *Jackson v. Metropolitan Edison Co.,* 419 U.S. 345, 352–53, 95 S. Ct. 449, 454 (1974). "The performance of a function which serves the public or which is 'affected with a public interest' does not suffice under this test. Rather, the activity must be one which is traditionally associated with sovereignty." *Miller v. Indiana Hospital,* 562 F. Supp. 1259, 1278 (W.D. Pa. 1983).

c. ***Flagg Brothers v. Brooks* and Its Significance on the Issue of State Action in Creditors' Remedies**

Probably the most significant case on the issue of state action in the exercise of creditors' remedies is *Flagg Brothers, Inc. v. Brooks,* 436 U.S. 149, 98 S. Ct. 1729 (1978). In this case Ms. Brooks had stored her family's household possessions in the warehouse of Flagg Brothers, Inc. She and Flagg Brothers disputed the amount of the storage charges. Finally, Flagg Brothers threatened to satisfy its claim by selling the furniture under the authority of Article 7 of the Uniform Commercial Code. U.C.C. § 7–209(1) gives a warehouseman a "lien * * * on the goods * * * in his possession for charges for storage * * *." This lien "may be enforced by public or private sale of the goods * * * at any time or place and on any terms which are commercially reasonable, after notifying all persons known to claim an interest in the goods." U.C.C. § 7–210(1). Ms. Brooks sought to enjoin the sale and recover damages by bringing suit under 42 U.S.C.A. § 1983, arguing that the sale would violate the due process and equal protection clauses of the Fourteenth Amendment. The question presented to the Court was whether a sale by a warehouseman pursuant to U.C.C. § 7–210 is attributable to the state so as to constitute state action. Writing for the majority, Justice Rehnquist answered clearly and flatly, "no."

No state official is involved in a U.C.C. § 7–210 sale. Therefore, Ms. Brooks argued for state action on the basis of the public function and nexus rubrics. The argument for public function was this: "[T]he resolution of private disputes is a traditional function of civil government, and * * * the State in § 7–210 has delegated this function to Flagg Brothers." 436 U.S. at 157, 98 S. Ct. at 1734. Rehnquist's response indicates that this reading of the public function doctrine is too broad. The doctrine applies only when the power delegated to a private actor is a power that traditionally has been reserved *exclusively* to the government. The doctrine is thus inapplicable to this case because the settling of disputes between creditors and debtors has never been an exclusive function of government. Rehnquist's sweeping conclusion is that the "entire field of activity" involving commercial liens and other creditors' remedies is beyond the scope of the public function rubric of state action. *Id.* at 162, 98 S. Ct. at 1736.

Ms. Brooks also argued for state action under the nexus test by arguing that the state had authorized and encouraged the challenged activity of the warehouseman. She relied principally on the enactment of U.C.C. § 7–210 by the state, which statute not only recognizes but also regulates in some detail the incidents of a warehouseman's sale. Rehnquist rejected this argument almost summarily because the state by enacting the law has not *compelled* the warehouseman's sale of Ms. Brooks' goods. The state may have made the remedy possible, but choosing to pursue it was a purely private decision which thus did not implicate the state.

With respect to creditors' remedies, state regulation is seldom more extensive than that associated with a warehouseman's lien; and in no case is a creditor forced or any more encouraged to pursue an authorized remedy. *Flagg Brothers* therefore suggests the general inapplicability of the nexus rubric of state action to the whole range of creditors' remedies. But see Note, *Creditors' Remedies as State Action,* 89 Yale L. J. 538 (1980). There will be exceptions, of course. See, e.g., *Goichman v. Rheuban Motors, Inc.,* 682 F.2d 1320 (9th Cir. 1982); *Stypmann v. City and County of San Francisco,* 557 F.2d 1338 (9th Cir. 1977) (there is sufficiently close nexus between state and conduct of garage keeper who asserted lien on vehicle towed and stored at direction of police enforcing traffic laws). The symbiotic relationship test is generally inapplicable, too, because in the ordinary case there surely is not an inextricable interdependence in the overall relationship between a creditor and the state.

The bottom line may well be that, ordinarily, the exercise of a creditors' remedy involves state action only if a government officer participates by performing a significant role in her official capacity. Consequently, a great many creditors' remedies are not limited by the due process requirements of the Fourteenth Amendment. This is most certainly true of special rights of creditors under state law such as a wage assignment, a bank's right of setoff (see supra Chapter IX.B.), the artisan's lien (see supra Chapter IX.C.), the rights of possession and sale by an Article 9 secured party (see U.C.C. §§ 9–503 & 9–504), and a real estate mortgagee's power of nonjudicial sale. Indeed, some lower court had held even before *Flagg Brothers* that the Fourteenth Amendment did not protect a debtor against these remedies. See, e.g., *Parks v. Mr. Ford,* 556 F.2d 132 (3d Cir. 1977) (artisan's right to retain goods); *Adams v. Southern Cal. First Nat. Bank,* 492 F.2d 324 (9th Cir. 1973), cert. denied, 419 U.S. 1006, 95 S. Ct. 325 (1974) (secured party's right to repossess collateral under U.C.C. § 9–503); *Donahoo v. Household Fin. Corp.,* 472 F. Supp. 353 (E.D. Mich. 1979) (wage assignment); *Cramer v. Metropolitan Sav. and Loan Ass'n,* 401 Mich. 252, 258 N.W.2d 20 (1977), cert. denied, 436 U.S. 958, 98 S. Ct. 3072 (1978) (nonjudicial mortgage foreclosure); *North Carolina Nat. Bank v. Burnette,* 297 N.C. 524, 256 S.E.2d 388 (1979) (sale of collateral by secured party); *Kruger v. Wells Fargo Bank,* 11 Cal. 3d 352, 521 P.2d 441, 113 Cal. Rptr. 449 (1974) (bank's right of set-off); *Garfinkle v. Superior Court,* 21 Cal. 3d 268, 578 P.2d 925, 146 Cal. Rptr. 208 (1978), appeal dismissed, 439 U.S. 949, 99 S. Ct. 343 (1978), reh'g denied, 439 U.S. 1104, 99 S. Ct. 886 (1979) (power of sale in deed of trust).

2. SIGNIFICANT TAKING

A debtor is not entitled to due process protection against a creditors' remedy simply because the remedy involves state action. The Fourteenth Amendment applies only when the state is involved in a *significant* taking of property, which means an interest encompassed by the Fourteenth Amendment's protection of property. Although "the range of interests protected by procedural due process is not infinite," *Board of Regents v. Roth,* 408 U.S. 564, 570, 92 S. Ct. 2701, 2705 (1972), the range is nevertheless wide.

a.   **Length of Deprivation Immaterial**
Obviously, the taking is significant when the state through execution process sells a debtor's property in satisfaction of a judgment against her. Yet, a taking cognizable under the Fourteenth Amendment is not limited to cases in which the debtor's rights in property are extinguished. The Fourteenth Amendment also protects against the interim seizure of personal property through a provisional, prejudgment remedy such as replevin, attachment or garnishment.

For example, in *Sniadach v. Family Fin. Corp.,* 395 U.S. 337, 89 S. Ct. 1820 (1969), the debtor complained about the lack of due process in the prejudgment garnishment of her bank account. The seizure did not finally deprive the debtor of her money. It only impounded the account in the event the plaintiff won judgment in the main action on the debt. If the defendant prevailed, the account was released so that the garnishment may have effected only a temporary deprivation. In the case *Fuentes v. Shevin,* 407 U.S. 67, 92 S. Ct. 1983 (1972), the replevin of a debtor's household goods similarly effected only a provisional, possibly temporary, taking. Nevertheless, in both cases the Court held that the takings were encompassed within the Fourteenth Amendment's protection. The rule is that even "a temporary, nonfinal deprivation of property is nonetheless a 'deprivation' in the terms of the Fourteenth Amendment, * * * which draws no bright lines around three-day, 10–day or 50–day deprivations of property. * * * [T]he length and consequent severity of a deprivation * * * is not decisive of the basic right to [due process] of some kind." Id. at 85–86, 92 S. Ct. at 1996–97.

b.   **Right to Recover Possession by Posting Bond Immaterial**
In *Sniadach* and *Fuentes,* the Court also concluded that, in determining if there has been a taking protected by due process, it is irrelevant that the debtor could regain possession of property seized through a provisional creditors' remedy by posting a forthcoming or discharging bond which guarantees the debtor's performance of an adverse judgment. "When officials * * * seize one piece of property from a person's possession and then agree to return it if he surrenders another, they deprive him of property whether or not he has the funds, the knowledge and the time needed to take advantage of the recovery provision." *Fuentes v. Shevin,* 407 U.S. at 85, 92 S. Ct. at 1997.

c.   **Lack of Full Title Immaterial**
Also irrelevant in deciding if there has been a taking in terms of the Fourteenth Amendment is the debtor's lack of full legal title to the property. In *Fuentes,* the creditor had retained title to the goods which it seized through replevin. In Uniform Commercial Code terminology, the creditor had an Article 9 security interest in the goods. No matter. "The Fourteenth Amendment's protection of 'property' * * * has never been interpreted to safeguard only the rights of undisputed ownership." Id. at 86, 92 S. Ct. at 1997. See also *Federal Deposit Ins. Corp. v. Morrison,* 747 F.2d 610 (11th Cir. 1984), cert. denied, 474 U.S. 1019, 106 S. Ct. 568 (1985). What mattered in *Fuentes* was that, notwithstanding the creditor's interest in the property, the debtor had ac-

quired the interest in continued posesssion and use of the goods, and this interest was sufficiently significant to warrant due process protection.

d. Nature of Property Immaterial

The *Sniadach* case involved a taking of wages, "a specialized type of property presenting distinct problems in our economic system." *Sniadach v. Family Fin. Corp.*, 395 U.S. 337, 340, 89 S. Ct. 1820, 1822 (1969). A taking of wages "may impose tremendous hardship on wage earnings with families to support," id. at 340, 89 S. Ct. at 1822, and "may as a practical matter drive a wage-earning family to the wall." Id. at 341–42, 89 S. Ct. at 1822–23. Nevertheless, in determining whether there has been a taking of property encompassed by the Fourteenth Amendment, the Court has made clear that it will not consider the nature of the property or the status of the debtor. Thus, a consumer debtor is entitled to due process when "nothing more than an assortment of household goods"—which are not "absolute necessities of life"—are replevied by a secured party. "The Fourteenth Amendment speaks of 'property' generally. And under our free enterprise system, an individual's choices in the marketplace are respected however unwise they may seem to someone else. It is not the business of a court adjudicating due process rights to make its own critical evaluation of those choices and protect only the ones that, by its own lights, are 'necessary.'" *Fuentes v. Shevin*, 407 U.S. 67, 88, 90, 92 S. Ct. 1983, 1998, 1999 (1972).

Similarly, due process must accompany a garnishment of property even though the target is the bank account of a corporation rather than the income or other property of a consumer. "It may be that consumers deprived of household appliances will more likely suffer irreparably than corporations deprived of bank accounts, but the probability of irreparable injury in the latter case is sufficiently great that some procedures are necessary to guard against the risk of initial error. We are no more inclined now than we have been in the past to distinguish among different kinds of property in applying the Due Process Clause." *North Georgia Finishing, Inc. v. Di-Chem, Inc.*, 419 U.S. 601, 608, 95 S. Ct. 719, 723 (1975).

e. Restriction on Free Alienability May Not Be Protected Taking

Although *Sniadach* and *Fuentes* establish that the Fourteenth Amendment generously shields a wide range of property interests as well as property ownership, not every interim seizure of a debtor's property results in a taking that merits due process protection. Consider, for instance, the case in which real estate is subjected to a construction lien. See Chapter IX.D, supra. The effect is to restrict the debtor's ability to alienate the property because purchasers would take subject to the lien. Nevertheless, this restriction on free alienability does not amount to a constitutionally protected deprivation of property. In theory, the debtor retains the right to sell the property. Moreover, the lien does not deprive the debtor of the rights of possession and use. *Spielman-Fond, Inc. v. Hanson's Inc.*, 379 F. Supp. 997 (D. Ariz. 1973), aff'd mem., 417 U.S. 901, 94 S. Ct. 2596 (1974); *South Central Dist. of Pentecostal Church of God of America, Inc. v. Bruce-Rogers Co.*, 269 Ark. 130, 599 S.W.2d 702 (1980);

Home Building Corp. v. Ventura Corp., 568 S.W.2d 769 (Mo. 1978). The same is true whenever real estate is seized pursuant to a prejudgment attachment. *Matter of Northwest Homes of Chehalis, Inc.,* 526 F.2d 505 (9th Cir. 1975), cert. denied, 425 U.S. 907, 96 S. Ct. 1501 (1976). There are a few cases to the contrary, see, e.g., *Connolly Development, Inc. v. Superior Court,* 17 Cal. 3d 803, 132 Cal. Rptr. 477, 553 P.2d 637 (1976), appeal dismissed, 429 U.S. 1056, 97 S. Ct. 778 (1977); and the recent trend among courts is to decide that the filing of a lis pendens, which like a construction lien or attachment of realty only restricts the free alienability of land, involves a significant taking of property which is protected by the Fourteenth Amendment. *Chrysler Corp. v. Fedders Corp.,* 670 F.2d 1316 (3d Cir. 1982); *Williams v. Bartlett,* 189 Conn. 471, 457 A.2d 290 (1983); *Hercules Chemical Co., Inc. v. VCI, Inc.,* 118 Misc.2d 814, 462 N.Y.S.2d 129 (1983); cf. *Lewis Service Center, Inc. v. Mack Financial Corp.,* 696 F.2d 66 (8th Cir. 1982) (restriction on alienation of personalty caused by temporary restraining order is a deprivation entitled to due process protection); but compare *United Sav. & Loan Ass'n v. Scruggs,* 181 N.J. Super. 52, 436 A.2d 559 (1981) (no taking by filing of lis pendens if property subject to pre-existing lien of creditor).

B. MINIMUM DUE PROCESS WITH RESPECT TO PREJUDGMENT REMEDIES

After deciding that the Fourteenth Amendment protects a debtor's rights against a creditor's remedy, the next issue is whether the remedy provides the procedural safeguards required by due process. The question, in other words, is what process is due.

There is no certain set of procedures that must be followed whenever the Fourteenth Amendment applies. The necessary procedural safeguards depend on the nature of the case and also on a balancing of the parties' interests and the interests of the government or the public generally. See, e.g., *Cleveland Board of Education v. Loudermill,* 470 U.S. 532, 105 S.Ct. 1487 (1985). In the area of prejudgment creditors' remedies, however, the following general framework seems to emerge from a huge number of lower court cases interpreting the major Supreme Court precedents, which are *Sniadach v. Family Finance Corp.,* 395 U.S. 337, 89 S. Ct. 1820 (1969); *Fuentes v. Shevin,* 407 U.S. 67, 92 S. Ct. 1983 (1972); *Mitchell v. W.T. Grant Co.,* 416 U.S. 600, 94 S. Ct. 1895 (1974); and *North Georgia Finishing, Inc. v. Di-Chem, Inc.,* 419 U.S. 601, 95 S. Ct. 719 (1975).

1. GENERAL RULE OF PRESEIZURE NOTICE AND HEARING

"For more than a century the central meaning of procedural due process has been clear: 'Parties whose rights are to be affected are entitled to be heard; and in order that they may enjoy that right they must be notified.'" *Fuentes v. Shevin,* 407 U.S. 67, 80, 92 S. Ct. 1983, 1994 (1972). Thus, the most basic elements, i.e., the "essential requirements," of due process are notice and an opportunity to respond at "some kind of hearing." *Cleveland Board of Education v. Loudermill,* 470 U.S. 532, 105 S.Ct. 1487 (1985). The most meaningful time for a hearing, of course, is before the deprivation. Therefore, consistent with the decisions in *Snia-*

dach and *Fuentes,* lower courts have established as a general rule that a seizure of a debtor's property through a creditor's exercise of a prejudgment remedy must be preceded by notice to the debtor of the impending seizure and an opportunity for the debtor to be heard, before the seizure, in opposition to it.

2. EXCEPTION WHEN THERE ARE OVERRIDING CREDITOR INTERESTS

In *Mitchell v. W.T. Grant Co.,* 416 U.S. 600, 94 S. Ct. 1895 (1974), a creditor with a lien on goods it had sold to the debtor sued in Louisiana to collect the purchase price of the property. At the beginning of the action, the creditor invoked the remedy of sequestration, a form of attachment. In asking for the issuance of a writ of sequestration, the creditor reported reason to believe that the debtor would dispose of the goods during the pendency of the debt action. A writ was issued ex parte directing the sheriff to seize the goods pendente lite as security for the judgment the creditor expected to win in the main action on the debt. Relying on *Sniadach* and *Fuentes,* the debtor argued that the sequestration procedure violated the Fourteenth Amendment inasmuch as there was no provision for preseizure notice and hearing. The Supreme Court rejected this argument.

The Court in *Mitchell* held that, when a creditor has a preexisting interest of her own in the property to be seized and the value of her interest is threatened if the debtor is allowed to continue in possession, the property can constitutionally be seized without prior notice and hearing so long as other procedural safeguards adequately protect the interests of the debtor by adequately guarding against an erroneous or arbitrary seizure. Ex parte seizure is thus approved on two conditions:

- An analysis of the realities of the circumstances affecting the property, and a balancing of the debtor's and creditor's interests, must support the conclusion that the creditor is entitled to "somewhat more protection" than she would receive under a procedural scheme requiring preseizure notice and hearing; and

- The procedures nevertheless cannot discount the importance of the debtor's interest and must effect a "constitutional accommodation" of the conflicting interests of both parties.

a. When Is a Creditor Entitled to "Somewhat More Protection"?

1) Preexisting Interest Plus Overt Threat to Collateral
The *Mitchell* case itself is authority that preseizure notice and hearing are not necessary when *the creditor has a preexisting interest in the property to be seized and there are facts suggesting that the debtor might dispose of or harm the property.*

2) Threat to General Assets
In the case *North Georgia Finishing, Inc. v. Di-Chem, Inc.,* 419 U.S. 601, 95 S. Ct. 719 (1975), the Court declared unconstitutional Georgia's prejudgment garnishment statute that had been used to freeze ex parte a corporation's bank account. The Court suggested that the statute, which did not provide preseizure notice and hearing, would have passed muster under the Fourteenth Amendment if the statute had provided other procedural

safeguards that adequately accommodated the debtor's interests along with the creditor's. In *North Georgia,* however, the creditor did not have a pre-existing interest in the property that was taken. It was a general, un-secured creditor which would be forced to rely on the debtor's assets gen-erally in satisfaction of a judgment. The creditor did contend in its application for the writ of garnishment that the bank account would be lost unless it was seized. The strong implication is that prior notice and hearing are not required of a prejudgment remedy even though the credi-tor is unsecured if *actions of the debtor threaten to diminish the general pool of assets to which the creditor must look for satisfaction of the judg-ment she expects to win.* Lower courts routinely hold that attachment statutes and other prejudgment remedies are not unconstitutional for fail-ing to provide prior notice and hearing in cases where the remedy issued because of a substantiated belief that the debtor might destroy, injure, or dispose of property that could be used to satisfy a creditor's judgment. See, e.g., *Springdale Farms, Inc. v. McIlroy Bank & Trust,* 281 Ark. 371, 663 S.W.2d 936 (1984) (attachment); *First Nat. Bank v. Southwest Yacht & Marine Supply Corp.,* 101 N.M. 431, 684 P.2d 517 (1984). There is authori-ty that prior notice and hearing cannot be excused even when the debtor threatens to dispose of her assets unless her plan is coupled with an in-tent to defraud creditors or otherwise to frustrate satisfaction of their claims. Compare *International State Bank v. Gamer,* 281 N.W.2d 855 (Minn. 1979) and *M.W. Ettinger, Inc. v. Anderson,* 360 N.W.2d 394 (Minn. App. 1985) with *Olson v. Ische,* 330 N.W.2d 710 (Minn. 1983).

3)   Preexisting Interest in Absence of Overt Threat to Collateral
A hard case that the courts have not resolved is whether preseizure notice and hearing are required whenever *the creditor has a preexisting interest in the property to be seized but there is no threat that the debtor will harm or dispose of the property.* In evaluating the realities and balancing the interests of the parties in *Mitchell,* the Court observed: "Wholly aside from whether the buyer, with possession and power over the property, will destroy or make away with the goods, the buyer in possession of consumer goods will undeniably put the property to its intended use, and the resale value of the merchandise will steadily decline as it is used over a period of time. * * * Clearly, if [the debtor's] payments cease and possession and use by the buyer continue, the seller's interest in the property as se-curity is steadily and irretrievably eroded until the time at which the full hearing is held." Thus, depreciation of the creditor's collateral is a reality to be considered, but whether this reality is sufficient in itself to dispense with preseizure notice and hearing has not been directly decided.

The Court in *Mitchell* suggests, however, that a creditor is entitled to somewhat more protection solely for the reason that she has a preexisting interest in the property seized. *Fuentes* was a case in which the creditor had a security interest in property which was replevied. There was no al-legation of threatened injury or disposition. The Court in *Fuentes* did de-clare the replevin statute unconstitutional because it did not provide for preseizure notice and hearing. Yet, in *Mitchell* the Court explained the *Fuentes* result in terms of the inadequacy of the replevin statute's other procedural safeguards compared to those of the sequestration statute approved in *Mitchell*. The clear inference is the reasoning of *Fuentes* is overruled and that prior notice and hearing are not required in a case such as *Fuentes*. The only explanation in terms of the *Mitchell* approach is that the existence of a preexisting interest in property to be seized is a sufficient reality in itself to entitle the creditor to somewhat more protection.

4) Debtor's Nonresidency
Many states provide for ex parte attachment solely on the basis that *the debtor is a nonresident*. Is the debtor's nonresidency sufficient reason in itself to excuse prior notice and hearing? Probably not. Indeed, harm or risk to the local property is perhaps lessened for the very reason that the debtor lives elsewhere.

A different question is whether allowing attachment solely on the basis of the debtor's nonresidency violates the privileges and immunities clause of the Constitution. The Second Circuit thinks not. *ITC Entertainment, Ltd. v. Nelson Film Partners,* 714 F.2d 217 (2d Cir. 1983) (upholding New York statute that authorizes attachment against resident debtor only upon a showing that she is attempting fraudulently to conceal or dispose of her assets and that authorizes attachment against nonresident without such a showing).

5) Government Acting to Protect Public Good
The easiest case for excusing preseizure notice and hearing involves a government pursuing some remedy that effects a seizure of an individual's property in order to protect the public's interests. *Calero-Toledo v. Pearson Yacht Leasing Co.,* 416 U.S. 663, 94 S. Ct. 2080 (1974) (upholding a Puerto Rican law providing for ex parte seizure and forfeiture of property used in connection with the violation of drug laws); *Fuentes v. Shevin,* 407 U.S. 67, 82, 92 S. Ct. 1983, 1995 (1972) (no prior hearing required in extraordinary circumstances as when seizure is directly necessary to secure an important governmental or general public interest) (dictum); *Goichman v. Rheuban Motors, Inc.,* 682 F.2d 1320 (9th Cir. 1982) (state towing vehicles in enforcement of traffic laws); *State v. Turner,* 110 Mich. App. 228, 312 N.W.2d 418 (1981) (state need not give prior notice and hearing when seeking restraining order to prevent a debtor from disposing of her property pending a hearing to determine if she has property which ought to be subjected to state's claim against her).

b. **What Procedures Effect a "Constitutional Accommodation" of Interests?**
The Court suggests in *Mitchell* and *North Georgia* that a prejudgment remedy constitutionally accommodates the interests of both the debtor and creditor if it provides the following procedural safeguards:

- The application for the writ must make a verified showing by petition or affidavit of "specific facts" the nature of the creditor's claim, its amounts, and the grounds relied on for the issuance of the writ. The affidavit must go "beyond mere conclusory allegations and clearly [set] out the facts entitling the creditor to [the remedy]," and it must be made by one having personal knowledge of the facts.

- "[T]he requisite showing must be made to a judge, and judicial authorization obtained."

- The creditor must post a bond to guarantee the debtor against damage or expense in the event the exercise of the remedy is shown to be mistaken or improvident.

- The debtor may regain possession of the property by putting up her own bond to protect the seller.

- "[T]he debtor may immediately have a full hearing on the matter of possession following the execution of the writ, thus cutting to a bare minimum the time of creditor or court-supervised possession."

- At the post-seizure hearing the burden is on the creditor either to prove the grounds upon which the writ is issued or, at least, to demonstrate probable cause for the writ.

- "[S]hould the writ be dissolved there are 'damages for the wrongful issuance of a writ' and for attorney's fees 'whether the writ is dissolved on motion or after trial on the merits.'"

The Supreme Court has not held that each of the procedural safeguards in the form reported here must be present in order to effect a constitutional accommodation of both parties' interests in a case where prior notice and hearing are excused. Indeed, in *Calero-Toledo v. Pearson Yacht Leasing Co.,* 416 U.S. 663, 94 S. Ct. 2080 (1974), a case decided the same day as *Mitchell,* the Court upheld a forfeiture law that provided fewer procedural safeguards than the sequestration statute approved in *Mitchell.* The *Calero-Toledo* case is very exceptional, however, because the seizure was effected by a government pursuing the important public interest of enforcing drug laws. Remember that deciding what process is due depends on a balancing of interests, and there is an inverse relationship between the significance of the creditor's interests and the extent and nature of procedural safeguards provided the debtor. The interests of the person seeking to take property of an individual weigh very heavily in the balance when the taker is a government acting to protect the public good. In addition to *Calero-Toledo,* see, e.g., *Goichman v. Rheuban Motors, Inc.,* 682 F.2d 1320 (9th Cir. 1982) (post-seizure hearing may be delayed a bit when state tows vehicles in enforcement of traffic laws); *State v. Turner,* 110 Mich. App. 228, 312 N.W.2d 418 (1981) (full panoply of *Mitchell* safeguards not necessary when state seeks restraining order to prevent a debtor from disposing of her property pending a hearing to determine if she has property which ought to be subjected to state's claim against her).

In judging the constitutional validity of creditors' remedies in cases between private parties, lower courts tend to look for all of the procedural safeguards mentioned in *Mitchell* and *North Georgia* as if the Supreme Court in those two cases had prescribed a detailed checklist of necessary procedures that must be satisfied in every respect. See, e.g., *Springdale Farms, Inc. v. McIlroy Bank & Trust,* 281 Ark. 371, 663 S.W.2d 936 (1984) (upholding attachment statute); *First Nat. Bank v. Southwest Yacht & Marine Supply Corp.,* 101 N.M. 431, 684 P.2d 517 (1984) (upholding replevin statute); *Peebles v. Clement,* 63 Ohio St. 2d 314, 408 N.E.2d 689 (1980) (declaring attachment statute unconstitutional); *General Electric Credit Corp. v. Hatch,* 3 Ohio App. 3d 80, 443 N.E.2d 1054 (1982) (replevin statute unconstitutional). Occasionally, in judging the constitutional validity of a prejudgment remedy, a court will add judicially to the law's black letter so that the local law provides all of the procedural safeguards mentioned in *Mitchell* and *North Georgia.* The Supreme Court has invited this sort of creative interpretation. *Carey v. Sugar,* 425 U.S. 73, 96 S. Ct. 1208 (1976) (directing federal district court to abstain from declaring attachment statute in violation of due process clause unless state courts have an opportunity to construe law so as to remove any constitutional problems).

In a rare case, a court will find that a local procedural scheme is constitutional even though it fails to match exactly the *Mitchell* safeguards. For instance, several courts have concluded that due process a la *Mitchell* does not require a judge to authorize a remedy such as attachment or replevin so long as the decision is made by a qualified official with the power to exercise some discretion in the matter. See, e.g., *Jonnett v. Dollar Sav. Bank,* 530 F.2d 1123, 1130 n.15 (3d Cir. 1976); *Springdale Farms, Inc. v. McIlroy Bank & Trust,* 281 Ark. 371, 663 S.W.2d 936 (1984); but see, e.g., *Guzman v. Western State Bank,* 516 F.2d 125, 131 (8th Cir. 1975); *Peebles v. Clement,* 63 Ohio St. 2d 314, 408 N.E.2d 689 (1980); see also *Lewis Service Center, Inc. v. Mack Financial Corp.,* 696 F.2d 66 (8th Cir. 1982) (TRO procedure not unconstitutional solely because plaintiff not required to post a bond inasmuch as defendant remains in possession of property); *Rocky B. Fisheries, Inc. v. North Bend Fabrication & Mach., Inc.,* 66 Or. App. 625, 676 P.2d 319 (1984), review denied, 297 Or. 82, 679 P.2d 1367 (1984), app. denied, 469 U.S. 802, 105 S. Ct. 57 (1984) (state maritime lien not unconstitutional in failing to provide, as did sequestration statute in *Mitchell,* written post-seizure notice because law presumes that ship captain will notify the ship owner).

3. HARD CASE: CREDITOR WITH IMPORTANT INTERESTS BUT IMPACT OF SEIZURE ON DEBTOR SEVERE

Due process ordinarily requires notice and hearing before the exercise of a prejudgment creditors' remedy. Prior notice and hearing are not necessary, however, and other procedural safeguards such as those approved in *Mitchell* will suffice, if the creditor's interests in immediate possession of the property override the debtor's interest in continued possession. Balancing these conflicting interests always is difficult, especially when the creditor's interests in immediate possession are pressing but taking the property from the debtor would cause a severe impact on the debtor. Suppose, for example, that the creditor has a security interest in the mobile home in which debtor resides. The debtor had defaulted in loan payments to the creditor. The creditor thus seeks to replevy the home from the debtor. Is the debtor entitled to prior notice and hearing? There is a good argument that the reasoning of *Mitchell* excuses preseizure notice and hearing when the creditor has a preexisting interest in the property to be taken. On the other hand, the mobile home is the debtor's home. She has no other residence. Taking it from her actually may force her onto the streets. Thus, more than in the usual case, there is greater need for procedural safeguards to protect against an arbitrary and erroneous seizure of the debtor's property. In this sort of case, the balancing of interests probably favors the debtor so that due process is satisfied with nothing less than notice and hearing before the property is taken. See generally *Sniadach v. Family Finance Corp.,* 395 U.S. 337, 89 S. Ct. 1820 (1969) (ex parte garnishment of wages unconstitutional because it would impose tremendous hardship on debtor and family and, as a practical matter, "drive [them] to the wall"); *Guzman v. Western State Bank,* 516 F.2d 125 (8th Cir. 1975) (attachment by secured party of debtor's mobile home was unconstitutional in absence of preseizure notice and hearing).

Yet, the debtor's hands must be clean in order to merit this extraordinary protection. Despite the importance to her and her livelihood of the property to be seized, the debtor probably is not entitled to prior notice and hearing if she deliberately threatens harm to the collateral for the purpose of frustrating satisfaction of the creditor's claim. See generally *International State Bank v. Gamer,* 281 N.W.2d 855 (Minn. 1979) (ex parte attachment of income-producing property constitutional when debtor threatens conduct that would defeat security interest in the property).

C. MINIMUM DUE PROCESS WITH RESPECT TO POSTJUDGMENT REMEDIES

In the case *Endicott-Johnson Corp. v. Encyclopedia Press, Inc.,* 266 U.S. 285, 45 S. Ct. 61 (1924), the Court considered what protection the Fourteenth Amendment affords a debtor against the seizure of her property in satisfaction of a judgment against her. The Court decided that due process does

> not require that a defendant who has been granted an opportunity to be heard and has had his day in court, should, after a judgment has been rendered against him, have a further notice and hearing before supplemental proceedings are taken to reach his property in satisfaction of the judgment. Thus, in the absence of a statutory requirement, it is not essential that he be given notice before the issuance of an execution against his tangible property; after the rendition of the judgment he must take "notice of what will follow," no further notice being "necessary to advance justice."

> There is no more reason why the judgment debtor should be entitled to notice before the issue of an execution provided by statute as supplemental process to im-

pound, in satisfaction of the judgment, choses in action due to him which cannot be reached by an ordinary execution.

Id. at 288, 45 S. Ct. at 63.

Many courts have considered the continuing vitality of *Endicott* in light of *Sniadach* and its progeny. The majority of them have concluded that *Endicott* is no longer the final word on the due process rights of judgment debtors. To determine what procedural safeguards are required of postjudgment remedies, the courts balance the conflicting interests of the parties, as well as governmental interests. There is no doubt that winning judgment on the debt strengthens the interests of the creditor and correspondingly weakens the interests of the debtor. As a result, the courts all agree that, generally, a debtor is not entitled to a hearing prior to seizure of her property through execution and postjudgment garnishment. See, e.g., *Brown v. Liberty Loan Corp.,* 539 F.2d 1355 (5th Cir. 1976), cert. denied, 430 U.S. 949, 97 S. Ct. 1588 (1977); *Huggins v. Deinhard,* 134 Ariz. 98, 654 P.2d 32 (App. 1982); but compare *Landrigan v. McElroy,* 457 A.2d 1056 (R.I. 1983) (a postjudgment body execution of the debtor herself unconstitutional in absence of prior notice and hearing on debtor's ability to pay the judgment).

Yet, a growing number of courts have decided that, when the taking involves possibly exempt property, the debtor is minimally entitled to simultaneous notice of the seizure, which notice should alert the debtor to her exemptions and to the procedure for protecting them, and also to an immediate post-seizure hearing a la *Mitchell* at which the debtor can claim her exemptions out of property that has been seized. The leading case is *Finberg v. Sullivan,* 634 F.2d 50 (3d Cir. 1980) (involved garnishment of income required for the basic expenditures of living); see also *Clay v. Edward J. Fisher, Jr., M.D., Inc.,* 584 F. Supp. 730 (S.D. Ohio 1984); *Dionne v. Bouley,* 583 F. Supp. 307 (D. R.I. 1984), aff'd as modified, 757 F.2d 1344 (1st Cir. 1985); *Harris v. Bailey,* 574 F. Supp. 966 (W.D. Va. 1983); *Deary v. Guardian Loan Co., Inc.,* 534 F. Supp. 1178 (S.D. N.Y. 1982); *Warren v. Delaney,* 98 A.D.2d 799, 469 N.Y.S.2d 975 (1983); but see *Floyd v. Bowen,* 833 F.2d 529 (5th Cir. 1987), reh. denied, 838 F.2d 1214 (1988); *Reigh v. Schleigh,* 784 F.2d 1191 (4th Cir.1986) (slams *Finberg*), cert. denied, 479 U.S. 847, 107 S. Ct. 167 (1986), vacating, 595 F. Supp. 1535 (D. Md. 1984); *Brown v. Liberty Loan Corp.,* 539 F.2d 1355 (5th Cir. 1976), cert. denied, 430 U.S. 949, 97 S. Ct. 1588 (1977).

Of course, whether the remedy is pre- or postjudgment, due process does not establish a rigid set of procedural requirements. In deciding what the Fourteenth Amendment demands of a postjudgment remedy, a court is free to consider variable factors such as the nature of the property to be seized, the significance of the creditor's interests, the type of remedy being pursued, and the nature of the deprivation. See generally, e.g., *Duranceau v. Wallace,* 743 F.2d 709 (9th Cir. 1984) (state as assignee of right to past-due child support payments garnishing portion of debtor-spouse's tort recovery); *Gedeon v. Gedeon,* 630 P.2d 579 (Colo. 1981) (upholding summary process for recording foreign judgment); *Peterson v. Montana Bank,* ___ Mont. ___, 687 P.2d 673 (1984) (debtor entitled to adequate notice prior to execution sale); *Northwest South Dakota Prod. Cr. Ass'n v. Dale,* 361 N.W.2d 275 (S.D. 1985) (threats to destroy property).

Also, the Fourteenth Amendment does not require any safeguards whatsoever in the pursuit of a postjudgment remedy if the taking involves a property interest not encompassed by the due process clause. *Casa del Rey v. Hart,* 31 Wash. App. 532, 643 P.2d 900 (1982) (levy of execution on real property does not effect a significant taking of property). Undoubtedly, however, whenever an execution lien on any kind of property is enforced through a sale of the property that will extinguish the debtor's rights, adequate prior notice of the sale is required. *Peterson v. Montana Bank,* ___ Mont. ___, 687 P.2d 673 (Mont. 1984). Regarding the adequacy of notice of a forced sale of property that will extinguish a person's rights in property, see generally *Mennonite Board of Missions v. Adams,* 462 U.S. 791, 103 S. Ct. 2706 (1983) (notice of sale of property for nonpayment of taxes by publication and posting fails to satisfy due process); *Cate v. Archon Oil Co.,* 695 P.2d 1352 (Okl. 1985) (due process violated where property was sold at execution upon notification by publication and public posting of notice); *Hornbuckle v. Burns,* 69 Or. App. 272, 686 P.2d 418 (1984) (due process does not require that debtors be notified of right to redeem property sold under execution process); *Miebach v. Colasurdo,* 35 Wash. App. 803, 670 P.2d 276 (1983), rev'd on other grounds, 102 Wash. 2d 170, 685 P.2d 1074 (1984) (posting of notice of sheriff's sale on door of debtor's residence satisfied due process in light of evidence that debtor read the notice and therefore had actual notice).

D. WAIVER OF DUE PROCESS RIGHTS

Even though a creditor pursues a remedy that implicates the state in a significant taking of a debtor's property, the debtor is not entitled to due process protection if she has effectively waived her Fourteenth Amendment rights. *D.H. Overmyer Co. v. Frick,* 405 U.S. 174, 92 S. Ct. 775 (1972) (waiver by express agreement, which case is fully explored in this Black Letter, supra, Chapter I); *United States v. Ford,* 551 F. Supp. 1101 (N.D. Miss. 1982) (implied waiver by conduct). To be effective, however, the waiver must be "voluntarily, intelligently and knowingly made." *Fuentes v. Shevin,* 407 U.S. 67, 92 S. Ct. 1983 (1972); *D.H. Overmyer Co. v. Frick,* 405 U.S. 174, 92 S. Ct. 775 (1972); *County of Ventura v. Tillett,* 133 Cal. App. 3d 105, 183 Cal. Rptr. 741 (1982), cert. denied, 460 U.S. 1051, 103 S. Ct. 1497 (1983); *Cheidem Corp. v. Farmer,* 449 A.2d 1061 (Del. Super. 1982). This means that, at a minimum, the language of waiver must be clear; the debtor must be aware of the significance of the waiver; and the parties must be of equal bargaining strength. A waiver of due process rights in the fine print of an adhesion contract is undoubtedly unenforceable. *Fuentes v. Shevin,* 407 U.S. 67, 92 S. Ct. 1983 (1972); *Rau v. Cavenaugh,* 500 F. Supp. 204 (D. S.D. 1980).

REVIEW QUESTIONS

1. A debtor is entitled to procedural due process under the Fourteenth Amendment when a bank as creditor provisionally seizes the debtor's car through the process of attachment. The debtor is not entitled to due process, however, if the bank exercises its equitable right of setoff against the debtor's checking account. Explain why the debtor would be protected by the Fourteenth Amendment in the case of attachment but not in the case of setoff.

2. Under what theories can the conduct of a private party be characterized as state action for purposes of the Fourteenth Amendment?

3. A debtor is entitled to procedural due process upon the provisional seizure of her car at the commencement of a replevin action against her. There is much authority holding, however, that the debtor would not be entitled to due process upon the attachment of real estate belonging to her at the commencement of an action to enforce a debt against her. Explain why the debtor would be protected by the Fourteenth Amendment in one case but not the other.

4. In the case *Sniadach v. Family Finance Corp.*, the Supreme Court held that notice and hearing must precede the garnishment of a debtor's wages. Five years later, in *Mitchell v. W.T. Grant Co.*, the Court held that prior notice and hearing were not required upon the attachment of a debtor's goods as long as the debtor had an opportunity to respond soon after the seizure. Did *Mitchell* overrule *Sniadach?*

5. When is a contractual waiver of due process rights enforceable?

*

XV

OTHER SOURCES OF DUE PROCESS PROTECTION

Analysis

A. *Fifth Amendment Due Process*
    1. *Federal Action*
    2. *What Process Is Due*
B. *State Constitutional Law*
C. *Contractual Due Process*

The Fourteenth Amendment to the United States Constitution is the most significant source of procedural due process guarantees for debtors. See supra Chapter XIV. There are other sources, however, which are discussed in this chapter. The Fifth Amendment to the Constitution affords a debtor due process when the federal government acts to derpive her of property. State constitutions also are a source of procedural guarantees. The typical state charter contains a due process clause. Finally, the contract between a debtor and creditor can provide the debtor with procedural safeguards that are not required by law.

A. FIFTH AMENDMENT DUE PROCESS

The Fifth and Fourteenth Amendments to the United States Constitution are alike in providing that no person shall be deprived of life, liberty, or property without due process of law. The two due process clauses are different in that the Fourteenth Amendment restrains the states, see supra Chapter XIV.A.1., while the Fifth Amendment limits the federal government and the District of Columbia.

1. FEDERAL ACTION
a. In General: Refer to State Action Rubrics
The Fifth Amendment restricts "only the Federal Government and not private persons." *Public Utilities Com'n v. Pollak,* 343 U.S. 451, 461, 72 S. Ct. 813, 820 (1952). Therefore, in deciding if there has been a violation of the Fifth Amendment due process clause, the first issue is whether the taking involves federal action. "The standards utilized to find federal action * * * [are] identical to those employed to detect 'state action'." *Wenzer v. Consolidated Rail Corp.,* 464 F. Supp. 643, 647 (E. D. Pa. 1979), aff'd without opin., 612 F.2d 576 (3d Cir. 1979); see also *Gerena v. Puerto Rico Legal Services, Inc.,* 697 F.2d 447, 449 (1st Cir. 1983); *Warren v. Government Nat. Mortgage Ass'n,* 611 F.2d 1229, 1232 (8th Cir.1980), cert. denied, 449 U.S. 847, 101 S. Ct. 133 (1980). Regarding the tests for finding state action for purposes of the Fourteenth Amendment, see supra Chapter XIV.A.1. Thus, federal action exists in the exercise of a creditor's remedy whenever a federal officer in her official capacity, or a federal instrumentality, actively participates in some significant way. A taxpayer is therefore entitled to Fifth Amendment due process when IRS officials or other representatives of the United States seize her property in enforcement of a federal tax lien; and a farmer is entitled to the same when the Farmers Home Administration extrajudicially forecloses a security agreement covering personal property or a real estate mortgage. *Johnson v. United States Department of Agriculture,* 734 F.2d 774 (11th Cir. 1984); *Rau v. Cavenaugh,* 500 F. Supp. 204 (D. S.D. 1980); but see *Arcoren v. Peters,* 829 F.2d 671 (8th Cir. 1987) (implying that there is no federal action when the FmHA or other government agency exercises its rights as an Article 9 secured party or otherwise acts in the capacity of a commercial lender pursuant to a security agreement).

Even if a private creditor acts alone in the pursuit of a remedy, her conduct will constitute federal action if there is a symbiotic relationship between the creditor and the United States; there is a close nexus between the remedy and the federal government; or the creditor in pursuing the remedy is exercising a public function. See supra Chapter XIV.A.1.b.

b. Nonjudicial Mortgage Foreclosure
1) Private Lender With Federal Guaranty

    a) Fourteenth Amendment Inapplicable
A recurring issue arising from the intersection of creditors' rights and Fifth Amendment due process is whether federal action exists when a federally guaranteed mortgage is foreclosed nonjudicially by a private creditor. In *Fitzgerald v. Cleland,* 498 F. Supp. 341 (D. Me. 1980), aff'd in part and rev'd in part, 650 F.2d 360 (1st Cir. 1981), mortgagors argued that their due process rights had been violated when a bank foreclosed the mortgage which was guaranteed by the Veterans

Administration. They relied on the Fourteenth Amendment as one source of due process protection. This reliance was misplaced. Non-judicial foreclosure of a real estate mortgage by a private actor is not state action even though the remedy is authorized and regulated by state statute. 498 F. Supp. at 346–48. Accord, *Charmicor v. Deaner,* 572 F.2d 694 (9th Cir. 1978); *Garfinkle v. Superior Court,* 21 Cal.3d 268, 146 Cal. Rptr. 208, 578 P.2d 925 (1978), appeal dismissed, 439 U.S. 949, 99 S. Ct. 343 (1978), reh'g denied, 439 U.S. 1104, 99 S. Ct. 886 (1979); *Cramer v. Metropolitan Sav. & Loan Ass'n,* 401 Mich. 252, 258 N.W.2d 20 (1977), cert. denied, 436 U.S. 958, 98 S. Ct. 3072 (1978); *Federal Nat. Mortgage Ass'n v. Scott,* 548 S.W.2d 545 (Mo. 1977), appeal dismissed, 436 U.S. 924, 98 S.Ct. 2816 (1978); *Edmundson Investment Co. v. Florida Treco, Inc.,* 633 S.W.2d 599 (Tex. Civ. App. 1982); *Kennebec, Inc. v. Bank of the West,* 88 Wash. 2d 718, 565 P.2d 812 (1977); *Dennison v. Jack,* 304 S.E.2d 300 (W. Va. 1983).

b) Fifth Amendment Inapplicable

The mortgagors in *Fitzgerald* also relied on the Fifth Amendment as a source of due process protection. They argued that the Veterans Administration, certainly a federal instrumentality, was involved in the foreclosure because of the many federal regulations to which the bank, as the principal on the VA guaranty, was subject. The court in *Fitzgerald* concluded, however, as have other courts, "that foreclosure by a private lender of a mortgage in a federal mortgage guaranty program does not involve federal action simply because the lender is subject to extensive federal regulation." 498 F. Supp. at 349; accord, *Rank v. Nimmo,* 677 F.2d 692, 702 (9th Cir.1982), cert. denied, 459 U.S. 907, 103 S.Ct. 210 (1982); compare *United States v. Whitney,* 602 F. Supp. 722, 733 n.11 (W.D.N.Y. 1985) (Fifth Amendment implicated when VA participated in denial of debtor's due process rights during judicial foreclosure instigated by private creditor).

2) Fannie Mae or Ginnie Mae as Mortgagee

The Federal National Mortgage Association (FNMA), also known as Fannie Mae, was created and chartered by the federal government for the purpose of maintaining a secondary market for home mortgages. Although FNMA is technically a private corporation whose stock is traded on the New York Stock Exchange, the President of the United States appoints a third of its board of directors, and the Secretary of Housing and Urban Development exercises certain supervisory powers over the corporation. When FNMA acts to foreclose nonjudicially a mortgage it holds, is the mortgagor entitled to Fifth Amendment due process protection? No. The leading case is *Northrip v. Federal Nat. Mortgage Ass'n,* 527 F.2d 23 (6th Cir. 1975). The court treated Fannie Mae as a private actor rather than a federal instrumentality, and refused to attribute its actions to the federal government despite the significant government involvement in, and regulation of, the workings of the corporation. Accord, *Roberts v. Cameron-Brown Co.,* 556 F.2d 356 (5th Cir. 1977); *Federal Nat. Mortgage Ass'n v.*

Scott, 548 S.W.2d 545 (Mo. 1977), appeal dismissed, 436 U.S. 924, 98 S. Ct. 2816 (1978).

The Government National Mortgage Association (GNMA), also known as Ginnie Mae, is a separate private corporation which the federal government created and chartered for the purpose of taking over certain functions formerly carried out by FNMA, including the liquidation of mortgages. Unlike FNMA, however, GNMA is wholly-owned by the federal government, and for all practical purposes is part of the Department of Housing and Urban Development. Nevertheless, in the case *Warren v. Governmental Nat. Mortgage Ass'n,* 611 F.2d 1229 (8th Cir. 1980), cert. denied, 449 U.S. 847, 101 S. Ct. 133 (1980), the court held that the Fifth Amendment did not afford a debtor due process protection when GNMA extrajudicially foreclosed under a deed of trust. Although conceding that, "as a matter of statutory and organizational form * * * GNMA could perhaps be viewed as more 'governmental' than its counterpart FNMA," id. at 1233 n.8, the court decided to treat Ginnie Mae as a private actor in line with the treatment of FNMA in the *Northrip* case. Id. The justification for this treatment was the desire of Congress to disassociate FNMA and GNMA from the federal government. Id.

The court in *Warren* then held that, despite the federal ownership and extensive federal regulation of GNMA, the corporation's extrajudicial foreclosure of a mortgage could not be attributed to the federal government because the nexus or link between the government's supervision of GNMA and the challenged activity was insufficiently close. Heavy governmental regulation of a private actor does not result in attributing all of the actor's conduct to government. " 'The government must be involved *with the activity* that causes the actual injury.' " Id. at 1234 (emphasis in original). There is no significant connection between government and GNMA's foreclosure in this case because "the power of sale clause as contained in the deed of trust is a contractual power having its genesis in the deed of trust itself and as such exists independent of any statute otherwise governing it." Id. at 1233–34. Moreover, regardless of the source of the right to foreclose, GNMA was not performing a delegated public function because "mortgage foreclosures through power of sale agreements such as the one at issue here are not in and of themselves powers of a governmental nature."

The courts in cases such as *Warren* and *Northrip* may be right in deciding that nonjudicial foreclosures by FNMA and GNMA qua private persons are not attributable to the government. The courts clearly are wrong, however, in characterizing FNMA and GNMA as private persons on the basis of the desire of Congress to disassociate the corporations' activities from the federal government. Surely the Constitution does not permit government to legislatively disavow its own conduct for due process purposes. Characterizing a person as a private actor or as a part of government is terribly important, of course, because there can be no question of government action when the government itself engages in the challenged activity. Conduct of governmental officials acting individually, or collectively as an agency or other unit of government, is government action for due process purposes under both the Fifth and Fourteenth Amendments regardless of the source of the right to engage in the conduct and whether or not the challenged activity historically is performed only by the sovereign.

3) United States Acting as Commercial Lender
The cases holding that non-judicial foreclosure by FNMA or GNMA involves no federal action were the foundation of a wider rule recently suggested in *Arcoren v. Peters,* 829 F.2d 671 (8th Cir. 1987). The court in *Arcoren* read those cases broadly, and used them to support the conclusion that federal action is absent when the government acts in the capacity of a commercial lender pursuant to a security agreement. Thus, a debtor is not entitled to due process protection when the Farmers Home Administration (FmHA), as an Article 9 secured party, exercises its rights to repossess and dispose of collateral. This conclusion is unprecedented and unsupported by the cases the court relied on. The FNMA and GNMA cases decided that both organizations are private persons, and that the agencies' conduct in nonjudicially foreclosing on collateral is not attributable to the United States under the public function rubric. Undoubtedly, however, the FmHA is a federal instrumentality, and the court in *Arcoren* does not decide otherwise. In effect, therefore, the court in *Arcoren* turns the public function doctrine inside out by reasoning that conduct by an agency of the United States is not federal action, for purposes of the Fifth Amendment, when the agency exercises a power not traditionally associated with sovereignty, such as the power to repossess collateral pursuant to a security agreement.

c. **National Banks**
A bank is not considered a federal instrumentality for purposes of the Fifth Amendment solely because it is federally chartered. Moreover, a national bank's conduct in pursuing creditors' remedies does not amount to federal action simply because the bank is heavily regulated by a variety of federal agencies. Federal regulation of a private actor triggers Fifth Amendment due process protection only when the challenged conduct and the federal regulation are directly and substantially linked. *Warren v. Governmental Nat. Mortgage Ass'n,* 611 F.2d 1229 (8th Cir.1980), cert. denied, 449 U.S. 847, 101 S. Ct. 133 (1980).

2. **WHAT PROCESS IS DUE**
a. **In General—Usual Balancing Approach**
The approach to deciding what process is due under the Fifth Amendment is no different from that used when the Fourteenth Amendment due process clause applies: The procedures must effect a constitutional accommodation of the interests of the parties and the government in line with the teachings of *Sniadach v. Family Fin. Corp.,* 395 U.S. 337, 89 S.Ct. 1820 (1969), and its prog-

eny. See supra Chapter XIV.B. Accordingly, although notice and hearing prior to a governmental seizure is the preferred practice, the opportunity to be heard can be delayed until soon after the taking when there are overriding creditor or government interests and adequate other procedural safeguards to protect the interests of the debtor. See generally *Calero-Toledo v. Pearson Yacht Leasing Co.,* 416 U.S. 663, 94 S. Ct. 2080 (1974); *Mitchell v. W.T. Grant Co.,* 416 U.S. 600, 94 S. Ct. 1895 (1974).

b. Maritime Attachment

Maritime attachment is a creditors' remedy that is frequently challenged under the Fifth Amendment due process clause. The Federal Rules of Civil Procedure authorize ex parte attachment of a debtor's property with respect to "any admiralty or maritime claim [against a person] * * * if the defendant shall not be found within the district", F.R.C.P. Supplemental Rule B, and also in an *in rem* action against a vessel to enforce "any maritime lien." F.R.C.P. Supplemental Rule C. Levy is effected by federal officers on process issued from federal court. The majority of courts facing the issue have held that maritime attachment under either Rule B or C does not violate Fifth Amendment due process even though there is no prior notice and hearing, *Polar Shipping Ltd. v. Oriental Shipping Corp.,* 680 F.2d 627 (9th Cir. 1982); *Amstar Corp. v. S/S Alexandros T.,* 664 F.2d 904 (4th Cir. 1981); *Merchants Nat. Bank v. Dredge General G.L. Gillespie,* 663 F.2d 1338 (5th Cir. 1981), cert. dismissed, 456 U.S. 966, 102 S.Ct. 2263 (1982); and some courts have gone so far as to say that the Fifth Amendment is satisfied even though the debtor or ship owner is not afforded the full panoply of other procedural safeguards outlined by the Supreme Court in *Mitchell. Trans-Asiatic Oil Ltd. v. Apex Oil Co.,* 743 F.2d 956 (1st Cir. 1984); *Schiffahrtsgesellschaft v. A. Bottacchi,* 732 F.2d 1543 (11th Cir. 1984), on reh'g, 773 F.2d 1528 (11th Cir.1985); cf. *Rocky B. Fisheries, Inc. v. North Bend Fabrication & Mach., Inc.,* 66 Or. App. 625, 676 P.2d 319 (1984), rev. denied, 297 Or. 82, 679 P.2d 1367 (1984), appeal dismissed, 469 U.S. 802, 105 S. Ct. 57 (1984) (upholding state maritime lien law which does not require sending notice to vessel owner on assumption that vessel captain will notify owner of seizure). The courts reason that the interests of the creditor in a typical admiralty case are extremely weighty. Jurisdiction over the debtor herself may be difficult or impossible to acquire, and only the debtor's ship or cargo is within the creditor's reach. Yet,

> a ship's ability to dock, unload cargo, and fill its hold with goods intended for another destination—all within 24 hours—imposes tremendous pressure on creditors desiring to attach a vessel or property located aboard. "A ship may be here today and gone tomorrow * * *." Worse yet, as the ship sails, so does the debtor. The frustrated creditor, much like Evangeline, the poor Acadian girl separated from her lover, is tragically left to roam the shores awaiting the debtor's next arrival.
>
> * * *
>
> In this atmosphere, [maritime attachment] restores order and attempts to protect the *creditor's rights*. It draws debtors from otherwise impene-

trable fortresses. It commands a speedy clarification of vital facts underlying both prior disputes and the current seizure. It compels adjudication. Otherwise, pursuit of such unresolvable disputes "would in many cases amount to a denial of justice."

Schiffahrtsgesellschaft v. A. Bottacchi, 732 F.2d 1543, 1547–48 (11th Cir. 1984), on reh'g, 773 F.2d 1528 (1985). For other cases like this one dealing with attachment under F.R.C.P. Supplemental Rule B, see Annot., 63 A.L.R. Fed. 651 (1983).

B.   STATE CONSTITUTIONAL LAW

The typical state constitution has its own clause guaranteeing that no person shall be deprived of life, liberty, or property without due process of law. Even though a creditor's remedy may pass muster under the Fourteenth Amendment as interpreted by the Supreme Court, the remedy may be invalid for failing to satisfy a local due process clause as interpreted by the state's highest court. The local high court, not the United States Supreme Court, is the final arbiter of the state constitution even when the constitutional provision at issue reads exactly like some part of the United States Constitution. A state through its own law is generally free to require greater due process protection of debtors' rights in a wider range of circumstances than does the Fourteenth Amendment so long as the federal constitutional rights of creditors are not thereby impaired.

For example, in *Sharrock v. Dell Buick-Cadillac, Inc.,* 45 N.Y.2d 152, 408 N.Y.S.2d 39, 379 N.E.2d 1169 (1978), the New York Court of Appeals considered the constitutionality of the state artisan's lien law which allowed a garageperson to enforce her lien for repair and storage charges by means of a nonjudicial public sale of the vehicle in her possession. Regarding artisans' liens, see Chapter IX.C. supra. The law was challenged as violative of the due process clauses of the state and federal constitutions. Just as the Fourteenth Amendment due process clause applies only when there is state action, see Chapter XIV.A.1., some state involvement in the challenged activity is also required to trigger due process protection under state constitutions. See, e.g., *Martin v. Heady,* 103 Cal. App. 3d 580, 163 Cal. Rptr. 117 (1980); *Reinersten v. Porter,* 242 Ga. 624, 250 S.E.2d 475 (1978); *Jensen v. Schreck,* 275 N.W.2d 374 (Iowa 1979); *North Carolina Nat. Bank v. Burnette,* 297 N.C. 524, 256 S.E.2d 388 (1979); *Helfinstine v. Martin,* 561 P.2d 951 (Okl. 1977).

The court in *Sharrock* essentially conceded that, in light of the decision in *Flagg Bros. v. Brooks,* 436 U.S. 149, 98 S. Ct. 1729 (1978), the enforcement of the lien involved insufficient state action to invoke the Fourteenth Amendment. This conclusion, however, did not stop the court from considering if the artisan's lien law violated state due process. "[T]he mere fact that an activity might not constitute State action for purposes of the Federal Constitution does not perforce necessitate that the same conclusion be reached when that conduct is claimed to be violative of the State Constitution. Indeed, on innumerable occasions this court has given our State Constitution an independent construction, affording the rights and liberties of the citizens of this State even more protection than may be secured under the United States Constitution."   45 N.Y.2d at

156, 379 N.E.2d at 1173, 408 N.Y.S.2d at 43. The court was equally generous in *Shar-rock,* finding that New York was so closely connected with the artisan's lien as to trigger application of the state due process clause and holding that the clause was violated because the law failed to provide the debtor with a meaningful opportunity to be heard.

In a later case, the New York warehouseman's lien law, U.C.C. § 2–710, also was held unconstitutional under the state due process clause. *Svendsen v. Smith's Moving and Trucking Co.,* 76 A.D.2d 504, 431 N.Y.S.2d 94 (1980), aff'd, 54 N.Y.2d 865, 444 N.Y.S.2d 904, 429 N.E.2d 411 (1981), cert. denied, 455 U.S. 927, 102 S. Ct. 1292 (1982). The Supreme Court reviewed this very same law in *Flagg Bros.* and decided that there was too little state involvement to trigger Fourteenth Amendment due process protection.

Other creditors' remedies that may well escape scrutiny under the Fourteenth Amendment due to lack of state action, or lack of a significant taking of property have been held unconstitutional nevertheless for failing to satisfy state due process requirements. See, e.g., *Martin v. Heady,* 103 Cal. App. 3d 580, 163 Cal. Rptr. 117 (1980) (sale provisions of aircraft lien law unconstitutional under due process provision of California Constitution); *Roundhouse Constr. Corp. v. Telesco Masons Supplies Co.,* 168 Conn. 371, 362 A.2d 778 (1975), vacated, 423 U.S. 809, 96 S. Ct. 20 (1975) (to consider if judgment based on federal or state constitutional grounds), reaffirmed, 170 Conn. 155, 365 A.2d 393 (1976) (decided on both federal and state due process clauses), cert. denied, 429 U.S. 889, 97 S. Ct. 246 (1976) (construction lien law); *Fox v. First Bank,* 32 U.C.C. Rep. Serv. 1682, aff'd on reargument, 33 U.C.C. Rep. Serv. 1166 (Super. Ct. 1982) (right of secured creditor to repossess and dispose of personal property collateral under Retail Installment Sales Financing Act); but see, e.g., *South Central Dist. of the Pentecostal Church of God of America, Inc. v. Bruce-Rogers Co.,* 269 Ark. 130, 599 S.W.2d 702 (1980) (construction lien law valid under state due process clause); *Helfinstine v. Martin,* 561 P.2d 951 (Okl. 1977) (secured party's right of repossession under U.C.C. Article 9 valid under state constitution); *Crouse v. First Union Trust Bank,* 86 A.D.2d 978, 448 N.Y.S.2d 329 (1982) (U.C.C. §§ 9–503 & 9–504 are not unconstitutional under state constitution).

C. CONTRACTUAL DUE PROCESS

A debtor can freely negotiate for the inclusion in her credit contract of procedural safeguards not required by law of the remedies that a creditor might pursue. For example, neither the Fourteenth nor Fifth Amendment applies when an Article 9 secured creditor who is a private party exercises her right to repossess collateral upon the debtor's default. See, e.g., *Penney v. First Nat. Bank,* 385 Mass. 715, 433 N.E.2d 901 (1982) (no government action). Thus, prior notice of the taking is not required by due process. Moreover, nothing in Article 9 requires such notice. See, e.g., *Teeter Motor Co. v. First Nat. Bank,* 260 Ark. 764, 543 S.W.2d 938 (1976). Yet, the parties to a security agreement can provide for notice not otherwise required by law. See U.C.C. §§ 1–102(2); 9–501(1) & (2); 9–503 ("Unless otherwise agreed * * *."). Thus, if the creditor acts without giving the notification prescribed by the parties' contract, she is liable to the debtor for damages. Of course, the bargaining position of most debtors is such that contract negotiations more often result in their agreeing to give up procedural rights provided by law, not in their getting creditors to create rights by contract.

REVIEW QUESTIONS

1. T or F There are different tests under the due process clauses of the Fifth and Fourteenth Amendments for determining when a private person's conduct amounts to government action.

2. T or F The Fifth Amendment due process clause applies whenever a federally chartered savings and loan association enforces a mortgage through a private sale of the real estate.

3. T or F The Fifth Amendment does not require giving the owner of a vessel notice and an opportunity for a hearing prior to the prejudgment attachment of the vessel in an action in federal court to enforce a maritime lien.

4. In the case *Flagg Bros. v. Brooks,* the Supreme Court held that a debtor was not entitled to due process protection when a warehouseman's lien was enforced against her property. Later, however, in the case *Svendsen v. Smith's Moving & Trucking Co.,* the New York Court of Appeals decided that due process must be afforded in the enforcement of such a lien. How are these two cases reconciled?

*

PART FIVE

BANKRUPTCY

The remainder of this Black Letter focuses on bankruptcy. Several very basic differences exist between bankruptcy law and state debtor-creditor law:

First, and most obvious, bankruptcy law is federal law, although it sometimes refers to and incorporates state law.

Second, state law puts a premium on prompt action by creditors: The first creditor to attach the debtor's property, the first creditor to execute on the property, etc., is the one most likely to be paid. Bankruptcy law, on the other hand, emphasizes equality of treatment rather than a race of diligence. While bankruptcy law does not provide equal treatment for all creditors, all creditors within a single class are treated the same. After the commencement of a bankruptcy case, a creditor generally cannot improve its position vis-a-vis other creditors by obtaining a lien on the assets of the debtor. Similarly, a creditor's ability to improve its position before bankruptcy is considerably limited by bankruptcy law.

Third, the prospects for debtor relief are much greater in bankruptcy. The concept of "discharge" is unique to bankruptcy. While no debtor is guaranteed a bankruptcy discharge, most debtors who file for bankruptcy do receive a discharge. "One of the primary purposes of the bankruptcy act is 'to relieve the honest debtor from the weight of oppressive indebtedness and permit him to start afresh * * *.'" *Local Loan Co. v. Hunt,* 292 U.S. 234, 244, 54 S. Ct. 695, 699 (1934).

Finally, the vocabulary of bankruptcy law is different from the vocabulary in state law. Both ordinary terms such as "debtor" and "insolvent" and more technical terms such as "inventory" and "notice and hearing" are given special and unique meanings by the federal Bankruptcy Code. As you work with this law, it is very important that you always check for definitions of the statutory terms.

XVI

OVERVIEW OF BANKRUPTCY

Analysis

A.   WHAT IS BANKRUPTCY LAW?

The law of bankruptcy is federal law. It is primarily, though not completely, statutory law.

1.   STATUTES
There are two main federal bankruptcy statutes, and the more recent statute has been significantly amended twice by two other enactments.

a.   Bankruptcy Act of 1898
The Bankruptcy Act of 1898 (commonly referred to as the "Act") governs bankruptcy cases filed prior to October 1, 1979.

b.   Bankruptcy Reform Act of 1978 (a/k/a Bankruptcy Code)
The principal source of modern bankruptcy law is the Bankruptcy Reform Act of 1978, which is commonly referred to as the "Bankruptcy Code." It governs bankruptcy cases filed since October 1, 1979. Inasmuch as most pending bankruptcy cases have been filed since that date, this Black Letter focuses on the Bankruptcy Code, as amended, rather than the Bankruptcy Act.

1)   Amendments
The Bankruptcy Code has been twice amended in major ways by the Congress.

   a)   Bankruptcy Amendments and Federal Judgeship Act of 1984
   Bankruptcy cases pending on or filed after July 10, 1984, are subject to most of the 1984 amendments relating to bankruptcy jurisdiction; bankruptcy cases filed after October 7, 1984, are subject to the 1984 changes in the substantive law of bankruptcy.

   b)   Bankruptcy Judges, United States Trustees, and Family Farmer Bankruptcy Act of 1986
   The substantive changes relating to "family farmers" apply only to cases filed since November 26, 1986.

2)   Divisions
The Bankruptcy Code divides the substantive law of bankruptcy into the following chapters:

Chapter 1 General Provisions, Definitions and Rules of Construction

Chapter 3 Case Administration

Chapter 5 Creditors, the Debtor, and the Estate

Chapter 7 Liquidation

Chapter 9 Adjustment of the Debts of a Municipality

Chapter 11 Reorganization

Chapter 12 Adjustment of Debts of a Family Farmer with Regular Annual Income

Chapter 13 Adjustment of the Debts of an Individual With Regular Income

Chapter 15 United States Trustees

The provisions in Chapters 1, 3, and 5 apply in every bankruptcy case, unless otherwise specified.

2. RULES

It is also necessary to deal with the Bankruptcy Rules. Pursuant to the authority of 28 USC section 2075, the United States Supreme Court promulgated Bankruptcy Rules. These rules, not the Federal Rules of Civil Procedure, "govern procedure in United States Bankruptcy Courts," Rule 1001. The Bankruptcy Rules are divided into ten parts. Each part governs a different stage of the bankruptcy process.

3. STATE LAW

Bankruptcy law also includes state law. While principles of federal supremacy and the inability of states to impair the obligations of contracts preclude state legislatures from enacting bankruptcy laws, the Bankruptcy Code often expressly incorporates state law. See, e.g., sections 522(b), 544(b). Additionally, in applying the Bankruptcy Code, reference is commonly made to state common-law concepts.

B. FORMS OF BANKRUPTCY RELIEF

This Black Letter deals with two basic forms of bankruptcy relief—liquidation and rehabilitation—under four chapters of the Bankruptcy Code—Chapter 7, Chapter 11, Chapter 12, and Chapter 13. The focus, however, is on Chapters 7, 11, and 13. Chapter 12, which is limited to family farm bankruptcy, is a temporary law that is set to expire October 1, 1993. Moreover, the typical law school course that covers bankruptcy does not include coverage of Chapter 12.

1. LIQUIDATION—CHAPTER 7

Chapter 7 is entitled "Liquidation." The title is descriptive. In a Chapter 7 case, the trustee collects the non-exempt property of the debtor, converts that property to cash, and distributes the cash to the creditors. The debtor gives up all of the non-exempt property she owns at the time of the filing of the bankruptcy petition in the hope of obtaining a discharge. A discharge releases the debtor from any further personal liability for her pre-bankruptcy debts.

Example: B owes C $2,000. B files a bankruptcy petition. C only receives $300 from the liquidation of B's assets. If B receives a bankruptcy discharge, C will be precluded from pursuing B for the remaining $1,700.

As the preceding paragraph implies, every liquidation case under the bankruptcy laws does not result in a discharge. Section 727(a), considered infra at pages 466–68, lists a number of grounds for withholding a discharge. And, even if the debtor is able to obtain a discharge, she will not necessarily be freed from all creditors' claims. Section 523, considered infra at pages 471–75, sets out exceptions to discharge.

The vast majority of bankruptcy cases are Chapter 7 cases. The term "bankruptcy" is often used to describe liquidation proceedings under the bankruptcy laws. References to "bankruptcy" in this Black Letter should generally be regarded as references to liquidation cases.

2. REHABILITATION—CHAPTERS 11, 12 AND 13

Chapters 11, 12, and 13 generally deal with rehabilitation, not liquidation, of the debtor's assets. In a rehabilitation case under the bankruptcy laws, creditors usually look to future earnings of the debtor, not the property of the debtor at the time of the initiation of the bankruptcy, to satisfy their claims. The debtor retains its assets and makes payments to creditors, usually from post-petition earnings, pursuant to a court approved plan.

Chapter 11, like Chapter 7, is available to all forms of debtors: individuals, partnerships and corporations. Chapter 11 is considered infra at pages 481–96. Chapter 13 can be used only by individuals with a "regular income" (as defined in section 101(27)) who have unsecured debts of less than $100,000 and secured debts of less than $350,000. Chapter 13 is considered infra at pages 497–509. Chapter 12 is modeled after Chapter 13 but differs from Chapter 13 in important respects, including eligibility. Chapter 12 is limited to debtors with a regular income from farming operations (regardless of whether the debtor is an individual, a corporation, or a partnership) having less than $1.5 million in debts (80% of which must arise from farming operations).

C. BANKRUPTCY COURTS AND BANKRUPTCY JUDGES

1. UNDER THE BANKRUPTCY ACT OF 1898

The Bankruptcy Act of 1898 provided for "bankruptcy referees." Originally, the judicial role of bankruptcy referees was relatively minor. The referee was primarily an administrator and supervisor of bankruptcy cases, not a judicial officer. Amendments to the Bankruptcy Act of 1898 made the bankruptcy referee more of a judicial officer. In 1973, the Bankruptcy Rules changed the title of the office from "bankruptcy referee" to "bankruptcy judge."

The 1898 Act used the term "courts of bankruptcy." A court of bankruptcy could be either the court of a federal district judge or the court of a bankruptcy judge. Any federal district court could be a "court of bankruptcy." Any judicial power conferred by the Bankruptcy Act of 1898 on the "court" could be exercised by either a federal district judge or a bankruptcy judge; any judicial power conferred by the Bankruptcy Act of 1898 on the "judge" could be exercised only by the federal district judge.

2. UNDER THE BANKRUPTCY CODE

Both the original enactment in 1978 and amendments to it deal with the bankruptcy court system separately from the substantive law of bankruptcy. The substantive law of bankruptcy is now in Title 11 of the United States Code; the law relating to bankruptcy judges is in Title 28.

Title 28 nowhere uses the term "bankruptcy referee." Section 152 of Title 28 provides for "bankruptcy judges" to be appointed by the United States courts of appeals. Section 151 of Title 28 states that these bankruptcy judges "shall constitute a unit of the district court to be known as the bankruptcy court." Note that under Title 28 as amended in 1984, the bankruptcy court is not really a separate court; rather, it is a part of the district court.

Accordingly, the grant of jurisdiction over bankruptcy matters is to the district court, 28 USC section 1334. The federal district judges then refer bankruptcy matters to the bankruptcy judges pursuant to 28 USC section 157.

It is important to understand the differences between 28 USC 1334 and 28 USC 157. Section 1334 grants jurisdiction over bankruptcy cases and proceedings; all grants of jurisdiction are to the district court. Neither the phrase "bankruptcy court" nor the phrase "bankruptcy judge" appears in section 1334. Remember, however, that the bankruptcy judge is a unit of the district court under section 151. Accordingly, a grant of jurisdiction to the "district court" does not preclude the bankruptcy judge from playing a role in bankruptcy litigation.

Section 157 spells out the role that the bankruptcy judge is to play in bankruptcy litigation. Section 157 is entitled "Procedures" and deals with referral of matters from the "district court" to the bankruptcy judge. Section 157 is not a jurisdictional provision; it does not grant jurisdiction to the bankruptcy judges.

In summary, section 1334 speaks to what district courts can do and is jurisdictional. Section 157 deals with what the bankruptcy judges can do and is procedural.

The allocation of judicial power and responsibility over bankruptcy matters is one of the most controversial and complex areas of bankruptcy law and practice. You will probably find it easier to deal with the bankruptcy jurisdiction issues after gaining some understanding of the substantive law of bankruptcy. Accordingly, bankruptcy jurisdiction issues are reserved for the last chapter of this Black Letter.

D. TRUSTEES

In every Chapter 7 case, every Chapter 12, every Chapter 13, and some Chapter 11 cases, there will be not only a bankruptcy judge but also a bankruptcy trustee. (In Chapter 11, the bankruptcy court decides whether it is necessary to appoint a trustee, section 1104.)

A bankruptcy trustee, who is usually a private citizen rather than an employee of the government, is "the representative of the estate," section 323. The filing of a bankruptcy petition is said to create an estate consisting generally of the property of the debtor as of the time of the bankruptcy filing. This estate is treated as a separate legal entity, distinct from the debtor. The bankruptcy trustee is the person who sues, or may be sued, on behalf of the estate.

1. CHAPTER 7 CASES
There is a bankruptcy trustee in every Chapter 7 case.

a. Selection of Trustee
Promptly after the "order for relief" in a Chapter 7 case, the United States trustee must appoint an "interim trustee" for the case, section 701. (The position and role of the United States trustee are discussed later in this chapter of the Black Letter.) In selecting an interim trustee, the United States trustee is limited to private citizens who are members of a "panel" of private trustees established and maintained by the Director of the Administrative Office of the United States Courts. This interim trustee will serve at least until the first meeting of creditors.

At the first meeting of creditors, the creditors may elect a new trustee to replace the interim trustee if creditors holding at least 20% in amount of certain, unsecured claims vote in the election, section 702(c). This percentage requirement is designed to insure that trustees are elected only in cases in which there is significant creditor interest and to discourage election of trustees at the urging of attorneys for creditors who hope to be attorneys for the trustee, as was often the practice under the Bankruptcy Act of 1898. If the creditor interest in the case is sufficient to permit election of a trustee, the creditors are not required to select a trustee who is a member of the panel of private trustees.

If the creditors do not elect a trustee, the interim trustee becomes the trustee and serves in that capacity for the duration of the case.

b. Powers and Duties
The powers and duties of a bankruptcy trustee vary from chapter to chapter. The duties of a bankruptcy trustee in a Chapter 7 case (which you should remember is a liquidation proceeding) include:

- collecting the "property of the estate," i.e., debtor's property as of the time of the filing of the bankruptcy petition

- challenging certain pre-bankruptcy and post-bankruptcy transfers of the property of the estate

- selling the property of the estate

- objecting to creditors' claims that are improper

- in appropriate cases, objecting to the debtor's discharge, section 704.

2. CHAPTER 13 CASES
There is also a bankruptcy trustee in every Chapter 13 case.

a. Selection
Creditors do not have the right to elect a trustee in Chapter 13. The United States trustee always appoints the trustee in Chapter 13 cases. Generally, the United States trustee will appoint one or more individuals to serve as trustee

for all Chapter 13 cases locally. Such trustees are generally referred to as "standing trustees."

b. Powers and Duties

Remember that Chapter 13 contemplates rehabilitation, not liquidation. In the typical Chapter 13 case, the debtor retains his or her assets and makes payments to creditors from post-petition earnings pursuant to a court-approved plan. The bankruptcy trustee in a Chapter 13 case is in part a disbursing agent who supervises the debtor's performance of the plan. The duties of a Chapter 13 trustee are set out in section 1302: essentially the duties of a Chapter 13 trustee are the same as a Chapter 7 trustee except, of course, that a Chapter 13 trustee does not collect and liquidate the property of the estate.

3. CHAPTER 11 CASES

While there is a bankruptcy trustee in every Chapter 7 case and every Chapter 13 case, there is rarely a bankruptcy trustee in a Chapter 11 case. In Chapter 11, a bankruptcy trustee will be appointed only if the bankruptcy judge decides, after notice and hearing, that there is "cause" or the "appointment is in the interests of creditors, any equity security holders, and other interests of the estate."

Remember also that Chapter 11, like Chapter 13, contemplates rehabilitation, not liquidation, and that Chapter 11, unlike Chapter 13, is available to corporations and partnerships as well as individuals. The typical Chapter 11 case involves a business that continues to operate after the bankruptcy petition is filed. If a bankruptcy trustee is named in such a case, he or she will take over the operation of the business. As noted above, generally there will not be a trustee in a Chapter 11 case. The debtor will usually remain in control of the business after the filing of a Chapter 11 petition; such a debtor is referred to as a "debtor in possession." Chapter XXVII of this Black Letter deals with Chapter 11 trustees and debtors in possession in more detail.

4. CHAPTER 12 CASES

There will be a trustee in every Chapter 12 case whose duties are similar to those of a Chapter 13 trustee. A Chapter 12 debtor remains in possession of her property and has the rights and powers of a Chapter 11 debtor in possession, unless the debtor is removed for reasons similar to those for removing a Chapter 11 debtor in possession (e.g., fraud, incompetence, gross mismanagement).

E. UNITED STATES TRUSTEES

There was no such thing as a United States trustee until the 1978 bankruptcy legislation. During the debate on bankruptcy legislation, considerable concern was expressed over the bankruptcy judges' involvement in the administration of bankruptcy cases. While both the House and the Senate seemed to agree that the bankruptcy judge should not perform administrative functions, there was disagreement over who should. The compromise was an experimental United States trustee program involving parts of 17 states and the District of Columbia. Through the 1986 Amendments, Congress made permanent and nationwide the the United States trustee program.

The U.S. Attorney General appoints a United States trustee for each of 21 geographical regions within the country. The term of each appointment is five years. The Attorney General is also authorized to appoint one more assistant United States trustees in any region where the public interest so requires. Moreover, in a region where the number of Chapter 12 or 13 cases so warrants, the United States trustee for the region is empowered to appoint people to serve as standing trustees.

Essentially, the United States trustee and her assistants perform appointing and other administrative tasks that the bankruptcy judge would otherwise have to perform, including the appointment and supervision of private trustees in chapter cases. Thus, United States trustees are not intended as substitutes for private bankruptcy trustees. Rather, United States trustees are more like substitutes for the bankruptcy judge with respect to supervisory and administrative details.

REVIEW QUESTIONS

1. T or F   Some states have bankruptcy laws.

2. T or F   An individual debtor cannot file a petition for relief under Chapter 11.

3. T or F   There is a trustee in every bankruptcy case.

4. How does the United States trustee differ from a bankruptcy trustee?

XVII

COMMENCEMENT AND DISMISSAL OF A BANKRUPTCY CASE

A. COMMENCEMENT

A bankruptcy case begins with the filing of a petition with the bankruptcy court, section 301. Generally, the debtor files the petition. Such debtor-initiated cases are often referred to as "voluntary." Creditors have a limited right to initiate "involuntary" bankruptcy cases against the debtor under Chapters 7 and 11.

1. VOLUNTARY CASES

A voluntary bankruptcy case is commenced when an eligible debtor files a petition. No formal adjudication is necessary; the filing operates as an "order for relief," section 301.

Section 301 deals with the commencement of voluntary cases under Chapter 7, 11, 12, or 13. It provides that a bankruptcy petition may be filed by any "entity that may be a debtor under such chapter." Section 109 sets out who is eligible to be a debtor under each chapter. Accordingly it is necessary to consider paragraphs (b), (d), (e), and (f) of section 109.

a. Eligibility Requirements

1) Chapter 7 Cases

Section 109(b) contains two limitations on the availability of Chapter 7 (liquidation) relief to a debtor:

- The debtor must be a "person." "Person" is defined in section 101(33) as including partnerships and corporations. A sole proprietorship would not be a "person."

- The debtor may not be a railroad, insurance company, or banking institution. Railroads are eligible for bankruptcy relief only under subchapter IV of Chapter 11; insurance companies and banking institutions are excluded from relief under the Bankruptcy Code because their liquidations are governed by other state and federal regulatory laws.

2) Chapter 11 Cases

With two exceptions, any person who is eligible to file a petition under Chapter 7 is also eligible to file a petition under Chapter 11, section 109(d).

- The first exception is railroads. As noted above railroads are eligible for Chapter 11, but not Chapter 7.

- The second exception is stockbrokers and commodity brokers; they are eligible for Chapter 7, but not Chapter 11.

3) Chapter 13 Cases

There are three significant limitations in section 109(e) on the availability of Chapter 13:

- The debtor must be an individual. A Chapter 13 petition may not be filed by a corporation or a partnership.

- The individual must have "income sufficiently stable and regular to enable such individual to make payments under a (Chapter 13 plan)," sections 101(27), 109(e). This includes not only wage earners, but also self-employed individuals, and individuals on welfare, pensions, or investment income.

- The debtor must have "non-contingent, liquidated" unsecured debts totalling less than $100,000 and "non-contingent, liquidated" secured debts of less than $350,000. (These debt limitations are considered again on page 498.)

4) Chapter 12 Cases

Only a family farmer with regular annual income may be a debtor under Chapter 12, section 109(f), and there are further restrictions:

- First, the debtor's annual income must be sufficiently stable and regular to enable her to make payments under a plan under Chapter 12, section 101(18).

- Second, when the family debtor is an individual or an individual and her spouse, their aggregate debts must not exceed $1.5 million, and at least 80% of the debts and 50% of their gross income must come from farming operations, section 101(17).

- Third, when the family farmer is a corporation or partnership, (1) more than 50% of the outstanding stock must be held by the same family which conducts the farming operation; (2) more than 80% of the value of the assets must be related to the farming operation; (3) the farmer's aggregate debts must not exceed $1.5 million, of which 80% or more arises out of the farming operations; and (4) any stock that is issued must not be publicly traded, section 101(17).

b. Insolvency Not Required

While too much debt makes a debtor ineligible for Chapter 13, too many assets does not make a debtor ineligible for Chapter 7, 11, or 13. Please note that insolvency is not a condition precedent to any form of voluntary bankruptcy action. A debtor may file a petition under Chapter 7, 11, or 13 even though solvent.

c. Joint Petitions

A husband and a wife may file a single joint petition for voluntary relief under any chapter that is available to each spouse. If a husband and a wife jointly file under Chapter 13, their aggregate debts are subject to the $100,000/$350,000 limits. Joint filing also may affect the property that can be claimed as exempt. See section 522(b).

d. Frequent-Filer Disqualification

As the preceding pages examining paragraphs (b), (d), and (e) of section 109 indicate, there are debtors that are eligible for some chapters of bankruptcy relief but not eligible for others. Additionally, there are individual debtors who are not eligible for relief under any chapter.

New section 109(f) adds what could be roughly called a "frequent filing" limitation. Under section 109(f), an individual debtor is not eligible to be a debtor under either 7, 11, or 13, if he or she was a debtor in a bankruptcy case within the last 180 days that was:

- dismissed by the court for failure of the debtor to abide by court orders or appear before the court, or

- dismissed on motion of the debtor following the filing of a request for relief from the automatic stay. Note that section 109(f) does not bar an individual who has completed a Chapter 7, 11, or 13 case from immediately filing for bankruptcy again.

e. Filing Fee

A debtor who files a bankruptcy petition must pay a filing fee: $60 for Chapter 7 or 13, $200 for Chapter 11, 28 U.S.C.A. § 1930(a). The court may dismiss the bankruptcy case for non-payment of fees, sections 707 and 1307. No provision is made for *in forma pauperis* bankruptcy.

2. INVOLUNTARY CASES

Debtors can be forced into bankruptcy by creditors filing involuntary petitions (petitions for involuntary bankruptcy) against them. Such a petition itself, however, does not entitle the creditors to relief. An order of relief against the debtor results only if she fails to answer the creditors' petition or a ground for bankruptcy is found to exist.

a. Limitations on Involuntary Petitions

Section 303 deals with bankruptcy petitions filed by creditors. It contains a number of significant limitations on involuntary petitions:

- Creditors may file involuntary petitions under Chapter 7 or 11 but not Chapter 12 or 13.

- Certain debtors are protected from involuntary petitions. Insurance companies, banking institutions, farmers, and charitable corporations may not be subjected to involuntary petitions.

- The petition must be filed by the requisite number of creditors. Generally, three creditors with unsecured claims totalling at least $5,000 must join in the petition. If, however, the debtor has less than twelve unsecured creditors, a single creditor with an unsecured claim of $5,000 is sufficient.

b. Grounds for Involuntary Relief

While the filing of an involuntary petition effects a commencement of the case, it does not operate as an adjudication, i.e., an order for relief, as it does in a voluntary case. (Reminder: All bankruptcy cases, both voluntary and involuntary, commence when the petition is filed. Numerous Bankruptcy Code provisions refer to and focus on this event. In voluntary cases, the order for relief also dates from the time when the petition is filed. In involuntary cases, the order for relief occurs at a later time. See Rules 1011, 1013.) In a involuntary case, the debtor has the right to file an answer and controvert the bankruptcy. If the debtor does not timely answer the petition, "the court shall order relief," section 303(h). If the debtor does timely answer the petition, the court "shall order relief against the debtor" only if one of the two grounds for involuntary relief are established. These grounds are:

1) Equitable Insolvency
   The first basis for involuntary relief is that the debtor is generally not paying debts as they come due. This is sometimes referred to as "equitable insolvency"; it is different from the definition of insolvency in section 101(29).

2) Receiver or Other Representative Taking Charge of Debtor's Property
   The alternative basis for involuntary relief is that within 120 days before the petition was filed, a general receiver, assignee, or custodian took possession of substantially *all* of the debtor's property or was appointed to take charge of substantially *all* of the debtor's property. The appointment of a receiver to take possession of Greenacre in a mortgage foreclosure action would not be a basis for involuntary relief because less than substantially all of the debtor's property is involved.

c. Procedures After Filing and Before Order for Relief

Usually there will be an interval of at least several weeks between the filing of an involuntary petition and the order of relief against the debtor. During this period, the debtor may continue to buy, use, or sell property and to operate its business, section 303(f). Sections 502(f) and 507(a)(2) protect third parties who deal with a debtor after an involuntary petition has been filed. These provisions are considered infra at page 449.

During the period after filing and before a decision on an order for relief, the bankruptcy court may appoint an interim trustee to take possession of the debtor's property or operate the debtor's business "if necessary to preserve the property of the estate or to prevent loss to the estate," section 303(g). If an interim trustee is appointed, the debtor may regain possession by posting a bond.

d. Remedies for Unfounded Petitions

Notwithstanding the protection of section 303(f), the filing of an involuntary petition adversely affects the debtor's financial reputation and business operations. Section 303(i) attempts to protect debtors from unfounded petitions by setting out the following remedies in cases in which an involuntary petition is dismissed after litigation:

- The court may grant judgment for the debtor against the petitioning creditors for costs and a reasonable attorney's fee.

- If an interim trustee took possession of the debtor's property, the court may grant judgment for "any damages proximately caused by the taking."

- If the petition was filed in "bad faith," the court may award "any damages proximately caused by such filing," including damages for loss of business and also punitive damages.

B. DISMISSAL

The bankruptcy court may dismiss or suspend a voluntary bankruptcy case even though it was filed by an eligible debtor. And, the bankruptcy court may dismiss or suspend an involuntary bankruptcy case even though all of the requirements of section 303 are satisfied. Each bankruptcy relief chapter has its own dismissal provision, and section 305 provides overarching additional reasons for dismissal that apply in every kind of case. In addition, the bankruptcy court may dismiss a bankruptcy case for failure to pay filing fees.

1. CHAPTER 7 CASES
Section 707 governs dismissal of Chapter 7 cases and provides for dismissal upon motion "for cause" and sua sponte by the court.

a. For Cause
Under section 707(a), the standard a bankruptcy court is to apply in ruling on a motion to dismiss is "for cause"; section 707(a) gives two examples of cause." This "cause" standard applies to motions to dismiss filed by the debtor as well as motions to dismiss filed by creditors. A debtor who files a Chapter 7 petition does not have an absolute right to have the bankruptcy case dismissed.

b. Sua Sponte
Under section 707(b), a bankruptcy court can act sua sponte and dismiss a Chapter 7 case if:

- the debtor is an individual

- the debts are "primarily consumer debts"

- "granting relief would be a substantial abuse of the provisions of this chapter."

Section 707(b) was added in 1984. It is not yet clear from the cases what "substantial abuse" means.

2. CHAPTER 11 CASES
In Chapter 11, like Chapter 7, the standard a bankruptcy court is to apply to a motion to dismiss is "for cause." Again, the statute sets out examples of cause, section 1112(b). Again, the "cause" standard applies to both debtor and creditor motions.

3. CHAPTER 12 AND CHAPTER 13 CASES
In Chapters 12 and 13, unlike Chapters 7 and 11, a debtor is given an absolute right to have his or her Chapter 13 case dismissed, section 1307(b). Motions to dismiss filed by creditors in a Chapter 13 case are subject to the "for cause" standard. Section 1307(c) sets out examples of "cause."

4. SECTION 305 DISMISSALS
In Chapter 7, 11, 12, and 13 cases, a debtor or creditors can also base a motion to dismiss on section 305. Section 305 empowers the bankruptcy court to dismiss or suspend a case if there is a foreign bankruptcy pending concerning the debtor or if

"the interests of creditors and the debtor would be better served by such dismissal or suspension."

Example: D, Inc., is generally not paying its debts as they come due. D, Inc. is trying to negotiate a workout with its creditors. Three of D, Inc.'s creditors are dissatisfied with the terms proposed in the workout and file an involuntary Chapter 11 petition against D, Inc. The bankruptcy court may decide to dismiss this petition if D, Inc. is making progress in negotiating a workout with its creditors.

A section 305 dismissal must be preceded by "notice and a hearing." The decision to dismiss (or not to dismiss) is not appealable. If an involuntary petition is dismissed under section 305, the petitioning creditors are not liable for costs, attorneys' fees or damages under section 303(i).

REVIEW QUESTIONS

1. D, an individual, wants to file a voluntary Chapter 7 petition. What must she establish in order to file?

2. Farmer F has not paid for feed C supplied. C learns that F is not paying any of his creditors. Can C file an involuntary Chapter 12 petition against F? An involuntary Chapter 7 petition?

3. D files a Chapter 7 petition. Two months after filing, D inherits $200,000. Can D now dismiss her petition?

4. T or F A Chapter 13 debtor has the right to dismiss his petition.

*

XVIII

STAY OF COLLECTION ACTIVITIES

Analysis

After the filing of a bankruptcy petition, a debtor needs immediate protection from the collection efforts of creditors. If the petition is a voluntary Chapter 7, the bankruptcy trustee needs time to collect the "property of the estate" and make pro rata distributions to creditors. If the petition is a voluntary Chapter 11, 12 or 13, the debtor needs time to prepare a plan. And, if the petition is an involuntary Chapter 7 or Chapter 11, the debtor needs time to controvert the petition. Moreover, since creditors will receive payment through the bankruptcy process or the plan of rehabilitation and some claims will be discharged, continued creditor actions would interfere with orderly bankruptcy administration.

Accordingly, the filing of a voluntary petition under Chapter 7, Chapter 11, Chapter 12, or Chapter 13, or the filing of an involuntary petition under Chapter 7 or Chapter 11 automatically "stays", i.e., restrains, creditors from taking further action against the debtor, the property of the debtor, or the property of the estate to collect their claims or enforce their liens, section 362.

There are four stay questions that lawyers (and law students) are most often asked:

1.   When does the automatic stay become effective?

2.   What is covered by the automatic stay?

3.   When does the automatic stay end?

4.   How can a creditor obtain relief from the stay?

A. TIME STAY ARISES

The automatic stay is triggered by the filing of a bankruptcy petition. It dates from the time of the filing, not from the time that a creditor receives notice or learns of the bankruptcy. If D files a bankruptcy petition on April 5, the stay becomes effective April 5. The stay dates from April 5 even if creditors do not learn of the bankruptcy until much later. If C, not knowing of D's bankruptcy, obtains a default judgment against D on April 29, the default judgment violates the automatic stay and is invalid.

B. SCOPE OF THE STAY

1. SECTION 362

Paragraph (a) of section 362 defines the scope of the automatic stay by listing all of the acts and actions that are stayed by the commencement of a bankruptcy case. It is comprehensive and includes virtually all creditor collection activity. Section 362(b) lists actions that are not stayed.

a. What Is Stayed

Subparagraphs (1), (2) and (8) of section 362(a) cover most litigation efforts of creditors directed at collecting pre-bankruptcy debts. Section 362(a)(1) stays creditors from filing collection suits after the bankruptcy petition is filed or from continuing collection suits that were commenced prior to bankruptcy. Section 362(a)(2) bars creditors from enforcing judgments obtained prior to bankruptcy. Section 362(a)(8) covers Tax Court proceedings concerning the debtor.

Subparagraphs (3), (4), (5), and (7) of section 362(a) stay virtually all types of secured creditor action against the property of the estate or property of the debtor. (Property of the estate is considered infra at pages 383–85.) Creditors are barred from obtaining liens, perfecting liens, enforcing liens after the bankruptcy petition is filed, and setting off debts owed the debtor.

Section 362(a)(6) stays "any act to collect * * *." This has been read as barring informal collection actions such as telephone calls demanding payments and dunning letters.

b. What Is Not Stayed

While paragraph (a) of section 362 indicates what is stayed, paragraph (b) lists various kinds of actions that are not stayed. For example, section 362(b)(2) provides a limited exception for alimony and child support claims. Such claims can be collected from property that is not "property of the estate."

c. Actions Against Third Persons

There is an important limitation on the scope of section 362 that is not dealt with in paragraph (b) of section 362. The automatic stay of section 362(a) only covers the debtor, property of the debtor, and property of the estate. It does not protect third parties.

Example: D borrows $3,000 from C and G guarantees repayment. If D files for bankruptcy, section 362(a) will stay C from attempting to collect from D. Section 362(a) will not, however, protect G.

2. SECTIONS 1201 AND 1301

While section 362(a) will not protect third persons such as G in the preceding example, section 1201 or 1301 might protect her. By reason of section 1301, the filing of a Chapter 12 or 13 petition automatically stays collection action against guarantors and other codebtors if

- the debt is a consumer debt and

- the codebtor is not in the credit business.

3. SECTION 105

Section 105 grants to bankruptcy courts the power to issue orders "necessary or appropriate to carry out the provisions of this title." Courts have used this section 105 power to stay or restrain creditor action.

a. Procedural Peculiarity

There is an important procedural difference between section 105 and sections 362, 1201, and 1301. An injunction or stay under section 105 will not be automatic. Rather, it will be granted according to the usual rules for injunctive relief.

b. Substantive Peculiarity

There is also an important substantive difference between section 105 and sections 362, 1201 and 1301. In acting under section 105, the bankruptcy court is not expressly limited by the restrictions in section 362, 1201 or 1301.

c. Application

If D, Inc. files for bankruptcy, can a court use section 105 to enjoin creditors from proceeding against P who personally guaranteed D, Inc.'s debts? There is dicta in numerous cases that a court has the power under section 105 to protect third parties but very few such holdings. Most of the cases refer to and quote from *In re Otero Mills, Inc.,* 21 B.R. 777 (Bkrtcy.N.M.1982), which sets out three requirements that must be satisfied before a court enjoins a creditors actions against a codebtor:

- "irreparable harm to the bankruptcy estate if the injunction does not issue;

- strong likelihood of success on the merits; and

- no harm or minimal harm to the other party or parties."

21 B.R. at 779.

C. TERMINATION OF THE STAY

Paragraph (c) of section 362 describes two situations in which the automatic stay terminates automatically.

1. PROPERTY NO LONGER ESTATE PROPERTY

Section 362(c)(1) provides that the automatic stay ends as to particular property when the property ceases to be property of the estate.

Example: C has a mortgage on D Corp.'s building. D Corp. files a bankruptcy petition. C is stayed from foreclosing its mortgage. The bankruptcy trustee sells D Corp.'s office building to X. C is no longer stayed from foreclosing its lien.

Property also ceases to be property of the estate when it is abandoned to the debtor under section 554. Notwithstanding the language of section 362(c)(1), abandonment does not terminate the stay. The stay continues by reason of section 362(a)(5). See *In re Cruseturner,* 8 B.R. 581, 7 B.C.D. 235 (Bkrtcy.Utah 1981).

2. CASE CLOSED OR DISMISSED OR DEBTOR DISCHARGED

Section 362(c)(2) provides that the automatic stay ends when the bankruptcy case is closed or dismissed or the debtor receives a discharge. The typical Chapter 7 bankruptcy can be completed in a matter of months. In Chapter 11 cases, however, there can be a gap of several years between the filing of the petition and discharge. Accordingly, unless some action is taken, the stay can last several years.

D. RELIEF FROM THE STAY

A bankruptcy court may grant relief from the automatic stay on request of a "party in interest," section 362(d). The relief will not always take the form of termination of the stay. Section 362(d) provides for relief "such as by terminating, annulling, modifying, or conditioning such stay." The Rules provide that the "request" in section 362 takes the form of a motion, Rules 4001(a), 9014. The facts of the reported cases make clear that the "party in interest" in section 362 litigation is typically a creditor, usually a secured creditor.

What must a creditor allege in its motion and establish in its proof in order to obtain relief from the stay? The grounds for relief from stay are set out in section 362(d).

1. **SECTION 362(d)(1)**

The most general statutory ground for relief from the stay is "for cause," section 362(d)(1). There is very little case law on what constitutes "cause" for purposes of section 362(d)(1). Most of the reported section 362(d)(1) cases involve the specific example of cause set out in the statute: "lack of adequate protection of an interest in property of such party in interest."

The quoted language raises four questions: (1) who is "the party in interest" (2) what is "the interest in property" (3) from what is it being protected and (4) how much protection is "adequate protection."

a. **Party in Interest**

The party in interest is the person seeking relief from the stay. Again, typically, the party in interest under section 362(d)(1) will be a secured creditor.

b. **Interest in Property**

What is protected is the secured creditor's interest in property, not the secured party's claim.

> *Example:* D owes C $100,000 and C has a mortgage on land worth $60,000. Section 362(d)(1) contemplates adequate protection of C's lien position, rather than C's right to the payment of $100,000.

c. **Protection Against What**

The questions of from what the interest in property is to be protected and how much protection is adequate protection are closely related.

The Supreme Court recently dealt with the questions in *United States Savings Association v. Timbers of Inwood Forest Associates, Ltd.,* __ U.S. __, 108 S.Ct. 626 (1988). There the Chapter 11 debtor, an apartment complex limited partnership, owed more than $4.3 million to a creditor, C, that had a deed of trust on the apartment complex. The collateral was worth at most $4.25 million and was not depreciating. C was an undersecured or partly secured creditor.

C moved for relief from the stay, contending that it was entitled to "lost opportunity costs." More specifically, C argued,

- part of its "interest in property" is the right to seize and sell the property when the debtor defaults;

- thus, if D had not filed for bankruptcy, C could seize and sell the equipment for $4.25 million;

- C could then lend this $4.25 million to another debtor and receive interest on the new $4.25 million loan;

- accordingly, in order to provide "adequate protection" of C's "interest in the property" as required by section 362(d)(1), the automatic stay should be conditioned on D making monthly payments to C equal to the amount that C would be receiving in interest payments on a new loan of $4.25 million. In sum, D should be compelled to pay C for its "lost opportunity costs."

Looking to legislative history and statutory language such as section 506, the Court rejected this argument.

d. Adequate Protection
1) What Is It?

Section 361 does not define "adequate protection"; rather, section 361 specifies three non-exclusive methods of providing adequate protection.

a) Periodic Cash Payments

The first method of adequate protection specified is periodic cash payments to the lien creditor equal to the decrease in value of the creditor's interest in the collateral.

Example: If C has a security interest in D's car and D files a bankruptcy petition, D can meet the adequate protection burden of section 362 by making cash payments equal to the depreciation on the car, section 361(1).

b) Additional or Substitute Lien

Section 361(2) indicates that adequate protection may take the form of an additional lien or substitute lien on other property.

Example: P files a Chapter 11 petition. C has a perfected security in P's equipment. P needs to use the encumbered equipment to continue operating its business in order to accomplish a successful Chapter 11 reorganization. Such use will, however, decrease the value of the equipment and C's lien in the equipment. Under section 361(2) adequate protection may take the form of a lien on other property owned by P. The new collateral does not necessarily have to be equipment.

c) Indubitable Equivalent

Section 361(3) grants the debtor-in-possession or trustee considerable flexibility in providing adequate protection. Section 361(3) recognizes such other protection, other than providing an administrative expense claim, that will result in the secured party's realizing the "indubitable equivalent" of the value of its interest in the collateral. The term "indubitable equivalent" is not statutorily defined.

2) Uncertainty Due to Process of Negotiating Adequate Protection

In summary, there is uncertainty as to (1) the importance of the "indubitable equivalent" language in section 361, and (2) the requirements of the "adequate protection" language in section 362(d). This uncertainty is attributable in part to the practice of negotiating rather than litigating section 362(d)(1) issues and in part to what is decided in section 362(d)(1) litigation. Section 362(d)(1) does not contemplate that the bankruptcy judge will decide what is adequate protection and mandate that it be provided. Rather, in section 362(d)(1) litigation the bankruptcy judge merely decides whether what the bankruptcy trustee or debtor in protection has offered is adequate protection.

3) When Adequate Protection Proves Inadequate

What if (i) there is section 362(d)(1) litigation, (ii) the bankruptcy judge decides that the debtor is providing adequate protection and (iii) the "adequate protection" proves to be inadequate? To illustrate, X has a perfected security interest in the inventory of Oscar De Lah Rentals Corp., O. O files a Chapter 11 petition. At the time of the petition, O owes X $100,000, and the encumbered inventory has a value of $60,000. X requests relief from the stay. The court concludes that O's offer of a personal guarantee by G was "adequate protection," was the "indubitable equivalent." This conclusion turns out to be wrong. When O's Chapter 11 reorganization fails, G is insolvent. The value of the inventory now securing O's $100,000 claim is worth only $20,000. Obviously, X can not sue the bankruptcy judge. What can X do?

Section 507(b) applies when "adequate protection" proves to be inadequate. It grants an administrative expense priority for the losses. (The significance of an administrative expense priority is considered infra at pages 451–52.) In the Oscar De Lah Rentals hypo, X would have a $40,000 administrative expense priority claim.

2. SECTION 362(d)(2)

Under section 362(d)(2) a lien creditor can obtain relief from the stay if

- the debtor does not have any equity in the encumbered property, AND

- the encumbered property is not necessary to an effective reorganization.

The application of section 362(d)(2)(A) would not seem to present any difficult legal issues: generally equity is measured by the difference between the value of the property and the encumbrances against it. If, for example, property has a value of $100,000 and is subject to a $120,000 lien, "the debtor does not have any equity in such property."

A creditor cannot obtain relief from the stay merely by establishing no equity. Note the conjunction "and" connecting the no equity test of section 362(d)(2)(A) and section 362(d)(2)(B).

a. **How Should Property Be Valued for Purposes of Section 362(d)(2)(A)?**
    Congress deliberately left unanswered the question whether property should be valued at a liquidation value, going concern value, or some other value, section 506.

b. **Which Liens Are to Be Considered for Purposes of Section 362(d)(2)(A)?**
    Assume, for example, that the debtor's land is valued at $300,000. X has a $250,000 lien on the land. Y has a $75,000 lien on the same land. Only X requests relief from the stay. Most courts would find no equity under these facts; the dominant view is that "equity" in section 362(d)(2)(A) refers to the difference between the value of the property and all encumbrances against it. Other courts, however, refuse to include liens junior to the creditor requesting relief.

c. **Issues in Section 362(d)(2)(B)**
    There are at least two separate issues raised by the language of section 362(d)(2)(B).

    First, is the property "necessary?" Does the individual debtor need the encumbered car in order to get to her job so that she can make her Chapter 13 payments? Does the business debtor need the encumbered equipment in order to manufacture goods so that it can make its Chapter 11 payments? Courts have been much more aggressive in deciding that an individual Chapter 13 debtor does not need a car than in deciding a business Chapter 11 debtor does not need equipment.

    Even if the collateral is necessary for the debtor's rehabilitation efforts, there is a second issue. Can the debtor reorganize? Is there a realistic possibility of an "effective reorganization?" Dicta in the recent Supreme Court decision in *United Savings Association of Texas v. Timbers of Inwood Forest Associates, Ltd.,* ___ U.S.___, 108 S.Ct. 626 (1988), suggests that this is a meaningful test: "What this requires is not merely a showing that if there is conceivably to be an effective reorganization, this property will be needed for it, but that the property is essential for an effective reorganization THAT IS IN PROSPECT."

3. **RELATIONSHIP BETWEEN SECTIONS 362(d)(1) AND 362(d)(2)**
    Note that section 362(d)(1) and section 362(d)(2) are connected by the conjunction "or." A creditor is entitled to relief from the stay if it is able to establish grounds for relief under either section 362(d)(1) or section 362(d)(2). If, for example, a creditor is able to establish the lack of adequate protection, it is entitled to relief from the stay even though the property is necessary to an effective reorganization.

4. **BURDEN OF PROOF IN SECTION 362(d) LITIGATION**
    Section 362(g) allocates the burden of proof in stay litigation. The creditor or other party requesting the relief has the burden on the issue of whether the debtor has an equity in the property. The debtor or bankruptcy trustee has the burden on all other issues.

REVIEW QUESTIONS

1. D files a bankruptcy petition on January 15. C, a creditor of D, does not learn of the filing until January 22 and does not receive official notice of the filing until February 3. When is the stay effective against C?

2. C obtained a judgment against D and had the sheriff seize property of D. The sheriff's sale is scheduled for April 5. D files a bankruptcy petition of April 4. Does the automatic stay affect the scheduled sheriff's sale? What if C does not know of the filing and the sale is held?

3. D files a bankruptcy petition. After the bankruptcy, D is involved in an automobile accident with V. Does the bankruptcy filing prevent V from proceeding against D? Against D's insurance company?

4. D files a bankruptcy petition. D owes S $400,000. S has a security interest in equipment. The equipment is worth $300,000 and depreciating at a rate of $2,000 a month. Can S invoke section 362(d)(1) and recover its collateral?

5. T or F   An unsecured creditor cannot obtain relief from the automatic stay under section 362(d)(1).

*

Analysis

A. WHY PROPERTY OF THE ESTATE IS AN IMPORTANT CONCEPT

The filing of a bankruptcy petition automatically creates an "estate," section 541(a). "Property of the estate" is one of the most important, most basic bankruptcy concepts. For example:

- A number of the general provisions in Chapters 3 and 5 use the phrase "property of the estate." For example, the automatic stay bars a creditor from collecting a pre-petition or post-petition claim from property of the estate, section 362(a)(3), (4).

- In a Chapter 7 case, "property of the estate" is collected by the bankruptcy trustee and sold; the proceeds of the sale of the property of the estate are then distributed to creditors, sections 704, 726. In other words, the loss of property of the estate is the primary cost of Chapter 7 bankruptcy to the debtor; the receipt of the pro-

383

ceeds from the sale of property of the estate is the primary benefit creditors derive from a Chapter 7 bankruptcy.

- In a Chapter 11, 12 or 13 case, the debtor retains the property of the estate. Nevertheless, it is necessary to determine what is property of the estate even in a Chapter 11, 12 or 13 case. In Chapter 11, 12 and 13 cases, the value of the property of the estate determines the minimum amount that must be offered to non-assenting general creditors in the plan of rehabilitation, sections 1129(a)(7), 1225(a)(4), and 1325(a)(4).

B.   WHAT IS PROPERTY OF THE ESTATE

The seven numbered subparagraphs of section 541(a) specify what property becomes property of the estate. Paragraph (1) is by far the most comprehensive and significant. Section 541(a)(1) provides, very broadly, that property of the estate includes "all legal or equitable interests of the debtor in property as of the commencement of the case," i.e., all property of the debtor as of the time of the filing of the bankruptcy petition.

Property of the estate thus includes both real property and personal property, both tangible property and intangible property, both property in the debtor's possession and property in which the debtor has an interest that is held by others. Third parties are statutorily required to return such property to the bankruptcy trustee or debtor-in-possession, sections 542 and 543.

1.   LIMITATIONS
Section 541(a)(1) contains two significant limitations on what constitutes property of the estate.

a.   Interests of the Debtor
Property of the estate is limited to "interests *of the debtor* in property."

> *Example:*   Mr. Rourke and Tatoo own an island as tenants in common. Mr. Rourke files a Chapter 7 petition. Only Mr. Rourke's limited interest in the island would be property of the estate. (Nevertheless, the entire island can be sold under section 363(h), (i), and (j)).

b.   Upon Commencement of the Case
Estate property is limited to the debtor's interests in property that she owns "as of the commencement of the case". "Commencement of the case" is synonymous with filing of the petition, sections 301, 303. Thus, property that the debtor acquired prior to the petition becomes property of the estate; property acquired after the petition generally is not property of the estate.

> *Example:*   If Ben Walton files a Chapter 7 petition on October 2, the money he earns for playing the piano at the Dew Drop Inn after October 2 is not "property of the estate."

2. EXCEPTIONS COVERING POST–PETITION PROPERTY

There are four significant exceptions to the rule that property acquired after the filing of a bankruptcy petition remains the debtor's property and is not property of the estate.

a. Certain Property Acquired Within 180 Days After Filing

Property of the estate includes property that the debtor acquires or becomes entitled to within 180 days after the filing of the petition by:

- bequest, devise, or inheritance

- property settlement or a divorce decree

- as beneficiary of a life insurance policy, section 541(a)(5).

b. Earnings of Property

Property of the estate also includes the post-petition earnings from property of the estate, section 541(a)(6). If, for example the Ropers file a Chapter 7 petition, the apartments that they own would be property of the estate, and post-petition rents from the apartments would be property of the estate.

c. Proceeds

Property of the estate includes property received from a conversion of property of the estate.

Example: Assume that James Rockford files a Chapter 11 petition and that the next day his mobile home is destroyed by a tidal wave. Any insurance proceeds would be property of the estate.

d. Chapters 12 and 13

In a Chapter 12 or 13 case, property of the estate includes wages earned and other property acquired by the debtor after the Chapter 12 or 13 filing, sections 1207 and 1306.

REVIEW QUESTIONS

1. T or F   Property of the estate is an important concept only in Chapter 7 cases.

2. D Corp., files a bankruptcy petition. Does property of the estate include the assets of its principal shareholder, P?

3. D, an artist, files for Chapter 7 relief. Are the earnings from work done after the Chapter 7 filing property of the estate?

4. D owns Blackacre. M has a mortgage on Blackacre. D files a Chapter 12 petition. Is Blackacre property of the estate?

*

XX

EXEMPTIONS IN BANKRUPTCY

Analysis

A. WHAT PROPERTY IS EXEMPT

Under non-bankruptcy law, Jim Rockford's mobile home would probably be exempt property. (Non-bankruptcy exemption law is considered supra at pages 223–54). Under the Bankruptcy Code, all pre-bankruptcy property in which the debtor has an interest becomes property of the estate, but an individual debtor is permitted to exempt certain property from property of the estate, section 522(b)(1).

1. CHOICE OF EXEMPTION LAWS

In bankruptcy, an individual debtor may assert the exemptions to which she is entitled under the laws of the state of her domicile and under federal laws other than Title 11, section 522(b)(2). Some of the items that may be exempted under federal laws other than Title 11 include: social security payments, 42 U.S.C.A. 407; civil service retirement benefits, 5 U.S.C.A. 729, 2265; veterans benefits, 45 U.S.C.A. 352(E). *Alternatively,* individual debtors may claim the Title 11 schedule of exemptions set out in section 522(d).

2. NO CHOICE IN STATE THAT HAS "OPTED OUT"

The Title 11 schedule of exemptions, described in section 522(d), is only available to individual debtors that reside in states that have not enacted "opt out" legislation pursuant to section 522(b)(1). Under section 522(b)(1), a state legislature can enact legislation precluding resident debtors from electing to utilize section 522(d). Most states have enacted such "opt out" legislation.

3. LIMITATIONS ON CHOICE

Even in states that have not "opted out" there are statutory limitations on the debtor's choice of exemption statutes.

a. All or Nothing

A debtor cannot select some exemptions from state law and some exemptions from section 522(d). He or she must choose either the non-bankruptcy exemptions or section 522(d).

b. Joint Cases

Under the 1984 amendments, section 522(b), husbands and wives in joint cases filed under section 302 or in individual cases which are being jointly administered under Bankruptcy Rule 1015(b) must both elect either the non-bankruptcy exemptions or the section 522(d) exemptions. While under section 522(m) each spouse will be entitled to separate exemptions, it will not be possible for one to choose section 522(d) exemptions while the other chooses non-bankruptcy exemptions.

In states that have not opted out, it may be disadvantageous for a husband and wife to file a joint petition. By filing two individual petitions and paying two $60 filing fees, a married couple may be able to increase the amount of their property that will be exempt.

4. WAIVERS OF EXEMPTIONS

The Bankruptcy Code expressly deals with the effect of a debtor's contracting away his or her exemptions. Such a contract has no effect. Whether an individual debtor elects to claim under non-bankruptcy exemption law or under section 522(d), waivers of exemption are not enforceable, section 522(e).

5. CONVERTING NON–EXEMPT PROPERTY TO EXEMPT PROPERTY

The Bankruptcy Code does not expressly deal with the consequences of a debtor converting non-exempt property into exempt property on the eve of bankruptcy. What if, just before filing for bankruptcy, D takes funds from her bank account, non-exempt property under relevant law, and invests the money in an exempt homestead? While the Bankruptcy Code does not answer this question, both legislative history and case law suggest that the property will be exempt. Some of the cases are mentioned supra at pages 189–90.

B. SIGNIFICANCE OF EXEMPT PROPERTY IN BANKRUPTCY

1. KEEPING PROPERTY

Generally, an individual debtor is able to retain his or her exempt property. Exempt property is not distributed to creditors in the bankruptcy case and is protected from the claims of most creditors after the bankruptcy case.

After bankruptcy, there are only four groups of creditors who have recourse to property set aside as exempt in a bankruptcy case:

- Creditors with tax claims excepted from discharge by section 523(a)(1);

- Creditors with domestic claims excepted from discharge by section 523(a)(5);

- Creditors whose claims arise after the filing of the bankruptcy petition;

- Creditors with liens on exempt property that are neither avoided nor extinguished through redemption.

Also, if the debtor chooses the section 522(d) set of exemptions, post-petition creditors will be able to reach items not exempted under relevant state law.

2. AVOIDING ENCUMBRANCES THROUGH INVALIDATION—§ 522(f)

Some liens on exempt property that are valid outside of bankruptcy can be invalidated because of bankruptcy. The general invalidation provisions, which are discussed infra at Chapter 21, are applicable to liens on exempt property. More importantly, section 522(f) empowers the debtor to avoid judicial liens on any exempt property and to avoid non-possessory, non-purchase money security interests in certain household goods, tools of trade, and health aids.

Example: Assume that the list of property that an individual claims as exempt includes a stereo system and an automobile. If a creditor has an attachment or execution lien on the stereo, the debtor may avoid the lien, section 522(f)(1). If a creditor has a security interest in the stereo, the security interest may be avoided unless it is either possessory or purchase money, section 522(f)(2). If a creditor has an attachment lien or execution lien on the automobile, the debtor may avoid the lien. If, on the other hand, a creditor has a security interest in the automobile, the debtor cannot avoid the lien unless—under the applicable exemption law—the automobile is a tool or implement of trade. It may be such a tool under state exemption law; it probably is not a tool or implement of trade under section 522(d).

a. When § 522(f) Applies
Section 522(f) applies in every personal bankruptcy, and is available to the debtor even if she elects to claim exemptions under non-bankruptcy law instead of section 522(d).

b. What Liens and Security Interests Are Affected

1) Judicial Liens
Section 522(f) can be used to avoid any judicial lien on exempt property.

2) Certain Security Interests
Section 522(f) does not invalidate every security interest. It reaches only security interests, i.e., consensual liens, that:

- are non-possessory, and

- are non-purchase money, and

- encumber exempt property *of a type mentioned in section 522(f)(2).*

c. Limits on Practical Significance of § 522(f)
There are two non-bankruptcy developments that limit the practical significance of section 522(f).

1) FTC Rule
The Federal Trade Commission has promulgated a trade regulation rule that makes obtaining a nonpossessory, non-purchase money security interest in household goods an unfair trade practice.

2) Change in State Exemption Law
Probably in reaction to § 522(f), some states have revised their exemption laws by providing that property encumbered by nonpossessory, non-purchase money security interests cannot be claimed as exempt. If a state has both opted out and adopted such a definition of exempt property, arguably its resident debtors can make no effective use of section 522(f). Under section 522(f), the debtors may avoid only judicial liens on property that is exempt. Some cases have held that if under state law property subject to liens cannot be exempt, then bankruptcy law section 522(f) cannot be used to avoid the liens.

3. EXTINGUISHING SECURITY INTERESTS THROUGH REDEMPTION—§ 722
Possessory security interests in exempt personal property, purchase money security interests in exempt personal property, and security interests in exempt personal property not covered by section 522(f) may be extinguished through "redemption." Section 722 authorizes an individual debtor to redeem or extinguish a lien on exempt personal property by paying the lienor the value of the property encumbered. The Code does not expressly indicate whether the section 722 payment must be in cash. The courts, however, consistently read section 722 as requiring cash payment.

> ***Example:*** D owes C $3000. C has a security interest in D's Buick. If D files a bankruptcy petition and the value of the Buick is only $1200, D can eliminate C's interest by paying C $1200.

In theory, section 722 applies to all liens on "tangible personal property intended for personal, family, or household use" that secure "a dischargeable consumer debt." So, there is considerable overlap between section 522(f) and section 722, except that section 722 does not apply to liens on tools of the trade. In practice, however, a debtor will not invoke section 722 to redeem property from liens which can be avoided under section 522(f).

REVIEW QUESTIONS

1. T or F   Only an individual can claim exempt property.

2. T or F   Only a Chapter 7 debtor can claim exempt property.

3. T or F   In states that have not "opted out," paragraph (d) of section 522 determines what property is exempt.

4. D files a Chapter 7 petition. D owes S $1,200. S has a non-purchase money security interest on D's furniture. The furniture has a value of no more than $500. Can D extinguish S's lien by redeeming the furniture for $500? Should D?

*

XXI

AVOIDING PRE-BANKRUPTCY TRANSFERS

> G. Reclamation Under U.C.C. Section 2–702
>   1. Right Under the Uniform Commercial Code
>   2. Bankruptcy's Effect on the Right

Some transfers that are valid outside of bankruptcy can be invalidated by a bankruptcy trustee. The Bankruptcy Code empowers the bankruptcy trustee to invalidate certain pre-bankruptcy transfers. These invalidation provisions reach both absolute transfers such as payments of money, gifts, and sales, and security transfers such as creation of mortgages and security interests.

Consider first the invalidation of an absolute transfer. When the bankruptcy trustee invalidates a pre-bankruptcy absolute transfer, the property becomes property of the estate, sections 550 and 541(a)(3). Assume that D owes C $1,000. D repays $800 of the $1,000 debt. D later files for bankruptcy. At the time of bankruptcy, C has a $200 claim against D, and the $600 is not property of the estate. If the bankruptcy trustee is able to void the payment, the $800 will be property of the estate and C will have a $1,000 claim against D.

Avoidance of a security transfer has similar effects. When the bankruptcy trustee invalidates a security transfer, the encumbered property becomes property of the estate free from encumbrances. Assume for example that D borrows $1,000 from S and grants S a security interest in equipment worth $1,000. At the time of bankruptcy, S has a $1,000 secured claim against D and only D's limited interest in the equipment is property of the estate. If the bankruptcy trustee is able to void the grant of the security interest, the unencumbered equipment will be property of the estate and S will have an unsecured $1,000 claim against D.

The various invalidation provisions reflect certain basic bankruptcy policies. The provisions and underlying policies are considered below.

A. PREFERENCES (SECTION 547)

Common law does not condemn a preference. Under common law, a debtor even an insolvent debtor, may treat certain creditors more favorably than other similar creditors. Although D owes X, Y, and Z $1,000 each, D may pay X's claim in full before paying any part of Y's claim or Z's claim.

Some state statutes void certain transfers because of their preferential character. The trustee may take advantage of such statutes by virtue of his powers under section 544(b): if the state anti-preference provision protects any actual creditor of the debtor, it protects the bankruptcy trustee. Section 544(b) is considered infra at pages 408–13.

Moreover, and much more important, bankruptcy law itself condemns certain preferences through § 547. A House report that accompanied a draft of the Code explained the rationale for such a bankruptcy policy as follows:

"The purpose of the preference section is twofold. First, by permitting the trustee to avoid pre-bankruptcy transfers that occur within a short period before bankruptcy, creditors are discouraged form racing to the courthouse to dismember the debtor during his slide into bankruptcy. The protection thus afforded the debtor often enables him to work his way out of a difficult financial situation through cooperation with all of his creditors. Second, and more important, the preference provisions facilitate the prime bankruptcy policy of equality of distribution among creditors of the debtor. Any creditor that received a greater payment than others of his class is required to disgorge so that all may share equally."

House Report 95–595 at 117–78.

1. ELEMENTS OF A PREFERENCE—§ 547(b)

Section 547(b) sets out the elements of a preference; the bankruptcy trustee may void any transfer of property of the debtor if he or she can establish:

- the transfer was "to or for the benefit of a creditor"; and

- the transfer was made for or on account of an "antecedent debt", i.e., a debt owed prior to the time of the transfer; and

- the debtor was insolvent at the time of the transfer; and

- the transfer was made within 90 days before the date of the filing of the bankruptcy petition, or was made between 90 days and 1 year before the date of the filing of the petition to an "insider", which term is defined in section 101 (An insider includes relatives of an individual debtor and directors of a corporate debtor.); and

- the transfer has the effect of increasing the amount that the transferee would receive in a Chapter 7 case.

Each of these requirements is now considered in turn.

a. To or for the Benefit of a Creditor

The term "creditor" essentially means someone who has a claim against the debtor, i.e., someone the debtor owes money. Thus, a true gift is not a preference because the debtor has not made a transfer of her property to or for the benefit of a creditor.

b. Antecedent Debt

A transfer is not a preference unless it is made for or on account of an antecedent debt, which essentially means an obligation existing prior to the time of the transfer.

c. Insolvency

The third requirement—insolvency of the debtor at the time of transfer—is made easy by section 547(f)'s creation of a rebuttable presumption of insolvency for the 90 days immediately preceding the filing of the bankruptcy petition.

d. 90–Day or One-Year Period

In determining whether the transfer was made within 90 days of the filing of the petition, look to Bankruptcy Rule 9006 which provides that the day on which the transfer occurred is not included. If under state law, a transfer is not fully effective against third parties until public notice of the transfer has been given and such public notice is not timely given, then section 547(e) deems the transfer to have occurred at the time public notice was given. The use of section 547 to invalidate transfers not recorded in a timely fashion is considered infra at pages 416–20.

In determining whether the transfer was made to an "insider" so that the relevant time period is one year, not merely 90 days, look to the Bankruptcy Code section 101(28)'s definition of insider.

Remember that the presumption of insolvency is limited to the 90 days immediately preceding the bankruptcy petition. Accordingly, in order to invalidate a transfer that occurred more than 90 days before the filing of the bankruptcy petition the trustee must establish that (i) the transferee was an "insider"; and (ii) the debtor was insolvent at the time of the transfer.

e. Improvement in Position

The fifth element, which essentially tests whether the transfer improved the creditor's position, will be satisfied unless the creditor was fully secured before the transfer or the property of the estate is sufficiently large to permit 100% payment to all unsecured claims.

Example: Assume that D makes a $1,000 payment to C, a creditor with a $10,000 unsecured claim, on January 10. On February 20, D files a bankruptcy petition. The property of the estate is sufficient to pay each unsecured creditor 50% of its claim. An unsecured creditor with a $10,000 claim will thus receive $5,000. C, however, will receive a total of $5,500 from D and D's bankruptcy unless the January 10th transfer is avoided. ($1,000 + 50% x (10,000−1,000)). Accordingly, the bankruptcy trustee may avoid the January 10th transfer under section 547(b) to "facilitate the prime bankruptcy policy of equality of distribution among creditors."

2. APPLYING § 547(b)

The following examples illustrate the application of section 547(b).

Examples: On February 2, D borrows $7,000 from C and promises to repay the $7,000 on March 2. D repays C on March 2d as promised. On May 24, D files a bankruptcy petition. The bankruptcy trustee can recover the $7,000 payment from C. See section 547(b); see also section 550.

On February 2, D borrows $7,000 from C. D repays C on March 2. On June 6, D files a bankruptcy petition. The bankruptcy trustee cannot recover the $7,000 from C under section 547(b). Section 547(b)(4) is not satisfied because more than 90 days.

On February 2, D borrows $7,000 from C. On March 2, X, a friend of D's, pays C the $7,000 D owed. On May 24, D files a bankruptcy petition. The bankruptcy trustee cannot recover the $7,000 from C under section 547(b). The payment was not a "transfer of an interest of the debtor in property."

On January 10, D borrows $10,000 from C and grants C a security interest in its equipment. At all relevant times, the equipment has a value of $20,000. On March 3, D repays C $3,000 of the $10,000. On April 4, D files a bankruptcy petition. The bankruptcy trustee can not avoid the March 3 payment under section 547(b). Section 547(b)(5) is not satisfied. Note that C had a security interest. Note also that the value of the collateral securing C's claim was greater than the amount of the claim. (See section 506. Under this provision, the amount of a secured claim is limited by the value of the collateral.) In a Chapter 7 case, the holder of a secured claim will receive either its collateral or its value up to the amount of the debt. Accordingly, even if the payment had not been made, S as a fully secured creditor would have been paid in full. A pre-bankruptcy payment to a fully secured creditor is not a preference.

On February 2, D borrows $200,000 from S and S records a mortgage on Redacre, real property of D's. At all relevant times, Redacre has a value of $140,000. On April 5, D repays $40,000 of the loan. On May 6, D files a bankruptcy petition. The property of the estate is sufficient to pay each unsecured creditor 10% of its claim. The trustee may avoid the April 5 payment and recover the $40,000 for the estate. All of the elements of section 547(b) including section 547(b)(5) are satisfied. If the transfer had not been made, S would have received $146,000. If the transfer is not avoided, S will receive $182,000. [$140,000 secured claim + $40,000 payment + $2,000 on remaining $20,000 unsecured claim.]

On March 3, D borrows $300,000 from S. On April 4, S demands security for the loan and D gives S a mortgage on Redacre. Redacre has a fair market value of $400,000. On May 5, D files a bankruptcy petition. The property of the estate is sufficient to pay each unsecured creditor 20% of its claim. The trustee may avoid the April 4 mortgage so that Redacre is property of the estate free and clear of S's lien. Again all of the elements of section 547(b) are satisfied. The transfer would enable S to receive $300,000. If the transfer had not been made, S would receive only $60,000. [Section 547(b) invalidates liens to secure past unsecured debts.]

On April 4, D borrows $40,000 from S and gives S a security interest in equipment. The equipment has a fair market value of $30,000. On June 6, D files a bankruptcy petition. The trustee may not avoid the April 4 security interest. The April 4 transfer was for present consideration, not "for or on account of an antecedent debt." Section 547 does not invalidate liens to secure new debts.

3.   EXCEPTIONS—§ 547(c)

Section 547(b) sets out the elements of a voidable preference. Section 547(c) excepts certain pre-petition transfers from the operation of section 547(b). If a transfer comes within one of section 547(c)'s exceptions, the bankruptcy trustee will not be able to invalidate the transfer even though the trustee can establish all of the requirements of section 547(b).

a.   Contemporaneous New Value

The first exception is for a transfer that

- was intended to be for new value, not an antecedent debt, and

- did in fact occur at a time "substantially contemporaneous" with the time that the debt arose, section 547(c)(1).

Example: D borrows $5,000 from C on April 5. Both parties then intend the loan to be a secured loan, secured by a pledge of D's X Corp. stock. On April 9, D pledges her X Corp. stock by delivering the certificates to C. On May 6, D files a bankruptcy petition. The bankruptcy trustee will not be able to void the April 9 pledge under section 547. The transfer is for an antecedent debt but is protected by section 547(c)(1).

Note that section 547(c)(1) requires both that the transfer actually be a "substantially contemporaneous exchange" and that the parties so intended.

Example: Assume that C makes a loan to D that both C and D intend to be a 180 day loan. Later that same day C first learns that D is in financial difficulty and so demands and obtains repayment. Section 547(c)(1) could not apply to the repayment. While the transfer actually was a "substantially contemporaneous exchange," it was not so intended. If bankruptcy occurs within 90 days, the trustee can avoid the payment under section 547(b).

b.   Payments in the Ordinary Course of Business

While section 547(c)(1) can apply to either an absolute or a security transfer, section 547(c)(2) protects only absolute transfers: payments. Section 547(c)(2) looks to both the nature of the debt and the nature of the payment. In order to come under the protection of section 547(c)(2):

- the debt must be in the ordinary course of business (business debtor) or financial affairs (non-business debtor) of both the debtor and the creditor; *and*

- the payment must be in the ordinary course of business or financial affairs of both the debtor and the creditor; *and*

- the payment must be made according to ordinary business terms.

Example: D receives her water bill for January water use on February 2. D and most water customers regularly pay their water bills by check before the end of the month. D pays her water bill by check on February 14. Section 547(c)(2) applies.

c. Enabling Loans

The third exception protects "enabling loans." Section 547(c)(3) requires that:

- the creditor gives the debtor "new value" to acquire certain real or personal property;

- the debtor signs a security agreement giving the creditor a security interest in the property;

- the debtor in fact uses the "new value" supplied by the creditor to acquire the property; and

- the creditor perfects its security interest no later than ten days after the debtor receives possession.

Example: On April 4, F borrows $14,000 from S to buy a new tractor and signs a security agreement that describes the tractor. S files a financing statement. On April 20, F uses S's $14,000 to buy a new tractor. On May 5, F files a bankruptcy petition. F's bankruptcy trustee may not avoid S's security interest. It is true that all of the elements of section 547(b) are satisfied. (The creation of a lien is a transfer of property of the debtor. It was, of course, "to or for the benefit of a creditor." And, it was "for or on account of an antecedent debt." "For purposes of this section, a transfer is not made until the debtor has acquired rights in the property transferred," section 547(e)(3). The other elements of section 547(b) are discussed supra on pages 395–96.) It is also true, however, that all of the elements of section 547(c)(3) are also satisfied, and thus the transfer is not voidable.

d. Subsequent Value

Section 547(c)(4) provides a measure of protection for a creditor who receives a preference and "after such transfer" extends further unsecured credit.

Example: On June 6, C lends D $6,000. On July 7, D repays $4,000. On August 8, C lends D an additional $3,000. On September 9, D files a bankruptcy petition. The bankruptcy trustee can recover only $1,000. The July 7 payment of $4,000 was a preference under section 547(b). The trustee's recovery, however, is reduced by the amount of the August 8 unsecured advance of $3,000, section 547(c)(4).

Note that under section 547(c)(4), the sequence of events is of critical significance. The additional extension of credit must occur after the preferential transfer. If on June 6, C lends D $6,000; on July 7, C lends D an additional

$3,000; on August 8, D repays $4,000, and on September 9, D files a bankruptcy petition, the trustee could recover $4,000 under section 547.

e. Floating Liens

1) What Is a Floating Lien

Section 547(c)(5) creates a limited exception from preference attack for certain Article 9 floating liens. U.C.C. Article 9 provides a mechanism for establishing a "floating lien." Such liens are most commonly used in financing accounts or inventory which normally "turn-over" in the ordinary course of the debtor's business.

To illustrate, assume that on January 10, Credit Co., C, lends Department Store, D, $100,000 and takes a security interest in the store's inventory. Obviously, C wants D to sell its inventory so that it can repay the loan. It is equally obvious that as inventory is sold, the collateral securing C loan decreases unless C's lien "floats" to cover the proceeds from the sale of the inventory and/or cover new inventory that D later acquires. Accordingly, the security agreement that D signs on January 10 will probably contain an after-acquired property clause, that is, will probably grant C a security interest not only in the inventory that D now owns but also in the inventory that D later acquires.

2) Why Is It a § 547(b) Preference

Even though D only signs this one security agreement, section 547 views D as making numerous different transfers of security interests. Under section 547(e)(3), "For purposes of this section, a transfer is not made until the debtor has acquired rights in the property transferred." This means that every time D acquires additional inventory there is a new transfer for purposes of section 547. Thus, if D acquires new inventory on March 3 and files for bankruptcy within the next 90 days, it would seem that the trustee can invalidate C's security interest in the March 3 inventory because there was

- a transfer of property of the debtor to a creditor

- for an antecedent debt [The debt was incurred on January 10. As noted above, section 547(e)(3) dates the transfer of the security interest in the March 3 inventory as March 3.]

- presumption of insolvency [Remember section 547(f).]

- transfer made within 90 days of the bankruptcy petition

- transfer increased bankruptcy distribution to C (unless C was already fully secured.)

3) How § 547(c)(5) Saves It

In the above problem, section 547(c)(5) will usually protect C. Under this provision, a creditor with a security interest in inventory or accounts or other receivables is subject to a preference attack only to the extent that it improves its position during the 90–day period before bankruptcy. The test is a two-point test and requires determination of the secured creditor's position 90 days before the petition and on the date of the petition. [If new value was first given after 90 days before the case, the date on which it was first given substitutes for the 90-day point.]

There are seven steps involved in applying section 547(c)(5)'s "two-step" test:

1 Determine the amount of debt on the date of the bankruptcy petition.

2 Determine the value of the debtor's accounts and/or inventory encumbered by the secured creditor's lien on the date of the petition.

3 Subtract # 2 from # 1.

4 Determine the amount of debt 90 days before the petition.

5 Determine the value of the debtor's accounts and/or inventory encumbered by the secured creditor's lien 90 days before the petition.

6 Subtract # 5 from # 4.

7 Subtract the answer in # 3 from the answer in # 6. This is the amount of the preference.

The following hypotheticals illustrate the application of section 547(c)(5).

Examples: At the time of its bankruptcy petition, D owes C $100,000 and has inventory with a value of $60,000. C has a security interest in all of D's inventory. 90 days before bankruptcy, D owed C $90,000 and had inventory with a value of $70,000. All of D's inventory was acquired within the last 90 days. Under these facts, C has not improved its position. Under these facts, C's security interest will be protected by section 547(c)(5).

At the time of its bankruptcy petition, D owes C $100,000 and has inventory with a value of $75,000. C has a security interest in all of D's inventory. 90 days before bankruptcy, D owed C $90,000 and had inventory with a value of $30,000. All of D's inventory was acquired within the last 90 days. Under these facts, the bankruptcy trustee may reduce C's secured claim from $75,000 to $40,000. There was a $35,000 reduction in the amount by which the claim exceeded the collateral. (90–30)–(100–75) The $75,000 security claim is thus reduced by this $35,000 improvement in position.

Compare the two preceding examples. Which fact situation is more common? How often in the "real world" will a debtor in financial difficulty acquire additional inventory or generate an increased amount of accounts?

It is submitted that in the usual situation section 547(c)(5) completely protects a security interest in after-acquired inventory or accounts, that is, in the usual situation the "except" language of section 547(c)(5) is inapplicable.

Examples: D files a bankruptcy petition on April 22. At the time of the bankruptcy petition, D owes S $200,000. S has a security interest in D's inventory of oriental rugs which then have a value of $200,000. On January 22, 90 days before the bankruptcy petition was filed, D owed S $200,000, and the rugs had a fair market value of $150,000. D did not acquire any additional rugs after January 22; the value of D's rugs increased because of market considerations. The trustee has no section 547 rights against S. There is no transfer to invalidate. S's improvement in position was not "to the prejudice of other creditors holding an unsecured claim."

D Manufacturing Co., D, files a bankruptcy petition on April 4. At the time of the filing of the bankruptcy, D owes C Credit Corp., C, $40,000. C has a valid-in-bankruptcy security interest in all of D's equipment. The security agreement between D and C has an after-acquired property clause. On the date of the filing of the petition, D's equipment has a fair market value of $31,000. On January 4, 90 days before the filing of the bankruptcy petition, D owed C $40,000 and D's equipment had a fair market value of $32,000. On February 2, D sold a piece of equipment for $6,000. (D used the $6,000 to pay taxes.) On March 3, D bought other equipment for $5,000. The trustee can limit S's security interest to the equipment owned on January 4. The March 3 "transfer" is a preference under section 547(b). (Remember, that March 3 is the date that the transfer of a security interest in the new equipment is deemed made for purposes of section 547, section 547(e)(3).) The March 3 "transfer" of a security interest in equipment is not protected by section 547(c)(5) because it only applies to security interests in inventory or accounts.

f. Statutory Liens

Section 547(c)(6) exempts "statutory liens" from the scope of section 547. Statutory liens are covered by section 545, which is explained on pages 421–22, infra.

"Statutory lien" is defined in section 101(45) as a lien "arising solely by force of statute." Section 101(45) expressly provides that neither a security interest nor a judicial lien is a "statutory lien." While there are statutes providing for security interests and judicial liens, neither a security interest nor a judicial lien arises "solely by force of statute." A security interest will always require an agreement; a judicial lien will always require court action.

Example: C Construction Co. is building a warehouse for D. Under relevant state statutes, a builder can obtain a construction lien. C takes the steps required by the state law and obtains a construction lien on the warehouse to secure payment for the work that it has done. If D files for bankruptcy, the bankruptcy trustee will not be able to attack the construction lien under section 547.

g. Small Consumer Transfers
Section 547(c)(7) was added in 1984. It applies only if

- the debtor is an individual and

- his or her debts are "primarily" consumer debts and

- the aggregate value of all property covered by the transfer is less than $600.

Example: D owes C $1,200 and pays her $400 four days before filing for bankruptcy, the bankruptcy trustee will not be able to recover the $400 from C under section 547.

B. SETOFFS (SECTION 553)

1. WHAT IS SETOFF
At times, a party is both a creditor and a debtor of another party. Assume, for example, that Stephen Weed, W, has a checking account at Kane Citizens Bank, B, with a $1,000 balance. W borrows $4,000 from B to buy a new car. B is in the position of a creditor of W's on the car loan; B, however, is in the position of a debtor of W's on the checking account. B is thus both W's creditor and W's debtor.

In attempting to collect the $4,000 loan from W, B may assert its right of setoff. "Set-off is the cancellation of cross demands between two parties. The term is commonly used to cover both judicially supervised setoffs and automatic extinction of cross-demands." Zubrow, *Integration of Deposit Account Financing Into Article 9 of the Uniform Commercial Code: A Proposal for Legislative Reform,* 68 Minn.L. Rev. 899, 901, n. 3 (1984).

The use of setoff is not limited to banks. Bank setoff is, however, the most common setoff transaction. Accordingly, this book will deal with setoff primarily in a banking context.

2. BANKRUPTCY AVOIDANCE OF SETOFF
Suppose that Kane Citizens Bank, B, asserts its right of setoff against Stephen Weed, W. B will thereby reduce W's checking account balance from $1,000 to 0 and reduce the amount owed by W on the $4,000 loan to $3,000. What if Stephen Weed files a bankruptcy petition one day after the setoff? Can the bankruptcy trustee recover the $1,000 from Kane Citizens Bank? If one day before the filing of a bankruptcy petition, W withdraws $1,000 from his savings account and uses that

$1,000 to reduce his indebtedness to B, the trustee can recover the $1,000 under section 547. Is there any reason to treat B's setoff differently?

Section 547 does not apply to setoffs. Section 553 is the only provision of the Bankruptcy Code that limits pre-petition setoffs. It contains a number of limitations on setoffs:

a. "Mutual Debt"
The debts must be between the same parties in the same right or capacity. For example, a claim against a "bankrupt" as an administratrix cannot be set off against a debt owed to the "bankrupt" as an individual. (*Aside:* The Bankruptcy Code uses the term "debtor", not the term "bankrupt". Nevertheless, in discussing setoffs in which each party is the debtor of the other, it seems less confusing to use the term "bankrupt" to identify the party that filed a voluntary bankruptcy petition (or the party whose creditors filed an involuntary bankruptcy petition).)

b. "Arose Before the Commencement of the Case"
Both the debt owed to the "bankrupt" and the claim against the "bankrupt" must have preceded the filing of the bankruptcy petition.

c. "Disallowed" (§ 553(a)(1))
Certain claims against a "bankrupt" are disallowed. See section 502 considered infra at pages 447–50. A claim that is disallowed under section 502 may not be used as the basis for a setoff.

> *Example:* A owes B $4,000. B files a bankruptcy petition. The debt from A to B is property of the estate. The trustee attempts to collect the $4,000 from A. A only pays the trustee $3,000. A alleges that it had set off a $1,000 claim it had against B prior to the bankruptcy filing. If that $1,000 claim would be barred by the statute of limitations in a state collection action, it would be disallowed under section 502(b)(1) and the setoff would be disallowed under section 553(a)(1).

d. "Acquired" Claims (§ 553(a)(2))
Certain acquired claims cannot be setoff. Assume for example, that B is insolvent; A owes B $4,000; B owes C $1,000. Because B is insolvent C's $1,000 claim is of little value to C. C would be willing to sell its claim against B to A for less than $1,000. A would be willing to buy C's claim for less than $1,000 if it could then assert that claim as a setoff to reduce its debt to B from $4,000 to $3,000.

Under section 553(a)(2), claims against the "bankrupt" acquired from a third party may not be set off against a debt owed to the "bankrupt" if:

- the claim was acquired within 90 days before the bankruptcy petition or after the bankruptcy petition, and

- the "bankrupt" was insolvent when the claim was acquired. [Section 553(c) creates a rebuttable presumption of insolvency.]

e. Build-Ups (§ 553(a)(3))
Section 553(a)(3) precludes a setoff by a bank if:

- money was deposited by the "bankrupt" within 90 days of the bankruptcy petition, and

- the "bankrupt" was insolvent at the time of the setoff (Remember section 553(c)'s presumption of insolvency.), and

- the purpose of the deposit was to create or increase the right of setoff.

Example: X Bank makes a loan to D Corp. Payment of the loan is guaranteed by P, the president of D Corp. D Corp. suffers financial reverses. X Bank pressures D Corp. and P to increase the balance of the corporation's general bank account. D Corp. moves $100,000 from other banks to its X Bank account before filing its bankruptcy petition. Section 553(a)(3) would preclude X Bank from taking the $100,000 by way of setoff.

f. Improvement in Position (§ 553(b))
Section 553(b) is similar to section 547(c)(5), considered supra at pages 400–02. Both are designed to prevent an improvement in position within 90 days of bankruptcy. Application of section 553(b) requires the following simple computations:

\# 1 Determine amount of claim against the debtor 90 days before the date of the filing of the petition. (If there is no "insufficiency" (as defined in section 553(b)(2)) 90 days before the petition, examine the 89th day, then the 88th day, etc. until a day is found that has an "insufficiency." Computations \# 1–\# 3 will then focus on that day.)

\# 2 Determine the "mutual debt" owing to the "bankrupt" by the holder of such claim 90 days before the filing of the petition.

\# 3 Subtract \# 2 from \# 1 to determine the "insufficiency."

\# 4 Determine the amount of the debt on the date that the right of setoff was asserted.

\# 5 Determine the amount of the setoff.

\# 6 Subtract \# 5 from \# 4 to determine the insufficiency.

\# 7 Subtract the answer in \# 6 from the answer in \# 3, to determine what part, if any, of the amount setoff the trustee may recover.

The following examples illustrate the application of section 553(b):

Examples: D files a Chapter 13 petition. 90 days before the petition, D owes B Bank $100,000 and has $40,000 on deposit. 10 days before the petition, B exercises its right of setoff. At that time, D owes B Bank $70,000 and the account has a $60,000 balance. There was a $60,000 ($100,000—$40,000) "insufficiency" 90 days before the bankruptcy petition was filed. At the time of the setoff, the "insufficiency" was only $10,000 ($70,000—$60,000). There was a $50,000 improvement in position ($60,000—$10,000). The bankruptcy trustee may recover from B Bank $50,000 of the amount of offset under section 553(b).

D files a Chapter 7 petition. 90 days before the petition, D owes $200,000 to B Bank and has $200,000 on deposit at B Bank. 88 days before the petition D withdraws $80,000 from the account; 5 days days before the petition, B exercises its right of setoff. At that time, D owes B $70,000 and has $60,000 on deposit in B Bank. The trustee may recover $60,000 from B Bank. On the first date within the 90 day period that there was an "insufficiency," it was an insufficiency of $80,000. At the time of the setoff, the "insufficiency" was only $10,000 ($70,000—$60,000). There was an improvement in position of $70,000 ($80,000—$10,000). Nevertheless, the trustee may recover only $60,000 under section 553(b). "The amount so offset" establishes the ceiling for recovery under section 553(b).

3. EFFECT OF BANKRUPTCY STAY

The filing of a bankruptcy petition automatically stays any further setoffs. Section 553 subjects the right of setoff to limitations provided in sections 362 and 363. Section 362(a)(7) stays setoffs. Thus, in order, to exercise a right of setoff after the filing of the bankruptcy petition it is necessary to obtain relief from the stay. Section 362(d), considered supra at pages 377–80, governs relief from the stay.

If a stay is terminated or modified to permit a post-petition setoff, the setoff will be limited by section 553(a) requirements # 1–# 5, discussed supra pages 404–05. Section 553(b) applies only to pre-petition setoffs.

C. FRAUDULENT TRANSFERS

1. SECTION 548

The Bankruptcy Code, like non-bankruptcy law, invalidates fraudulent conveyances. Indeed, the Bankruptcy Code's main fraudulent conveyance provision, section 548, is very much like the non-bankruptcy fraudulent conveyance statutes considered supra at pages 181–202.

a. Based on UFCA

Section 548 is based on the Uniform Fraudulent Conveyances Act. Section 548(a)(1) corresponds to section 7 of the UFCA; it empowers the trustee to invalidate transfers made with actual intent to hinder, delay or defraud creditors.   Section 548(b) is similar to the partnership provisions of section 8(a) of the UFCA. Under section 548(b), the trustee of a bankrupt partnership may avoid a transfer of partnership property to a general partner if the partnership was or thereby became insolvent.   The consideration given the partnership by the partner is irrelevant since a general partner is individually liable for the payment of the partnership's debts.   Transfers by a partnership to a non-partner are governed by section 548(a).

Section 548(a)(2) resembles UFCA sections 4 and 7; it provides for avoidance of transfers where the debtor received less than a "reasonably equivalent value" and (i) was insolvent or became insolvent as a result of the transaction, or (ii) was engaged in business or was about to engage in a business transaction for which his remaining property was unreasonably small capital; or (iii) intended to incur or believed that he would incur debts beyond his ability to pay.

REMINDERS: You may remember that there is a presumption of insolvency in section 547.   If so, you also remember that the presumption of insolvency in section 547 is limited to section 547: "for purposes of this section," section 547(f).

You may also remember that the Bankruptcy Code has its own definition of insolvency in section 101.   Section 101 compares the amount of the debtor's debts with the value of her non-exempt property.   What is the practical significance, if any, of this reminder?   In states with liberal exemptions, most individuals are insolvent for purposes of section 548.

Final recollection for now.   The UFCA uses essentially the same definition of insolvency.

b.   Differences From UFCA

Section 548 differs from the UFCA in several significant respects:

- Section 548 applies to transfers of both non-exempt and exempt property. The UFCA is limited to transfers of non-exempt property.

- The test in section 548(a)(2) is "reasonably equivalent value."   The test in section 4 of the UFCA is "fair consideration."   The "fair consideration" standard requires an inquiry into both the amount of consideration and the parties' good faith.   Section 548's use of "reasonably equivalent value" eliminates a good faith requirement from the value determination.   However, the "good faith" of the transferee remains significant under section 548.   Section 548(c) protects a transferee who takes "for value and in good faith."   Accordingly, the practical significance of the use of "reasonably equivalent value" instead of "fair consideration" is the elimination of any inquiry into the good faith of the transferor in determining whether a trustee can recover property under section 548(a)(2).

  In contrast, the transferor's good faith (or lack of good faith) is, of course, a very important factor in determining whether the trustee may invalidate a transfer under section 548(a)(1): "made such transfer * * * with actual intent to hinder, delay or defraud."

- Section 548 eliminates the requirement of actual unpaid creditors as to whom the transfer was fraudulent. Under the UFCA a transfer by an insolvent not for fair consideration may be set aside only by creditors who were creditors at the time of the transfer. Under section 548(a)(2), such a transfer may be avoided even though all who were creditors at the time of the transfer have been paid.

- The UFCA does not have its own statute of limitations. States generally have a three to six year limitations period for actions to invalidate fraudulent conveyances. Under section 548, the bankruptcy trustee may only reach transfers made within one year of the filing of the bankruptcy petition.

- For purposes of section 548, a transfer will be deemed made when it becomes so far perfected that a bona fide purchaser from the debtor could not acquire an interest in the property transferred superior to the interest of the transferor, section 548(d). The problems of determining the date that a transfer will be deemed made are considered at pages 420–21 infra.

The one-year period of section 548 is not a true statute of limitations. It does not require that the trustee's action to invalidate the transfer be commenced within one year of the time the transfer was made. If the transfer was made within one year of the date of the filing of the bankruptcy petition, the bankruptcy trustee has up until the closing or dismissal of the case or two years after his or her appointment, whichever first occurs, to commence the invalidation action, section 546.

> *Example:* Assume that in June of 1988, Mrs. Lupner gave her daughter Lisa a new piano as a graduation present. Mrs. Lupner was insolvent at the time of the gift. On August 1, 1989, Mrs. Lupner files a bankruptcy petition. By the date of bankruptcy, Mrs. Lupner has repaid all of her June, 1988 creditors except Todd DilaMuca whom she owed $10. Mrs. Lupner's bankruptcy trustee will not be able to recover the piano under section 548. The transfer was a fraudulent conveyance (a transfer for less than "reasonably equivalent value" while insolvent) but it was made more than a year prior to the bankruptcy petition.

2.   SECTION 544(b)

Section 548 is not the only provision in the Bankruptcy Code that invalidates fraudulent conveyances. The trustee may also use section 544(b) to invalidate fraudulent conveyances.

a. Incorporates State Law

Section 544(b) does not specifically provide for the invalidation of fraudulent conveyances. Rather it empowers the bankruptcy trustee to avoid any pre-bankruptcy transfer that is voidable under applicable law by a creditor holding an unsecured claim that is allowable. (Section 502 governs allowance of claims. Section 502 is considered infra at pages 447–50.)

Section 544(b) incorporates state fraudulent conveyance law into the Bankruptcy Code. If, outside of bankruptcy, the transfer would be governed by a Statute of Elizabeth fraudulent conveyance statute, section 544(b) is a Statute of Elizabeth statute; if the state statute is the UFCA, then section 544(b) is UFCA.

Example: In the Lupner problem, the June gift of a piano would be a fraudulent conveyance, under non-bankruptcy law, as to Todd DilaMuca. Todd DilaMuca was a creditor holding an unsecured claim that is allowable. Accordingly, the bankruptcy trustee may use section 544(b) to recover the piano.

Section 544(b) reflects not only the state substantive law of fraudulent conveyances but also the state limitations period for fraudulent conveyances. The state limitations period determines which transfers may be challenged, not when the challenge must be made. Section 546 again gives the trustee time after his or her appointment to commence the action.

Example: D makes a fraudulent conveyance in January of 1988. State law imposes a five-year limitation period on fraudulent conveyance actions. If D files a bankruptcy petition in December of 1989 that satisfies or tolls the state law limitations period, D's bankruptcy trustee will have the additional section 546 period to commence a fraudulent conveyance action.

b. Trustee in Better Position Than Actual Creditor: *Moore v. Bay*

While the existence of the trustee's section 544(b) avoiding powers depends upon the existence of an avoiding power held by an actual creditor, the extent of the trustee's section 544(b) avoidance powers is greater than the power of the actual creditor. In the Lupner problem, under state fraudulent conveyance law, if Lisa Lupner paid Todd DilaMuca $10, she could keep the piano. Under section 544(b), Lisa is not so fortunate. Legislative history clearly indicates that section 544(b) retains the rule of *Moore v. Bay,* 284 U.S. 4, 52 S.Ct. 3 (1931).

Under the rule of *Moore v. Bay,* the trustee is not limited in his recovery by the amount of the claim of the actual creditor. A transfer which is voidable by a single, actual creditor, may be avoided entirely by the trustee, regardless of the size of the actual creditor's claim. Thus Lisa may not keep the piano by simply paying the bankruptcy trustee $10.

3. COMPARISON OF SECTIONS 548 AND 544(b)

The Lupner hypothetical points up the similarities and differences of sections 548 and 544(b).

These provisions are also compared by the following chart:

548	544(b)
1. Essentially UFCA	1. UFCA or Statute of Elizabeth, whichever is the state law
2. Reaches transfers made within one year of bankruptcy petition [limitations period is measured from the time the transfer is *deemed* made. See pages 420–21 infra]	2. Reaches all transfers made with state limitations period [limitations period is measured from the time the transfer was actually made]
3. Elements of fraudulent conveyance tested as of time that transfer was *deemed* made. See pages 420–21 infra	3. Elements of fraudulent conveyance tested as of time that the fraudulent conveyance was actually made
4. Transferee that takes for value and in good faith protected	4. Transferee that takes for value and in good faith protected
5. No requirement of actual creditor as to whom conveyance is fraudulent	5. Voidable only if transfer is fraudulent as to an actual creditor with an unsecured, allowable claim
6. Complete invalidation	6. Complete invalidation

4. FORECLOSURE SALES AS FRAUDULENT TRANSFERS

There is currently considerable controversy over fraudulent conveyance challenges in bankruptcy to pre-bankruptcy foreclosure sales. This controversy is discussed earlier in the chapter on fraudulent conveyances under state law. See supra pages 195–98. Please "re-read." You may very well see this kind of problem on a final examination!

D. TRANSFERS NOT TIMELY RECORDED OR PERFECTED

A bankruptcy trustee may avoid certain pre-petition transfers that are not timely recorded or perfected. A failure to record or a delay in recording can adversely affect other creditors. If creditor X does not record its lien on D's property, creditor Y might not know that D's property is encumbered. Relying on the mistaken belief that D holds his property free from liens, Y might extend credit, refrain from obtaining a lien, or forebear from instituting collection proceedings.

State law requires recordation or other public notice of a number of transfers. Real estate recording statutes require the recording of deeds and real property mortgages. Article 6 of the Uniform Commercial Code requires that creditors be notified in advance of any bulk transfer. Section 2–326 of the Code calls for public notice of sales on consignment. And, Article 9 of the Uniform Commercial Code calls for public notice, (perfection) of security interests.

The Bankruptcy Code does not have its own public notice requirements. It does not simply invalidate all transfers not recorded within 10 days or 90 days. Rather, the Bankruptcy Code makes use of the notoriety requirements of state law in the following invalidation provisions: sections 544, 547 and 545.

1. SECTION 544(b)

Section 544(b) empowers the bankruptcy trustee to invalidate any transfer that under non-bankruptcy law is voidable as to any actual creditor of the debtor with an unsecured, allowable claim. (Note: Most creditors' claims are allowable. Section 502, particularly section 502(b), indicates the extent to which claims are disallowed. Section 502 is considered infra at pages 447–50.)

In applying section 544(b), it is thus necessary to determine:

- whether non-bankruptcy law public notice requirements have been timely satisfied;

- which persons are protected by the non-bankruptcy requirement of public notice;

- if any actual creditor of the debtor with an unsecured allowable claim comes within the class of persons protected by such state law.

The following hypotheticals illustrate the application of section 544(b):

Examples: On January 10, D makes a bulk transfer to X. X fails to give notice to C, one of D's creditors. Under U.C.C. section 6–104, such failure to notify renders the transfer "ineffective" against C. On March 3, D files a bankruptcy petition. On that date, C is still one of D's unsecured creditors. The bankruptcy trustee will be able to invalidate the January 10 transfer to X. The applicable public notoriety requirement, section 6–104, was not timely satisfied. Section 6–104 protects all creditors of the transferor whose claims arose before the bulk transfer. C is such a creditor. C is an actual creditor of the debtor-transferor with an unsecured, allowable claim. Since the transfer is ineffective as to C, the bankruptcy trustee can invalidate the transfer. (Remember that under section 544(b), the bankruptcy trustee is not limited by the amount of the actual creditor's claim. A transaction which is voidable (or ineffective) as to a single actual creditor can be completely avoided by the trustee, regardless of the size of that creditor's claim. See page 409 supra.)

On January 10, D borrows $10,000 from M and gives M a mortgage on Redacre. On February 2, C lends D $10,000. On March 3, M records its mortgage. On July 7, D files a bankruptcy petition. On the date of the perfection, D still owes $10,000 to M and

$10,000 to C. D's bankruptcy trustee will not be able to invalidate M's mortgage. The public notoriety requirements were not timely satisfied. M delayed in recording its mortgages. Most real property recording statutes only protect purchasers and/or lien creditors. C is not within the class of persons protected by the applicable recording statute. Section 544(b) empowers the trustee to invalidate transfers that are invalid as to actual creditors such as C. Since C cannot invalidate the transfer, the bankruptcy trustee cannot invalidate the transfer under section 544(b).

On January 10, D borrows $10,000 from S and gives S a security interest in equipment. On February 2, C lends D $10,000. On March 3 S perfects its security interest. On July 7, D files a bankruptcy petition. On the date of the petition, D still owes $10,000 to S and $10,000 to C. D's bankruptcy trustee will not be able to invalidate S's security interest. The public notoriety requirements of the UCC were not timely satisfied. S delayed in perfecting its security interest. Article 9's perfection requirements, however, protect only certain gap secured creditors and buyers. C is not within the class of persons protected by the applicable recording statute. Section 544(b) empowers the bankruptcy trustee to avoid transfers that are invalid as to actual creditors. Since no actual creditor can invalidate the transfer, the bankruptcy trustee can not invalidate the transfer.

On January 10, D borrows $10,000 from S and gives S a security interest in equipment. On February 2, L obtains an execution lien on the same equipment. On March 2, S perfects its security interest. On July 7, D files a bankruptcy petition. On the date of the petition, D is still indebted to S and L. The bankruptcy trustee will not be able to invalidate S's security interest. Again, the public notoriety requirements of the UCC were not timely satisfied. Article 9's perfection requirements do protect a lien creditor such as L, section 9–301. L is a holder of a secured claim. Section 544(b) only gives the bankruptcy trustee the invalidation powers of any actual holders of unsecured claims. While L has the power to invalidate S's security interest, the bankruptcy trustee does not have L's invalidation powers.

As the last three of these examples illustrate, the use of section 544(b) to invalidate pre-petition transfers that were not timely recorded is severely limited. Section 544(b) gives the trustee the invalidation powers of any actual unsecured creditors. Most recording statutes protect lien creditors or bona fide purchasers, but not unsecured creditors.

NOTE ON PRESEVATION OF INVALIDATED LIENS: Under section 544(b), the bankruptcy trustee may assert the rights of an actual lien creditor whose lien has been invalidated. Under section 551, all avoided transfers are preserved. The preservation, however, is generally of no practical significance.

Preservation of an invalidated lien benefits only the bankruptcy estate, not the lien creditor. Where an invalidated lien is preserved, the trustee is able to assert the status of that lien creditor in attacking other liens on the property. If there are no other creditors with liens on the same property, or if all such other liens are superior to the lien that the trustee avoids, nothing is gained by preserving the invalidated lien. Preservation of a lien is of practical significance only where there are other liens on the property, subordinate to the lien avoidable by the trustee, that the trustee may not attack in any other manner.

Example: On February 2, S lends D $20,000 and takes a security interest in D's equipment. On March 3, X, another creditor of D, obtains an execution lien on the equipment. On March 13, S perfects its security interest. On March 23, D files a bankruptcy petition. X defeats S, section 9–301. The bankruptcy trustee, T, defeats X if D was insolvent on March 3, section 547, (considered supra at page 395 et seq.). X's lien is preserved under section 551. T may then assert the rights of X to invalidate S's security interest under section 544(b). Note that the trustee could also use section 547 to invalidate S's lien if D was insolvent on March 13, see page 416 et seq. infra. The rule that, under section 544(b), the trustee may assert the rights of an actual lien creditor whose lien has been invalidated is of very limited practical significance.

2. SECTION 544(a)

Section 544(b) looks to the rights of actual creditors of the debtor; section 544(a) focuses on the rights of hypothetical lien creditors and bona fide purchasers of real property. Section 544(a) empowers the bankruptcy trustee to invalidate any transfer that under non-bankruptcy law is voidable as to a creditor who extended credit and obtained a lien on the date of the filing of the bankruptcy petition or is voidable as to a bona fide purchaser of real property whether or not such a creditor or purchaser actually exists. In applying section 544(a), it is thus necessary to determine whether:

- non-bankruptcy law public notice requirements have been timely satisfied;

- a creditor who extended credit and obtained a lien on the date that the bankruptcy petition was filed, or a bona fide purchaser of real property on the date of the bankruptcy petition, comes within the class of persons protected by such state law.

The following examples illustrate the application of section 544(a):

Examples: On January 10, D borrows $10,000 from M and gives M a mortgage on Redacre. On February 2, D files a bankruptcy petition. As of the date of the petition, M had not recorded its mortgage. D's bankruptcy trustee may invalidate M's mortgage under section 544(a). The public notice requirements of the state real property recording statutes were not satisfied. Real property recording statutes typically protect bona fide purchasers. Since the mortgage was unrecorded on the date that the bankruptcy petition was filed, M's mortgage would be ineffective as against a bona fide purchaser of Redacre on the date that the petition was filed. Section 544(a) gives the bankruptcy trustee the same powers as a person who was a bona fide purchaser on the date that the bankruptcy petition was filed.

On January 10, D borrows $10,000 from S and gives S a security interest in equipment. On February 2, D files a bankruptcy petition. S fails to perfect its security interest prior to February 2. The bankruptcy trustee will be able to invalidate S's security interest under section 544(a). The applicable public notice requirement was not satisfied. Article 9's perfection requirements protect creditors with judicial liens, section 9–301. Since the security interest was unperfected on the date that the bankruptcy petition was filed, S's security interest would be subordinate to the claim of a creditor who obtained a judicial lien on the date that the petition was filed, section 9–301. Section 544(a) gives the trustee the same invalidation powers as a person who extended credit and obtained a judicial lien on the date that the bankruptcy petition was filed. (NOTE: Even though the Uniform Commercial Code uses the term "subordinate" instead of "voidable", a security interest that would be "subordinate" to a creditor who obtained a judicial lien on the date of the filing of the bankruptcy petition is "voidable" by the bankruptcy trustee.)

On January 10, D borrows $10,000 from S to buy equipment and gives S a purchase money security interest in the equipment. On January 18, D files a bankruptcy petition. On January 19, S perfects its security interest. (NOTE: The filing of a bankruptcy petition stays or stops most creditor collection efforts. Section 362(a), considered supra at pages 374–75, defines the scope of the stay, by listing the acts that are stayed by the commencement of the bankruptcy case. Section 362(a)(4) stays lien perfection. Section 362(b) lists exceptions to the automatic stay. Section 362(b)(3) excepts perfection of security interests within ten days of bankruptcy.) The bankruptcy trustee may not invalidate S's security interest. Section 544(a) empowers the bankruptcy trustee to invalidate security interests that would be subordinate to the claims of a creditor who obtained a judicial lien on the date that the petition was filed. By reason of U.C.C. section 9–301(2), S's purchase money security interest would be effective as against a creditor who obtained a lien on January 18, the date that the bankruptcy petition was filed. Section 9–301(2) provides in part: "If the secured party files with respect to a purchase money security interest before or within ten days after the debtor receives possession of the collateral, he takes priority over the rights of * * * a lien creditor which arise between the time the security interest attaches and the time of filing." This "ten-day grace period" is also effective against a bankruptcy trustee, see section 546(b). Accordingly, S's purchase money security interest is effective against the bankruptcy trustee.

On January 10, Dudley Doright, D, borrows $10,000 from Snidely Whiplash, S and gives S a security interest in equipment. On December 29, S properly files his financing statement. On December 30, D files a bankruptcy petition. The bankruptcy trustee may not invalidate S's security interest under section 544(a). The public notice requirements of Article 9 were not timely satisfied; S delayed in perfecting its security interest for almost a year. Article 9's perfection requirements protect "gap" lien creditors and buyers. In this hypothetical, the bankruptcy trustee has the right of a lien creditor, but not a gap lien creditor. Section 544(a) gives the bankruptcy trustee the invalidation powers of a creditor who obtained a judicial lien as of the date of the bankruptcy petition. On the date of the bankruptcy petition, December 30, S's security interest was perfected. A perfected security interest is effective against lien creditors, cf. sections 9–201, 9–301. Accordingly, S's security interest may not be invalidated under section 544(a). (WARNING: The bankruptcy trustee will probably be able to invalidate S's security interest under some other provision of the Bankruptcy Code. If D was insolvent on December 29, the bankruptcy trustee may invalidate S's security interest under section 547. The applicability of section 547 to transfers not timely perfected or recorded is considered infra at pages 416–20.)

These examples suggest three general rules for the use of section 544(a) in invalidating transfers:

- If the transfer has been recorded or otherwise perfected prior to the date that the bankruptcy petition was filed, the trustee will not be able to invalidate the transfer under section 544(a).

- Except as noted in the next rule, if the transfer was not recorded or otherwise perfected by the date that the bankruptcy petition was filed, the bankruptcy trustee will be able to invalidate the transfer under section 544(a).

- The bankruptcy trustee will not be able to invalidate a purchase money security interest perfected within ten days after the delivery of the collateral to the debtor even if the debtor files a bankruptcy petition in the gap between the creation of the security interest and perfection.

3.   COMPARISON OF SECTIONS 544(a) AND 544(b)

	544(a)	**544(b)**
I. STATUS (federal law) A. Necessity of protected actual creditor with allowable claim	NOT NECESSARY	NECESSARY
B. Effect of amount of actual creditor's claim	IRRELEVANT	IRRELEVANT
II. PRACTICAL SIGNIFICANCE OF STATUS (non-bankruptcy law) A. Real property transfers	1. Recording statute protects either creditors or purchasers 2. Transfers not recorded at time bankruptcy petition filed may be avoided	1. Recording statute must protect unsecured creditors 2. Transfers not timely recorded may be invalidated if an actual creditor with an unsecured allowable claim extended credit in the gap
B. Personal property transfers governed by UCC	Article 9 security interests not perfected at the date of filing of the bankruptcy petition may be invalidated	Subject to the very limited exception noted on the bottom of p. 411. Section 544(b) may not be used to invalidate Article 9 security interests. Section 544(b) may be used to invalidate a bulk transfer if an actual creditor with unsecured, allowable claim failed to receive the notice required by Article 6

4.   SECTION 547(e)

a.   Dealing With Delays in Perfection Through Preference Law: Deeming Time of Perfection as Time of Transfer

In the Dudley Doright/Snidely Whiplash hypothetical on page 415, the bankruptcy trustee was not able to invalidate Snidely's security interest under section 544(a) notwithstanding Snidely's long delay in giving public notice of his lien. Should Doright's bankruptcy trustee be able to invalidate Snidely's lien? Yes, but the Code uses an odd method to achieve the result: preference law of section 547, which is discussed supra at pages 394–98. Review that discussion before going ahead.

Basically, the Bankruptcy Code's method is to "deem" that for purposes of applying the requirements of section 547(b) (discussed supra at pages 394–98) the date of transfers not timely recorded is the date of perfection, not the date of actual transfer.

b. Local Law Determines Means of Perfection
Section 547 does not specify the means of perfection. Rather, section 547(e)(1) provides that for purposes of section 547, transfers shall be perfected when effective under non-bankruptcy law against certain specified third parties. In a transfer of real property other than fixtures, the third parties are bona fide purchasers, i.e., the date of perfection is the date that the transfer is effective against bona fide purchasers. Non-bankruptcy law generally requires that transfers of interests in real property other than fixtures be recorded in order to be effective against bona fide purchasers.

A transfer of personal property or fixtures is perfected for purposes of section 547 when it is effective against a creditor with a judicial lien. Absolute transfers of personal property are generally effective against subsequent lien creditors of the transferor without any recording.

Examples: A pays B $1,000. This transfer is effective against subsequent lien creditors of A without any recording.

X sells 200 widgets to Y. Again, the transfer is effective as against subsequent lien creditors of the transferor without recordation.

Security transfers, i.e., liens, on personal property or fixtures are not effective against subsequent judicial lien creditors of the transferor without recordation or other perfection.

Example: D gives S a security interest in equipment to secure a debt. Under UCC section 9–301(1)(b), S's security interest is not superior to the rights of a subsequent judicial lien creditor of D until S perfects.

c. How All This Works
The Doright/Whiplash example illustrates the practical significance of statutorily delaying the effective date of the transfer until public notice of the transfer has been given.

Example: Remember Doright borrowed $10,000 from Snidely on January 10 and gave Snidely a security interest in equipment which Snidely perfected on December 29. Doright filed a bankruptcy petition on December 30. At first, it might seem that section 547 is not applicable because it appears that the security transfer from Doright to Snidely was not for an antecedent indebtedness and did not occur within 90 days of the bankruptcy petition. For purposes of section 547, however, the transfer will be deemed made on December 29, not January 10. [Under section 9–301, Snidely's security interest would not be effective as against subsequent judicial lien creditors until that date. Accordingly, by reason of section 547(e), the transfer is deemed not made until that date.] Thus, the "December 29 transfer" would be within 90 days of the bankruptcy petition. Thus, the "December 29 transfer" would be for an antecedent indebtedness, i.e., the $10,000 loaned on January 10. Thus, the trustee would be able to invalidate S's security under section 547 if D was insolvent on December 29. [Remember section 547(f) creates a rebuttable presumption of insolvency.]

This example illustrates that a delay in perfection can result in a security interest actually given for present consideration being deemed made for an antecedent indebtedness and thus a section 547 preference.

d. Grace Period

In the Dudley Doright hypothetical, over eleven months elapsed between the granting of the security interest and the perfecting of the security interest. What if the delay was eleven weeks? Eleven days? Eleven hours? Is there some sort of "grace period" in section 547?

Section 547(e) does not require immediate perfection; it provides a ten-day "grace period" for perfection. Section 547(e)(2) describes three situations:

- First, section 547(e)(2)(A) deals with transfers perfected within ten days. Such a transfer will be deemed made at the time of the transfer. A transfer deemed made at the time of the transfer is not vulnerable to attack by the bankruptcy trustee under section 547.

- Second, section 547(e)(2)(B) deals with transfers not perfected within ten days. Such a transfer will be deemed made at the time of perfection. A transfer deemed made at a point in time later than the time of the transfer is vulnerable to attack by the bankruptcy trustee under section 547.

- Third, section 547(e)(2)(C) deals with the effect of filing a bankruptcy petition during the ten-day "grace period." Under such facts, the transfer will be deemed made at the time of the transfer if it is perfected within ten days of the transfer or will be deemed made at the time of the filing of the bankruptcy petition if it is not perfected within ten days.

The operation of section 547(e) is illustrated in the following five examples:

Examples: On January 10, S lends D $10,000 and obtains a security interest in D's equipment. S perfects this security interest on January 19. For purposes of section 547, the security transfer will be deemed to have occurred on January 10, section 547(e)(2)(A). S perfected within ten days after the transfer so the transfer is deemed made when it was actually made, January 10. Not a transfer for an antecedent debt. A January 10 transfer for a January 10 debt. Not a preference.

On January 10, D borrows $10,000 from S and grants S a security interest in its equipment. S perfects its security interest on February 2. S did not perfect within ten days so that for purposes of the elements of section 547(b), the transfer will be deemed to have occurred when it was finally perfected, February 2. A transfer for an antecedent debt. A February 2 transfer for a January 10 debt. Possibly a preference.

On January 10, S lends D $10,000 and obtains a non-purchase money security interest in D's equipment. D files a bankruptcy petition on January 15. S perfects its security interest on January 19. For purposes of section 547, the security transfer will be deemed to have occurred on January 10, section 547(e)(2)(A), section 547(e)(2)(C)(ii). [Same facts as the first example in this set except that D filed a bankruptcy petition before the security interest was perfected.] CAUTION: This hypothetical raises not only section 547(e) issues but also issues under section 362 and section 544. Section 362(a)(4) bars the perfection of liens after the filing of a bankruptcy petition. Section 362(b)(3), however, creates an exception for perfection "accomplished within the period provided under section 547(e)(2)(A)." Accordingly, it would seem that the perfection did not violate the automatic stay. Accordingly, it would seem that the bankruptcy trustee will not be able to avoid the security interest under section 547. The bankruptcy trustee, however, will be able to avoid the security interest under section 544(a). Remember, that under section 544(a), the trustee has the rights and powers of a creditor that had a judicial lien as of the time of the bankruptcy filing. At that time, the security interest was unperfected. An unperfected security interest is subordinate to a judicial lien creditor under section 9–301 and thus is avoidable by the bankruptcy trustee under section 544(a).

On January 10, S lends D $10,000 and obtains a security interest in D's equipment. D files a bankruptcy petition on January 15. S perfects its security interest on February 2. For purposes of section 547, the security transfer will be deemed to have occurred on January 15, section 547(e)(2)(C). Transfers not perfected within ten days are deemed made at the date of the bankruptcy petition if the filing of the petition preceded perfection. [Same facts as the second example on this set except that D filed a bankruptcy petition before the security interest was filed.]

On January 20, M lends D $10,000 and obtains a mortgage on Redacre. The applicable state recording statute contains a twenty-day grace period. M records its mortgage on February 2, D files a bankruptcy petition on March 3. For purposes of section 547, the security transfer will be deemed to have occurred on February 2. Section 547(e) recognizes only a ten-day grace period. M failed to perfect within that ten-day period. Accordingly, the time of the transfer will be deemed to be the date of perfection.

5. SECTION 548(d)

Section 548(d) is similar to section 547(e). Section 547(e) fixes the time when a transfer is deemed made for purposes of the preference invalidation provisions of section 547. Section 548(d) fixes the time when a transfer is deemed made for purposes of the fraudulent conveyance invalidation provisions of section 548 (discussed supra at pages 406–08): when the transfer is so far perfected that no subsequent bona fide purchaser of the property from the debtor can acquire rights in the property superior to those of the transferee.

The purpose of section 548(d) is to prevent a fraudulent conveyance from escaping invalidation by being kept secret for over a year.

Example: On January 10, 1988, D, an insolvent, gives Redacre to X. X does not record the deed until November 11, 1989. On December 12, 1989, D files a bankruptcy petition. Remember, section 548 has a one-year limitations period. (This one-year limitation period and the other requirements of section 548 are considered supra at pages 406–08.) The transfer of Redacre was actually made more than one year before the bankruptcy petition was filed. The transfer, however, was not effective against a subsequent bona fide purchaser until it was recorded on November 11. Accordingly, under section 548(d), the transfer is deemed made on November 11, 1989. Without section 548(d), the bankruptcy trustee could not invalidate the gift by an insolvent D under section 548.

The transfer from D to X in this example paragraph was a "true" fraudulent conveyance: a transfer by an insolvent without "reasonably equivalent value." Section 548(d), however, also may enable the bankruptcy trustee to invalidate some transfers that are not "true" fraudulent conveyances, that is, transfers in which there has been merely a delay in recordation or perfection. Consider the following illustration.

Example: Wallace Cleaver, W, gives Redacre to his brother Theodore, T, in 1986. W is solvent at that time. T, however, does not record the transfer until June of 1988. At that time, W is insolvent. In July of 1988, W files a bankruptcy petition. The bankruptcy trustee will be able to use section 548(a)(2) to invalidate the 1986 gift of Redacre.

Note that T's delay in recordation is crucial to the bankruptcy trustee's section 548 case. At the time that the gift is actually made, the donor, W, is solvent. There are no legal problems with people who are solvent making gifts. This happens every Chanukah and Christmas. Gifts are fraudulent conveyances when made by people who are insolvent.

While the donor, W, was solvent when the gift was actually made, he is insolvent when the gift is deemed made under section 548(d), which is the time the transfer is perfected against bona fide purchasers from the transferor. Section 548(d), like section 547(e), enables the trustee to test all aspects of the transaction as of the time of recordation rather than as of the time of the actual transfer. Since W was insolvent when the transfer is deemed made at the time of recordation, the transfer was fraudulent as a transfer by an insolvent without reasonably equivalent value.

6. **SECTION 545(2)**

Section 545(2) invalidates statutory liens that are not perfected or enforceable on the date of the petition against a hypothetical bona fide purchaser. Section 546(b) recognizes any applicable state law "grace period." If under state law, the statutory lien may still be perfected and that perfection relates back to a pre-bankruptcy petition date, then the bankruptcy trustee will not be able to invalidate the lien.

Section 545(2) is of very limited practical significance. First, most statutory liens satisfy section 545(2)'s bona fide purchaser test. Second, statutory liens are also subject to section 544(a) which can be used to invalidate any statutory lien on real property that is voidable by a hypothetical bona fide purchaser and any statutory lien on personal property that is voidable by a hypothetical lien creditor.

E. LANDLORDS' LIENS

Sections 545(3) and 545(4) are the easiest invalidation provisions to read, understand and apply.

"The trustee may avoid the fixing of a statutory lien on the property of the debtor to the extent that such lien * * *

(3) is for rent

(4) is a lien of distress for rent."

Note that the provisions only invalidate STATUTORY landlord liens, i.e., liens for rent arising "solely by force of a statute." If the lease agreement creates an Article 9 security interest in property of the lessee, this contractual lien is not affected by section 545.

When a landlord requires its tenant to sign a security agreement giving the landlord a security interest in property of the tenant to secure rental payments, the landlord has, of course, obtained a lien. This lien held by the landlord is not however, a "landlord's lien"; it is a security interest. Not all liens securing claims by landlords are "landlord's liens." (Only Chuck Berry would be inclined to call a security interest obtained by Mabel, "Mabelline.")

F. DISGUISED PRIORITIES

Section 507 of the Bankruptcy Code is a priority provision; it sets out the order in which the various unsecured claims against the debtor are to be satisfied. It displaces any state priority statutes. (Section 507 is considered infra at pages 450–54.)

Section 545 protects this federal priority scheme from disruption by state priority provisions that are "disguised" as statutory liens. Section 545 reaches spurious statutory liens which are in reality merely priorities.

When is a statutory lien more like a priority than a lien? Remember that a priority does not arise until distribution of a debtor's assets on insolvency. Accordingly, section 545(1) provides for invalidation of a statutory lien which first becomes effective upon the bankruptcy or insolvency of the debtor.

G. RECLAMATION UNDER UCC SECTION 2–702

1. RIGHT UNDER THE UNIFORM COMMERCIAL CODE

When a buyer fails to pay for goods it accepts, the seller has a legal right to recover the contract price, UCC section 2–709. This legal right is of limited practical significance if the buyer is insolvent. Accordingly, the Uniform Commercial Code grants unpaid credit sellers a right to recover the goods. Section 2–702 of the Uniform Commercial Code empowers a seller to "reclaim" the goods if:

- credit sale, and

- buyer insolvent when goods received, and

- written misrepresentation of solvency within three months before delivery or the demand for reclamation is made within ten days of the buyer's receipt of the goods.

Case law has created a similar right of reclamation for sellers paid with bad checks. The right of reclamation of a "cash" seller who has been paid by a check that is subsequently dishonored is based on U.C.C. sections 2–507 and 2–511. See *In re Samuels & Co., Inc.*, 526 F.2d 1238 (5th Cir. 1976).

2. BANKRUPTCY'S EFFECT ON THE RIGHT
a. No Effect if Section 546(c) or (d) Satisfied

What is the effect of the bankruptcy of the buyer on the seller's right of reclamation? Sections 546(c) and (d) deal with this question. Section 546 does not create a right of reclamation. Instead, it sets out the effect of bankruptcy on a right of reclamation created under non-bankruptcy law.

[Note: Section 546(d) was added in 1984. It deals with the effect of bankruptcy on the non-bankruptcy reclamation rights of farmers who have sold grain to storage facilities and fishermen who have sold fish to processing facilities. Section 546(d) has the same general requirements as section 546(c). Accordingly, this outline discusses only section 546(c).]

Section 546(c) has four requirements:

- The seller has a right of reclamation under non-bankruptcy law.

- The buyer received the goods while insolvent.

- The sale was in the ordinary course of the seller's business.

- The seller makes a written reclamation demand within ten days of the buyer's receipt of the goods.

If a seller has complied with these four requirements, the bankruptcy trustee cannot invalidate the seller's right of reclamation under section 544(a) (considered supra at page 413), section 545 (considered supra at page 422), section 547 (considered supra at page 394), or section 549 (considered infra at page 428).

WARNING! The first requirement of section 546(c) is that the seller enjoy a right of reclamation under non-bankruptcy law. The requirements for reclamation under U.C.C. section 2–702 are similar to, but not identical with, the requirements of section 546(c). The two provisions differ in the following respects:

- Section 546(c) requires that the sale in question be "in the ordinary course of such seller's business." Section 2–702 does not.

- While both provisions require insolvency of the buyer at the time of receipt of the goods, the definition of insolvent in section 101(29) of the Bankruptcy Code is significantly different from the definition of insolvent in section 1–201(23) of the UCC.

- Section 546(c) requires a demand in writing. Section 2–702 does not.

- Section 546(c) requires that the seller demand reclamation "before ten days [Does this mean 9 days?] after" receipt. Section 2–702 imposes a ten-day limitation unless there has been a written misrepresentation of solvency within three months before delivery.

The requirements of section 546 cannot be satisfied, of course, unless the different requirements of UCC section 2–702 have been met.

b. Exceptions
1) Vulnerability to Section 544(b)
Section 546(c) does not protect the seller's right of reclamation from invalidation based on section 544(b), Section 544(b) is considered supra at pages 408–13. If other unsecured creditors have rights superior to the seller's right of reclamation, the trustee may assert these rights under section 544(b) to defeat the seller's right of reclamation. If a secured creditor has rights superior to the seller's right of reclamation, the trustee may assert these rights only if the trustee is able to avoid the lien of the secured creditor and preserve it for the benefit of the estate.

2)   Alternative Relief
Even though the seller complies with section 546, and her right of reclamation is safe from section 544(b), the bankruptcy court may nevertheless deny reclamation if it protects the seller by either granting its claim arising from the sale of goods an administrative expense priority or securing the claim by a lien.

Under section 546(d), the bankruptcy court may only deny reclamation if it secures the farmer or fisherman's reclamation claim by a lien.

c.   **Result if Section 546 Not Satisfied**
What if a seller with a non-bankruptcy reclamation claim fails to satisfy the four requirements of section 546(c)? While the Bankruptcy Code does not deal with the question directly, the cases consistently hold that the bankruptcy trustee can avoid the reclamation rights of a seller who fails to comply with section 546(c).

REVIEW QUESTIONS

1. T or F   The debtor can avoid pre-bankruptcy transfers under sections 544, 545, 547, and 548.

2. D Corp., owes C $20,000. P, the principal shareholder of D Corp., pays C the $20,000. D Corp., files a bankruptcy petition 89 days later. Is there a voidable preference?

3. D Corp., owes C $300,000. D Corp., pays C $90,000. Four months later, D Corp., files a bankruptcy petition. Is there a voidable preference?

4. Same facts as # 3 except that P, the principal shareholder of D Corp., had guaranteed payment to C.

5. D owes C $500,000. C has a mortgage on Redacre. Redacre has a value of $550,000. Sixty days before filing for bankruptcy, D pays C $300,000. Is there a preference?

6. Same facts as # 5 except that Redacre is only worth $300,000.

7. D, a lawyer, bought supplies from C on credit. C billed D at the end of the month and D paid by the 15th. Two months later, D filed a Chapter 11 petition. Was the payment to C a preference?

8. T or F   D owes B Bank $80,000. D has an account at B Bank with a $60,000 balance. B Bank exercises its right of setoff. D files a bankruptcy petition the next day. D can avoid the setoff under section 547.

9. T or F   S foreclosed its mortgage on D's building and bought the building at the foreclosure sale by bidding in its claim. Two months later, S sold the building to T for a substantial profit. Thirteen months after the foreclo-

sure sale, D filed a bankruptcy petition. D's bankruptcy trustee cannot recover from either S or T under section 548.

10. 1/10, S obtained a purchase money security interest in D's farm equipment. Under state law, S had 20 days to perfect. D files for bankruptcy on 1/23. S perfects its security interest on 1/28. Can the bankruptcy trustee avoid S's security interest?

*

XXII

POST–BANKRUPTCY TRANSFERS

Analysis

The prior chapter deals with avoidance of transfers that occurred prior to the time that the bankruptcy petition was filed. Sections 544, 545, 547 and 548 apply only to pre-bankruptcy transfers. None of these provisions can be used to avoid an unauthorized transfer of property of the estate that occurs after the bankruptcy petition is filed. Section 549 applies to post-bankruptcy transfers of estate property.

A. THE PROBLEM OF POST–PETITION TRANSFERS

The date of the filing of the bankruptcy petition is critically important in bankruptcy law. Subject to limited exceptions noted on pages 384–85, only the property of the debtor as of the date of the filing of the petition becomes property of the estate. Generally, property acquired by the debtor after the bankruptcy petition has been filed remains property of the debtor.

The date of the filing of the petition is significant not only in determining what property becomes property of the estate but also in determining when the property becomes property of the estate. The filing of a bankruptcy petition—voluntary or involuntary— creates the estate.

The date of the filing of the bankruptcy petition is not, however, the date that the debtor loses possession of her property, not even in Chapter 7 cases. While section 701 provides for the appointment of an interim trustee in Chapter 7 cases "promptly after the order for relief," there will be some delay before the trustee takes possession of the property.

During the hiatus between the filing of the bankruptcy petition and the bankruptcy trustee's taking possession of the property of the estate, the debtor will usually have possession and control of the property of the estate. At times, the debtor will, after the filing of the petition, transfer property of the estate to some third party. Assume, for example, that B files a Chapter 7 petition on January 10. On January 12, B sells her summer home to X. On January 13, B sells her boat to Y. Obviously, B should not have made these post-bankruptcy transfers. Obviously, the trustee has a cause of action against B for conversion. Obviously, the trustee can claim any proceeds from the post-bankruptcy transfers as property of the estate. And, obviously the claim against the debtor and the right to remaining proceeds will usually be of limited practical significance. The significant inquiry is whether the trustee can recover the summer house from X and/or the boat from Y. Should the bankruptcy laws protect X and/or Y?

B. GENERAL RULE REGARDING AVOIDANCE OF POST–PETITION TRANSFERS

Section 549(a) provides that, as a general rule, the trustee can avoid any unauthorized post-petition transfer of estate property. In other words, transferees such as X and Y are unprotected and are accountable for the property.

C. EXCEPTIONS PROTECTING TRANSFEREES

Section 549 protects X and Y in certain circumstances. Before considering these circumstances, remember that section 549 protects only the transferee, not the debtor-transferor.

1. **AUTHORIZED TRANSFERS**

A post-bankruptcy transfer will be effective against the bankruptcy trustee if the transfer was authorized by the Bankruptcy Code or by the bankruptcy court. For this reason, post-bankruptcy transfers in Chapter 11 cases are effective. Sales by a Chapter 11 debtor-in-possession or trustee are authorized by section 363. [Section 363 governs post-petition/pre-confirmation transactions. After confirmation, the property is no longer property of the estate, section 1142. Section 549 only applies to post-bankruptcy transfers of property of the estate.]

2. **INVOLUNTARY CASES**

Section 549(b) validates transfers by the debtor that occur after the filing of an *involuntary* bankruptcy petition and before the order for relief to the extent that the transferee gave value to the debtor after the filing of the bankruptcy petition.

Examples: On February 22, D's creditors file an involuntary petition. On February 25, D sells her stove to X for $300. The trustee may not recover the stove from X. X is protected by section 549(b).

Same facts, except that D knew of the involuntary petition. Same result. Section 549(b) protects post-petition transfers "notwithstanding any notice or knowledge of the case that the transferee has."

On January 10, C lends D $1,000. On February 2, D's creditors file an involuntary petition. On February 15, D transfers his stereo to C in satisfaction of the January 10 debt. The trustee can recover the stereo from C. The stereo was transferred to satisfy a debt that arose before the petition. The transferee did not give value to the debtor after the filing of the bankruptcy petition. The transferee is not protected by section 549(b).

On April 4, the creditors of D file an involuntary petition. On April 14, D sells Greenacre to Y for $40,000. The trustee may not recover Greenacre from Y. Section 549(b) protects transferees of both personalty and realty.

3. **TRANSFERS OF REAL ESTATE**

Section 549(c) protects post-petition transfers of *realty* from trustee avoidance. A transfer of real property by the debtor after the filing of a voluntary petition or after an order for relief in an involuntary case will be effective against the bankruptcy trustee if:

- the transfer occurs and is properly recorded before a copy of the bankruptcy petition is filed in the real estate records for the county where the land is located, and

- the transferee is a buyer or lienor for fair equivalent value without knowledge of the petition.

Example: On February 2, B files a voluntary petition. On February 3, B sells land in White County to Y for $10,000, the "fair equivalent value" of the land. Y has no "knowledge of the commencement of the case." Y properly files the transfer in the White County real estate records on February 4. A copy of the bankruptcy petition is filed in the real estate records for White County on February 5. The trustee cannot avoid the transfer. Y is protected by section 549(c).

WARNING! There is no personal property counterpart of section 549(c). Personal property of the debtor transferred by the debtor after the filing of a voluntary petition can be recovered from the transferee unless the transfer was authorized by the Bankruptcy Code or by the bankruptcy court.

D. POST–PETITION TRANSFERS OF ESTATE PROPERTY BY THIRD PARTIES

Some post-petition transfers of property of the estate are made by persons holding property of the debtor, not the debtor herself. For example, on January 11, D files a voluntary bankruptcy petition. As of that date, D has $1,000 in her checking account at B Bank. This checking account becomes property of the estate on January 11. On January 13, B Bank honors a $300 check issued by D to X on January 7 and charges D's account.

B Bank was protected under the Bankruptcy Act of 1898. See *Bank of Marin v. England,* 385 U.S. 99, 87 S.Ct. 274 (1966). B Bank is protected under the Bankruptcy Code by way of section 542.

Under section 542(c), a third person who in good faith transfers property of the estate after the filing of the petition is protected from the bankruptcy trustee if the third party had "neither notice nor actual knowledge of the commencement of the case." Accordingly, if B Bank has neither actual knowledge nor notice of D's petition, it will not be liable to the bankruptcy trustee.

WARNING! Note that section 542(c) only protects B Bank, the party who transfers the property of the estate; it does not protect X, the transferee. The trustee has a right to recover the $300, which is property of the estate, from X. This is the point of the reference to section 542(c) in section 549(a)(2)(A). Even though section 542(c) protects the person who transfers property of the estate post-petition, section 549 empowers the trustee to recover the property from the transferee.

REVIEW QUESTIONS

1.   D files a Chapter 7 petition on January 5. D sells her boat to T on January 9 for $10,000. T knows of the bankruptcy filing. Can the trustee recover the $10,000 from D?

2.   Same facts as # 1. Can the trustee recover the boat from T even if T did not know of D's bankruptcy?

3. D Furniture Store, Inc., D, files a Chapter 11 petition on April 5. On April 6, D sells furniture to T in the ordinary course of its business. A trustee is later appointed. Can the bankruptcy trustee recover the furniture from T under section 549? What if T knew of D's bankruptcy filing?

4. D has a bank account at X Bank. D issues a check to Y. D files for Chapter 7 relief. After the bankruptcy filing, the check clears, i.e., is paid by X Bank. What are the rights, if any, of the trustee?

*

XXIII

EFFECT OF BANKRUPTCY ON SECURED CLAIMS

Analysis

A. WHAT IS A SECURED CLAIM

The Bankruptcy Code deals with "claims," not creditors. Accordingly, under the Bankruptcy Code there will be creditors with secured claims instead of secured creditors.

A creditor has a secured claim if it holds a lien on or has a right of setoff against "property of the estate." The claim is secured only to the extent of the value of "such creditor's interest in the estate's interest in such property," section 506(a).

Examples: Suture Self, Inc. (S), a do-it-yourself health care center, owes X $100,000 and Y $200,000. Both X and Y have mortgages on S's building. X's mortgage has priority over Y's under state law. S files for bankruptcy. The building has a value of $160,000. Under these facts, X would have a $100,000 secured claim; Y would have a secured claim of $60,000 and an unsecured claim of $140,000. (NOTE: In law school hypotheticals, the teacher gets to decide what the value of the collateral is. "Real lawyers" do not enjoy that luxury. The question of the value of the collateral is difficult and important. The Bankruptcy Code does not provide a method for valuing collateral. Section 506 states that value is to be determined by the court on a case-by-case basis in light of the purpose of the valuation and of the proposed disposition of the property.)

Sunshine Cab Co. obtains a $2,000 judgment against Bobby Wheeler and causes the sheriff to execute on personal property belonging to Wheeler. The personal property subject to Sunshine's execution lien has a value of $800. Sunshine has a $800 secured claim and a $1,200 unsecured claim.

Bates Motel, Inc. owes Fairvale Bank & Trust $30,000 on an unsecured loan. Bates Motel, Inc. has $9,000 on deposit in the bank. Fairvale Bank & Trust has a $9,000 secured claim and a $21,000 unsecured claim.

[The answer to the third example assumes that Fairvale Bank & Trust has a right of setoff under state law. The answers to the first and second examples assume that the liens are valid in bankruptcy.]

B. INVALIDATION OF LIENS

Some liens that are valid outside of bankruptcy can be invalidated in a bankruptcy case. Section 522(f), empowers the debtor to invalidate certain liens on certain exempt property. Sections 544, 545, 547, 548, and 549, empower the bankruptcy trustee to invalidate certain transfers that create liens.

Example: Assume that S lends D $10,000 and obtains a security interest in D's inventory. S does not file a financing statement or otherwise perfect its security interest. Under section 9–203 of the Uniform Commercial Code, S has a valid security interest. Under section 9–201, this unperfected security interest is effective between S and D and is effective against most third parties. For example, S's right to D's inventory is superior to the rights of any of D's unsecured creditors. If, however, D files a bankruptcy petition, S's unperfected security interest may be invalidated by the trustee under section 544(a) so that S will simply have an unsecured claim for $10,000. Section 544(a) gives the bankruptcy trustee the rights and powers of a creditor who obtains a judicial lien at the time the bankruptcy petition was filed. At the time the bankruptcy petition was filed, S's security interest was unperfected. An unperfected security interest is ineffective as against a creditor with a judicial lien, UCC section 9–301. Accordingly, S's unperfected security interest is ineffective as against the bankruptcy trustee. Section 544(a) is considered supra at pages 413–16.

Note the effect of lien invalidation. All that is eliminated is the lien. The creditor's claim remains. Lien invalidation converts a secured claim into an unsecured claim.

C. OVERVIEW OF IMPACT OF BANKRUPTCY ON SECURED CLAIMS

In thinking about the impact of bankruptcy on secured claims, a law student or lawyer should focus on two questions:

- How can the debtor's bankruptcy filing adversely affect the holder of a secured claim?

- How can a secured claim be satisfied when the debtor is in bankruptcy?

D. WHAT CAN HAPPEN TO SECURED CLAIMS DURING BANKRUPTCY

Most liens cannot be avoided under sections 522(f), 544, 545, 547, 548, or 549. What effect does bankruptcy have on a creditor that holds a valid-in-bankruptcy lien? This question is particularly important in Chapters 11, 12 and 13 cases for two reasons:

- a Chapters 11, 12 or 13 case often lasts three years or more;

- in Chapter 13 cases and in most Chapters 11 and 12 cases, the debtor remains in possession of encumbered property.

1. DELAY IN REALIZING ON COLLATERAL
Recall that the automatic stay of section 362 prevents a creditor from enforcing its lien against property of the estate or property of the debtor. Accordingly, a creditor will not be able to sell or even seize encumbered property from a debtor who is in bankruptcy without obtaining relief from the automatic stay.

2. DEBTOR'S USE, LEASE, OR SALE OF COLLATERAL
Section 363 provides for continued use, lease, or sale of encumbered property during bankruptcy. The lien holder is protected by section 363's adequate protection requirements. Section 363 is considered infra at pages 485–87.

3. LOSS OF PRIORITY
Section 364(d) empowers the bankruptcy court to approve the debtor's granting a post-petition creditor a lien on encumbered property that has priority over all pre-petition liens.

Example: X makes a $600,000 construction loan to D and obtains and records a first mortgage on the project. D is unable to complete the building with the $600,000 provided by X. D is unable to obtain additional financing. D is able to file for Chapter 11. Y is willing to loan D the $200,000 needed to finish the building if its mortgage has priority over X's. Under section 364(d), the bankruptcy court can authorize D's granting Y, the later-in-time post-petition lender, a lien that has priority over X's.

Section 364(d) imposes three requirements on the granting of such a "super-priority":

- there must be "notice and a hearing,"

- the debtor-in-possession or trustee is unable to obtain credit otherwise, and

- the holder of the pre-petition lien is adequately protected.

4. LIMITATIONS ON FLOATING LIENS
a. After-Acquired Original Collateral
In commercial credit transactions, security agreements usually provide that the collateral includes property that the debtor later acquires. Such after-acquired property clauses are expressly permitted by section 9–204 of the UCC; but after-acquired property clauses are expressly cut off in bankruptcy by section 552(a).

Example: On January 10, S extends credit to and obtains and perfects a security interest in all of D's inventory, now owned or later acquired. On March 3, D acquires additional inventory. On March 4, D files a Chapter 11 petition and continues operating its business. On April 7, D acquires additional inventory. In bankruptcy, S's claim would be secured by the January 10 inventory and by the March 3 inventory. It would not be secured by the April 7 inventory. Section 552(a) states that a security agreement entered into before the commencement of the case does not reach property acquired after the commencement of the case other than proceeds.

b. Proceeds
Under U.C.C. Article 9, a security interest automatically floats to proceeds, section 9–306(2). The Bankruptcy Code generally recognizes a security interest in post-petition proceeds from pre-petition collateral, section 552(b).

Example: If D sold inventory on March 5, the identifiable proceeds from this post-petition sale of pre-petition property would be subject to S's security interest.

5. RETURN OF REPOSSESSED PROPERTY
Section 542(a) compels the holder of a secured claim that has taken possession of its collateral prior to bankruptcy to return it to the debtor when she files a bankruptcy petition. Assume, for example, that S extended credit to D and obtained and perfected a security interest in D's inventory. D defaulted. S repossessed the inventory. D then filed for Chapter 11 relief. Reading section 362(a)(4) should

leave you convinced that S cannot sell the inventory without obtaining relief from the stay. Reading section 542 should leave you confused.

Section 542(a) compels the turnover of "property that the trustee may use, sell, or lease under section 363" "unless such property is of inconsequential value or benefit to the estate." What is the antecedent of the pronoun "such"? If it is "property that the trustee may use, sell, or lease under section 363," then it is necessary to look at section 363. Section 363 provides for the use, sale, or lease of "property of the estate." Section 363's use of the term "property of the estate" is probably misleading. Section 363 does more than just authorize the use, sale, or lease of property of the estate, i.e., the debtor's interest in property. Instead, section 363 authorizes the use, sale, or lease of property in which the debtor has an interest. In any event, it is thus necessary to look at section 541 which describes property of the estate in terms of the "interest of the debtor in property." What is the interest of the debtor in inventory that has been repossessed? A right of redemption under section 9–506? A right to any surplus produced by a forced sale under 9–504? Are these rights of "inconsequential value" for purposes of section 542?

The Supreme Court worked through these questions in *United States v. Whiting Pools, Inc.,* 462 U.S. 198, 103 S. Ct. 2309 (1983), and concluded that section 542 requires that a creditor, who seized its collateral prior to bankruptcy, turn over the property to a Chapter 11 debtor. *Whiting Pools* involved a seizure by the IRS of property subject to a tax lien. It seems clear from dicta in *Whiting Pools* that the Court would reach a similar result if a private creditor seized property subject to its security interest.

E. SATISFACTION OF SECURED CLAIMS

1. OVERVIEW
a. Recovery of Collateral
If the holder of a secured claim recovers its collateral, the secured claim is extinguished. Assume, for example, that D owes S $22,000 and S has a security interest on equipment worth $10,000. D files a Chapter 7 bankruptcy petition. If the trustee turns over the equipment to S, S no longer has a secured claim. S still has a $12,000 claim, but the claim is an unsecured claim.

Chapters 7, 11, and 13 all permit satisfaction of a secured claim by surrender of the collateral. Neither Chapter 7, nor Chapter 11, nor Chapter 13 requires the satisfaction of a secured claim by surrender of the collateral.

b. Payment of Amount Equal to the Value of the Collateral
If the holder of a secured claim does not recover its collateral, it should receive a payment equal to the value of the collateral. In a Chapter 7 case, this payment should be in cash unless the holder of the secured claim agrees to periodic payments pursuant to a section 524 reaffirmation agreement. Chapters 11 and 13 both contemplate periodic payments to holders of secured claims pursuant to the court approved plan.

2. CHAPTER 7

There are six different ways that a Chapter 7 case can result in the holder of a secured claim obtaining either the collateral or its cash value.

a. Obtaining Relief from the Automatic Stay

Under state law, a secured creditor can generally realize on its lien by foreclosure. In bankruptcy, a holder of a secured claim can foreclose its lien only after it has obtained relief from the automatic stay of section 362.

b. Abandonment by the Bankruptcy Trustee

Section 521(4) requires the debtor to surrender all property of the estate to the trustee. Assume, for example, that James Kirk, K, files a Chapter 7 petition. Mr. Spock is appointed as trustee. K owes Federation Bank, F, $100,000. F has a properly perfected security interest in K's ship. The ship has a value of $80,000. If K files for Chapter 7 relief, section 521(3) requires that the ship be surrendered to Mr. Spock.

Because the amount of F's secured claim is greater than the value of the ship, the ship is of "inconsequential value" to the estate. Section 554 authorizes a bankruptcy trustee to abandon any property that is burdensome to the estate or of inconsequential value to the estate. Thus, Mr. Spock can abandon the ship. According to the legislative history, "abandonment may be to any party with a possessory interest in the property abandoned," H.R.Rep. 995, 377 (1977). Some courts have relied on this language and on the language in section 362(a)(5) to hold that encumbered property must be abandoned to the debtor not to a creditor with a lien on the property. Even if Spock abandons the ship to K, K can then release the ship to F.

c. Sale of the Collateral by the Bankruptcy Trustee and Distribution of the Proceeds from This Sale to the Holder of the Secured Claim

In certain, limited situations, the trustee is empowered to sell encumbered property free and clear of all liens, see section 363(f). For example, Mr. Spock can sell K's ship if the sale yields more than F's $100,000 secured claim, section 363(f)(3). The proceeds of any such sale will first be used to cover the costs of the sale, sections 363(j), 506(c). The first $100,000 of net proceeds will be paid to F.

d. Redemption by Payment by the Debtor

Section 722 empowers individual Chapter 7 debtors to extinguish liens on certain property by paying the holder of the secured claim an amount equal to the value of the encumbered property. Please read section 722. Note that section 722 would apply to the Federation lien only if (1) the ship was "intended primarily for personal, family, or household use" (i.e. not an enterprise), (2) the debt was a "dischargeable consumer debt," and (3) the ship had been exempted or abandoned.

e. Payments Pursuant to a Reaffirmation Agreement

A debtor who has filed for bankruptcy relief can agree to continue paying some of his pre-bankruptcy debts after the bankruptcy case. For example, K can agree to pay F $20,000 a year for the next 4 years. Such an agreement is commonly referred to as a reaffirmation agreement. Not all reaffirmation agreements are legally enforceable. Section 524 controls reaffirmation agreements. Section 524 is considered infra at page 477.

f. Voluntary Return by Trustee

If encumbered property of a Chapter 7 debtor is not foreclosed by a holder of a secured claim after it obtains relief from the stay under section 362(d), or abandoned under section 554, or sold by the trustee under section 363(f), or redeemed under section 722, or covered by a section 524 reaffirmation agreement, then section 725 controls its disposition. Please read section 725. "The purpose of this section is to give the court appropriate authority to ensure that collateral or its proceeds is returned to the proper secured creditor." H.R. Rep., No. 995, 382; S.Rep. 989, 96. Section 725 contemplates that Mr. Spock release K's ship to F.

3. CHAPTERS 11 AND 13

What the holder of a secured claim receives in a Chapter 11 case or a Chapter 13 case depends on the provisions of the plan. A Chapter 11 plan can modify the rights of the holder of any secured claim, section 1123(b)(1). A Chapter 13 plan can modify the rights of the holder of any secured claim other than a claim secured "only by a security interest in real property that is the debtor's principal residence," section 1322(b)(2). There are, however, statutory limits on the modification of the rights of holders of secured claims. Unless the holder is willing to settle for less, the plan must provide for either (1) the surrender of the collateral to the holder of the secured claim, or (2) payments to the secured creditor that have a present value equal to the value of the collateral, sections 1129(b)(2) & 1325(a)(5). In Chapter 11, the payments under the plan to a nonassenting secured creditor must also total "at least the allowed amount of such a claim," section 1129(b)(2)(A). Understanding this requirement requires an understanding of section 1111(b). All of this understanding will take place in Chapter XXVII, infra.

Assume, for example, that D owes S $220,000. S has a mortgage on Blueacre. If Blueacre is worth $180,000, D's Chapter 11 or Chapter 13 plan must either surrender Blueacre to S or propose to pay S an amount that has a present value of $180,000. Obviously, a plan that provides for 36 monthly payments of $5,000 would not meet this standard. $180,000 over 36 months does not have a present value of $180,000. Obviously, Chapters 11 and 13 contemplate that a secured creditor that is being paid in installments will receive interest on its secured claim. What is not obvious from either the statute or cases is what the rate of interest should be. Some cases have looked to the contract rate of interest; some have looked to the current market rate on comparable credit transactions; some have looked to other factors.

Example: In January of 1988, D borrows $10,000 from C and agrees to pay 14% interest on the debt until it is repaid. D grants C a mortgage on Blueacre. In February of 1989, D files a Chapter 11 petition. At the time of the bankruptcy filing, D owes C $12,000 in principal and unpaid, accrued interest, and Blueacre has a value of $8,000. Accordingly,

C has an $8,000 secured claim and a $4,000 unsecured claim, section 506(a). D's Chapter 11 plan is confirmed in March of 1990. C's $8,000 secured claim does not accrue interest from the date of bankruptcy filing in February of 1989 until the time of confirmation in March of 1990. Only a claim that is fully secured draws interest from the time of the filing of the petition to the date of confirmation of the plan, section 506(b). C's $8,000 secured claim will, however, draw interest from the time of confirmation of the plan until it is fully satisfied. It is not clear whether this interest will be 14% or some other rate.

To summarize, (1) only a claim that is fully secured will draw interest from the time of the bankruptcy filing until the confirmation of a plan; and (2) any claim that is paid in installments will draw interest from the time of the confirmation of the plan until the time of the last plan payment.

F. POSTPONEMENT OF TAX LIENS IN CHAPTER 7 CASES

A government's claim for taxes is usually secured by a statutory lien. (Federal tax liens are considered supra at pages 271–82.) Such a statutory lien will not always be valid in bankruptcy. For example, an unfiled federal tax lien can be avoided by the trustee under section 544(a). The explanation is that an unfiled federal tax lien is not valid as against a creditor with a judicial lien, IRC 6323(a). Section 544(a) gives the bankruptcy trustee the rights and powers of a creditor that obtained a judicial lien as of the date of the bankruptcy filing. Accordingly, if the federal tax lien had not been filed prior to bankruptcy, the bankruptcy trustee can invalidate the tax lien under section 544(a). Section 544(a) is considered supra at pages 413–16.

If the government has not obtained a tax lien prior to bankruptcy or if the tax lien has been avoided under section 544, the tax claim will be an unsecured claim. Such an unsecured claim is governed by section 507(a)(7), not section 724.

Section 724 only applies if (1) Chapter 7 bankruptcy and (2) claim for taxes secured by a valid-in-bankruptcy tax lien. Section 724(b) postpones the payment of such a tax claim until the complete payment of all claims entitled to priority under section 507(a)(1)–(6). The priority provisions of section 507 are considered infra at pages 451–54. In 1984, Congress amended section 507 by adding a new sixth priority and postponing taxes to a seventh priority. Congress neglected to amend section 724 to conform to this change until 1986. See section 724(b)(2).

Examples: The debtor has property worth $4,000. This property is subject to a properly recorded tax lien for $3,000. The debtor also has $3,000 of debts entitled to priority under section 507(a)(1)–(6) and $5,000 of unsecured debts. The distribution in Chapter 7 would be $3,000 to the section 507(a)(1)–(6) claimants and $1,000 to the tax lienor. [See section 724(b)(5).]

Same facts except that the property is also subject to a $2,000 security interest. Under non-bankruptcy law, the security interest is junior in right to the nonpossessory tax lien. The distribution in Chapter 7 would be

$3,000 to section 507(a)(1)–(6) claimants and $1,000 to the junior security interest. [See section 724(b)(4)]. Note that the junior secured creditor is receiving exactly the same amount that it would have received if section 724(b) had not been applicable. Section 724(b) results in different claims being paid prior to the junior, non-tax lien, but the amount so paid is not affected by section 724(b).]

Same facts as the second of these examples except that the amount of the claims entitled to a section 507(a)(1)–(6) priority is $6,000. The distribution in Chapter 7 would be $3,000 to section 507(a)(1)–(6) claimants and $1,000 to the junior security interest.

Same facts as the second example except that the amount of the claims entitled to a section 507(a)(1)–(6) priority is only $1,400. The distribution in Chapter 7 would be $1,400 to section 507(a)(1)–(6) claimants, $1,600 to the tax lienor, and $1,000 to the junior security interest. [See section 724(b)(3).]

Same facts as the first example in this set except that the property is real property and is also subject to a $3,000 mortgage. Under non-bankruptcy law, this mortgage is senior in right to the tax lien. The distribution in bankruptcy would be $3,000 for the senior mortgage and $1,000 to section 507(a)(1)–(6) claimants. [See section 724(b)(1).]

The above combinations do not exhaust all possible section 724(b) problems. In resolving other section 724(b) problems remember that the amount distributed to a claim secured by a non-tax lien is neither increased nor decreased by the application of section 724(b); such creditors should receive the same distribution they would receive if section 724(b) were not applicable.

REVIEW QUESTIONS

1. T or F D Corp. owes S $100,000. P, the president of D Corp., has guaranteed payment and has pledged her D Corp. stock to secure payment. D Corp. files a bankruptcy petition. If the pledged D Corp. stock is worth $65,000, S has a $65,000 secured claim.

2. D owed S $200,000 and had a security interest in D's equipment. On default, S repossessed the equipment and sold it to T. The sale completely complied with the requirements of state law. One day after the sale, D filed a Chapter 11 petition. The debtor-in-possession needs the equipment to operate. Can the debtor-in-possession recover the equipment from T?

3. T or F The trustee in bankruptcy can abandon encumbered property to the secured party.

4. T or F The bankruptcy trustee can sell property free and clear of liens.

CHAPTER 7 AND UNSECURED CLAIMS

Analysis

A. WHAT IS A CLAIM

Generally, the Bankruptcy Code deals with "claims," not creditors. The term "claim" is defined in section 101(4), and has alternative components of "right to payment" or "equitable remedy for breach of performance."

1. RIGHT TO PAYMENT

It is clear from section 101(4)(A) that any right to payment is a "claim." The right to payment can be contingent, unliquidated, unmatured, and disputed and still be a claim.

Examples: C buys goods from D Corp. The goods are defective. D Corp. files a bankruptcy petition before C files a law suit. C has a claim.

D borrows $2,000 from C. X guarantees repayment of the loan. D files for bankruptcy. Both C and X have claims.

2. EQUITABLE REMEDY

Section 101(4)(B) dealing with rights to equitable remedies is less clear. Some, but not all, rights to equitable remedies are claims. The test is whether the right to an equitable remedy "gives rise to a right to payment." What does this mean?

It would seem that an order restraining an individual from seeing his wife or a corporation from polluting the water would not give rise to a right to payment, that is, would not be a "claim." What about an order requiring a business to clean up a waste site?

In *Ohio v. Kovacs,* 469 U.S. 274, 105 S.Ct. 705 (1985), the Court concluded that an injunction order that obligated Kovacs to clean up a dump site was a "claim." In so holding, the Court emphasized that a receiver had been appointed prior to bankruptcy and that after his appointment "the only performance sought from Kovacs was the payment of money." 105 S.Ct. at 710.

B. WHAT IS AN UNSECURED CLAIM

A claim is unsecured if the creditor has not obtained a consensual, judicial, or statutory lien or if the value of the property subject to the lien is less than the amount of the creditor's claim.

Examples: C provides diaper service to D. D files a bankruptcy petition. At the time of the bankruptcy petition, D owes C $100 for diaper service. C has an unsecured claim.

D Corp. borrows $2,000,000 from C and grants C a mortgage on Redacre. At the time of D Corp.'s bankruptcy it still owes C $2,000,000 and the encumbered property has a value of $800,000. S is a creditor with a $1,200,000 unsecured claim. [S is also a creditor with an $800,000 secured claim. The rights of holders of secured claims in a Chapter 7 case are considered supra at pages 435–41.]

C. COLLECTION OF UNSECURED CLAIMS FROM THE DEBTOR

Under section 362, the filing of a Chapter 7 petition operates as a "stay." This automatic stay prevents a creditor from collecting its unsecured claim from the debtor until the bankruptcy case is closed. The automatic stay and relief therefrom are considered supra in Chapter XVIII.

Under section 727, the bankruptcy court generally grants the debtor a "discharge." This discharge prevents a creditor from collecting its claim from the debtor after the bankruptcy case is closed. The discharge and exceptions thereto are considered in Chapter XXVI infra.

The section 362 stay coupled with the section 727 discharge makes it necessary for most holders of unsecured claims to look to the "property of the estate" for the satisfaction of their claims.

D. SATISFACTION OF UNSECURED CLAIMS IN CHAPTER 7 CASES

We now know:

- what an unsecured claim is, and

- that the automatic stay generally precludes collection of unsecured claims from the debtor during the bankruptcy case, and

- that the discharge generally bars collection of unsecured claims from the debtor after the bankruptcy case.

We need to determine, therefore, how to collect on unsecured claims in a Chapter 7 bankruptcy case. It thus becomes necessary to learn:

- what property is distributed to holders of unsecured claims in a Chapter 7 case, and

- which holders of unsecured claims are eligible to participate in the distribution of this property, and

- what is the order of distribution, i.e., which claims are paid first.

1. WHAT PROPERTY IS DISTRIBUTED TO HOLDERS OF UNSECURED CLAIMS IN CHAPTER 7 CASES

In a Chapter 7 case, the bankruptcy trustee has a statutory duty to sell the "property of the estate," section 704(1). The net proceeds received from the liquidation of the "property of the estate" is to be distributed to the holders of unsecured claims. Such claimants do not, however, receive the net proceeds from the sale of all of the "property of the estate":

- Some "property of the estate" will be turned over to the debtor as exempt property, section 522.

- Some "property of the estate" will be transferred after the filing of the bankruptcy petition to third parties protected by section 549.

- Some "property of the estate" will be subject to liens that are valid in bankruptcy. Encumbered property or the proceeds thereof must be first used to satisfy the holders of secured claims, section 725.

- Some "property of the estate" must be used to satisfy the administrative expenses of the bankruptcy proceeding.

Subject to these four exceptions, holders of unsecured claims receive the net proceeds from the bankruptcy trustee's sale of the "property of the estate."

2. WHICH HOLDERS OF UNSECURED CLAIMS PARTICIPATE IN THE DISTRIBUTION OF PROPERTY OF THE ESTATE

a. Proof of Claim

In a case under Chapter 7 of the Bankruptcy Code, the debtor will file a list of creditors, section 521. The court will then send notice of the Chapter 7 case to the listed creditors, section 342. The creditors that wish to participate in the distribution of the proceeds of the liquidation of the "property of the estate" must file a proof of claim, sections 501, 726.

Most of the requirements as to form, content, and procedure for proofs of claim are found in the Bankruptcy Rules. For example, there is no statutory language governing the time for filing a proof of claim. Section 501 simply speaks of "timely filing." Rule 3002(c) governs the time for filing a proof of claim in a Chapter 7 case or a Chapter 13 case. In Chapter 11 cases, a creditor is required to file a proof of claim only if its claim is scheduled as disputed, contingent, or unliquidated, section 1111(a); Rule 3003(b)(1).

Section 501(c) authorizes the debtor to file a proof of claim for a creditor who does not timely file. This provision is primarily intended to protect the debtor if the claim of the creditor is nondischargeable. When no proof of claim is filed, there will be no bankruptcy distribution to the holder of the claim. If no bankruptcy distribution is made to the holder of a claim excepted from discharge, the debtor will have to pay the claim in full after the bankruptcy case is closed. If, however, the debtor files a proof of claim, the holder of the nondischargeable claim will participate in the bankruptcy distribution and the post-bankruptcy liability of the debtor to the creditor will be reduced by the amount of distribution.

Example: Assume that David Lee Roth, D, files a Chapter 7 petition. He owes California Bank, C, $10,000. C made the loan to D because of a false financial statement; its claim against D is excepted from discharge. (Section 523(a)(2) excepts from discharge claims based on credit extended in reliance on a false financial statement. Section 523(a)(2) is considered infra at pages 472–73.) If no proof of claim is filed by or for C, it will have a $10,000 claim against D after the close of the Chapter 7 case. If, however, D files a proof of claim for C Bank, its post-bankruptcy claim against him will be reduced by the amount C receives in the bankruptcy distribution.

b. Allowance

In a Chapter 7 case, the proceeds of the liquidation of the property of the estate are not distributed to all holders of unsecured claims against the debtor. Rather, the distribution is only made to unsecured creditors whose claims are "allowed," section 726.

Under the Bankruptcy Act of 1898, only claims that were both allowable and provable were permitted to participate in the bankruptcy distribution. The requirement of provability excluded certain tort claims and certain other contingent and unliquidated claims from sharing in the distribution of the proceeds from the liquidation of the bankrupt estate, section 63. The Bankruptcy Code eliminates the requirement of provability. Tort claims and other contingent and unliquidated claims may participate in the bankruptcy distribution, cf. sections 502(b)(1), 502(c).

If a proof of claim has been filed, the claim is deemed allowed "unless a party in interest objects," section 502(a). The statute does not define "party in interest"; clearly, another creditor or the bankruptcy trustee is a "party in interest" for purposes of objections to allowance of a claim.

1) **Reasons for Objecting to Allowance**
   Section 502(b) sets out nine grounds for disallowing claims:

   - If the claim is unenforceable against the debtor or the property of the debtor by reason of any agreement or applicable law, it will not be allowed, section 502(b)(1).

     A non-recourse loan is an example of an agreement which makes a claim unenforceable. UCC section 2–302 is an example of a law which makes a claim unenforceable.

   - A claim for "unmatured" interest will be disallowed, section 502(b)(2).

     Generally, interest stops accruing when a bankruptcy petition is filed. Only claims that are secured by collateral that has a value greater than the amount of the claim will accrue interest after the filing of a bankruptcy petition, section 506(b).

     Example: D borrows $1,000 from C; the loan agreement provides for 14% interest. At the time of the bankruptcy filing, D owes $1,444. C's allowable claim will be $1,444; it will not draw the 14% interest after the bankruptcy filing.

   - If a claim is for an ad valorem property tax, it will be disallowed to the extent that the claim exceeds the value of the estate's interest in the property, section 502(b)(3).

   - If the claim is for services of the debtor's attorney or an "insider," it will be disallowed to the extent the claim exceeds the reasonable value of such services, section 502(b)(4). "Insider" is defined in section 101(28). "Insider" includes the relatives of an individual debtor; the partners of a partnership debtor; and the officers, directors, and other persons in control of a corporate debtor.

- If the claim is for post-petition alimony or child support, it will not be allowed, section 502(b)(5). These claims are excepted from discharge under section 523(a)(5).

The following example illustrates the application of sections 502(b)(5) and 523(a)(5).

> *Example:* H and W are divorced in January of 1989. The divorce decree orders H to pay alimony of $1,000 a month. H files a bankruptcy petition on December 31, 1989. He owes W $2,000 for November and December alimony. W's claims for $2,000 of unpaid 1989 alimony is allowable. Section 502(b)(5) only disallows a claim for alimony that is "unmatured on the date of the filing of the petition." Accordingly, W's claim for post-petition alimony is disallowed. If W's claim for $2,000 of unpaid 1989 alimony is not fully satisfied by the bankruptcy distribution, W may attempt to collect any deficiency from H personally. Section 523(a)(5) excepts alimony claims from the bankruptcy discharge. Accordingly, H's bankruptcy discharge will not affect W's right to collect post-petition alimony from H personally.

- If the claim is that of a landlord for future rent, it will be limited to the greater of one year's payments or 15% of the payments for the balance of the lease, not to exceed three years' payments in total, section 502(b)(6).

Note that section 502(b)(6) only limits the allowance of claims for future rentals by a lessor of real property. It does not affect a claim for rentals due on or before the filing of the bankruptcy petition. It does not affect a claim for rentals under a lease of personal property. Nor does the section not limit the amount of a claim for future rents of personal property. Section 547(e) suggests that the Bankruptcy Code considers "fixtures" to be real property. If so, section 502(b)(6) would apply to a claim by a lessor of equipment that was installed in such a manner as to become a fixture under state law.

Note also that section 502(b)(6) does not guarantee an allowable claim for back rent plus a minimum of one year's rent; rather, it places a ceiling on the allowance of rent claims.

> *Example:* D rents a building from C and signs a 20–year lease at a monthly rental rate of $5,000. At the time that D files her bankruptcy petition, she owes C $10,000 in back rent. If D immediately rejects the lease and C then relets the

building to X for $6,000 a month, C's allowable claim will be limited to the $10,000 in back rent.

- Section 502(b)(7) imposes a similar limitation on the allowable claim for termination of an employment contract: no more than back wages due at the time of the bankruptcy filing and one year's future compensation.

- If the claim is a federal tax claim which arises because the state unemployment tax is paid late and so no federal tax credit is allowed, the federal claim will be treated the same as if the credit had been allowed in full in the federal return, which means the federal tax claim would be disallowed, section 502(b)(8).

2) Contingent or Unliquidated Claims
The fact that a claim is contingent or unliquidated at the time that the bankruptcy petition is filed does not affect its allowance. The court may either delay bankruptcy distribution until the claim is fixed in amount, or, if liquidation of the claim would "unduly delay the administration of the case," estimate the amount of the claim, section 502(c).

Example: V files a $100,000 tort suit against T. T immediately files a bankruptcy petition. V then files a proof of claim. V's claim is allowable. The court may either delay distribution to T's creditors and the closing of T's bankruptcy case until V's tort claim has been litigated, or the court may estimate the amount of V's claim.

Section 502(c) does not indicate which judge shall do the estimating for purposes of allowance. 28 USC 157(b)(2)(B) states that "estimation of contingent or unliquidated personal injury tort or wrongful death claims against the estate for the purposes of distribution" is not a "core proceeding." This provision is considered in the chapter on allocation of judicial power over bankruptcy.

3) Pre- Versus Post-Petition Claims
Generally, only claims that arise before the bankruptcy petition are allowable. If, for example, D files a voluntary bankruptcy petition on January 11, and C lends D $100 on February 2, C's claim is not allowable.

There are four exceptions to the rule that only claims that predate the bankruptcy petition are allowable in Chapter 7.

- In an involuntary case, claims arising in the ordinary course of the debtor's business after the commencement of the case but before the earlier of the appointment of a trustee or the order for relief will be allowed as if the claim had arisen before the bankruptcy petition, section 502(f).

- Claims arising from the rejection of an executory contract or unexpired lease of the debtor are allowed as if the claim had arisen before the date of the filing of the petition, section 502(g).

- A claim arising from the recovery of property because of a voidable transfer will be determined and allowed as though it were a pre-petition claim, section 502(h).

  > *Example:* Assume that on January 11, D repays C the $1,000 he owes her. On February 2, D files a bankruptcy petition. On May 5, D's bankruptcy trustee recovers the $1,000 from C as a section 547 preference. Under section 502(h), C has an allowable claim for $1,000.

- A claim that does not arise until after the commencement of the case for a tax entitled to the seventh priority shall be treated as if the claim had arisen before the date of the filing of the petition, section 502(i).

In Chapter 13 cases, certain post-petition taxes and consumer debts are allowable, section 1305(a).

4) Reconsideration
    Before a case is closed, a claim that has been allowed may be reconsidered for cause and reallowed or disallowed according to the equities of the case, section 502(j).

3. ORDER OF DISTRIBUTION

There are a number of statements in reported cases, law review articles, and legal texts praising the theme of equality of distribution to creditors in bankruptcy proceedings. Such statements must be using the term "equality" in the *Animal Farm* sense: In bankruptcy, some creditors are clearly "more equal" than others. Some unsecured claims must be fully satisfied before any distribution is made to other unsecured claims.

Section 726 establishes the rules for distribution in a Chapter 7 case to the holders of unsecured claims. Basically, the distribution is to be as follows:

- priorities under section 507 (section 507 is considered below)

- allowed unsecured claims which were either timely filed or tardily filed by a creditor who did not know of the bankruptcy

- allowed unsecured claims which were tardily filed by creditors with notice or actual knowledge of the bankruptcy

- fines and punitive damages

- post-petition interest on pre-petition claims

Each claim of each of the five classes must be paid in full before any claim in the next class receives any distribution. Each claimant within a particular class shares pro rata if the proceeds from the liquidation of the property of the estate is insufficient to satisfy all claims in that class.

Example: Assume that $20,000 is available to pay holders of unsecured claims and the following unsecured claims:

- $11,000 claims entitled to priority under section 507

- $4,800 claim by X that was timely filed

- $7,200 claim by Y that was timely filed

- $3,000 claim by Z that was not timely filed even though Z knew of the bankruptcy proceedings.

The distribution would be:

- $11,000 to holders of priority claims;

- $3,600 to X [The first $11,000 must be used to pay priority claims. The remaining $9,000 ($20,000–$11,000) must be distributed pro rata to $12,000 ($4,800 + $7,200) of timely filed claims. Accordingly, each timely filed claim will be paid at the rate of 75 cents on the dollar. ($9,000–$12,000). Accordingly, X will receive $3,600 for its $4,800 claim.];

- $5,400 to Y.

In the very unlikely event that the sale of the "property of the estate" yields enough to satisfy every claim in each of the five "classes" listed above, the surplus is paid to the debtor.

a.   Priorities

The task of distributing the proceeds from the sale of the property of the estate is complicated by the fact that claims do not come neatly labelled "claims entitled to priority under section 507." Instead, it is necessary to determine which claims are entitled to priority under section 507.

Section 507 establishes seven classes of priority claims. Each claim of a class must be paid in full before any claim in the next class receives any distribution. After all of the priority claims have been fully satisfied, distributions are made to unsecured claims that are timely filed, section 726(a)(2).

1)   Administrative Expenses

In the typical Chapter 7 case, administrative expenses allowed under section 503(b) and fees and charges assessed against an estate under Chapter 123 of Title 28 are accorded first priority, section 507(a)(1). Administrative expenses include the costs of maintaining, repairing, storing, and selling the property of the estate; taxes the trustee incurs in administering property of the estate; the trustee's fee; the debtor's attorney's fees; the trustee's attorney's fee; and limited expenses of certain creditors.

a) Superpriority

Section 364(c) empowers the bankruptcy court to authorize a bankruptcy trustee or debtor-in-possession to obtain credit or incur debt that has a priority over all administrative expenses. Section 364(c) is considered infra at page 485. Section 507(b) grants a holder of a secured claim whose "adequate protection" proved to be less than adequate a "superpriority" over all administrative expenses. "Adequate protection" is considered supra at pages 378–79; section 507(b) is considered supra at page 379. These provisions apply only if the bankruptcy trustee or a Chapter 11 debtor-in-possession is authorized to operate the business. In the typical Chapter 7 case, the bankruptcy trustee is not authorized to operate the business. Accordingly, in a typical Chapter 7 case, sections 364(c) and 507(b) do not apply. Accordingly, in a typical Chapter 7 case, administrative expenses are accorded a first priority after indefeasible liens.

b) Pro Rata Sharing

In the typical Chapter 7 case, each section 507(a)(1) administrative expense claimant shares pro rata if the proceeds from the sale of the property of the estate is less than the total amount of all claims entitled to this priority. If the proceeds from the sale of the property of the estate is more than the total amount of all claims entitled to a first priority, second priority claims are next paid.

c) Converted Cases

Some Chapter 7 cases start as Chapter 11 or Chapter 13 cases and are converted to Chapter 7, sections 1112, 1307. In such a case, the administrative expenses incurred in the Chapter 7 liquidation are paid in full before any payment is made for the administrative expenses incurred while the case was under Chapter 11 or 13, section 726(b).

2) Ordinary Business Expenses

In an involuntary case, the second priority is accorded to claims arising in the ordinary course of the debtor's business after the commencement of the case but before the earlier of the appointment of a trustee or the order for relief.

Example: The creditors of an all-night Chinese restaurant, Wok Around the Clock, Inc., W, file an involuntary Chapter 7 petition on January 11. On January 12, C makes his usual weekly delivery of vegetables to W. C's claim will be entitled to a second priority under section 507(a)(2).

Section 507(a)(2) only applies in involuntary bankruptcy cases. If all second priority claims are satisfied, it is necessary to look to the third priority.

3) Wage Claims

Section 507(a)(3) grants a third priority to wage claims. This third priority includes claims for vacation pay, severance pay, and sick leave pay. It is subject to two limitations:

- Time—only compensation earned within 90 days before the bankruptcy petition. (If the debtor's business ceased operations before the bankruptcy petition, the 90 day period is measured from the cessation of business operations.)

- Amount—only $2,000 per employee.

Example: Assume that D files a Chapter 7 petition on December 31. It owes C $5,000 for November and December salary. $2,000 of C's wage claim would be entitled to a third priority under section 507(a)(3); the remaining $3,000 of his claim would be a general unsecured claim.

4) Employee Benefit Plans

Claims for contributions to employee benefit plans receive a fourth priority under section 507(a)(4). This priority for fringe benefits is also subject to time and amount limitations:

- Time—only for services rendered within 180 days of the bankruptcy petition. (If the debtor's business ceased operations before the bankruptcy petition, the 180 days is measured from the cessation of business operation.)

- Amount—[$2,000 x number of employees]—total payment to employees under section 507(a)(3) + total payments to other employee benefit plans.

Note that payments under section 507(a)(4) will be made to the benefit plan, not directly to individual employees. Note also that section 507(a)(4) focuses on the aggregate of other payments to all employees covered by the plan, not the payments to an individual employee.

5) Farmers and Fishermen

Section 507(a)(5) grants farmers a fifth priority for claims against grain storage facilities and fishermen a fifth priority against fish processing facilities. This priority is limited to $2,000 per individual claimant.

6) Consumers

Section 507(a)(6) grants a sixth priority to consumers who made a money deposit for property or services that were never provided. If, for instance, D pays $2,500 for five years of dance lessons at C Dance Studios, Inc., and C files a Chapter 7 petition before providing dance lessons, $900 of D's claim will be entitled to a sixth priority. The sixth priority is limited in amount to $900 per claimant.

7)   Tax Claims
Certain specified tax claims enjoy a seventh priority. (Remember that under section 724(b), a tax claim secured by an indefeasible lien is paid after certain priority claims. Section 724(b) is considered supra at pages 440–41.)

Taxes entitled to this seventh priority include:

- income taxes for the three tax years immediately preceding the filing of the bankruptcy petition;

  The three-year period is measured from the last date including extensions for filing a return to the date of the bankruptcy petition. If, for example, D files a bankruptcy petition on April 15, 1990, claims for taxes for 1989, 1988, and 1987 would be entitled to a priority. If, however, D files a bankruptcy petition on December 7, 1990, only claims for taxes for 1989 and 1988 would be entitled to a priority.

  property taxes assessed before the filing of the bankruptcy petition and last payable without a penalty one year before that date; and

- if the debtor is an employer, taxes withheld from employees' paychecks.

b.   **Subordination**
Section 507, the priority provision, has the effect of moving certain specified claims to the head of the line. Section 510, the subordination provision, has the effect of moving some claims further back in the line. Section 726, which governs the order of distribution in a Chapter 7 case, is prefaced, "Except as provided in section 510."

1)   Required Subordination
Section 510 requires subordination in two instances:

- when there is a subordination agreement that would be enforceable under non-bankruptcy law, section 510(a)

- when a seller or purchaser of equity securities seeks damages or rescission, section 510(b).

2)   Discretionary Subordination
Additionally, the court has the discretion after notice and hearing to subordinate any claim to another claim or claims "under principles of equitable subordination," section 510(c). According to legislative history, these equitable principles are defined by case law. A student note summarized the case law on equitable subordination as follows:

"The federal courts have employed equity powers to subordinate claims valid under state law in two broad classes of cases. Where a claimant has engaged in inequitable conduct toward other claimants, the bankruptcy court will often subordinate his claim. * * * Secondly, courts have subordinated valid claims of persons holding positions of control whose actions have caused damage to the estate."

Note, *Bankruptcy: Power to Subordinate on Equitable Grounds Claims Valid Under State Law,* 67 Colum.L.Rev. 583, 587 (1967).

REVIEW QUESTIONS

1. T or F D owes S $100,000. If S has a security interest in D's equipment, S does not have an unsecured claim.

2. D owes your client C $2,000. C learns that D has filed a Chapter 7 petition. Should C file a proof of claim?

3. 1/15/89, D borrows $300,000 from C. The loan agreement provides that D will pay C $330,000 on 1/15/90. On 7/15/89, D files a Chapter 11 petition. What is the amount of C's claim?

4. D Mfg Co. manufactures snowmobiles. It gives a two-year warranty. D Mfg Co. files a Chapter 7 petition. What are the rights of a person who bought a snowmobile within two years of the Chapter 7 filing?

5. 1/15, D files a Chapter 7 petition. On 2/2, D injures C in an automobile accident. What is the effect of D's bankruptcy on C?

6. T or F D leases a building from L for three years. One year later, D files a Chapter 7 petition. L will have an unsecured claim for back rents plus one year's rent.

*

XXV

LEASES AND EXECUTORY CONTRACTS

Analysis

457

The effect of bankruptcy on a debtor's leases and executory contracts is governed primarily by section 365. Under section 365, a bankruptcy trustee can either

- reject a lease or executory contract;

- assume and retain a lease or executory contract;

- assume and assign a lease or executory contract.

In order to understand section 365 and assess these three options, a law student or lawyer must be able to answer the following questions:

- First, what is the effect of rejecting a lease or executory contract, or assuming a lease or executory contract?

- Second, what is the procedure for rejecting or assuming a lease or executory contract?

- Third, what are the limitations, if any, on rejecting a lease or executory contract?

- Fourth, what are the limitations, if any, on assuming or assigning a lease or executory contract?

- Fifth, what is an executory contract?

A. EFFECT OF REJECTION, ASSUMPTION, ASSIGNMENT

Floyd Lawson, L, leases a building for his barbershop from Mayberry Realty Corp., M. The lease agreement provides for a ten-year term and monthly rentals of $250. L files a bankruptcy petition. What is the effect of the bankruptcy trustee or debtor-in-possession rejecting the lease? Assuming the lease? Assigning the lease?

1. REJECTION

If the lease is rejected, L has no further right to use the building for his barbershop. If the lease is rejected, L has no further personal liability on the lease. The rejection of the lease is, of course, a breach of the lease, section 365(g). M will have an allowable unsecured claim against the bankrupt estate for back rent and future rentals, sections 502(g) & 502(a)(6). The amount that M will receive on this unsecured claim will depend on the property of the estate in a Chapter 7 case and will depend on the provisions of the plan in a Chapter 11 or Chapter 13 case.

2. ASSUMPTION

If the lease is assumed, the leasehold continues to be an asset of the estate. L can continue to operate his barbershop in the building. Assumption covers the burdens of the lease as well as the benefits. By assuming the lease, the trustee or debtor-in-possession is obligating the estate to make all payments under the lease. This obligation is a first priority administrative expense.

Compare the Bankruptcy Code's treatment of the debtor's landlord with its treatment of the debtor's secured creditor. If a Chapter 11 or Chapter 13 debtor wants to retain a building that she is leasing, the debtor must continue to make all payments called for by the lease. Section 365 does not provide for the alteration or modification of leases; under section 365, the lease is either rejected or assumed, as is.

In contrast, if a Chapter 11 or Chapter 13 debtor wants to keep a building that is subject to a mortgage, the debtor can "impair or modify" the rights of the mortgagee in her plan, sections 1123(b)(1) & 1322(b)(2).

Example: D Corp. files a Chapter 11 petition. D is using two buildings. It is leasing one of the buildings from X at a rental of $2,000 a month. Y is financing D's purchase of the other building. The Y loan agreements grant Y a mortgage on the building and call for monthly payments of $3,000. D can keep the leased building only if it continues to pay X $2,000. D has greater flexibility with respect to retention of the building subject to Y's mortgage.

3. ASSUMPTION AND ASSIGNMENT

What if the trustee or debtor-in-possession assumes the barbershop lease and sells the lease to Aunt Bea Taylor who wants to open an adult bookstore in the building? Such an assignment "relieves the trustee and the estate from any liability for any breach of such contract or lease occurring after such assignment," section 365(k). After the assignment, M can look only to Aunt Bea for the payment of the post-assignment obligations under the lease.

B. PROCEDURE FOR REJECTION OR ASSUMPTION

Section 365(a) contemplates court approval of rejection or assumption. Rule 6006 provides that the assumption or rejection is a contested matter governed by Rule 9014. Neither the Code nor the Rules indicate what standard the court should apply in determining whether to grant or withhold its approval. Most, but not all, cases seem to apply a business judgment test.

1. CHAPTER 7 CASES

There is a 60–day rule in Chapter 7 cases. Leases and executory contracts that are not assumed within 60 days after the order for relief are deemed rejected, section 365(d)(1).

2. CHAPTERS 11 AND 13

Section 365(d)(4) provides the same 60–day time limit in Chapter 11 and Chapter 13 cases for leases of non-residential real property. There is no time limit in Chapter 11 and Chapter 13 cases for the assumption or rejection of residential leases, personal property leases, or other executory contracts. Such leases and contracts can be assumed or rejected in the Chapter 11 or Chapter 13 plan or can be assumed or rejected prior to the formulation of the plan, sections 365(d)(2), 1123(b)(2), 1322(b)(7).

C. LIMITATIONS ON THE REJECTION OF A LEASE OR EXECUTORY CONTRACT

There are five situations in which the power of a trustee or debtor-in-possession to reject a lease or executory contract is limited:

1. DEBTOR IS LANDLORD

Section 365(h) limits the effect of rejection of a lease of real property when the debtor is the landlord. A trustee for a debtor who owns rental real property may not use section 365 to evict tenants. Even if the trustee decides to reject the debtor/lessor's leases, the tenant has a right to remain in possession.

Example: Hulk Hogan invests some of his earnings in an office building where your law firm rents an office. If the Hulkster later files for bankruptcy and rejects the lease, your firm can still remain in possession of the leasehold.

The trustee for the debtor/lessor may, however, use rejection to terminate some of the services required by the lease, such as maintenance. The lessee may then offset any damages caused by such termination against its rent obligation.

2. TIMESHARE CONTRACT

Sections 365(h) and (i) provide similar limitations on a debtor/seller's rejection of a timeshare contract.

3. LAND SALES CONTRACT

Section 365(i) provides similar limitations on the debtor/seller's rejection of an installment land sales contract.

4. INTELLECTUAL PROPERTY LICENSES

In 1988, Congress added section 365(n) which provides similar limitations on a debtor/licensor's rejection of an intellectual property license.

5. COLLECTIVE BARGAINING CONTRACTS AND RETIREMENT BENEFITS

Section 1113 limits the rejection of collective bargaining contracts in Chapter 11 cases. Paragraph (f) of section 1113 prohibits a debtor/employer from unilaterally changing a pre-bankruptcy collective bargaining agreement. Paragraph (e) provides for court approval of interim changes pending court action on a request to reject a collective bargaining agreement. Paragraph (b) requires post-petition negotiations with and disclosures to the union as a condition precedent to rejection of the collective bargaining agreement. And, paragraph (c) sets out the standard the court is to apply in ruling on a motion to reject a collective bargaining agreement.

In June of 1988, Congress added section 1114 which similarly limits rejection of retirement benefits.

D. LIMITATIONS ON ASSUMPTION AND ASSIGNMENT

1. **LEASES AND EXECUTORY CONTRACTS THAT CANNOT BE ASSUMED OR ASSUMED AND ASSIGNED**
There are some leases and executory contracts that cannot be assumed and assigned.

   a. **Terminated Before Bankruptcy**
   A lease or contract that has terminated before bankruptcy cannot be assumed.

   Example: D leases Blackacre from L. D defaults. L takes the steps required by state law to evict D and terminate the lease. D later files for bankruptcy. D cannot assume the lease. Regardless of religious views, there is no such thing as a born-again lease.

   The 1984 amendments added section 365(c)(3) that prohibits the assumption of a lease of non-residential real property that has terminated prior to the order for relief. It can be questioned whether this was a necessary addition. There are numerous pre-1984 cases holding that terminated leases cannot be assumed.

   b. **Loan Commitment**
   A loan commitment or other financing arrangement cannot be assumed, section 363(c)(2).

   Example: C agrees to provide D with a $250,000 line of credit. D files a bankruptcy petition before drawing on this line of credit. D cannot assume this executory contract and compel C to loan the $250,000.

   c. **Contract Not Assignable by State Law**
   Contracts that are not assignable under state law are not assignable in bankruptcy, section 365(c)(1).

   Example: Batman contracts to patrol the streets of Gotham City. Batman later files a bankruptcy petition, Batman cannot assign this contract to Madonna.

   Contract clauses that specifically prohibit or limit the assumption and assignment of leases and executory contracts in bankruptcy will not be effective. The trustee or debtor-in-possession can assume a lease even though the lease agreement provides in the lease for automatic termination or a right of termination because of bankruptcy or insolvency, section 365(e).

2. **REQUIREMENTS FOR ASSUMPTION AND ASSIGNMENT**
Paragraph (b) of section 365 sets out the requirements for assumption of a lease or executory contract. Note that paragraph (b) only applies if there has been a default other than breach of a provision relating to bankruptcy filing or insolvency.

   Example: Kinky Friedman's Kosher Fried Chicken, Inc., K, rents a space in Underground Atlanta. K files a bankruptcy petition. At the time of the bankruptcy petition, K is current on all of its obligations under the lease. If K decides to assume the lease, section 365(b) does not apply.

The principal requirement of section 365(b) is "adequate assurance." Section 365(b) requires "adequate assurance" of future performance and a cure of all defaults or "adequate assurance" that all defaults will be promptly cured. The term "adequate assurance" is not statutorily defined. Section 365(b)(3) indicates what constitutes "adequate assurance" if the lease covers real property that is a part of a "shopping center." The term "shopping center" is not statutorily defined. Because of section 365(b)(3), a lessor of a shopping center enjoys greater protection than a lessor of other real property.

"Adequate assurance" is also a condition precedent to assignment of a lease or executory contract. Remember that after assignment, the other party to the lease or executory contract can look only to the assignee for the performance of the debtor's post-assignment obligations under the lease or contract. To protect the non-bankrupt party, section 365(f)(2) requires that the assignee provide "adequate assurance" of future performance as a condition to any assignment.

The "adequate assurance" standard sounds similar to, but is apparently different from, the standard applied in stay litigation. Section 362(d) protects the holder of secured claims by requiring "adequate protection" of the creditor's *interest in the collateral*. Section 365(b) protects the lessor of property by requiring "adequate assurance" of the *lease obligations*.

E. DEFINITION OF EXECUTORY CONTRACT

Section 365 applies to leases and executory contracts. The Bankruptcy Code does not define the term "lease." There is probably no need for a definition. When there is a problem as to whether a "lease" of personal property is a disguised credit sale, bankruptcy courts look to the definition of "security interest" in UCC section 1–201(37).

Similarly, the Bankruptcy Code does not define the phrase "executory contract." The most frequently cited and most thorough discussion of executory contracts in bankruptcy is a two-part, 142–page article written prior to the enactment of the Bankruptcy Code by Professor Vern Countryman. Professor Countryman concludes that an executory contract for purposes of bankruptcy is one that is so far unperformed on both sides that the failure of either party to complete her performance would be a material breach excusing further performance from the other party. See Countryman, *Executory Contracts In Bankruptcy,* 57 Minn.L.Rev. 439 (1973); 58 Minn.L.Rev. 479 (1974). Most of the reported cases under the Bankruptcy Act of 1898 and the Bankruptcy Code seem to follow the Countryman definition. There are, however, cases that use a different definition of "executory contract."

REVIEW QUESTIONS

1. D files a Chapter 7 bankruptcy petition. She is renting an apartment; she would like to remain in that apartment. Should the trustee assume the lease?

2. D files a bankruptcy petition. She wants to reject the lease. What should she do?

3. D files a Chapter 11 petition. She is renting a building that she uses to operate her business. Prior to her Chapter 11 filing, she had missed three rental payments? Can D still assume the lease?

4. D develops new technology and obtains the protection of the patent/copyright laws. D later grants a long-term exclusive license of the process to T. The agreement contains performance obligations for D as well as payment obligations for T. D files a bankruptcy petition. Can D reject the license agreement? What are the consequences of such rejection?

*

XXVI

DISCHARGE

Analysis

Most individuals who file voluntary bankruptcy petitions expect that the bankruptcy case will wipe out all of their debts. These expectations are not always realized. Bankruptcy "discharges" *certain* debtors from *certain* debts.

465

As the last sentence suggests, there are three major discharge issues:

- Which debtors receive a discharge?

- Which debts are discharged?

- What is the effect of a discharge?

A. WHICH DEBTORS RECEIVE A DISCHARGE (MAINLY, OBJECTIONS TO DISCHARGE)

1. CHAPTER 7

a. Importance of Determining Eligibility for Discharge

In counseling a beleaguered individual debtor about Chapter 7, it is very important to ascertain her eligibility for discharge—to determine whether any of the grounds for withholding discharge can be established by the bankruptcy trustee or a creditor. If the debtor is denied a discharge, she loses two ways: The debtor will leave the bankruptcy case without her section 541 property yet owing the same debts that she owed at the time of the filing of the bankruptcy case less any distribution that creditors received from the trustee.

b. Grounds for Withholding Discharge

The grounds for withholding a discharge, i.e., objections to discharge, are set out in section 727(a). These ten grounds are exclusive. Unless the bankruptcy trustee or a creditor can establish one of these ten objections, the debtor in a Chapter 7 case will receive a bankruptcy discharge of certain of her debts.

1) Corporation or Partnership

Section 727(a)(1) denies a discharge to corporations and partnerships. Only an individual is eligible to receive a discharge in a case under Chapter 7 of the Bankruptcy Code. This rule is intended to prevent "trafficking in corporate shells and partnerships." Generally, the owners of a bankrupt corporation do not need a bankruptcy discharge. Since the corporation is a separate legal entity, they are protected from personal liability for the corporation's debts.

BE AWARE, however, that a corporation may receive a discharge under Chapter 11, section 1141(d), or Chapter 12, section 1228.

2) Certain Fraudulent Conveyances

A fraudulent conveyance may be the basis for an objection to discharge. Section 727(a)(2) denies a discharge to a debtor who transfers property "with an intent to hinder, delay or defraud" within the twelve months immediately preceding the filing of the bankruptcy petition or after the filing of the bankruptcy petition. Note the intent requirement of section 727(a)(2). There are other "kinds" of fraudulent conveyances in section 548.

3) Failing to Preserve Record
An objection to discharge may be based on the unjustified failure to keep or preserve financial records, section 727(a)(3). A section 727(a)(3) objection raises the following issues of fact:

- Has the debtor failed to keep financial records?

- Is such failure "justified under all of the circumstances of the case"?

- Is it still possible to ascertain the debtor's financial condition and business transactions?

The standards applied in resolving these fact questions will reflect the nature of the debtor's business and his assets and liabilities.

4) Depriving Trustee of Property or Information
Section 727(a)(4) lists four acts which tend to deprive the bankruptcy trustee of property of the estate or of information necessary to discover or collect property of the estate:

- making a false oath or account in connection with the bankruptcy case;

- presenting or using a false claim against the estate;

- receiving or giving consideration for action or inaction in the bankruptcy proceeding; or

- withholding books and records from the bankruptcy trustee.

Proof that the debtor "knowingly and fraudulently" committed one of these acts will bar discharge. Proof that the debtor "knowingly and fraudulently" committed one of these acts will also subject the debtor to criminal sanctions: a fine of not more than $5,000 and/or imprisonment for not more than five years, 18 U.S.C.A. section 152. The standard of proof under 18 U.S.C.A. is beyond a reasonable doubt; section 727(a)(4) merely requires a preponderance of the evidence. Accordingly, section 727(a)(4) focuses on commission of the act, not conviction for the crime.

5) Failing to Explain Loss of Assets
The fifth ground for denial of discharge is the failure to explain "satisfactorily" any loss or deficiency of assets, section 727(a)(5). Section 727(a)(5) focuses on the truth of the debtor's explanation, not on the wisdom of his or her expenditures.

6) Refusal to Testify
Under section 727(a)(6), a debtor may be denied discharge if he refuses to testify after having been granted immunity or after improperly invoking the constitutional privilege against self-incrimination.

7) Acts Affecting Bankruptcy of Insider
The seventh ground for withholding discharge is the debtor's commission of any act specified in section 727(a)(2)–(6) no more than a year before the filing of the bankruptcy petition in connection with another bankruptcy case concerning an "insider," section 727(a)(7). The term "insider" is defined in section 101(28). An individual's relatives, partners, partnership or corporation all come within the definition.

8) Recent Discharge in Chapter 7 or 11 Case
If a debtor has received a discharge in a Chapter 7 or Chapter 11 case in the past six years, she will be denied discharge, section 727(a)(8).

9) Recent Discharge in Chapter 13 Case
If a debtor has received a discharge in a Chapter 13 case within the past six years she will be denied a discharge unless (a) payments under the plan totalled at least 100% of the allowed unsecured claims, or (b) payments under the plan totalled at least 70% of the allowed unsecured claims and the plan was proposed in good faith and was the debtor's "best effort," section 727(a)(9).

Note: Under sections 727(a)(8) and (9), the six years are measured from filing date to filing date. So, if X obtains a bankruptcy discharge on April 5, 1986, in a bankruptcy case filed on December 7, 1985, section 727(a)(9) would not bar X's bankruptcy discharge in a Chapter 7 case filed on December 8, 1991. Also, Section 727(a)(8) and section 727(a)(9) only limit the availability of a discharge in a Chapter 7 case. They do not affect the debtor's right to file a voluntary petition or creditors' right to file involuntary petitions.

10) Waiver of Discharge
Section 727(a)(10) recognizes certain waivers of discharge. A debtor's waiver will bar discharge only if it is:

* in writing, and

* executed after the filing of the bankruptcy petition, after the order for relief, and

* approved by the court.

c. **Procedure for Withholding Discharge**
1) Somebody Must Object to Discharge
Remember that section 727(a) is not self-executing. The bankruptcy trustee or a creditor must object to discharge, section 727(c)(1). The time for and form of objection are governed by Rules 4004 and 7001.

2) Time for Filing Objection
Rule 4004 sets the time for filing complaints objecting to discharge. Any such complaint must be filed within 60 days of the first date set for the meeting of creditors. The court may "for cause" extend the time for fil-

ing a complaint objecting to discharge on motion of a party in interest. Such a motion, however, must be filed within the 60–day period.

3) Trial

If an objection to discharge is filed, the bankruptcy court tries the issue of the debtor's right to a discharge. Such a trial is an "adversary proceeding" governed by Part VII of the Bankruptcy Rules, Rule 4004(d). If no objection to discharge is filed, and the debtor has not waived his right to a discharge, has not failed to attend the meeting of creditors, and has paid the filing fees, the court shall grant the discharge, section 727(a), Rule 4004(c).

d. Hearing After Determination Whether to Grant Discharge

After the court has determined whether to grant a discharge, the court must hold a hearing and the debtor must appear in person, section 524(d). The hearing must be held within 30 days of the order granting or denying a discharge. Rule 4008. At the hearing, the court informs the debtor that a discharge has been granted, or why a discharge has not been granted.

2. CHAPTER 11
a. In General

In Chapter 11, the confirmation of the plan operates as a discharge, section 1141(d). The following example points out the practical significance of this rule:

Example: D Corp. owes X $100,000. D Corp.'s Chapter 11 plan proposes to pay X $70,000 over three years. On confirmation, D's only obligation to X is to pay it $70,000 over three years as provided in the plan. The remainder of the debt has been discharged.

b. Grounds for Denying Discharge

The grounds for denying a discharge in a Chapter 11 case are different from the grounds for denying a discharge in a Chapter 7 case. A Chapter 11 debtor will be denied a discharge only if all of the following requirements are satisfied:

* the plan provides for liquidation of all or substantially all of the property of the estate; AND

* the debtor does not engage in business after consummation of the plan; AND

* the debtor would be denied a discharge if the case were in Chapter 7, section 1141(d)(3).

The following examples illustrate the application of section 1141(d)(3):

Examples: D Corp. files a Chapter 11 petition. Its Chapter 11 plan provides for the sale of all of its assets, distribution of the proceeds from the sale to creditors, and termination of business operations. D Corp. would not receive a discharge.

D Inc.'s Chapter 11 plan provides for the sale of six stores and continued operations of five stores. If its plan is confirmed, D Inc. will receive a discharge.

D, an individual who owns and operates several small businesses as sole proprietorships, files a Chapter 11 petition. D's Chapter 11 plan provides for the continued operation of these businesses. Because of her "bankruptcy history," D would be denied a Chapter 7 discharge under section 727(a)(9). If her Chapter 11 plan is confirmed, D will receive a discharge.

3. CHAPTERS 12 AND 13

In Chapter 12 and 13 cases, unlike Chapter 11 cases, the confirmation of the plan does not effect a discharge. In Chapter 12 and Chapter 13, the question of whether a debtor will receive a discharge cannot be resolved until the debtor either completes her payments under the plan or completes her efforts to make payments under the plan, sections 1228 and 1328.

Sections 1228(a) and 1328(a) make mandatory the discharge of a debtor who has completed all of the payments required by her Chapter 12 or 13 plan. Sections 1228(b) and 1328(b) give the court discretion to grant a "hardship" discharge to a debtor who has failed to make all of the payments required by her Chapter 12 or 13 plan. Sections 1228(b) and 1328(b) list three factors that the court should consider in exercising this discretion. Section 727 is not included in the list; section 727 is not applicable in Chapter 12 or 13 cases.

In Chapter 13 cases (but *not* Chapter 12 cases) a discharge under paragraph (a) is more comprehensive than a discharge under paragraph (b). As indicated on pages 504–05, infra, more debts are excepted from a section 1328(b) discharge.

B. WHICH OBLIGATIONS ARE AFFECTED BY A BANKRUPTCY DISCHARGE (MAINLY, EXCEPTIONS TO DISCHARGE)

Even when the debtor receives a discharge, she is not necessarily freed from all of her obligations. Certain obligations are not affected by a discharge. In determining whether a discharge affects an obligation, it is necessary to consider the following three questions.

- IS THE OBLIGATION A "DEBT" AS THAT TERM IS DEFINED IN SECTION 101?

Sections 727(b), 1141(d), and 1328 discharge the debtor from "debts."

Remember that section 101 defines "debt" in terms of a "claim" and that section 101's definition of "claim" is very broad. Virtually all of a debtor's obligations will come within the term "debt." Current cases are raising a couple of issues in this regard. In the *Manville* cases, the courts are wrestling with the question of whether people who are developing asbestosis because of exposure to Manville products, but are not yet aware of the disease, have "claims." In *Kovacs* and other environmental cases, the courts are considering whether clean-up obligations give rise to "debts."

- IF SO, WHEN DID THE OBLIGATION BECOME A DEBT?

Subject to limited exceptions, a Chapter 7 discharge reaches only "debts that arose before the date of the order for relief," section 727(b). A Chapter 11 discharge covers debts that "arose before the date of such confirmation," section 1141(d)(1)(A). A Chapter 12 or 13 discharge reaches debts "provided for by the plan," section 1228, 1328(a), (c). This includes pre-petition debts and post-petition debts that come under section 1305.

- IS SECTION 523 APPLICABLE?

Section 523 excepts certain debts from the operation of a discharge. Section 523 applies in all Chapter 7 cases, in Chapter 11 cases involving individual debtors, and in Chapter 13 cases in which the debtor receives a section 1328(b) "hardship discharge," sections 727(b), 1141(d)(2), and 1328(c).

The next several pages cover section 523 and point up the extent to which Chapters 7, 11, 12, and 13 differ with respect to debts affected by a discharge.

1. CHAPTER 7
a. Debts That Are Discharged
In a Chapter 7 case, a discharge relieves a debtor from personal liability for debts that are both

- incurred prior to the time of the order for relief and

- not within one of the ten exceptions to discharge set out in section 523.

b. Debts That Are Excepted From Discharge
It is very important to understand the difference between section 727(a) objections to discharge and section 523(a) exceptions to discharge. If an objection to discharge has been established, all creditors may attempt to collect the unpaid balance of their claims from the debtor. If a creditor establishes an exception to discharge, only that creditor may attempt to collect the unpaid portion of its claim from the debtor; all other pre-petition claims remain discharged. Proof of an objection to discharge benefits all creditors; proof of an exception to discharge benefits only the creditor who establishes the exception.

Section 523(a) sets out ten exceptions to discharge.

1) Taxes
Bankruptcy affords very little relief to the delinquent taxpayer. Most taxes are not discharged in bankruptcy. Section 523(a)(1) excepts from the bankruptcy discharge all income and excise taxes for the three tax years immediately preceding bankruptcy. Taxes that are entitled to a priority

are excepted from discharge, section 523(a)(1)(A). Section 507(a) provides a priority for taxes for "a taxable year ending on or before the date of the filing of the petition for which a return, if required, is last due, including extensions, after three years before the date of the filing of the petition." And, taxes more than three years old are non-dischargeable if (a) a return was not filed, or (b) a return was filed within two years of the filing of the bankruptcy petition, or (c) a "fraudulent return" was filed.

2) Debts for Property Obtained Through Fraud
a) Generally
Section 523(a)(2) excepts from discharge debts for money, property, or services obtained through fraud, false pretenses, or false representations. Section 523(a)(2) replaces section 17(a)(2) of the Bankruptcy Act of 1898. Section 17(a)(2) was the most frequently invoked exception to discharge, usually by lending institutions, finance companies, credit unions, or credit sellers contending that the debtor obtained money or goods through fraud in that she failed to disclose all existing debts in the financial data form she submitted when she applied for credit.

b) False Financial Statements
Section 523(a)(2)(B) deals specifically with false financial statements. A creditor seeking an exception to discharge based on the debtor's providing false or incomplete financial information must establish:

- a materially false written statement respecting the financial condition of the debtor or an "insider";

- its *reasonable* reliance on the statement;

- the debtor's intent to deceive.

Section 523(a)(2)(B) presents hard problems of proof for a creditor. Merely establishing the falsity of the debtor's financial data will not be sufficient. The creditor will also have to establish its reliance, the reasonableness of such reliance, and, most difficult of all, the debtor's intent to deceive.

c) Consumer Debts
The 1984 amendment to section 523(a)(2) seems to add exceptions from discharge for certain consumer obligations for luxury goods and services and for certain cash advances. Note, however, that new section 523(a)(2)(C) provides that such debts are "presumed to be nondischargeable." How can this presumption be rebutted? Section 523(a)(2)(C) begins with the phrase "for purposes of subparagraph (A) of this subsection." Section 523(a)(2)(A) deals with false representations. When a person buys something on credit, he impliedly represents (1) an ability to pay and (2) an intent to repay. Section 523(a)(2)(C) seems to presume that with respect to the described luxury purchases and cash advances the debtor lacks that ability and/or intent. Ac-

cordingly, it would seem that the debtor can avoid section 523(a)(2)(C)'s exception from discharge by showing that he had both the ability and the intent to repay at the time of the transaction.

d) **Unjustified Assertion of Exception to Discharge for Consumer Debt**
It is necessary to read section 523(d) together with section 523(a)(2). A creditor who unsuccessfully asserts a section 523(a)(2) exception to the discharge of a consumer debt may be required to pay the debtor's costs, including an attorney's fee. Section 523(d)'s test is whether the creditor was "not substantially justified." Even if the position of the creditor was "not substantially justified," it can avoid section 523(d) liability if "special circumstances would make the award unjust."

3) **Unscheduled Debts**
Unscheduled debts are excepted from discharge by section 523(a)(3). A creditor needs to know that its debtor is involved in a bankruptcy case. Only a creditor that timely files a proof of claim shares in the distribution of the "property of the estate." How does a creditor learn that its debtor is in bankruptcy? Section 521 requires the debtor to file a schedule of liabilities, and the bankruptcy court sends a notice to each creditor on the list. A creditor whose debt was not scheduled will not receive notice; a creditor that does not receive notice will not file a proof of claim unless it otherwise knows of the bankruptcy case; a creditor that does not file a proof of claim will not be paid from the property of the estate. Accordingly, section 523(a)(3) excepts from discharge a debt not timely scheduled unless the creditor had notice or actual knowledge of the bankruptcy case.

4) **Liabilities as Fiduciary**
Section 523(a)(4) excepts from bankruptcy discharge liabilities from "fraud or defalcation while acting in a fiduciary capacity." It also makes nondischargeable all embezzlement and larceny liabilities, whether the debtor is a fiduciary or not.

5) **Domestic Obligations**
Section 523(a)(5) makes certain domestic obligations nondischargeable: child support and alimony for the maintenance or support of a spouse. The debt may have been incurred in connection with a property settlement so long as it is actually in the nature of alimony, maintenance, or child support. Liabilities which are a part of a property settlement which are not in the nature of alimony, maintenance or child support are dischargeable.

6) **Liabilities for Willful and Malicious Injury**
Section 523(a)(6) excepts from the operation of the bankruptcy discharge any debt arising from the debtor's "willful and malicious" injury of person or property.

a) Meaning of "Willful and Malicious"
There is considerable confusion as to the meaning of the limiting phrase "willful and malicious." The exact same phrase was used in the exception to discharge provisions in the Bankruptcy Act of 1898. The Supreme Court in *Tinker v. Colwell,* 193 U.S. 473, 24 S.Ct. 505 (1904), held that those provisions excepted a criminal conversation judgment stating that "a willful disregard of what one knows to be his duty, * * * which necessarily causes injury and is done intentionally may be said to be done willfully and maliciously."

Since section 523(a)(6) uses the same language as the Bankruptcy Act of 1898, it would seem that *Tinker v. Colwell* would be authority for the meaning of "willful and malicious" in section 523(a)(6). However, the Committee reports that accompanied a late draft of the Bankruptcy Code expressly rejects *Tinker v. Colwell.*

b) Unauthorized Sales of Collateral
Most of the litigation under section 523(a)(6) involves an unauthorized sale of encumbered property by the debtor. For example, S has a security interest in D's tractor. The security agreement provides that D shall not sell the tractor without prior written authorization from S. D makes an unauthorized sale of the tractor, spends the proceeds, and files for bankruptcy. While this sale is an injury to property for purposes of section 523(a)(6), is it "willful and malicious"?

There is a line of cases that read section 523(a)(6) as requiring a conscious intent to harm the creditor; these cases hold that an unauthorized sale of encumbered property is not "willful and malicious." Other cases interpret section 523(a)(6) as merely requiring that the debtor know that his action will harm the creditor; these cases hold that an unauthorized sale of encumbered property is "willful and malicious."

7) Governmental Fines
Fines, penalties, or forfeitures that the debtor owes to a governmental entity are nondischargeable unless the debt is compensation for an actual pecuniary loss or a tax penalty on a dischargeable tax, section 523(a)(7).

On the other hand, claims for fines, penalties, and forfeitures have a very low priority in bankruptcy, section 726(a)(4).

8) Education Debts
Section 523(a)(8) contains an exception to discharge for certain educational debts: the debtor's obligations on a student loan made or guaranteed by a governmental unit or a nonprofit institution may be discharged in bankruptcy only if the bankruptcy petition was filed more than five years after the commencement of the repayment period unless the court finds that repayment of the loan will "impose undue hardship on the debtor and the debtor's dependents."

9) DWI Debts
Section 523(a)(9), added in 1984, excepts from discharge obligations incurred as a result of the debtor's driving while intoxicated. Note, however, the exact statutory language, particularly the word "judgment." It can at least be argued that section 523(a)(9) does not apply if D files for bankruptcy before a judgment is entered against her assessing liability for damages caused as a result of her driving while intoxicated.

10) Debts Covered by Previous Bankruptcy in Which Discharge Not Granted
Section 523(a)(10) excepts from discharge debts that were or could have been listed in a prior case in which the debtor did not receive a discharge.

Compare section 523(a)(9) with section 523(b). Section 523(a)(9) denies dischargeability; section 523(b) provides for dischargeability. Section 523(a)(9) looks to debts from a prior bankruptcy case in which a discharge was withheld (i.e., objection to discharge under section 727) for reasons other than the six-year bar. Section 523(b) applies when there was a prior bankruptcy case in which a discharge was granted but certain debts were excepted from the discharge because of a "time problem," such as the three-year tax period or the five-year educational loan period. If there is no longer a time period problem, then the debts that were nondischargeable in the earlier case are now dischargeable.

Examples: 8/85, D files a bankruptcy petition. D denied a discharge because of falsification of records, section 727(a)(3). Four years later, D again files a bankruptcy petition; any of the pre–1985 debts still unpaid are excepted from discharge by section 523(a)(9).

9/85, X files a bankruptcy petition. X receives a discharge; X's debt to Y is not discharged because it was not timely scheduled; 9/87, X again files a bankruptcy petition; if X's debt to Y is still unpaid and is now timely scheduled, the debt can be discharged, section 523(b).

c. **Procedure for Asserting Exceptions**
Exceptions to discharge based on section 523(a)(2), (4), or (6) must be asserted in bankruptcy court. Unless the creditor's motion is timely made, the debt is discharged.

When a creditor is relying on section 523(a)(1), (3), (5), (7), (8), (9), or (10), there is no requirement that the matter be heard in bankruptcy court. If no request is filed with the bankruptcy court, the dischargeability issue may arise in connection with the creditor's collection efforts in a nonbankruptcy forum.

Example: D owes C $1,000. D files a bankruptcy petition. D fails to list her debt to C on her schedule of liabilities. D receives a bankruptcy discharge. Six months later, C sues D in state court for the

$1,000. If D asserts her bankruptcy discharge as a defense, C can counter by asserting a section 523(a)(3) exception to discharge.

Rule 4007(c) sets a deadline for filing complaints contending that a particular debt is excepted from discharge by section 523(a)(2), (4), or (6). It is similar to the rule for filing complaints objecting to discharge, i.e., it sets a deadline of 60 days following the first date set for the meeting of creditors. This 60–day time period can be extended if a motion is filed before the expiration of the 60–day period. See Rules 4007(c) and 9006(b)(1). A motion filed after the expiration of the 60–day period will not be successful. The bankruptcy court does not have the discretion to extend the time to file a section 523(c) complaint after the expiration of the 60 days. See Rule 9006(b)(3). A creditor or the debtor may at "any time" file a complaint with the bankruptcy court to determine whether a particular debt is excepted from discharge by section 523(a)(1), (3), (5), (7), (8), or (9), Rule 4007(b). If no such complaint is filed with the bankruptcy court, the dischargeability issue may arise in connection with the creditor's collection efforts in a non-bankruptcy forum.

2. CHAPTER 11

The answer to the question which debts are affected by a discharge is different in Chapter 11 than in Chapter 7 in two significant respects.

- First, recall that a Chapter 7 discharge is generally limited to debts that arose before the date of the order for relief, section 727. A Chapter 11 discharge reaches debts that arose before the date of confirmation of the plan.

- Second, every Chapter 7 discharge is subject to the exceptions to discharge of section 523. In Chapter 11, section 523 only applies if the debtor is an individual, section 1141(d)(2). Section 523 does not apply if the Chapter 11 debtor is a corporation or a partnership.

3. CHAPTER 13 CASES AND CHAPTER 12 CASES

In Chapter 13 cases, the answer to the question which debts are covered by the discharge depends on the nature of the Chapter 13 discharge. If the debtor has made all of the payments required by the plan and received a discharge under section 1328(a), the discharge affects all debts provided for by the plan except

- claims for alimony and child support and

- certain long term obligations such as a house mortgage on which the payments extend beyond the term of the plan, section 1328(a). (Note that section 1328(a), unlike section 523(a)(1), does not except unpaid taxes from the operation of a discharge. Section 1328(a) should be read together with section 1322(a)(2) which in essence requires that all Chapter 13 plans provide for full payment of the taxes covered by section 523(a)(1).)

As noted earlier, the "hardship" discharge under section 1328(b) and *all* discharges under Chapter 12 are not as comprehensive as the section 1328(a) discharge. If the debtor receives a discharge under section 1328(b) or under section 1228(a) or (b), all of the exceptions to discharge in section 523 apply, section 1328(c).

C. EFFECT OF A DISCHARGE

1. WHAT A DISCHARGE DOES

a. Protection From Personal Liability

A discharge protects the debtor from any further personal liability on discharged debts. Section 524(a) provides that a discharge voids a judgment on discharged debts and enjoins any legal "action" to collect such a debt from the debtor or property of the debtor. A discharge also bars extrajudicial collection "acts" such as dunning letters or telephone calls to collect discharged debts.

b. Protection From Reaffirmation Agreements

A reaffirmation agreement is an agreement to pay a debt dischargeable in bankruptcy. Under contract law principles, an express promise to pay a debt that has been discharged in bankruptcy is enforceable even though there is no consideration or detrimental reliance to support the promise. Sections 524(c) and (d) limit the enforceability of reaffirmation agreements by

- requiring that the agreement be executed before the discharge is granted, section 524(c)(1);

- giving the debtor a right to rescind, section 524(c)(4);

- requiring that the agreement include a clear and conspicuous statement of the right to rescind, section 524(c)(2);

- requiring the agreement be filed with the court, section 524(c)(3);

- requiring a hearing if the debtor is an individual, section 524(d).

If the debtor was represented by an attorney in negotiating the reaffirmation agreement, section 524(c)(3) also requires an affidavit from the attorney. The affidavit must state that (1) the debtor was "fully informed," (2) the agreement was "voluntary," and (3) the agreement does not impose an "undue hardship." If the debtor was represented by an attorney in negotiating the reaffirmation agreement, the judge does not scrutinize the substance of the agreement. If an individual debtor was not represented by an attorney in negotiating the reaffirmation agreement, the judge must test the reaffirmation agreement by the standards set out in section 524(a)(6) unless the debt was fully secured by real property.

In sum:

- sections 524(c)(1), (2), (3), and (4) apply to all reaffirmation agreements.

- section 524(d)'s hearing requirement applies only if the debtor is an individual.

- section 524(c)(3)'s affidavit requirement applies only if debtors are represented by attorneys in reaffirmation negotiations;

- section 524(c)(6) applies only to individual debtors not represented by attorneys in negotiating the reaffirmation agreements.

c.   Protection from Discrimination by a Governmental Unit or an Employer

Subject to very limited exceptions, a governmental unit may not deny a debtor a license or a franchise or otherwise discriminate against a debtor *"solely because"* the debtor

- filed for bankruptcy,

- was insolvent prior to and/or during bankruptcy, or

- refuses to pay debts *discharged* by his, her or its bankruptcy, section 525(a).

The 1984 amendments added similar protection from discrimination by employers. A private employer cannot fire an employee or "discriminate with respect to employment" *"solely because"* (i) the employee filed for bankruptcy, (ii) was insolvent prior to or during the bankruptcy, or (iii) refuses to pay debts *discharged* by his or her bankruptcy, section 525(b).

The italicized language in the preceding paragraphs emphasizes the limitations on the protection from discrimination provided by section 525. If an employer dismisses an employee because of lack of financial ability and responsibility, can it consider the employee's bankruptcy along with other information? If a debtor's educational loans are excepted from discharge, can a state college withhold her transcript until the educational loans are paid?

2.   WHAT A DISCHARGE DOES *NOT* DO

A discharge does not cancel or extinguish debts. It only protects the debtors from further personal liability on the debt.

a.   No Protection of Codebtors

Section 524(e) limits the protection of the discharge to the debtor. A bankruptcy discharge does not automatically affect the liability of other parties such as codebtors or guarantors. For example, the discharge of an insured tortfeasor does not affect the liability of the insurance company.

b.   No Effect on Liens

A bankruptcy discharge has no effect on a lien. See, e.g., *Long v. Bullard,* 117 U.S. 617, 6 S.Ct. 917 (1886); *United Presidential Life Ins. Co. v. Barker,* 31 B.R. 145 (N.D.Tex.1983). This rule is important primarily with respect to abandoned or exempt property.

> *Example:*   D owes C $10,000. The debt is secured in part by D's car which is worth $6,000. D files for relief under Chapter 7. The trustee abandons the car to the debtor under section 554. D receives a discharge. The discharge does not extinguish C's security interest. If D is in default, C can repossess the car under U.C.C. section 9–503. The discharge does, however, wipe out C's rights against D personally. If C repossesses and resells the car, C can not obtain a deficiency judgment against D.

3. DISCHARGE AND A DEBTOR'S LEGALLY IMPOSED PUBLIC OBLIGATIONS

a. Obligations to Dispose of Toxic Waste

The effect of a bankruptcy discharge on a debtor's obligations to the public under state law, such as state environmental laws, may depend on the fundamental question whether such an obligation is a "claim." A discharge affects "debts", sections 727(b), 1141(d), 1328. Debt is defined in section 101 as "liability on a claim," and "claim" is defined in section 101 as "right to payment" or "right to equitable remedy for breach." Recently, the Supreme Court dealt with this issue.

In *Ohio v. Kovacs,* 469 U.S. 274, 105 S.Ct. 705 (1985), the Supreme Court held that a Chapter 7 debtor's obligation to clean-up toxic wastes gave rise to a "claim" within the meaning of the Bankruptcy Code and could be discharged. Kovacs had been the chief executive officer of a corporation that operated a waste disposal site in Ohio. Ohio sued the corporation and Kovacs, alleging violation of the environmental laws. Kovacs later signed a consent judgment, requiring him to remove all industrial wastes from the site within twelve months. Because of Kovacs' noncompliance with the order, the state court appointed a receiver who was directed to take control of all of Kovacs' assets and clean up the site. Kovacs then filed for bankruptcy.

In holding that a bankruptcy discharge relieved Kovacs of his duty to clean up toxic wastes, the Supreme Court emphasized Kovacs' lack of control over the site because of the appointment of a receiver. "What the receiver wanted from Kovacs after bankruptcy was money to defray cleanup costs." 469 U.S. at 284, 105 S.Ct. at 710. "On the facts before it and with the receiver in control of the site, we cannot fault the Court of Appeals for concluding that the cleanup order had been converted into an obligation to pay money, an obligation that was dischargeable in bankruptcy." 469 U.S. at 285, 105 S.Ct. at 711. "[W]e do not address what the legal consequences would have been had Kovacs been taken into bankruptcy before a receiver was appointed." Id.

b. Court-Ordered Restitution in Criminal Cases

Some courts had similarly decided that dischargeable debts include court-ordered restitution imposed in connection with a criminal defendant's sentence. In *Kelly v. Robinson,* 479 U.S. 36, 107 S.Ct. 353 (1986), however, the Court decided that even if such an obligation is a "debt," it is excepted from discharge by section 523(a)(7), which excepts a debt that is a "fine, penalty, or forfeiture payable to and for the benefit of a governmental unit, and is not compensation for actual pecuniary loss." The court reasoned that neither of the section's qualifying clauses—"to or for the benefit of a government unit" nor "not compensation for pecuniary loss"—was triggered by the restitution order. Although the victim gets the money, the real purpose is to benefit society as a whole. Moreover, the decision to order restitution does not really turn on the victim's injury; rather, it turns on the "penal goals of the State and the situation of the defendant."

REVIEW QUESTIONS

1. T or F Every debtor receives a discharge.

2. T or F A corporate debtor cannot receive a discharge in a Chapter 7 case.

3. T or F Discharge under Chapter 13 can be more favorable to the debtor than discharge under Chapter 7, 11 or 12.

4. T or F Discharge does not affect a debtor's liability for taxes.

5. H and W are divorced and H is ordered to pay alimony to W. H later obtains a bankruptcy discharge. While W is notified of the bankruptcy, she does not litigate discharge or dischargeability in the bankruptcy case. After the bankruptcy, H stops paying W alimony. Advise W.

6. D buys a car from S on credit and grants S a security interest in the car. D later files a bankruptcy petition and receives a discharge. In the bankruptcy, D claims the car as exempt property. After the discharge, D stops making car payments to S. Can S still repossess the car?

XXVII

CHAPTER 11

Analysis

The Bankruptcy Act of 1898 contains four separate chapters for the reorganization of businesses: Chapter VIII which deals with railroad reorganizations; Chapter IX which covers corporate reorganizations; Chapter XI for the arrangement of unsecured debts by corporations, partnerships and individuals; and Chapter XII which is available to non-corporate debtors who own encumbered real estate. Chapter 11 of the Bankruptcy Code replaces these four chapters. It contains some principles from each of the above chapters and some new concepts. Chapter 13 is also available to certain business debtors, i.e., "individuals with a regular income" and less than $100,000 of unsecured debts and $350,000 of secured debts. Chapter 13 is considered infra at pages 497–509.

A. COMMENCEMENT OF THE CASE

1. FILING THE PETITION

A case under Chapter 11 is commenced by the filing of a petition. The petition may be filed by either the debtor or creditors.

a. Voluntary Petition

Insolvency is not a condition precedent to a voluntary Chapter 11 petition. With two exceptions, any "person" that is eligible to file a voluntary bankruptcy petition under Chapter 7 is also eligible to file a petition under Chapter 11.

- The first exception is stockbrokers and commodity brokers: They are eligible for Chapter 7, but not Chapter 11.

- The second exception is railroads: Railroads are eligible for Chapter 11, but not Chapter 7.

If the Chapter 11 petition has been filed by an eligible debtor, no formal adjudication is necessary. The filing of the petition operates as an "order for relief," section 301.

b. Involuntary Petition

The requirements for a creditor-initiated Chapter 11 case are the same as the requirements for an involuntary Chapter 7 case, section 303. These requirements are discussed supra at pages 368–69.

2. NOTIFYING AND ORGANIZING THE CREDITORS

a. List of Creditors and Notice

How will creditors learn of a Chapter 11 filing? Sections 521 and 342 provide a partial answer. Section 521 obligates the debtor to file a list of creditors. Section 342 requires appropriate notice of the order for relief. Rule 2002 governs the content of and time for the notice.

b. Proof of Claim

Generally, a creditor whose claim is included on a Chapter 11 debtor's list of creditors will not have to file a proof of claim. Unless the claim is scheduled as disputed, contingent, or unliquidated, a proof of claim is "deemed" filed by section 1111(a). Rules 3001 and 3003 govern the filing of a proof of claim in a Chapter 11 case.

c.   Creditors' Meeting
The Bankruptcy Code requires a meeting of creditors, section 341. Section 343 indicates that the debtor is to be examined under oath at the meeting. Section 341(c) prohibits the bankruptcy judge from presiding at or attending the meeting. This prohibition is consistent with the Bankruptcy Code's goal of limiting the judge to adjudicatory functions. At a creditors' meeting, the judge might obtain a great deal of extraneous information without the constraints of adversarial trial procedure.

d.   Creditors' Committee
In most Chapter 11 cases, the debtor has hundreds if not thousands of creditors. It would not be practical for the Chapter 11 debtor to attempt to negotiate with each creditor individually. Accordingly, section 1102 directs the bankruptcy court to appoint a committee of unsecured creditors as soon as practicable after the order for relief. A prepetition creditors' committee will be continued if it was "fairly chosen and is representative of the different kinds of claims to be represented," section 1102(b)(1). In the absence of any such prepetition committee, the court is instructed to appoint the seven largest unsecured creditors willing to serve, section 1102(b). On request of a party in interest and after notice and hearing, the court may change the membership or size of a committee if it is not sufficiently representative, section 1102(c).

A creditors' committee performs a number of functions. It may:

* consult with the trustee or debtor-in-possession concerning the administration of the case;

* investigate the debtor's acts and financial condition;

* participate in the formulation of the plan;

* request the appointment of a trustee;

* "perform such other services as are in the interest of those represented," section 1103(c).

The creditors' committee may also appear at various hearings as a party in interest, section 1109(b). And, the committee may file a plan in those situations where the debtor ceases to have the exclusive right to do so, section 1121.

B.   OPERATION OF THE BUSINESS

Successful rehabilitation of a business under Chapter 11 generally requires the continued operation of the business. No court order is necessary in order to operate the debtor's business after the filing of a Chapter 11 petition. Section 1108 provides: "Unless the court * * * orders otherwise, the trustee may operate the debtor's business."

1. WHO OPERATES THE BUSINESS

a. Debtor-in-possession

Notwithstanding section 1108's use of the word "trustee," the debtor will remain in control of the business in most Chapter 11 cases. Pre-bankruptcy management will continue to operate the business as a "debtor-in-possession" unless a request is made for the appointment of a trustee and the court, after notice and a hearing, grants the request.

b. Trustee

Section 1104 sets out the grounds for the appointment of a trustee. A trustee is to be appointed if

- there is cause (fraud, dishonesty, mismanagement, or incompetence) or

- the appointment of a trustee is "in the interest of creditors, any equity security holders, and other interests of the estate."

Section 1104 specifically instructs the court to disregard the number of shareholders or the amount of assets and liabilities of the debtor in deciding whether to appoint a trustee.

If a trustee is appointed, she must be "disinterested," as defined in section 101(13). The duties of a trustee are enumerated in section 1106. Essentially, the trustee has responsibility for the operation of the business and formulation of the Chapter 11 plan.

c. Examiner

If a trustee is not appointed, the court may appoint an "examiner." Section 1104(b) sets out the requirements for the appointment of an examiner:

- a trustee was not appointed, and

- appointment of an examiner was requested by a party in interest, and

- the debtor's nontrade, nontax, unsecured debts exceed $5,000,000, or "such appointment is in the interests of creditors, any equity security holders, and other interests of the estate."

An "examiner" does not operate the business. Rather he investigates the competence and honesty of the debtor and files a report of the investigation, sections 1104(b), 1106(b).

2. OBTAINING CREDIT

One of the first problems confronting a debtor-in-possession or a Chapter 11 trustee is financing the operation of the business pending the formulation and approval of a plan of rehabilitation. Obtaining credit is essential to almost every Chapter 11 case. Section 364 deals with obtaining credit. It provides a number of inducements to third parties to extend credit to a debtor that has filed a Chapter 11 petition.

a. Priority in Payment Over Pre-Petition Creditors

A post-petition unsecured credit transaction in the Chapter 11 debtor's "ordinary course of business" automatically has administrative expense priority over pre-petition creditors, section 364(a). The court may, after notice and hearing, provide administrative expense priority for credit transactions that are not in the ordinary course of business, section 364(b).

Note the two differences between paragraphs (a) and (b) of section 364. First, paragraph (a) applies to ordinary course of business credit transactions; paragraph (b) applies if the credit transaction is not in the ordinary course of the debtor's business. Second, paragraph (b) requires "notice and hearing"; there is no notice and hearing requirement in paragraph (a).

b. Priority in Payment Over Administrative Expenses Plus Collateral

If priority over pre-petition unsecured creditors is not a sufficient inducement, the bankruptcy court may, after notice and hearing, authorize obtaining credit with:

- priority over other administrative expenses, or

- a lien on the debtor's unencumbered property, or

- a lien on the debtor's encumbered property, section 364(c).

c. Superpriority in Collateral

Section 364(d) is the "last resort" provision. If the debtor is unable to otherwise obtain credit, the court may authorize the debtor to grant its post-petition creditors a "superpriority," i.e., a lien on encumbered property that is equal or senior to existing liens. The court may authorize such a "superpriority" only if there is "adequate protection" of the pre-petition secured creditors' interests.

3. USE OF ENCUMBERED PROPERTY

In the typical Chapter 11 case, most of the personal and real property that the debtor owns *at the time of* the filing of the Chapter 11 petition is encumbered by liens.

a. Immunity of Post-Petition Property From Pre-Petition Liens

1) General Rule

The personal and real property that the debtor acquires *after* the filing of the Chapter 11 petition is generally protected from pre-petition liens. Property acquired by the debtor after it files a Chapter 11 petition will not be "subject to any lien resulting from any security agreement entered into by the debtor before the commencement of the case," section 552(a). After-acquired property clauses are not recognized in cases under the Bankruptcy Code.

Example: Reems Organ Co. files a Chapter 11 petition. If First Bank has contracted for a security interest in "all of Reems' inventory, now owned or hereafter acquired," section 552(a) will limit

First Bank's lien to organs manufactured by Reems before the Chapter 11 petition was filed.

2) Exception for Proceeds

First Bank's lien will probably also reach the proceeds from the sale of such pre-petition organs. The Bankruptcy Code does recognize a right to "proceeds, product, offspring, rents, or profits," section 552(b). Under section 552(b), a pre-petition security interest continues to reach proceeds acquired after the bankruptcy petition was filed "except to any extent that the court, after notice and a hearing and based on the equities of the case, orders otherwise."

The "equities of the case" exception covers situations where property of the estate is used in converting the collateral into proceeds. If, for example, Reems incurs costs of $1,000 in selling organs for $7,000, the court may limit First Bank's lien on the proceeds to $6,000.

b. Effect of Stay on Reaching Collateral

Section 362(a), considered supra at pages 374–75, stays a creditor with a lien on the property of a Chapter 11 debtor from repossessing the encumbered property. Section 362(d), considered supra at pages 376–80, provides for relief from the stay in limited situations.

c. Rules as to Use of Collateral

Section 363 empowers the debtor-in-possession or trustee to continue using, selling, and leasing encumbered property. The interest of the lien creditor is safeguarded by section 363's requirement of "adequate protection," section 363(e). (The concept of "adequate protection" is dealt with by section 361. Section 361 is dealt with on pages 378–80.)

1) Non-Cash Collateral

Encumbered property that is not "cash collateral", as defined in section 363(a), may be used, sold, or leased in the ordinary course of business without a prior judicial determination of "adequate protection," section 363(c)(1). Section 363(c)(1) is applicable only if "the business of the debtor is authorized to be operated." In a Chapter 11 case, the trustee or debtor-in-possession is authorized to operate the business "unless the court orders otherwise," section 1108.

On "request" of the lien creditor, the court shall condition the use, sale, or lease of encumbered property so as to provide "adequate protection," section 363(e).

Example: If D Department Stores, Inc., D, files a Chapter 11 petition and C Bank, C, has a perfected security interest in D's inventory, D may continue to sell inventory in the ordinary course of business. D will not have to obtain court permission in order to make such sales; rather, C will have the burden of requesting the court to prohibit or condition such sales so as to provide "adequate protection" of C's security interest.

Notice and a hearing on the issue of "adequate protection" are required before a Chapter 11 debtor uses, sells, or leases encumbered property in a manner that is not in the ordinary course of business, section 363(b). Remember that "notice and hearing" means "such notice as is appropriate in the particular circumstances, and such opportunity for a hearing as is appropriate in the particular circumstances," section 102(1)(A).

Example: If D, after filing its Chapter 11 petition, decides to discontinue its furniture department and wants to make a bulk sale of its furniture inventory, C must be first given notice and the opportunity for a hearing on the issue of "adequate protection."

2) Cash Collateral

Encumbered "cash collateral" may only be used if the court, after notice and hearing on adequate protection, authorizes such use, section 363(c)(2). "Cash collateral" is defined in section 363(a): "cash, negotiable instruments, documents of' title, securities, deposit accounts, or other cash equivalents." A bank account is "cash collateral"; accounts receivable are not. Accordingly, D may not withdraw funds from its bank account to pay employees or the utilities without bankruptcy court authorization; and, D may not spend the cash it receives from post-petition sales of inventory without such authorization. Unless the debtor-in-possession or trustee is authorized to use cash collateral, all such cash collateral coming into possession of the debtor-in-possession or trustee must be segregated and accounted for, section 363(c)(4).

C. PREPARATION OF THE PLAN OF REHABILITATION

1. WHO PREPARES THE PLAN

A Chapter 11 plan may be filed at the same time as the petition or any time thereafter.

a. When Trustee Not Appointed

Unless a trustee has been appointed, the debtor initially has the exclusive right to file a Chapter 11 plan. "Only the debtor may file a plan until after 120 days after the date of the order for relief under this chapter," section 1121(b). If the debtor does file a plan within this 120 day period, no other plan may be filed during the first 180 days of the case, section 1121(c)(3). Section 1121(d) empowers the bankruptcy court to extend or reduce the 120–day and 180–day periods.

Note that the time is measured from the date of the order of relief, not the date that the Chapter 11 plan was filed.

> *Example:* Assume that D files a Chapter 11 petition on January 12, and files its Chapter 11 plan on February 22. No other plan may be filed until after July 11 (180 days from January 12).

b.   When Trustee Is Appointed

If a trustee is appointed, the trustee, the debtor, a creditor, the creditors' committee, and any other party in interest may file a plan, section 1121(c). More than one plan may be filed.

c.   When Debtor Fails to File Plan

Similarly, if the debtor fails to file a plan and obtain creditor acceptances within the specified time periods, any party in interest may file a plan and more than one plan may be filed. Acceptance of a Chapter 11 plan by creditors is considered infra at pages 489–92.

d.   Important Role of Creditors' Committee

No matter who files the plan, the creditors' committee will probably play a major role in formulating the plan, cf. section 1103(c)(3).

2.   TERMS OF THE PLAN

Section 1123 governs the provisions of a Chapter 11 plan. Subparagraph (a) sets out the mandatory provisions of a Chapter 11 plan ("shall"); subparagraph (b) of section 1123 indicates the permissive provisions of a Chapter 11 plan ("may").

a.   Rights Altered

A Chapter 11 plan may alter the rights of unsecured creditors, secured creditors, and/or shareholders.

b.   Classes of Claims

Section 1123 contemplates that the plan will divide creditors' claims into classes and treat each claim in a particular class the same.

Section 1122 governs classification of claims in Chapter 11 plans.

- Section 1122(b) authorizes the segregation of all small claims into a single class if "reasonable and necessary for administrative convenience."

  NOTE: A Chapter 11 debtor will often find it advantageous to pay small claims in full. A class of claims that receives full cash payment on the effective date of the plan is not "impaired," section 1124(3)(A). A class that is not impaired under a plan is deemed to have accepted the plan, and solicitation of acceptances with respect to such class is not required, section 1126(f).

- Section 1122(a) provides the general test for "inclusion"—for determining whether a claim can be included in the same class. All claims within a class must be "substantially similar." Section 1122(a) does not provide any test for "exclusion"—for determining whether a claim must be included in the same class. No language in section 1122 expressly limits the discretion of the drafter of the plan in placing "substantially similar" claims in different classes.

> ***Example:*** Assume that X, Y, and Z are creditors of Chapter 11 debtor, D. If D's plan places all three creditors' claims in the same class, section 1122(a) controls. It is clear from section 1122(a) that D cannot place the claims of X, Y, and Z in a single class unless all three claims are "substantially similar." If, however, D's Chapter 11 plan places each creditors claim in a separate class, section 1122(a) does not control. What limits D's discretion in placing claims in a separate class is not clear from the Bankruptcy Code.

3. FUNDING FOR THE PLAN

Compliance with the requirements of section 1123 is not the difficult part of preparing a plan for the rehabilitation of a business under Chapter 11. Rather, the hard questions are how much creditors will be offered by the plan and how the plan will be effectuated. There are several sources of funding:

a. Loans

Chapter 11 debtors often use money borrowed from third parties to make distributions to creditors under Chapter 11 plans.

b. Sale of Assets

Sale of assets is another major source for Chapter 11 payments. A Chapter 11 plan may provide for the sale of all or substantially all of the debtor's assets, section 1123(b)(4).

c. Securities

Often, a Chapter 11 plan offers creditors the debtor's debt or equity securities, rather than cash. Generally, the issuance of a security requires expensive and time-consuming federal and state registration. Section 1145(a)(1) exempts the issuance of the debtor's securities under a Chapter 11 plan from federal and state registration requirements. A creditor's resale of a security received under a Chapter 11 is also exempted from federal and state registration requirements, section 1145(b). Section 4(1) of the Securities Act of 1933 states in essence that transactions by any person who is not an "issuer, underwriter, or dealer" need not be registered. Section 1145(b)(2) provides an exemption to creditors who resell securities obtained under a Chapter 11 plan by indicating that such creditors are not "underwriters."

D. ACCEPTANCE

1. DISCLOSURE

"The premise underlying * * * Chapter 11 * * * is the same as the premise of the securities law. If adequate disclosure is provided to all creditors and stockholders whose rights are to be affected, then they should be able to make an informed judgment of their own, rather than having the court or the Securities and Exchange Commission inform them in advance whether the proposed plan is a good plan," H.R. 95–595, p. 226. Accordingly, the bankruptcy court does not review a Chapter 11 plan before it is submitted to creditors and shareholders for vote. Instead, the bankruptcy court reviews the information provided to creditors and shareholders to insure that their judgment is an "informed judgment."

Section 1125 requires full disclosure before postpetition solicitation of acceptances of a Chapter 11 plan. Two items are especially important in making full disclosure:

a. Copy of Plan
Creditors and shareholders must be provided with a copy of the plan or a summary of the plan.

b. Written Disclosure Statement
Creditors and shareholders must be also be provided with "a written disclosure statement approved, after notice and a hearing, by the court as containing adequate information." Section 1125(b).

"Adequate information" is defined in section 1125(a) as information which it is "reasonably practicable" for this debtor to provide to enable a "hypothetical reasonable investor" who is typical of the holders of the claims or interests to make an informed judgment on the plan. What constitutes "adequate information" thus depends on the circumstances of each case, on factors such as:

• the condition of the debtor's books or records,

• the sophistication of the creditors and stockholders, and

• the nature of the plan.

2. WHO VOTES
a. People With "Allowed" Claims and Interests
Both creditors and shareholders vote on Chapter 11 plans. According to section 1126(a), creditors with claims "allowed under section 502" and shareholders with interests "allowed under section 502" vote on Chapter 11 plans.

b. "Double-Deeming"
1) Determining Whether Claim or Interest "Allowed"
The statutory requirement of "allowed under section 502" is generally satisfied by the Bankruptcy Code's "double-deeming." In a Chapter 11 case, section 1111 deems filed a claim or interest that is scheduled and is not shown as disputed, contingent, or unliquidated. And, section 502 deems allowed any claim or interest that is filed and not objected to by a party in interest.

2) Eliminating Voting by Certain Classes of Claims or Interests
Statutory "deeming" also eliminates voting by two classes of claims or interests. First, if a class is to receive nothing under the plan, it is deemed to have rejected the plan, and its vote need not be solicited, section 1126(g). Second, if a class is not "impaired" under the plan, the class is

deemed to have accepted the plan and again its vote need not be solicited, section 1126(f).

3. IMPAIRMENT OF CLAIMS

The concept of "impairment" is unique to Chapter 11. Section 1124 is entitled "Impairment of Claims or Interests." Under section 1124 a class of claims or interests is impaired unless

- the legal, equitable, and contractual rights of the holder are left "unaltered;" (If the plan in any way changes the rights of the holder, it alters and thus impairs the holder. It is not necessary to determine whether the change adversely affects the holder.) or

- the only alteration of legal, equitable, or contractual rights is reversal of an acceleration on default by curing the default and reinstating the debt; or

- cash payment to (A) a creditor on the effective date of the plan is equal to the allowed amount of the claim; or (B) cash payment to a shareholder on the effective date of the plan is equal to the greater of the share's redemption price and its liquidation preference.

4. 1111(b) ELECTIONS

Section 1111(b), like section 1124, deals with a concept that is unique to Chapter 11. Generally, a creditor whose debt is only partially secured has two claims—a secured claim measured by the value of its collateral and an unsecured claim for the remainder, section 506(a).

Example: C's $100,000 claim against D is secured by real property owned by D that is valued at $70,000. Under section 506(a), C has a $70,000 secured claim and a $30,000 unsecured claim. Under section 1111(b), C can elect to have a $100,000 secured claim and no unsecured claim.

Note: Section 1111(b) provides for election by classes of secured claims, not by individual holders of secured claims. Generally, each holder of a secured claim will be in a separate class. Note also that some classes of secured claims are not eligible to make a section 1111(b) election.

Let's use this example to consider the advantages and the disadvantages of a section 1111(b) election:

a. Advantages of Section 1111(b) Election

- If C makes the section 1111(b) election, its secured claim will be impaired under section 1124(3), considered above, unless the Chapter 11 plan provides for a cash payment of $100,000.

- If C makes the section 1111(b) election, section 1129(b), considered infra at pages 493–94, requires that C be paid at least $100,000 under the plan.

b.   Disadvantages of Section 1111(b) Election
  - If C makes the section 1111(b) election, it will not be able to vote its
    $30,000 unsecured claim. C's negative vote might prevent D from ob-
    taining the necessary creditor acceptance.

  - If C makes the section 1111(b) election, it will not participate in the distri-
    bution to holders of unsecured claims.

5.   NEEDED MAJORITIES
a.   Class of Claims
A class of claims has accepted a plan when more than one half in number
and at least two thirds in amount of the allowed claims actually voting on the
plan approve the plan, section 1126(c). The following example illustrates the
application of section 1126(c):

Example: D files a Chapter 11 petition. D's schedule of creditors shows 222
different creditors and $1,000,000 of debt. D's Chapter 11 plan di-
vides creditors into four classes. Class 3 consists of 55 creditors,
with claims totalling $650,000. Only 39 of the creditors in Class 3
vote on the plan. Their claims total $450,000. If at least 20 Class
3 creditors (more than 1/2 of 39) with claims totalling at least
$300,000 (2/3 of 450,000) vote for D's plan, the plan has been ac-
cepted by Class 3.

b.   Class of Interests
A class of interests has accepted a plan when at least two thirds in amount of
the allowed interests actually voting on the plan approve the plan, section
1126(d).

E.   CONFIRMATION

Section 1128 requires that the bankruptcy court hold a hearing on confirmation and
give parties in interest notice of the hearing so that they might raise objections to confirmation.

While it is possible for more than one plan to be filed and accepted, only one plan
may be confirmed. If more than one plan meets the confirmation standards of section
1129, the court "shall consider the preferences of creditors and equity security holders
in determining which plan to confirm," section 1129(c).

Subparagraphs (a), (b), and (d) of section 1129 contain the confirmation standards. Section 1129(d) prohibits confirmation of a plan whose "principal purpose" is the avoidance
of taxes or the avoidance of registration of securities. Subparagraph (a) and (b) are discussed below.

1.   STANDARDS FOR CONFIRMATION
a.   Plans Accepted by Every Class
Subject to the limited exception of sections 1129(c) and 1129(d), a plan that has
been accepted by every class of claims and every class of interests must be

confirmed by the bankruptcy court if the 11 enumerated requirements of section 1129(a) are satisfied. Section 1129(b) does not apply to plans that have been accepted by every class of claims and every class of interests.

Most of the requirements of section 1129(a) are easy to understand, easy to apply. Two of the requirements are somewhat complex.

1) Best Interests of Creditors
   Section 1129(a)(7) creates a "best interests of creditors" test. It requires that each dissenting member of a class, including dissenting members of classes that approve the plan, receive at least as much under the plan as it would have received in a Chapter 7 liquidation. Section 1129(a)(7) looks to the value of the distribution under the plan as of the effective date of the plan. If for example the plan calls for payment to creditor X of $100 a month for 20 months, the value of the payment to X "as of the effective date of the plan" is clearly less than $2,000.

2) Priority Claims
   Section 1129(a)(9) provides special treatment for priority claims. A holder of an administrative expense claim or a claim for certain postpetition expenses in an involuntary case must be paid in cash on the effective date of the plan unless the claim holder otherwise agrees, section 1129(a)(9)(A). Wage claims, claims for fringe benefits, and certain claims of consumer creditors must be paid in cash on the effective date of the plan unless the class agrees to accept deferred cash payments that have a present value equal to the amount of the claims, section 1129(a)(9)(B). Each priority tax claim must receive deferred cash payments that have a present value equal to the amount of the claim, section 1129(a)(9)(C).

b. **Plans Accepted by Less Than Every Class**
   1) Additional Requirements
      Plans accepted by less than every class can be confirmed only if the additional requirements of section 1129(b) are satisfied. Section 1129(b) requires that

      - at least one impaired class of claims has accepted the plan;
      - the plan does not discriminate unfairly;
      - the plan is fair and equitable.

      This last requirement, "fair and equitable," is the most troubling.

   2) "Fair and Equitable"
      Section 1129(b)(2) sets out three different tests for determining whether a plan is "fair and equitable" depending on whether the dissenting class is a secured claim, unsecured claim, or ownership interest.

a) As to Secured Claims

The section 1111(b) election, considered supra at pages 491–92, affects whether a Chapter 11 plan is fair and equitable to a holder of a secured claim. Section 1129(b)(2)(A)(i) requires that

- the holder of the secured claim retain its lien,

- the payments at least equal the amount of the allowed secured claim, and

- the payments have a present value equal to the value of the collateral.

The following example points out the relationship between these three requirements and section 1111(b).

Example: Assume that D owes C $100,000. C has a lien on D's equipment that has a value of $85,000. D files for Chapter 11 relief. C makes a section 1111(b) election. C does not accept the plan. The plan will be fair and equitable with respect to C if (1) it provides that the security interest will remain on D's equipment to secure the entire $100,000 debt, (2) C is paid at least $100,000 over the life of the plan, and (3) the deferred payments to be made to C under the plan have a present value of at least $85,000.

b) As to Unsecured Claims

The "fair and equitable" standard is satisfied with respect to a dissenting class of unsecured claims if junior claims and interests neither receive nor retain anything, section 1129(b)(2)(B)(ii).

Example: D Corp. files for Chapter 11 relief. Its Chapter 11 plan provides for payment of 70 cents on the dollar to a class of holders of unsecured claims and for its stockholders to retain their D Corp. stock. This plan is not "fair and equitable" under section 1129(b)(2)(B)(ii). Stockholders are junior to the dissenting class and stockholders are retaining property under the plan.

In other words, a plan is not fair and equitable unless dissenting unsecured creditors have absolute priority over any junior class of claims, which is not the case if unsecured creditors receive less than full payment and a junior class receives or retains property under the plan. Supreme Court case law created a capital contribution exception to this *absolute priority rule* in *Case v. Los Angeles Lumber Products Co.*, 308 U.S. 106, 60 S.Ct. 1 (1939). By contributing new capital, shareholders could retain an ownership interest in a Chapter 11 corporation in a cram down. In *Northwest Bank Worthington v. Ahlers*, ___ U.S. ___, 108 S.Ct. 963 (1988), the Court rejected an expansion of the new contribution of capital exception so as to permit farmers to retain ownership of their farms by contributing future labor. And, in a footnote, the Court raised a question as to the continued viability of the capital contribution exception.

A comprehensive consideration of the other "fair and equitable" provisions in section 1129(b) is beyond the scope of this basic student outline.

2. EFFECT OF CONFIRMATION

a. Plan Governs Obligations

After confirmation of a Chapter 11 plan, the debtor's performance obligations are governed by the terms of the plan. The provisions of a confirmed Chapter 11 plan bind not only the debtor but also the debtor's creditors and shareholders "whether or not such creditor, equity security holder, or general partner has accepted the plan," section 1141(a). Subject to limitations noted below, confirmation of a Chapter 11 plan operates as a discharge, section 1141(d). The following example illustrates the possible application of sections 1141(a) and 1141(d).

Example: D's confirmed Chapter 11 plan provides for monthly payments to creditors. Each creditor in Class 2 is to receive 5% of its claim each month for 15 months. After making two payments under the plan, D defaults. At the time of the filing of the petition D owed C $10,000. C has received $1,000 under the plan. C's claim against D is now limited to $6,500. (75% × $10,000−1,000).

b. Limitations on Discharge

Chapter 11 withholds discharge from some debtors and some debts. The plan may limit discharge, section 1141(d)(1). The order of confirmation may limit discharge, section 1141(d)(1). The exceptions to discharge in section 523 are applicable to individual debtors, section 1141(d)(2). The objections to discharge in section 727 are applicable only if

- the plan provides for the sale of all or substantially all of the debtor's property, and

- the debtor does not engage in business after the consummation of the plan, section 1141(d)(3).

The following chart compares Chapter 11 discharge rules with those of Chapter 7, considered supra at pages 466–70.

	Chapter 7	Chapter 11
Corporations, Partnerships	Not eligible for discharge	Eligible for discharge unless plan is a liquidating plan and the debtor terminates business
Section 523	Applicable to individuals	Applicable to individuals
Grounds for withholding discharge	Section 727	1. provision in plan, 2. provision in confirmation order, 3. Section 727 *if* a. liquidating plan, and b. termination of business operations

REVIEW QUESTIONS

1. T or F There is a trustee in every Chapter 11 case.

2. T or F A Chapter 11 debtor-in-possession must obtain court approval before borrowing money or selling assets.

3. D files a Chapter 11 petition. Your client, C, one of D's creditors, wants D to liquidate. Can C file a creditor's plan providing for the immediate liquidation of D?

4. D files for Chapter 11 relief. Her plan divides claims into classes: Class 1 for claims of less than $5,000 and Class 2 for claims of $5,000 or more. The plan proposes to pay Class 1 claims in full, over three years. Does D have to solicit and obtain acceptances from Class 1 claims?

5. T or F In Chapter 11 cases, unlike Chapter 7 cases, the debtor is not required to treat all unsecured claims the same.

6. D owes C $100,000. D files a Chapter 11 petition. Her Chapter 11 plan provides inter alia for the payment of the $60,000 to D. D's plan is confirmed. D is unable to make the payments called for by the plan. Advise C.

XXVIII

CHAPTER 13

Analysis

A. ELIGIBILITY

Chapter 13 of the Bankruptcy Code replaces Chapter XIII of the Bankruptcy Act of 1898. Chapter XIII was limited to a "wage earner," i.e., "an individual whose principal income is derived from wages, salary, or commissions."

Chapter 13 of the Bankruptcy Code is open to more debtors, except that neither a stockbroker nor a commodity broker may file a petition under Chapter 13, section 109(e). Subject to limited exceptions, the source of income is not an eligibility test. A debtor may file for Chapter 13 relief if she:

- IS AN INDIVIDUAL, and

Chapter 13 is not available to corporations or partnerships.

- HAS A "REGULAR INCOME," and

The phrase "individual with a regular income" is statutorily defined in section 101(27) as "an individual whose income is sufficiently stable and regular to enable such individual to make payments under a plan under Chapter 13 of this title."

- HAS FIXED UNSECURED DEBTS OF LESS THAN $100,000 AND FIXED SECURED DEBTS OF LESS THAN $350,000, section 109(e).

Note that the debt limitation does not include contingent, unliquidated claims. For example, Dr. Frank Burns is sued for $400,000 for malpractice on April 4. He could still file a Chapter 13 petition on April 5.

B. COMMENCEMENT OF THE CASE

1. BY FILING VOLUNTARY PETITION
Chapter 13 is similar to Chapter 7 and Chapter 11 in that the case begins with the filing of a bankruptcy petition, section 301. Chapter 13 is different from Chapter 7 and Chapter 11 in that only the debtor may file a Chapter 13 petition. There are no involuntary, i.e., creditor-initiated, Chapter 13 cases.

2. STAY TRIGGERED
The filing of a Chapter 13 petition triggers the automatic stay of section 362. Section 362 is discussed supra at pages 373–81. A Chapter 13 petition also stays civil collection activities directed against codebtors of the individual who filed the petition, section 1301.

C. CODEBTOR STAY

Section 1301 restrains a creditor from attempting to collect a debt from the codebtor of a Chapter 13 debtor. The following example illustrates the application of section 1301's codebtor stay:

Example: D borrows money from C to buy a pair of contact lenses. Her mother, M signs the note as a comaker. D later incurs financial problems and files a Chapter 13 petition. Section 362 stays C from attempting to collect from D; section 1301 stays C from attempting to collect from M.

1. APPLICABILITY OF STAY
Section 1301's stay of collection activities directed at codebtors is applicable only if:

- the debt is a consumer debt, and
- the codebtor is not in the credit business.

2. TERMINATION OF STAY
This codebtor stay automatically terminates when the case is closed, dismissed, or converted to Chapter 7 or 11.

3. RELIEF FROM STAY
Section 1301(c) sets out three grounds for relief from the codebtor stay. Section 1301(c) requires notice and hearing and requires the court to grant relief if any of the three grounds are established.

a. Codebtor Got the Consideration
First, the stay on collection from the codebtor will be lifted if the codebtor, not the Chapter 13 debtor, received the consideration for the claim, section 1301(c)(1).

Example: If in the preceding example, M, not D, filed for Chapter 13 relief, C could petition for relief under section 1301(c)(1) so that it could attempt to collect from D.

Section 1301(c)(1) also covers the situation in which the Chapter 13 debtor is merely an accommodation indorser.

b.   Claim Not Paid Under Debtor's Plan
Second, when the Chapter 13 plan has been filed, a creditor may obtain relief from the codebtor stay to the extent that "the plan filed by the debtor proposes not to pay such claim," section 1301(c)(2).

Example: D still owes C $200. D's Chapter 13 plan proposes to pay each holder of an unsecured claim 70 cents on the dollar. As soon as the plan is filed, D can obtain relief from the stay so that it can obtain $60 from M.

A motion to lift the stay under section 1301(c)(2) is deemed granted unless the debtor or codebtor files a written objection within 20 days, section 1301(d).

c.   Irreparable Harm
Third, section 1301(c)(3) requires the court to grant relief from the codebtor stay to the extent that "such creditor's interest would be irreparably harmed by continuation of such stay." The running of a state statute of limitations is not a basis for relief under section 1301(c)(3). Section 108(c) guarantees the creditor at least 30 days after the termination of the stay to file a state collection action against the codebtor.

D.   TRUSTEES

1.   APPOINTMENT
There will be a trustee appointed in every Chapter 13 case, section 1302(a).

Chapter 13 trustees are appointed by United States trustees. (The United States trustee is considered at pages 363–64 supra.) In most regions, the United States trustee appoints a standing trustee for Chapter 13 cases. Where there is no standing trustee, the United State trustee "shall appoint one disinterested person to serve as trustee in the case or the United States trustee may serve as a trustee in the case," section 1302(a).

2.   DUTIES AND POWERS
The trustee in a Chapter 13 case is an active trustee. Section 1302 imposes a number of duties on a trustee in a Chapter 13 case. Operation of the debtor's business is not one of the duties there enumerated. If a debtor engaged in business files a Chapter 13 petition, section 1304(b) contemplates that the business will be operated by the debtor, not by the trustee, "unless the court orders otherwise."

Moreover, a Chapter 13 trustee probably has all of the avoidance powers discussed in Chapter XXI, supra. The Bankruptcy Code does not clearly indicate whether a Chapter 13 trustee can assert the avoidance provisions. The statutory arguments for a Chapter 13 trustee being able to avoid preferences and other pre-bankruptcy transfers are these:

- section 103, which indicates that provisions in Bankruptcy Code Chapter 5 (such as section 547) are applicable in Chapters 7, 11, and 13;

- use of the word "trustee" in section 547 and the other avoidance provisions.

The statutory argument for a Chapter 13 trustee not being able to avoid preferences and other pre-bankruptcy transfers focuses on section 1302(b)'s exclusion of section 704(1). If a Chapter 13 trustee is not empowered to "collect the property of the estate," is she able to avoid pre-bankruptcy transfers?

An excellent law review article by Professor Ralph Peeples considers this question and properly concludes that a Chapter 13 trustee should be able to assert the avoidance provisions. Peeples, *Five Into Thirteen: Lien Avoidance in Chapter 13*, 61 N.C.L.Rev. 849 (1983).

Even if a Chapter 13 trustee *can* avoid transfers, questions remain as to whether she *will* or *must* do so.

E. PREPARATION OF THE CHAPTER 13 PLAN

1. WHO FILES

Only a debtor may file a Chapter 13 plan, section 1321. The court may dismiss a Chapter 13 case or convert it to Chapter 7 for "failure to file a plan timely under section 1321 of this title," section 1307(c)(3). The Code leaves the question of the meaning of "timely"—how many days the debtor has to file such a plan—to the rules.

2. CONTENTS

Section 1322 governs the contents of a Chapter 13 plan. Subsection (a) of section 1322 specifies what the plan must provide; subsection (b) specifies what the plan may provide.

a. What Plan Must Provide

A Chapter 13 plan must provide for full payment in cash of all claims entitled to priority under section 507, unless the holder of the claim otherwise agrees, section 1322(a)(2).

b. What Plan May Provide

1) For Less Than Full Payment of Unsecured Claims

A Chapter 13 plan may provide for less than full payment to other unsecured claims. It may not, however, arbitrarily pay some holders of unsecured claims less than others. Rather, the plan must either treat all unsecured claims the same or classify claims and provide for the same treatment of each unsecured claim within a particular class, sections 1322(a)(3), 1322(b)(4).

2) For Modifying Secured Claims

A Chapter 13 plan may also modify the rights of most holders of secured claims. It may modify the rights of creditor A who has a security interest on the Chapter 13 debtor's car. It may modify the rights of Creditor B who has a mortgage on the Chapter 13 debtor's store. It may not, however, modify the rights of Creditor C who has mortgage only on the Chapter 13 debtor's principal residence, section 1322(b)(2). Note, however, the word "only" in section 1322(b)(2). If C loaned D 100,000 and obtained a mortgage on both D's residence and D's store, it would seem that the plan could modify D's rights.

3. FUNDING

In the typical Chapter 13 case, the source of the payments proposed by the plan will be the debtor's wages. This is not, however, a statutory requirement. Section 1322(a)(1) only requires that the plan provide for submission of "such portion of future earnings * * * of the debtor to the supervision and control of the trustee as is necessary for the execution of the plan." Payments under the plan may also be funded by sale of property of the estate, section 1322(b)(8).

4. PAYMENT PERIOD

Section 1322(c) limits the payment period under a Chapter 13 plan to three years, except that the court may "for cause" approve a payment period of as long as five years.

F. CONFIRMATION OF THE CHAPTER 13 PLAN

In Chapter 13, creditors do not vote on the plan. Chapter 13 requires only court approval, i.e., confirmation. A creditor can object to confirmation, section 1324.

1. STANDARDS FOR CONFIRMATION

The standards for judicial confirmation of a Chapter 13 plan are set out in section 1325.

a. Satisfy Bankruptcy Law
Section 1325(a)(1) requires that the plan satisfy the provisions of Chapter 13 and other applicable bankruptcy law requirements.

b. Payment of Filing Fee
Section 1325(a)(2) conditions confirmation on payment of the $60 filing fee.

c. Good Faith
Section 1325(a)(3) sets out a "good faith" standard. This is the most often invoked basis for withholding confirmation.

d. Best Interests of Creditors
Section 1325(a)(4) protects the holders of unsecured claims by imposing a "best interests of creditors" test: the present value of the proposed payments to a holder of an unsecured claim must be at least equal to the amount that the creditor would have received in a Chapter 7 liquidation.

The following example illustrates the practical significance of the "present value" language in section 1325(a)(4).

> *Example:* Assume these facts: D owes C $1,000; D files a Chapter 13 petition. If D had filed a Chapter 7 petition, the sale of the property of the estate would have yielded a sufficient sum to pay all priority creditors in full and pay unsecured creditors like C 36 cents on the dollar. D's Chapter 13 petition proposes to pay C $10 a month for 36 months. This plan does not satisfy the requirement of section 1325(a)(4). Payment of $360 over a thirty-six month period does not have a "present value" of $360. This hypothetical is probably somewhat unrealistic. In the typical Chapter 7 case, an unsecured creditor would receive little if anything. Accordingly, in the typical Chapter 13 case, section 1325(a)(4) will be easily satisfied.

Section 1325(a)(4) now must be read together with section 1325(b) which was added in 1984. New section 1325(b) requires that a Chapter 13 plan either provide for payment in full of all claims or commit all of the debtor's "disposable income" for three years to payments under the plan. The phrase "disposable income" is defined in section 1325(b)(2). The following example illustrates the application of section 1325(b):

> *Example:* D files a Chapter 13 petition. She earns $1,200 a month. $900 of the $1,200 is "reasonably necessary" to support and maintain D and her dependents. D's Chapter 13 plan must commit $300 a month for 36 months.

What if D's income or living expenses change so that her "disposable income" changes? Section 1325(b) seems to require the court to determine what D's disposable income will be over the next three years. If there is an unanticipated change, then the debtor or a creditor can request a modification of the plan under section 1329.

e. Protection of Secured Claims

Section 1325(a)(5) protects the holders of secured claims "provided for by the plan" by requiring one of the following:

- acceptance of the plan by such a creditor; or

- continuation of the lien and proposed payments to such a creditor of a present value that at least equals the value of the collateral; or

- surrender of the collateral to the creditor.

f. Ability to Perform

Section 1325(a)(6) requires a determination of ability to perform; it requires that the debtor "will be able to make all payments under the plan and to comply with the plan."

2. BINDING EFFECT

A confirmed Chapter 13 plan is binding on the debtor and all of his creditors, section 1327(a). Unless the plan or the order confirming the plan otherwise provides, confirmation of a plan vests all of the "property of the estate" in the debtor free and clear of "any claim or interest of any creditor provided for by the plan," section 1327(c).

3.   PERFORMANCE
After confirmation, the plan is put into effect with the debtor generally making the payments provided in the plan to a Chapter 13 trustee who acts as a disbursing agent.

4.   MODIFICATION
A Chapter 13 plan can be modified after confirmation. Section 1329 expressly provides for postconfirmation modification on request of the debtor, the trustee, or the holder of an unsecured claim. The 1984 amendments added the language that expressly empowers an unsecured creditor to request modification of a Chapter 13 plan. This suggests that if the income of a Chapter 13 debtor increases after she has obtained confirmation of her plan but before she completes the payments under the plan, a creditor can request that payments under the plan be increased.

G.   DISCHARGE

1.   WHEN GRANTED
After completion of the payments provided for in the Chapter 13 plan, the debtor receives a discharge, section 1328(a).

2.   EXCEPTIONS
A section 1328(a) discharge is not subject to all of the exceptions from discharge set out in section 523. The only debts excepted from a section 1328(a) discharge are:

- allowed claims not provided for by the plan,

- certain long-term obligations specifically provided for by the plan, and

  > *Note:*   A Chapter 13 plan may not provide for a payment period of more than five years, section 1322(c). Some of the debtor's debts may have a longer payment period. Assume, for example, that D buys a new mobile home on January 10, 1990. She obtains financing from B Bank; the note provides for payments of $300 a month for 120 months. On March 30, 1991, D files a Chapter 13 petition. Her Chapter 13 plan provides for payments of $300 a month to B Bank for the 36 months of the plan, cf. section 1322(b)(5). On completion of the plan, D's obligation to B Bank for the remaining payments is excepted from discharge by section 1328(a)(1).

- claims for alimony and child support.

3.   HARDSHIP DISCHARGE
The bankruptcy court may grant a discharge in a Chapter 13 case even though the debtor has not completed payments called for by the plan. Section 1328(b) empowers the bankruptcy court to grant a "hardship" discharge if:

- the debtor's failure to complete the plan was due to circumstances for which she "should not justly be held accountable;" and

- the value of the payments made under the plan to each creditor at least equals what that creditor would have received under Chapter 7; and

- modification of the plan is not "practicable."

A section 1328(b) "hardship" discharge is not as comprehensive as a section 1328(a) discharge. A "hardship" discharge is limited by all of the section 523(a) exceptions to discharge, section 1328(c).

4. EFFECT ON DISCHARGE IN SUBSEQUENT CASES
If a debtor receives a discharge under either section 1328(a) or section 1328(b), he may not receive a discharge in a Chapter 7 case filed within six years of the date that the Chapter 13 case was filed unless payments under the plan totalled at least 70% of the allowed unsecured claims, and the plan was the "debtor's best effort," section 727(a)(9). A discharge under section 1328(a) or section 1328(b) does not affect the debtor's right to future Chapter 13 relief.

H. DISMISSAL AND CONVERSION

1. UPON DEBTOR'S REQUEST
A debtor who files a Chapter 13 petition may change his mind. He may at any time request the bankruptcy court to dismiss the case or convert it to a case under Chapter 7, sections 1307(a), (b).

2. UPON CREDITOR'S REQUEST
The bankruptcy court may also dismiss a Chapter 13 case or convert it to a case under Chapter 7 on request of a creditor. The statutory standard for such creditor-requested conversion or dismissal is "for cause." Section 1307(c) sets out eight examples of "cause."

3. BY COURT
Section 1307(d) gives a bankruptcy court the power to convert from Chapter 13 to Chapter 11 before confirmation of the plan on request of a party in interest and after notice and hearing. Section 1307(e) protects farmers from creditor-requested conversions from Chapter 13 to Chapter 7 or Chapter 11.

4. TREATMENT OF POST–PETITION CLAIMS AND PROPERTY UPON CONVERSION
Converting a case from Chapter 13 to Chapter 7 raises questions about the treatment of post-petition claims and post-petition property.

a. Claims
Assume that D files a Chapter 13 petition on January 15 and converts to Chapter 7 on April 5. What about the claims against D that arise from January 15 to April 5? According to sections 1305 and 348(d), claims arising in the period between filing of the Chapter 13 petition and conversion to Chapter 7 are allowable claims and cases have consistently so held.

b.   Property

The treatment of property acquired between January 15 and April 5 is less clear. Is it property of the estate? If D had filed a Chapter 7 petition, the property that D acquired after January 15 would not be property of the estate, section 541. However, property acquired after the filing of a Chapter 13 case is property of the estate under section 1306. Under section 348, the conversion from 13 to 7 does not "effect a change in the date of the filing of the petition." It is not clear, however, whether section 348 means that D should be regarded as having filed a Chapter 13 case on January 15 or a Chapter 7 case on that date. Cases are divided as to whether property acquired in the gap between filing for Chapter 13 relief and conversion to Chapter 7 is property of the estate.

I.   COMPARISON OF CHAPTERS 7 AND 13

Only a debtor may file a Chapter 13 petition. Each debtor who files a Chapter 13 petition could instead have filed a Chapter 7 petition. Before filing, the debtor's attorney should carefully compare Chapters 7 and 13. The following chart provides such a comparison:

	Chapter 7	Chapter 13
1. Automatic Stay	Automatic stay of section 362 protects the debtor from creditors' collection efforts	Automatic stay of section 362 protects the debtor from creditor's collection efforts. Automatic stay of section 1301 protects co-debtors
2. Loss of Property	"Property of the estate" as described in section 541 is distributed to creditors	Except as provided in the plan or in the order of confirmation, debtor keeps "property of the estate"
3. Availability of Discharge	Section 727(a) lists ten grounds for objection to discharge	Section 727 is inapplicable. Discharge depends on completion of payments required by the plan, section 1328(a). Section 1328(b) provides for a "hardship" discharge to a debtor who makes some but not all payments required by the plan

	Chapter 7	Chapter 13
4. Debtors Excepted From Discharge	Section 523(a) excepts nine classes of claims from the operation of a discharge	A section 1328(a) discharge is only subject to the exception for alimony and child support. A section 1328(b) discharge is subject to all of section 523(a)'s exceptions to discharge
5. Effect on Future Chapter 7 Relief	A debtor who receives a discharge in a Chapter 7 case may not obtain a discharge in another Chapter 7 case for six years	A Chapter 13 discharge does not affect the availability of discharge in a future Chapter 7 case if the Chapter 13 plan was the debtor's "best effort" and paid 70% of all general claims
6. Whether debtor's post-petition earnings are property of the estate	No, section 541(a)(6)	Yes, section 1306
7. Debtor's ability to terminate the case	"Only for cause", section 707	"On request of the debtor at any time," section 1307(b)
8. Relief from taxes	Ability to satisfy taxes not a condition to discharge; most taxes unaffected by discharge	Subject to limited exceptions, plan must provide for full payment of all taxes, section 1322(a)(2); payment of taxes may be deferred over five year life of plan; no exception from discharge
9. Amount required to be distributed to holders of claims	Property of the estate, section 541	Plan controls; confirmation requires that holders of claims receive at least as much as they would in 7 and that plan commits all disposable income, sections 1325(a)(4); 1325(b).

J. COMPARISON OF CHAPTERS 11 AND 13

Any debtor who files a Chapter 13 petition could instead have filed a Chapter 11 petition. Accordingly, before filing, the debtor's attorney should carefully compare Chapters 11 and 13.

1. ADVANTAGES OF CHAPTER 13 OVER CHAPTER 11
Chapter 13 would seem to offer an eligible debtor the following advantages:

- Codebtors are protected by the automatic stay, section 1301.

- A business debtor desiring to continue operating his or her business is probably less likely to be replaced by a trustee in Chapter 13 than in Chapter 11. Section 1303 sets out the duties of a Chapter 13 trustee. It does not mention operating the business. The phrase in section 1304(b), "Unless the court orders otherwise," is, however, statutory authority for the court turning over the operation of the debtor's business to the Chapter 13 trustee.

- Only the debtor may file a plan in Chapter 13.

- Chapter 13 makes no provision for creditors' committees.

- Chapter 13 does not require creditor acceptance of a plan of rehabilitation.

- The objections to discharge set out in section 727 do not apply in Chapter 13. These objections do apply in Chapter 11 liquidation cases, section 1141(d)(3).

- A Chapter 13 discharge can be more comprehensive than a Chapter 11 discharge. If a debtor completes her payments under the Chapter 13 plan and receives a discharge under section 1328(a), she will not be affected by the exceptions to discharge in section 523. If an individual debtor receives a Chapter 11 discharge, she will be affected by the exceptions to discharge in section 523, section 1141(d)(2).

2. ADVANTAGES OF CHAPTER 11 OVER CHAPTER 13
There are, however, also reasons for an individual debtor to use Chapter 11 rather than Chapter 13:

- In Chapter 11, the plan can modify the payment obligations on the debtor's home mortgage, section 1123(b)(1). A Chapter 13 plan cannot modify the payment obligations on the debtor's home mortgage, section 1322(b)(2).

- Classification of claims in a Chapter 13 plan cannot "discriminate unfairly," section 1322(b)(1). Classification of claims in a Chapter 11 plan is subject to a "discriminate unfairly" test only if the requisite majority of that class fails to accept the plan, sections 1122, 1129(b)(1).

- A Chapter 13 plan must either pay all claims in full or commit all of the debtor's "disposable income" for the next three years to the plan, section 1325(b). There is no comparable requirement in Chapter 11.

- A debtor receives a discharge "earlier" in Chapter 11 than in Chapter 13. A debtor receives a Chapter 11 discharge when her plan is confirmed, section 1141(d). In Chapter 13, confirmation does not effect a discharge. A Chapter 13 debtor does not receive a discharge until she has completed payments under the plan or has been excused from making payments because of hardship, section 1328.

REVIEW QUESTIONS

1. D is a lawyer. She is a sole practitioner. Is she eligible for Chapter 13 relief?

2. S has a mortgage on D's home. The mortgage payments are $600 a month. D files a Chapter 13 petition. What is the effect if any of the Chapter 13 filing on S?

3. T or F   Creditors do not vote on Chapter 13 plans.

4. T or F   After a Chapter 13 plan is confirmed, the trustee takes possession of the property of the estate.

5. D owes educational debts from law school. Can she avoid paying these debts by filing for Chapter 13 relief?

*

ALLOCATION OF JUDICIAL POWER OVER BANKRUPTCY MATTERS

Analysis

The question of which court has the power to adjudicate the litigation that arises in bankruptcy can be an important one. Many attorneys that represent parties with claims against the bankrupt or parties against whom the bankrupt has claims prefer to litigate in some forum other than the bankruptcy court. Some believe that the bankruptcy judge has a pro-debtor bias; others are simply more comfortable or more familiar with state court procedures.

In considering the question of which court has the power to adjudicate the litigation that arises in bankruptcy, it is helpful to consider the kinds of matters that can arise in bankruptcy.

- Some will involve only bankruptcy law. For example, D files a Chapter 13 petition. C, a creditor of D, files a motion to dismiss alleging that D does not meet the eligibility standards of section 109(e) in that D owes more than $350,000 of unsecured debt. D's answer raises the question of whether section 109(e) includes disputed debts.

- Other matters will involve both bankruptcy law and non-bankruptcy law. For example, D files a Chapter 7 petition. C files a secured claim that describes its Article 9 security interest. The bankruptcy trustee takes the position that C's security interest is invalid. If this is litigated, it will probably involve both the Bankruptcy Code's invalidation provisions and the Uniform Commercial Code's perfection provisions.

- And, still other matters will not involve substantive bankruptcy law. For example, D, Inc., a Chapter 11 debtor, files a breach of contract claim against X.

A. HISTORY

The allocation of judicial power over bankruptcy matters has been and still is one of the most controversial bankruptcy issues. A general familiarity with prior statutory schemes and prior controversies is helpful to understanding the present situation.

1. **1898 ACT**
    a. **Central Notion of "Summary Jurisdiction"**
        Under the Bankruptcy Act of 1898, bankruptcy courts had limited jurisdiction. This jurisdiction was commonly referred to as "summary jurisdiction." The phrase "summary jurisdiction" is somewhat misleading. First, it incorrectly implies that under the Bankruptcy Act of 1898, bankruptcy courts had a second, non-summary form of jurisdiction. Summary jurisdiction is the only form of jurisdiction that a bankruptcy judge possessed under the Bankruptcy Act of 1898. Bankruptcy courts had only summary jurisdiction; other courts had plenary jurisdiction. Second, it incorrectly implies that in resolving controversies the bankruptcy judge always conducted summary proceedings.

    b. **Reach of Summary Jurisdiction**
        Summary jurisdiction extended to

        - all matters concerned with the administration of the bankruptcy estate and

- some disputes between the bankruptcy trustee and third parties involving rights to money and other property in which the bankrupt estate claimed an interest.

The tests for deciding which disputes with third parties were within the bankruptcy judge's summary jurisdiction turned on issues such as whether

- the property in question was in the actual possession of the bankrupt at the time of the commencement of the case,

- the property in question was in the constructive possession of the bankrupt at the time of the commencement of the case, and

- the third party actually or impliedly consented to bankruptcy court jurisdiction.

There was considerable uncertainty over which disputes were within the summary jurisdiction of the bankruptcy court. This uncertainty gave rise to considerable litigation.

2.   1978 CODE
Apparently for the above reasons, Congress in 1978 decided to create a bankruptcy court with pervasive jurisdiction. Apparently for political reasons, Congress also decided that this bankruptcy court should not be an Article III court.

a.   Meaning of Article III Court
As you recall from your constitutional law course in law school or civics in high school, Article III of the Constitution vests the judicial power of the United States in the United States Supreme Court and such inferior tribunals as Congress might create. To insure the independence of the judges appointed under Article III (the so-called constitutional courts), Article III provides them with certain protections. These include tenure for life, removal from office only by congressional impeachment, and assurance that their compensation will not be diminished. The constitutional courts created under Article III include the United States Supreme Court, the United States Courts of Appeal, and the United States District Courts. The United States Customs Court (now the Court of International Trade) is an Article III court; its judges may be, and often are, assigned to hear cases in the district courts and the courts of appeals.

b.   Contrast Legislative Courts
Congress, in the exercise of its legislative powers enumerated in Article I of the Constitution, may create other inferior federal tribunals, the so-called legislative courts. Judges of these legislative courts need not be granted tenure for life. In addition, they can be removed by mechanisms other than congressional impeachment, and their salaries are subject to congressional reduction. Historically, these Article I legislative courts and their judges have been granted jurisdiction over limited and narrowly defined subject matters, like the Tax Court. In other instances, jurisdiction has been limited to narrowly defined ge-

ographical territories, such as the territorial courts, the District of Columbia courts, etc.

c. **Bankruptcy Judges: Article III Powers Without Article III Protection**
In enacting the 1978 Code, Congress gave bankruptcy judges none of the protections found in Article III of the Constitution. Nevertheless, in enacting the 1978 Code, Congress gave bankruptcy judges much of the power and responsibilities of an Article III judge. Since bankruptcy debtors can be just about any kind of individual or business entity, this meant that litigation in the bankruptcy courts could deal with almost every facet of business and personal activity.

3. ***MARATHON PIPE LINE* DECISION**
The 1978 grant of pervasive jurisdiction to a non-Article III bankruptcy court was successfully challenged in the *Marathon* case.

a. **Facts**
Northern Pipeline, a Chapter 11 debtor, filed a breach of contract lawsuit against Marathon Pipe Line in bankruptcy court. There was no question as to whether the bankruptcy court had jurisdiction over this lawsuit under 28 USC section 1471(c). Marathon Pipe Line did, however, question whether section 1471(c) conferred Article III judicial power on non-Article III courts in violation of the separation of powers doctrine and filed a motion to dismiss. The bankruptcy judge refused to dismiss; he was reversed by the district judge. On direct appeal, a divided Supreme Court sustained Marathon's challenge in *Northern Pipeline Constr. Co. v. Marathon Pipe Line Co.,* 458 U.S. 50, 102 S.Ct. 2858 (1982).

b. **Holding**
The Court in *Marathon* was so divided that there was no majority opinion. Justice Brennan's opinion was joined by three other justices. Additionally, two justices concurred in the result. The holding of these six is perhaps best summarized in footnote 40 of Justice Brennan's plurality opinion which indicates that (1) the 1978 legislation does grant the bankruptcy court the power to hear Northern Pipeline's breach of contract claim, (2) the bankruptcy court, a non-Article III court, cannot constitutionally be vested with jurisdiction to decide such state law claims, and (3) this grant of authority to the bankruptcy court is not severable from the remaining grant of authority to the bankruptcy court.

c. **Decision**
The Supreme Court in *Marathon* stayed the entry of any judgment until October 4, 1982, to allow Congress time to enact new legislation allocating judicial power over bankruptcy matters. When Congress failed to act, the stay was extended to December 24, 1982. Again, Congress failed to act.

4. EMERGENCY RULE

a. Rule of District Courts

In December of 1982, all of the district courts adopted an Emergency Rule on allocation of judicial power over bankruptcy matters. The Rule was proposed by the Director of the Administrative Office of the United States Courts at the instruction of the Judicial Conference. The Emergency Rule was based on questionable assumptions such as the assumption that the district courts still had bankruptcy jurisdiction after *Marathon.* Nevertheless, all of the courts of appeal that considered constitutional challenges to the Rule upheld its validity.

b. What Rule Provided

The Emergency Rule provided for a general reference from the district court to the bankruptcy court of all bankruptcy litigation covered by section 28 USC 1471. Paragraph (d)(3) of the Rule created a special category of proceedings, "civil proceedings that, in the absence of a petition in bankruptcy, could have been brought in a district court or a state court"; in such "related proceedings," the bankruptcy court could not enter a judgment unless the parties consented, but, like a special master, was to submit findings and a proposed judgment to be reviewed by the district court.

5. 1984 AMENDMENTS

After *Marathon,* Congress was urged to solve the constitutional dilemma by establishing bankruptcy courts as Article III courts. Congress rejected this solution. Instead, the 1984 amendments make the bankruptcy court a part of the federal district court, confer jurisdiction in bankruptcy on the district court, and allocate judicial power in bankruptcy matters between the federal district judge and the bankruptcy judge. It is easy for any lawyer or law student to criticize the provisions allocating judicial power over bankruptcy matters. It is more difficult (but probably more important) for a lawyer or law student to understand how these provisions operate.

B. OPERATION OF 1984 AMENDMENTS

In understanding the 1984 amendments allocating judicial powers over bankruptcy matters, it is necessary to understand three separate, new sections to Title 28: sections 151, 1334, and 157.

1. BANKRUPTCY COURT AS PART OF THE DISTRICT COURT, SECTION 151

Section 151 refers to a bankruptcy judge and a bankruptcy court as a "unit" of the district court. It is important to keep this reference in mind when reading other sections in Title 28 dealing with the allocation of judicial power in bankruptcy matters. When the term "district court" appears in section 1334 or section 157, it could be referring to the United States district judge and/or the bankruptcy judge. After all, the bankruptcy judge is a part of the district court, i.e., a "unit" of the district court.

2.   GRANTS OF JURISDICTION TO THE DISTRICT COURT, SECTION 1334(a) AND (b)

a.   Jurisdiction Over "Cases"

Section 1334(a) vests original and exclusive juridiction in the district court over all cases arising under the Bankruptcy Code. "Case" is a term of art used in both the Bankruptcy Code and the Bankruptcy Rules. "Case" refers to the entire Chapter 7, 9, 11, or 13 case, not just some controversy that arises in connection with it.

b.   Jurisdiction Over "Proceedings"

The term "case" is to be distinguished from the term "proceeding." A specific dispute that arises during the pendency of a case is referred to as a "proceeding." Section 1334(b) provides that the district courts have original but not exclusive jurisdiction over all civil proceedings "arising under title 11, or arising in or related to cases under title 11."

Example: If the Sunshine Cab Co. files a Chapter 11 petition, section 1334(a) gives the district court jurisdiction over Sunshine's Chapter 11 case itself. And, section 1334(b) gives the district court jurisdiction over a complaint filed by Sunshine's trustee alleging that payments to Louie De Palma were preferential or a complaint filed against Sunshine by Elaine Nardo alleging sex discrimination.

3.   ROLE OF THE BANKRUPTCY COURT, SECTION 157

Clearly, section 1334 confers jurisdiction over bankruptcy matters to the district court. It is equally clear that most federal district judges have neither the time nor the inclination to exercise this jurisdiction. Accordingly, section 157 empowers the district judge to refer bankruptcy matters to the bankruptcy judge.

Note the title of section 157, "Procedures." As this title suggests, section 157 is not a jurisdictional provision. It does not confer jurisdiction on the bankruptcy judge. Rather, it deals with the procedural role that the bankruptcy judge, a unit of the district court under section 151, is to play in exercising the jurisdiction conferred by section 1334 on the district court.

a.   "Core" Versus "Non-Core" Proceedings

Section 157 differentiates between "core" and "non-core" proceedings. A nonexclusive list of core proceedings is set out in section 157(b)(2). [Sunshine Cab's section 547 action against Louie is an easy example of a core proceeding.] Generally, in core proceedings, the bankruptcy judge conducts the trial or hearing and enters a final judgment.

Obviously, if a matter is not a core proceeding, it is a "non-core proceeding." "Non-core proceeding" is neither defined nor illustrated in the statute. [Elaine's sex discrimination action against the Sunshine Cab Co. is an obvious example of a non-core proceeding.] In non-core proceedings, the bankruptcy judge still can hold the trial or hearing, but generally cannot issue a final judgment. She instead submits proposed findings of fact and law to the district court for review, section 157(c)(1).

b.   Who Determines Whether Proceeding Is "Core" or "Non-Core"
The bankruptcy judge is empowered to determine whether a matter is a core proceeding or a non-core proceeding, section 157(b)(3). Note that a determination that a proceeding is non-core does not mean that the matter is withdrawn from the bankruptcy judge. Remember that a bankruptcy judge can hear non-core proceedings and prepare findings of facts and law.

c.   District Court Judge's Withdrawal of Case or Proceeding From Bankruptcy Judge
Section 157(d) authorizes the district judge to withdraw a case or proceeding from a bankruptcy judge. (Note: Section 157(d) uses the phrase "district court." In this context, however, it would seem that "district court" should be limited to the district judge. How can a bankruptcy judge decide that she should withdraw a reference to herself?)

The first sentence of section 157(d) provides for permissive withdrawal "for cause shown." The second sentence of section 157(d) requires withdrawal of a proceeding on timely motion of a party if both the Bankruptcy Code and another federal law must be considered. Note the statutory phrase "requires consideration of both." What does this mean? *In re White Motors Corp.*, 42 B.R. 693, 12 B.C.D. 235 (N.D.Ohio 1984), the federal district court concluded that section 157(d) mandates withdrawal only if the resolution of the dispute requires a "substantial and material" consideration of non-bankruptcy law. The obvious questions the *White Motors* decision raise are (1) what is the statutory basis for a "substantial and material" test, and (2) what is "substantial and material"?

4.   ABSTENTION UNDER SECTION 1334(c)
Withdrawal under section 157(d) moves a matter from the bankruptcy judge to the federal district judge. Abstention under section 1334 moves the litigation from the federal courts to a state court.

a.   Permissive
Section 1334(c)(1) provides for permissive abstention. If the district court believes that abstention would be "in the interest of justice" or "in the interest of comity with State courts or respect for State law," it has the option of abstaining.

b.   Mandatory
Section 1334(c)(2) provides for mandatory abstention. The district court must abstain if the following requirements of section 1334(c)(2) are satisfied:

• A party to the proceeding must timely file a motion to abstain.

   Section 1334(c)(2), unlike section 157(d), makes no provision for the court to act on its own motion. Nor does section 1334(c)(2) indicate what "timely" means.

• The proceeding is based on a state-law claim or cause of action.

- The matter is a "related to" proceeding, as contrasted with an "arising under" or "arising in" proceeding.

  Section 1334(b) uses all three of these phrases. Section 1334(c)(2) limits mandatory abstention to its certain "related to" proceedings. There is no statutory definition of "arising under," "arising in," or "related to." Obviously, Sunshine Cab's preference action against Louie is an example of "arising under", that is, it is a cause of action created by the Bankruptcy Code. Obviously, Elaine's sex-discrimination action against Sunshine Cab is either "arising in" or "related to." It is not obvious from existing case law whether Elaine's action is "arising in" or "related to."

- The action could not have been commenced in federal court in the absence of the jurisdiction conferred by section 1334.

  If there is any other basis for federal court jurisdiction, mandatory abstention is not available. This requirement means that mandatory abstention would not be available in the *Northern Pipeline* case because of the diversity of citizenship between the parties.

- An action is commenced in state court.

  There is a question as to whether this means that the state court action must be pending at the time of the bankruptcy filing.

- The state court action can be timely adjudicated.

C. QUESTIONS ABOUT ALLOCATION OF JUDICIAL POWER UNDER THE 1984 AMENDMENTS

As is obvious from the above discussion of the operation of the 1984 amendments, there are a number of still unanswered questions about the allocation of judicial power over bankruptcy matters. In addition to the questions raised above, consider:

- What constitutes "consent" for purposes of section 157(c)(2)?

- Can the bankruptcy judge's "core"/"non-core" determination under section 157(b)(3) be appealed?

- Can the district court act sua sponte under the second sentence of section 157(d)? [Note the first sentence of section 157(d) expressly mentions "on its own motion."]

- When does "district court" include the bankruptcy judge? In section 1334(c), can a bankruptcy judge decide a mandatory abstention motion? In section 157(b)(5), can the bankruptcy judge try a personal injury claim and submit proposed findings of fact and conclusions of law? In section 157(d), can the bankruptcy judge play any role in withdrawal motions?

- Do the references to "personal injury tort" in sections 157(b)(2)(B) and 157(b)(5) and 1411 include products claims that are based on a breach of UCC warranty theory?

- Are the 1984 provisions on allocation of judicial power in bankruptcy constitutional? Are the *Northern Pipeline* tests—whatever they are—satisfied?

REVIEW QUESTIONS

1. T or F The bankruptcy judge has jurisdiction over bankruptcy proceedings; the district judge has jurisdiction over bankruptcy cases.

2. T or F A bankruptcy judge can hear both core and non-core proceedings.

3. T or F Withdrawal of the reference moves the case from federal court to state court.

4. T or F Judge Wapner would be a good bankruptcy judge.

*

ANSWERS TO REVIEW QUESTIONS

I. INCREASING THE ODDS OF A CREDITOR'S JUDGMENT

1. A cognovit judgment is entered without giving the debtor notice or an opportunity for a hearing, which due process rights the debtor purportedly waived in signing the contract containing a cognovit clause. The key issue in determining the validity of the judgment, therefore, is the validity of the waiver, i.e., whether it was voluntarily, intelligently, and knowingly made.

2. Jurisdiction is lacking because the only contact between the defendant and Minnesota is the presence in that state of an intangible right which the insurer owes the defendant. Under *Shaffer,* the presence of property in a state is not ordinarily a sufficient contact in and of itself to support judicial jurisdiction of any kind. This question and answer is based on *Rush v. Savchuk,* 444 U.S. 320, 100 S. Ct. 571 (1980).

3. *False*   Suing a debtor in a forum distant from her residence may be an unfair and deceptive trade practice under the Federal Trade Commission Act. Moreover, the forum court may decline to exercise jurisdiction under the doctrine of *forum non conveniens.*

4. *False*   There must be a substantial or, at least, reasonable relationship between the chosen state and the parties or their transaction; the parties' choice of law cannot override application of the law of a state having a materially greater interest than the chosen state in having its law applied; and the

choice cannot offend a statute of the forum state that dictates to the court how the applicable law will be chosen.

II. JUDGMENT LIENS

1. In most states, a lien of judgment does not arise until the judgment is docketed or otherwise indexed or recorded as prescribed by statute.

2. The lien does not reach any of D's property in County Z unless and until C dockets her judgment there.

3. In most states, registry laws protect judgment lienors. Thus, D's unrecorded conveyance to Z would not be effective as to C whose judgment lien would attach to the property and have priority over Z's claim as purchaser.

4. C can enforce her lien against B because subsequent transferees of property that is encumbered by a judgment lien take their interests subject to the lien. This rule applies not only against an immediate transferee from the judgment debtor, but also against successive transferees. The lien does not attach, however, to the proceeds of either sale of the property.

5. In most states, O's lien on the lake property would rank ahead of P's under the usual rule that priority between judgment lienors inter se is determined according to the order in which their judgments were docketed. As to the after-acquired property, however, the liens would be of equal rank, or priority would be given the lienor who first levies on the property.

6. The answer depends on whether the revivor action in State A is a continuation of the original proceeding or a separate lawsuit that creates a new judgment. If the former, enforcement of the judgment in State B is barred because ten years has lapsed since the judgment was obtained. If the latter, a fresh ten-year period of limitation began to run from the time of renewal and thus the judgment is enforceable because the period of limitation has not expired.

III. ENFORCING JUDGMENTS THROUGH EXECUTION

1. *False.* The sheriff acts to enforce a money judgment only when directed to do so by a writ of execution or other appropriate process.

2. A writ of execution is issued by the clerk of the court that rendered the judgment or by the clerk of any court in which the judgment has been docketed.

3. Any of the debtor's nonexempt, tangible personal property and also most of her nonexempt interests in real estate can be seized and sold through execution.

4. *False.* Property seized through execution usually is held by the sheriff until such time as she sells it.

5. The return date of a writ of execution is the day on which the sheriff must report how successful she has been in satisfying the judgment or what property she has seized toward that end. The writ of execution generally expires on its return date and thereafter will no longer support levy on the debtor's property. A new or *alias* writ must be issued.

6. The sheriff returns the writ *nulla bona* if she is unable to locate any leviable property of the debtor.

7. The basic rules are that levy on a certificated security requires actual seizure by the sheriff and that levy on uncertificated securities is accomplished by notifying the person who controls transfer of the property.

8. *False.* In most states the right of redemption applies only to real property. Personal property cannot be redeemed.

9. *False.* The general rule is that mere inadequacy of price is insufficient in itself to justify setting aside an execution sale.

10. Neither real nor personal property is immune from levy and sale under execution simply because it is encumbered by a mortgage or other security interest.

11. The general rule is that a buyer at an execution sale acquires only such title as the debtor had, which would mean that the buyer takes subject to the mortgage. The buyer will take free of the mortgage, however, if the encumbrance was unrecorded and (1) the recording laws protect buyers of real estate at execution sales or (2) the execution creditor through whom she claims is entitled to priority over the mortgagee.

12. In the majority of states, the lien of execution attaches and dates from the time the sheriff levies on property. In a minority of states, the lien dates from the time the writ of execution is delivered to the sheriff.

13. The lien of judgment arises when the judgment is docketed. The execution lien attaches only after the process of execution has been initiated, either at the time when the writ of execution is delivered to the sheriff or when the sheriff actually levies on property. The lien of judgment reaches only real estate. The lien of execution attaches to both real estate and personal property.

14. Uniform Commercial Code Article 9 governs the priority dispute. Under this statute, C is a "lien creditor," U.C.C. § 9–301(3). The usual rule is that a secured party loses to a lien creditor whose acquires her lien before the security interest is perfected. U.C.C. § 9–301(1)(b). Under this rule, C would win. An exception applies, however, when the security interest is a purchase money security interest as defined in U.C.C. § 9–107. Local Bank's interest is a purchase money security interest. Thus, because of U.C.C. § 9–301(2), Local Bank prevails if its interest was perfected within ten days of D taking possession of the equipment, notwithstanding that C's lien arose before Local Bank's interest was perfected.

15. *True.* Federal law provides that district court judgments shall be enforced through execution process in accordance with the practice and procedure of the state in which the district court is held.

IV. FINDING PROPERTY OF THE DEBTOR

1. A creditor's bill is an equitable remedy designed specifically to aid in discovering hidden assets of a judgment debtor and in applying hard to reach assets to the creditor's judgment.

2. An individual creditor pursues a creditor's bill alone. The remedy is referred to as a general creditors' bill if the creditor files the action on behalf of herself and other creditors of the debtor.

3. There is authority that an equitable lien survives the expiration of a judgment lien.

4. A creditor's bill is a judge-made equitable remedy providing for the discovery of a debtor's assets and the application of the property to a creditor's judgment. Supplemental proceedings have the same general purpose but are creatures of statute that have largely displaced the creditor's bill. A creditor's bill is a separate action, but supplemental proceedings are a continuation of the creditor's original action against the debtor.

5. There are two broad types of supplemental proceedings. One type is supplemental discovery which provides for discovery against persons who might have information that could be useful in locating nonexempt property of a judgment debtor. The other type is supplemental relief which provides for applying to the creditor's judgment whatever property is discovered.

6. Much of the relief available through a creditor's bill is also available through supplemental proceedings, except that the latter remedy cannot everywhere be used, as can the former, to set aside a fraudulent conveyance by the debtor.

V. GARNISHMENT

1. Garnishment typically begins with the judgment creditor, the garnishor, filing with the court an affidavit describing the judgment, complaining that the judgment is unsatisfied, and alleging that a third person, the garnishee, is indebted to, or holds property of, the judgment debtor. The judge or the court clerk then issues a garnishment summons that is served on the garnishee and the judgment debtor.

2. The jurisdictions differ with respect to the consequence of a garnishee failing to answer a garnishment summons. The garnishee risks liability for (1) the full amount of the garnishor's judgment against the debtor; (2) the amount or value of the debtor's property that the judgment creditor alleged was in the garnishee's hands; or (3) the actual damages suffered by the garnishor as a result of the garnishee's neglect in not answering the summons.

3. The garnishee is accountable for the amount of the garnishable wages paid to the debtor.

4. The maximum garnishable amount is $45 a week. Weekly disposable earnings total $180, which is computed as follows: ($900 a month gross pay—$180 [taxes + social security]) / 4 weeks = $180. The cost of health insurance is not subtracted because, unlike taxes and social security, it is not a deduction required by law to be withheld.

5. The absolute maximum would be $117 a week (65% of D's disposable weekly earnings) if D is not supporting a new or another former spouse or a dependent child and if the garnishment is to enforce a support payment which is more than three months delinquent.

6. *True.*

7. The employer risks civil liability (including reinstatement of the employee and payment of back-pay) enforced by the United States Secretary of Labor and also criminal liability ($1000 fine and/or one year imprisonment).

8. Bank is liable for the amount of the check only if it had a reasonable time to act on the garnishment before it paid the check.

9. Creditor A's garnishment is entitled to priority because it was first served on the garnishee.

10. The answer changes in favor of Creditor B in a state such as New York which gives priority to a support garnishment over a garnishment for a contract debt without regard to time of service.

11. *True.* The Congress has waived sovereign immunity for the Postal Service.

12. The answer changes unless the garnishment is for the enforcement of an award for child support or alimony.

VI. FRAUDULENT CONVEYANCES

1. Because of D's subjective intention to hinder or delay her creditors, the conveyance of the stock is actually fraudulent not only against existing creditors such as A, whose claim existed at the time of the conveyance, but also against future creditors such as B whose claim arose after the conveyance.

2. The answers are altogether different. The conveyance is neither actually nor constructively fraudulent against any of D's creditors. The conveyance is not actually fraudulent because there is no subjective intention to hinder, delay, or defraud creditors. Despite D's insolvency, there is no constructive fraud because fair consideration was given in exchange for the conveyance of the stock.

3. The conveyance is constructively fraudulent under laws such as UFCA § 4 if D was insolvent at the time of the conveyance or, as a result of the conveyance, was

rendered insolvent. Yet, the conveyance is voidable only by creditors whose claims existed at the time of the conveyance. Future creditors are not protected against this kind of fraudulent conveyance.

4. The conveyance is not constructively fraudulent inasmuch as D was solvent at all times. Nevertheless, the lack of fair consideration and the familial relationship are badges of fraud indicating, and perhaps giving rise to a presumption of, actual fraudulent intention.

5. The mortgage was given for less than fair consideration if the amount of the loan was disproportionately small as compared with the value of the collateral. In this event, the lack of fair consideration coupled with D's insolvency would render the secured transaction constructively fraudulent under laws such as UFCA § 4. Under the new UFTA, however, a creditor cannot attack a security transfer on the ground that the value of the property transferred is disproportionate to the debt secured.

6. The answer is "no" under state law because of the traditional rule that a foreclosure sale of collateral conducted according to law cannot be attacked as a fraudulent conveyance solely on the basis of inadequacy of price. The answer might be different under federal bankruptcy law because of the *Durrett* decision.

7. There is no actual fraud, and the conveyance to A is not constructively fraudulent because there was fair consideration. Fair consideration is given when an antecedent debt is satisfied. The conveyance to A amounted to nothing more than a preference, which under traditional law is not subject to attack as a preference.

8. The answer is the same under traditional law. Mere preferences are not avoidable as fraudulent conveyances even if the preferred creditor is a relative. The answer might be different under the new UFTA, which renders constructively fraudulent a preferential transfer to an insider, including a relative, if the insider had reasonable cause to believe that the debtor was insolvent. UFTA § 5(b).

9. The traditional rule is that a conversion of nonexempt property to exempt property is not vulnerable as a fraudulent conveyance regardless of the debtor's motive or financial condition.

10. The remedies generally available to protected creditors for curing a fraudulent conveyance are (1) restraining any further disposition of the property, appointing a receiver to take charge of it, or obtaining other judicial orders designed to protect the property; (2) ignoring the conveyance and seizing the property through attachment or execution when such remedies are otherwise available; and (3) suing to set aside the conveyance.

11. R can defeat the action to set aside the conveyance by establishing that she was an innocent purchaser for fair consideration. R was not such a purchaser, however, if the real estate was worth only half the stock's value. Fair consideration requires the exchange of property having equivalent values. Nevertheless, if R made the exchange without actual fraudulent intent, she made retain the stock as security for return of the less than fair consideration she gave.

12. **No.** Only in exceptional cases does traditional law provide for the recovery of damages against the transferee of property which has been fraudulently conveyed. The answer may change under the new UFTA, which appears to allow the recovery of damages in any case where a fraudulent conveyance could be set aside by a creditor.

VII. BULK SALES

1. The sale is unaffected by the failure to comply with Article 6 because the statute is inapplicable. Article 6 does not govern when the principal business of the enterprise whose assets are sold is something other than the sale of inventory from stock.

2. Notice of the bulk sale must be given to the transferor's creditors, and the proceeds of the sale must be applied to their claims.

3. The sale is not ineffective under Article 6 unless B had knowledge that the list was inaccurate in not including State Bank.

4. The answer is different. The sale is ineffective.

5. The sale is voidable by State Bank which can sue to set aside the sale and have the property applied in satisfaction of its claim; or, if attachment, execution or other process is otherwise available to the bank, it can proceed to levy on the property as if the sale had not taken place. Additionally or alternatively, State Bank can pursue any other legal or equitable remedy that is available under local law, such as the appointment of a receiver to take control of the property.

6. As a general rule, a bulk sale that is ineffective against the transferee of the goods also is ineffective against those who claim through the transferee. An important exception is that an innocent purchaser for value from the transferee, which probably describes the buyers of the snowmobiles from B, takes free of a defect in the transferee's title that results from noncompliance with Article 6.

VIII. SHIELDING EXEMPT PROPERTY

1. The common limitations on exemptions of personal property are: the debtor must be a resident of the state and head of a family or household, the debtor must need the property, and the property's value must not exceed a sum specified by statute.

2. The kinds of claims and debts enforceable against exempt personal property include: debts for necessaries of life; claims for alimony and support; tort claims; purchase money debts; and tax claims.

3. *False.*

4. *True.*

5. The two most important reasons are these: First, the state law may protect a larger part of her wages. Second, Title III provides no protection whatsoever once wages have been paid to an employee. State law ordinarily continues to shield exempt income received by a debtor even after she deposits it into a bank account.

6. The proceeds of a matured policy paid to a beneficiary usually are exempt from the claims of her creditors and those of the insured. The insured's creditors ordinarily can reach the proceeds of a policy paid to the insured's estate. The present value of an unmatured policy of insurance, such as the policy's cash surrender value, typically is exempt from the claims of the policy owner's creditors.

7. **No.** For property to qualify as an exempt homestead, there must be a dwelling which the debtor occupies as her home.

8. The country place could be claimed as a homestead only if D and her family occupied it rather than the city house as their usual residence.

9. **Yes.** So long as the place is and continues to be the bona fide residence of the debtor and her family, the property qualifies for the homestead exemption despite its use partly, or even chiefly, as income-producing rental or commercial property.

10. **No.** The homestead exemption is available in most states only to a debtor who heads a "household" or a "family," which means that a person or people must reside with the debtor and depend on her partly or fully for support.

11. The usual answer is "no," unless prior to the sale D had abandoned the place as her homestead.

12. Most states by statute shield such proceeds for a short period of time to allow the debtor to acquire a new homestead.

IX. SPECIAL RIGHTS UNDER STATE LAW

1. *False.* A credit seller has a right to reclaim only if the buyer was insolvent when she received the goods, and even in this case the right to reclaim is conditioned on the seller demanding the goods within ten days after the buyer's receipt of them. See U.C.C. § 2–702(2).

2. She cannot reclaim as a disappointed cash seller. The taking of a postdated check means that the transaction was a credit sale rather than a sale on a cash basis. See U.C.C. § 2–511 comment 6. Thus, Seller can reclaim the goods only if the buyer was insolvent when she received the property and Seller makes a timely demand for return of the goods. See U.C.C. § 2–702(2).

3. The secured party usually has the better right because, as a good faith purchaser for value, she acquires her interest free of any right of reclamation whether the seller is a disappointed cash seller claiming the goods under U.C.C. §§ 2–507 and 2–511 or a credit seller claiming them under U.C.C. § 2–702(2).

4. A bank can exercise its right of setoff only to satisfy matured debts. Thus, the bank can offset D's account in the amount of the third installment. Whether the bank can offset the account for the whole balance of the loan depends on whether the loan agreement contains, and the bank invokes, an acceleration clause by which a default in one installment makes the entire loan due and payable.

5. **No.** To the extent that D's debt has matured, the bank can offset the funds in the joint account that belong to D.

6. The universal rule is that, if the bank had notice that the funds in the account belonged to B, the account could not be offset to satisfy a debt owed by A. If the bank was ignorant of B's claim to the funds, the majority rule allows the offset. The minority, or equitable rule, allows the offset only if the bank had changed its position in reliance, or if for some other reason the equities favor the bank.

7. Under the common law, R has the right to retain the property until she is paid. Most states by statute have given an artisan the additional remedy of selling the property in satisfaction of her claim.

8. R's lien is entitled to priority unless the lien is statutory and the statute expressly gives priority to the bank's security interest. U.C.C. § 9–310.

9. The construction lien laws in many states do not limit a landowner's maximum exposure to the price she agreed to pay the contractor for the improvement, and there is no credit given the landowner for payments made to the contractor. Thus, if the landowner has paid the contractor in full but none of the laborers or suppliers have been paid, each of them can assert a lien on the real estate. The landowner must satisfy these liens or lose the property through a foreclosure sale to enforce the liens.

10. Bank should look in the local public records where construction lien claims usually are indexed among the real estate records or in their own special filing system. In addition, Bank should look at the real estate. If work on an improvement has begun, construction liens thereafter arising will in many states relate back to the beginning of the project and take priority over a mortgage recorded after that time.

X. FEDERAL TAX LIEN

1. The answer is (a), (b) & (c). Filing a notice of tax lien is important for priority over third parties' claim, but filing is unimportant and totally unnecessary to the creation and enforcement of the tax lien against the taxpayer.

2. *True and False.* A federal tax lien cannot arise until the government has made a demand for payment of the assessed taxes and the taxpayer has refused to pay. Yet, once these conditions have been satisfied, the lien relates back to, and dates from, the time of the assessment.

3. *False.*

4. X takes the set free of the lien. See 26 U.S.C.A. § 6323(b)(3).

5. S's security interest is entitled to priority. See 26 U.S.C.A. § 6323(a), which gives priority to a security interest that is perfected before the tax lien is filed.

6. The answer is different: the tax lien is entitled to priority.

7. S has priority as to the accounts arising on May 5 because of the 45–day rule of 26 U.S.C.A. § 6323(c), which protects perfected security interests in after-acquired commercial financing security including accounts. The IRS wins as to the accounts arising on June 6 because the security interest attaches more than 45 days after the tax lien was filed.

8. The IRS has priority as to all of the equipment. Security interests attaching to property after the filing of a tax lien notice ordinarily are subordinate to the tax lien. There is an exception in § 6323(c) for after-acquired commercial financing security, but equipment is not commercial financing security.

9. S's interest expands by $5000 when the additional loan is made. Ordinarily, this expansion would be subordinate to a previously filed tax lien. In this problem, however, the collateral is accounts which are commercial financing security, and thus the expansion is protected from the tax lien under the 45–day rule of § 6323(c). S has priority as to both the original loan and the later advance for a total of $15,000. This answer assumes that S was ignorant of the federal tax lien when the future advance was made.

10. The future advance is protected by the 45–day rule of § 6323(d), which protects future advances that expand security interests in any kind of collateral. This answer assumes that S was ignorant of the federal tax lien when the future advance was made.

XI. ATTACHMENT

1. The answer is "false" for most states. Attachment ordinarily is limited to actions in which money damages are sought *and* in which certain extenuating circumstances, i.e., *grounds of attachment,* are present.

2. The usual procedural prerequisites to the issuance of a writ of attachment are: the plaintiff must commence suit; an affidavit of attachment must be presented to the issuing officer; the plaintiff must post bond; and, in about half the states, the defendant must be notified that attachment is sought and be given a pre-seizure opportunity for a hearing.

3. Attached property ordinarily is not sold unless and until the attaching creditor wins judgment against the defendant. An exception is made when the property is perishable, threatens to decline speedily in value, or is unduly expensive to hold.

4. The defendant can move to vacate or discharge the attachment; she can post a bond and thereby regain possession of the attached property; and she can challenge the sufficiency of plaintiff's bond.

5. The posting of either type of bond allows the defendant to regain possession of property that has been seized from her pursuant to attachment. If a discharging or dissolution bond is posted, another consequence is that the property is released from the lien of attachment.

6. In most states, an attachment lien dates from the time of the sheriff's levy.

7. A's claim is entitled to priority.

8. B has priority. U.C.C. § 9–301(1)(b).

XII. REPLEVIN

1. The replevin remedy is an incident of the replevin action. The action is a suit for the return of specific goods and chattels to which the plaintiff has an immediate and exclusive right to repossession. The remedy is an ancillary procedure whereby the sheriff provisionally takes the property from the defendant pending outcome of the action.

2. *True.* The determinative issue in a replevin action is whether the plaintiff has an immediate right to possession of the property as against the defendant. This issue does not necessarily turn on ownership.

3. *False.* In most states the replevin remedy is available in any replevin action when the plaintiff can demonstrate the probability that she is entitled to possession of the property as against the defendant.

4. If the defendant does not post bond to keep possession of the property, it is delivered to the plaintiff who keeps it pendente lite.

5. **Yes.** A successful plaintiff is entitled to damages resulting from the defendant's wrongful taking or detention, which include damages for loss of use and depreciation in value. A successful defendant can recover damages she suffered as a result of the property taken from her provisionally through the plaintiff's use of the replevin remedy. Whichever party is successful, the victor in an appropriate case may recover damages equalling the value of the property instead of recovering the property itself.

XIII. LIS PENDENS

1. **Yes.** Because of the lis pendens effect, C is bound by the outcome of the litigation between A and B so that she stands in the same position as her grantor, B, and takes the property subject to the judgment rendered against B.

2. C would not take subject to the equitable lien in a state where the lis pendens effect is limited by statute and is made dependent on the filing of a notice of lis pendens. Even in such a state, however, C would take subject to the equitable lien if she had actual knowledge of the litigation with respect to the property pending between A and B.

3. C would not take subject to the equitable lien under the general rule that the notice and binding effect of lis pendens does not affect persons who acquired their interest prior to the filing of the notice of lis pendens. In some states, however, C would take subject to the lien if the conveyance to her was not recorded until after the lis pendens notice was filed.

XIV. FOURTEENTH AMENDMENT PROTECTION

1. Attachment involves state action because of the active and substantial participation of public officials. Setoff is a purely private action that is not attributable to the state. The Fourteenth Amendment restrains state action only.

2. The major theories or tests are: the symbiotic relationship test; the nexus test; and the public function test.

3. The seizure of a car involves a significant taking of property because the debtor loses the rights of use and possession. The attachment of real estate results only in restricting the free alienability of the property, which many courts hold is not a taking encompassed by the Fourteenth Amendment.

4. *Mitchell* did not overrule *Sniadach*. Due process requires a constitutional accommodation of the interests of both debtor and creditor. These interests will vary from case to case, which means that the requirements of due process will vary. In *Sniadach,* the debtor's interests outweighed those of the creditor. In *Mitchell,* the creditor's interests were heavier. This difference in the facts, i.e., in the balancing of interests, not a difference in law, accounts for the different procedures required in the two cases.

5. A contractual waiver of due process rights is enforceable only if it was "voluntarily, intelligently, and knowingly" made.

XV. OTHER SOURCES OF DUE PROCESS PROTECTION

1. *False.* The tests are the same.

2. *False.* Nonjudicial foreclosure of a mortgage by a federally chartered savings and loan is not conduct attributable to the federal government. The Fifth Amendment limits only government action, not conduct by private persons.

3. *True.* The Fifth Amendment due process clause applies but does not require prior notice and hearing. The interests of the creditor outweigh those of the vessel's owner.

4. *Flagg Bros. v. Brooks* was decided under the due process clause of the Fourteenth Amendment. The *Svendsen* case was decided under the due process clause of a state constitution. A state's highest appellate court, not the United States Supreme Court, is the final arbiter of its state constitution. Notwithstanding the Supremacy Clause of the United States Constitution, the local document can be interpreted as limiting a wider range of creditors' remedies.

XVI. OVERVIEW OF BANKRUPTCY

1. *False.* Bankruptcy law is federal law.

2. *False.* Chapter 11 is not limited to corporations and partnerships. Individuals can file for Chapter 11 relief.

3. *False.* There is not a trustee in most Chapter 11 cases.

4. The United States Trustee is an employee of the federal government with responsibility for the administration of bankruptcy generally. In Chapter 7 and 11 cases, the trustee has responsibility for the particular case. In Chapters 12 and 13, there are generally standing trustees with responsibility for all 12 or 13 cases in that district.

XVII. COMMENCEMENT AND DISMISSAL

1. There is nothing that D has to establish as a condition precedent to filing for relief under Chapter 7. Chapter 7 does not have an insolvency requirement.

2. **No.** Farmers are protected from involuntary bankruptcy, section 303.

3. Perhaps not. A Chapter 7 debtor does not have a right to dismiss his case. The statutory standard is "cause." Numerous reported cases have denied motions to dismiss by Chapter 7 debtors.

4. *True.*

XVIII. STAY OF COLLECTION ACTIVITIES

1. The stay becomes effective as soon as the petition is filed. Knowledge or notice of the case is irrelevant.

2. The automatic stay would bar the continuation of the collection process. If the sale is held in violation of the stay, it is void or voidable.

3. **No.** The automatic stay only affects efforts to collect prepetition claims from the debtor or property of the debtor, section 362(a)(1).

4. S can argue that its interest in the collateral is not being adequately protected, i.e., it is depreciating. That does not, however, mean that S will recover the collateral.

Note the various forms of relief from the stay under section 362(d)(1). The debtor could propose that the stay be conditioned on making monthly payments measured by the amount of the depreciation.

5. *False.* An unsecured creditor can move for and receive relief under section 362(d) (1). Note that the general standard of section 362(d)(1) is cause.

XIX. PROPERTY OF THE ESTATE

1. *False.* Property of the estate is an important concept in cases under Chapter 7, 11, 12, or 13. While generally a Chapter 11, 12, or 13 debtor retains possession of property of the estate, her sale and use of it is subject to court control under section 363. Moreover, property of the estate is a relevant consideration in plan confirmation.

2. **No.** Absent piercing the corporate veil.

3. An individual's earnings from post-petition services are not property of the estate, section 541(a)(6).

4. Blackacre is not property of the estate. D's interest in Blackacre is property of the estate.

XX. EXEMPTIONS IN BANKRUPTCY

1. *True.*

2. *False.*

3. *False.* In the few states that have not opted out, a debtor can choose either non-bankruptcy exemption law or the exemptions in section 522(d).

4. While D can redeem the furniture under section 722 by paying the $500, D should instead use section 522(f)(2) to avoid the non-purchase money security interest.

XXI. AVOIDING PRE–BANKRUPTCY TRANSFERS

1. *False.* These provisions set out the trustee's avoidance powers.

2. **No.** Section 547(b) deals with transfer of property of the debtor.

3. **No.** 90 days.

4. Preference period for insiders is one year. P is an insider. P is also a creditor of D; guarantee gives rise to a claim. While the transfer was to C, it was for the benefit of P.

5. Paying on a fully secured claim is not a preference, section 547(b)(5).

6. Paying on a partly secured claim can be a preference unless there is a release of collateral.

7. Yes, the payment was a preference. All of the requirements of section 547(b) are satisfied. The payments cannot be recovered, however, because of section 547(c)(2) and possibly section 547(c)(7).

8. Section 553 governs setoffs. If the trustee is going to challenge a pre-bankruptcy setoff, she must use section 553.

9. *True.* Section 548 has a one year limitation period. Remember that section 544(b) provides an alternative base for challenging fraudulent conveyances.

10. **Yes.** While section 546(b) incorporates state grace periods into section 544(a), section 547(e) establishes a federal ten-day rule.

XXII. POST–BANKRUPTCY TRANSFERS

1. Yes, but * * *. How likely is it that D still has the $10,000? That is why the section 549 rights against T are so important.

2. **Yes.** The general rule of section 549 is that the trustee can avoid post-bankruptcy transfers. None of the exceptions to this general rule are applicable to this transfer of personal property in a voluntary case.

3. Generally, in Chapter 11 cases, there is not a trustee. Assuming that a trustee was later appointed, she could not avoid this transfer. It was authorized under section 363 of the Bankruptcy Code.

4. Under state law, the issuance of a check does not effect a transfer of funds. The transfer occurs when the check was honored. Since the check was not honored prior to the bankruptcy filing, the funds in the account were property of the estate. Honoring the check was a post-petition transfer. Section 542(c) protects the bank if it did not have notice or knowledge. The trustee can pursue Y, the payee.

XXIII. EFFECT OF BANKRUPTCY ON SECURED CLAIMS

1. *False.* Section 506 looks to the value of the property of the debtor that secures the debt. Here the stock is property of a third party.

2. **No.** Section 542 deals with turnover of property of the estate, i.e., property in which the debtor has an interest. After the foreclosure sale, D has no interest in the property.

3. *False.* Property is abandoned to the debtor.

4. *True.*

XXIV.   CHAPTER 7 AND UNSECURED CLAIMS

1. *False.*   If the value of the collateral is less than $100,000, S also has an unsecured claim.

2. **Yes.**   Filing a proof of claim is a condition precedent to participating in the bankruptcy distribution.   Filing a proof of claim has no effect on discharge or dischargeability.

3. The loan agreement provides for interest.   Interest stops running on unsecured claims as of the time of the bankruptcy filing.

4. The consumer's rights under the warranty comes within the Bankruptcy Code's definition of "claim."   The Code provides for estimation of such claims but does not provide for the estimation mechanism.

5. The Chapter 7 bankruptcy only affects pre-petition claims.   C is free to proceed against D outside of bankruptcy.

6. *False.*   The one year rule for leases only establishes a ceiling for claims for future rentals not the amount of such claims.   Absent bankruptcy, how much could L recover.   Perhaps, L was able to lease the property immediately at a higher rental rate.

XXV.   LEASES AND EXECUTORY CONTRACTS

1. Section 365 doesn't really work well here.   It contemplates either rejection or assumption.   If the trustee rejects the lease, it is a breach.   If the trustee assumes the lease, it is a administrative expense obligation of the estate.   Some imaginative judges use section 554 abandonment here.

2. Note that section 365(a) calls for bankruptcy judge approval.   Recall also the time limits in Chapter 7 and in other chapters for nonresidential real property leases.

3. Yes, but ∗ ∗ ∗ D will have to satisfy the adequate assurance requirements of section 365(b).

4. This is similar to the facts in *Lubrizol Enterprises v. Richmond Metal Finishers,* 756 F.2d 1043 (4th Cir. 1985).   There D was able to reject the contract and recover the technology.   Could it be argued that the transfer of the technology was "executed"? Alternatively, could it be argued that the effect of rejection should be similar to the effect of a breach under state law?   Under state law, if D breached, it would not be able to recover the technology.

XXVI.   DISCHARGE

1. *False.*

2. *True.*

3. ***True.***   Most exceptions to discharge do not apply to the debtor who receives a discharge under section 1328(a).

4. ***False.***   Most taxes are excepted from discharge.

5. W can sue in state court. She will not be affected by the automatic stay because of the discharge. And, in the state court action, she can, if necessary, assert her section 523(a)(5) exception to discharge.

6. **Yes.**   The discharge affects only D's personal liability; it does not extinguish the lien.

XXVII. CHAPTER 11

1. ***False.***

2. ***False.***   Ordinary course transactions do not require prior court approval, sections 363, 364.

3. Creditors can file a plan in Chapter 11 cases. It can be a liquidating plan. Creditors can file a plan even though the debtor has filed a plan. Absent the appointment of a trustee, the debtor has a period in which only she can file the plan, section 1121.

4. Class 1 claims are being impaired. While they are being paid in full, the payment is not in cash. Accordingly, it is necessary to solicit acceptances from Class 1 claimants.

5. ***True.***

6. The confirmation of the plan effects a discharge. Accordingly, C's claim against D is now limited to the unpaid portion of the plan's $60,000 obligation.

XXVIII. CHAPTER 13

1. Yes, if her income is "regular" as defined in section 101 and she does not exceed the debt limits of section 109.

2. In a Chapter 13 plan, a debtor cannot change payment obligations on a debt secured solely by her principal residence.

3. ***True.***

4. ***False.***

5. Possibly. A debtor who obtains a discharge under section 1328(a) is not subject to the educational debt exception to discharge.

XXIX. ALLOCATION OF JUDICIAL POWER OVER BANKRUPTCY

1. *False.*

2. *True.*   She can render final judgments only in core proceedings.

3. *False.*   Withdrawal is all about the role of the bankruptcy judge and the district court judge.

PRACTICE EXAMINATION

Three types of questions might appear on a final examination in a debtor-creditor course: (1) pure creditors' rights questions that involve only issues of state law and non-bankruptcy federal law; (2) pure or core bankruptcy questions; and (3) questions combining creditors' rights and bankruptcy issues. Teachers of debtor-creditor law tend to favor the third type because those kinds of questions are efficient testing tools (i.e., can kill two birds with one stone), and also because real-life bankruptcy problems typically involve mixed questions of bankruptcy and non-bankruptcy law. So be on guard: A problem set in bankruptcy may harbor important issues of state and federal creditors' rights law. Another warning: Debtor-creditor teachers especially like bankruptcy problems dealing with the trustee's avoiding powers, and can go absolutely nuts mixing avoiding powers with state creditors' rights law.

Here is a very straightforward, relatively simple, practice final examination which asks 15 questions totalling 100 points. As far as we know, this examination has never been given anywhere; but each of the questions has appeared on final examinations in one or more law schools. (That's right—law teachers share exam questions.) Some of the questions are objective; others are short essay. You should be prepared to explain fully all of your answers, including answers to the objective questions.

This examination, like any real law school final exam, is "comprehensive" only in the sense that it can potentially cover any issue in the course. As will be true of an actual debtor-creditor exam, however, this practice examination tests only a very narrow selection of issues that you will study in class or in reading this Black Letter or other secondary source. Be forewarned that the selection here might not mirror (or even be close) to your teacher's choice of issues on the final exam she prepares especially for you. Good luck!

Instructions: [Most teachers would give you three hours to take the examination, and would allow you to consult the Bankruptcy Code and other relevant federal statutes (such as the federal tax lien law). Some teachers (probably not most of them) would also allow you to consult state statutory law that was covered in the course.]

QUESTION 1
(10 points)

D owes the federal government $40,000 in back taxes; and in January, the IRS made a tax assessment against D.

In February, J obtained a $40,000 judgment against D, and in March docketed this judgment in Travis County.

The IRS filed a tax lien notice there in April.

In May, D bought land worth $50,000 in Travis County.

List the questions that should be considered in determining which lien, the tax lien or J's judgment lien, has priority to the Travis County land.

QUESTION 2
(5 points)

C won a $1.5 million judgment against Ace, Inc., and garnished First Bank where Ace maintained a deposit account containing $500,000. At the time, Ace owed the Bank $400,000. To what extent, if any, is the Bank, as garnishee, accountable to C? Explain you answer, and state any assumptions on which it is based.

QUESTION 3
(5 points)

D owned a townhouse in Hennepin County where she lived most of the time, and a lakeside vacation home in Clever County. J won a judgment against D and docketed it in Clever County. Thereafter, D changed her principal place of residence to Clever County and began living permanently in the vacation home. The townhouse had been destroyed in a bad storm. The loss was covered by insurance, but D decided to invest the insurance proceeds rather than replace the townhouse. Can J get the vacation home, or the insurance proceeds, or both?   Explain.

QUESTION 4
(10 points)

A. With the actual intent to defraud her creditors, D sells everything she owns to various innocent buyers who pay substantial value for the property, and then D skips the country with the proceeds. Circle the best answer:

(a) These sales can be set aside because of D's actual intent to defraud.

(b) These sales cannot be set aside because they are not fraudulent conveyances.

(c) These sales cannot be set aside due to the buyers' innocence.

B. D is insolvent. She needs cash. To get cash quickly, she makes a bargain-basement sale of her vacation home to a real estate company which paid less than fair market value for the property but did so in good faith. Circle the best answer:

(a) The sale cannot be set aside because it is not fraudulent.

(b) The sale cannot be set aside because the buyer acted in good faith.

(c) The sale can be set aside as constructively fraudulent.

QUESTION 5
(5 points)

S has long supplied various paper products to D who operates a cafe. D is now in financial trouble and has recently defaulted in paying the $10,000 past-due, unsecured account owed S. S is worried because D has begun to sell her assets to solve, temporarily, the cash-flow problems of the business. Thus, S decides to sue D to collect the account. Identify from the following list which one or more pre-judgment remedies are likely available to S?

(a) Attachment   (c) Replevin   (e) All of them.
(b) Garnishment (d) Lis pendens (f) None of them.

QUESTION 6
(5 points)

Seller shipped goods to Buyer. After shipment but before Buyer actually received the goods, Buyer purported to resell the goods to User. Buyer and User entered into a sales contract covering the identified goods, and User made a substantial downpayment. Seller, however, stopped delivery of the goods because Buyer's check for the purchase price bounced. Whose claim to the goods is superior, the Seller's or User's? Explain.

QUESTION 7
(5 points)

O hired C, a general contractor, to construct a building on land owned by O. Work on the project began on June 1 when the foundation was dug. C subcontracted the plumbing work to P who started work on October 5. On June 10, Bank recorded a mortgage on the property to secure a loan to finance construction. P performed fully for C, but was not paid for her work. P thus asserted a construction lien on the building and in doing so fully complied with local law to claim and enforce such a lien. Is P's lien entitled to priority over Bank's mortgage?

QUESTION 8
(5 points)

Seller, a New York company, supplies business equipment to buyers on credit. Seller wishes to ensure that any litigation between it and a buyer, with respect to a contract between them, will take place in New York. Identify in the following list the kind of clause(s) that Seller should include in the sales contract in an attempt to prevent a buyer from suing elsewhere.

a.   Cognovit

b.   Choice-of-law clause

c.   Warrant of attorney

d.   Confession-of-judgment clause

e.   Due process waiver

f.   Consent-to-jurisdiction clause

g.   All of the above

h.   None of the above

QUESTION 9
(10 points)

Dr. D is a dermatologist who privately practices medicine in the downstairs portion of her duplex. She lives upstairs. Because of bad investments, she is presently unable to pay all of her debts. She comes to you for legal advice.

A. If Dr. D files a Chapter 7 petition, can she claim her duplex as exempt property? Her pre-petition earnings? Her post-petition earnings?

B. If Dr. D files a Chapter 11 petition, will her post-petition earnings be property of the estate?

C. Assume that Dr. D files a Chapter 13 petition on August 18. On August 28, she pays $2,000 to C Medical Supplies, Inc. on a long-standing debt. On September 9, Dr. D converts her Chapter 13 case to a Chapter 7 case. Can the bankruptcy trustee recover the $2,000 from C Medical Supplies, Inc.?

QUESTION 10
(5 points)

X owes D a debt of $70,000 that is fully secured. D owes C $40,000 that is only partly secured. D and X agree that X will pay C the $40,000 that D owes C, and that the amount that X owes D will be reduced by $40,000. X makes the agreed upon $40,000 payment to C. A month later, D files a Chapter 7 petition. Can the bankruptcy trustee recover the $40,000 payment from C?

QUESTION 11
(5 points)

In December, 1988, D, a farmer, prepares a deed to 25 acres of her farm, puts the deed in a box which she wraps, and gives the package to S, D's daughter, as a Christmas present. The effect is to render S insolvent. S does not record the deed until

January, 1989. D files a Chapter 12 bankruptcy petition 91 days after the deed was recorded. Can D's gift of the land be avoided?

QUESTION 12
(10 points)

A. D and X are both in the chemical business. Each sells chemicals to the other on credit. D has just filed a Chapter 11 petition.

Exactly 90 days before D's filing, D owed X $40,000, and X owed D $60,000. Exactly 70 days before D's filing, X paid D the $60,000 debt. Exactly 45 days before D's filing, D paid X the $40,000 debt.

What are the effects, if any, of D's bankruptcy on the two payments between D and X?

B. D and X are both in the chemical business. Each sells chemicals to the other on credit. D has just filed a Chapter 7 petition.

Exactly 90 days before D's filing, D owed X $40,000, and X owed D $60,000. Exactly 35 days before the filing, X exercised its right of setoff against D under state law and sent D a check for $20,000.

What is the effect, if any, of D's bankruptcy?

QUESTION 13
(10 points)

A. D files a Chapter 11 petition on March 3. On March 5, D receives a bill from Dr. C for medical services rendered on February 20. D wants to pay the bill immediately. What are the possible bankruptcy law consequences, if any, of D paying the bill? Of Dr. C hounding D for payment if the bill is not paid?

B. You represent X Store and Bank. D is one of the suppliers for X Store. D has filed a Chapter 11 petition. Advise X Store as to the possible legal risks, if any, in continuing to buy goods from D. Advise Bank on how it can collect the loan made to D that is secured by D's inventory.

QUESTION 14
(5 points)

On January 10, D charged two round-trip, first-class tickets to Europe in March on Delta Airline. The tickets cost $3500, and their price was charged to D's Delta Airline credit card. D received the two tickets and a bill for $3500 payable within 25 days.

On February 2, before D had used the tickets or paid for them, she filed a Chapter 7 petition.

Discuss the significance of concluding that the tickets are executory contracts.

QUESTION 15
(5 points)

D asked Witte's Garage to repair her valuable sports car. Witte fixed it, but D failed to pay the repair charges. D filed Chapter 7. Must Witte surrender D's car to the trustee in bankruptcy? Does the answer depend on whether Witte has an artisan's lien on the car? Do the answers to the first and second questions determine whether Witte can sell the car and apply the proceeds in satisfaction of the repair bill?

APPENDIX C

TEXT CORRELATION CHART

Black Letter Creditors' Rights And Bankruptcy	Baird & Jackson: Bankruptcy Law (2d ed.)	Eisenberg: Bankruptcy And Debtor-Creditor	Epstein, Landers & Nickles: Debtors And Creditors (3d ed.)	Jordan & Warren: Bankruptcy	King & Cook: Creditors' Rights, Debtors' Protection, And Bankruptcy	Riesenfeld: Creditors' Remedies And Debtors' Protection (4th ed.)	Warren & Westbrook: The Law Of Debtors And Creditors	White: Bankruptcy And Creditors' Rights
Chapter I Increasing The Odds Of A Creditor's Judgment	—	—	689–701	—	—	400–14	—	—
Chapter II Judgment Liens	—	—	48–55	—	113–18	51–80 89–148	40–41	511–27
Chapter III Enforcing Judgments Through Execution	—	349–82	28–48	—	119–64	51–89 149–204	44–55	529–37
Chapter IV Finding Property Of The Debtor	—	—	58–65	—	108, 117	266–88	—	—
Chapter V Garnishment	—	—	65–86	—	165–237	204–39	55–68	546–56
Chapter VI Fraudulent Conveyances	—	279–328	86–108	—	347–408	347–89	120–39	711–43
Chapter VII Bulk Sales	—	328–44	108–18	—	—	—	—	743–54
Chapter VIII Shielding Exempt Property	—	382–406	127–44	—	409–506	289–333	100–20	471–509
Chapter IX Special Rights Under State Law	—	—	509–95	—	70–106	—	141–47 627–57	572–613

Black Letter Creditors' Rights And Bankruptcy	Baird & Jackson: Bankruptcy Law (2d ed.)	Eisenberg: Bankruptcy And Debtor–Creditor	Epstein, Landers & Nickles: Debtors And Creditors (3d ed.)	Jordan & Warren: Bankruptcy	King & Cook: Creditors' Rights, Debtors' Protection, And Bankruptcy	Riesenfeld: Creditors' Remedies And Debtors' Protection (4th ed.)	Warren & Westbrook: The Law Of Debtors And Creditors	White: Bankruptcy And Creditors' Rights
Chapter X Federal Tax Lien	—	407–25	599–640	—	281–346	—	—	613–15
Chapter XI Attachment	—	259–79	145–64	—	165–235	240–65	—	537–46
Chapter XII Replevin	—	—	170–78	—	—	—	—	—
Chapter XIII Lis Pendens	—	—	164–70	—	170	—	—	527–29
Chapter XIV Fourteenth Amendment Protection	—	—	645–83	—	200–37	12–51	72–100	766–71
Chapter XV Other Sources Of Due Process Protection	—	—	683–89	—	—	—	—	—
Chapter XVI Overview Of Bankruptcy	20–46	452–57	704–12	17–26	576–80	455–64	169–78	29–94
Chapter XVII Commencement And Dismissal Of A Bankruptcy Case	47–122	458–66	713–33	—	581–658	464–87	—	—
Chapter XVIII Stay Of Collection Activities	362–450	524–48	744–62	—	1031–95	540–91	192–202 403–30	95–125
Chapter XIX Property Of The Estate	171–218 817–49	467–79	734–40	27–52	933–46	504–39	180–88	—
Chapter XX Exemptions In Bankruptcy	850–906	480–501	741–43	53–80	826–42	592–627 721–62	204–18	471–509
Chapter XXI Avoiding Pre-Bankruptcy Transfers	219–360	687–772	899–960	300–582	848–932	648–713	459–90 521–45	221–80 643–46
Chapter XXII Post–Bankruptcy Transfers	—	—	961–63	—	—	714–20	—	—
Chapter XXIII Effect Of Bankruptcy On Secured Claims	—	583–92	830–78	208–30	—	771–79	280–303	—
Chapter XXIV Chapter 7 And Unsecured Claims	123–70 547–600	592–632	798–799 811–29	81–112 231–46 273–99	947–1030	780–800	—	—
Chapter XXV Leases And Executory Contracts	451–520	549–82	879–98	819–94	1097–74	629–40	492–520	164–220
Chapter XXVI Discharge	729–816	634–86	763–97	113–207 247–72	777–825	801–63	226–76	—
Chapter XXVII Chapter 11	601–728	807–94	973–1030	680–964	—	864–89	371–696	281–60
Chapter XXVIII Chapter 13	907–40	773–806	—	625–79	—	890–902	277–370	417–70

Black Letter Creditors' Rights And Bankruptcy	Baird & Jackson: Bankruptcy Law (2d ed.)	Eisenberg: Bankruptcy And Debtor–Creditor	Epstein, Landers & Nickles: Debtors And Creditors (3d ed.)	Jordan & Warren: Bankruptcy	King & Cook: Creditors' Rights, Debtors' Protection, And Bankruptcy	Riesenfeld: Creditors' Remedies And Debtors' Protection (4th ed.)	Warren & Westbrook: The Law Of Debtors And Creditors	White: Bankruptcy And Creditors' Rights
Chapter XXIX Allocation Of Judicial Power Over Bankruptcy Matters	941–96	895–954	964–72	995–1058	658–776	488–503	699–720	—

*

APPENDIX D

GLOSSARY

A

Abandonment Conduct of a debtor that results in the loss of the homestead exemption and that usually involves moving away from the place with the present or subsequently formed intention never to occupy it again as a home. Also, a bankruptcy term that describes a trustee's release of property of the estate to the debtor.

Acceptance Vote of creditors in requisite number and amount for a Chapter 11 plan.

Adequate Assurance Standard applied in determining whether a debtor in default on a lease or other executory contract can assume under section 365.

Adequate Protection Phrase used in several sections of the Bankruptcy Code to describe protection afforded to holders of secured claims. More specifically, the lack of adequate protection of the creditor's interest in its collateral is a basis for relief from stay under section 362(d)(1);

adequate protection is also the standard for creditor protection from sale or use or encumbrance of the collateral under sections 363 and 364. While adequate protection is not statutorily defined, section 361 sets out examples of adequate protection.

Affidavit A sworn statement of facts or allegations made to or before a person authorized by law to administer oaths.

Alias Writ of Execution A second writ of execution issued to enforce a judgment that was not fully satisfied by the sheriff acting under the first or original writ.

Artisans' Lien A lien that arises by law to secure payment of a person who cares for, repairs, or otherwise enhances the value of goods.

Attachment An extraordinary, pre-judgment, statutory remedy which is ancillary to the main suit, has nothing to do with the merits of the action, and is a summary, anticipatory method of impounding defendant's assets to facilitate collection of the judgment against her, if and when a judgment is obtained.

Attachment Lien See Lien of Attachment.

Automatic Stay Bar on collection efforts, judicial and extrajudicial, directed to the debtor or the property of the debtor. The automatic stay becomes effective as soon as the bankruptcy petition is filed.

B

Badge of Fraud A circumstance or other fact accompanying a transfer of property that the courts recognize as an especially reliable indicator of the transferor's actual intention to hinder, delay, or defraud creditors in making the transfer.

Bankrupt No such person under the Bankruptcy Code. "Debtor" is the term used.

Bankruptcy Judge A judicial officer of the district court.

Bulk Sale A transfer out of the ordinary course of a major part of the inventory of the transferor whose business is the sale of goods from stock, which transfer is regulated by Uniform Commercial Code Article 6 so as to protect creditors of the transferor.

C

Cash Surrender Value The amount of money that the owner of an insurance policy can receive from the insurer in lieu of continued insurance coverage.

Choice of Law A contractual provision wherein the parties designate the state whose law will govern disputes arising out of their agreement.

Claim and Delivery See Replevin.

Cognovit A device, usually in the form of a contractual provision, by which a debtor consents in advance to the creditor's obtaining judgment on the debt without giving the debtor notice of the suit to enforce the debt or an opportunity for a hearing on the matter.

Confession of Judgment Often used as a synonym for cognvoit, but also can refer to a debt-or's consent to entry of a judgment against her in any kind of proceeding, including a proceeding of which she was notified and in which she had a right to be heard.

Confirmation Judicial approval of a Chapter 11, 12, or 13 plan.

Construction Lien A lien that arises by law and attaches to real estate to secure payment of a person who improved the property through the rendering of labor or other services or the furnishing of materials or other supplies. Another name for this lien is mechanics' lien.

Core Proceeding Undefined term that covers the kind of cases that a bankruptcy judge can decide, absent withdrawal of the reference.

Cram Down Colloquial expression that describes court confirmation of a Chapter 11, 12 or 13 plan, notwithstanding creditor opposition.

Creditor's Bill A judge-made, equitable remedy, known also as a creditors' suit, that is a separate action following judgment against a debtor which is designed to uncover nonexempt assets of the debtor and to apply them in satisfaction of the judgment, including property fraudulently conveyed by the debtor.

Creditors' Committee Representatives of creditors in Chapter 11 cases.

Creditors' Suit See Creditor's Bill.

D

Debtor In bankruptcy law, person who files a voluntary petition or person against whom an involuntary petition is filed; in other words, the "bankrupt."

Debtor-in-Possession Debtor in a Chapter 11 or Chapter 12 case. To illustrate, in a Chapter 11 case either the debtor will remain in control of its business or assets or a trustee will be appointed to take control of the business or assets.

Delivery Bond A guaranteed undertaking by a defendant whose property has been seized through attachment promising that, in exchange for return of the property to her pending resolution of the main action, she will surrender the property or its value in satisfaction of judgment against her. Another name for this bond is "forthcoming bond."

Detinue Another name for Replevin, although technically an ancestor of replevin describing in early common law a case in which goods had been delivered under a bailment and the bailee refused to redeliver after proper request.

Discharging Bond Same as a delivery bond except that not only does it permit defendant to regain possession of attached property, it also effects a release of the property from the lien of attachment. Another name for this bond is "dissolution bond."

Dissolution Bond. See Discharging Bond.

Distress Early common-law process which allowed a creditor to seize property of a debtor and hold the property as security for the debtor's obligation, as a landlord might do when a tenant defaulted in paying rent.

Docket A book or set of records in which a judge or clerk of court notes briefly all the proceedings in a case.

Dormancy Lapse in the executability of a judgment, and also in the effectiveness of the judgment lien, which is cured through revival of the judgment.

E

Elegit A judicial writ, which is no long used, that directed the satsifaction of a judgment through transfer of the debtor's personal property to the creditor at an appraised price, and, if this was insufficient, assignment of the use of one half of the debtor's land to the creditor as tenant by the *elegit* for a term based on an appraisal of its value.

Equitable Right of Setoff Self-help cancellation of cross demands. A remedy that is most often used by banks to unilaterally offset the general deposit accounts of a customer to satisfy matured debts the customer owes the bank.

Exceptions to Discharge Debts not affected by a bankruptcy discharge.

Execution Modern process whereby a state official (usually a sheriff) is directed by way of an appropriate judicial writ to seize and sell so much of the debtor's nonexempt property as is necessary to satisfy a judgment.

Execution Lien See Lien of Execution.

Executory Contracts Undefined term in bankruptcy law describing transactions subject to section 365. In bankruptcy, an executory contract can be assumed or rejected, but not modified.

Exemption or Exempt Property An item of, or interest in, property that is not subject to seizure and sale on process to secure or enforce a judgment against a debtor.

Ex Parte Refers to a proceeding in which a court takes action upon the application of only one side to a controversy without notifying the other side or giving the other side an opportunity to be heard with respect to the action.

F

Fair Consideration A term of fraudulent conveyance law describing whatever is given in exchange for a conveyance of debtor's property whenever the exchange involves property or other things having substantially equivalent values.

Fieri Facias (Fi. Fa.) Judicial writ directing sheriff to satisfy a judgment from the debtor's property; in its original form, the writ directed the seizure and sale of goods and chattels only, but eventually was enlarged to permit levy on real property, too; largely synonymously with modern writ of execution.

Foreign Attachment Refers to the use of the pre-judgment remedy of attachment against the property of a defendant who is not a resident of the jurisdiction where the main action is pending.

Forthcoming Bond See Delivery Bond.

Forum Non Conveniens Doctrine of civil procedure empowering a trial court to decline to exercise judicial jurisdiction if trying the case elsewhere would be more appropriate.

Forum-Selection Clause A contract provision through which the parties set the venue for litigation between them.

Full Faith and Credit Art. IV, § 1 of the United State Constitution which mandates that valid civil judgments in one state or territory are entitled to enforcement in any other state or territory.

G

Garnishment A procedure, which sometimes is called "trustee process," for reaching obligations owed to the debtor or property of the debtor in a third party's possession.

Garnishment Lien See Lien of Garnishment.

Garnishee Third-party defendant in a garnishment proceeding who holds property of, or owes an obligation to, a debtor, which property or obligation the debtor's creditor seeks by way of the proceeding to reach and apply in satisfaction of her claim against the debtor.

Garnishor Creditor who initiates garnishment for the purpose of reaching property or credits of a debtor held or owed by a third person who is the garnishee.

Grounds for Attachment Certain extenuating circumstances that must be present before a plaintiff can have a defendant's property seized through the remedy of attachment, which grounds typically include the defendant threatening to remove her property from the jurisdiction or to dispose of her property.

H

Holder of Claim Creditor. If D owes C $300,000 and D files a bankruptcy petition, D will be a debtor and C will be the holder of a claim.

Holder of a Secured Claim Creditor with a lien on property of the debtor or a right of setoff against property of the debtor. The amount of a secured claim is limited by both the debt and the value of the collateral. If D owes C $300,000 and the debt is secured by inventory, the amount of C's secured claim will depend on the value of inventory. If inventory is valued at $200,000, then C's secured claim will only be $200,000. Under these facts, C will also have an unsecured claim for $100,000. A single credit transaction can be the basis for two claims: a secured claim and an unsecured claim.

Holder of an Unsecured Claim A creditor that does not have a lien or right of setoff against the debtor's property or a creditor that has a lien on or right of setoff against property of the debtor that has a value less than the amount of the debt.

Homestead or Homestead Exemption Generally refers to exempt real property which by statute is beyond the reach of creditors because the debtor resides there with a family which depends on her for support.

I

In Custodia Legis In custody of the law, as when a defendant's property is seized through the remedy of attachment and is held by the sheriff pending resolution of the main action between the parties.

In Personam Jurisdiction A type of judicial jurisdiction that supports a judgment binding the persons who are before the court.

In Rem Jurisdiction A type of judicial jurisdiction that supports a judgment determining the interests of all persons in property upon which the court acts.

Involuntary Case Bankruptcy case initiated by creditors' filing a petition.

J

Judicial Jurisdiction That which empowers a court to exercise judicial power and render valid and enforceable judgments.

Judgment Lien An encumbrance that arises by law when a judgment for the recovery of money is docketed and that attaches to the debtor's real estate located in the county where the judgment is docketed.

L

Levy The process whereby a sheriff or other state official empowered by writ or other judicial directive actually seizes, or otherwise brings within her control, a judgment debtor's property which is taken to secure or satisfy the judgment.

Lien of Attachment An encumbrance on property seized through the pre-judgment remedy of attachment that is inchoate when it first arises, usually upon the sheriff's levy of the property, and that becomes final and perfected upon judgment for the attaching creditor in the action who caused attachment to issue. For purposes of priority against third parties' claims to the property, a lien of attachment perfected by judgment dates from the time the lien first arose.

Lien of Execution An encumbrance that attaches by operation of law to a judgment debtor's real and personal property when the property is subjected to execution process and that gives the execution creditor a priority over subsequent transferees of the property and also over prior unrecorded conveyances of interests in the property.

Lien of Garnishment Encumbrance on property of a debtor held by a garnishee that attaches in favor of the garnishing creditor when garnishment summons is served upon the garnishee and that also impounds credits owed by the garnishee to the debtor so that they must be paid to the garnishing creditor.

Lis Pendens A common-law doctrine, now codified in many states so as to condition its effect on the filing of a notice, that binds a purchaser or encumbrancer of property to the results of any pending lawsuit which may affect the title to, any lien on, or possession of the property.

M

Mechanics' Lien See Construction Lien.

N

Nulla Bona Return A sheriff's return of a writ of execution indicating that she has been unable to find any leviable property of the judg-

ment debtor to seize and sell in satifaction of the judgment.

O

Objections to Discharge Grounds for withholding a discharge in a Chapter 7 case.

Order of Delivery Writ issued in furtherance of replevin remedy which directs sheriff to seize disputed property from person in possession of it. Other names include Writ of Possession and Writ of Replevin.

P

Pendente Lite During the lawsuit or litigation.

Pluries Writs of Execution Third and subsequent writs of execution issued to enforce a judgment that was not satisfied by the sheriff acting under the original and alias writs of execution.

Preference Except where defined more specifically by statute, a transfer of an insolvent debtor's property for or on account of an antecedent debt so that the preferred creditor receives more in satisfaction of her claim than other creditors with similar claims.

Priority Unsecured claims that by statute receive more favorable treatment in bankruptcy than other unsecured claims. In a Chapter 7 distribution, priority claims must be paid first. In a Chapter 11 plan, priority claims must be paid in full.

Probate Homestead Refers to the rights of a debtor's spouse and minor children to continue to possess and use a homestead after the debtor's death even though they have no interest in the property themselves notwithstanding the claims of heirs or devisees and free from the claims of the debtor's creditors.

Proof of Claim Filing required of creditors in cases under Chapters 7, 12, and 13.

Purchase Money (Encumbrance, Interest, Mortgage) A claim to property securing repayment of value given so as to enable acquisition of property.

Q

Quasi in Rem Jurisdiction A type of judicial jurisdiction that supports a judgment binding the interests of particular persons in property upon which the court acts.

R

Reaffirmation Post-petition agreement to pay pre-petition obligations. Court approval is required.

Receiver A person appointed by a court for the purpose of preserving property of a debtor pending an action against her, or applying the property in satisfaction of a creditor's claim, whenever there is danger that, in the absence of such an appointment, the property will be lost, removed or injured.

Reclaim or Reclamation A seller's very limited right under Uniform Commercial Code Article 2 to retrieve goods delivered to a buyer as when, in a cash transaction, the buyer pays with a worthless check or, in a credit transaction, the buyer is insolvent when she receives the goods.

Redemption The right of a debtor, and sometimes of a debtor's other creditors, to repurchase from a buyer at a forced sale property of the debtor that was seized and sold in satisfaction of a judgment or other claim against the debtor, which right usually is limited to forced sales of real property. Also, a bankruptcy term for extinguishing a lien on exempt property by making a cash payment equal to the value of the property.

Renewal of or Renewing a Judgment A judgment is a form of a debt. If this debt is not paid, the creditor can bring an action on it. This action sometimes is referred to as a renewal of a judgment. Renewal, however, is a new lawsuit, separate from the action that originally produced the judgment; the suit must be commenced before expiration of the statute of limitation governing the enforcement of judgments; and, if the creditor prevails, she obtains a new judgment and a fresh judgment lien. Moreover, the statute of limitation governing the enforcement of judgments begins running anew.

Replevin Refers to a civil action for possession of property wrongfully taken or detained by the defendant; refers also to a provisional remedy that is an incident of a replevin action which allows the plaintiff at any time before judgment to take the disputed property from the defendant and hold the property pendente lite. Other names for replevin include Claim and Delivery, Detinue, Revendication, and Sequestration.

Replevin in Cepit Replevin action in case where defendant has both wrongfully taken and wrongfully detained the property. Compare Replevin in Detinet.

Replevin in Detinet Replevin action in case where defendant rightfully obtained possession of property but wrongfully detains it. Compare Replevin in Cepit.

Return of Execution Writ The report of a sheriff to the court issuing a writ of execution on how successful the sheriff has been in enforcing the writ, which report typically must be made within 60 or 90 days following issuance of the writ.

Revendication The civil law equivalent of Replevin.

Revival of Judgment or Revivor A summary proceeding designed to substantiate and revitalize a dormant judgment. A revivor proceeding ordinarily is thought of as a continuation of the action that produced the judgment and not as a separate action producing its own judgment and judgment lien.

S

Scire Facias A judicial writ directing a debtor to appear and show cause why a dormant judgment against her should not be revived.

Sequestration In the law of creditors' rights, most often refers to an equitable form of attachment, although occasionally used (or misused) to identify a replevin-like process; very broad meaning implies any setting aside of a person's property to answer for the demands of another.

Set Off Refers generally to the right of any person to reduce the amount of her debt to another by any sum the other person owes her and includes the right of a bank to debit a customer's general deposit account in the amount of a debt which the customer owes the bank.

Sovereign Immunity Common-law principle that forbids suit against a government without the government's consent.

Statute of 13 Elizabeth The source of modern fraudulent conveyance law that was enacted by Parliament in 1570 and condemned any conveyance of a debtor's property made with the actual intention to hinder, delay, or defraud the debtor's creditors.

Summary Jurisdiction Phrase that describes the jurisdiction of bankruptcy courts under the Bankruptcy Act of 1898.

Supplemental or Supplementary Proceedings Post-judgment remedies provided by statute or procedural rules that allow discovery against persons who might have information on the whereabouts of nonexempt assets of the debtor (Supplemental Discovery) and that facilitate application of these assets in satisfaction of the judgment (Supplemental Relief).

T

Trustee Representative of the creditors, generally a private citizen, not an employee of the federal government. There will be a trustee in every Chapter 7, 12, and 13 case and some Chapter 11 cases. Her powers and duties vary from chapter to chapter. The trustee is generally appointed by the United States Trustee.

Creditors can elect a trustee to replace an appointed trustee.

Trustee Process See Garnishment.

U

U.C.C. or UCC Uniform Commercial Code.

UFCA Uniform Fraudulent Conveyance Act (1919), which half the states have adopted.

UFTA Uniform Fraudulent Transfer Act (1984), which is the successor to the UFCA.

United States Trustee Federal government official that preforms appointing and other administrative tasks that a bankruptcy judge would otherwise have to perform. Chapter 15 of the Bankruptcy Code details the duties and powers of the United States Trustee.

V

Voluntary Case Bankruptcy case initiated by a debtor's filing a petition.

W

Writ A command or order from a court directing and empowering a sheriff or other officer to perform some act such as bringing a person before the court or seizing property against which further action may be required.

Writ of Execution Formal, written command of a court directing a sheriff or other state official to enforce a judgment through process of execution.

Writ of Possession See Order of Delivery.

*

APPENDIX E

TABLE OF CASES

APPENDIX F

TABLE OF STATUTES

†